CR
WHO'S WHO
2008

Looking Ahead by
SIR IAN BOTHAM
PCA President

Foreword by
MATTHEW HOGGARD

Edited by
CHRIS MARSHALL

Statistics by
RICHARD LOCKWOOD

Photographs by
GETTY IMAGES

This edition first published in the UK in 2008 by Green Umbrella Publishing

www.gupublishing.co.uk

Publishers: Jules Gammond and Vanessa Gardner

ISBN: 978-1-906229-63-4

Editor (for Green Umbrella Publishing): Kirsty Ennever
Picture research: Ellie Charleston
Quiz compiled by Chris Marshall
Cover design by Kevin Gardner
Printed and bound in the UK by
Butler & Tanner, Frome

ACKNOWLEDGEMENTS

Cover photographs by Getty Images, 101 Bayham Street, London, NW1 0AG

The publishers would also like to thank the county clubs, the players and their families for their assistance in helping to assemble the information and photographs in this book.

Extra information has also been gathered from the pages of *Wisden Cricketers' Almanack*, *The Wisden Cricketer*, *The Times*, *The Sunday Times*, Cricinfo.com and CricketArchive.com

Thanks also to the following for providing additional photographs: Andrew Hignell/Glamorgan Cricket Archives, Archant, Bucks Free Press, David Griffin, Derby Evening Telegraph, Empics, Galvineyes, Kent CCC, Lancashire CCC/Ken Grime, Leicestershire CCC, MCC, Middlesex CCC, Nigel Stockley, Northamptonshire CCC, Paul Hughes/Loughborough Town CC, Somerset CCC, Surrey CCC, Sussex CCC, SWpix, Uxbridge CC, Worcestershire CCC, www.durhamccc.co.uk, www.eastbournecricketclub.co.uk, www.philbrittphotography.co.uk, Yorkshire CCC

CONTENTS

LOOKING AHEAD
by Sir Ian Botham

The arrival of *The Cricketers' Who's Who* always prompts that realisation in me that a new season is about to begin. I need to start gathering my thoughts, predicting which clubs and which players will succeed and reminding myself about who achieved what last year. The *Who's Who* is an invaluable aid to that process.

I'm heading off to New Zealand in a couple of days as I write this. I've only been back from Sri Lanka for a few weeks. That's the nature of the international schedule these days, and if it's gruelling for us commentators, imagine what it's like for the players. Every time I see a comment on player burn-out I think about what it's like to play for England today – I loved to tour, but everyone's different and the boys are away from home an enormous amount of time. What's really needed is a good definitive study of the issue and ICC should get on with it so we can all know whether it exists and, if it does, what we can do about it.

Another element that will be addressed this coming season will be our domestic structure. After a false start called the Domestic Structure Review Group, ECB have come up with a brand new idea called the Domestic Structure Review Group. They will recommend the changes that need to be brought in to take English cricket through its next TV deal starting in 2010, so it's pretty important. Naturally, this links into the burn-out and the heavy scheduling issue I wrote about earlier. Obviously we need to get rid of 40-over cricket – it serves no purpose at all and the players overwhelmingly agree. Less cricket with more quality – that's what needs to happen and a lot of people will be watching ECB and their new DSRG to see if they can actually get it right.

I'm really excited about the 2008 season. We had such a cracking down-to-the-wire end to the LV County Championship last year that there must be nine teams out there believing they can win it. We've also got an array of quality players – just browse through this book – and I think we're going to see some amazing performances. Let's hope the weather isn't as influential this year, and here's to days of sunshine and intense competition.

Good luck to the players.

Sir Ian Botham
PCA President

FOREWORD
by Matthew Hoggard

As I write this, I'm gearing up to challenge New Zealand in their backyard before they come over to ours this summer. One of the benefits of playing cricket is travelling to interesting places around the world. It can certainly broaden the mind, but then cricket can offer so much on so many levels.

As a recent dad and the Team England Ambassador for the Cricket Foundation's *Chance to shine* campaign, I now truly appreciate what cricket can do for children. For me it is the ultimate team game. You're given a clear role, against which you can set personal objectives, whilst always being aware that they need to be in line with the team's overall aims. It's what makes great teams in my view – everyone having a personal focus, whilst sharing common goals.

That's why it's essential that we ensure that competitive cricket is reintroduced into our state schools. It's the reason why I have nominated *Chance to shine* as my Benefit Year charity in 2008. I urge all the players in this book and everyone involved in cricket to do whatever they can to help, so that our game can become even stronger, and more importantly children may be given their *Chance to shine*.

Matthew Hoggard
February 2008

Editor's Notes

The cricketers listed in this volume include all those who played 1st XI cricket for a first-class county at least once last season, in first-class or one-day (including Twenty20) cricket, and all those registered (at the time of going to press at the beginning of February) to play for the 18 first-class counties in 2008. The umpires' section contains the officials making up the first-class list for 2008, plus Mark Benson, who is on the ICC Elite Panel.

All players' statistics are complete to the end of the last English season (the Stop press section for individual players notes subsequent highlights) and cover first-class, List A and Twenty20 fixtures played that season. Such matches that took place elsewhere in the cricket-playing world during the period, such as ODIs played in Ireland and Scotland and the Twenty20 World Championship in South Africa, do not feature in the players' season statistics but are recorded in their career tables. Test, ODI and Twenty20 International tallies for umpires are up to and including 25 January 2008.

Within the season statistics tables, List A refers to the English domestic one-day competitions and limited-over games such as those between the counties and sides touring England. In addition, just as a player's first-class figures include Test matches, which are also extracted and listed separately, so his List A figures include One-Day Internationals, which are pulled out and appear separately in the same way. Furthermore, in the career tables the List A category contains figures of all the official 'full-length' one-day games in which a player has taken part worldwide. The categories 20/20 Int (Twenty20 Internationals) and 20/20 (all Twenty20 matches) operate in similar fashion to the corresponding first-class and one-day categories.

Numbers of hundreds given in the statistics tables include all multiples (200s, 300s etc.). Tallies of multiple hundreds for players and also of one-day hundreds and one-day five-wicket innings for umpires who are former players are shown in the body of the entry, since these cannot be found in the statistics tables. Statistics for 2007 are not given for players whose appearances that season were only for teams other than a county – e.g. universities (excluding international cricketers on tours to England). These appearances are, however, reflected in their career statistics and reference is made in the Extras section to the team for which they played.

Figures about 1000 runs, 50 wickets and 50 dismissals in a season refer to matches in England only. The figures for batting and bowling averages refer to the full first-class English list for 2007, followed in brackets by the 2006 figures. Inclusion in the batting averages depends on a minimum of six completed innings and an average of at least

10.00; a bowler has to have taken at least ten wickets for inclusion in the bowling averages. Season strike rates for bowlers are allocated according to the same criterion and can be found in the table of 2007 bowling averages at the end of the book. 'Strike rate' refers to a bowler's record of balls bowled per wicket taken.

In the Overseas tours section, the layout 'England to Pakistan 2005-06 (one-day series)', for example, indicates that a player was selected for only the one-day portion of the tour; the layout 'England to Zimbabwe (one-day series) 2004-05', on the other hand, indicates that the tour consisted of a one-day series only.

The following abbreviations apply in the text: ODI means One-Day International; Twenty20 Int means Twenty20 International; * means not out. In statistics tables FC means all first-class matches, including figures for Test matches; List A – 'full-length' one-day matches classified as such by the ICC (e.g. Friends Provident Trophy, NatWest Pro40 and limited-overs matches against touring sides), including figures for One-Day Internationals; 20/20 Int – Twenty20 Internationals; 20/20 – all 'official' Twenty20 matches, including figures for Twenty20 Internationals and Twenty20 matches between counties and touring sides. Some further abbreviations appear this year in the Best batting and Best bowling sections. These identify particular grounds in cities and towns that boast more than one. A list of the abbreviations featured and the grounds to which they refer is set out opposite.

Please note that Worcestershire ceased awarding caps in 2001 and now present 'colours' to each player who appears for the county in the Championship; that beginning in 2004 Gloucestershire have awarded caps to players on making their first first-class appearance for the county; that Durham ceased awarding caps after the 2005 season, replacing the cap system with grades of player seniority.

A book of this complexity and detail has to be prepared some months in advance of the new cricket season, and occasionally there are recent changes in a player's circumstances or the structure of the game which cannot be included in time. Many examples of facts, statistics and even opinions which can quickly become outdated in the period between the compilation of the book and its publication, months later, will spring to the reader's mind, and I ask him or her to make the necessary commonsense allowance and adjustments.

Chris Marshall, February 2008

GROUND ABBREVIATIONS

Abu Dhabi (SZ) – Sheikh Zayed Stadium
Brisbane (AB) – Allan Border Field
Bulawayo (AC) – Bulawayo Athletic Club
Chittagong (B) – Bir Shrestha Shahid Ruhul Amin Stadium
(Chittagong Divisional Stadium)
Christchurch (VG) – Village Green
Colombo (Bur) – Burgher Recreation Club Ground
Colombo (CCC) – Colts Cricket Club Ground
Colombo (PP) – Police Park Ground
Colombo (PSS) – P Saravanamuttu Stadium
Colombo (RPS) – R Premadasa Stadium
Colombo (SSC) – Sinhalese Sports Club Ground
Delhi (KS) – Karnail Singh Stadium
Harare (A) – Alexandra Sports Club
Harare (T) – Takashinga Sports Club
Johannesburg (WM) – Walter Milton Oval, University of Witwatersrand
Karachi (UBL) – United Bank Limited Sports Complex
Lahore (C) – Lahore City Cricket Association Ground
Melbourne (SK) – St Kilda Cricket Club Ground (Junction Oval)
Paarl (PCC) – Paarl Cricket Club Ground
Portsmouth (BP) – Benjamin's Park
Pretoria (LCD) – LC de Villiers Oval
Pretoria (SCC) – Sinovich Park
Rajkot (MS) – Madhavrao Scindia Cricket Ground
Rawalpindi (KRL) – Khan Research Laboratory Ground
Stellenbosch (US) – Stellenbosch University Ground
Toronto (MSE) – Maple Leaf South-East Ground, King City

THE PLAYERS

KOLPAK

If a cricketer is a national of a country that has an Association Agreement with the EU (such as South Africa or Zimbabwe) and also has a valid UK work permit, he enjoys the same right to work within the EU as an EU citizen and may be eligible to play county cricket as a domestic (that is, non-overseas) player. Cricketers playing in England under this system are commonly referred to as Kolpak players, after the Kolpak ruling, a judgement in the European Court of Justice that found in favour of Maros Kolpak, a Slovakian handball goalkeeper who challenged his status as a non-EU player in Germany.

SOUTH AFRICA AND NEW ZEALAND

Throughout the book there are 100 quiz questions relating to Test and ODI encounters over the years between England and the tourists to these shores in 2008: South Africa and New Zealand.

thewisden cricketer

Love cricket?

Read *The Wisden Cricketer* – the world's no.1 cricket magazine

Every month you'll find...

- **The biggest interviews** with the likes of Kevin Pietersen, Brian Lara, Steve Harmison, Ian Botham and Rahul Dravid
- **Top analysis** from experts such as Sky Sports commentators Nasser Hussain and David Lloyd
- **The best cricket writing** from around the world
- **Fantastic competitions** to win anything from Test match tickets to exotic holidays
- **News, views and gossip** from every county dressing room
- **Relive the greatest moments** in cricket with our regular Eyewitness feature

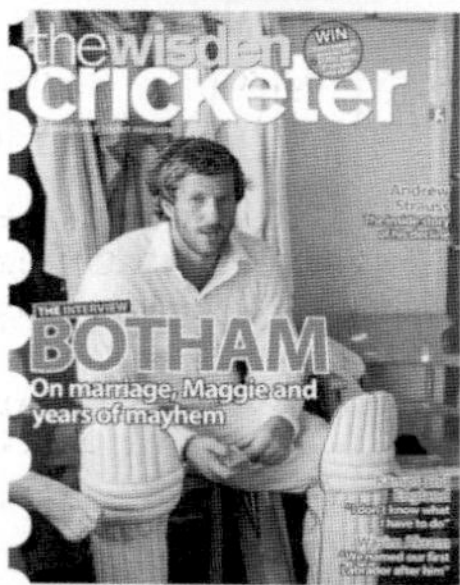

3 ISSUES FOR JUST £1

Take advantage of our special introductory subscription offer and pay just £1 for your first 3 issues. If you like what you see, your subscription will continue at the special low rate of just £18.75 every six issues – saving you 16% on the cover price.

To order, call 0844 815 0864, quoting ref. CWW08

ABDUL RAZZAQ Worcestershire

Name: Abdul Razzaq
Role: Right-hand bat, right-arm fast-medium bowler
Born: 2 December 1979, Lahore, Pakistan
Height: 5ft 11in
County debut: 2002 (Middlesex), 2007 (Worcestershire)
County cap: 2002 (Middlesex), 2007 (Worcestershire colours)
Test debut: 1999-2000
ODI debut: 1996-97
Twenty20 Int debut: 2006
1st-Class 200s: 1
Education: Furqan Model Secondary School, Lahore
Overseas tours: Pakistan U19 to West Indies 1996-97, to South Africa 1996-97, to Australia 1997-98, to South Africa (U19 World Cup) 1997-98; Pakistan A to England 1997, to New Zealand 1998-99; Pakistan to Sri Lanka 1996-97, to UK, Ireland and Netherlands (World Cup) 1999, to Australia 1999-2000, to West Indies 1999-2000, to Sri Lanka 2000, to Kenya (ICC Knockout Trophy) 2000-01, to England 2001, to Bangladesh 2001-02, to Sharjah (v West Indies) 2001-02, to Sri Lanka (ICC Champions Trophy) 2002-03, to Sri Lanka and Sharjah (v Australia) 2002-03, to South Africa 2002-03, to Africa (World Cup) 2002-03, to New Zealand 2003-04, to England (ICC Champions Trophy) 2004, to Australia 2004-05, to India 2004-05, to West Indies 2004-05, to Sri Lanka 2005-06, to Scotland and England 2006, to India (ICC Champions Trophy) 2006-07, plus other one-day series and tournaments in India, South Africa, Toronto, Sharjah, Bangladesh, Singapore, New Zealand, Morocco, Kenya, Sri Lanka, England, Netherlands and Abu Dhabi; Asian Cricket Council XI to Australia (Tsunami Relief Fund) 2004-05, to South Africa (Afro-Asia Cup) 2005-06
Overseas teams played for: Several in Pakistan, including Lahore City 1996-97 – 1998-99, Zarai Taraqiati Bank 2003-04 –
Extras: Formerly known as Abdur Razzaq. Returned figures of 2-68/7-51 on first-class debut for Lahore City v Karachi Whites in the final of the Quaid-e-Azam Trophy at Thatta 1996-97. Took hat-trick (Kaluwitharana, Herath, Pushpakumara) in the second Test v Sri Lanka at Galle 2000, becoming only the second Pakistan bowler, after Wasim Akram (twice), to take a hat-trick in Tests. FICA Young Player of the Year 2001. His series and match awards include Man of the [Test and ODI] Series v West Indies 2001-02, Man of the [ODI] Series v Sri Lanka 2005-06 and Man of the Match v Sri Lanka at Jaipur in the ICC Champions Trophy 2006-07 (4-50/24-ball 38*). Was an

overseas player with Middlesex in 2002 and 2003; was a temporary overseas player with Worcestershire during the 2007 season as a replacement for Phil Jaques and Doug Bollinger
Best batting: 203* Middlesex v Glamorgan, Cardiff 2002
Best bowling: 7-51 Lahore City v Karachi Whites, Thatta 1996-97

2007 Season

	M	Inn	NO	Runs	HS	Avg	100	50	Ct	St	Balls	Runs	Wkts	Avg	BB	5I	10M
Test																	
FC	3	5	1	172	78	43.00	-	1	1	-	405	219	6	36.50	2-35	-	-
ODI																	
List A	4	4	1	73	35 *	24.33	-	-	-	-	138	154	5	30.80	2-19	-	
20/20 Int																	
20/20																	

Career Performances

	M	Inn	NO	Runs	HS	Avg	100	50	Ct	St	Balls	Runs	Wkts	Avg	BB	5I	10M
Test	46	77	9	1946	134	28.61	3	7	15	-	7008	3694	100	36.94	5-35	1	-
FC	108	168	26	4792	203 *	33.74	8	23	28	-	17154	10071	307	32.80	7-51	10	2
ODI	231	198	49	4465	112	29.96	2	22	31	-	9797	7658	246	31.13	6-35	3	
List A	285	244	58	5626	112	30.24	2	30	42	-	12437	9929	330	30.08	6-35	3	
20/20 Int	2	2	1	27	17 *	27.00	-	-	-	-	36	58	3	19.33	3-30	-	
20/20	12	11	2	327	63	36.33	-	2	3	-	258	329	15	21.93	3-30	-	

ACKERMAN, H. D. Leicestershire

Name: Hylton Deon (HD) Ackerman
Role: Right-hand bat, right-arm medium bowler
Born: 14 February 1973, Cape Town, South Africa
Height: 5ft 11in **Weight:** 13st
County debut: 2005
County cap: 2005
Test debut: 1997-98
1000 runs in a season: 2
1st-Class 200s: 2
1st-Class 300s: 1
Place in batting averages: 159th av. 27.80 (2006 5th av. 75.33)
Parents: Hylton and Dawn
Wife and date of marriage: Katherine, 25 April 2004
Family links with cricket: Father (H. M. Ackerman) played first-class cricket in South Africa and also for Northamptonshire
Education: Rondebosch Boys' High School, South Africa

Overseas tours: South Africa U24 to Sri Lanka 1995; Western Province to Australia 1995-96, to Zimbabwe 1996-97; South Africa A to England 1996, to Sri Lanka 1998, to Zimbabwe 2004; South Africa to Zimbabwe 2001-02; Leicestershire to Pakistan and India 2005
Overseas teams played for: Western Province 1993-94 – 2002-03; Gauteng 2003-04; Lions 2004-05; Cape Cobras 2005-06; Warriors 2006-07 –
Career highlights to date: 'Being picked for South Africa in 1998'
Cricket moments to forget: 'Being dropped from South African team'
Cricket superstitions: 'None'
Cricketers particularly admired: Steve Waugh
Other sports followed: Football (Manchester United), 'all sport'
Favourite band: Snow Patrol
Relaxations: 'Golf, movies, reading'
Extras: Scored maiden first-class double century (202*) v Northerns at Centurion in the SuperSport Series 1997-98, in the process breaking Barry Richards's record for the most first-class runs by a South African in a domestic season (ended 1997-98 with 1373 at 50.85). Scored century (145) for South Africa A v Sri Lanka A at Matara 1998, winning Man of the Match award. Man of the SuperSport Series 2000-01. His other domestic awards include Man of the Match v Griqualand West at Kimberley (81) and v KwaZulu-Natal at Durban (86*), both in the Standard Bank Cup 2003-04. Captain of Leicestershire 2005. Scored 309* v Glamorgan at Cardiff 2006, setting a new record for the highest individual first-class score by a Leicestershire player; also scored 62 in second innings to set a new record individual match aggregate for the county (371). Leicestershire Cricketer of the Year 2006. Is not considered an overseas player
Opinions on cricket: 'Young players are good for the game, but let's not forget that mature, older players still have a lot to offer. People are too quick to push young players and get rid of experienced ones.'
Best batting: 309* Leicestershire v Glamorgan, Cardiff 2006

2007 Season

	M	Inn	NO	Runs	HS	Avg	100	50	Ct	St	Balls	Runs	Wkts	Avg	BB	5I	10M
Test																	
FC	15	26	0	723	153	27.80	3	1	15	-	0	0	0		-	-	-
ODI																	
List A	14	14	0	476	83	34.00	-	5	8	-	0	0	0		-	-	
20/20 Int																	
20/20	5	5	1	157	66	39.25	-	1	-	-	0	0	0		-	-	

Career Performances

	M	Inn	NO	Runs	HS	Avg	100	50	Ct	St	Balls	Runs	Wkts	Avg	BB	5I	10M
Test	4	8	0	161	57	20.12	-	1	1	-	0	0	0		-	-	-
FC	178	298	27	11729	309 *	43.28	31	64	144	-	102	57	0		-	-	-
ODI																	
List A	185	178	23	5095	114 *	32.87	1	37	69	-	48	52	0		-	-	
20/20 Int																	
20/20	35	35	4	1224	87	39.48	-	11	10	-	0	0	0		-	-	

ADAMS, A. R. — Nottinghamshire

Name: <u>André</u> Ryan Adams
Role: Right-hand bat, right-arm fast-medium bowler
Born: 17 July 1975, Auckland, New Zealand
Height: 5ft 11in **Weight:** 14st 7lbs
Nickname: Dre, Doctor
County debut: 2004 (Essex), 2007 (Nottinghamshire)
County cap: 2004 (Essex)
Test debut: 2001-02
ODI debut: 2000-01
Twenty20 Int debut: 2004-05
Place in batting averages: (2006 119th av. 32.85)
Place in bowling averages: 101st av. 35.78 (2006 102nd av. 39.52)
Parents: Felise du Chateau and Keith Adams
Wife and date of marriage: Ardene, 5 April 2003
Children: Danté, 24 February 2004
Family links with cricket: 'Parents West Indian!'
Education: West Lake Boys, Auckland

Overseas tours: New Zealand to Sharjah (ARY Gold Cup) 2000-01, to Australia 2001-02 (VB Series), to Sharjah (Sharjah Cup) 2001-02, to Pakistan 2002, to Africa (World Cup) 2002-03, to Sri Lanka 2003 (Bank Alfalah Cup), to England 2004 (NatWest Series), to Bangladesh 2004-05 (one-day series), to Zimbabwe 2005-06 (Videocon Tri-Series), to South Africa (one-day series) 2005-06
Overseas teams played for: Takapuna, Auckland; Auckland 1997-98 –
Career highlights to date: 'Test victory against England in final game (Auckland) in 2002, my Test debut'
Cricket moments to forget: 'Losing to India in 2003 World Cup'
Cricket superstitions: 'None'
Cricketers particularly admired: Viv Richards, Michael Holding
Other sports followed: Rugby (Auckland Blues, All Blacks)
Favourite band: Ryan Edwards
Relaxations: Xbox
Extras: Member of New Zealand team to 1998 Indoor Cricket World Cup. Leading wicket-taker in 1999-2000 Shell Cup one-day competition (28; av. 13.50). His ODI match awards include Man of the Match v India at Queenstown 2002-03 (5-22) and v West Indies at Port Elizabeth in the 2002-03 World Cup (35*/4-44). An overseas player with Essex July to September 2004 and in 2005 and 2006. Scored maiden first-class century (91-ball 124) v Leicestershire at Leicester 2004 in his first Championship innings and batting at No. 9. Took Championship hat-trick (Burns, Jayasuriya, Hildreth) v Somerset at Taunton 2005. Was a temporary overseas player with Nottinghamshire during the 2007 season as a replacement for David Hussey
Best batting: 124 Essex v Leicestershire, Leicester 2004
Best bowling: 6-25 Auckland v Wellington, Auckland 2004-05

2007 Season

	M	Inn	NO	Runs	HS	Avg	100	50	Ct	St	Balls	Runs	Wkts	Avg	BB	5I	10M
Test																	
FC	4	6	1	104	33	20.80	-	-	1	-	823	501	14	35.78	4-74	-	-
ODI																	
List A	2	2	0	14	9	7.00	-	-	2	-	66	77	2	38.50	2-33	-	
20/20 Int																	
20/20																	

Career Performances

	M	Inn	NO	Runs	HS	Avg	100	50	Ct	St	Balls	Runs	Wkts	Avg	BB	5I	10M
Test	1	2	0	18	11	9.00	-	-	1	-	190	105	6	17.50	3-44	-	-
FC	78	104	9	2380	124	25.05	3	10	49	-	15378	7524	292	25.76	6-25	10	1
ODI	42	34	10	419	45	17.45	-	-	8	-	1885	1643	53	31.00	5-22	1	
List A	119	87	21	1190	90 *	18.03	-	1	31	-	5483	4353	153	28.45	5-7	3	
20/20 Int	4	2	1	13	7	13.00	-	-	1	-	77	105	3	35.00	2-20	-	
20/20	20	16	5	224	54 *	20.36	-	1	4	-	396	501	27	18.55	3-27	-	

ADAMS, C. J. Sussex

Name: Christopher (Chris) John Adams
Role: Right-hand bat, right-arm medium bowler, slip fielder, county captain
Born: 6 May 1970, Whitwell, Derbyshire
Height: 6ft **Weight:** 13st 7lbs
Nickname: Grizzly, Grizwold
County debut: 1988 (Derbyshire), 1998 (Sussex)
County cap: 1992 (Derbyshire), 1998 (Sussex)
Benefit: 2003 (Sussex)
Test debut: 1999-2000
ODI debut: 1998
1000 runs in a season: 9
1st-Class 200s: 4
Place in batting averages: 44th av. 46.81 (2006 40th av. 50.75)
Parents: John and Eluned (Lyn)
Wife and date of marriage: Samantha Claire, 26 September 1992
Children: Georgia Louise, 4 October 1993; Sophie Victoria, 13 October 1998
Family links with cricket: Brother David played 2nd XI cricket for Derbyshire and Gloucestershire. Father played for Yorkshire Schools and uncle played for Essex 2nd XI
Education: Chesterfield Boys Grammar School; Repton School
Qualifications: 6 O-levels, NCA coaching awards, Executive Development Certificate in Coaching and Management Skills
Overseas tours: Repton School to Barbados 1987; England NCA North to Northern Ireland 1987; England XI to New Zealand (Cricket Max) 1997; England to South Africa and Zimbabwe 1999-2000; Sussex to Grenada 2001, 2002; Blade to Barbados 2001
Overseas teams played for: Takapuna, New Zealand 1987-88; Te Puke, New Zealand 1989-90; Primrose, Cape Town, South Africa 1991-92; Canberra Comets, Australia 1998-99; University of NSW, Australia 2000-01
Cricket moments to forget: 'The death of Umer Rashid in Grenada [2002]'
Cricketers particularly admired: Ian Botham
Other sports played: Golf, football, 'dabbled a bit with ice hockey'
Other sports followed: Football ('Arsenal!')
Relaxations: 'Family time'
Extras: Represented English Schools U15 and U19, MCC Schools U19 and, in 1989, England YC. Took two catches as 12th man for England v India at Old Trafford in 1990. Set Derbyshire record for the highest score in the Sunday League (141*) v Kent at Chesterfield 1992. Sussex Player of the Year 1998 and 1999. Set individual one-day record score for Sussex of 163 (off 107 balls) v Middlesex in the National League at

Arundel 1999. Sussex 1st XI Fielder of the Season 2000. BBC South Cricketer of the Year 2001. One of *Wisden*'s Five Cricketers of the Year 2004. Scored 200 against Northamptonshire at Hove 2004, in the process becoming the third batsman (after Mark Ramprakash and Carl Hooper) to score a century against all 18 counties. Captain of Sussex since 1998

Best batting: 239 Derbyshire v Hampshire, Southampton 1996

Best bowling: 4-28 Sussex v Durham, Riverside 2001

2007 Season

	M	Inn	NO	Runs	HS	Avg	100	50	Ct	St	Balls	Runs	Wkts	Avg	BB	5I	10M
Test																	
FC	15	24	2	1030	193	46.81	3	3	27	-	24	9	0		-	-	-
ODI																	
List A	11	9	1	226	70	28.25	-	1	4	-	0	0	0		-	-	
20/20 Int																	
20/20	9	9	3	229	56 *	38.16	-	1	2	-	0	0	0		-	-	

Career Performances

	M	Inn	NO	Runs	HS	Avg	100	50	Ct	St	Balls	Runs	Wkts	Avg	BB	5I	10M
Test	5	8	0	104	31	13.00	-	-	6	-	120	59	1	59.00	1-42	-	-
FC	321	523	38	19061	239	39.30	48	91	391	-	3276	1922	41	46.87	4-28	-	-
ODI	5	4	0	71	42	17.75	-	-	3	-	0	0	0		-	-	
List A	357	336	56	11176	163	39.91	20	69	165	-	1391	1217	32	38.03	5-16	1	
20/20 Int																	
20/20	34	30	6	738	63	30.75	-	2	9	-	0	0	0		-	-	

1. Who were the captains at The Oval in 1965 when England and South Africa met in their final official Test before the latter's isolation?

ADAMS, J. H. K. Hampshire

Name: James (Jimmy) Henry Kenneth Adams
Role: Left-hand opening bat, left-arm medium bowler
Born: 23 September 1980, Winchester
Height: 6ft 1in **Weight:** 14st 7lbs
Nickname: Bison, Nugget, Hippy, HC
County debut: 2002
County cap: 2006
1000 runs in a season: 1
1st-Class 200s: 1
Place in batting averages: 68th av. 40.68 (2006 61st av. 45.11)
Parents: Jenny and Mike
Marital status: Single
Family links with cricket: 'Dad played a bit for Kent Schoolboys. Brothers Ben and Tom, Hampshire age groups'
Education: Sherborne School; Loughborough University
Qualifications: BSc Human Biology, ECB Levels I and II coaching
Career outside cricket: 'House husband would be ideal'
Off-season: 'Hopefully go off in the New Year but not a lot until then; probably coaching and sorting house out'
Overseas tours: West of England to West Indies 1995; England U19 to Sri Lanka (U19 World Cup) 1999-2000; Sherborne School to Pakistan
Overseas teams played for: Woodville, Adelaide 1999-2000; Melville, Perth 2000-01; Bayswater-Morley, Perth 2004-05
Career highlights to date: 'Maiden hundred and county cap'
Cricket moments to forget: 'Kidderminster, June 2000'
Cricket superstitions: 'Routines more than anything – I like a long breakfast, though'
Cricketers particularly admired: 'M. Parker, R. Smith, B. Lara …'
Young players to look out for: Liam Dawson, Hamza Riazuddin, Ben Howell
Other sports played: 'Bit of five-a-side, but not as much in terms of other sport as I'd like'; hockey (Dorset age group when 14)
Other sports followed: 'Most sports' – football (Aston Villa), NFL
Favourite band: 'Zeppelin, Rose Hill Drive, Pumpkins etc.'
Relaxations: 'Music, reading and food'
Extras: Played in U15 World Cup 1996. Hampshire Young Player of the Year 1998. Represented England U19 2000. Played for Loughborough UCCE 2002-04 (captain 2003), scoring a century in each innings (103/113) v Kent at Canterbury 2002. Represented British Universities 2002-04 (captain 2003). Scored maiden

Championship century (168*) as Hampshire scored 404-5 to beat Yorkshire at Headingley 2006

Opinions on cricket: 'Twenty20 pulls the crowds and draws a younger audience which is great, but I think the powers that be may bleed it dry in an attempt to maximise profits. All pretty good in general.'

Best batting: 262* Hampshire v Nottinghamshire, Trent Bridge 2006

Best bowling: 2-16 Hampshire v Durham, Riverside 2004

2007 Season

	M	Inn	NO	Runs	HS	Avg	100	50	Ct	St	Balls	Runs	Wkts	Avg	BB	5I	10M
Test																	
FC	11	20	1	773	110	40.68	1	5	10	-	240	137	3	45.66	2-37	-	-
ODI																	
List A	6	5	1	110	38	27.50	-	-	2	-	54	55	1	55.00	1-34	-	
20/20 Int																	
20/20	5	2	0	12	12	6.00	-	-	2	-	30	53	0		-	-	

Career Performances

	M	Inn	NO	Runs	HS	Avg	100	50	Ct	St	Balls	Runs	Wkts	Avg	BB	5I	10M
Test																	
FC	64	115	11	3516	262 *	33.80	4	17	47	-	769	527	10	52.70	2-16	-	-
ODI																	
List A	14	13	1	217	40	18.08	-	-	6	-	55	61	1	61.00	1-34	-	
20/20 Int																	
20/20	12	5	2	45	17 *	15.00	-	-	3	-	36	60	0		-	-	

2. Who became the fourth batsman in Test history to score a double century in consecutive matches, in the second Test between England and South Africa at Lord's in 2003?

ADSHEAD, S. J. — Gloucestershire

Name: Stephen John Adshead
Role: Right-hand bat, wicket-keeper
Born: 29 January 1980, Worcester
Height: 5ft 8in **Weight:** 13st
Nickname: Adders, Top Shelf
County debut: 2000 (Leicestershire), 2003 (Worcestershire), 2004 (Gloucestershire)
County cap: 2003 (Worcestershire colours), 2004 (Gloucestershire)
Place in batting averages: 168th av. 26.29 (2006 147th av. 29.86)
Parents: David and Julie
Wife: Becky
Family links with cricket: Father and brother club cricketers in Worcester; mother keen spectator
Education: Brideley Moor HS, Redditch
Qualifications: 9 GCSEs, 3 A-levels, ECB Level 2 coaching
Career outside cricket: Coaching
Overseas tours: Leicestershire to Potchefstroom, South Africa 2001
Overseas teams played for: Fish Hoek, Cape Town 1998-99; Witwatersrand Technical, Johannesburg 1999-2000; Central Hawke's Bay, New Zealand 2000-01
Career highlights to date: 'Winning C&G final at Lord's 2004'
Cricket moments to forget: 'The whole 2002 season was a fairly miserable one'
Cricket superstitions: 'None'
Cricketers particularly admired: Alec Stewart, Steve Waugh
Young players to look out for: Steve Davies
Favourite band: U2
Relaxations: 'Spending as much time as possible with my wife Becky; gym, eating'
Extras: Scored 187-minute 57* to help save match v Lancashire at Cheltenham 2004
Best batting: 148* Gloucestershire v Surrey, The Oval 2005

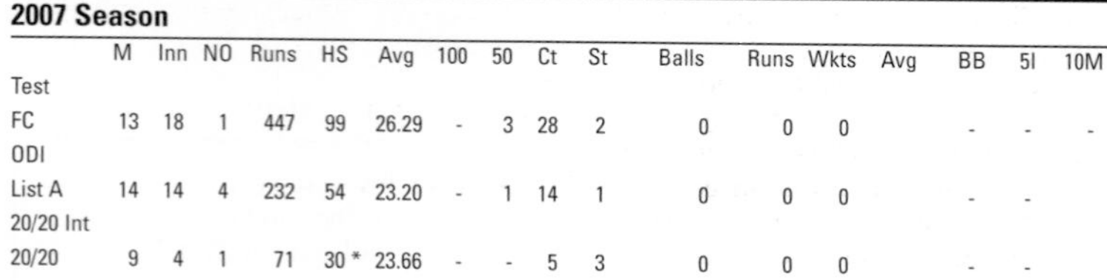

2007 Season

	M	Inn	NO	Runs	HS	Avg	100	50	Ct	St	Balls	Runs	Wkts	Avg	BB	5I	10M
Test																	
FC	13	18	1	447	99	26.29	-	3	28	2	0	0	0		-	-	-
ODI																	
List A	14	14	4	232	54	23.20	-	1	14	1	0	0	0		-	-	
20/20 Int																	
20/20	9	4	1	71	30 *	23.66	-	-	5	3	0	0	0		-	-	

Career Performances

	M	Inn	NO	Runs	HS	Avg	100	50	Ct	St	Balls	Runs	Wkts	Avg	BB	5I	10M
Test																	
FC	65	107	17	2765	148 *	30.72	1	17	161	14	0	0	0		-	-	-
ODI																	
List A	69	63	14	1028	77 *	20.97	-	4	79	26	0	0	0		-	-	
20/20 Int																	
20/20	33	21	7	310	81	22.14	-	1	12	14	0	0	0		-	-	

AFZAAL, U. Surrey

Name: Usman Afzaal
Role: Left-hand bat, slow left-arm bowler
Born: 9 June 1977, Rawalpindi, Pakistan
Height: 6ft **Weight:** 12st 7lbs
Nickname: Saeed, Gulfraz, Usy Bhai, Trevor
County debut: 1995 (Nottinghamshire), 2004 (Northamptonshire)
County cap: 2000 (Nottinghamshire), 2005 (Northamptonshire)
Test debut: 2001
1000 runs in a season: 6
Place in batting averages: 99th av. 35.62 (2006 41st av. 50.57)
Parents: Firdous and Shafi Mahmood
Marital status: Single
Family links with cricket: Older brother Kamran played for NAYC and for Nottinghamshire U15-U19 ('top player'); younger brother Aqib played for Notts and England U15; 'Uncle Mac and Uncle Raja great players'
Education: Manvers Pierrepont School; South Notts College
Qualifications: Coaching certificates
Overseas tours: Nottinghamshire to South Africa; England U19 to West Indies 1994-95, to Zimbabwe 1995-96; 'the great ZRK tour to Lahore, Pakistan' 2000; England A to West Indies 2000-01; England to India and New Zealand 2001-02
Overseas teams played for: Victoria Park, Perth
Career highlights to date: 'Playing for England in the Ashes [2001]'
Cricket moments to forget: 'Every time I get out'
Cricketers particularly admired: David Gower, Saeed Anwar, Ian Botham, Clive Rice, Uncle Raja and Uncle Mac
Other sports played: Indoor football

Other sports followed: Football ('a bit of Man U')
Relaxations: 'Praying; spending time with friends and family; listening to Indian music'
Extras: Played for England U15 and U17. Won Denis Compton Award 1996. Took wicket (Adam Gilchrist) with third ball in Test cricket v Australia at The Oval 2001. C&G Man of the Match award for his 3-8 (from four overs) and 64* v Ireland at Clontarf 2002. Left Northamptonshire at the end of the 2007 season and has joined Surrey for 2008
Best batting: 168* Northamptonshire v Essex, Northampton 2005
Best bowling: 4-101 Nottinghamshire v Gloucestershire, Trent Bridge 1998

2007 Season

	M	Inn	NO	Runs	HS	Avg	100	50	Ct	St	Balls	Runs	Wkts	Avg	BB	5I	10M
Test																	
FC	8	16	0	570	73	35.62	-	5	3	-	18	10	1	10.00	1-5	-	-
ODI																	
List A	6	6	0	309	132	51.50	1	1	1	-	24	41	0			-	-
20/20 Int																	
20/20	6	5	0	108	54	21.60	-	1	-	-	0	0	0			-	-

Career Performances

	M	Inn	NO	Runs	HS	Avg	100	50	Ct	St	Balls	Runs	Wkts	Avg	BB	5I	10M
Test	3	6	1	83	54	16.60	-	1	-	-	54	49	1	49.00	1-49	-	-
FC	190	330	34	11129	168 *	37.59	26	56	90	-	7485	4118	79	52.12	4-101	-	-
ODI																	
List A	155	144	21	4541	132	36.91	5	30	39	-	1065	1008	39	25.84	3-4	-	
20/20 Int																	
20/20	31	28	5	490	64 *	21.30	-	2	5	-	48	66	2	33.00	2-15	-	

AGA, R. G. — Sussex

Name: Ragheb Gul Aga
Role: Right-hand bat, right-arm medium-fast bowler; all-rounder
Born: 10 July 1984, Nairobi, Kenya
Height: 6ft 3in **Weight:** 13st 3lbs
Nickname: Rags
County debut: 2007 (one-day)
ODI debut: 2004
Parents: Munawar and Zeenat
Marital status: Single
Education: Hillcrest Secondary School, Kenya; Brighton University (Eastbourne Campus)

Qualifications: 'Sport and exercise scientist – specialist area environmental physiology'
Career outside cricket: 'BDM MKK Sports. Eastbourne College hockey coach'
Off-season: 'Staying at home – working on improving my game with coaches at SCCC'
Overseas tours: Kenya U19 to New Zealand (U19 World Cup) 2001-02 (c); Kenya to West Indies (Carib Beer Cup) 2003-04, to England (ICC Champions Trophy) 2004; Kenya VI to Hong Kong 2004, plus other tours with Kenya U19 and Kenya
Career highlights to date: 'Man of the Match v India A in Nairobi [2004] – 4-18 to win match'
Cricket moments to forget: 'First club game, aged 16 – ran out club captain'
Cricketers particularly admired: Jacques Kallis, Chris Cairns, Wasim Akram
Young players to look out for: Andy Hodd
Other sports played: Hockey (Eastbourne 1st XI – Player of the Season 2006-07; Eastbourne U21 captain – Sussex Cup winners 2005)
Other sports followed: Football (Spurs), rugby (Leicester Tigers)
Injuries: Out for two weeks with a shoulder impingement
Relaxations: 'Cooking (and eating), reading'
Extras: Made first-class debut for Kenya v Jamaica in Grenada in the Carib Beer Cup 2003-04. Man of the Match v India A in the Kenya Triangular Tournament in Nairobi 2004 (17-ball 16 followed by 4-18). Appointed stand-in captain of Kenya for the semi-final of the ICC Inter-Continental Cup v Scotland in Abu Dhabi 2004. Brighton University Sporting Hall of Fame: Achievement in Cricket (with Kenya) 2006. Eastbourne CC 1st XI Player of the Season 2007
Best batting: 43 Kenya v Namibia, Nairobi (AK) 2004
Best bowling: 4-71 Kenya v Guyana, Georgetown 2003-04

2007 Season

	M	Inn	NO	Runs	HS	Avg	100	50	Ct	St	Balls	Runs	Wkts	Avg	BB	5I	10M
Test																	
FC																	
ODI																	
List A	1	0	0	0	0		-	-	-	-	48	64	1	64.00	1-64	-	
20/20 Int																	
20/20																	

Career Performances

	M	Inn	NO	Runs	HS	Avg	100	50	Ct	St	Balls	Runs	Wkts	Avg	BB	5I	10M
Test																	
FC	8	16	2	138	43	9.85	-	-	6	-	799	436	13	33.53	4-71	-	-
ODI	2	2	0	1	1	.50	-	-	-	-	78	87	2	43.50	2-17	-	
List A	10	9	0	68	16	7.55	-	-	3	-	342	336	11	30.54	4-14	-	
20/20 Int																	
20/20																	

AHMED, J. S. — Essex

Name: Jahid Sheikh Ahmed
Role: Right-hand bat, right-arm medium-fast bowler
Born: 20 February 1986, Chelmsford
Height: 5ft 11in **Weight:** 11st 7lbs
Nickname: J, Jarhead, Jay-Z
County debut: 2005
Parents: Sheikh Faruque Ahmed
Marital status: Single
Education: St Peter's High School; University of East London ('third and last year – Sports Science')
Qualifications: GCSEs, A-levels
Career outside cricket: 'University'
Off-season: 'University, gym, training; tour to Dubai'
Overseas tours: Essex to South Africa 2006
Career highlights to date: 'Getting 4-32 against Sri Lanka 2006' *(List A debut)*
Cricketers particularly admired: Brett Lee
Young players to look out for: Stuart Broad
Other sports played: Badminton, football; cross country (Essex)
Other sports followed: Football (Arsenal)
Favourite band: 2Pac and the Outlawz
Relaxations: 'Listening to music, going out, chilling with friends, snooker, swimming pool, sauna and jacuzzi'
Extras: Essex Academy 2004. Community award from Bangladeshi channel, presented by the High Commissioner. 'First British Bengali to play first-class cricket in this country'
Opinions on cricket: 'Standard of the game is very high. Kolpak players good for short term but not long term. One overseas player is good.'

Best batting: 14* Essex v Worcestershire, Worcester 2005
Best bowling: 2-41 Essex v Middlesex, Chelmsford 2007

2007 Season

	M	Inn	NO	Runs	HS	Avg	100	50	Ct	St	Balls	Runs	Wkts	Avg	BB	5I	10M
Test																	
FC	3	3	2	14	7 *	14.00	-	-	2	-	171	143	3	47.66	2-41	-	-
ODI																	
List A	2	2	2	1	1 *		-	-	2	-	30	32	0		-	-	
20/20 Int																	
20/20																	

Career Performances

	M	Inn	NO	Runs	HS	Avg	100	50	Ct	St	Balls	Runs	Wkts	Avg	BB	5I	10M
Test																	
FC	5	4	3	28	14 *	28.00	-	-	3	-	459	360	6	60.00	2-41	-	-
ODI																	
List A	6	2	2	1	1 *		-	-	2	-	240	202	10	20.20	4-32	-	
20/20 Int																	
20/20	2	0	0	0	0		-	-	-	-	36	56	2	28.00	1-25	-	

AHMED, M. Worcestershire

Name: Mehraj Ahmed
Role: Right-hand bat, right-arm fast bowler
Born: 5 January 1989, Birmingham
Weight: 13st 3lbs
Nickname: Maz
County debut: No first-team appearance
Parents: Altaf and Nassim
Marital status: Single
Education: Kingsbury School; Josiah Mason College
Qualifications: Level 1 Maths, Level 2 English
Career highlights to date: 'Playing for England'
Cricket moments to forget: 'None'
Cricket superstitions: 'I wear my silver chain round my neck'
Cricketers particularly admired: Waqar Younis
Young players to look out for: Aneesh Kapil

Other sports played: Football, rugby ('just for college')
Other sports followed: Football (Manchester United)
Injuries: Out for six weeks with a side strain
Favourite band: G-Unit
Relaxations: 'Listening to music'
Extras: Bowling has been clocked at 87mph. Player of the year three times for club
Opinions on cricket: 'I love the game and it can't get any better at the moment.'

ALI, K. — Worcestershire

Name: Kabir Ali
Role: Right-hand bat, right-arm medium-fast bowler
Born: 24 November 1980, Birmingham
Height: 6ft **Weight:** 12st 7lbs
Nickname: Kabby, Taxi
County debut: 1999
County colours: 2002
Test debut: 2003
ODI debut: 2003
50 wickets in a season: 4
Place in batting averages: 273rd av. 11.10 (2006 261st av. 12.00)
Place in bowling averages: 27th av. 24.44 (2006 36th av. 29.02)
Parents: Shabir Ali and M. Begum
Marital status: Single
Family links with cricket: Father played club cricket. Cousins Moeen and Omar also play for Worcestershire. Cousin Kadeer plays for Gloucestershire
Education: Moseley School; Wolverhampton University
Qualifications: GNVQ Leisure and Tourism, coaching
Overseas tours: Warwickshire U19 to Cape Town 1998; ECB National Academy to Australia and Sri Lanka 2002-03; England to Australia 2002-03 (VB Series), to South Africa 2004-05 (one-day series), to Pakistan 2005-06 (one-day series), to India 2005-06 (one-day series); England VI to Hong Kong 2003, 2004, 2005, 2006; England A to West Indies 2005-06; England Lions to India 2007-08
Overseas teams played for: Midland-Guildford, Perth; Rajasthan, India 2006-07
Career highlights to date: 'Playing for England'
Cricketers particularly admired: Wasim Akram, Glenn McGrath
Young players to look out for: Moeen Ali, Omar Ali, Atif Ali
Other sports played: Football, snooker
Other sports followed: Football, snooker

Relaxations: 'Playing snooker and spending time with family and friends'
Extras: Warwickshire Youth Young Player of the Year award. Represented England U19. NBC Denis Compton Award for the most promising young Worcestershire player 2000. Junior Royals Player of the Year 2001. Worcestershire Player of the Year 2002. PCA Young Player of the Year 2002, 2003. Made Test debut in the fourth Test v South Africa at Headingley 2003, taking a wicket (Neil McKenzie) with his fifth ball. Worcestershire Young Player of the Year 2003. Don Kenyon Award 2003. Player of the Final in the Hong Kong Sixes 2004
Best batting: 84* Worcestershire v Durham, Stockton 2003
Best bowling: 8-50 Worcestershire v Lancashire, Old Trafford 2007
Stop press: Forced to withdraw from England Lions tour of India 2007-08 with an ankle injury

2007 Season

	M	Inn	NO	Runs	HS	Avg	100	50	Ct	St	Balls	Runs	Wkts	Avg	BB	5I	10M
Test																	
FC	14	19	0	211	39	11.10	-	-	1	-	2393	1369	56	24.44	8-50	3	2
ODI																	
List A	16	9	3	64	22 *	10.66	-	-	2	-	654	603	29	20.79	5-46	1	
20/20 Int																	
20/20	7	6	2	67	25 *	16.75	-	-	-	-	125	163	9	18.11	3-18	-	

Career Performances

	M	Inn	NO	Runs	HS	Avg	100	50	Ct	St	Balls	Runs	Wkts	Avg	BB	5I	10M
Test	1	2	0	10	9	5.00	-	-	-	-	216	136	5	27.20	3-80	-	-
FC	97	133	19	2002	84 *	17.56	-	7	24	-	16657	9929	359	27.65	8-50	16	4
ODI	14	9	3	93	39 *	15.50	-	-	1	-	673	682	20	34.10	4-45	-	
List A	146	88	24	975	92	15.23	-	3	25	-	6259	5371	216	24.86	5-36	2	
20/20 Int																	
20/20	16	12	3	152	49	16.88	-	-	5	-	327	431	19	22.68	3-18	-	

3. Who became the first South Africa player to score a century in each innings of a Test (189/104*) at Trent Bridge in 1947?

ALI, K. Gloucestershire

Name: Kadeer Ali
Role: Right-hand opening bat, right-arm medium bowler
Born: 7 March 1983, Birmingham
Height: 6ft 2in **Weight:** 12st
Nickname: Kads, Kaddy, Rat
County debut: 2000 (Worcestershire), 2005 (Gloucestershire)
County cap: 2002 (Worcestershire colours), 2005 (Gloucestershire)
Place in batting averages: 115th av. 33.44 (2006 75th av. 39.71)
Parents: Munir Ali and Maqsood Begum
Marital status: Single
Family links with cricket: 'Father has cricket academy – "Streets to Arena". Cousin Kabir Ali plays for Worcestershire. Brothers Moeen and Omar Ali also play for Worcestershire'
Education: Handsworth Grammar; Moseley Sixth Form College
Qualifications: 5 GCSEs, Level 1 coach
Off-season: 'Training in Bristol'
Overseas tours: England U19 to India 2000-01, to Australia and (U19 World Cup) New Zealand 2001-02; England A to Malaysia and India 2003-04
Overseas teams played for: WA University, Perth 2002-03; Lahore Model Town CC, Pakistan 2005; PTCL, Pakistan 2005-06
Career highlights to date: 'Playing in Twenty20 finals day; playing in the final against Kent. Playing against Australia'
Cricket moments to forget: 'My debut against Glamorgan – got a pair'
Cricket superstitions: 'None'
Cricketers particularly admired: Graeme Hick, Younus Khan
Young players to look out for: Moeen Ali, Omar Ali, Aatif Ali
Other sports played: Football, snooker
Other sports followed: Football (Birmingham City FC)
Favourite band: Yusuf Islam (formerly Cat Stevens)
Relaxations: 'Cinema; relaxing with friends and family'
Extras: Young Player awards at Warwickshire CCC. Represented England U19 2000-02; England U19 Player of Series v India U19 2002. NBC Denis Compton Award for the most promising young Worcestershire player 2001, 2002. ECB National Academy 2003-04. Became first player to hit a ball over the Basil D'Oliveira Stand at Worcester, v New Zealanders 2004. Gloucestershire Young Player of the Year and Players' Player of the Year 2007

Opinions on cricket: 'Twenty20 is definitely the way forward.'
Best batting: 145 Gloucestershire v Northamptonshire, Northampton 2006
Best bowling: 1-4 Gloucestershire v Glamorgan, Bristol 2005

2007 Season

	M	Inn	NO	Runs	HS	Avg	100	50	Ct	St	Balls	Runs	Wkts	Avg	BB	5I	10M
Test																	
FC	16	28	1	903	140	33.44	2	4	8	-	0	0	0		-	-	-
ODI																	
List A	14	14	0	590	114	42.14	2	3	4	-	0	0	0		-	-	
20/20 Int																	
20/20	6	6	2	167	47 *	41.75	-	-	-	-	0	0	0		-	-	

Career Performances

	M	Inn	NO	Runs	HS	Avg	100	50	Ct	St	Balls	Runs	Wkts	Avg	BB	5I	10M
Test																	
FC	65	118	5	3041	145	26.91	3	18	32	-	456	289	3	96.33	1-4	-	-
ODI																	
List A	41	41	1	1231	114	30.77	2	8	6	-	63	59	1	59.00	1-4	-	
20/20 Int																	
20/20	12	12	2	289	53	28.90	-	1	3	-	0	0	0		-	-	

ALI, M. M. — Worcestershire

Name: Moeen Munir Ali
Role: Left-hand bat, right-arm off-spin bowler; batting all-rounder
Born: 18 June 1987, Birmingham
Height: 6ft **Weight:** 11st
Nickname: Mo
County debut: 2005 (Warwickshire), 2007 (Worcestershire)
County colours: 2007 (Worcestershire)
Place in batting averages: (2006 211th av. 19.66)
Parents: Munir Ali and Maqsood Begum
Marital status: Single
Family links with cricket: Brother Kadeer plays for Gloucestershire; younger brother Omar and cousin Kabir are also at Worcestershire. Father has 'Streets to Arena' cricket academy
Education: Moseley School

Qualifications: GCSEs and Leisure and Tourism
Off-season: 'Training with the EPP [England Performance Programme] Squad up to Christmas'
Overseas tours: 'Streets to Arena' to Pakistan 2002; England U19 to India 2004-05, to Bangladesh 2005-06, to Sri Lanka (U19 World Cup) 2005-06 (c); England Performance Programme to India 2007-08
Overseas teams played for: Claremont-Nedlands, Perth 2003-04
Career highlights to date: 'Winning Pro40 in 2007. Scoring a hundred off 46 balls [v Northamptonshire at Kidderminster in the Pro40 2007]'
Cricket moments to forget: 'Don't have any'
Cricket superstitions: 'None'
Cricketers particularly admired: Saeed Anwar, Graeme Hick, Kumar Sangakkara
Young players to look out for: Omar Ali, Atif Ali, Mehraj Ahmed
Other sports followed: Football (Liverpool)
Favourite band: Yusuf Islam (formerly Cat Stevens)
Relaxations: 'Praying'
Extras: Represented England U15 2002. Won five Warwickshire youth awards from age of 11. Represented England U19 2004, 2005, 2006
Opinions on cricket: 'The quicker the game gets the better, but four-day cricket is also very important.'
Best batting: 85 Worcestershire v Sussex, Hove 2007
Best bowling: 2-50 Warwickshire v Lancashire, Edgbaston 2006

2007 Season

	M	Inn	NO	Runs	HS	Avg	100	50	Ct	St	Balls	Runs	Wkts	Avg	BB	5I	10M
Test																	
FC	3	5	0	180	85	36.00	-	2	-	-	126	106	0		-	-	-
ODI																	
List A	11	11	0	359	100	32.63	1	2	2	-	120	107	4	26.75	2-45	-	
20/20 Int																	
20/20	4	3	0	33	12	11.00	-	-	-	-	0	0	0		-	-	

Career Performances

	M	Inn	NO	Runs	HS	Avg	100	50	Ct	St	Balls	Runs	Wkts	Avg	BB	5I	10M
Test																	
FC	10	15	0	414	85	27.60	-	5	4	-	584	439	3	146.33	2-50	-	-
ODI																	
List A	20	19	1	532	100	29.55	1	4	3	-	244	222	5	44.40	2-45	-	
20/20 Int																	
20/20	4	3	0	33	12	11.00	-	-	-	-	0	0	0		-	-	

ALI, O. M. — Worcestershire

Name: Omar Munir Ali
Role: Left-hand bat, right-arm medium bowler
Born: 29 August 1988, Birmingham
Height: 5ft 11in **Weight:** 11st 7lbs
Nickname: Omz, Omzy
County debut: No first-team appearance
Parents: Munir Ali and Maqsood Begum
Marital status: Single
Family links with cricket: 'Father runs cricket academy ("Streets to Arena"); Kadeer Ali (Gloucestershire), Moeen Ali (Worcestershire) – brothers; Kabir Ali (Worcestershire) – cousin'
Education: Moseley School
Qualifications: GCSEs
Off-season: 'Training with Worcestershire'
Overseas tours: 'Tour to Pakistan 2005; tours to Dubai 2004, 2006'
Career highlights to date: 'Representing Worcestershire second team'
Cricketers particularly admired: Brian Lara, Saeed Anwar, Mark Ramprakash
Young players to look out for: Moeen Ali, Aatif Ali, Behram Ali
Other sports played: Football, snooker
Other sports followed: Football (Birmingham City)
Favourite band: Usher, Ne-Yo, Timbaland, Massari, B2K, Sizzla
Relaxations: 'Chilling with friends/family'
Extras: Scored unbeaten double century against Shropshire U17. Played for Herefordshire in Minor Counties competitions 2005
Opinions on cricket: 'Everyone seems to enjoy the Twenty20 – brings in big crowds, which is good to see.'

4. Which current Warwickshire fast bowler made his Test debut in the fourth Test between England and South Africa at Headingley in 2003, scoring 59?

ALLENBY, J. Leicestershire

Name: James (Jim) Allenby
Role: Right-hand bat, right-arm medium bowler, county vice-captain
Born: 12 September 1982, Perth, Australia
Height: 6ft **Weight:** 13st 8lbs
Nickname: Jimmy, Jay, Jay Bay, Ducktails
County debut: 2005 (one-day), 2006 (first-class)
Place in batting averages: 108th av. 34.31
Place in bowling averages: 128th av. 44.13
Parents: Michael and Julie
Marital status: 'Unmarried'
Family links with cricket: 'Great-grandfather played at Yorkshire/Hampshire'
Education: Christ Church Grammar School, Perth
Qualifications: Level 1 coach
Off-season: 'Playing and coaching cricket in Perth, WA; going to the beach!'
Overseas teams played for: Claremont-Nedlands CC, Perth 1993 –
Career highlights to date: 'Playing in and winning Twenty20 [2006]. Hundred (103*) and 68* on Championship debut [v Essex at Leicester 2006]'
Cricket moments to forget: 'A bit of the 2007 season!'
Cricket superstitions: 'Put gear on same way each time I bat'
Cricketers particularly admired: Steve Waugh, Dean Jones, Paul Nixon
Young players to look out for: David Brown, Stewart Walters
Other sports followed: Football (Leeds United)
Favourite band: Powderfinger
Relaxations: 'Playing golf, swimming/surfing at beach'
Extras: Set record individual score for Western Australia in U19 cricket (180) v Northern Territory 2000-01. Played for Durham Board XI in the 2003 C&G. Set new record for highest individual score in the Durham County League (266*) playing for Brandon 2005. Scored 103* and 68* on Championship debut v Essex at Leicester 2006. Appointed vice-captain of Leicestershire at the end of August 2007. Is not considered an overseas player
Opinions on cricket: 'Twenty20 has made the game more watchable for everyone.'
Best batting: 103* Leicestershire v Essex, Leicester 2006
Best bowling: 5-125 Leicestershire v Gloucestershire, Bristol 2007

2007 Season

	M	Inn	NO	Runs	HS	Avg	100	50	Ct	St	Balls	Runs	Wkts	Avg	BB	5I	10M
Test																	
FC	16	26	4	755	93	34.31	-	5	15	-	1262	662	15	44.13	5-125	1	-
ODI																	
List A	14	13	2	386	91 *	35.09	-	3	7	-	372	308	13	23.69	5-43	1	
20/20 Int																	
20/20	5	5	1	54	43	13.50	-	-	1	-	42	79	2	39.50	1-8	-	

Career Performances

	M	Inn	NO	Runs	HS	Avg	100	50	Ct	St	Balls	Runs	Wkts	Avg	BB	5I	10M
Test																	
FC	18	30	6	994	103 *	41.41	1	6	17	-	1310	685	15	45.66	5-125	1	-
ODI																	
List A	28	25	6	530	91 *	27.89	-	3	13	-	711	551	21	26.23	5-43	1	
20/20 Int																	
20/20	21	17	6	207	64	18.81	-	1	10	-	180	262	10	26.20	2-22	-	

AMBROSE, T. R. Warwickshire

Name: Timothy (Tim) Raymond Ambrose
Role: Right-hand bat, wicket-keeper
Born: 1 December 1982, Newcastle, New South Wales, Australia
Height: 5ft 7in
Nickname: Shambrose, Freak, Mole
County debut: 2001 (Sussex), 2006 (Warwickshire)
County cap: 2003 (Sussex), 2007 (Warwickshire)
1st-Class 200s: 1
Place in batting averages: 58th av. 43.10 (2006 111th av. 34.07)
Parents: Raymond and Sally
Marital status: Single
Family links with cricket: Cousin played Sydney first grade; father captain of local grade D4 team
Education: Merewether Selective High, NSW
Career outside cricket: Greenkeeping
Overseas tours: Sussex to Grenada 2001, 2002; England Performance Programme to India 2007-08; England to New Zealand 2007-08

Overseas teams played for: Wallsend, NSW 2000; Nelson Bay, NSW 2001; Newcastle, NSW 2002
Career highlights to date: 'Winning the Championship 2003. Maiden first-class century, 149 v Yorkshire [2002]'
Cricketers particularly admired: Alec Stewart, Ian Healy, Steve Waugh, Mushtaq Ahmed
Other sports played: Football, squash, golf, rugby league, rugby union, AFL, 'I'll have a go at anything'
Other sports followed: Rugby league (Newcastle Knights), Australian Rules (Sydney Swans), football (Tottenham Hotspur)
Favourite band: Jeff Buckley, Ben Harper, Jack Johnson
Relaxations: Guitar, music
Extras: Captained Newcastle (NSW) U16 1999 Bradman Cup winning side. Played for New South Wales U17. Won NSW Junior Cricketer of the Year three years running. C&G Man of the Match award for his 95 v Buckinghamshire at Beaconsfield 2002. Scored maiden first-class double century (251*) v Worcestershire at Worcester 2007, in the process sharing with Heath Streak (66) in a new Warwickshire record partnership for the sixth wicket (226). Represented England Lions 2007
Best batting: 251* Warwickshire v Worcestershire, Worcester 2007

2007 Season

	M	Inn	NO	Runs	HS	Avg	100	50	Ct	St	Balls	Runs	Wkts	Avg	BB	5I	10M
Test																	
FC	16	23	3	862	251 *	43.10	1	4	39	-	0	0	0		-	-	-
ODI																	
List A	16	15	5	652	135	65.20	2	2	20	3	0	0	0		-	-	
20/20 Int																	
20/20	8	8	1	252	77	36.00	-	1	2	2	0	0	0		-	-	

Career Performances

	M	Inn	NO	Runs	HS	Avg	100	50	Ct	St	Balls	Runs	Wkts	Avg	BB	5I	10M
Test																	
FC	72	113	9	3627	251 *	34.87	4	22	145	14	6	1	0		-	-	-
ODI																	
List A	77	71	10	1872	135	30.68	2	8	88	11	0	0	0		-	-	
20/20 Int																	
20/20	20	17	4	435	77	33.46	-	2	11	7	0	0	0		-	-	

ANDERSON, J. M. Lancashire

Name: James Michael Anderson
Role: Left-hand bat, right-arm fast-medium bowler
Born: 30 July 1982, Burnley
Height: 6ft 2in **Weight:** 13st
Nickname: Jimmy
County debut: 2001 (one-day), 2002 (first-class)
County cap: 2003
Test debut: 2003
ODI debut: 2002-03
Twenty20 Int debut: 2006-07
50 wickets in a season: 2
Place in bowling averages: 81st av. 33.34
Parents: Michael and Catherine
Wife and date of marriage: Daniella (Lloyd), February 2006
Family links with cricket: Father and uncle played for Burnley
Education: St Theodore's RC High School and Sixth Form – both Burnley
Qualifications: 10 GCSEs, 3 A-levels, Level 2 coaching award
Off-season: Touring with England
Overseas tours: Lancashire to Cape Town 2002; ECB National Academy to Australia 2002-03; England to Australia 2002-03 (VB Series), to Africa (World Cup) 2002-03, to Bangladesh and Sri Lanka 2003-04, to West Indies 2003-04, to Zimbabwe (one-day series) 2004-05, to South Africa 2004-05, to Pakistan 2005-06, to India 2005-06, to India (ICC Champions Trophy) 2006-07, to Australia 2006-07, to West Indies (World Cup) 2006-07, to South Africa (World 20/20) 2007-08, to Sri Lanka 2007-08, to New Zealand 2007-08; England A to West Indies 2005-06
Career highlights to date: 'ODI hat-trick. Two five-fors at Lord's'
Cricket moments to forget: 'Ashes 2006-07'
Cricketers particularly admired: Allan Donald, Darren Gough, Peter Martin
Young players to look out for: Jonathan Clare
Other sports played: Golf (12 handicap), football, tennis
Other sports followed: Football (Burnley, Arsenal), 'interested in all sports'
Favourite band: Oasis, U2
Relaxations: 'Reading, music'
Extras: Represented England U19 2001. Took 50 first-class wickets in his first full season 2002. NBC Denis Compton Award for the most promising young Lancashire player 2002. Took Championship hat-trick (Robinson, Hussain, Jefferson) v Essex at Old Trafford 2003. Recorded a five-wicket innings return (5-73) on Test debut in the

first Test v Zimbabwe at Lord's 2003. Became the first England bowler to take an ODI hat-trick (Abdul Razzaq, Shoaib Akhtar, Mohammad Sami) v Pakistan at The Oval in the NatWest Challenge 2003. Cricket Writers' Club Young Player of the Year 2003. His series and match awards include England's Man of the [Test] Series v India 2007 and two Man of the Match awards in the 2002-03 World Cup. England 12-month central contract 2007-08

Opinions on cricket: 'Twenty20 has taken all forms of the game to a new level, but we should be very wary of overkill.'

Best batting: 37* Lancashire v Durham, Old Trafford 2005

Best bowling: 6-23 Lancashire v Hampshire, Rose Bowl 2002

2007 Season

	M	Inn	NO	Runs	HS	Avg	100	50	Ct	St	Balls	Runs	Wkts	Avg	BB	5I	10M
Test	3	5	2	22	16	7.33	-	-	3	-	878	498	14	35.57	5-42	1	-
FC	9	8	2	23	16	3.83	-	-	4	-	1905	1067	32	33.34	5-42	2	-
ODI	10	5	4	15	11 *	15.00	-	-	4	-	563	468	19	24.63	4-23	-	
List A	17	7	6	23	11 *	23.00	-	-	6	-	869	689	26	26.50	4-23	-	
20/20 Int	2	0	0	0	0		-	-	-	-	48	64	3	21.33	2-37	-	
20/20	5	0	0	0	0		-	-	-	-	105	147	4	36.75	2-37	-	

Career Performances

	M	Inn	NO	Runs	HS	Avg	100	50	Ct	St	Balls	Runs	Wkts	Avg	BB	5I	10M
Test	19	28	17	123	21 *	11.18	-	-	7	-	3659	2264	60	37.73	5-42	3	-
FC	66	76	36	362	37 *	9.05	-	-	25	-	11499	6741	228	29.56	6-23	10	1
ODI	76	31	16	104	15	6.93	-	-	17	-	3831	3077	113	27.23	4-23	-	
List A	121	50	31	192	15	10.10	-	-	24	-	5905	4619	178	25.94	4-23	-	
20/20 Int	7	2	2	1	1 *		-	-	-	-	162	230	7	32.85	2-24	-	
20/20	23	5	4	22	16	22.00	-	-	2	-	487	693	20	34.65	2-24	-	

ANDREW, G. M. — Worcestershire

Name: Gareth Mark Andrew

Role: Left-hand bat, right-arm medium-fast bowler

Born: 27 December 1983, Yeovil

Height: 6ft **Weight:** 14st

Nickname: G-Train, Brad, Sobers

County debut: 2003 (Somerset)

Parents: Peter and Susan

Marital status: Single

Family links with cricket: Father and younger brother club cricketers

Education: Ansford Community School; Richard Huish College, Taunton

Qualifications: 10 GCSEs, 3 A-levels, Level 1 coach

Overseas tours: West of England U15 to West Indies 1999; England U17 to Australia 2001; Somerset Academy to Western Australia 2002; 'Aus Academy' to Perth 2003
Overseas teams played for: Swanbourne CC, Perth 2002-03; Glenelg CC, Adelaide 2005-06, 2006-07
Career highlights to date: 'Twenty20 champions 2005, division two winners 2007, Pro40 promotion 2007 – all with Somerset'
Cricket moments to forget: 'Whenever bowling in the Twenty20'
Cricket superstitions: 'Always put my boots on the right feet'
Cricketers particularly admired: Ian Botham, Andrew Flintoff, Chris Cairns
Young players to look out for: Joss Buttler, Rob Travers
Other sports played: Football (Bruton Town FC, Yeovil District U11-U16, Castle Cary AFC)
Other sports followed: Football (Yeovil Town, Man Utd)
Favourite band: Red Hot Chili Peppers
Extras: Represented England U19 v South Africa U19 2003. Left Somerset at the end of the 2007 season and has joined Worcestershire for 2008
Best batting: 44 Somerset v Sri Lanka A, Taunton 2004
Best bowling: 4-63 Somerset v Sri Lanka A, Taunton 2004

2007 Season

	M	Inn	NO	Runs	HS	Avg	100	50	Ct	St	Balls	Runs	Wkts	Avg	BB	5I	10M
Test																	
FC																	
ODI																	
List A	2	2	0	8	7	4.00	-	-	1	-	90	117	2	58.50	1-42	-	
20/20 Int																	
20/20	6	3	1	21	12 *	10.50	-	-	1	-	136	177	5	35.40	1-20	-	

Career Performances

	M	Inn	NO	Runs	HS	Avg	100	50	Ct	St	Balls	Runs	Wkts	Avg	BB	5I	10M
Test																	
FC	11	14	1	163	44	12.53	-	-	5	-	1337	989	28	35.32	4-63	-	-
ODI																	
List A	43	25	6	180	33	9.47	-	-	13	-	1411	1477	42	35.16	4-48	-	
20/20 Int																	
20/20	30	14	4	71	12 *	7.10	-	-	9	-	535	780	28	27.85	4-22	-	

ANYON, J. E. — Warwickshire

Name: James Edward Anyon
Role: Left-hand bat, right-arm fast-medium bowler
Born: 5 May 1983, Lancaster
Height: 6ft 2in **Weight:** 13st 7lbs
Nickname: Jimmy
County debut: 2005
Place in batting averages: 228th av. 18.09
Place in bowling averages: 131st av. 44.50 (2006 63rd av. 32.61)
Parents: Peter and Christine
Marital status: Single
Family links with cricket: 'Dad used to play village cricket'
Education: Garstang High School; Preston College; Loughborough University
Qualifications: GCSEs, 3 A-levels, BSc Sports Science with Management, Level 1 coaching
Overseas teams played for: Claremont-Nedlands, Perth 2004-05
Career highlights to date: 'Bowling at Brian Lara'
Cricketers particularly admired: Glenn McGrath, Michael Atherton
Young players to look out for: Moeen Ali
Other sports played: Football, golf
Other sports followed: Football (Man Utd, Preston North End)
Favourite band: Nuse
Extras: Young Player of the Year awards at Preston CC. Bowler of the Year award at Farsley CC (Bradford League) 2004. Played for Loughborough UCCE 2003, 2004. Took Twenty20 hat-trick (Durston, Andrew, Caddick) v Somerset at Edgbaston 2005
Best batting: 37* Warwickshire v Durham, Riverside 2007
Best bowling: 5-83 Warwickshire v Nottinghamshire, Edgbaston 2006

2007 Season

	M	Inn	NO	Runs	HS	Avg	100	50	Ct	St	Balls	Runs	Wkts	Avg	BB	5I	10M
Test																	
FC	14	16	5	199	37 *	18.09	-	-	3	-	2245	1424	32	44.50	4-55	-	-
ODI																	
List A	5	1	1	3	3 *		-	-	3	-	180	210	7	30.00	3-46	-	
20/20 Int																	
20/20	5	0	0	0	0		-	-	-	-	90	110	8	13.75	2-15	-	

Career Performances

	M	Inn	NO	Runs	HS	Avg	100	50	Ct	St	Balls	Runs	Wkts	Avg	BB	5I	10M
Test																	
FC	36	48	19	311	37 *	10.72	-	-	11	-	5559	3354	82	40.90	5-83	1	-
ODI																	
List A	31	8	3	16	12	3.20	-	-	7	-	1144	1066	31	34.38	3-41	-	
20/20 Int																	
20/20	18	3	3	16	8 *		-	-	3	-	309	433	24	18.04	3-6	-	

AZHAR MAHMOOD Kent

Name: Azhar Mahmood Sagar
Role: Right-hand bat, right-arm fast-medium bowler; all-rounder
Born: 28 February 1975, Rawalpindi, Pakistan
Height: 6ft **Weight:** 13st 5lbs
Nickname: Aju
County debut: 2002 (Surrey)
County cap: 2004 (Surrey)
Test debut: 1997-98
ODI debut: 1996
1st-Class 200s: 1
Place in batting averages: 154th av. 28.00 (2006 87th av. 37.50)
Place in bowling averages: (2006 94th av. 37.45)
Parents: Mohammed Aslam Sagar and Nusrat Perveen
Wife and date of marriage: Ebba Azhar, 13 April 2003
Education: FG No. 1 High School, Islamabad
Qualifications: 'A-level equivalent'
Overseas tours: Pakistan Youth to New Zealand 1994-95; Pakistan A to Bangladesh 1996, to England 1997; Pakistan to India (Pepsi Independence Cup) 1997, to South Africa and Zimbabwe 1997-98, to Bangladesh (Wills International Cup) 1998-99, to India 1998-99, to UK, Ireland and Netherlands (World Cup) 1999, to Australia 1999-2000, to Sri Lanka 2000, to Kenya (ICC Knockout Trophy) 2000-01, to New Zealand 2000-01, to England 2001, to Bangladesh 2001-02, to Zimbabwe 2002-03, to Africa (World Cup) 2002-03, to New Zealand 2003-04, to England (ICC Champions Trophy) 2004, to South Africa 2006-07 (one-day series), to West Indies (World Cup) 2006-07, plus other one-day tournaments in Toronto, Kenya, Sharjah, Bangladesh, Singapore, Australia, Morocco and England

Overseas teams played for: Islamabad; United Bank; Rawalpindi; Pakistan International Airlines; Habib Bank 2006-07
Career highlights to date: 'First Test match (debut) against South Africa in 1997 in Pakistan (Rawalpindi). I scored 128* in the first innings and 50* in the second, plus two wickets – Man of the Match'
Cricket moments to forget: 'World Cup 1999 – final against Australia (which we lost)'
Cricket superstitions: 'None'
Other sports played: Snooker, basketball, kite flying
Other sports followed: Football (Man U)
Relaxations: 'Listening to music, training, spending time with my family'
Extras: Scored 128* and 50* on Test debut in the first Test v South Africa at Rawalpindi 1997-98; during first innings shared with Mushtaq Ahmed (59) in a stand of 151, equalling the world tenth-wicket record in Tests. Scored century (136) in the first Test v South Africa at Johannesburg 1997-98, becoming the first Pakistan player to score a Test century in South Africa and achieving feat of scoring a century on Test debuts home and away. Took 6-18 v West Indies in the Coca-Cola Champions Trophy in Sharjah 1999-2000 and 5-28 v Sri Lanka in the final of the same competition, winning the Man of the Match award on both occasions. An overseas player with Surrey at the start of the 2002 season and 2003-07. Left Surrey during the 2007 season and has joined Kent for 2008 as a non-overseas player
Best batting: 204* Surrey v Middlesex, The Oval 2005
Best bowling: 8-61 Surrey v Lancashire, The Oval 2002

2007 Season

	M	Inn	NO	Runs	HS	Avg	100	50	Ct	St	Balls	Runs	Wkts	Avg	BB	5I	10M
Test																	
FC	3	6	0	168	69	28.00	-	1	2	-	522	278	3	92.66	3-73	-	-
ODI																	
List A	6	6	0	136	63	22.66	-	1	5	-	291	226	12	18.83	4-39	-	
20/20 Int																	
20/20	7	7	4	111	39 *	37.00	-	-	-	-	109	162	4	40.50	2-37	-	

Career Performances

	M	Inn	NO	Runs	HS	Avg	100	50	Ct	St	Balls	Runs	Wkts	Avg	BB	5I	10M
Test	21	34	4	900	136	30.00	3	1	14	-	3015	1402	39	35.94	4-50	-	-
FC	145	226	27	6251	204 *	31.41	8	32	122	-	24217	12644	494	25.59	8-61	19	3
ODI	143	110	26	1521	67	18.10	-	3	37	-	6242	4813	123	39.13	6-18	3	
List A	254	202	44	3341	101 *	21.14	2	12	78	-	11251	8606	269	31.99	6-18	5	
20/20 Int																	
20/20	35	34	10	684	65 *	28.50	-	2	8	-	650	801	37	21.64	4-20	-	

BALCOMBE, D. J. Hampshire

Name: David John Balcombe
Role: Right-hand bat, right-arm fast-medium bowler
Born: 24 December 1984, City of London
Height: 6ft 4in
Nickname: Balcs, Spalko
County debut: 2006 (one-day), 2007 (first-class)
Place in batting averages: 185th av. 24.00
Place in bowling averages: 135th av. 47.90
Parents: Peter and Elizabeth
Marital status: Single
Education: St John's School, Leatherhead; Durham University
Qualifications: 9 GCSEs, 3 A-levels, BA (Hons) 2.1, Level 1 coaching award
Off-season: 'Spending six months in Perth, Western Australia, training and playing'
Overseas tours: Surrey Academy to Perth 2004; MCC A to Canada 2005; Hampshire to Cape Town 2007
Overseas teams played for: Midland-Guildford CC, Western Australia 2003-04; Mount Lawley CC, Western Australia 2005-06
Career highlights to date: 'Taking maiden first-class five-wicket return against Durham CCC. Making my Championship and Pro40 debuts for Hampshire last season'
Cricket moments to forget: 'Bowling two overs for 35 in a one-day game'
Cricket superstitions: 'Left equipment on first – i.e. left shoe, left pad'
Cricketers particularly admired: Shane Warne
Young players to look out for: Robbie Williams, Richard Morris, Chris Benham, Liam Dawson
Other sports followed: Rugby (London Wasps), football (Arsenal)
Favourite band: Five for Fighting, Kings of Leon
Relaxations: 'Sleeping, films'
Extras: Played for Durham UCCE 2005-07 (awarded cap for performances in 2005). Represented British Universities 2006. Recorded best match figures by a Hampshire bowler in a 2nd XI game – 14-88 (8-40/6-48) v Gloucestershire 2nd XI at The Rose Bowl 2007
Opinions on cricket: 'It is continuously moving forward and developing. It is an exciting time to be involved in the game – with new regulations allowing only one overseas player and fewer non-qualified players, younger players will inevitably be given more opportunities.'
Best batting: 73 DUCCE v Leicestershire, Leicester 2005
Best bowling: 5-112 DUCCE v Durham, Durham 2005

2007 Season

	M	Inn	NO	Runs	HS	Avg	100	50	Ct	St	Balls	Runs	Wkts	Avg	BB	5I	10M
Test																	
FC	5	8	2	144	29	24.00	-	-	3	-	755	479	10	47.90	3-58	-	-
ODI																	
List A	1	1	0	2	2	2.00	-	-	-	-	30	19	0		-	-	
20/20 Int																	
20/20																	

Career Performances

	M	Inn	NO	Runs	HS	Avg	100	50	Ct	St	Balls	Runs	Wkts	Avg	BB	5I	10M
Test																	
FC	12	17	3	271	73	19.35	-	1	5	-	1934	1320	27	48.88	5-112	1	-
ODI																	
List A	1	1	0	2	2	2.00	-	-	-	-	30	19	0		-	-	
20/20 Int																	
20/20	1	1	0	3	3	3.00	-	-	-	-	12	15	0		-	-	

BALLANCE, G. S. — Yorkshire

Name: Gary Simon Ballance
Role: Left-hand top-order bat, occasional right-arm leg-spin bowler
Born: 22 November 1989, Harare, Zimbabwe
Nickname: Gazza
County debut: 2006 (one-day, Derbyshire)
Parents: Simon and Gail
Marital status: Single
Family links with cricket: 'Father – Zimbabwe Country Districts.' Is nephew of David Houghton, former captain of Zimbabwe
Education: Peterhouse, Zimbabwe; Harrow School
Overseas tours: Zimbabwe U19 to Sri Lanka (U19 World Cup) 2005-06
Career highlights to date: 'Making 73 for Derbyshire first team against Hampshire [2006]'
Cricket superstitions: 'None'
Cricketers particularly admired: Andy Flower, Shane Warne
Other sports played: Golf, tennis, rugby

Other sports followed: Football (Liverpool)
Favourite band: Blink-182, The Killers
Relaxations: 'Watching TV'
Extras: Man of the Match v England U19 at Colombo in the U19 World Cup 2005-06 (3-21/47). Made Derbyshire one-day debut aged 16 v West Indies A in a 50-over match at Derby 2006, scoring 48; made Pro40 debut v Hampshire at The Rose Bowl 2006, scoring 73. Left Derbyshire at the end of the 2007 season and has joined Yorkshire for 2008

2007 Season

	M	Inn	NO	Runs	HS	Avg	100	50	Ct	St	Balls	Runs	Wkts	Avg	BB	5I	10M
Test																	
FC																	
ODI																	
List A	1	1	0	2	2	2.00	-	-	-	-	0	0	0		-	-	
20/20 Int																	
20/20																	

Career Performances

	M	Inn	NO	Runs	HS	Avg	100	50	Ct	St	Balls	Runs	Wkts	Avg	BB	5I	10M
Test																	
FC																	
ODI																	
List A	4	4	0	129	73	32.25	-	1	1	-	0	0	0		-	-	
20/20 Int																	
20/20																	

5. Who scored his maiden Test hundred (104) at the age of 39 in the second Test between England and South Africa at Headingley in 1994?

BANERJEE, V. Gloucestershire

Name: Vikram Banerjee
Role: Left-hand bat, left-arm orthodox spin bowler
Born: 20 March 1984, Bradford
Height: 6ft **Weight:** 11st
Nickname: Banners
County debut: 2006
County cap: 2006
Place in bowling averages: 133rd av. 45.30 (2006 145th av. 57.21)
Parents: Biren and Shyamli
Marital status: Single
Education: King Edward's School, Birmingham; Cambridge University
Qualifications: 12 GCSEs, 4 A-levels, BA (Econ), coaching Level 2
Overseas tours: ECB Emerging Players to Mumbai (World Cricket Academy) 2006-07
Overseas teams played for: Shivaji Park Gymkhana, Mumbai 2003
Career highlights to date: 'Winning at Lord's in 2005 Varsity Match. First wicket for Gloucestershire (Mark Butcher)'
Cricket moments to forget: 'Innings defeat to Somerset on debut'
Cricket superstitions: 'Right pad on first'
Cricketers particularly admired: Viv Richards, Sachin Tendulkar, Bishan Bedi
Other sports followed: Football (Aston Villa)
Favourite band: U2, Status Quo, Sting, Jack Johnson, Coldplay
Relaxations: 'Movies, reading, spending time with mates'
Extras: Cambridge Blue 2004-06. Played for Cambridge UCCE 2006. ECB National Skills Set. NBC Denis Compton Award for the most promising young Gloucestershire player 2006
Best batting: 29 Cambridge University v Oxford University, Fenner's 2005
Best bowling: 4-38 Gloucestershire v Northamptonshire, Gloucester 2007

2007 Season

	M	Inn	NO	Runs	HS	Avg	100	50	Ct	St	Balls	Runs	Wkts	Avg	BB	5I	10M
Test																	
FC	11	15	10	46	11 *	9.20	-	-	3	-	2093	1178	26	45.30	4-38	-	-
ODI																	
List A																	
20/20 Int																	
20/20																	

Career Performances

	M	Inn	NO	Runs	HS	Avg	100	50	Ct	St	Balls	Runs	Wkts	Avg	BB	5I	10M
Test																	
FC	20	30	13	185	29	10.88	-	-	5	-	3962	2267	42	53.97	4-38	-	-
ODI																	
List A																	
20/20 Int																	
20/20																	

BANKS, O. A. C. — Somerset

Name: Omari Ahmed Clemente Banks
Role: Right-hand bat, right-arm off-spin bowler; all-rounder
Born: 17 July 1982, Anguilla, Leeward Islands
County debut: 2001 (Leicestershire)
Test debut: 2002-03
ODI debut: 2002-03
Overseas tours: West Indies U19 to England 2001; West Indies A to England 2006; West Indies to Zimbabwe and South Africa 2003-04, to England 2004, to Sri Lanka 2005, to Pakistan 2006-07
Overseas teams played for: Leeward Islands 2000-01 –
Extras: Played for Leicestershire 2nd XI in 2000 and 2001, making one first-class appearance for the county against the Pakistani tourists at Leicester. First cricketer from the island of Anguilla to play Test cricket for West Indies. In only his second Test, scored 47* as West Indies chased down a Test record fourth innings target of 418 in the fourth Test v Australia in St John's 2002-03. His awards include Man of the Match v Jamaica in the Busta Cup 2000-01 (7-70/3-78 plus 43) and v Jamaica in the Carib Beer Cup 2006-07 (100 plus 2-88/1-3), both at grounds on St Kitts. Is not considered an overseas player
Best batting: 100 Leeward Islands v Jamaica, Cayon 2006-07
Best bowling: 7-70 Leeward Islands v Jamaica, Molyneaux 2000-01
Stop press: Man of the Match v Jamaica (62/2-46) and v West Indies U19 (2-18/55*), both in Guyana in the KFC Cup 2007-08

2007 Season (did not make any first-class or one-day appearances)

Career Performances

	M	Inn	NO	Runs	HS	Avg	100	50	Ct	St	Balls	Runs	Wkts	Avg	BB	5I	10M
Test	10	16	4	318	50 *	26.50	-	1	6	-	2401	1367	28	48.82	4-87	-	-
FC	56	87	14	1754	100	24.02	1	9	32	-	11625	5908	159	37.15	7-70	6	1
ODI	5	5	0	83	33	16.60	-	-	-	-	270	189	7	27.00	2-24	-	
List A	45	39	11	833	77 *	29.75	-	5	12	-	2084	1457	56	26.01	4-23	-	
20/20 Int																	
20/20																	

BARNES, M. W. Warwickshire

Name: Michael William Barnes
Role: Right-hand bat, wicket-keeper
Born: 3 April 1985, Frimley, Surrey
Height: 5ft 11in **Weight:** 11st
Nickname: Barnesy, Barndog, Barno, 'anything with a Barn!'
County debut: 2007
Parents: Sharon and Doug
Marital status: Single
Family links with cricket: 'Dad used to play'
Education: Bohunt School, Liphook; South Downs College
Qualifications: 11 GCSEs
Overseas tours: West of England U15 to West Indies 2000
Overseas teams played for: Westville CC, South Africa 2006
Career highlights to date: 'First hundred, against Middlesex. Winning 2nd XI Trophy with Warwickshire and joining the Bears'
Cricket moments to forget: 'Any dropped catches'
Cricket superstitions: 'Must wink at the number 14 after I've seen the number 13 – very strange but I can't help it'
Cricketers particularly admired: Alec Stewart, Ricky Ponting, Matthew Scott
Other sports played: Football (Chelsea and West Ham Youth teams)
Other sports followed: Football (Chelsea), Australian Rules football (Essendon Bombers), 'England in anything'
Favourite band: Aerosmith, Jimmy Barnes
Relaxations: 'Watching TV (*Family Guy*), golf'

Extras: Took hat-trick of stumpings at the age of 12. Took five catches in Yorkshire's only innings on first-class debut at Edgbaston 2007. Released by Warwickshire at the end of the 2007 season

Opinions on cricket: 'Needs to be taken into the present time and not be dragged down by old-fashioned opinions.'

2007 Season

	M	Inn	NO	Runs	HS	Avg	100	50	Ct	St	Balls	Runs	Wkts	Avg	BB	5I	10M
Test																	
FC	1	0	0	0	0		-	-	5	-	0	0	0		-	-	-
ODI																	
List A	1	1	1	1	1*		-	-	5	-	0	0	0		-	-	
20/20 Int																	
20/20																	

Career Performances

	M	Inn	NO	Runs	HS	Avg	100	50	Ct	St	Balls	Runs	Wkts	Avg	BB	5I	10M
Test																	
FC	1	0	0	0	0		-	-	5	-	0	0	0		-	-	-
ODI																	
List A	1	1	1	1	1*		-	-	5	-	0	0	0		-	-	
20/20 Int																	
20/20																	

6. Who had match figures of 15-45 but also bagged a pair opening the innings for England v South Africa at Port Elizabeth in 1895-96?

BATTY, G. J. Worcestershire

Name: Gareth Jon Batty
Role: Right-hand bat, off-spin bowler, county vice-captain; all-rounder
Born: 13 October 1977, Bradford, Yorkshire
Height: 5ft 11in **Weight:** 12st 7lbs
Nickname: Batts, Boris, Red, Terry, Stuta
County debut: 1997 (Yorkshire), 1998 (one-day, Surrey), 1999 (first-class, Surrey), 2002 (Worcestershire)
County colours: 2002 (Worcestershire)
Test debut: 2003-04
ODI debut: 2002-03
50 wickets in a season: 2
Place in batting averages: 172nd av. 25.63 (2006 58th av. 46.50)
Place in bowling averages: 112th av. 40.07 (2006 69th av. 33.46)
Parents: David and Rosemary
Marital status: Single
Family links with cricket: Father was Yorkshire Academy coach; brother played for Yorkshire and Somerset
Education: Bingley Grammar; Worcester College
Qualifications: 9 GCSEs, BTEC Art and Design, coaching certificate
Career outside cricket: Property development and coaching
Off-season: 'Training'
Overseas tours: England U15 to South Africa 1993; England U19 to Zimbabwe 1995-96, to Pakistan 1996-97; ECB National Academy to Australia and Sri Lanka 2002-03; England to Bangladesh and Sri Lanka 2003-04, to West Indies 2003-04, to Zimbabwe (one-day series) 2004-05, to South Africa 2004-05, to India 2005-06 (one-day series); England A to West Indies 2005-06
Overseas teams played for: Marist Newman, Australia 1999
Career highlights to date: 'Making England debut'
Cricket moments to forget: 'Whenever we lose'
Cricket superstitions: 'None'
Cricketers particularly admired: Adam Hollioake, Alec Stewart 'to name but two'
Young players to look out for: Daryl Mitchell, Steve Davies
Other sports played: Golf, rugby
Other sports followed: Rugby league (Leeds Rhinos), 'all sports'
Favourite band: Rick Astley
Relaxations: 'Property and spending time with family and friends'
Extras: *Daily Telegraph* Young Player of the Year 1993. Surrey Supporters' Club Most Improved Player Award and Young Player of the Year Award 2001. Surrey CCC

Young Player of the Year Award 2001. ECB 2nd XI Player of the Year 2001. Leading all-rounder in the inaugural Twenty20 Cup 2003. Made Test debut in the first Test v Bangladesh at Dhaka 2003-04, taking a wicket (Alok Kapali) with his third ball. Vice-captain of Worcestershire since 2005. ECB National Academy 2005-06
Opinions on cricket: 'Wickets in general are batter-friendly. Would be good to see it evened out. Keep the kids interested at all costs.'
Best batting: 133 Worcestershire v Surrey, The Oval 2004
Best bowling: 7-52 Worcestershire v Northamptonshire, Northampton 2004

2007 Season

	M	Inn	NO	Runs	HS	Avg	100	50	Ct	St	Balls	Runs	Wkts	Avg	BB	5I	10M
Test																	
FC	14	22	3	487	84	25.63	-	3	7	-	2937	1523	38	40.07	6-106	3	-
ODI																	
List A	17	10	2	147	36 *	18.37	-	-	4	-	587	460	8	57.50	3-47	-	
20/20 Int																	
20/20	7	5	1	38	16	9.50	-	-	1	-	72	95	4	23.75	2-28	-	

Career Performances

	M	Inn	NO	Runs	HS	Avg	100	50	Ct	St	Balls	Runs	Wkts	Avg	BB	5I	10M
Test	7	8	1	144	38	20.57	-	-	3	-	1394	733	11	66.63	3-55	-	-
FC	107	166	30	3639	133	26.75	2	18	75	-	21425	10410	318	32.73	7-52	13	1
ODI	7	5	1	6	3	1.50	-	-	4	-	362	294	4	73.50	2-40	-	
List A	150	120	25	1599	83 *	16.83	-	4	55	-	5867	4382	129	33.96	4-27	-	
20/20 Int																	
20/20	33	30	6	361	87	15.04	-	1	9	-	546	779	25	31.16	3-38	-	

7. Which current county captain found himself facing a hat-trick ball batting at No. 6 within 15 minutes of the start of his Test debut in the first Test at Johannesburg in 1999-2000?

BATTY, J. N. — Surrey

Name: Jonathan Neil Batty
Role: Right-hand bat, wicket-keeper
Born: 18 April 1974, Chesterfield
Height: 5ft 10in **Weight:** 11st 6lbs
Nickname: JB
County debut: 1997
County cap: 2001
1000 runs in a season: 1
50 dismissals in a season: 4
Place in batting averages: 51st av. 43.86 (2006 99th av. 35.34)
Parents: Roger and Jill
Marital status: Single
Family links with cricket: Father played to a high standard of club cricket
Education: Wheatley Park; Repton; Durham University (St Chad's); Keble College, Oxford
Qualifications: 10 GCSEs, 4 A-levels, BSc (Hons) in Natural Sciences, Diploma in Social Studies (Oxon)
Overseas tours: Repton School to Netherlands 1991; MCC to Bangladesh 1996; Surrey to South Africa 1997, 2001
Overseas teams played for: Mount Lawley CC, Perth 1997-2002
Career highlights to date: 'Winning three County Championships'
Cricket moments to forget: 'None!'
Cricketers particularly admired: David Gower, Alec Stewart, Jack Russell
Other sports played: Golf, squash
Other sports followed: Football (Nottingham Forest)
Relaxations: Reading, listening to music, movies
Extras: Represented Combined Universities 1994, 1995. Oxford Blue 1996. Surrey Supporters' Club Most Improved Player 2002, 2003. BBC Radio London Listeners' Cricketer of the Year 2003. Became second wicket-keeper (after Kent's Steve Marsh in 1991) to take eight catches in an innings (a new Surrey record) and score a century (129) in the same match, v Kent at The Oval 2004. Achieved double of 1000 (1025) runs and 50 (53) dismissals in first-class cricket 2006. Captain of Surrey 2004
Best batting: 168* Surrey v Essex, Chelmsford 2003
Best bowling: 1-21 Surrey v Lancashire, Old Trafford 2000

2007 Season	M	Inn	NO	Runs	HS	Avg	100	50	Ct	St	Balls	Runs	Wkts	Avg	BB	5I	10M
Test																	
FC	15	25	3	965	154 *	43.86	4	3	42	5	0	0	0		-	-	-
ODI																	
List A	15	14	2	331	52 *	27.58	-	2	28	2	0	0	0		-	-	
20/20 Int																	
20/20	8	7	3	84	49	21.00	-	-	7	4	0	0	0		-	-	

Career Performances	M	Inn	NO	Runs	HS	Avg	100	50	Ct	St	Balls	Runs	Wkts	Avg	BB	5I	10M
Test																	
FC	159	243	30	7235	168 *	33.96	16	34	420	56	78	61	1	61.00	1-21	-	-
ODI																	
List A	163	131	24	2385	158 *	22.28	1	12	166	27	0	0	0		-	-	
20/20 Int																	
20/20	42	35	13	467	59	21.22	-	2	30	16	0	0	0		-	-	

BEER, W. A. T. Sussex

Name: William (Will) Andrew Thomas Beer
Role: Right-hand bat, leg-spin bowler
Born: 8 October 1988, Crawley
Height: 5ft 9in **Weight:** 12st
Nickname: Ferret, Beero
County debut: No first-team appearance
Parents: Andrew and Sarah
Marital status: Single
Family links with cricket: 'Dad and Uncle Robin both played for Horsham 1st XI for many years'
Education: Reigate Grammar School
Qualifications: 3 A-levels
Off-season: 'Playing abroad'
Overseas teams played for: Western Province CC, Cape Town 2007-08
Career highlights to date: 'Five wickets v Hants in 2nd XI Championship 2007. Playing for England U17'
Cricket moments to forget: 'Getting out first ball in first ever county game, for Sussex U10'
Cricket superstitions: 'None'

Cricketers particularly admired: Shane Warne
Young players to look out for: Ben Brown, Matt Machan
Other sports played: Golf, squash (Sussex U15)
Other sports followed: Football (Manchester United), rugby, golf
Favourite band: Maroon 5
Relaxations: 'Listening to music'
Extras: Sussex Academy Player of the Year 2006

BELL, I. R. Warwickshire

Name: Ian Ronald Bell
Role: Right-hand bat, right-arm medium bowler
Born: 11 April 1982, Coventry
Height: 5ft 10in **Weight:** 11st
Nickname: Belly
County debut: 1999
County cap: 2001
Test debut: 2004
ODI debut: 2004-05
Twenty20 Int debut: 2006
1000 runs in a season: 2
1st-Class 200s: 2
Place in batting averages: 87th av. 37.76 (2006 22nd av. 59.41)
Parents: Terry and Barbara
Marital status: Single
Family links with cricket: Brother Keith played for England U18, Staffordshire and Warwickshire 2nd XI
Education: Princethorpe College, Rugby
Overseas tours: Warwickshire U19 to Cape Town 1998-99; England U19 to New Zealand 1998-99, to Malaysia and (U19 World Cup) Sri Lanka 1999-2000, to India 2000-01 (c); England A to West Indies 2000-01, to Sri Lanka 2004-05 (c); ECB National Academy to Australia 2001-02, to Sri Lanka 2002-03; England to Zimbabwe (one-day series) 2004-05, to South Africa 2004-05, to Pakistan 2005-06, to India 2005-06, to India (ICC Champions Trophy) 2006-07, to Australia 2006-07, to West Indies (World Cup) 2006-07, to Sri Lanka 2007-08, to New Zealand 2007-08
Overseas teams played for: University of Western Australia, Perth 2003-04
Cricketers particularly admired: Michael Atherton, Steve Waugh, Alec Stewart, Nick Knight
Other sports played: Football (was at Coventry City School of Excellence), rugby, golf

Other sports followed: Football (Aston Villa), rugby union (Northampton Saints)
Relaxations: Golf, listening to music
Extras: Played for England U14, U15, U16, U17; captained England U19. NBC Denis Compton Award for the most promising young Warwickshire player 1999, 2000, 2001. Gray-Nicolls Trophy for Best Young Schools Cricketer 2000. Cricket Society's Most Promising Young Cricketer of the Year Award 2001. Recorded maiden one-day century (125) and maiden one-day five-wicket return (5-41) v Essex at Chelmsford in the NCL 2003. Scored maiden first-class double century (262*) v Sussex at Horsham 2004, in the process setting with Tony Frost (135*) a new Warwickshire record partnership for the seventh wicket (289*). Cricket Writers' Club Young Cricketer of the Year 2004. PCA Young Player of the Year award 2004. ECB National Academy 2004-05. Made ODI debut in the first ODI v Zimbabwe at Harare 2004-05, scoring 75 and winning Man of the Match award. His other match and series awards include Man of the Match in the fourth ODI v Pakistan at Trent Bridge 2006 (86*) and Player of the [ODI] Series v India 2007. Appointed MBE in 2006 New Year Honours as part of 2005 Ashes-winning England team. Recalled to the Test side for series v Pakistan 2006, scoring three hundreds (100*, 106*, 119) in successive Tests. ICC Emerging Player of the Year award 2006. England 12-month central contract 2007-08
Best batting: 262* Warwickshire v Sussex, Horsham 2004
Best bowling: 4-4 Warwickshire v Middlesex, Lord's 2004

2007 Season

	M	Inn	NO	Runs	HS	Avg	100	50	Ct	St	Balls	Runs	Wkts	Avg	BB	5I	10M
Test	7	12	1	417	109 *	37.90	1	3	5	-	0	0	0		-	-	-
FC	9	14	1	491	109 *	37.76	1	4	6	-	0	0	0		-	-	-
ODI	10	10	1	507	126 *	56.33	1	3	6	-	0	0	0		-	-	
List A	13	13	1	552	126 *	46.00	1	3	6	-	0	0	0		-	-	
20/20 Int																	
20/20																	

Career Performances

	M	Inn	NO	Runs	HS	Avg	100	50	Ct	St	Balls	Runs	Wkts	Avg	BB	5I	10M
Test	30	54	6	2035	162 *	42.39	6	14	28	-	108	76	1	76.00	1-33	-	-
FC	115	197	18	7710	262 *	43.07	19	43	72	-	2719	1490	47	31.70	4-4	-	-
ODI	54	52	4	1890	126 *	39.37	1	13	14	-	88	88	6	14.66	3-9	-	
List A	146	139	12	4642	137	36.55	3	36	47	-	1290	1138	33	34.48	5-41	1	
20/20 Int	2	2	0	36	22	18.00	-	-	1	-	0	0	0		-	-	
20/20	20	19	4	282	66 *	18.80	-	1	8	-	132	186	3	62.00	1-12	-	

BENHAM, C. C. Hampshire

Name: Christopher (Chris) Charles Benham
Role: Right-hand bat, right-arm off-spin bowler
Born: 24 March 1983, Frimley, Surrey
Height: 6ft 2in **Weight:** 'It varies'
Nickname: Cut-snake, Togo, Benoit, Benny
County debut: 2004
Place in batting averages: 201st av. 22.28 (2006 113th av. 33.60)
Parents: Frank and Sandie
Marital status: Single
Family links with cricket: 'Both older brothers, Nick and Andy, played local club cricket'
Education: Yateley Comprehensive School; Yateley Sixth Form College; Loughborough University
Qualifications: 10 GCSEs, 3 A-levels, BSc (Hons) 2.1 Sport and Exercise Science
Off-season: 'Playing grade cricket for Casey-South Melbourne October to March'
Overseas tours: West of England U15 to West Indies 1998
Overseas teams played for: Perth CC 2004-05; Casey-South Melbourne 2007-08
Career highlights to date: '158 (off 130 balls) in Pro40 play-off match v Glamorgan at The Rose Bowl, September 2006, which we won to gain promotion to first division'
Cricket moments to forget: 'Getting a king pair in a pre-season friendly match against Essex in 2005'
Cricket superstitions: 'There's a few!'
Cricketers particularly admired: Ricky Ponting, Sachin Tendulkar, Shane Warne, John Crawley, Darren Lehmann, Mark Ramprakash
Young players to look out for: Benny Howell, Liam Dawson
Other sports played: Football (school, district and county sides; trials with Swindon and Crystal Palace), tennis, golf
Other sports followed: Football (Reading FC), 'follow all sports'
Favourite band: Newton Faulkner
Relaxations: 'Reading, music, PlayStation, "Champ Man"'
Extras: Played for ESCA U15 and England U16. Played for Loughborough UCCE 2002, 2004. Represented British Universities 2004. Scored 74 on Championship debut v Derbyshire at Derby 2004. NBC Denis Compton Award for the most promising young Hampshire player 2006. Scored 130-ball 158 v Glamorgan at The Rose Bowl in Pro40 play-off 2006, winning Man of the Match award
Best batting: 95 Hampshire v Warwickshire, Rose Bowl 2006

2007 Season

	M	Inn	NO	Runs	HS	Avg	100	50	Ct	St	Balls	Runs	Wkts	Avg	BB	5I	10M
Test																	
FC	9	14	0	312	76	22.28	-	1	10	-	0	0	0		-	-	-
ODI																	
List A	12	12	0	319	111	26.58	1	1	3	-	0	0	0		-	-	
20/20 Int																	
20/20	7	7	2	132	45	26.40	-	-	-	-	0	0	0		-	-	

Career Performances

	M	Inn	NO	Runs	HS	Avg	100	50	Ct	St	Balls	Runs	Wkts	Avg	BB	5I	10M
Test																	
FC	27	45	1	1135	95	25.79	-	6	24	-	30	37	0		-	-	-
ODI																	
List A	24	23	1	806	158	36.63	3	4	7	-	0	0	0		-	-	
20/20 Int																	
20/20	15	13	2	252	59	22.90	-	1	4	-	0	0	0		-	-	

BENKENSTEIN, D. M. — Durham

Name: Dale Martin Benkenstein
Role: Right-hand bat, right-arm off-break or medium bowler, county captain
Born: 9 June 1974, Harare, Zimbabwe
County debut: 2005
ODI debut: 1998-99
1000 runs in a season: 3
1st-Class 200s: 2
Place in batting averages: 21st av. 55.56 (2006 36th av. 51.72)
Place in bowling averages: (2006 101st av. 39.42)
Family links with cricket: Father, Martin, and two brothers, Brett and Boyd, played first-class cricket
Education: Michaelhouse, KwaZulu-Natal
Overseas tours: KwaZulu-Natal to Australia (Champions Cup) 2000-01; South Africa U24 to Sri Lanka 1995; South Africa A to Sri Lanka 1998, to West Indies 2000; South Africa to Malaysia (Commonwealth Games) 1998-99, to Bangladesh (Wills International Cup) 1998-99, to New Zealand 1998-99, to Sri Lanka (ICC Champions Trophy) 2002-03, plus one-day series and tournaments in Kenya, India and Sharjah

Overseas teams played for: Natal/KwaZulu-Natal 1992-93 – 2003-04; Dolphins 2003-04 –
Extras: Captained Natal Schools and South Africa Schools and has played ODI cricket for South Africa. One of *South African Cricket Annual*'s five Cricketers of the Year 1997. Was captain of KwaZulu-Natal, leading the side to the double (SuperSport Series and Standard Bank Cup) in 1996-97 and 2001-02. Has won numerous domestic awards, including Man of the Match in the final of the Standard Bank Cup 2001-02 at Durban (77*) and in the final of the SuperSport Series 2005-06 at Durban (151). Scored century (125) v Middlesex at Lord's 2006, in the process sharing with Gareth Breese (110) in a new record fifth-wicket partnership for Durham (222). Scored century (151) v Yorkshire at Headingley 2006, in the process sharing with Ottis Gibson (155) in a new record seventh-wicket partnership for Durham (315). Captain of Durham since 2006. Is not considered an overseas player
Best batting: 259 KwaZulu-Natal v Northerns, Durban 2001-02
Best bowling: 4-16 Dolphins v Warriors, Durban 2005-06

2007 Season

	M	Inn	NO	Runs	HS	Avg	100	50	Ct	St	Balls	Runs	Wkts	Avg	BB	5I	10M
Test																	
FC	16	28	5	1278	117	55.56	3	8	5	-	354	202	2	101.00	1-24	-	-
ODI																	
List A	19	17	7	560	97 *	56.00	-	4	7	-	267	240	6	40.00	2-51	-	
20/20 Int																	
20/20	6	5	0	58	23	11.60	-	-	1	-	6	11	0		-	-	

Career Performances

	M	Inn	NO	Runs	HS	Avg	100	50	Ct	St	Balls	Runs	Wkts	Avg	BB	5I	10M
Test																	
FC	175	266	33	10897	259	46.76	27	56	123	-	6101	2999	84	35.70	4-16	-	-
ODI	23	20	3	305	69	17.94	-	1	3	-	65	44	4	11.00	3-5	-	
List A	240	215	54	5742	107 *	35.66	1	33	86	-	2663	2197	76	28.90	4-16	-	
20/20 Int																	
20/20	33	32	5	621	56 *	23.00	-	2	13	-	252	326	14	23.28	3-10	-	

BENNING, J. G. E. Surrey

Name: James Graham Edward Benning
Role: Right-hand bat, right-arm medium bowler; batting all-rounder
Born: 4 May 1983, Mill Hill, London
Height: 5ft 11in **Weight:** 13st
Nickname: Benno
County debut: 2002 (one-day), 2003 (first-class)
Place in batting averages: 160th av. 27.70 (2006 63rd av. 44.36)
Parents: Sandy and David
Marital status: Single
Family links with cricket: 'Dad played for Middlesex'
Education: Caterham School
Qualifications: 12 GCSEs, 3 AS-levels
Overseas tours: Surrey YC to Barbados 1999-2000, to Sri Lanka 2002
Overseas teams played for: North Dandenong, Australia 2001-02
Cricket moments to forget: 'Dropping two catches in front of a lively crowd at Canterbury, live on Sky'
Cricket superstitions: 'Order in which I put my kit on'
Cricketers particularly admired: Alec Stewart, Adam Hollioake
Other sports played: Rugby, football
Other sports followed: Football (Watford)
Favourite band: 'Listen to almost all music apart from thrash metal'
Relaxations: 'Going to the gym, music, spending time around friends'
Extras: Played for England U15-U19. First recipient of Ben Hollioake Scholarship. NBC Denis Compton Award for the most promising young Surrey player 2003. Scored maiden Championship century from 100 balls (finishing with 112) v Gloucestershire at The Oval 2006 on his 23rd birthday. Carried bat for 146-ball 189* as Surrey fell two short of Gloucestershire's 339-8 at Bristol in the C&G 2006. Scored 134-ball 152 v Gloucestershire at The Oval in the Friends Provident 2007, in the process sharing with Alistair Brown (176) in a Surrey record one-day partnership (294) as the county posted a world record List A total of 496-4
Best batting: 128 Surrey v OUCCE, The Parks 2004
Best bowling: 3-57 Surrey v Kent, Tunbridge Wells 2005

2007 Season

	M	Inn	NO	Runs	HS	Avg	100	50	Ct	St	Balls	Runs	Wkts	Avg	BB	5I	10M
Test																	
FC	8	11	1	277	51	27.70	-	1	5	-	102	91	0		-	-	-
ODI																	
List A	14	14	1	414	152	31.84	1	-	9	-	54	84	2	42.00	1-14	-	
20/20 Int																	
20/20	8	8	0	195	69	24.37	-	1	4	-	0	0	0		-	-	

Career Performances

	M	Inn	NO	Runs	HS	Avg	100	50	Ct	St	Balls	Runs	Wkts	Avg	BB	5I	10M
Test																	
FC	28	45	4	1442	128	35.17	4	6	13	-	933	794	11	72.18	3-57	-	-
ODI																	
List A	61	60	3	1960	189*	34.38	2	12	20	-	854	951	28	33.96	4-43	-	
20/20 Int																	
20/20	38	38	1	878	88	23.72	-	6	11	-	30	43	2	21.50	1-7	-	

BERG, G. K. — Middlesex

Name: Gareth Kyle Berg
Role: Right-hand bat, right-arm medium-fast bowler; all-rounder
Born: 18 January 1981, Cape Town, South Africa
Height: 6ft **Weight:** 13st 5lbs
Nickname: Bergy, Ice, Ford
County debut: No first-team appearance
Parents: Gina and Richard
Wife and date of marriage: Kelly, 1 April 2004
Children: Roman, 17 July 2007
Family links with cricket: 'Grandfather put cricket bat and ball in my hand at early age of three years old'
Education: South African College School (SACS)
Qualifications: Level 2 cricket coach, Level 1 hockey coach, Level 1 rugby coach, Level 1 athletics coach
Career outside cricket: Professional sports coach in schools
Off-season: 'Looking after my son Roman all winter, watching him grow up'

Career highlights to date: 'Playing alongside Hansie Cronje and Shaun Pollock in a friend's benefit game'
Cricket moments to forget: 'Being left out of South Africa U15 World Cup squad one week before the World Cup in England'
Cricket superstitions: 'Always put my right boot and pad on first. Look at the sun when stepping on to the field'
Cricketers particularly admired: Steve Waugh, Herschelle Gibbs
Young players to look out for: Steven Finn
Other sports played: Football (Western Province), rugby
Other sports followed: Football (Man Utd 'since three years old')
Favourite band: Red Hot Chili Peppers, Oasis, Beatles, Dean Martin
Relaxations: 'Surfing, sleeping'
Extras: Played for Western Province Academy and Western Province B. Has played for Northamptonshire 2nd XI and Middlesex 2nd XI in the 2nd XI Championship. Plays for Radlett CC
Opinions on cricket: 'Love all the new formats that are coming out, which allow more specialist players to shine! Specialist forms of the game!'

BICHEL, A. J. — Essex

Name: Andrew (Andy) John Bichel
Role: Right-hand bat, right-arm fast bowler
Born: 27 August 1970, Laidley, Queensland, Australia
Height: 5ft 11in **Weight:** 14st 7lbs
Nickname: Bic, Andre
County debut: 2001 (Worcestershire), 2005 (Hampshire), 2006 (Essex)
County cap: 2001, colours 2002 (both Worcestershire), 2007 (Essex)
Test debut: 1996-97
ODI debut: 1996-97
50 wickets in a season: 1
Place in batting averages: 12th av. 60.25 (2006 83rd av. 37.85)
Place in bowling averages: 7th av. 20.53 (2006 52nd av. 30.96)
Parents: Trevor and Shirley
Wife and date of marriage: Dionn, 18 April 1997
Children: Keegan, 26 October 1999; Darcy, 24 October 2002

Family links with cricket: 'Family had strong representation in Queensland country cricket. Uncle Don played for Queensland'
Education: Laidley High; Ipswich College of TAFE (engineering and construction)
Qualifications: Carpenter and joiner; project management experience; cricket coaching
Overseas tours: Queensland Academy to South Africa 1994; Australian Academy to South Africa 1996; Australia A to Scotland and Ireland 1998; Australia to South Africa 1996-97, to England 1997, to New Zealand (one-day series) 1997-98, to Malaysia (Commonwealth Games) 1998-99, to West Indies 1998-99, to South Africa 2001-02, to Kenya (PSO Tri-Nation Tournament) 2002, to Sri Lanka (ICC Champions Trophy) 2002-03, to Sri Lanka and Sharjah (v Pakistan) 2002-03, to Africa (World Cup) 2002-03, to West Indies 2002-03, to India (TVS Cup) 2003-04; FICA World XI to New Zealand 2004-05
Overseas teams played for: Laidley Blue Dogs 1980-92; South Brisbane 1992 –; Queensland 1992-93 –
Career highlights to date: 'World Cup 2003, Australia v England – 7-20 and 34 not out'
Cricket moments to forget: 'Losing any game is never good. Phone call from Trevor Hohns [Australia's then chairman of selectors] to say I would be left out of the team'
Cricket superstitions: 'Don't like people talking about how well they are playing'
Cricketers particularly admired: Brian Lara, Dennis Lillee, Steve Waugh
Young players to look out for: Mitchell Johnson, Chris Hartley, Tim Phillips, Ravi Bopara
Other sports played: Rugby league (Toowoomba RL first grade aged 17-20), tennis (first grade LTA), golf
Other sports followed: Rugby league (Brisbane Broncos), AFL (Brisbane Lions), football (West Ham)
Favourite band: U2, INXS, Cold Chisel, Coldplay
Relaxations: 'Fishing, beach, family, golf'
Extras: Sheffield Shield Player of the Year 1996-97. Queensland Player of the Year 1998-99, 2005-06. An overseas player with Worcestershire 2001-02, 2004. Won the Dick Lygon Award 2001 as Worcestershire's Player of the Year; was also the Worcestershire Supporters' Association Player of the Year 2001 and the winner of the inaugural Don Kenyon Award. Man of the Match v South Africa at Sydney in the VB Series 2001-02 (5-19) and v England at Port Elizabeth in the World Cup 2002-03 (34* following 7-20 – the third best bowling return in ODI history – for which he also won the Wisden International one-day performance award 2003). Named Australia's State Player of the Year at the 2005 Allan Border Medal awards. Was a temporary overseas player with Hampshire during the 2005 season, scoring 138 on debut v Gloucestershire at Cheltenham and in the process sharing with Nic Pothas (139) in a new Hampshire record partnership for the eighth wicket (257). Named Man of the Series in the Pura Cup 2005-06. An overseas player with Essex 2006-07. Has same birthday as the late Sir Donald Bradman

Opinions on cricket: 'Cricketers of today must make sure they develop their games to entertain the public.'
Best batting: 148 Essex v Nottinghamshire, Chelmsford 2007
Best bowling: 9-93 Worcestershire v Gloucestershire, Worcester 2002

2007 Season

	M	Inn	NO	Runs	HS	Avg	100	50	Ct	St	Balls	Runs	Wkts	Avg	BB	5I	10M
Test																	
FC	8	12	4	482	148	60.25	2	2	7	-	1306	842	41	20.53	7-36	3	1
ODI																	
List A	7	6	3	118	43 *	39.33	-	-	3	-	318	274	12	22.83	4-22	-	
20/20 Int																	
20/20	8	6	0	76	35	12.66	-	-	1	-	168	198	8	24.75	3-34	-	

Career Performances

	M	Inn	NO	Runs	HS	Avg	100	50	Ct	St	Balls	Runs	Wkts	Avg	BB	5I	10M
Test	19	22	1	355	71	16.90	-	1	16	-	3336	1870	58	32.24	5-60	1	-
FC	183	242	25	5694	148	26.23	8	23	89	-	36873	19791	766	25.83	9-93	36	7
ODI	67	36	13	471	64	20.47	-	1	19	-	3257	2463	78	31.57	7-20	2	
List A	235	161	40	2491	100	20.58	1	5	73	-	11433	8362	320	26.13	7-20	4	
20/20 Int																	
20/20	29	22	7	364	58 *	24.26	-	1	11	-	619	822	33	24.90	4-23	-	

8. Which sometime Nottinghamshire all-rounder scored a whirlwind 80 and took 5-31 as New Zealand registered their first Test victory at The Oval in 1999?

BIRCH, D. J. — Derbyshire

Name: Daniel (Dan) John Birch
Role: Left-hand bat, right-arm medium bowler
Born: 21 January 1981, Nottingham
Height: 6ft 3in **Weight:** 16st
Nickname: Birchy
County debut: 2007
Place in batting averages: 112th av. 33.71
Marital status: Single
Family links with cricket: 'Dad John Birch played for Notts CCC in 1970s and 1980s and was [Notts] manager'
Education: Kimberley Comprehensive
Career outside cricket: 'Manager and coach at John Birch Sports Centre Ltd'
Overseas teams played for: Frankston Peninsula CC, Melbourne 2002-03
Cricketers particularly admired: Shane Warne, Brian Lara
Other sports followed: Football (Nottingham Forest)
Relaxations: 'Weight training, fishing, pub'
Extras: Scored century (130) on first-class debut v Cambridge UCCE at Fenner's 2007. Scored Derbyshire Premier League record 224* for Sandiacre v Alvaston & Boulton 2007
Best batting: 130 Derbyshire v CUCCE, Fenner's 2007

2007 Season

	M	Inn	NO	Runs	HS	Avg	100	50	Ct	St	Balls	Runs	Wkts	Avg	BB	5I	10M
Test																	
FC	4	7	0	236	130	33.71	1	1	1	-	0	0	0		-	-	-
ODI																	
List A	8	8	0	199	60	24.87	-	1	2	-	0	0	0		-	-	
20/20 Int																	
20/20	1	1	0	8	8	8.00	-	-	-	-	0	0	0		-	-	

Career Performances

	M	Inn	NO	Runs	HS	Avg	100	50	Ct	St	Balls	Runs	Wkts	Avg	BB	5I	10M
Test																	
FC	4	7	0	236	130	33.71	1	1	1	-	0	0	0		-	-	-
ODI																	
List A	8	8	0	199	60	24.87	-	1	2	-	0	0	0		-	-	
20/20 Int																	
20/20	1	1	0	8	8	8.00	-	-	-	-	0	0	0		-	-	

BIRT, T. R. Derbyshire

Name: Travis Rodney Birt
Role: Left-hand bat, 'right-arm fast bowler', wicket-keeper 'sometimes'
Born: 9 December 1981, Sale, Victoria, Australia
Height: 5ft 11in **Weight:** 14st
Nickname: Trevor
County debut: 2006
1000 runs in a season: 1
Place in batting averages: 82nd av. 38.43 (2006 50th av. 48.13)
Parents: Rod and Wendy
Marital status: Single
Family links with cricket: 'Uncle still dominates local cricket in Melbourne'
Education: Catholic College, Sale, Victoria
Career outside cricket: 'Helicopter pilot'
Overseas tours: Commonwealth Bank Centre of Excellence to India 2004
Overseas teams played for: Tasmania 2003-04 –
Career highlights to date: 'Deceiving HD Ackerman with my lack of pace and removing his middle stump with my first ball in one-day cricket'
Cricket moments to forget: 'In Under 12s I dropped the same batsman three times in four balls'
Cricket superstitions: 'Left pad first; bottom strap followed by the top strap'
Young players to look out for: Tim Paine
Other sports followed: Football (Man United)
Favourite band: Linkin Park
Relaxations: 'PlayStation, shopping'
Extras: Represented Australia U19 2000-01. Set then record for the highest individual score for Tasmania in a List A match with his 145 v South Australia at Hobart in the

ING Cup 2004-05, also winning Man of the Match award. His other match awards include Man of the Match v New South Wales at Hobart in the Pura Cup 2005-06 (160). Represented Australia A in the Top End Series 2006, scoring century (130) v India A at Cairns. An overseas player with Derbyshire 2006-07
Best batting: 181 Derbyshire v Gloucestershire, Bristol 2006
Best bowling: 1-24 Derbyshire v Surrey, The Oval 2006

2007 Season

	M	Inn	NO	Runs	HS	Avg	100	50	Ct	St	Balls	Runs	Wkts	Avg	BB	5I	10M
Test																	
FC	13	24	1	884	162	38.43	2	5	22	-	21	26	0		-	-	-
ODI																	
List A	14	14	2	257	47	21.41	-	-	4	-	1	4	0		-	-	
20/20 Int																	
20/20	6	6	0	115	40	19.16	-	-	1	-	0	0	0		-	-	

Career Performances

	M	Inn	NO	Runs	HS	Avg	100	50	Ct	St	Balls	Runs	Wkts	Avg	BB	5I	10M
Test																	
FC	58	107	6	4002	181	39.62	9	24	40	-	172	145	2	72.50	1-24	-	-
ODI																	
List A	62	62	3	1599	145	27.10	2	7	21	-	91	89	5	17.80	2-15	-	
20/20 Int																	
20/20	12	12	1	165	40	15.00	-	-	3	-	0	0	0		-	-	

BLACKWELL, I. D. — Somerset

Name: Ian David Blackwell
Role: Left-hand bat, slow left-arm bowler; all-rounder/'team ball shiner'
Born: 10 June 1978, Chesterfield
Height: 6ft 2in
Nickname: Blackie, Donk, Chilli, Blackpiece, Doncarney, Le Donk
County debut: 1997 (Derbyshire), 2000 (Somerset)
County cap: 2001 (Somerset)
Test debut: 2005-06
ODI debut: 2002-03
1000 runs in a season: 2
1st-Class 200s: 1
Place in batting averages: 77th av. 39.23
Place in bowling averages: 63rd av. 29.65
Parents: John and Marilyn
Wife and date of marriage: Elizabeth, 30 September 2006

Family links with cricket: 'Dad played for Derbyshire Over 50s a few years ago but prefers to watch now'
Education: Manor School; Brookfield Community School
Qualifications: 9 GCSEs, 2 A-levels, Level 2 coaching award ('completing Level 3 this winter')
Career outside cricket: 'None as yet'
Off-season: 'Training in Taunton. Plenty of Wii action'
Overseas tours: Somerset to Cape Town 2000, 2001; England VI to Hong Kong 2001; England to Sri Lanka (ICC Champions Trophy) 2002-03, to Australia 2002-03 (VB Series), to Africa (World Cup) 2002-03, to Bangladesh and Sri Lanka 2003-04 (one-day series), to West Indies 2003-04 (one-day series), to Pakistan 2005-06 (one-day series), to India 2005-06; ECB National Academy to Australia 2002-03

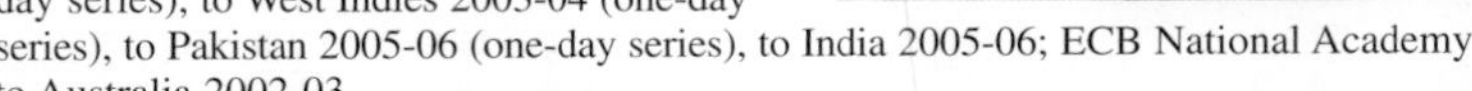

Overseas teams played for: Delacombe Park CC, Melbourne 1997, 1999; Spotswood CC, Melbourne
Career highlights to date: 'Playing for England. Winning the C&G Trophy 2001; winning the Twenty20 2005; promoted as champions of division two 2007'
Cricket moments to forget: 'All my noughts for England'
Cricket superstitions: 'Always chew gum'
Cricketers particularly admired: Ricky Ponting, Graeme Smith, Marcus Trescothick, Andrew Caddick, Peter Trego, James Hildreth, Viv Richards, Brian Lara
Young players to look out for: Tom Westley, Alex Wakely, Adil Rashid
Other sports played: Golf (6 handicap – 'more like 12 now'), football (Sheffield Wednesday Young Owls)
Other sports followed: Football (Chesterfield FC – 'Up the Spireites!')
Injuries: Out for three weeks with bruising on the bone of a knee
Favourite band: Eminem 'but any music really'
Relaxations: 'PS2 and the Wii'
Extras: Became first batsman in Championship history to score two centuries (103/122) in a match batting at No. 7, v Northants at Northampton 2001. Scored 134-ball double century (finishing with 247*) v Derbyshire at Taunton 2003, the fastest double century on record by an Englishman in terms of balls received. Won the Walter Lawrence Trophy 2005 (fastest first-class century of the season) for his 67-ball hundred (finishing with 107) v Derbyshire at Taunton. Captain of Somerset July 2005-2006, although absent injured for most of the 2006 season
Opinions on cricket: 'Would like to see one of the league one-day competitions axed and the knockout cup brought back. If you play poorly, you're out and you play less

cricket. If you keep winning, you don't mind the extra games. More Twenty20 cricket and day/night games.'
Best batting: 247* Somerset v Derbyshire, Taunton 2003
Best bowling: 7-90 Somerset v Glamorgan, Taunton 2004
7-90 Somerset v Nottinghamshire, Trent Bridge 2004

2007 Season

	M	Inn	NO	Runs	HS	Avg	100	50	Ct	St	Balls	Runs	Wkts	Avg	BB	5I	10M
Test																	
FC	15	19	2	667	141	39.23	1	5	2	-	1947	860	29	29.65	3-8	-	-
ODI																	
List A	15	15	1	436	97	31.14	-	3	5	-	641	509	18	28.27	3-39	-	
20/20 Int																	
20/20	2	1	1	42	42 *		-	-	-	-	48	37	1	37.00	1-12	-	

Career Performances

	M	Inn	NO	Runs	HS	Avg	100	50	Ct	St	Balls	Runs	Wkts	Avg	BB	5I	10M
Test	1	1	0	4	4	4.00	-	-	-	-	114	71	0		-	-	-
FC	130	196	15	7039	247 *	38.88	17	34	47	-	19276	9098	217	41.92	7-90	7	-
ODI	34	29	2	403	82	14.92	-	1	8	-	1230	877	24	36.54	3-26	-	
List A	209	191	17	4730	134 *	27.18	3	28	53	-	7027	5626	159	35.38	5-26	1	
20/20 Int																	
20/20	23	22	5	396	82	23.29	-	1	8	-	446	511	19	26.89	4-26	-	

9. Who became the first New Zealand batsman to carry his bat in a Test match, v England at Lord's in 1969?

BLAKE, A. J. Kent

Name: Alexander (Alex) James Blake
Role: Left-hand bat, right-arm medium-fast bowler; all-rounder
Born: 25 January 1989, Bromley, Kent
Height: 6ft 1in **Weight:** 14st
Nickname: Blakey, Butler, Brakey
County debut: 2007 (one-day)
Parents: Andrew and Michelle
Marital status: Single
Education: Hayes Secondary School
Qualifications: 8 GCSEs, 3 A-levels, Level 1 hockey coach
Off-season: 'Training and playing club cricket in Perth, Western Australia'
Overseas tours: England U19 to Malaysia 2006-07
Overseas teams played for: Balcatta CC, Perth 2007-08
Career highlights to date: 'Making my debut for Kent against Surrey in a Pro40 floodlit game on Sky Sports'
Cricket moments to forget: 'Being hit for three consecutive sixes by Inzamam-ul-Haq (Pro40 Kent v Yorkshire 2007)'
Cricket superstitions: 'Turn left at top of bowling mark'
Cricketers particularly admired: Brian Lara, Steve Waugh, Jacques Kallis
Young players to look out for: Daniel Bell Drummond
Other sports played: Hockey (HSBC HC)
Other sports followed: Football (Tottenham Hotspur)
Favourite band: The Fray, Kaiser Chiefs
Relaxations: 'Music, poker, TV'
Extras: Kent Academy Scholar of the Year 2005, 2006. Kent League Young Player of the Year 2007. Borough of Bromley Sports Personality of the Year 2007

2007 Season

	M	Inn	NO	Runs	HS	Avg	100	50	Ct	St	Balls	Runs	Wkts	Avg	BB	5I	10M
Test																	
FC																	
ODI																	
List A	3	2	2	15	11 *		-	-	-	-	72	61	1	61.00	1-25	-	
20/20 Int																	
20/20																	

Career Performances

	M	Inn	NO	Runs	HS	Avg	100	50	Ct	St	Balls	Runs	Wkts	Avg	BB	5I	10M
Test																	
FC																	
ODI																	
List A	3	2	2	15	11 *		-	-	-	-	72	61	1	61.00	1-25	-	
20/20 Int																	
20/20																	

BOJE, N. — Northamptonshire

Name: Nico (Nicky) Boje
Role: Left-hand bat, slow left-arm bowler; all-rounder
Born: 20 March 1973, Bloemfontein, South Africa
Nickname: Bodge
Height: 5ft 10in
County debut: 2002 (Nottinghamshire), 2007 (Northamptonshire)
Test debut: 1999-2000
ODI debut: 1995-96
Twenty20 Int debut: 2005-06
Place in batting averages: 61st av. 41.83
Place in bowling averages: 23rd av. 23.87
Family links with cricket: Older brother Eduard (E.H.L.) Boje played for Orange Free State 1989-90 – 1990-91
Education: Grey College, Bloemfontein

Overseas tours: South Africa A to Zimbabwe 1994-95, to England 1996, to Sri Lanka 1998-99 (vc), to Australia 2002-03; South Africa U24 to Sri Lanka 1995-96; South Africa to Zimbabwe 1995-96 (one-day series), to India 1996-97, to Bangladesh (Wills International Cup) 1998-99, to New Zealand 1998-99, to UK, Ireland and Netherlands (World Cup) 1999, to India 1999-2000, to Sri Lanka 2000, to Kenya (ICC Knockout Trophy) 2000-01, to West Indies 2000-01, to Australia 2001-02, to Sri Lanka (ICC Champions Trophy) 2002-03, to New Zealand 2003-04, to Sri Lanka 2004, to England (ICC Champions Trophy) 2004, to West Indies 2004-05, to Australia 2005-06, to Sri Lanka 2006, plus other one-day series and tournaments in Sharjah, Australia, Singapore, Morocco and England; South Africa VI to Hong Kong 2006 (c)
Overseas teams played for: Orange Free State/Free State 1990-91 – 2002-03; Eagles 2003-04 – 2006-07
Other sports played: Rugby, tennis

Extras: Represented South Africa Schools 1989-91. Attended South Africa Academy. One of *South African Cricket Annual*'s five Cricketers of the Year 2001. Represented South Africa in the 2002-03 World Cup. Represented African XI in the Afro-Asia Cup 2005-06. His series and match awards include Man of the [ODI] Series v New Zealand 2000-01 (had scores of 105*, 64 and 129 in the first three ODIs), Man of the Match in the second Test v India at Bangalore 1999-2000 (85 as nightwatchman plus 5-83 in India's second innings) and Man of the Match in the seventh ODI v Australia at Cape Town 2001-02 (49/5-21); Man of the Match in the final of the 2006 Hong Kong Sixes. Was Nottinghamshire's overseas player in 2002. Retired from international cricket in December 2006. Was a temporary overseas player with Northamptonshire during the 2007 season as a replacement for Johannes van der Wath; has returned for 2008 as a non-overseas player. Scored century (125), then followed up with second innings figures of 6-110 v Leicestershire at Leicester 2007
Best batting: 125 Northamptonshire v Leicestershire, Leicester 2007
Best bowling: 8-93 Eagles v Dolphins, Durban 2005-06

2007 Season

	M	Inn	NO	Runs	HS	Avg	100	50	Ct	St	Balls	Runs	Wkts	Avg	BB	5I	10M
Test																	
FC	4	7	1	251	125	41.83	1	1	1	-	817	382	16	23.87	6-110	1	-
ODI																	
List A	6	6	1	146	74 *	29.20	-	1	5	-	260	207	11	18.81	3-30	-	
20/20 Int																	
20/20																	

Career Performances

	M	Inn	NO	Runs	HS	Avg	100	50	Ct	St	Balls	Runs	Wkts	Avg	BB	5I	10M
Test	43	62	10	1312	85	25.23	-	4	18	-	8620	4265	100	42.65	5-62	3	-
FC	175	261	48	7059	125	33.14	6	42	104	-	36665	15874	499	31.81	8-93	22	2
ODI	115	71	18	1414	129	26.67	2	4	33	-	4541	3415	96	35.57	5-21	1	
List A	247	172	45	3379	129	26.60	2	13	75	-	10568	7548	232	32.53	5-21	1	
20/20 Int	1	0	0	0	0		-	-	-	-	24	27	1	27.00	1-27	-	
20/20	19	14	5	267	52 *	29.66	-	1	5	-	330	412	14	29.42	3-31	-	

BOLLINGER, D. E. Worcestershire

Name: Douglas (Doug) Erwin Bollinger
Role: Left-hand bat, left-arm fast-medium bowler
Born: 24 July 1981, Sydney, Australia
Height: 6ft 3½in
Nickname: Eagle
County debut: 2007
Place in bowling averages: 132nd av. 44.56
Overseas tours: New South Wales to India 2005-06; Australia A to Pakistan 2007-08
Overseas teams played for: New South Wales 2002-03 –
Extras: Represented Australia A v South Africa A 2002-03 and Australia Centre of Excellence in the Cricket Australia Emerging Players Tournament 2006. Became only the fourth bowler to achieve a hat-trick in the Australian domestic one-day competition, v South Australia (Cameron, Smith, Ferguson) at Canberra in the ING Cup 2004-05. Man of the Match v Queensland at Brisbane in the ING Cup 2005-06 (4-31). Recorded maiden first-class five-wicket innings return (5-73) v Tasmania at Hobart in the final of the Pura Cup 2006-07. Was an overseas player with Worcestershire 2007
Best batting: 31* New South Wales v Queensland, Brisbane 2006-07
Best bowling: 5-15 Australia A v Pakistan A, Lahore 2007-08
Stop press: Man of the Match v Tasmania at Sydney in the Pura Cup 2007-08 (6-68/6-63)

2007 Season

	M	Inn	NO	Runs	HS	Avg	100	50	Ct	St	Balls	Runs	Wkts	Avg	BB	5I	10M
Test																	
FC	7	8	2	38	21	6.33	-	-	-	-	1146	713	16	44.56	4-82	-	-
ODI																	
List A	9	3	1	12	7	6.00	-	-	2	-	390	348	11	31.63	3-36	-	
20/20 Int																	
20/20	4	1	0	5	5	5.00	-	-	-	-	60	105	2	52.50	1-35	-	

Career Performances

	M	Inn	NO	Runs	HS	Avg	100	50	Ct	St	Balls	Runs	Wkts	Avg	BB	5I	10M
Test																	
FC	36	44	20	180	31 *	7.50	-	-	12	-	6181	3530	88	40.11	5-15	2	-
ODI																	
List A	36	12	7	36	7 *	7.20	-	-	9	-	1717	1362	45	30.26	4-24	-	
20/20 Int																	
20/20	5	1	0	5	5	5.00	-	-	-	-	72	141	2	70.50	1-35	-	

BOPARA, R. S. — Essex

Name: Ravinder (Ravi) Singh Bopara
Role: Right-hand bat, right-arm medium bowler; batting all-rounder
Born: 4 May 1985, London
Height: 5ft 10in **Weight:** 12st 7lbs
Nickname: Puppy, Bops
County debut: 2002
County cap: 2005
ODI debut: 2006-07
1st-Class 200s: 1
Place in batting averages: 13th av. 60.00 (2006 100th av. 35.28)
Place in bowling averages: 130th av. 44.41 (2006 129th av. 45.00)
Parents: Baldish and Charanjit
Marital status: Engaged
Education: Brampton Manor School
Off-season: 'Hopefully playing for England'
Overseas tours: England U19 to Australia 2002-03, to Bangladesh (U19 World Cup) 2003-04; England A to West Indies 2005-06, to Bangladesh 2006-07; England to Australia 2006-07 (C'wealth Bank Series), to West Indies (World Cup) 2006-07, to Sri Lanka 2007-08, to New Zealand 2007-08 (one-day series)
Overseas teams played for: Rockingham-Mandurah CC, Perth 2004
Career highlights to date: 'Winning Sri Lanka [ODI] series away from home [2007-08]'
Cricket moments to forget: 'Any injuries, especially broken thumb'
Cricketers particularly admired: Sachin Tendulkar, Jacques Kallis
Injuries: Quad strain ('missed West Indies series'); broken thumb ('missed Twenty20 World Championship')
Relaxations: 'Music, pets'

Extras: Played for Development of Excellence XI (South) v West Indies U19 2001. Represented England U19 2003 and 2004. C&G Man of the Match award v Devon at Exmouth 2005 (65*). Scored 135 v Australians in a two-day game at Chelmsford 2005. Represented England A v Sri Lankans and v Pakistanis 2006. ECB National Academy 2005-06, 2006-07. Man of the Match v Sri Lanka in Antigua in the World Cup 2006-07 (52)
Best batting: 229 Essex v Northamptonshire, Chelmsford 2007
Best bowling: 5-75 Essex v Surrey, Colchester 2006
Stop press: Made Test debut in the first Test v Sri Lanka at Kandy 2007-08

2007 Season

	M	Inn	NO	Runs	HS	Avg	100	50	Ct	St	Balls	Runs	Wkts	Avg	BB	5I	10M
Test																	
FC	12	18	2	960	229	60.00	3	4	5	-	842	533	12	44.41	3-60	-	-
ODI	5	4	1	81	43 *	27.00	-	-	2	-	43	46	0		-	-	
List A	17	16	3	520	101	40.00	1	3	5	-	396	389	15	25.93	3-13	-	
20/20 Int																	
20/20	5	4	1	134	55	44.66	-	1	1	-	86	87	5	17.40	2-22	-	

Career Performances

	M	Inn	NO	Runs	HS	Avg	100	50	Ct	St	Balls	Runs	Wkts	Avg	BB	5I	10M
Test																	
FC	60	97	15	3206	229	39.09	6	12	40	-	4099	2831	58	48.81	5-75	1	-
ODI	14	12	4	253	52	31.62	-	1	3	-	139	121	3	40.33	2-43	-	
List A	86	79	20	1894	101 *	32.10	2	11	24	-	1756	1575	56	28.12	3-13	-	
20/20 Int																	
20/20	30	23	3	413	83	20.65	-	2	7	-	362	470	19	24.73	3-18	-	

BORRINGTON, P. M. Derbyshire

Name: Paul Michael Borrington
Role: Right-hand opening bat, right-arm off-spin bowler, occasional wicket-keeper
Born: 24 May 1988, Nottingham
Height: 5ft 10in **Weight:** 10st 4lbs
Nickname: Borrers, Boz, Bozza
County debut: 2005
Parents: Tony and Sheila
Marital status: Single
Family links with cricket: Father played for Derbyshire 1970-82
Education: Chellaston School; Repton School (sixth form); Loughborough University
Qualifications: GCSEs, A-levels
Career outside cricket: 'Second-year student at Loughborough University'

Off-season: 'Studying and preparing for the 2008 season'
Overseas tours: Derbyshire U15 to South Africa 2003; England U16 to South Africa 2004; Repton School to Sri Lanka 2005; Derbyshire Academy to South Africa 2007
Career highlights to date: 'Captaining the Midlands to victory in the 2003 Bunbury Festival. First-class debut v Leicestershire at the age of 17'
Cricket moments to forget: 'Leaving a straight ball on my first-class debut'
Cricket superstitions: 'None'
Cricketers particularly admired: Michael Vaughan
Young players to look out for: 'The current Derbyshire Academy'
Other sports played: Football, occasional golf
Other sports followed: Football (Crewe Alexandra)
Favourite band: Razorlight
Relaxations: 'Spending time with my friends'
Extras: NBC Denis Compton Award for the most promising young Derbyshire player 2005. Derbyshire Academy Player of the Year 2006
Best batting: 50 Derbyshire v Northamptonshire, Derby 2007

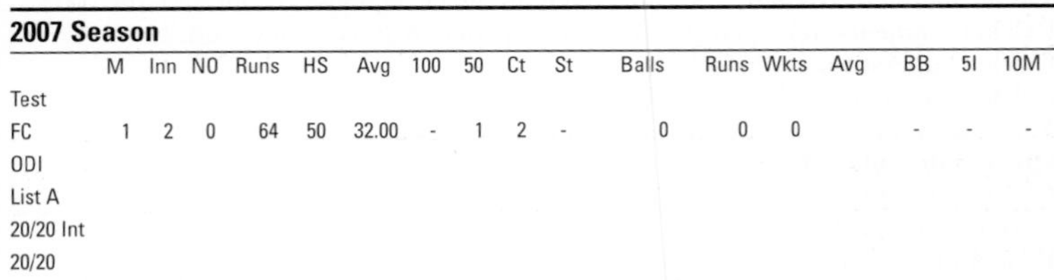

2007 Season

	M	Inn	NO	Runs	HS	Avg	100	50	Ct	St	Balls	Runs	Wkts	Avg	BB	5I	10M
Test																	
FC	1	2	0	64	50	32.00	-	1	2	-	0	0	0		-	-	-
ODI																	
List A																	
20/20 Int																	
20/20																	

Career Performances

	M	Inn	NO	Runs	HS	Avg	100	50	Ct	St	Balls	Runs	Wkts	Avg	BB	5I	10M
Test																	
FC	4	6	0	152	50	25.33	-	1	2	-	0	0	0		-	-	-
ODI																	
List A																	
20/20 Int																	
20/20																	

BOTHA, A. G. Warwickshire

Name: Anthony (Ant) Greyvensteyn Botha
Role: Left-hand bat, slow left-arm bowler
Born: 17 November 1976, Pretoria, South Africa
Height: 6ft **Weight:** 12st 7lbs
Nickname: Boats
County debut: 2004 (Derbyshire), 2007 (Warwickshire)
County cap: 2004 (Derbyshire)
50 wickets in a season: 1
Place in batting averages: 217th av. 20.31 (2006 177th av. 24.73)
Place in bowling averages: 60th av. 29.43 (2006 98th av. 38.75)
Parents: Elise and Ian
Marital status: Single
Education: Maritzburg College; Natal Tech
Qualifications: Marketing Manager Diploma
Overseas tours: South Africa U19 to India 1995-96
Overseas teams played for: Natal/KwaZulu-Natal 1995-96 – 1998-99; Easterns 1999-2000 – 2002-03; Joondalup CC, Perth 2005-06
Career highlights to date: 'Winning the four-day championship with Easterns 2002'
Cricket moments to forget: 'Getting badly injured in 2004 against Yorkshire'
Cricket superstitions: 'None'
Cricketers particularly admired: Steve Waugh, Jonty Rhodes
Young players to look out for: Greg Smith (Derbyshire)
Other sports played: Hockey, tennis
Other sports followed: Football (Liverpool), Super 14 rugby (Sharks)
Favourite band: Live
Relaxations: 'Watersports, beach'
Extras: Represented South African Schools 1995. Played for South Africa Academy 1997. Scored maiden first-class century (103) v Durham UCCE at Derby 2004, then took 5-55 in the DUCCE second innings to become the first Derbyshire player since 1937 to score a century and record a five-wicket innings return in the same first-class match. C&G Man of the Match award v Durham at Riverside 2005 (4-44/34*). Left Derbyshire towards the end of the 2007 season and joined Warwickshire. Is England-qualified
Best batting: 156* Derbyshire v Yorkshire, Derby 2005
Best bowling: 8-53 Natal B v Northerns B, Centurion 1997-98

2007 Season

	M	Inn	NO	Runs	HS	Avg	100	50	Ct	St	Balls	Runs	Wkts	Avg	BB	5I	10M
Test																	
FC	16	23	1	447	101	20.31	1	2	12	-	3318	1619	55	29.43	6-101	3	-
ODI																	
List A	15	12	4	267	54 *	33.37	-	2	5	-	475	425	13	32.69	3-52	-	
20/20 Int																	
20/20	6	5	0	82	26	16.40	-	-	1	-	111	127	9	14.11	4-14	-	

Career Performances

	M	Inn	NO	Runs	HS	Avg	100	50	Ct	St	Balls	Runs	Wkts	Avg	BB	5I	10M
Test																	
FC	100	160	22	3336	156 *	24.17	4	14	74	-	17917	8703	260	33.47	8-53	8	1
ODI																	
List A	109	84	25	1328	60 *	22.50	-	4	46	-	3942	3177	107	29.69	5-60	1	
20/20 Int																	
20/20	25	19	5	224	26	16.00	-	-	7	-	477	566	27	20.96	4-14	-	

BOYCE, M. A. G. Leicestershire

Name: Matthew (Matt) Andrew Golding Boyce
Role: Left-hand opening bat, right-arm medium bowler
Born: 13 August 1985, Cheltenham
Height: 5ft 10in **Weight:** 11st 4lbs
Nickname: Boycey, Ferret
County debut: 2006
Parents: Anne and Andrew
Marital status: Single
Family links with cricket: 'Father played recreational cricket for over 20 years and coached youth cricket for ten years. Aunt played for Cambridge University. Brother played for Oakham School for three years in 1st XI'
Education: Oakham School; Nottingham University
Qualifications: 2.1 in Management and Economics
Off-season: 'In Australia at Darren Lehmann's academy'
Overseas teams played for: Hoppers Crossing, Melbourne 2003-04

Career highlights to date: 'First-class debut and one-day debut. Scoring a double century [150-ball 225 for Rutland Championship side v Peterborough 2004]'
Cricket moments to forget: 'Going out to bat against Northants without a box on!'
Cricket superstitions: 'None'
Cricketers particularly admired: Graham Thorpe, Mark Ramprakash, Paul Nixon
Young players to look out for: Tom New, Josh Cobb
Other sports played: Rugby (Oakham School *Daily Mail* Cup winner), hockey (Midlands U14 and U16),
Injuries: Out for two weeks with a damaged shoulder nerve
Favourite band: The Fray, The Wallflowers
Relaxations: 'Poker, socialising, relaxing in general!'
Extras: County Council Special Award for Youth Cricket. *Rutland Times* Young Cricketer of the Year. Sporting Moment of the Year 2004 (225; *see above*). Rutland League Teenage Cricketer of the Year. Leading batsman in Leicestershire League
Opinions on cricket: 'In a game where so much is said about Kolpak players [*see page 13*], I believe the best young English players will still come through. Chances are for taking, not giving.'
Best batting: 6 Leicestershire v Pakistanis, Leicester 2006

2007 Season

	M	Inn	NO	Runs	HS	Avg	100	50	Ct	St	Balls	Runs	Wkts	Avg	BB	5I	10M
Test																	
FC	1	1	0	5	5	5.00	-	-	-	-	0	0	0		-	-	-
ODI																	
List A	1	1	0	36	36	36.00	-	-	-	-	0	0	0		-	-	
20/20 Int																	
20/20																	

Career Performances

	M	Inn	NO	Runs	HS	Avg	100	50	Ct	St	Balls	Runs	Wkts	Avg	BB	5I	10M
Test																	
FC	2	3	0	15	6	5.00	-	-	-	-	0	0	0		-	-	-
ODI																	
List A	1	1	0	36	36	36.00	-	-	-	-	0	0	0		-	-	
20/20 Int																	
20/20																	

BRAGG, W. D. — Glamorgan

Name: William (Will) David Bragg
Role: Left-hand bat, wicket-keeper
Born: 24 October 1986, Gwent, South Wales
Height: 5ft 10in **Weight:** 12st 6lbs
Nickname: Braggy, Milf, Braggpot, Pottsy
County debut: 2007
Parents: Susan and Steven
Marital status: Single
Family links with cricket: 'Father and brother have both played for local sides (Malpas CC)'
Education: Rougemont Independent School; Cardiff University
Qualifications: 11 GCSEs, 4 A-levels
Career highlights to date: 'Playing for Glamorgan'
Cricket moments to forget: 'Dropping easy catches'
Cricket superstitions: 'Put box on last'
Cricketers particularly admired: Matthew Maynard, Alan Jones, Brian Lara
Young players to look out for: Tom Maynard, Ben Wright, Mike O'Shea, James Harris
Other sports played: Rugby (for school), football (Gwent County)
Other sports followed: Football (Tottenham)
Favourite band: Razorlight
Extras: Scored most runs by any batsman for Wales U15. Played for Wales Minor Counties in the C&G 2005 and in Minor Counties competitions 2004-06
Opinions on cricket: 'One-day cricket seems to pull in the crowds, exciting. Four-day cricket seems far slower and more boring.'
Best batting: 24 Glamorgan v Somerset, Taunton 2007

2007 Season

	M	Inn	NO	Runs	HS	Avg	100	50	Ct	St	Balls	Runs	Wkts	Avg	BB	5I	10M
Test																	
FC	2	4	0	51	24	12.75	-	-	-	-	0	0	0		-	-	-
ODI																	
List A																	
20/20 Int																	
20/20																	

Career Performances

	M	Inn	NO	Runs	HS	Avg	100	50	Ct	St	Balls	Runs	Wkts	Avg	BB	5I	10M
Test																	
FC	2	4	0	51	24	12.75	-	-	-	-	0	0	0		-	-	-
ODI																	
List A	1	1	1	41	41 *		-	-	1	-	0	0	0		-	-	
20/20 Int																	
20/20																	

BREESE, G. R. Durham

Name: Gareth Rohan Breese
Role: Right-hand bat, right-arm off-spin bowler; all-rounder
Born: 9 January 1976, Montego Bay, Jamaica
Height: 5ft 8in **Weight:** 13st
Nickname: Briggy
County debut: 2004
Test debut: 2002-03
Place in batting averages: 241st av. 16.11 (2006 203rd av. 21.48)
Place in bowling averages: (2006 136th av. 48.03)
Parents: Brian and Jean
Marital status: Single
Family links with cricket: Father played league cricket in Somerset and Wales; also played representative cricket for two parishes in Jamaica as wicket-keeper/batsman. He is currently the cricket operations officer of the Jamaica Cricket Association
Education: Wolmer's Boys School, Kingston; University of Technology, Kingston
Qualifications: Level 2 coach, Diploma in Hotel and Resort Management
Overseas tours: West Indies U19 to Pakistan and Bangladesh 1995-96; Jamaica to Malaysia (Commonwealth Games) 1998-99; West Indies A to England 2002; West Indies to India 2002-03
Overseas teams played for: Jamaica 1995-96 – 2005-06
Career highlights to date: 'Playing at the highest level and representing Durham over the last four seasons'
Cricket moments to forget: 'My two Test innings'
Cricket superstitions: 'None'

Cricketers particularly admired: Jimmy Adams, Courtney Walsh, Delroy Morgan (Jamaica), Dale Benkenstein, Gordon Muchall
Young players to look out for: Gordon Muchall, Nick Cook, Ben Harmison
Other sports played: Pool
Relaxations: 'My computer; music, shopping; hanging out with team-mates/friends'
Extras: Represented West Indies U19 1994-95. Second-highest wicket-taker in the Busta Cup 2000-01 with 36 (av. 15.11) and in 2001-02 with 44 (av. 20.18). Captain of Jamaica in first-class cricket 2003-04 and in one-day cricket 2004-05. Scored 165* as Durham made 453-9 to beat Somerset at Taunton 2004. Scored century (110) v Middlesex at Lord's 2006, in the process sharing with Dale Benkenstein (125) in a new record fifth-wicket partnership for Durham (222). Is a British passport-holder and is not considered an overseas player
Best batting: 165* Durham v Somerset, Taunton 2004
Best bowling: 7-60 Jamaica v Barbados, Bridgetown 2000-01

2007 Season

	M	Inn	NO	Runs	HS	Avg	100	50	Ct	St	Balls	Runs	Wkts	Avg	BB	5I	10M
Test																	
FC	5	10	1	145	53	16.11	-	1	6	-	504	368	5	73.60	3-102	-	-
ODI																	
List A	19	12	2	217	68 *	21.70	-	1	3	-	739	611	25	24.44	5-49	1	
20/20 Int																	
20/20	6	3	1	12	6	6.00	-	-	1	-	103	87	8	10.87	3-5	-	

Career Performances

	M	Inn	NO	Runs	HS	Avg	100	50	Ct	St	Balls	Runs	Wkts	Avg	BB	5I	10M
Test	1	2	0	5	5	2.50	-	-	1	-	188	135	2	67.50	2-108	-	-
FC	110	178	19	4086	165 *	25.69	3	26	91	-	17810	8266	273	30.27	7-60	12	3
ODI																	
List A	105	76	16	1146	68 *	19.10	-	3	45	-	4118	3076	112	27.46	5-49	1	
20/20 Int																	
20/20	25	20	4	133	24 *	8.31	-	-	9	-	469	513	29	17.68	4-14	-	

BRESNAN, T. T. — Yorkshire

Name: Timothy (Tim) Thomas Bresnan
Role: Right-hand bat, right-arm fast bowler; all-rounder
Born: 28 February 1985, Pontefract
Height: 6ft 1in **Weight:** 14st 7lbs
Nickname: Brez, Brezzie, Tikka
County debut: 2001 (one-day), 2003 (first-class)
County cap: 2006
ODI debut: 2006
Twenty20 Int debut: 2006
Place in batting averages: 38th av. 48.50 (2006 184th av. 24.18)
Place in bowling averages: 91st av. 34.02 (2006 61st av. 32.06)
Parents: Julie and Ray
Marital status: Single
Family links with cricket: 'Dad played local league cricket'
Education: Castleford High School; Pontefract New College
Qualifications: 11 GCSEs, UKCC 2 cricket coaching, Advanced Scuba Diver Level II
Overseas tours: Yorkshire U16 to Cape Town 2001; England U17 to Australia 2000-01; England U19 to Australia and (U19 World Cup) New Zealand 2001-02, to Australia 2002-03, to Bangladesh (U19 World Cup) 2003-04; England VI to Hong Kong 2006; England A to Bangladesh 2006-07; England Performance Programme to India 2007-08
Overseas teams played for: Sutherland CC, Sydney 2005-06
Career highlights to date: 'Making England debut, Lord's 2006'
Cricket moments to forget: 'First big injury, June 2006'
Cricket superstitions: 'None'
Cricketers particularly admired: Ian Botham
Young players to look out for: Jack Hughes
Other sports played: Golf
Other sports followed: Football (Sheffield United)
Favourite band: Razorlight, Snow Patrol
Relaxations: 'PlayStation, cinema'
Extras: Bunbury Festival Best All-rounder and Most Outstanding Player 2000. Made one-day debut v Kent at Headingley 2001 aged 16 years 102 days, making him the youngest player to represent Yorkshire since Paul Jarvis in 1981. NBC Denis Compton Award for the most promising young Yorkshire player 2002, 2003. Represented England U19 2002 and 2003. Scored maiden first-class century (116) v Surrey at The

Oval 2007, in the process sharing with Jason Gillespie (123*) in a new record ninth-wicket partnership for Yorkshire (246)
Best batting: 126* England A v Indians, Chelmsford 2007
Best bowling: 5-42 Yorkshire v Worcestershire, Worcester 2005

2007 Season

	M	Inn	NO	Runs	HS	Avg	100	50	Ct	St	Balls	Runs	Wkts	Avg	BB	5I	10M
Test																	
FC	16	21	7	679	126 *	48.50	3	2	6	-	2124	1157	34	34.02	4-10	-	-
ODI																	
List A	16	11	4	182	33	26.00	-	-	2	-	599	565	15	37.66	3-22	-	
20/20 Int																	
20/20	8	5	1	50	25 *	12.50	-	-	3	-	108	146	5	29.20	2-9	-	

Career Performances

	M	Inn	NO	Runs	HS	Avg	100	50	Ct	St	Balls	Runs	Wkts	Avg	BB	5I	10M
Test																	
FC	59	79	14	1671	126 *	25.70	3	8	22	-	8605	4730	145	32.62	5-42	2	-
ODI	4	4	1	51	20	17.00	-	-	1	-	150	169	2	84.50	1-38	-	
List A	108	74	21	971	61	18.32	-	1	30	-	4357	3693	95	38.87	4-25	-	
20/20 Int	1	1	1	6	6 *		-	-	-	-	12	20	0		-	-	
20/20	30	21	8	273	42	21.00	-	-	10	-	536	680	31	21.93	3-21	-	

BROAD, S. C. J. — Nottinghamshire

Name: Stuart Christopher John Broad
Role: Left-hand bat, right-arm fast-medium bowler
Born: 24 June 1986, Nottingham
Height: 6ft 6in **Weight:** 13st
Nickname: Broady
County debut: 2005 (Leicestershire)
County cap: 2007 (Leicestershire)
ODI debut: 2006
Twenty20 Int debut: 2006
Place in batting averages: (2006 204th av. 21.46)
Place in bowling averages: 35th av. 25.08 (2006 53rd av. 31.06)
Parents: Carole and Chris
Marital status: Single
Family links with cricket: 'Dad played for Glos, Notts and England'

Education: Oakham School
Qualifications: 10 GCSEs, 3 A-levels
Overseas tours: Oakham School to South Africa 2000-01; England A to West Indies 2005-06, to Bangladesh 2006-07; England to Australia 2006-07 (C'wealth Bank Series), to West Indies (World Cup) 2006-07, to South Africa (World 20/20) 2007-08, to Sri Lanka 2007-08, to New Zealand 2007-08
Overseas teams played for: Hoppers Crossing CC, Melbourne 2004-05
Career highlights to date: 'England ODI debut v Pakistan 2006. Winning Twenty20 Cup 2006 with Leicestershire'
Cricket superstitions: 'Three warm-up balls before I bowl a new spell'
Cricketers particularly admired: Glenn McGrath, Shaun Pollock
Young players to look out for: Mark Collier
Other sports played: Hockey (Midlands age groups), golf
Other sports followed: Football (Nottingham Forest), rugby (Leicester Tigers)
Favourite band: Snow Patrol
Relaxations: 'PSP, playing golf, films'
Extras: Leicestershire Young Cricketers' Batsman of the Year 2003. Represented England U19 2005. Cricket Writers' Club Young Cricketer of the Year 2006. Cricket Society Most Promising Young Cricketer of the Year 2006. ECB National Academy 2005-06, 2006-07. Man of the Match in the fourth ODI v India at Old Trafford 2007 (4-51/45*). Left Leicestershire at the end of the 2007 season and has joined Nottinghamshire for 2008
Opinions on cricket: 'From what I've seen, Kolpak cricketers [*see page 13*] improve the standard of cricket in England, but it is good to see the ECB controlling the number of players that come over. The best youngsters still break through. Playing against better players can only make England stronger in the future because youngsters have to improve their game to compete.'
Best batting: 91* Leicestershire v Derbyshire, Leicester 2007
Best bowling: 5-67 Leicestershire v Derbyshire, Leicester 2007
Stop press: Made Test debut in the second Test v Sri Lanka in Colombo 2007-08

10. Which future Derbyshire player opened the batting for South Africa throughout the 1965 series against England?

2007 Season

	M	Inn	NO	Runs	HS	Avg	100	50	Ct	St	Balls	Runs	Wkts	Avg	BB	5I	10M
Test																	
FC	6	7	2	247	91 *	49.40	-	2	-	-	964	602	24	25.08	5-67	2	-
ODI	10	7	3	112	45 *	28.00	-	-	2	-	562	480	14	34.28	4-51	-	
List A	16	9	3	119	45 *	19.83	-	-	3	-	850	738	24	30.75	4-51	-	
20/20 Int	2	1	1	1	1 *		-	-	2	-	42	63	2	31.50	1-31	-	
20/20	3	1	1	1	1 *		-	-	2	-	60	91	4	22.75	2-28	-	

Career Performances

	M	Inn	NO	Runs	HS	Avg	100	50	Ct	St	Balls	Runs	Wkts	Avg	BB	5I	10M
Test																	
FC	33	40	11	643	91 *	22.17	-	4	8	-	5253	3181	112	28.40	5-67	6	-
ODI	16	11	7	126	45 *	31.50	-	-	4	-	812	697	19	36.68	4-51	-	
List A	31	15	8	155	45 *	22.14	-	-	6	-	1528	1340	41	32.68	4-51	-	
20/20 Int	8	4	2	6	3 *	3.00	-	-	3	-	180	282	9	31.33	3-37	-	
20/20	17	4	2	6	3 *	3.00	-	-	4	-	390	454	23	19.73	3-13	-	

BROPHY, G. L. — Yorkshire

Name: Gerard Louis Brophy
Role: Right-hand bat, wicket-keeper
Born: 26 November 1975, Welkom, South Africa
Height: 5ft 11in **Weight:** 12st
Nickname: Scuba, Broph
County debut: 2002 (Northamptonshire), 2006 (Yorkshire)
Place in batting averages: 117th av. 32.94 (2006 236th av. 15.68)
Parents: Gerard and Trish
Wife and date of marriage: Alison, 3 January 2004
Education: Christian Brothers College, Boksburg; Wits Technikon (both South Africa)
Qualifications: Marketing Diploma, Level 2 coach
Overseas tours: South Africa U17 to England 1993; South Africa Academy to Zimbabwe 1998-99
Overseas teams played for: Gauteng 1996-97 – 1998-99; Free State 1999-2000 – 2000-01

Career highlights to date: 'Captaincy of Free State 2000-01. First dismissal [in collaboration] with Allan Donald'
Cricket moments to forget: 'Messing up a live TV interview'
Cricket superstitions: 'Right pad on first and right glove on first'
Cricketers particularly admired: Ray Jennings, Ian Healy, Allan Donald, Hansie Cronje
Other sports played: Golf, rugby
Other sports followed: Golf, rugby
Favourite band: Coldplay
Relaxations: 'Fishing, travelling, braais, scuba diving'
Extras: Captained South Africa U17. Played for Ireland in the NatWest 2000. Holds a British passport and is not considered an overseas player
Best batting: 185 South Africa Academy v ZCU President's XI, Harare (S) 1998-99

2007 Season

	M	Inn	NO	Runs	HS	Avg	100	50	Ct	St	Balls	Runs	Wkts	Avg	BB	5I	10M
Test																	
FC	13	19	1	593	100 *	32.94	1	2	35	4	0	0	0		-	-	-
ODI																	
List A	11	10	1	297	66	33.00	-	2	8	3	0	0	0		-	-	
20/20 Int																	
20/20	8	8	2	151	44	25.16	-	-	3	-	0	0	0		-	-	

Career Performances

	M	Inn	NO	Runs	HS	Avg	100	50	Ct	St	Balls	Runs	Wkts	Avg	BB	5I	10M
Test																	
FC	76	121	15	3352	185	31.62	6	15	186	14	6	1	0		-	-	-
ODI																	
List A	78	62	10	1238	66	23.80	-	6	66	16	0	0	0		-	-	
20/20 Int																	
20/20	23	20	6	362	57	25.85	-	1	8	1	0	0	0		-	-	

11. Who was recalled to the England Test side for the match against South Africa at Headingley in 2003 more than ten years after his previous Test appearance?

BROWN, A. D. Surrey

Name: Alistair Duncan Brown
Role: Right-hand bat, right-arm off-spin bowler, occasional wicket-keeper
Born: 11 February 1970, Beckenham
Height: 5ft 10in **Weight:** 12st 7lbs
Nickname: The Lord
County debut: 1990 (one-day), 1992 (first-class)
County cap: 1994
Benefit: 2002
ODI debut: 1996
1000 runs in a season: 8
1st-Class 200s: 3
List A 200s: 2
Place in batting averages: 194th av. 23.08 (2006 30th av. 54.95)
Parents: Robert and Ann
Wife and date of marriage: Sarah, 10 October 1998
Children: Max Charles, 9 March 2001; Joe Robert, 11 March 2003
Family links with cricket: Father played for Surrey Young Amateurs in the 1950s
Education: Caterham School
Qualifications: 5 O-levels, Level II coach
Overseas tours: England VI to Singapore 1993, 1994, 1995, to Hong Kong 1997; England to Sharjah (Champions Trophy) 1997-98, to Bangladesh (Wills International Cup) 1998-99
Overseas teams played for: North Perth, Western Australia 1989-90
Career highlights to date: '118 v India at Old Trafford 1996; 203 v Hampshire at Guildford 1997; 268 v Glamorgan at The Oval 2002'
Cricket moments to forget: 'A great couple of days in Ireland!'
Cricket superstitions: 'Always get to the ground before 11 a.m.'
Cricketers particularly admired: Ian Botham, Viv Richards
Other sports played: Football, golf
Other sports followed: Football (West Ham United), rugby union (London Wasps)
Favourite band: Roachford, Snow Patrol
Relaxations: 'Golf and sleep (when the children allow)'
Extras: Man of the Match for his 118 against India in the third ODI at Old Trafford 1996. Recorded the highest-ever score in the Sunday League with 203 off 119 balls against Hampshire at Guildford in 1997 and received an individual award at the PCA dinner for that achievement. Joint winner (with Carl Hooper) of the EDS Walter Lawrence Trophy for the fastest first-class 100 of the 1998 season (72 balls v

Northants at The Oval). Surrey CCC Batsman of the Season 2001. Scored 160-ball 268 out of 438-5 v Glamorgan at The Oval in the C&G 2002; it set a new record for the highest individual score in professional one-day cricket worldwide and Brown also became the first batsman to have scored two double centuries in one-day cricket. Scored 154 v Lancashire at Old Trafford 2004 to complete full set of first-class hundreds against all 17 other counties. Scored 97-ball 176 v Gloucestershire at The Oval in the Friends Provident 2007, in the process sharing with James Benning (152) in a Surrey record one-day partnership (294) as the county posted a world record List A total of 496-4

Best batting: 295* Surrey v Leicestershire, Oakham School 2000
Best bowling: 3-25 Surrey v Somerset, Guildford 2006

2007 Season

	M	Inn	NO	Runs	HS	Avg	100	50	Ct	St	Balls	Runs	Wkts	Avg	BB	5I	10M
Test																	
FC	9	14	2	277	69	23.08	-	3	7	-	48	38	0		-	-	-
ODI																	
List A	15	14	0	411	176	29.35	1	2	3	-	66	86	2	43.00	1-24	-	
20/20 Int																	
20/20	8	8	0	124	31	15.50	-	-	2	-	0	0	0		-	-	

Career Performances

	M	Inn	NO	Runs	HS	Avg	100	50	Ct	St	Balls	Runs	Wkts	Avg	BB	5I	10M
Test																	
FC	240	379	41	14705	295 *	43.50	44	60	242	1	1188	630	5	126.00	3-25	-	-
ODI	16	16	0	354	118	22.12	1	1	6	-	6	5	0		-	-	
List A	369	354	17	10698	268	31.74	19	49	125	-	489	524	14	37.42	3-39	-	
20/20 Int																	
20/20	42	42	1	978	83	23.85	-	6	28	-	2	2	0		-	-	

BROWN, B. C. — Sussex

Name: Ben Christopher Brown
Role: Right-hand bat, wicket-keeper
Born: 23 November 1988, Crawley
Height: 5ft 8in **Weight:** 11st 10lbs
County debut: 2007
Parents: Diana and Chris
Marital status: Single
Education: Ardingly College
Qualifications: 9 GCSEs, 2 A-levels, Level 2 coaching, NVQ in Cricket
Off-season: 'Touring with England U19 to Sri Lanka and then on to Malaysia for U19 World Cup'

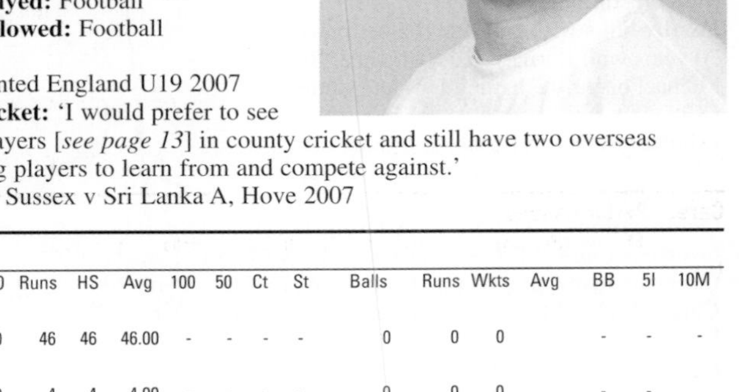

Overseas tours: Sussex Academy to Cape Town 2005; England U19 to Malaysia 2006-07, to Malaysia (U19 World Cup) 2007-08
Career highlights to date: 'Getting my first contract at Sussex'
Cricket moments to forget: 'Running into Billy Godleman and subsequently being run out for 0 on TV debut!'
Cricket superstitions: 'None'
Cricketers particularly admired: Alec Stewart, Adam Gilchrist
Young players to look out for: Matt Machan, Will Beer, Michael Thornely
Other sports played: Football
Other sports followed: Football (Chelsea FC)
Extras: Represented England U19 2007
Opinions on cricket: 'I would prefer to see fewer Kolpak players [*see page 13*] in county cricket and still have two overseas players for young players to learn from and compete against.'
Best batting: 46 Sussex v Sri Lanka A, Hove 2007

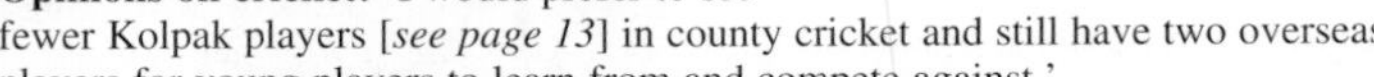

2007 Season

	M	Inn	NO	Runs	HS	Avg	100	50	Ct	St	Balls	Runs	Wkts	Avg	BB	5I	10M
Test																	
FC	1	1	0	46	46	46.00	-	-	-	-	0	0	0		-	-	-
ODI																	
List A	1	1	0	4	4	4.00	-	-	-	-	0	0	0		-	-	
20/20 Int																	
20/20																	

Career Performances

	M	Inn	NO	Runs	HS	Avg	100	50	Ct	St	Balls	Runs	Wkts	Avg	BB	5I	10M
Test																	
FC	1	1	0	46	46	46.00	-	-	-	-	0	0	0		-	-	-
ODI																	
List A	1	1	0	4	4	4.00	-	-	-	-	0	0	0		-	-	
20/20 Int																	
20/20																	

BROWN, D. O. Gloucestershire

Name: David Owen Brown
Role: Right-hand bat, right-arm medium bowler
Born: 8 December 1982, Burnley
Height: 6ft **Weight:** 13st 7lbs
Nickname: Wally, Browny
County debut: 2006
County cap: 2006
Place in batting averages: 244th av. 15.33
Parents: Peter and Valerie
Marital status: Single
Family links with cricket: 'Father played for 30 years with Burnley and Southgate. Brother Michael opens the batting for Hampshire CCC'
Education: Queen Elizabeth's Grammar School, Blackburn; Collingwood College, Durham University
Qualifications: 10 GCSEs, 4 A-levels, BA (Hons) Sport in the Community
Overseas tours: MCC B to Nepal 2003; MCC A to Canada 2005
Overseas teams played for: Claremont-Nedlands, Perth 2001-02; Perth CC 2005-06
Career highlights to date: 'Signing for Gloucestershire CCC. Playing for Durham University'
Cricket moments to forget: 'First-class debut v Notts for Durham University 2003 – got golden duck and went the distance. Any time I self-destruct'
Cricket superstitions: 'None'
Cricketers particularly admired: Dale Benkenstein, Andrew Flintoff, Ricky Ponting, James Anderson
Young players to look out for: Will Smith, Ali Maiden, David Balcombe, Jonathan Clare, James Allenby, Luke Ronchi, Lee Daggett
Other sports played: Golf, football
Other sports followed: Football (Burnley FC)
Favourite band: Dire Straits, Fleetwood Mac, Eagles, 'any "cheese"'
Relaxations: 'Championship Manager; watching *The Office*, *Alan Partridge*; golf, DVDs, cinema, socialising, sleeping'
Extras: Played for Durham UCCE 2003-05. Represented British Universities 2005. Struck 26-ball 63* on one-day debut v Surrey at Bristol in the C&G 2006
Best batting: 77 DUCCE v Leicestershire, Leicester 2005
Best bowling: 2-25 Gloucestershire v Northamptonshire, Gloucester 2007

2007 Season

	M	Inn	NO	Runs	HS	Avg	100	50	Ct	St	Balls	Runs	Wkts	Avg	BB	5I	10M
Test																	
FC	3	6	0	92	43	15.33	-	-	-	-	228	140	2	70.00	2-25	-	-
ODI																	
List A	9	8	2	126	33	21.00	-	-	2	-	204	185	8	23.12	3-29	-	
20/20 Int																	
20/20	5	3	0	24	14	8.00	-	-	1	-	36	35	3	11.66	1-11	-	

Career Performances

	M	Inn	NO	Runs	HS	Avg	100	50	Ct	St	Balls	Runs	Wkts	Avg	BB	5I	10M
Test																	
FC	14	24	0	590	77	24.58	-	4	7	-	1062	819	12	68.25	2-25	-	-
ODI																	
List A	11	10	3	203	63 *	29.00	-	1	2	-	234	232	8	29.00	3-29	-	
20/20 Int																	
20/20	14	11	1	162	36	16.20	-	-	3	-	36	35	3	11.66	1-11	-	

BROWN, D. R. Warwickshire

Name: Douglas (Dougie) Robert Brown
Role: Right-hand bat, right-arm fast-medium bowler; all-rounder
Born: 29 October 1969, Stirling, Scotland
Height: 6ft 2in **Weight:** 14st 7lbs
Nickname: Hoots
County debut: 1991 (one-day), 1991-92 (first-class)
County cap: 1995
Benefit: 2005
ODI debut: 1997-98
Twenty20 Int debut: 2007-08
1000 runs in a season: 1
50 wickets in a season: 4
1st-Class 200s: 1
Place in batting averages: (2006 208th av. 20.44)
Place in bowling averages: (2006 32nd av. 28.48)
Parents: Alastair and Janette
Children: Lauren, 14 September 1998
Family links with cricket: 'Both grandads played a bit'

Education: Alloa Academy; West London Institute of Higher Education (Borough Road College)
Qualifications: 9 O-Grades, 5 Higher Grades, BEd (Hons) Physical Education, ECB Level III coach
Career outside cricket: PE teacher
Overseas tours: Scotland XI to Pakistan 1988-89; England VI to Hong Kong 1997, 2001, 2003; England A to Kenya and Sri Lanka 1997-98; England to Sharjah (Champions Trophy) 1997-98, to West Indies 1997-98 (one-day series), to Bangladesh (Wills International Cup) 1998-99; Scotland to UAE (ICC Six Nations Challenge) 2003-04, to Ireland (ICC Trophy) 2005, to Bangladesh (one-day series) 2006-07, to Kenya (including ICC World Cricket League) 2006-07, to West Indies (World Cup) 2006-07, to South Africa (World 20/20) 2007-08
Overseas teams played for: Primrose, Cape Town 1992-93; Vredenburg Saldhana, Cape Town 1993-94; Eastern Suburbs, Wellington 1995-96; Wellington, New Zealand 1995-96; Namibia 2002-03
Career highlights: 'Playing first Lord's final v Northants 1995. England debut in Sharjah'
Cricket moments to forget: 'Phone call from David Graveney (chairman of selectors) saying you are dropped!'
Cricket superstitions: 'None'
Cricketers particularly admired: Ian Botham, Wasim Akram, Dermot Reeve 'and everyone who gives 100 per cent'
Other sports played: Golf
Other sports followed: Football (Alloa Athletic, 'and all the Midlands football teams')
Favourite band: Oasis, U2
Relaxations: 'Music, time with Lauren'
Extras: Played football at Hampden Park for Scotland U18. Has played first-class and one-day cricket (including ODI and Twenty20 Int) for Scotland; has also played ODI cricket for England. Scored 1118 runs and took 109 wickets in all first-team county cricket 1997. Vice-captain of Warwickshire 2002-03. Warwickshire All-rounder of the Year 2002. Scored 108 v Essex at Edgbaston in the C&G 2003, winning Man of the Match award and sharing with Ashley Giles (71*) in a competition record seventh-wicket partnership (170). Scored century (108*) then returned first innings figures of 5-53 v Northamptonshire at Northampton 2004. Took 500th first-class wicket for Warwickshire (Ed Smith), v Middlesex at Lord's 2006. Elected chair of the PCA, April 2007. Retired from county cricket at the end of the 2007 season and has taken up the post of Warwickshire Academy Director
Opinions on cricket: 'Still a great game!'
Best batting: 203 Warwickshire v Sussex, Hove 2000
Best bowling: 8-89 First-Class Counties XI v Pakistan A, Chelmsford 1997

2007 Season

	M	Inn	NO	Runs	HS	Avg	100	50	Ct	St	Balls	Runs	Wkts	Avg	BB	5I	10M
Test																	
FC																	
ODI																	
List A																	
20/20 Int																	
20/20	1	1	1	20	20 *		-	-	-	-	0	0	0		-	-	

Career Performances

	M	Inn	NO	Runs	HS	Avg	100	50	Ct	St	Balls	Runs	Wkts	Avg	BB	5I	10M
Test																	
FC	209	319	41	8511	203	30.61	10	44	130	-	30855	16177	567	28.53	8-89	21	4
ODI	25	24	6	319	50 *	17.72	-	1	4	-	953	919	22	41.77	3-37	-	
List A	314	256	42	4883	108	22.81	1	23	76	-	12942	9979	370	26.97	5-31	2	
20/20 Int	2	1	0	1	1	1.00	-	-	-	-	24	44	0		-	-	
20/20	30	22	2	244	37	12.20	-	-	9	-	504	655	23	28.47	3-21	-	

BROWN, J. F. — Northamptonshire

Name: Jason Fred Brown
Role: Right-hand bat, off-spin bowler
Born: 10 October 1974, Newcastle-under-Lyme
Height: 6ft **Weight:** 13st
Nickname: Cheese, Fish, Brownie
County debut: 1996
County cap: 2000
Benefit: 2008
50 wickets in a season: 3
Place in bowling averages: 120th av. 41.16 (2006 139th av. 50.42)
Parents: Peter and Cynthia
Wife and date of marriage: Sam, 26 September 1998
Children: Millie
Education: St Margaret Ward RC School, Stoke-on-Trent
Qualifications: 9 GCSEs, Level 1 coaching qualification
Overseas tours: Kidsgrove League U18 to Australia 1990; Northants CCC to Zimbabwe 1998, to Grenada 2000; England A to West Indies 2000-01; England to Sri Lanka 2000-01

Overseas teams played for: North East Valley, Dunedin, New Zealand 1996-97
Cricketers particularly admired: John Emburey, Carl Hooper
Other sports played: Golf
Other sports followed: Football (Port Vale)
Relaxations: 'Reading, listening to music'
Extras: Represented Staffordshire at all junior levels, in Minor Counties, and in the NatWest 1995. Once took 10-16 in a Kidsgrove League game against Haslington U18 playing for Sandyford U18. Took 100th first-class wicket in 23rd match, v Sussex at Northampton 2000, going on to take his 50th wicket of the season in the same game, only his seventh of the summer. Took 5-27 v Somerset at Northampton 2003, the best return by a Northants bowler in the Twenty20 Cup. C&G Man of the Match award for his 5-19 v Cambridgeshire at Northampton 2004
Best batting: 38 Northamptonshire v Hampshire, Northampton 2003
Best bowling: 7-69 Northamptonshire v Durham, Riverside 2003

2007 Season

	M	Inn	NO	Runs	HS	Avg	100	50	Ct	St	Balls	Runs	Wkts	Avg	BB	5I	10M
Test																	
FC	14	17	6	108	25	9.81	-	-	3	-	2723	1235	30	41.16	5-47	1	-
ODI																	
List A	13	3	2	9	6 *	9.00	-	-	2	-	628	514	8	64.25	2-35	-	
20/20 Int																	
20/20	7	0	0	0	0		-	-	2	-	108	116	6	19.33	3-16	-	

Career Performances

	M	Inn	NO	Runs	HS	Avg	100	50	Ct	St	Balls	Runs	Wkts	Avg	BB	5I	10M
Test																	
FC	119	140	57	616	38	7.42	-	-	24	-	29450	13210	404	32.69	7-69	22	5
ODI																	
List A	142	51	31	116	16	5.80	-	-	28	-	6788	4940	127	38.89	5-19	1	
20/20 Int																	
20/20	33	2	1	9	6 *	9.00	-	-	8	-	653	805	34	23.67	5-27	1	

BROWN, K. R. — Lancashire

Name: Karl Robert Brown
Role: Right-hand bat, right-arm medium bowler
Born: 17 May 1988, Bolton
Height: 5ft 10in **Weight:** 10st 11lbs
Nickname: Brownie, Charlie
County debut: 2006
Parents: Paul and Lorraine
Marital status: Single

Family links with cricket: Father a club cricketer for over 30 years and had two seasons as club professional at Clifton CC in the Bolton Association
Education: Hesketh Fletcher CE, Atherton, Lancashire
Qualifications: 8 GCSEs
Overseas tours: England U16 to South Africa 2003-04; England U19 to Bangladesh 2005-06, to Malaysia 2006-07
Cricket superstitions: 'None'
Cricketers particularly admired: Andrew Flintoff
Young players to look out for: Tom Smith
Other sports played: 'Used to play football'; golf
Other sports followed: Football (Bolton Wanderers), golf
Favourite band/music: Floorfillers 4
Relaxations: 'Watching Bolton Wanderers FC'
Extras: Lancashire Junior Player of the Year 2004. Represented England U19 2007
Best batting: 32 Lancashire v DUCCE, Durham 2006

2007 Season

	M	Inn	NO	Runs	HS	Avg	100	50	Ct	St	Balls	Runs	Wkts	Avg	BB	5I	10M
Test																	
FC	1	2	0	27	27	13.50	-	-	1	-	18	7	0		-	-	-
ODI																	
List A	1	1	0	1	1	1.00	-	-	-	-	0	0	0		-	-	
20/20 Int																	
20/20																	

Career Performances

	M	Inn	NO	Runs	HS	Avg	100	50	Ct	St	Balls	Runs	Wkts	Avg	BB	5I	10M
Test																	
FC	2	4	0	61	32	15.25	-	-	1	-	18	7	0		-	-	-
ODI																	
List A	1	1	0	1	1	1.00	-	-	-	-	0	0	0		-	-	
20/20 Int																	
20/20																	

BROWN, M. J. — Hampshire

Name: Michael James Brown
Role: Right-hand bat, wicket-keeper
Born: 9 February 1980, Burnley
Height: 6ft **Weight:** 12st
Nickname: Fagmo, Weasel, Stone, Dawson
County debut: 1999 (Middlesex), 2004 (Hampshire)
County cap: 2007 (Hampshire)
1000 runs in a season: 1
Place in batting averages: 57th av. 43.12 (2006 122nd av. 32.71)
Parents: Peter and Valerie
Marital status: Single
Family links with cricket: 'Father played league cricket for 30 years. Mum makes great tuna sandwiches.' Younger brother David played for DUCCE and is now with Gloucestershire
Education: Queen Elizabeth's Grammar School, Blackburn; Durham University
Qualifications: 10 GCSEs, 4 A-levels, 2.1 Economics/Politics
Career outside cricket: 'Stockbroking'
Off-season: 'Stockbroking internship at KBC Peel Hunt in London'
Overseas teams played for: Western Province CC, Cape Town 1998-99; Fremantle CC 2002-05; South Perth CC 2005-06
Career highlights to date: 'Durham 2007 – 56* and 126* gained draw for Hampshire'
Cricket moments to forget: 'Leaving straight balls'
Cricket superstitions: 'Always tap non-striker's end four times at end of over when at that end'
Cricketers particularly admired: Dale Benkenstein, Nic Pothas, Michael Yardy
Young players to look out for: Liam Dawson, Ben Howell
Other sports played: Football ('badly'), golf ('occasional bandit')
Other sports followed: Football (Burnley FC)
Injuries: 'Whole body knackered'
Favourite band: Goo Goo Dolls, Razorlight, The Killers, Oasis
Relaxations: 'Golf, shares'
Extras: Represented ECB U19 A v Pakistan U19 1998. Played for Durham UCCE and represented British Universities 2001, 2002. 'Was at non-striker's end as five wickets fell in one over, Middlesex 2nd XI v Glamorgan 2nd XI, July 2001.' Carried bat for 56* v Durham at Riverside 2007 (as Ottis Gibson took all ten Hampshire wickets), following up with 126* in the second innings (out of 262-9) to save the game

Opinions on cricket: 'Less cricket. More practice. Forget 50-over cricket and replace with 40-over cricket. All the players prefer it, but what do we know? ICC run by set of desk people rather than ex-cricketers.'
Best batting: 133 Hampshire v LUCCE, Rose Bowl 2006

2007 Season

	M	Inn	NO	Runs	HS	Avg	100	50	Ct	St	Balls	Runs	Wkts	Avg	BB	5I	10M
Test																	
FC	16	29	4	1078	126 *	43.12	3	5	14	-	0	0	0		-	-	-
ODI																	
List A	1	1	0	1	1	1.00	-	-	-	-	0	0	0		-	-	
20/20 Int																	
20/20	1	1	0	35	35	35.00	-	-	-	-	0	0	0		-	-	

Career Performances

	M	Inn	NO	Runs	HS	Avg	100	50	Ct	St	Balls	Runs	Wkts	Avg	BB	5I	10M
Test																	
FC	62	110	12	3199	133	32.64	6	18	54	-	0	0	0		-	-	-
ODI																	
List A	9	9	0	228	76	25.33	-	1	3	-	0	0	0		-	-	
20/20 Int																	
20/20	4	4	0	54	35	13.50	-	-	-	-	0	0	0		-	-	

BROWNING, R. J. — Northamptonshire

Name: Richard (Rich) James Browning
Role: Right-hand bat, right-arm medium-fast bowler
Born: 9 October 1987, Wolverhampton
Height: 6ft 3in **Weight:** 14st 11lbs
Nickname: Browndog
County debut: 2006 (one-day, Derbyshire)
Parents: Tim and Carolyn
Marital status: Single
Family links with cricket: 'Father once fielded for England in the 1980 Test match at Headingley against West Indies as Botham was injured. He and my grandfather also played decent standard club cricket'
Education: Wolverhampton Grammar School
Qualifications: 10 GCSEs, 3 A-levels, Level 2 cricket coaching

Overseas tours: Derbyshire Academy to Port Elizabeth 2006
Career highlights to date: 'Making my first-team debut [for Derbyshire] away to Worcestershire in a Pro40 game on Sky Sports'
Cricketers particularly admired: Andrew Flintoff, Glenn McGrath, Brett Lee
Young players to look out for: Moeen Ali, Chris Paget, Paul Borrington, Dan Redfern, Jake Needham
Other sports played: Football ('used to play Wolverhampton Schools')
Other sports followed: Football (Leeds United – 'grandfather used to play for them and Sheffield United in the 1960s')
Relaxations: 'Driving, listening to music and socialising with mates'
Extras: Represented England Schools v India U19 2006. Played for North Regional U19 in regional tournament at Loughborough 2006
Opinions on cricket: 'Game is becoming increasingly more well known and followed and I believe this is thanks to the excitement of the Twenty20 and Pro40 introductions. Keep it coming!'

2007 Season (did not make any first-class or one-day appearances)

Career Performances

	M	Inn	NO	Runs	HS	Avg	100	50	Ct	St	Balls	Runs	Wkts	Avg	BB	5I	10M
Test																	
FC																	
ODI																	
List A	1	1	0	2	2	2.00	-	-	-	-	18	26	0		-	-	
20/20 Int																	
20/20																	

BRUCE, J. T. A. — Hampshire

Name: James Thomas Anthony Bruce
Role: Right-hand bat, right-arm fast-medium bowler
Born: 17 December 1979, Hammersmith, London
Height: 6ft 1in **Weight:** 13st 12lbs
Nickname: Bula, Bear, Brucey
County debut: 2003
County cap: 2006
Place in bowling averages: 69th av. 30.74 (2006 39th av. 29.18)
Parents: Andrew and Claire
Marital status: Single
Family links with cricket: 'All three of my brothers played youth cricket for Hampshire'
Education: Eton College; Durham University
Qualifications: BA (Hons) Geography, Level 1 coaching

Off-season: 'Winter internship with Investec'
Overseas tours: West of England U15 to West Indies 1994; Eton College to South Africa 1997; Durham University to Cape Town 2000; Yellowhammers to Cape Town 2001; Eton Ramblers to India 2005; Stock Exchange CC to South Africa 2006
Overseas teams played for: Balmain Tigers, Sydney 2002-03; South Perth CC, Perth 2004, 2005
Career highlights to date: 'Playing in Friends Provident final 2007'
Cricket moments to forget: 'Having my box split in two by Mike Kasprowicz'
Cricket superstitions: 'Too many to mention'
Cricketers particularly admired: Robin Smith, Bruce Reid
Young players to look out for: Liam Dawson, Jack Shephard
Other sports played: Golf
Other sports followed: Rugby
Favourite band: Powderfinger
Relaxations: 'I like spending time on the beach, watching TV and sleeping'
Extras: Played for DUCCE in 2001 and 2002. Played for Cumberland in the C&G 2002
Opinions on cricket: 'Cricket should not be played when it's raining. Whether it's Twenty20 or not is irrelevant.'
Best batting: 32 Hampshire v Surrey, The Oval 2007
Best bowling: 5-43 Hampshire v Nottinghamshire, Rose Bowl 2006

2007 Season

	M	Inn	NO	Runs	HS	Avg	100	50	Ct	St	Balls	Runs	Wkts	Avg	BB	5I	10M
Test																	
FC	14	18	7	84	32	7.63	-	-	4	-	2117	1199	39	30.74	5-64	2	-
ODI																	
List A	10	3	2	17	11 *	17.00	-	-	2	-	426	357	11	32.45	2-27	-	
20/20 Int																	
20/20	7	2	1	12	8 *	12.00	-	-	5	-	108	156	4	39.00	2-21	-	

Career Performances

	M	Inn	NO	Runs	HS	Avg	100	50	Ct	St	Balls	Runs	Wkts	Avg	BB	5I	10M
Test																	
FC	49	57	23	243	32	7.14	-	-	14	-	6905	4225	124	34.07	5-43	3	-
ODI																	
List A	31	15	9	76	19 *	12.66	-	-	9	-	1232	976	44	22.18	4-18	-	
20/20 Int																	
20/20	20	6	2	30	12	7.50	-	-	11	-	288	391	15	26.06	3-20	-	

BURROWS, T. G. — Hampshire

Name: Thomas (Tom) George Burrows
Role: Right-hand bat, wicket-keeper
Born: 5 May 1985, Reading, Berkshire
Height: 5ft 8in **Weight:** 10st 10lbs
Nickname: TB
County debut: 2005 (*see* ***Extras***)
Parents: Tony and Victoria
Marital status: Single
Family links with cricket: 'My father was briefly on Gloucestershire groundstaff and played club cricket'
Education: Reading School; Solent University
Qualifications: 12 GCSEs, 4 AS-levels, 3 A-levels, Level 1 cricket coach
Overseas tours: MCC to Namibia and Uganda 2004-05
Overseas teams played for: Melville CC, Perth 2003-04
Career highlights to date: 'First-class debut v Kent, scoring 42 and putting on 131 with Shane Warne when we were 130-7'
Cricket moments to forget: 'Any dropped catch'
Cricket superstitions: 'Left pad on first'
Cricketers particularly admired: Adi Aymes, Jack Russell, Steve Waugh, John Crawley
Other sports played: Rugby, football
Other sports followed: Football (Chelsea), rugby (London Irish)
Favourite band: Gavin DeGraw
Relaxations: 'Watching films'
Extras: Appeared as substitute wicket-keeper for Hampshire v Yorkshire at The Rose Bowl 2002 but did not make full debut until 2005. Played for Berks in the C&G 2003
Best batting: 42 Hampshire v Kent, Canterbury 2005

2007 Season

	M	Inn	NO	Runs	HS	Avg	100	50	Ct	St	Balls	Runs	Wkts	Avg	BB	5I	10M
Test																	
FC	1	1	0	35	35	35.00	-	-	4	-	0	0	0		-	-	-
ODI																	
List A																	
20/20 Int																	
20/20																	

Career Performances

	M	Inn	NO	Runs	HS	Avg	100	50	Ct	St	Balls	Runs	Wkts	Avg	BB	5I	10M
Test																	
FC	4	6	0	139	42	23.16	-	-	14	-	0	0	0		-	-	-
ODI																	
List A	3	3	1	18	16	9.00	-	-	3	2	0	0	0		-	-	
20/20 Int																	
20/20	1	0	0	0	0		-	-	-	-	0	0	0		-	-	

BUTCHER, M. A. — Surrey

Name: Mark Alan Butcher
Role: Left-hand bat, right-arm medium bowler, county captain
Born: 23 August 1972, Croydon
Height: 5ft 11in **Weight:** 13st
Nickname: Butch, Baz
County debut: 1991 (one-day), 1992 (first-class)
County cap: 1996
Benefit: 2005
Test debut: 1997
1000 runs in a season: 8
1st-Class 200s: 2
Place in batting averages: 73rd av. 39.57 (2006 25th av. 58.60)
Parents: Alan and Elaine
Children: Alita, 1999
Family links with cricket: Father Alan played for Glamorgan, Surrey and England and is now coach with Surrey; brother Gary played for Glamorgan and Surrey; uncle Ian played for Gloucestershire and Leicestershire; uncle Martin played for Surrey
Education: Trinity School; Archbishop Tenison's, Croydon

Qualifications: 5 O-levels, senior coaching award
Career outside cricket: Singer, guitar player
Overseas tours: England YC to New Zealand 1990-91; Surrey to Dubai 1990, 1993, to Perth 1995; England A to Australia 1996-97; England to West Indies 1997-98, to Australia 1998-99, to South Africa 1999-2000, to India and New Zealand 2001-02, to Australia 2002-03, to Bangladesh and Sri Lanka 2003-04, to West Indies 2003-04, to South Africa 2004-05
Overseas teams played for: South Melbourne, Australia 1993-94; North Perth 1994-95
Cricketers particularly admired: Ian Botham, David Gower, Viv Richards, Larry Gomes, Graham Thorpe, Alec Stewart, Michael Holding
Other sports followed: Football (Crystal Palace)
Relaxations: Music, playing the guitar, novels, wine
Extras: Played his first game for Surrey in 1991 against his father's Glamorgan in the Refuge Assurance League at The Oval, the first-ever match of any sort between first-class counties in which a father and son have been in opposition. Captained England in the third Test v New Zealand at Old Trafford 1999, deputising for the injured Nasser Hussain. Scored match-winning 173* in the fourth Test v Australia at Headingley 2001, winning Man of the Match award, and was England's Man of the Series with 456 runs (more than any other batsman on either side) at an average of 50.66. His other Test awards include England's Man of the Series v Sri Lanka 2002 and v Zimbabwe 2003. Slazenger Sheer Instinct Award 2001 for the cricketer who has impressed the most in the recent season. Scored century in each innings (151/108) v Glamorgan at The Oval 2006, emulating achievement of his father, Alan (117*/114), in the corresponding fixture in 1984. Reached the final of BBC celebrity singing show *Just the Two of Us* in January 2007 with Sarah Brightman. Scored 179 at Hove 2007, in the process sharing with Mark Ramprakash (266*) in the highest partnership ever recorded against Sussex in the County Championship (403). Captain of Surrey since 2005
Best batting: 259 Surrey v Leicestershire, Leicester 1999
Best bowling: 5-86 Surrey v Lancashire, Old Trafford 2000

2007 Season

	M	Inn	NO	Runs	HS	Avg	100	50	Ct	St	Balls	Runs	Wkts	Avg	BB	5I	10M
Test																	
FC	14	21	2	752	179	39.57	2	2	14	-	39	28	0		-	-	-
ODI																	
List A	11	10	1	447	72 *	49.66	-	5	4	-	0	0	0		-	-	
20/20 Int																	
20/20	8	7	0	56	25	8.00	-	-	3	-	0	0	0		-	-	

Career Performances

	M	Inn	NO	Runs	HS	Avg	100	50	Ct	St	Balls	Runs	Wkts	Avg	BB	5I	10M
Test	71	131	7	4288	173 *	34.58	8	23	61	-	901	541	15	36.06	4-42	-	-
FC	269	460	36	17098	259	40.32	36	92	249	-	7703	4237	125	33.89	5-86	1	-
ODI																	
List A	185	166	30	4179	104	30.72	1	27	59	-	2527	2210	49	45.10	3-23	-	
20/20 Int																	
20/20	13	12	0	210	60	17.50	-	2	4	-	0	0	0		-	-	

CADDICK, A. R. Somerset

Name: Andrew Richard Caddick
Role: Right-hand bat, right-arm fast-medium bowler, county vice-captain
Born: 21 November 1968, Christchurch, New Zealand
Height: 6ft 5in **Weight:** 14st 13lbs
Nickname: Des, Shack
County debut: 1990 (one-day), 1991 (first-class)
County cap: 1992
Benefit: 1999
Test debut: 1993
ODI debut: 1993
50 wickets in a season: 11
100 wickets in a season: 1
Place in batting averages: 258th av. 13.36 (2006 230th av. 17.05)
Place in bowling averages: 17th av. 23.10 (2006 86th av. 35.85)
Parents: Christopher and Audrey
Wife and date of marriage: Sarah, 27 January 1995
Children: Ashton Faye, 24 August 1998; Fraser Michael, 12 October 2001
Education: Papanui High School, Christchurch, New Zealand
Qualifications: Qualified plasterer and tiler. Qualified helicopter pilot
Overseas tours: New Zealand YC to Australia (U19 World Cup) 1987-88, to England 1988; England A to Australia 1992-93; England to West Indies 1993-94, to Zimbabwe and New Zealand 1996-97, to West Indies 1997-98, to South Africa and Zimbabwe 1999-2000, to Kenya (ICC Knockout Trophy) 2000-01, to Pakistan and Sri Lanka 2000-01, to India (one-day series) and New Zealand 2001-02, to Sri Lanka (ICC Champions Trophy) 2002-03, to Australia 2002-03, to Africa (World Cup) 2002-03

Career highlights to date: 'Bowling West Indies out at Lord's [2000] and thus getting my name up on the board'
Cricketers particularly admired: Dennis Lillee, Richard Hadlee, Robin Smith, Jimmy Cook
Other sports followed: 'Mostly all'
Relaxations: Golf
Extras: Whyte and Mackay Bowler of the Year 1997. Took 105 first-class wickets (av. 19.82) in 1998 season. Leading wicket-taker in the single-division four-day era of the County Championship with 422 wickets (av. 22.48) 1993-99. Cornhill England Player of the Year 1999-2000. Took 5-16 from 13 overs as West Indies were bowled out for 54 in their second innings in the second Test at Lord's 2000. Took 5-14 in the fourth Test v West Indies at Headingley 2000, including four wickets (Jacobs, McLean, Ambrose, King) in an over. One of *Wisden*'s Five Cricketers of the Year 2001. Took 200th Test wicket (Craig McMillan) in the third Test v New Zealand at Auckland 2001-02. His international awards include England's Man of the [Test] Series v New Zealand 1999 and joint Man of the Match (with Gary Kirsten) in the third Test v South Africa at Durban 1999-2000 (7-46). Retired from ODI cricket in March 2003. Took 1000th first-class wicket (Joe Sayers) v Yorkshire at Taunton 2005. Returned career-best match figures of 12-71 (7-30/5-41) v Gloucestershire at Bristol 2007. Appointed vice-captain of Somerset for 2008
Best batting: 92 Somerset v Worcestershire, Worcester 1995
Best bowling: 9-32 Somerset v Lancashire, Taunton 1993

2007 Season

	M	Inn	NO	Runs	HS	Avg	100	50	Ct	St	Balls	Runs	Wkts	Avg	BB	5I	10M
Test																	
FC	16	13	2	147	51	13.36	-	1	2	-	3251	1733	75	23.10	7-30	4	1
ODI																	
List A	9	5	4	9	5	9.00	-	-	3	-	385	360	12	30.00	5-49	1	
20/20 Int																	
20/20	4	0	0	0	0		-	-	-	-	90	119	5	23.80	2-22	-	

Career Performances

	M	Inn	NO	Runs	HS	Avg	100	50	Ct	St	Balls	Runs	Wkts	Avg	BB	5I	10M
Test	62	95	12	861	49 *	10.37	-	-	21	-	13558	6999	234	29.91	7-46	13	1
FC	260	341	65	4104	92	14.86	-	9	85	-	57182	29815	1145	26.03	9-32	77	17
ODI	54	38	18	249	36	12.45	-	-	9	-	2937	1965	69	28.47	4-19	-	
List A	261	135	59	810	39	10.65	-	-	44	-	12779	9034	341	26.49	6-30	5	
20/20 Int																	
20/20	16	1	0	0	0	0.00	-	-	1	-	306	468	15	31.20	2-12	-	

CARBERRY, M. A. Hampshire

Name: Michael Alexander Carberry
Role: Left-hand bat, right-arm medium bowler
Born: 29 September 1980, Croydon
Height: 5ft 11in **Weight:** 14st 7lbs
Nickname: Carbs
County debut: 2001 (Surrey), 2003 (Kent), 2006 (Hampshire)
County cap: 2006 (Hampshire)
1000 runs in a season: 1
Place in batting averages: 31st av. 50.80 (2006 93rd av. 36.07)
Parents: Maria and Neville
Marital status: Single
Family links with cricket: 'My dad played club cricket'
Education: St John Rigby College
Qualifications: 10 GCSEs
Overseas tours: Surrey U17 to South Africa 1997; England U19 to New Zealand 1998-99, to Malaysia and (U19 World Cup) Sri Lanka 1999-2000; England A to Bangladesh 2006-07; England Performance Programme to India 2007-08; England Lions to India 2007-08
Overseas teams played for: Portland CC, Melbourne; University CC, Perth 2005
Career highlights to date: 'Every day is a highlight'
Cricket moments to forget: 'None'
Cricketers particularly admired: Ricky Ponting, Brian Lara
Relaxations: 'Sleeping'
Extras: Scored century (126*) for ECB U18 v Pakistan U19 at Abergavenny 1998. Represented England U19 1999, 2000. NBC Denis Compton Award for the most promising young Surrey player 1999, 2000. Scored century (137) on Kent debut v Cambridge UCCE at Fenner's 2003. Scored 112 as Kent scored a then county record fourth innings 429-5 to beat Worcestershire at Canterbury 2004. Scored career-best 192* as Hampshire scored 331-5 to beat Warwickshire with three balls to spare at The Rose Bowl 2007. Scored century in each innings (127/120) v Worcestershire at Kidderminster 2007. Scored century (113*) v Yorkshire at Headingley 2007, in the process passing 1000 first-class runs in a season for the first time
Best batting: 192* Hampshire v Warwickshire, Rose Bowl 2007
Best bowling: 2-85 Hampshire v Durham, Riverside 2006

2007 Season

	M	Inn	NO	Runs	HS	Avg	100	50	Ct	St	Balls	Runs	Wkts	Avg	BB	5I	10M
Test																	
FC	13	24	3	1067	192 *	50.80	5	3	2	-	180	125	2	62.50	1-13	-	-
ODI																	
List A	14	14	3	345	75 *	31.36	-	2	5	-	0	0	0		-	-	
20/20 Int																	
20/20	7	6	2	79	23	19.75	-	-	1	-	0	0	0		-	-	

Career Performances

	M	Inn	NO	Runs	HS	Avg	100	50	Ct	St	Balls	Runs	Wkts	Avg	BB	5I	10M
Test																	
FC	65	114	11	4152	192 *	40.31	11	20	28	-	612	490	7	70.00	2-85	-	-
ODI																	
List A	80	75	6	1730	88	25.07	-	14	27	-	42	41	1	41.00	1-21	-	
20/20 Int																	
20/20	32	29	7	587	90	26.68	-	4	11	-	0	0	0		-	-	

CARTER, N. M. — Warwickshire

Name: Neil Miller Carter
Role: Left-hand bat, left-arm fast-medium bowler
Born: 29 January 1975, Cape Town, South Africa
Height: 6ft 2in **Weight:** 15st 10lbs
Nickname: Carts
County debut: 2001
County cap: 2005
Place in batting averages: (2006 237th av. 15.62)
Place in bowling averages: 52nd av. 28.30 (2006 109th av. 40.94)
Parents: John and Heather
Marital status: Single
Education: Hottentots Holland High School; Cape Technikon; ITI; stock market training
Qualifications: Certified Novell Engineer, Level 2 coaching
Career outside cricket: Investing and stock market
Off-season: 'Buying and selling shares'

Overseas tours: SA Country Schools U15 to England 1992; Warwickshire to Cape Town 2001-03, to Grenada 2007
Overseas teams played for: Boland 1998-99 – 2003-04
Career highlights to date: 'Lord's finals and Championship win plus 2005 season'
Cricket moments to forget: 'Losing C&G final 2005'
Cricketers particularly admired: Allan Donald, Shaun Pollock
Young players to look out for: Chris Woakes, Moeen Ali
Other sports played: Swimming, golf, chess, Let it Ride
Other sports followed: Rugby union (Stormers in Super 14; Springboks), football (Sheffield Wednesday), baseball (LA Angels), ice hockey (Ducks)
Injuries: Out for the first two months of the season after a cartilage operation
Favourite band: Mike and the Mechanics
Relaxations: Gricing (steam train photography)
Extras: Won Man of the Match award in first one-day match for Warwickshire v Essex at Edgbaston in the C&G 2001 (4-21/43-ball 40). Warwickshire Player of the Year 2005 (1088 runs and 94 wickets in all cricket and, including Twenty20, equalled Allan Donald's club season record of 53 one-day wickets). Is England-qualified
Opinions on cricket: 'Ninety-six overs a day looks a good option, seeing that it would be difficult to reduce the number of four-day games. Extending the Friends Provident 50-over competition is also welcomed.'
Best batting: 103 Warwickshire v Sussex, Hove 2002
Best bowling: 6-63 Boland v Griqualand West, Kimberley 2000-01

2007 Season

	M	Inn	NO	Runs	HS	Avg	100	50	Ct	St	Balls	Runs	Wkts	Avg	BB	5I	10M
Test																	
FC	3	5	2	56	27	18.66	-	-	1	-	514	283	10	28.30	5-62	1	-
ODI																	
List A	4	4	0	146	92	36.50	-	1	-	-	178	149	5	29.80	3-23	-	
20/20 Int																	
20/20	8	7	1	111	58	18.50	-	1	-	-	162	199	10	19.90	3-29	-	

Career Performances

	M	Inn	NO	Runs	HS	Avg	100	50	Ct	St	Balls	Runs	Wkts	Avg	BB	5I	10M
Test																	
FC	74	101	21	1507	103	18.83	1	3	21	-	12205	7147	189	37.81	6-63	6	-
ODI																	
List A	124	103	12	1779	135	19.54	1	5	12	-	5502	4377	171	25.59	5-31	2	
20/20 Int																	
20/20	38	36	2	586	58	17.23	-	1	6	-	770	913	42	21.73	5-19	1	

CHAMBERS, M. A. Essex

Name: Maurice Anthony Chambers
Role: Right-hand bat, right-arm fast bowler
Born: 14 September 1987, Port Antonio, Jamaica
Height: 6ft 3in **Weight:** 13st
Nickname: Moza, Chungkid
County debut: 2005
Parents: Elain Lewis
Marital status: Single
Education: Homerton College of Technology; Sir George Monoux College
Career outside cricket: 'College and playing basketball with my mates'
Off-season: 'Getting myself fully fit and hopefully going on tour to Dubai in March'
Overseas tours: Essex Academy to India 2006-07; England U19 to Malaysia 2006-07
Career highlights to date: 'Playing for Essex 2nd XI v Middlesex [2006] and bowling 16 overs, 7 maidens, and taking 3 wickets for 25 runs'
Cricket moments to forget: 'Playing for England U19 v India, we were 8 wickets down with 2 balls to go and I was the last batsman. I told myself I was not going to pad up, and then my mate was out and I went in to bat with no Abdo Guard or gloves'
Cricketers particularly admired: Courtney Walsh, Curtly Ambrose, Stuart Broad, Brian Lara, Kevin Pietersen, Brett Lee
Young players to look out for: Mervyn Westfield, Jahid Ahmed, Steve Finn, Andrew Miller, Ben Wright
Other sports played: 'Play basketball at college for the fun of it'
Other sports followed: Football (Manchester United)
Injuries: Out for the whole of the 2007 season with a stress fracture in the lower back
Favourite band: 50 Cent
Relaxations: 'Music, shopping, football and playing PS2'
Extras: London Schools Cricket Association Bowler of the Year 2004. Jack Petchey Award 2004. Played for MCC Young Cricketers 2004. Wanstead CC Bowler of the Year
Opinions on cricket: 'It's a wonderful game and I love it.'
Best batting: 2* Essex v Derbyshire, Chelmsford 2005
Best bowling: 1-73 Essex v Derbyshire, Chelmsford 2005

2007 Season (did not make any first-class or one-day appearances)

Career Performances

	M	Inn	NO	Runs	HS	Avg	100	50	Ct	St	Balls	Runs	Wkts	Avg	BB	5I	10M
Test																	
FC	1	1	1	2	2*		-	-	-	-	96	84	1	84.00	1-73	-	-
ODI																	
List A																	
20/20 Int																	
20/20																	

CHANDERPAUL, S. Durham

Name: Shivnarine Chanderpaul
Role: Left-hand bat, leg-break bowler
Born: 16 August 1974, Demerara, Guyana
Nickname: Shiv
County debut: 2007
Test debut: 1993-94
ODI debut: 1994-95
Twenty20 Int debut: 2005-06
1st-Class 200s: 3
1st-Class 300s: 1
Place in batting averages: 4th av. 74.44
Wife: Amy
Overseas tours: West Indies U19 to England 1993; West Indies to India 1994-95, to New Zealand 1994-95, to England 1995, to Australia 1995-96, to India, Pakistan and Sri Lanka (World Cup) 1995-96, to Australia 1996-97, to Pakistan 1997-98, to Bangladesh (Wills International Cup) 1998-99, to South Africa 1998-99, to UK, Ireland and Netherlands (World Cup) 1999, to Bangladesh 1999-2000, to New Zealand 1999-2000, to England 2000, to Australia 2000-01, to Zimbabwe and Kenya 2001, to Sharjah (v Pakistan) 2001-02, to Sri Lanka (ICC Champions Trophy) 2002-03, to India and Bangladesh 2002-03, to Africa (World Cup) 2002-03, to Zimbabwe and South Africa 2003-04, to England 2004, to England (ICC Champions Trophy) 2004, to Sri Lanka 2005 (c), to Australia 2005-06 (c), to New Zealand 2005-06 (c), to India (ICC Champions Trophy) 2006-07, to Pakistan 2006-07, to England 2007, to South Africa (World 20/20) 2007-08, to Zimbabwe and South Africa 2007-08, plus other one-day tournaments and series in Sharjah, Singapore, Toronto, Bangladesh, Australia, Malaysia, India and Ireland

Overseas teams played for: Guyana 1991-92 – 2006-07
Extras: Scored century (104) as West Indies made a Test record 418 in the fourth innings to beat Australia in Antigua 2002-03, winning Man of the Match award. His other series and match awards include Man of the [Test] Series v India 2001-02 (562 runs; av. 140.50), West Indies Man of the [Test] Series v England 2004 (437 runs; av. 72.83) and 2007 (446 runs; av 148.66) and overall Man of the [ODI] Series v England 2007 (202 runs; av. 202.00). Represented West Indies in the 2006-07 World Cup. Captain of West Indies from March 2005 to April 2006, scoring a double century (203*) in his first Test in charge, v South Africa 2004-05 in his home country of Guyana. Was an overseas player with Durham for part of the 2007 season; has returned as overseas player for 2008
Best batting: 303* Guyana v Jamaica, Kingston 1995-96
Best bowling: 4-48 Guyana v Leeward Islands, Basseterre 1992-93

2007 Season

	M	Inn	NO	Runs	HS	Avg	100	50	Ct	St	Balls	Runs	Wkts	Avg	BB	5I	10M
Test	3	5	2	446	136 *	148.66	2	3	-	-	66	43	0		-	-	-
FC	7	12	3	670	136 *	74.44	2	5	4	-	114	66	0		-	-	-
ODI	3	3	2	202	116 *	202.00	1	1	-	-	0	0	0		-	-	
List A	9	7	3	465	116 *	116.25	1	4	-	-	0	0	0		-	-	
20/20 Int	1	1	0	41	41	41.00	-	-	-	-	0	0	0		-	-	
20/20	1	1	0	41	41	41.00	-	-	-	-	0	0	0		-	-	

Career Performances

	M	Inn	NO	Runs	HS	Avg	100	50	Ct	St	Balls	Runs	Wkts	Avg	BB	5I	10M
Test	104	178	24	7182	203 *	46.63	16	43	44	-	1680	845	8	105.62	1-2	-	-
FC	208	340	56	14757	303 *	51.96	41	73	128	-	4610	2434	56	43.46	4-48	-	-
ODI	222	208	29	6975	150	38.96	7	47	61	-	716	617	14	44.07	3-18	-	
List A	321	297	48	10055	150	40.38	8	72	94	-	1645	1346	56	24.03	4-22	-	
20/20 Int	4	4	0	115	41	28.75	-	-	2	-	0	0	0		-	-	
20/20	4	4	0	115	41	28.75	-	-	2	-	0	0	0		-	-	

CHAPPLE, G. — Lancashire

Name: Glen Chapple
Role: Right-hand bat, right-arm medium-fast bowler; all-rounder
Born: 23 January 1974, Skipton, Yorkshire
Height: 6ft 1in **Weight:** 13st
Nickname: Chappy
County debut: 1992
County cap: 1994
Benefit: 2004
ODI debut: 2006

50 wickets in a season: 4
Place in batting averages: 198th av. 22.53 (2006 126th av. 32.22)
Place in bowling averages: 12th av. 21.85 (2006 28th av. 27.41)
Parents: Mike and Eileen
Wife and date of marriage: Kerry, 31 January 2004
Children: Annie, 6 August 2003; Joe, 16 January 2006
Family links with cricket: Father played in Lancashire League for Nelson and was a professional for Darwen and Earby
Education: West Craven High School; Nelson and Colne College
Qualifications: 8 GCSEs, 2 A-levels
Overseas tours: England U18 to Canada (International Youth Tournament) 1991; England YC to New Zealand 1990-91; England U19 to Pakistan 1991-92, to India 1992-93; England A to India 1994-95, to Australia 1996-97; England VI to Hong Kong 2002, 2003, 2004, 2006
Cricket superstitions: 'None'
Cricketers particularly admired: Dennis Lillee, Robin Smith
Other sports followed: Football (Liverpool), golf
Favourite band: U2, Oasis, Stone Roses
Relaxations: 'Golf'
Extras: Set record for fastest century in first-class cricket (21 minutes; against declaration bowling) v Glamorgan at Old Trafford 1993. Man of the Match in the 1996 NatWest final against Essex at Lord's (6-18). Lancashire Player of the Year 2002. Returned match figures of 10-86 (7-53/3-33) v Durham at Blackpool 2007
Opinions on cricket: 'How long do people have to keep banging on about playing too much cricket? It's not difficult to see and it's annoying that nothing will change until my boots are in the bin! Cheers!'
Best batting: 155 Lancashire v Somerset, Old Trafford 2001
Best bowling: 7-53 Lancashire v Durham, Blackpool 2007

2007 Season

	M	Inn	NO	Runs	HS	Avg	100	50	Ct	St	Balls	Runs	Wkts	Avg	BB	5I	10M
Test																	
FC	12	16	1	338	88	22.53	-	2	4	-	2191	1027	47	21.85	7-53	1	1
ODI																	
List A	8	4	1	133	66	44.33	-	1	1	-	284	209	5	41.80	1-26	-	
20/20 Int																	
20/20	2	1	1	15	15 *		-	-	-	-	30	44	0		-	-	

Career Performances

	M	Inn	NO	Runs	HS	Avg	100	50	Ct	St	Balls	Runs	Wkts	Avg	BB	5I	10M
Test																	
FC	216	297	55	6023	155	24.88	6	27	72	-	36521	18352	651	28.19	7-53	25	2
ODI	1	1	0	14	14	14.00	-	-	-	-	24	14	0		-	-	
List A	252	142	36	1869	81 *	17.63	-	9	55	-	10793	8111	278	29.17	6-18	4	
20/20 Int																	
20/20	23	15	4	150	55 *	13.63	-	1	8	-	384	519	21	24.71	2-13	-	

CHEETHAM, S. P. Lancashire

Name: Steven Philip Cheetham
Role: Right-hand bat, right-arm fast bowler
Born: 5 September 1987, Oldham
Height: 6ft 5in **Weight:** 14st 5lbs
Nickname: Cheets
County debut: 2007
Parents: Philip and Joan
Marital status: Single
Education: Bury Grammar School
Qualifications: 10 GCSEs, 4 A-levels
Off-season: 'Playing cricket in Australia'
Overseas teams played for: Cheltenham CC, Melbourne 2007-08
Career highlights to date: 'First-team debut for Lancashire v Durham UCCE. Representing England U17'
Cricket moments to forget: 'Two seasons of injuries – stress fracture of back and double hernia'
Cricket superstitions: 'Always right pad on first'
Cricketers particularly admired: Marcus Trescothick, Chris Gayle, Brett Lee, Andrew Flintoff
Young players to look out for: Richard Jones, Steve Mullaney, Karl Brown
Other sports played: Football (Bury GS Old Boys)
Other sports followed: Football (Oldham Athletic)
Injuries: Out for six weeks with a double hernia
Favourite band: Arctic Monkeys, Oasis
Relaxations: 'Music'
Extras: Best figures of 5-11 for Radcliffe v Ramsbottom in the Inter League Club Challenge Trophy as a 17-year-old. Attended Dennis Lillee's MRF Pace Foundation, India 2007. Is a Lancashire Scholarship player and appeared in one first-class match for the county in 2007

Opinions on cricket: '[Would like] to see more young players from the academies come through the counties to represent both counties and England.'
Best bowling: 1-44 Lancashire v DUCCE, Durham 2007

2007 Season

	M	Inn	NO	Runs	HS	Avg	100	50	Ct	St	Balls	Runs	Wkts	Avg	BB	5I	10M
Test																	
FC	1	0	0	0	0		-	-	1	-	144	127	1	127.00	1-44	-	-
ODI																	
List A																	
20/20 Int																	
20/20																	

Career Performances

	M	Inn	NO	Runs	HS	Avg	100	50	Ct	St	Balls	Runs	Wkts	Avg	BB	5I	10M
Test																	
FC	1	0	0	0	0		-	-	1	-	144	127	1	127.00	1-44	-	-
ODI																	
List A																	
20/20 Int																	
20/20																	

CHERRY, D. D. — Glamorgan

Name: Daniel David Cherry
Role: Left-hand bat, right-arm spin bowler
Born: 7 February 1980, Newport, Gwent
Height: 5ft 9in **Weight:** 12st 6lbs
Nickname: Spikes, McNab, Kiwi, Banners, Rhino
County debut: 1998
1st-Class 200s: 1
Place in batting averages: 237th av. 16.50 (2006 134th av. 31.29)
Parents: David and Elizabeth
Marital status: Single
Family links with cricket: Father played club cricket for Cresselly CC and now coaches
Education: Tonbridge School, Kent; University of Wales, Swansea

Qualifications: 10 GCSEs, 3 A-levels, BA History, Level 2 coach
Career outside cricket: 'Criminal analysis or criminology'
Overseas tours: Tonbridge School to Australia 1996-97; Glamorgan to Cape Town 2002
Overseas teams played for: Doutta Stars, Melbourne 2002-03
Career highlights to date: 'Maiden first-class hundred (226 v Middlesex 2005)'
Cricket moments to forget: 'Getting hit on the hand by a Shoaib Akhtar beamer!'
Cricket superstitions: 'None'
Cricketers particularly admired: Michael Atherton, Graham Thorpe, Steve James
Young players to look out for: James Harris, Gareth Rees, Willy Bragg
Other sports played: Rugby, rackets (Public Schools doubles champion)
Other sports followed: Rugby (Neath-Swansea Ospreys), football (Everton)
Favourite band: Super Furry Animals
Relaxations: Reading true crime books, listening to music
Extras: Played for ECB U19 XI v Pakistan U19 1998. Awarded Glamorgan 2nd XI cap 2002. Glamorgan Young Player of the Year 2005. First Glamorgan player to score a double hundred as maiden first-class century (226 v Middlesex at Southgate 2005). Released by Glamorgan at the end of the 2007 season
Opinions on cricket: 'Work hard, back your ability and most importantly – enjoy it!'
Best batting: 226 Glamorgan v Middlesex, Southgate 2005

2007 Season

	M	Inn	NO	Runs	HS	Avg	100	50	Ct	St	Balls	Runs	Wkts	Avg	BB	5I	10M
Test																	
FC	7	12	0	198	48	16.50	-	-	3	-	12	5	0		-	-	-
ODI																	
List A																	
20/20 Int																	
20/20																	

Career Performances

	M	Inn	NO	Runs	HS	Avg	100	50	Ct	St	Balls	Runs	Wkts	Avg	BB	5I	10M
Test																	
FC	40	71	1	1824	226	26.05	3	4	12	-	52	18	0		-	-	-
ODI																	
List A	22	20	0	312	42	15.60	-	-	5	-	66	91	1	91.00	1-26	-	
20/20 Int																	
20/20	3	3	1	55	43 *	27.50	-	-	1	-	6	6	2	3.00	2-6	-	

CHILTON, M. J. — Lancashire

Name: Mark James Chilton
Role: Right-hand bat, right-arm medium bowler
Born: 2 October 1976, Sheffield
Height: 6ft 2in **Weight:** 13st 6lbs
Nickname: Chill, Peter, Roger, Dougie
County debut: 1997
County cap: 2002
1000 runs in a season: 1
Place in batting averages: 152nd av. 28.00 (2006 128th av. 31.91)
Parents: Jim and Sue
Wife and date of marriage: Hayley, 29 December 2006
Family links with cricket: 'Dad played local leagues'
Education: Manchester Grammar School; Durham University
Qualifications: BA (Hons) Business Economics, Level III coach
Off-season: 'Working with a bank'
Overseas tours: Manchester Grammar School to Barbados 1993-94, to South Africa 1995-96; Durham University to Zimbabwe 1997-98
Overseas teams played for: East Torrens, Adelaide 2000-01; North Sydney CC, Sydney 2002-03
Career highlights to date: 'Playing for and captaining Lancashire'
Cricket moments to forget: 'Losing C&G final 2006'
Cricket superstitions: 'None'
Cricketers particularly admired: John Crawley, David Gower
Young players to look out for: Gareth Cross, Steven Croft
Other sports played: Golf
Other sports followed: Football (Manchester United)
Favourite band: Oasis
Relaxations: 'Guitar'
Extras: Represented England U14, U15, U17. England U15 Batsman of the Year award 1992. Played for North of England v New Zealand U19 1996. Played for British Universities in 1997 Benson and Hedges Cup, winning the Gold Award against Sussex at Fenner's (34/5-26). Captain of Lancashire 2005-07
Opinions on cricket: 'We need to keep a system that allows opportunity at the right times for young, emerging England players and not get sucked into filling these gaps with cricketers from other countries. Quality, yes; quantity, no.'
Best batting: 131 Lancashire v Kent, Old Trafford 2006
Best bowling: 1-1 Lancashire v Sri Lanka A, Old Trafford 1999

2007 Season

	M	Inn	NO	Runs	HS	Avg	100	50	Ct	St	Balls	Runs	Wkts	Avg	BB	5I	10M
Test																	
FC	14	24	2	616	115	28.00	1	2	7	-	24	13	0		-	-	-
ODI																	
List A	11	11	1	206	77 *	20.60	-	1	3	-	0	0	0		-	-	
20/20 Int																	
20/20	6	3	1	30	12 *	15.00	-	-	2	-	0	0	0		-	-	

Career Performances

	M	Inn	NO	Runs	HS	Avg	100	50	Ct	St	Balls	Runs	Wkts	Avg	BB	5I	10M
Test																	
FC	143	233	16	6965	131	32.09	17	25	110	-	1311	664	10	66.40	1-1	-	-
ODI																	
List A	158	151	20	3885	115	29.65	4	19	49	-	1082	992	41	24.19	5-26	1	
20/20 Int																	
20/20	32	22	8	236	38	16.85	-	-	13	-	0	0	0		-	-	

CHOPRA, V. — Essex

Name: Varun Chopra
Role: Right-hand opening bat, right-arm swing/leg-spin bowler
Born: 21 June 1987, Barking, Essex
Height: 6ft 1in **Weight:** 12st 7lbs
Nickname: Chops, Tiddles
County debut: 2006
Place in batting averages: 151st av. 28.21 (2006 82nd av. 37.93)
Parents: Chander and Surinder
Marital status: Single
Education: Ilford County HS
Qualifications: 11 GCSEs, 4 A-levels
Off-season: 'Perth – Willetton CC; Essex pre-season to Dubai'
Overseas tours: England U19 to Bangladesh 2005-06 (c), to Sri Lanka (U19 World Cup) 2005-06; Essex to South Africa 2006, to Dubai 2007
Overseas teams played for: Willetton CC, Perth 2006-08
Career highlights to date: 'Captaining England U19. Man of Series v India U19 2006. Century [106 plus 50* in second innings] on Championship debut v Gloucestershire [at Chelmsford 2006]'

Cricket moments to forget: 'Any dropped catch. England U19 [World Cup] semi-final v India [2005-06]' (*England lost by 234 runs, having been bowled out for 58*)
Cricketers particularly admired: Sachin Tendulkar, Shane Warne, Andy Flower
Young players to look out for: Mervyn Westfield, Maurice Chambers
Other sports played: 'Football – Spot!'
Favourite band: Musiq Soulchild, Ginuwine, T.I., Lil Wayne, Kanye
Relaxations: 'Jamming with mates, poker, Pro Evo'
Extras: Lord's Taverners Player of the Year U13, U15, U19. Sony Sports Personality of the Year runner-up. Captained England U19 2005 and 2006; Man of the Match v Bangladesh U19 at Colombo in the quarter-finals of the U19 World Cup 2005-06 and Man of the Series v India U19 2006, scoring a century in each innings (123/164) in the second 'Test' at Taunton. Scored century (106) on Championship debut v Gloucestershire at Chelmsford 2006, in the process becoming the youngest player to score a Championship hundred for Essex
Best batting: 106 Essex v Gloucestershire, Chelmsford 2006

2007 Season

	M	Inn	NO	Runs	HS	Avg	100	50	Ct	St	Balls	Runs	Wkts	Avg	BB	5I	10M
Test																	
FC	16	26	3	649	86	28.21	-	5	15	-	30	25	0		-	-	-
ODI																	
List A	10	10	0	276	102	27.60	1	1	4	-	0	0	0		-	-	
20/20 Int																	
20/20	1	1	1	5	5 *		-	-	1	-	0	0	0		-	-	

Career Performances

	M	Inn	NO	Runs	HS	Avg	100	50	Ct	St	Balls	Runs	Wkts	Avg	BB	5I	10M
Test																	
FC	25	42	4	1218	106	32.05	1	9	22	-	30	25	0		-	-	-
ODI																	
List A	12	12	0	283	102	23.58	1	1	4	-	0	0	0		-	-	
20/20 Int																	
20/20	2	2	2	6	5 *		-	-	1	-	0	0	0		-	-	

CHOUDHRY, S. H. Warwickshire

Name: Shaaiq Hussain Choudhry
Role: Right-hand bat, slow left-arm bowler
Born: 3 November 1985, Sheffield, Yorkshire
Height: 5ft 10in **Weight:** 11st 7lbs
Nickname: Shak, Chouds
County debut: No first-team appearance
Parents: Sabir and Badar-u-Nasa
Marital status: Single
Education: Fir Vale School; Rotherham College of Arts and Technology; University of Bradford
Qualifications: 9 GCSEs, BTEC National Diploma, BSc (Hons) degree ('currently studying final year')
Off-season: 'In the coming years I would like to go and play some cricket abroad to gain experience and further my skills and knowledge of the game, as I have not had the opportunity to do this in the past due to educational commitments'
Overseas tours: MCC Universities to Ireland 2006; Bradford/Leeds UCCE to India 2007; British Universities to South Africa 2008
Career highlights to date: '54* against West Indians for MCC in 2007. Six wickets against Surrey CCC at The Oval [for Bradford/Leeds UCCE 2007]. As a cricket fan, I have grown up watching cricketers like Mark Ramprakash and Vikram Solanki, and having the opportunity to play against them and get their wickets was a huge personal achievement for me'
Cricket moments to forget: 'Getting hit out of the ground by Rikki Clarke at The Oval'
Cricketers particularly admired: Shane Warne, Muttiah Muralitharan, Michael Vaughan, Sachin Tendulkar
Other sports followed: 'Follow a little of most sports'
Injuries: Out for approximately four weeks with a torn ligament
Favourite band: Kanye West, Usher, Timbaland
Relaxations: 'Going to the gym, socialising with friends and family and listening to music'
Extras: Played for Bradford/Leeds UCCE 2006, 2007. Made first-class debut for MCC v West Indians at Durham 2007, scoring 54*
Opinions on cricket: 'I believe the game today is a faster-moving game as it is played in a more aggressive manner. I also think the standard of the game has developed and improved a great deal since I've been following it due to the help of the advanced technology that's around in this day and age.'
Best batting: 54* MCC v West Indians, Durham 2007

2007 Season (did not make any first-class or one-day appearances for his county)

Career Performances

	M	Inn	NO	Runs	HS	Avg	100	50	Ct	St	Balls	Runs	Wkts	Avg	BB	5I	10M
Test																	
FC	1	2	2	61	54 *		-	1	-	-	72	43	0		-	-	-
ODI																	
List A																	
20/20 Int																	
20/20																	

CLARE, J. L. Derbyshire

Name: Jonathan Luke Clare
Role: Right-hand bat, right-arm medium-fast bowler; all-rounder
Born: 14 June 1986, Burnley, Lancashire
Height: 6ft 3in **Weight:** 14st 2lbs
Nickname: JC, Sidewinder, Scream
County debut: 2007
Place in bowling averages: 6th av. 20.30
Parents: John and Elaine
Marital status: Single
Family links with cricket: Grandfather and father played club cricket for Burnley CC
Education: St Theodores RC High School
Qualifications: 11 GCSEs, 3 A-levels
Off-season: 'In the gym; watching the Clarets (Burnley FC); golf'
Overseas teams played for: Northern Districts, New Zealand; Hamilton Old Boys, New Zealand

Career highlights to date: 'Taking 5-90 on first-class debut v Notts'
Cricket superstitions: 'None'
Cricketers particularly admired: Dale Benkenstein, Steve Waugh
Young players to look out for: Dan Redfern, Karl Brown, Gary Ballance
Other sports played: Football, golf, darts
Other sports followed: Football (Burnley FC)
Favourite band: Arctic Monkeys, 'any Manchester music'
Relaxations: 'Socialising, betting, dodgeball'
Extras: Was member of Burnley U15 with three other players currently playing county/international cricket – David Brown (Gloucestershire), Michael Brown

(Hampshire), James Anderson (Lancashire/England). Recorded maiden first-class five-wicket return (5-90) on debut v Nottinghamshire at Chesterfield 2007
Opinions on cricket: 'More youth!'
Best batting: 22 Derbyshire v Northamptonshire, Derby 2007
Best bowling: 5-90 Derbyshire v Nottinghamshire, Chesterfield 2007

2007 Season

	M	Inn	NO	Runs	HS	Avg	100	50	Ct	St	Balls	Runs	Wkts	Avg	BB	5I	10M
Test																	
FC	2	3	0	42	22	14.00	-	-	-	-	296	203	10	20.30	5-90	1	-
ODI																	
List A	3	3	0	17	12	5.66	-	-	1	-	108	117	4	29.25	3-44	-	
20/20 Int																	
20/20																	

Career Performances

	M	Inn	NO	Runs	HS	Avg	100	50	Ct	St	Balls	Runs	Wkts	Avg	BB	5I	10M
Test																	
FC	2	3	0	42	22	14.00	-	-	-	-	296	203	10	20.30	5-90	1	-
ODI																	
List A	3	3	0	17	12	5.66	-	-	1	-	108	117	4	29.25	3-44	-	
20/20 Int																	
20/20																	

CLARK, S. R. — Hampshire

Name: Stuart Rupert Clark
Role: Right-hand bat, right-arm fast-medium bowler
Born: 28 September 1975, Sutherland, Sydney, Australia
Height: 6ft 5½in
Nickname: Sarfraz
County debut: 2004 (Middlesex), 2007 (Hampshire)
County cap: 2007 (Hampshire)
Test debut: 2005-06
ODI debut: 2005-06
Twenty20 Int debut: 2005-06
Place in batting averages: 278th av. 10.14
Place in bowling averages: 36th av. 25.08
Overseas tours: Australia A to South Africa 2002-03, to Pakistan 2005-06; Australia to England 2005, to New Zealand (one-day series) 2005-06, to South Africa 2005-06, to Bangladesh 2005-06, to Malaysia (DLF Cup) 2006-07, to West Indies (World Cup) 2006-07, to South Africa (World 20/20) 2007-08, to India (one-day series) 2007-08
Overseas teams played for: New South Wales 1997-98 –

Extras: Took 45 Pura Cup wickets (av. 23.27) 2001-02 and was New South Wales Player of the Year. Returned third best match figures by an Australian Test debutant (9-89 – 5-55/4-34) in the first Test v South Africa at Cape Town 2005-06, winning Man of the Match award and going on to win Man of the [Test] Series award (20 wickets; av. 15.85). Leading wicket-taker in the 2006-07 Ashes series (26 wickets; av. 17.03). His domestic match awards include Man of the Match v Western Australia at Perth in the ING Cup final 2002-03 (3-34) and v Western Australia at Perth in the Pura Cup 2006-07 (8-58/2-36, including first innings hat-trick – North, Voges, Magoffin). Was a temporary overseas player with Middlesex during the 2004 and 2005 seasons; was an overseas player with Hampshire during the 2007 season

Best batting: 62 New South Wales v South Australia, Adelaide 2006-07

Best bowling: 8-58 New South Wales v Western Australia, Perth 2006-07

2007 Season

	M	Inn	NO	Runs	HS	Avg	100	50	Ct	St	Balls	Runs	Wkts	Avg	BB	5I	10M
Test																	
FC	6	9	2	71	17	10.14	-	-	3	-	1052	602	24	25.08	7-82	1	-
ODI																	
List A	7	2	2	2	1 *		-	-	1	-	392	239	21	11.38	6-27	1	
20/20 Int																	
20/20																	

Career Performances

	M	Inn	NO	Runs	HS	Avg	100	50	Ct	St	Balls	Runs	Wkts	Avg	BB	5I	10M
Test	9	10	2	116	39	14.50	-	-	2	-	2048	837	47	17.80	5-55	1	-
FC	79	106	29	1092	62	14.18	-	1	23	-	16290	7926	294	26.95	8-58	12	1
ODI	25	8	5	59	16 *	19.66	-	-	7	-	1266	1133	36	31.47	4-54	-	
List A	119	36	14	186	26 *	8.45	-	-	26	-	6166	4477	165	27.13	6-27	1	
20/20 Int	8	0	0	0	0		-	-	4	-	192	204	13	15.69	4-20	-	
20/20	8	0	0	0	0		-	-	4	-	192	204	13	15.69	4-20	-	

CLARKE, R. Derbyshire

Name: Rikki Clarke
Role: Right-hand bat, right-arm fast-medium bowler, county captain; all-rounder
Born: 29 September 1981, Orsett, Essex
Height: 6ft 4½in **Weight:** 14st
Nickname: Clarkey, Crouchy
County debut: 2001 (one-day, Surrey), 2002 (first-class, Surrey)
County cap: 2005 (Surrey)
Test debut: 2003-04
ODI debut: 2003
1000 runs in a season: 1
1st-Class 200s: 1
Place in batting averages: 193rd av. 23.15 (2006 27th av. 57.05)
Place in bowling averages: 122nd av. 42.20 (2006 110th av. 41.40)
Parents: Bob and Janet
Marital status: Single
Family links with cricket: 'Dad played a bit but not any more'
Education: Broadwater; Godalming College
Qualifications: 5 GCSEs, GNVQ Leisure and Tourism
Overseas tours: Surrey U19 to Barbados; MCC Young Cricketers to Cape Town; England to Sri Lanka (ICC Champions Trophy) 2002-03, to Bangladesh and Sri Lanka 2003-04, to West Indies 2003-04, to India (ICC Champions Trophy) 2006-07; ECB National Academy to Australia and Sri Lanka 2002-03; England A to Sri Lanka 2004-05, to West Indies 2005-06
Career highlights to date: 'Playing for England'
Cricket moments to forget: 'None'
Cricket superstitions: 'Left pad first'
Cricketers particularly admired: Andrew Flintoff, Darren Gough
Young players to look out for: Jade Dernbach, James Benning
Other sports played: Snooker, poker
Other sports followed: Football (Tottenham)
Favourite band: Ne-Yo
Relaxations: 'Watching films and playing poker'
Extras: Named after former Tottenham Hotspur and Argentina footballer Ricky Villa. Represented England U17. Scored maiden first-class century (107*) on first-class debut v Cambridge UCCE at Fenner's 2002. NBC Denis Compton Award for the most promising young Surrey player 2002. Cricket Writers' Club Young Player of the Year 2002. Surrey Supporters' Young Player of the Year 2002. Surrey Sponsors' Young

Player of the Year 2002. Made ODI debut v Pakistan at Old Trafford in the NatWest Challenge 2003, taking the wicket of Imran Nazir with his first ball in international cricket. ECB National Academy 2004-05, 2005-06, 2006-07. Vice-captain of Surrey 2006 to June 2007. Scored 28-ball 82* v Gloucestershire at The Oval in the Friends Provident 2007 as Surrey posted a world record List A total of 496-4. Left Surrey at the end of the 2007 season and has joined Derbyshire for 2008 as captain
Best batting: 214 Surrey v Somerset, Guildford 2006
Best bowling: 4-21 Surrey v Leicestershire, Leicester 2003

2007 Season

	M	Inn	NO	Runs	HS	Avg	100	50	Ct	St	Balls	Runs	Wkts	Avg	BB	5I	10M
Test																	
FC	10	14	1	301	68 *	23.15	-	2	10	-	929	633	15	42.20	3-57	-	-
ODI																	
List A	6	6	1	217	82 *	43.40	-	2	6	-	240	229	6	38.16	2-40	-	
20/20 Int																	
20/20	6	5	2	49	22 *	16.33	-	-	-	-	70	87	2	43.50	1-16	-	

Career Performances

	M	Inn	NO	Runs	HS	Avg	100	50	Ct	St	Balls	Runs	Wkts	Avg	BB	5I	10M
Test	2	3	0	96	55	32.00	-	1	1	-	174	60	4	15.00	2-7	-	-
FC	76	122	13	4201	214	38.54	10	17	87	-	6616	4585	110	41.68	4-21	-	-
ODI	20	13	0	144	39	11.07	-	-	11	-	469	415	11	37.72	2-28	-	
List A	110	97	13	2161	98 *	25.72	-	11	46	-	2869	2728	71	38.42	4-49	-	
20/20 Int																	
20/20	33	31	8	510	79 *	22.17	-	2	14	-	429	522	25	20.88	3-11	-	

12. Which spinner had match figures of 11-147 for England against New Zealand in the first Test at Christchurch in 1991-92?

CLAYDON, M. E. Durham

Name: Mitchell Eric Claydon
Role: Left-hand bat, right-arm fast bowler
Born: 25 November 1982, Fairfield, Australia
Height: 6ft 4in **Weight:** 15st 9lbs
Nickname: Lips
County debut: 2005 (Yorkshire), 2007 (Durham)
Parents: Robert (Tosh) and Sue
Marital status: Single
Children: Lachlan Robert Bickhoff-Claydon, 25 February 2004
Family links with cricket: Father played for Markington CC in the Nidderdale League
Education: Westfields Sports High School, Sydney
Qualifications: Level 1 coaching
Career outside cricket: 'Real estate agent'
Overseas teams played for: Campbelltown-Camden Ghosts 1999 –
Career highlights to date: 'Being a part of Durham 2007, even though I only played one game'
Cricket moments to forget: 'While participating in a fielding drill consisting of high catches, I misjudged the height of the ball; the next thing I knew I was lying on the physio table with an ice pack on my forehead'
Cricket superstitions: 'Must wear my gold chain that has a photo of my sister who died in 2003'
Cricketers particularly admired: Steve Waugh
Young players to look out for: Ben Harmison, Mark Stoneman
Other sports played: Rugby league, rugby union
Other sports followed: Rugby league (West Tigers), football (Leeds United)
Injuries: 'Stress fracture L5 – never healed from 2006'
Favourite band: Denham Reagh
Relaxations: 'Surfing whilst home in Australia; golf'
Extras: Only player in history of Campbelltown-Camden Ghosts to have taken two first grade hat-tricks. Holds a British passport and is not considered an overseas player
Best batting: 38 Yorkshire v Durham, Riverside 2006
Best bowling: 3-26 Durham v DUCCE, Durham 2007

2007 Season

	M	Inn	NO	Runs	HS	Avg	100	50	Ct	St	Balls	Runs	Wkts	Avg	BB	5I	10M
Test																	
FC	2	1	1	14	14 *		-	-	-	-	318	219	6	36.50	3-26	-	-
ODI																	
List A																	
20/20 Int																	
20/20																	

Career Performances

	M	Inn	NO	Runs	HS	Avg	100	50	Ct	St	Balls	Runs	Wkts	Avg	BB	5I	10M
Test																	
FC	5	3	1	52	38	26.00	-	-	-	-	720	482	9	53.55	3-26	-	-
ODI																	
List A	7	2	0	15	9	7.50	-	-	-	-	342	293	8	36.62	2-41	-	
20/20 Int																	
20/20	7	2	2	14	12 *		-	-	2	-	139	188	5	37.60	2-6	-	

CLIFF, S. J. — Leicestershire

Name: Samuel (Sam) James Cliff
Role: Right-hand bat, right-arm medium-fast bowler
Born: 3 October 1987, Nottingham
Height: 6ft 2in **Weight:** 11st 8lbs
Nickname: Cliffy, Jacko
County debut: 2007
Parents: Colin Cliff and Julie Silverwood
Marital status: Single
Family links with cricket: 'Father plays village cricket "very well" and has scored over 60 centuries (he keeps reminding me)'
Education: Colonel Frank Seely Comprehensive, Calverton, Nottingham
Qualifications: 10 GCSEs
Career outside cricket: Painter and decorator
Off-season: 'Hopefully touring'
Overseas tours: Leicestershire Young Cricketers to India 2005-06
Career highlights to date: 'Getting a contract. Playing in the same amateur side as Luke Wright (Sussex and England)'
Cricket moments to forget: 'None yet!'

Cricket superstitions: 'A few little ones but nothing specific'
Cricketers particularly admired: Brett Lee, Luke Wright
Young players to look out for: Josh Cobb
Other sports played: Golf, football
Other sports followed: Ice hockey (Nottingham Panthers), football (Notts County), rugby (Nottingham)
Favourite band: Cascada
Relaxations: 'Socialising, watching live sport'
Extras: Played for Leicestershire Academy v England U19 2007. Played in Loughborough Town's Leicestershire County Cup winning side 2007, taking 2-13 from eight overs in the final v Market Harborough at Leicester
Opinions on cricket: 'Important to have "two strings to the bow" in today's game.'
Best batting: 11 Leicestershire v Northamptonshire, Leicester 2007
Best bowling: 1-28 Leicestershire v OUCCE, The Parks 2007

2007 Season

	M	Inn	NO	Runs	HS	Avg	100	50	Ct	St	Balls	Runs	Wkts	Avg	BB	5I	10M
Test																	
FC	2	3	2	21	11	21.00	-	-	-	-	168	126	1	126.00	1-28	-	-
ODI																	
List A																	
20/20 Int																	
20/20																	

Career Performances

	M	Inn	NO	Runs	HS	Avg	100	50	Ct	St	Balls	Runs	Wkts	Avg	BB	5I	10M
Test																	
FC	2	3	2	21	11	21.00	-	-	-	-	168	126	1	126.00	1-28	-	-
ODI																	
List A																	
20/20 Int																	
20/20																	

13. Who took a world record 11 catches as wicket-keeper in the second Test between England and South Africa at Johannesburg in 1995-96?

CLINTON, R. S. Surrey

Name: Richard Selvey Clinton
Role: Left-hand opening bat, right-arm medium bowler
Born: 1 September 1981, Sidcup, Kent
Height: 6ft 3in **Weight:** 15st 9lbs
Nickname: Clint
County debut: 2001 (Essex), 2004 (Surrey)
Parents: Cathy and Grahame
Marital status: Married
Family links with cricket: 'Father played for Surrey. Uncles, cousin and brother play high standard of club cricket in Kent Premier League'
Education: Colfes School, London; Loughborough University
Qualifications: 9 GCSEs, 3 A-levels
Overseas teams played for: Kensington CC, Adelaide; Valleys CC, Brisbane 2000-02
Cricket superstitions: 'Just a tried and tested routine'
Cricketers particularly admired: Graham Thorpe, Mark Butcher
Other sports played: Football, squash
Other sports followed: Motor racing (Formula One)
Favourite band: Aqua, The Sometime Maybes
Extras: Scored 36 and 58* on first-class debut v Surrey at Ilford 2001; scored 56 the following day on Norwich Union League debut v Durham at the same ground. Played for Loughborough UCCE 2004-06. Represented British Universities 2004, 2005, 2006. Joined Surrey during the 2004 season, scoring 73 on Championship debut v Worcestershire at The Oval
Best batting: 108* LUCCE v Essex, Chelmsford 2006
Best bowling: 2-30 Essex v Australians, Chelmsford 2001

2007 Season

	M	Inn	NO	Runs	HS	Avg	100	50	Ct	St	Balls	Runs	Wkts	Avg	BB	5I	10M
Test																	
FC	3	2	0	0	0	0.00	-	-	1	-	102	55	0		-	-	-
ODI																	
List A	1	1	0	2	2	2.00	-	-	1	-	0	0	0		-	-	
20/20 Int																	
20/20																	

Career Performances

	M	Inn	NO	Runs	HS	Avg	100	50	Ct	St	Balls	Runs	Wkts	Avg	BB	5I	10M
Test																	
FC	42	70	5	1837	108 *	28.26	4	9	24	-	295	207	2	103.50	2-30	-	-
ODI																	
List A	19	16	3	191	56	14.69	-	1	4	-	48	58	2	29.00	2-16	-	
20/20 Int																	
20/20																	

CLOUGH, G. D. — Nottinghamshire

Name: Gareth David Clough
Role: Right-hand bat, right-arm medium bowler; all-rounder
Born: 23 May 1978, Leeds
Height: 6ft **Weight:** 12st
Nickname: Garth, Banga
County debut: 1998 (Yorkshire), 2001 (Nottinghamshire)
Parents: David and Gillian
Marital status: Single
Education: Pudsey Grangefield
Qualifications: 9 GCSEs, 3 A-levels, Level 1 cricket coach
Overseas tours: Yorkshire to Durban and Cape Town 1999; Nottinghamshire to Johannesburg 2001-03
Overseas teams played for: Somerset West, Cape Town 1996-97; Deepdene Bears, Melbourne 1999-2000, 2001-02
Career highlights to date: '2006 Twenty20 finals day'
Cricket moments to forget: 'Result at end of Twenty20 final'
Cricketers particularly admired: Ian Botham, Steve Waugh
Young players to look out for: Samit Patel
Other sports played: Golf, football, poker, darts
Other sports followed: 'All sports'; football (Everton), rugby league (Leeds Rhinos)
Favourite band: Razorlight
Relaxations: 'Dining out, socialising with friends, golf'
Extras: Took 6-25 v Sussex at Trent Bridge in the Pro40 2006, the best one-day return by a Nottinghamshire bowler since 1994
Opinions on cricket: 'Just keeps on getting better and better.'
Best batting: 55 Nottinghamshire v India A, Trent Bridge 2003
Best bowling: 3-69 Nottinghamshire v Gloucestershire, Trent Bridge 2001

2007 Season

	M	Inn	NO	Runs	HS	Avg	100	50	Ct	St	Balls	Runs	Wkts	Avg	BB	5I	10M
Test																	
FC	1	2	0	9	7	4.50	-	-	-	-	156	82	4	20.50	3-72	-	-
ODI																	
List A	10	3	2	40	26 *	40.00	-	-	1	-	324	330	7	47.14	4-43	-	
20/20 Int																	
20/20	6	3	1	9	3 *	4.50	-	-	5	-	107	150	6	25.00	4-24	-	

Career Performances

	M	Inn	NO	Runs	HS	Avg	100	50	Ct	St	Balls	Runs	Wkts	Avg	BB	5I	10M
Test																	
FC	12	17	2	156	55	10.40	-	1	4	-	1218	766	16	47.87	3-69	-	-
ODI																	
List A	96	53	18	625	42 *	17.85	-	-	28	-	3224	2815	86	32.73	6-25	1	
20/20 Int																	
20/20	34	21	5	278	40 *	17.37	-	-	9	-	551	720	30	24.00	4-24	-	

COBB, J. J. — Leicestershire

Name: Joshua (<u>Josh</u>) James Cobb
Role: Right-hand bat, leg-spin bowler; 'batter that bowls'
Born: 17 August 1990, Leicester
Height: 6ft 1in **Weight:** 12st 6lbs
Nickname: Cobby
County debut: 2007
Parents: Russell and Sharon
Family links with cricket: 'Father ex-Leicestershire player'
Education: Bosworth College; Oakham School
Qualifications: GCSEs
Off-season: 'Going away to South Africa or Australia to develop my game'
Overseas tours: Leicestershire U14 to South Africa 2003; Leicestershire U19 to India 2006
Career highlights to date: 'Making first-class debut v Northamptonshire [2007] having just turned 17'
Cricket superstitions: 'Putting on left pad before right pad'
Cricketers particularly admired: Shane Warne, Darren Stevens, Paul Nixon

Young players to look out for: Shiv Thakor
Other sports played: Badminton (Leicestershire U13-15), football ('played in goal for Leicester District at U16')
Other sports followed: Football (Manchester United), rugby (Leicester Tigers)
Favourite band: D12
Relaxations: 'Listening to music, socialising with friends, playing sports and reading and writing books!'
Extras: Made 2nd XI Championship debut 2006. Played for Leicestershire Academy v Victoria Emerging Players at Leicester 2007, scoring 102*
Opinions on cricket: 'Should use more technology where possible, trying not to slow the game down in the process.'
Best batting: 21 Leicestershire v Northamptonshire, Leicester 2007

2007 Season

	M	Inn	NO	Runs	HS	Avg	100	50	Ct	St	Balls	Runs	Wkts	Avg	BB	5I	10M
Test																	
FC	1	2	0	23	21	11.50	-	-	-	-	54	44	0		-	-	-
ODI																	
List A																	
20/20 Int																	
20/20																	

Career Performances

	M	Inn	NO	Runs	HS	Avg	100	50	Ct	St	Balls	Runs	Wkts	Avg	BB	5I	10M
Test																	
FC	1	2	0	23	21	11.50	-	-	-	-	54	44	0		-	-	-
ODI																	
List A																	
20/20 Int																	
20/20																	

14. Whose 753 runs at an average of 94.12 recorded in 1947 remains the best aggregate for England in a Test series v South Africa?

COETZER, K. J. Durham

Name: Kyle James Coetzer
Role: Right-hand bat, right-arm medium bowler
Born: 14 April 1984, Aberdeen
Height: 5ft 11in
Nickname: Costa
County debut: 2004
Place in batting averages: 85th av. 38.26
Parents: Peter and Megan
Marital status: Single
Family links with cricket: 'All of my family plays, including two older brothers'
Education: Aberdeen Grammar School
Qualifications: Standard grades, 4 Intermediate 2s
Overseas tours: Scotland U19 to New Zealand (U19 World Cup) 2001-02, to Bangladesh (U19 World Cup) 2003-04 (c), plus other Scotland age-group and A tours; Scotland to UAE (ICC Inter-Continental Cup) 2004, to Ireland (ICC Trophy) 2005, to Barbados 2005-06; Durham to Dubai 2005, 2006, to Mumbai 2006
Overseas teams played for: Cape Town CC 2002-03, 2003-04, 2004, 2005-06; Gosnells CC 2005
Cricket moments to forget: 'Most of 2006 season'
Cricket superstitions: 'Touch bat in crease after "over" is called'
Cricketers particularly admired: Jacques Kallis, Michael Hussey
Young players to look out for: Andrew Smith, Moneeb Iqbal
Other sports played: Golf, basketball, football
Other sports followed: Football (Aberdeen, Arsenal)
Favourite band: Jack Johnson 'and a good mix of music'
Relaxations: 'Listening to music'
Extras: Man of the Match v Italy in the ECC U19 Championships at Deventer 2003 (146*). Has played for Scotland in first-class and one-day cricket, including NCL 2003 and C&G 2003, 2004 and 2006. Scored 67 on first-class debut, for Durham v Glamorgan at Cardiff 2004
Best batting: 153* Durham v DUCCE, Durham 2007

2007 Season

	M	Inn	NO	Runs	HS	Avg	100	50	Ct	St	Balls	Runs	Wkts	Avg	BB	5I	10M
Test																	
FC	14	26	3	880	153 *	38.26	2	2	14	-	0	0	0		-	-	-
ODI																	
List A	16	15	2	431	76	33.15	-	3	7	-	0	0	0		-	-	
20/20 Int																	
20/20	2	1	0	1	1	1.00	-	-	-	-	0	0	0		-	-	

Career Performances

	M	Inn	NO	Runs	HS	Avg	100	50	Ct	St	Balls	Runs	Wkts	Avg	BB	5I	10M
Test																	
FC	23	41	6	1336	153 *	38.17	3	4	14	-	54	22	0		-	-	-
ODI																	
List A	26	24	3	517	76	24.61	-	3	10	-	60	47	0		-	-	
20/20 Int																	
20/20	2	1	0	1	1	1.00	-	-	-	-	0	0	0		-	-	

COLLINGWOOD, P. D. Durham

Name: Paul David Collingwood
Role: Right-hand bat, right-arm medium bowler
Born: 26 May 1976, Shotley Bridge, Tyneside
Height: 5ft 11in **Weight:** 12st
Nickname: Colly
County debut: 1995 (one-day), 1996 (first-class)
County cap: 1998
Benefit: 2007
Test debut: 2003-04
ODI debut: 2001
Twenty20 Int debut: 2005
1000 runs in a season: 2
1st-Class 200s: 1
Place in batting averages: 52nd av. 43.85 (2006 70th av. 41.81)
Parents: David and Janet
Wife: Vicki
Children: Shannon, 2006

Family links with cricket: Father and brother play in the Tyneside Senior League for Shotley Bridge CC
Education: Blackfyne Comprehensive School; Derwentside College
Qualifications: 9 GCSEs, 2 A-levels
Overseas tours: Durham Cricket Academy to Sri Lanka 1996 (c); England VI to Hong Kong 2001, 2002; England to Zimbabwe (one-day series) 2001-02, to India and New Zealand 2001-02 (one-day series), to Australia 2002-03, to Africa (World Cup) 2002-03, to Bangladesh and Sri Lanka 2003-04, to West Indies 2003-04, to Zimbabwe (one-day series) 2004-05, to South Africa 2004-05, to Pakistan 2005-06, to India 2005-06, to India (ICC Champions Trophy) 2006-07, to Australia 2006-07, to West Indies (World Cup) 2006-07, to South Africa (World 20/20) 2007-08 (c), to Sri Lanka 2007-08 (ODI c), to New Zealand 2007-08 (ODI c)
Overseas teams played for: Bulleen CC, Melbourne 1995-96, 1996-97 ('won flag on both occasions'); Cornwall CC, Auckland 1997-98; Alberton CC, Johannesburg 1998-99; Richmond CC, Melbourne 2000-01
Cricket moments to forget: 'Being Matthew Walker's (Kent) first first-class wicket'
Cricket superstitions: 'Left pad on first, and wearing them on the wrong legs'
Cricketers particularly admired: Steve Waugh, Jacques Kallis, Glenn McGrath, Shane Warne
Other sports played: Golf (9 handicap)
Other sports followed: Football ('The Red and Whites' – Sunderland)
Extras: Took wicket (David Capel) with first ball on first-class debut against Northants, then scored 91 in Durham's first innings. Durham Player of the Year 2000. Joint (and first English) winner of the Jack Ryder Medal, awarded by the umpires, for his performances in Victorian Premier Cricket 2000-01. Scored 112* and took England ODI record 6-31 v Bangladesh at Trent Bridge in the NatWest Series 2005, winning Man of the Match award. His other match awards include Man of the Match v Sri Lanka at Perth in the VB Series 2002-03 (100) and in three consecutive matches (including the two finals) in the Commonwealth Bank Series 2006-07; Man of the Match in the first Twenty20 Int v West Indies at The Oval 2007 (79). Vice-captain of Durham 2005-06. Slazenger Sheer Instinct Award 2005. Appointed MBE in 2006 New Year Honours as part of 2005 Ashes-winning England team. Scored 206 in the second Test at Adelaide 2006-07, becoming the first England batsman to score a Test double century in Australia since Wally Hammond in 1936-37 and sharing with Kevin Pietersen (158) in a record fourth-wicket stand for England v Australia (310). One of *Wisden*'s Five Cricketers of the Year 2007. England one-day captain since June 2007. England 12-month central contract 2007-08
Best batting: 206 England v Australia, Adelaide 2006-07
Best bowling: 5-52 Durham v Somerset, Stockton 2005

2007 Season

	M	Inn	NO	Runs	HS	Avg	100	50	Ct	St	Balls	Runs	Wkts	Avg	BB	5I	10M
Test	7	13	1	556	128	46.33	2	2	10	-	323	160	5	32.00	2-24	-	-
FC	8	15	1	614	128	43.85	2	3	11	-	425	199	5	39.80	2-24	-	-
ODI	10	9	2	324	91 *	46.28	-	2	8	-	353	324	3	108.00	2-45	-	
List A	14	13	2	435	91 *	39.54	-	3	11	-	429	374	8	46.75	3-33	-	
20/20 Int	2	2	0	106	79	53.00	-	1	1	-	18	38	2	19.00	2-21	-	
20/20	2	2	0	106	79	53.00	-	1	1	-	18	38	2	19.00	2-21	-	

Career Performances

	M	Inn	NO	Runs	HS	Avg	100	50	Ct	St	Balls	Runs	Wkts	Avg	BB	5I	10M
Test	27	51	5	2016	206	43.82	5	6	37	-	773	425	6	70.83	2-24	-	-
FC	146	257	19	8573	206	36.02	19	40	157	-	8425	4241	105	40.39	5-52	1	-
ODI	131	119	27	3290	120 *	35.76	4	17	79	-	3266	2750	67	41.04	6-31	1	
List A	292	274	49	7450	120 *	33.11	6	43	153	-	7562	6066	172	35.26	6-31	1	
20/20 Int	11	11	0	250	79	22.72	-	1	2	-	132	205	11	18.63	4-22	-	
20/20	11	11	0	250	79	22.72	-	1	2	-	132	205	11	18.63	4-22	-	

COLLINS, P. T. — Surrey

Name: Pedro Tyrone Collins
Role: Right-hand bat, left-arm fast-medium bowler
Born: 12 August 1976, Boscobelle, Barbados
County debut: No first-team appearance
Test debut: 1998-99
ODI debut: 1999-2000
Family links with cricket: Half-brother Fidel Edwards plays for Barbados and West Indies
Overseas tours: West Indies A to South Africa 1997-98, to Bangladesh and India 1998-99; West Indies to Bangladesh 1999-2000, to New Zealand 1999-2000, to Zimbabwe and Kenya 2001, to Sri Lanka 2001-02, to Sharjah (v Pakistan) 2001-02, to Sri Lanka (ICC Champions Trophy) 2002-03, to India and Bangladesh 2002-03, to Africa (World Cup) 2002-03, to England 2004, to Australia (VB Series) 2004-05, to South Africa (World 20/20) 2007-08, to South Africa 2007-08, plus one-day tournament in Sharjah
Overseas teams played for: Barbados 1996-97 –

Extras: Man of the Match v Windward Islands in Dominica in the Carib Beer Cup 2006-07 (6-24/1-15). Played for Benwell Hill in the North East Premier League 2007. Is not considered an overseas player
Best batting: 25 Barbados v Trinidad and Tobago, Pointe-a-Pierre 2003-04
Best bowling: 6-24 Barbados v Windward Islands, Portsmouth (BP) 2006-07
Stop press: Took 7-11 v West Indies U19 at Berbice in the KFC Cup 2007-08, winning Man of the Match award

2007 Season (did not make any first-class or one-day appearances)

Career Performances

	M	Inn	NO	Runs	HS	Avg	100	50	Ct	St	Balls	Runs	Wkts	Avg	BB	5I	10M
Test	32	47	7	235	24	5.87	-	-	7	-	6964	3671	106	34.63	6-53	3	-
FC	99	124	30	607	25	6.45	-	-	26	-	17256	8692	335	25.94	6-24	7	-
ODI	30	12	5	30	10 *	4.28	-	-	8	-	1577	1212	39	31.07	5-43	1	
List A	63	25	8	122	55 *	7.17	-	1	12	-	3275	2348	96	24.45	5-43	1	
20/20 Int																	
20/20	3	1	0	1	1	1.00	-	-	-	-	58	45	4	11.25	3-13	-	

COMPTON, N. R. D. — Middlesex

Name: Nicholas (Nick) Richard Denis Compton
Role: Right-hand bat, right-arm off-spin bowler
Born: 26 June 1983, Durban, South Africa
Height: 6ft 1in **Weight:** 13st 1lb
Nickname: Compo, Lord
County debut: 2001 (one-day), 2004 (first-class)
County cap: 2006
1000 runs in a season: 1
Place in batting averages: 202nd av. 22.16 (2006 53rd av. 46.96)
Parents: Richard and Glynis
Marital status: Single
Family links with cricket: Grandfather Denis Compton played football and cricket for England
Education: Harrow School; Durham University
Qualifications: 3 A-levels, ECB coach Level 1
Overseas tours: England U19 to Australia and (U19 World Cup) New Zealand 2001-02; MCC to Canada 2005-06; England A to Bangladesh 2006-07

Overseas teams played for: University of Western Australia, Perth 2001; Berea Rovers, Durban; University of Cape Town
Career highlights to date: 'Reaching 100 at Lord's with a six v Kent to score my first Championship century [2006] – champagne moment!'
Cricket moments to forget: 'Relegation to second division [2006]'
Cricketers particularly admired: Rahul Dravid, Jacques Kallis, Steve Waugh, Ed Joyce
Young players to look out for: Billy Godleman, Steve Finn
Other sports played: Golf (6 handicap), waterskiing, represented Natal at junior level at tennis
Other sports followed: Football (Arsenal), Super 14 rugby union (Sharks)
Favourite band: The Killers
Extras: Played for Natal U13 and U15. Natal Academy award 1997. Middlesex U17 Batsman of the Season 1999. Middlesex U19 Player of the Season 2000. NBC Denis Compton Award for the most promising young Middlesex player 2001, 2002, 2006. Represented England U19 2002. Scored maiden first-class century (101) v OUCCE at The Parks 2006 and maiden Championship century (124) in the following match v Kent at Lord's 2006. Carried bat for 105* v Nottinghamshire at Lord's 2006, in the process passing 1000 first-class runs for the season in his first full season of county cricket. Is England-qualified
Opinions on cricket: 'A great time to be involved in English cricket.'
Best batting: 190 Middlesex v Durham, Lord's 2006
Best bowling: 1-94 Middlesex v Sussex, Southgate 2006

2007 Season

	M	Inn	NO	Runs	HS	Avg	100	50	Ct	St	Balls	Runs	Wkts	Avg	BB	5I	10M
Test																	
FC	11	18	0	399	67	22.16	-	3	6	-	24	20	0		-	-	-
ODI																	
List A	12	11	4	286	110 *	40.85	1	-	11	-	24	25	0		-	-	
20/20 Int																	
20/20	5	4	0	43	17	10.75	-	-	3	-	0	0	0		-	-	

Career Performances

	M	Inn	NO	Runs	HS	Avg	100	50	Ct	St	Balls	Runs	Wkts	Avg	BB	5I	10M
Test																	
FC	35	61	7	2060	190	38.14	6	9	18	-	66	123	1	123.00	1-94	-	-
ODI																	
List A	43	37	8	831	110 *	28.65	1	4	22	-	54	45	0		-	-	
20/20 Int																	
20/20	22	17	1	187	50 *	11.68	-	1	13	-	0	0	0		-	-	

COOK, A. N. Essex

Name: Alastair Nathan Cook
Role: Left-hand opening bat, right-arm off-spin bowler
Born: 25 December 1984, Gloucester
Height: 6ft 2in **Weight:** 12st 10lbs
Nickname: Ali, Cooky, Chef
County debut: 2003
County cap: 2005
Test debut: 2005-06
ODI debut: 2006
Twenty20 Int debut: 2007
1000 runs in a season: 3
Place in batting averages: 24th av. 54.70 (2006 11th av. 64.38)
Parents: Graham and Elizabeth
Marital status: Single
Family links with cricket: 'Dad played for village side; brothers play for Maldon CC'
Education: Bedford School
Qualifications: 9 GCSEs, 3 A-levels
Overseas tours: Bedford School to Barbados 2001; England U19 to Bangladesh (U19 World Cup) 2003-04 (c); England A to Sri Lanka 2004-05, to West Indies 2005-06; England to Pakistan 2005-06, to India 2005-06, to Australia 2006-07, to Sri Lanka 2007-08, to New Zealand 2007-08
Cricket moments to forget: 'Running myself out first ball in U15 World Cup game against India'
Cricket superstitions: 'A few!'
Cricketers particularly admired: Graham Thorpe, Andy Flower, Graham Gooch
Young players to look out for: James Hildreth, Mark Pettini
Other sports played: Squash, golf
Other sports followed: 'All sports'
Relaxations: 'Spending time with friends'
Extras: Played for England U15 in U15 World Cup 2000. Represented England U19 2003 and (as captain) 2004. Scored 69* on first-class debut v Nottinghamshire at Chelmsford 2003 and a further two half-centuries in his next two Championship matches. Had consecutive scores of 108*, 108* and 87 in the U19 World Cup 2003-04 in Bangladesh. NBC Denis Compton Award for the most promising young Essex player 2003. ECB National Academy 2004-05 (part-time), 2005-06. Scored 214 v Australians at Chelmsford in a two-day game 2005. Cricket Writers' Club Young Player of the Year 2005. PCA Young Player of the Year 2005, 2006. Called up as a replacement to the England tour of India 2005-06, scoring century (104*) on Test

debut in the first Test at Nagpur (following 60 in first innings). Scored maiden Ashes century (116) in the third Test at Perth 2006-07, becoming the first England player to score four Test hundreds before his 22nd birthday. Man of the Match in the first Test v West Indies at Lord's 2007 (105/65). England 12-month central contract 2007-08
Best batting: 195 Essex v Northamptonshire, Northampton 2005
Best bowling: 3-13 Essex v Northamptonshire, Chelmsford 2005
Stop press: Man of the Match in the fourth ODI v Sri Lanka in Colombo 2007-08 (80)

2007 Season

	M	Inn	NO	Runs	HS	Avg	100	50	Ct	St	Balls	Runs	Wkts	Avg	BB	5I	10M
Test	7	13	0	621	106	47.76	2	3	10	-	0	0	0		-	-	-
FC	11	20	0	1094	142	54.70	5	3	12	-	6	6	0		-	-	-
ODI	9	9	0	248	102	27.55	1	-	3	-	0	0	0		-	-	
List A	15	15	1	521	125	37.21	2	1	8	-	0	0	0		-	-	
20/20 Int	2	2	0	24	15	12.00	-	-	1	-	0	0	0		-	-	
20/20	2	2	0	24	15	12.00	-	-	1	-	0	0	0		-	-	

Career Performances

	M	Inn	NO	Runs	HS	Avg	100	50	Ct	St	Balls	Runs	Wkts	Avg	BB	5I	10M
Test	21	39	2	1658	127	44.81	6	6	19	-	0	0	0		-	-	-
FC	69	123	11	5297	195	47.29	17	25	71	-	156	117	3	39.00	3-13	-	-
ODI	11	11	0	328	102	29.81	1	-	3	-	0	0	0		-	-	
List A	40	39	4	1147	125	32.77	2	4	19	-	18	10	0		-	-	
20/20 Int	2	2	0	24	15	12.00	-	-	1	-	0	0	0		-	-	
20/20	4	4	0	35	15	8.75	-	-	1	-	0	0	0		-	-	

COOK, S. J. — Kent

Name: Simon James Cook
Role: Right-hand bat, right-arm fast-medium bowler
Born: 15 January 1977, Oxford
Height: 6ft 4in **Weight:** 13st
Nickname: Cookie, Donk, Chef
County debut: 1997 (one-day, Middlesex), 1999 (first-class, Middlesex), 2005 (Kent)
County cap: 2003 (Middlesex), 2007 (Kent)
Place in batting averages: 236th av. 16.77 (2006 253rd av. 14.00)
Place in bowling averages: 86th av. 33.63 (2006 66th av. 33.03)
Parents: Phil and Sue
Marital status: Single
Family links with cricket: Brothers played for Oxfordshire
Education: Matthew Arnold School
Qualifications: GCSEs, NVQ Business Administration II, Level 3 ECB coach

Career outside cricket: Coaching and property development
Overseas tours: Middlesex to South Africa 2000
Overseas teams played for: Rockingham, Perth 2001, 2002
Career highlights to date: 'Beating Australia in one-day game at Lord's; winning division two of NCL and equalling league record for wickets in a season (39)'
Cricket moments to forget: 'Being outside the circle in a one-day game when I was supposed to be in it. Danny Law was bowled, the ball went for four [off the stumps, making six no-balls in total] and he went on to win the game for Durham'
Cricket superstitions: 'None'
Cricketers particularly admired: Angus Fraser, Glenn McGrath

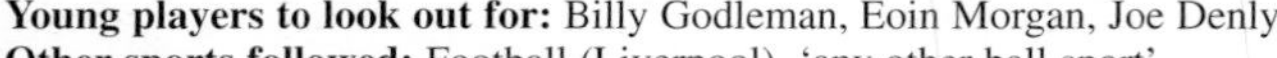

Young players to look out for: Billy Godleman, Eoin Morgan, Joe Denly
Other sports followed: Football (Liverpool), 'any other ball sport'
Player website: www.vcamcricket.co.uk
Extras: Scored career best 93* v Notts at Lord's 2001, helping Middlesex to avoid the follow-on, then took a wicket with the first ball of his opening spell. Equalled Adam Hollioake's record for the most wickets in a one-day league season (39) 2004
Best batting: 93* Middlesex v Nottinghamshire, Lord's 2001
Best bowling: 8-63 Middlesex v Northamptonshire, Northampton 2002

2007 Season

	M	Inn	NO	Runs	HS	Avg	100	50	Ct	St	Balls	Runs	Wkts	Avg	BB	5I	10M
Test																	
FC	12	14	5	151	50 *	16.77	-	1	4	-	1456	740	22	33.63	6-35	1	-
ODI																	
List A	16	10	3	121	49	17.28	-	-	5	-	797	624	27	23.11	4-25	-	
20/20 Int																	
20/20	11	1	1	25	25 *		-	-	-	-	239	275	17	16.17	3-21	-	

Career Performances

	M	Inn	NO	Runs	HS	Avg	100	50	Ct	St	Balls	Runs	Wkts	Avg	BB	5I	10M
Test																	
FC	103	133	18	1887	93 *	16.40	-	5	31	-	15817	8322	259	32.13	8-63	9	-
ODI																	
List A	151	98	31	1149	67 *	17.14	-	2	23	-	6768	5334	193	27.63	6-37	2	
20/20 Int																	
20/20	27	12	5	106	25 *	15.14	-	-	3	-	559	690	39	17.69	3-14	-	

CORK, D. G. — Lancashire

Name: Dominic Gerald Cork
Role: Right-hand bat, right-arm fast-medium bowler
Born: 7 August 1971, Newcastle-under-Lyme, Staffordshire
Height: 6ft 2½in **Weight:** 14st
Nickname: Corky
County debut: 1990 (Derbyshire), 2004 (Lancashire)
County cap: 1993 (Derbyshire), 2004 (Lancashire)
Benefit: 2001 (Derbyshire)
Test debut: 1995
ODI debut: 1992
50 wickets in a season: 7
1st-Class 200s: 1
Place in batting averages: 175th av. 25.30 (2006 188th av. 23.60)
Place in bowling averages: 88th av. 33.70 (2006 19th av. 25.50)
Parents: Gerald and Mary
Wife and date of marriage: Donna, 28 August 2000
Children: Ashleigh, 28 April 1990; Gregory, 29 September 1994
Family links with cricket: 'Father and two brothers played in the same side at Betley CC in Staffordshire'
Education: St Joseph's College, Trent Vale, Stoke-on-Trent; Newcastle College
Qualifications: 2 O-levels, Level 2 coach
Overseas tours: England YC to Australia 1989-90; England A to Bermuda and West Indies 1991-92, to Australia 1992-93, to South Africa 1993-94, to India 1994-95; England to South Africa 1995-96, to India and Pakistan (World Cup) 1995-96, to New Zealand 1996-97, to Australia 1998-99, to Pakistan and Sri Lanka 2000-01, to Sri Lanka (ICC Champions Trophy) 2002-03; England VI to Hong Kong 2005, 2006 (c)
Overseas teams played for: East Shirley, Christchurch, New Zealand 1990-91
Career highlights to date: 'Making my debut for England'
Cricket moments to forget: 'Every time the team loses'
Cricket superstitions: 'None'
Cricketers particularly admired: Kim Barnett, Mike Atherton, Ian Botham, Malcolm Marshall
Other sports played: Golf, football
Other sports followed: Football (Stoke City)
Favourite band: 'Anything R&B'

Relaxations: 'Listening to music'
Extras: Scored century (110) as nightwatchman for England Young Cricketers v Pakistan Young Cricketers at Taunton 1990. Took 8-53 before lunch on his 20th birthday, v Essex at Derby 1991. Selected for England A in 1991 – his first full season of first-class cricket. PCA Young Player of the Year 1991. Took 7-43 on Test debut against West Indies at Lord's 1995, the best innings figures ever by an England debutant. Took hat-trick (Richardson, Murray, Hooper) against the West Indies at Old Trafford in the fourth Test 1995. PCA Player of the Year 1995. Finished top of the Whyte and Mackay bowling ratings 1995. Cornhill England Player of the Year 1995-96. One of *Wisden*'s Five Cricketers of the Year 1996. Man of the Match in the second Test v West Indies at Lord's 2000; on his recall to the Test side he had match figures of 7-52 followed by a match-winning 33* in England's second innings. Derbyshire captain 1998-2003. Took Twenty20 hat-trick (Pietersen, Ealham, Patel) v Nottinghamshire at Old Trafford 2004
Best batting: 200* Derbyshire v Durham, Derby 2000
Best bowling: 9-43 Derbyshire v Northamptonshire, Derby 1995

2007 Season

	M	Inn	NO	Runs	HS	Avg	100	50	Ct	St	Balls	Runs	Wkts	Avg	BB	5I	10M
Test																	
FC	13	17	4	329	48 *	25.30	-	-	4	-	2165	1011	30	33.70	3-39	-	-
ODI																	
List A	9	7	2	123	39	24.60	-	-	2	-	324	256	5	51.20	2-26	-	
20/20 Int																	
20/20	2	2	1	26	23 *	26.00	-	-	1	-	36	71	1	71.00	1-42	-	

Career Performances

	M	Inn	NO	Runs	HS	Avg	100	50	Ct	St	Balls	Runs	Wkts	Avg	BB	5I	10M
Test	37	56	8	864	59	18.00	-	3	18	-	7678	3906	131	29.81	7-43	5	-
FC	278	407	54	8965	200 *	25.39	8	50	200	-	47271	23277	875	26.60	9-43	32	5
ODI	32	21	3	180	31 *	10.00	-	-	6	-	1772	1368	41	33.36	3-27	-	
List A	282	219	32	3995	93	21.36	-	19	105	-	13358	9452	343	27.55	6-21	4	
20/20 Int																	
20/20	29	25	3	267	28	12.13	-	-	6	-	426	510	22	23.18	4-16	-	

15. Which former Nottinghamshire, Durham and Lancashire batsman scored the fastest Test double hundred in terms of balls received (153 balls) in the first Test v England at Christchurch in 2001-02?

COSKER, D. A. Glamorgan

Name: Dean Andrew Cosker
Role: Right-hand bat, left-arm spin bowler
Born: 7 January 1978, Weymouth, Dorset
Height: 5ft 11in **Weight:** 12st 7lbs
Nickname: Lurks, The Lurker
County debut: 1996
County cap: 2000
Place in batting averages: (2006 231st av. 16.80)
Place in bowling averages: 74th av. 32.37 (2006 130th av. 45.03)
Parents: Des and Carol
Wife and date of marriage: Katie, 24 November 2006
Family links with cricket: 'Brother dabbled in Welsh League. Father still plays village cricket but refuses to give up the ghost'
Education: Millfield School
Qualifications: 10 GCSEs, 4 A-levels
Overseas tours: West of England U15 to West Indies 1993-94; Millfield School to Sri Lanka 1994-95; England U17 to Netherlands 1995; England U19 to Pakistan 1996-97; England A to Kenya and Sri Lanka 1997-98, to Zimbabwe and South Africa 1998-99; Glamorgan CCC to Cape Town and Jersey
Overseas teams played for: Gordon CC, Sydney 1996-97; Crusaders, Durban 2001-02
Cricketers particularly admired: Graham Gooch, Graham Thorpe
Young players to look out for: Gareth Rees, Richard Grant
Other sports played: Golf
Other sports followed: Football ('Spurs and the Swans')
Extras: England U15, U17 and U19. Played for U19 TCCB Development of Excellence XI v South Africa U19 1995. Leading wicket-taker on England A tour of Zimbabwe and South Africa 1998-99 (22; av. 22.90). Third youngest Glamorgan player to receive county cap
Best batting: 52 Glamorgan v Gloucestershire, Bristol 2005
Best bowling: 6-140 Glamorgan v Lancashire, Colwyn Bay 1998

2007 Season

	M	Inn	NO	Runs	HS	Avg	100	50	Ct	St	Balls	Runs	Wkts	Avg	BB	5I	10M
Test																	
FC	11	16	2	137	30	9.78	-	-	2	-	1830	939	29	32.37	5-69	1	-
ODI																	
List A	11	10	6	107	39 *	26.75	-	-	4	-	408	332	11	30.18	3-30	-	
20/20 Int																	
20/20	6	0	0	0	0		-	-	3	-	60	109	5	21.80	3-18	-	

Career Performances

	M	Inn	NO	Runs	HS	Avg	100	50	Ct	St	Balls	Runs	Wkts	Avg	BB	5I	10M
Test																	
FC	145	182	56	1624	52	12.88	-	1	94	-	27306	13241	347	38.15	6-140	3	-
ODI																	
List A	162	85	38	464	39 *	9.87	-	-	63	-	6960	5541	167	33.17	5-54	1	
20/20 Int																	
20/20	32	8	7	30	10 *	30.00	-	-	13	-	480	715	24	29.79	3-18	-	

COVERDALE, P. S. Northamptonshire

Name: Paul Stephen Coverdale
Role: Right-hand bat, right-arm medium-fast bowler
Born: 24 July 1983, Harrogate
Height: 5ft 10in **Weight:** 12st 6lbs
Nickname: Covers, Flaps, Drill Sergeant, Machine
County debut: 2007
Parents: Stephen and Jane
Marital status: Single
Family links with cricket: 'Father played for Yorkshire CCC and Cambridge University and is the former Chief Executive of Northamptonshire'
Education: Wellingborough School; Loughborough University
Qualifications: 9 GCSEs, 3 A-levels, BSc (Hons) Information Management and Business Studies, Level 1 coach
Career outside cricket: 'Since completing university have set up a sporting memorabilia and exhibitions company (CaptureSport), specialising in creating memorabilia products for sports personalities' testimonials and benefits and for clubs'

Overseas tours: Northamptonshire U19 to South Africa 2000
Overseas teams played for: Swanbourne, Perth 2002
Cricket moments to forget: 'Leaving a straight one first ball on a pair in a 2nd XI match a few years ago and then breaking my hand punching the dressing-room wall!'
Cricketers particularly admired: Allan Lamb, Steve Waugh, Matthew Hayden, Mike Hussey, Jacques Kallis
Other sports played: 'Pub golf'
Other sports followed: Rugby union (Northampton Saints), football (Aston Villa)
Favourite band: Bon Jovi, Dire Straits, Whitesnake
Player website: www.capturesport.com
Extras: Played county age groups, captaining at U14, U15, U17 and U19. Represented East England Schools U18. Played for Northamptonshire Board XI in the C&G 2001, 2002 and 2003. Represented English Universities in the Home Nations Tournament 2003. Captained English Universities 2004. Released by Northamptonshire at the end of the 2007 season
Best batting: 11 Northamptonshire v CUCCE, Fenner's 2007
Best bowling: 1-36 Northamptonshire v CUCCE, Fenner's 2007

2007 Season

	M	Inn	NO	Runs	HS	Avg	100	50	Ct	St	Balls	Runs	Wkts	Avg	BB	5I	10M
Test																	
FC	1	1	0	11	11	11.00	-	-	-	-	79	39	1	39.00	1-36	-	-
ODI																	
List A	1	0	0	0	0		-	-	-	-	18	21	0		-	-	
20/20 Int																	
20/20																	

Career Performances

	M	Inn	NO	Runs	HS	Avg	100	50	Ct	St	Balls	Runs	Wkts	Avg	BB	5I	10M
Test																	
FC	1	1	0	11	11	11.00	-	-	-	-	79	39	1	39.00	1-36	-	-
ODI																	
List A	4	3	0	33	19	11.00	-	-	3	-	114	69	1	69.00	1-21	-	
20/20 Int																	
20/20																	

16. During New Zealand's first innings of the first Test at Lord's in 1986, four players, two of whom were not on the teamsheet, kept wicket for England. Can you name them?

CRAWLEY, J. P. Hampshire

Name: John Paul Crawley
Role: Right-hand bat, occasional wicket-keeper
Born: 21 September 1971, Maldon, Essex
Height: 6ft 2in **Weight:** 13st 7lbs
Nickname: Creepy, Jonty, JC
County debut: 1990 (Lancashire), 2002 (Hampshire)
County cap: 1994 (Lancashire), 2002 (Hampshire)
Benefit: 2008 (Hampshire)
Test debut: 1994
ODI debut: 1994-95
1000 runs in a season: 10
1st-Class 200s: 6
1st-Class 300s: 2
Place in batting averages: 75th av. 39.36 (2006 7th av. 66.80)
Parents: Frank and Jean (deceased)
Marital status: Married
Family links with cricket: Father played in Manchester Association; brother Mark played for Lancashire and Nottinghamshire; brother Peter plays for Warrington CC and has played for Scottish Universities and Cambridge University; uncle was excellent fast bowler; godfather umpires in Manchester Association
Education: Manchester Grammar School; Trinity College, Cambridge; Open University Business School
Qualifications: 10 O-levels, 2 AO-Levels, 3 A-levels, 2 S-levels, BA in History, MA (Cantab), Professional Certificate in Management
Overseas tours: England YC to Australia 1989-90, to New Zealand 1990-91 (c); England A to South Africa 1993-94, to West Indies 2000-01; England to Australia 1994-95, to South Africa 1995-96, to Zimbabwe and New Zealand 1996-97, to West Indies 1997-98, to Australia 1998-99, 2002-03
Overseas teams played for: Midland-Guildford, Perth 1990
Cricketers particularly admired: Michael Atherton, Neil Fairbrother, Graham Gooch, Alec Stewart, David Gower, Allan Donald, Ian Salisbury
Other sports followed: Football (Manchester United), golf
Relaxations: 'Playing or trying to play the guitar'
Extras: Sir John Hobbs Silver Jubilee Memorial Prize 1987. Played for England YC 1989, 1990 and (as captain) 1991; first to score 1000 runs in U19 'Tests'. Lancashire vice-captain 1998. Topped English first-class batting averages for 1998 season (1851 runs; av. 74.04). Lancashire Player of the Year 1998. Lancashire captain 1999-2001.

Scored 272 on debut for Hampshire v Kent at Canterbury 2002, a Hampshire debut record. Captain of Hampshire 2003. Hampshire Player of the Year 2006
Best batting: 311* Hampshire v Nottinghamshire, Rose Bowl 2005
Best bowling: 1-7 Hampshire v Surrey, The Oval 2005

2007 Season

	M	Inn	NO	Runs	HS	Avg	100	50	Ct	St	Balls	Runs	Wkts	Avg	BB	5I	10M
Test																	
FC	15	27	5	866	113 *	39.36	1	6	4	-	12	22	0		-	-	-
ODI																	
List A	14	13	1	512	97 *	42.66	-	5	9	-	0	0	0		-	-	
20/20 Int																	
20/20																	

Career Performances

	M	Inn	NO	Runs	HS	Avg	100	50	Ct	St	Balls	Runs	Wkts	Avg	BB	5I	10M
Test	37	61	9	1800	156 *	34.61	4	9	29	-	0	0	0		-	-	-
FC	334	554	56	23637	311 *	47.46	53	129	211	1	215	283	2	141.50	1-7	-	-
ODI	13	12	1	235	73	21.36	-	2	1	1	0	0	0		-	-	
List A	300	286	23	8457	114	32.15	7	54	94	4	6	4	0		-	-	
20/20 Int																	
20/20	10	10	1	107	23	11.88	-	-	3	-	0	0	0		-	-	

CROFT, R. D. B. — Glamorgan

Name: Robert Damien Bale Croft
Role: Right-hand bat, off-spin bowler
Born: 25 May 1970, Morriston, Swansea
Height: 5ft 11in **Weight:** 13st 7lbs
Nickname: Crofty
County debut: 1989
County cap: 1992
Benefit: 2000
Test debut: 1996
ODI debut: 1996
50 wickets in a season: 9
Place in batting averages: 180th av. 24.79 (2006 131st av. 31.63)
Place in bowling averages: 85th av. 33.51 (2006 60th av. 32.00)
Parents: Malcolm and Susan
Wife: Marie
Children: Callum James Bale Croft

Family links with cricket: Father and grandfather played league cricket
Education: St John Lloyd Catholic School, Llanelli; Neath Tertiary College; West Glamorgan Institute of Higher Education
Qualifications: 6 O-levels, OND Business Studies, HND Business Studies, NCA senior coaching certificate
Overseas tours: England A to Bermuda and West Indies 1991-92, to South Africa 1993-94; England to Zimbabwe and New Zealand 1996-97, to West Indies 1997-98, to Australia 1998-99, to Sharjah (Coca-Cola Cup) 1998-99, to Sri Lanka 2000-01, 2003-04; England VI to Hong Kong 2003, 2005 (c)
Career highlights to date: 'Playing for England and winning the Championship with Glamorgan in 1997'
Cricket moments to forget: 'None. This career is too short to forget any of it'
Cricketers particularly admired: Ian Botham, Viv Richards, Shane Warne
Other sports played: 'Give anything a go'
Other sports followed: Football (Liverpool FC), rugby (Llanelli and Wales)
Interests/relaxations: 'Everything'
Extras: Captained England South to victory in International Youth Tournament 1989 and was voted Player of the Tournament. Glamorgan Young Player of the Year 1992. Scored Test best 37* in the third Test at Old Trafford 1998, resisting for 190 minutes to deny South Africa victory. Represented England in the 1999 World Cup. Honorary fellow of West Glamorgan Institute of Higher Education. Scored 69-ball 119 v Surrey at The Oval in the C&G 2002 as Glamorgan made 429 in reply to Surrey's 438-5. Glamorgan Player of the Year 2003 (jointly with Michael Kasprowicz) and 2004. Glamorgan vice-captain 2002-03; appointed captain during 2003, taking over from the injured Steve James; stood down as captain in mid-September 2006. Man of the Match in England's victory v Pakistan in the final of the Hong Kong Sixes 2003. Retired from international cricket in January 2004. Cricket Society's Wetherell Award 2004 for the leading all-rounder in English first-class cricket. Took 1000th first-class wicket (Niall O'Brien) v Northamptonshire at Northampton 2007 to become the first Welshman to have scored 10,000 runs and taken 1000 wickets in first-class cricket
Best batting: 143 Glamorgan v Somerset, Taunton 1995
Best bowling: 8-66 Glamorgan v Warwickshire, Swansea 1992

2007 Season

	M	Inn	NO	Runs	HS	Avg	100	50	Ct	St	Balls	Runs	Wkts	Avg	BB	5I	10M
Test																	
FC	16	26	2	595	115	24.79	1	1	10	-	3601	1877	56	33.51	6-44	5	1
ODI																	
List A	11	10	2	141	40 *	17.62	-	-	3	-	330	283	10	28.30	2-29	-	
20/20 Int																	
20/20	6	5	1	69	22	17.25	-	-	1	-	84	95	2	47.50	1-23	-	

Career Performances

	M	Inn	NO	Runs	HS	Avg	100	50	Ct	St	Balls	Runs	Wkts	Avg	BB	5I	10M
Test	21	34	8	421	37 *	16.19	-	-	10	-	4619	1825	49	37.24	5-95	1	-
FC	350	521	92	11317	143	26.38	7	49	169	-	77112	36201	1004	36.05	8-66	46	9
ODI	50	36	12	345	32	14.37	-	-	11	-	2466	1743	45	38.73	3-51	-	
List A	385	322	59	6268	143	23.83	4	31	92	-	17653	12751	394	32.36	6-20	1	
20/20 Int																	
20/20	33	23	5	394	62 *	21.88	-	2	15	-	648	851	33	25.78	3-32	-	

CROFT, S. J. — Lancashire

Name: Steven John Croft
Role: Right-hand bat, right-arm medium-fast bowler; all-rounder
Born: 11 October 1984, Blackpool
Height: 5ft 11in **Weight:** 14st
Nickname: Crofty
County debut: 2005
Place in batting averages: 220th av. 19.29
Parents: Elizabeth and Lawrence
Marital status: Single
Family links with cricket: Father played for local team
Education: Highfield High, Blackpool; Myerscough College
Qualifications: 10 GCSEs, First Diploma in Sports Studies, Level 2 cricket coach
Career outside cricket: Coaching
Overseas teams played for: St Kilda, Melbourne 2005-06
Career highlights to date: 'Signing for Lancashire CCC'
Cricket moments to forget: 'Duck on 2nd XI debut'
Cricket superstitions: 'Left pad on first'
Cricketers particularly admired: Andrew Flintoff, Stuart Law, Jacques Kallis
Young players to look out for: Karl Brown, Tom Smith, Gareth Cross
Other sports played: Football ('played for Blackpool town team and trialled at Oldham FC and Wimbledon FC')
Other sports followed: Football (Newcastle)
Favourite band: Oasis, The Killers, Blink-182
Relaxations: 'Socialising with friends; music, movies, sport'
Extras: Played for Lancashire Board XI in the C&G 2003. Only third amateur to score over 1000 runs in a season in the Northern Premier League

Best batting: 65 Lancashire v Sussex, Hove 2007
Best bowling: 3-40 Lancashire v Durham, Blackpool 2007

2007 Season

	M	Inn	NO	Runs	HS	Avg	100	50	Ct	St	Balls	Runs	Wkts	Avg	BB	5I	10M
Test																	
FC	11	19	2	328	65	19.29	-	2	12	-	474	286	6	47.66	3-40	-	-
ODI																	
List A	13	13	4	323	63	35.88	-	1	2	-	239	200	3	66.66	1-24	-	
20/20 Int																	
20/20	6	6	2	143	49	35.75	-	-	3	-	36	50	1	50.00	1-35	-	

Career Performances

	M	Inn	NO	Runs	HS	Avg	100	50	Ct	St	Balls	Runs	Wkts	Avg	BB	5I	10M
Test																	
FC	13	21	2	351	65	18.47	-	2	13	-	540	335	6	55.83	3-40	-	-
ODI																	
List A	23	21	5	474	63	29.62	-	2	9	-	414	399	11	36.27	4-59	-	
20/20 Int																	
20/20	14	14	3	245	49	22.27	-	-	8	-	122	171	5	34.20	2-10	-	

CROOK, A. R. — Northamptonshire

Name: Andrew (Andy) Richard Crook
Role: Right-hand bat, right-arm off-spin bowler
Born: 14 October 1980, Adelaide, South Australia
Height: 6ft 4in **Weight:** 14st 5lbs
Nickname: Crooky, Gonk
County debut: 2004 (Lancashire), 2007 (Northamptonshire)
Place in batting averages: 113th av. 33.62
Parents: Sue (mother) and Doug (stepfather); Martyn (father)
Marital status: Engaged to Louise
Children: Harriet, 2007
Family links with cricket: 'Brother, Steve, also at Northants'
Education: Rostrevor College
Overseas teams played for: South Australia 1998-99; Northern Districts, South Australia; East Torrens CC, Adelaide

Career highlights to date: '2005 Twenty20 finals day'
Cricket moments to forget: 'Being the last man out on my Old Trafford debut, and my wicket meant Lancashire were relegated to Division Two of the County Championship'
Cricketers particularly admired: Gary Kirsten
Young players to look out for: Karl Brown
Other sports followed: Football (Blackburn Rovers), AFL (Essendon Bombers)
Favourite band: Snow Patrol, U2, Counting Crows
Extras: Made first-class debut for South Australia v England XI at Adelaide 1998-99. Made new Lancashire record individual one-day score (162*), v Buckinghamshire at Wormsley in the C&G 2005, winning Man of the Match award. Is not considered an overseas player
Best batting: 88 Lancashire v OUCCE, The Parks 2005
Best bowling: 3-71 Lancashire v Essex, Old Trafford 2005

2007 Season

	M	Inn	NO	Runs	HS	Avg	100	50	Ct	St	Balls	Runs	Wkts	Avg	BB	5I	10M
Test																	
FC	5	9	1	269	72	33.62	-	2	4	-	102	60	0		-	-	-
ODI																	
List A	5	5	1	83	24 *	20.75	-	-	-	-	70	93	2	46.50	1-35	-	
20/20 Int																	
20/20																	

Career Performances

	M	Inn	NO	Runs	HS	Avg	100	50	Ct	St	Balls	Runs	Wkts	Avg	BB	5I	10M
Test																	
FC	10	16	1	469	88	31.26	-	3	8	-	882	569	7	81.28	3-71	-	-
ODI																	
List A	21	19	3	444	162 *	27.75	1	-	4	-	423	412	12	34.33	3-32	-	
20/20 Int																	
20/20	10	7	3	51	15	12.75	-	-	3	-	126	201	7	28.71	2-25	-	

17. Which pair of South African cricketing brothers – one a batsman, the other an off-spinner – called time on their Test careers after the fifth Test v England at The Oval in 1951?

CROOK, S. P. Northamptonshire

Name: <u>Steven</u> Paul Crook
Role: Right-hand bat, right-arm medium-fast bowler; all-rounder
Born: 28 May 1983, Adelaide, South Australia
Height: 5ft 11in **Weight:** 13st 3lbs
Nickname: Crooky, Crookster
County debut: 2003 (Lancashire), 2005 (Northamptonshire)
Place in batting averages: 167th av. 26.46 (2006 227th av. 17.25)
Place in bowling averages: 102nd av. 36.13 (2006 133rd av. 46.00)
Parents: 'Dad – Martyn, mum – Sue and stepfather – Doug'
Marital status: Single
Family links with sport: Brother Andrew also at Northamptonshire. Father, Martyn, played professional football
Education: Rostrevor College
Qualifications: Matriculation
Overseas tours: Lancashire to Cape Town 2003, 2004
Overseas teams played for: Northern Districts, South Australia
Career highlights to date: 'Playing semi-final of Twenty20 2004'
Cricket moments to forget: 'Getting beaten in semi of Twenty20 2004'
Cricketers particularly admired: Andrew Flintoff, Stuart Law
Young players to look out for: Tom Smith, Steve Croft, Andy Crook
Other sports followed: Football (Tottenham Hotspur FC)
Favourite band: The Doors, The Strokes
Relaxations: 'Hanging out with mates'
Extras: Attended South Australia Cricket Academy. Represented South Australia U13-U19. Selected for Australia U19 preliminary World Cup squad 2001-02. Is not considered an overseas player
Best batting: 97 Northamptonshire v Yorkshire, Northampton 2005
Best bowling: 4-56 Northamptonshire v Essex, Northampton 2007

2007 Season

	M	Inn	NO	Runs	HS	Avg	100	50	Ct	St	Balls	Runs	Wkts	Avg	BB	5I	10M
Test																	
FC	10	16	3	344	60	26.46	-	2	3	-	1390	831	23	36.13	4-56	-	-
ODI																	
List A	6	2	1	6	4	6.00	-	-	2	-	306	334	5	66.80	1-52	-	
20/20 Int																	
20/20	7	3	1	9	4	4.50	-	-	2	-	114	156	6	26.00	2-24	-	

Career Performances

	M	Inn	NO	Runs	HS	Avg	100	50	Ct	St	Balls	Runs	Wkts	Avg	BB	5I	10M
Test																	
FC	29	38	7	954	97	30.77	-	6	10	-	3574	2363	52	45.44	4-56	-	-
ODI																	
List A	25	16	2	152	23	10.85	-	-	6	-	882	908	18	50.44	4-20	-	
20/20 Int																	
20/20	18	11	2	133	27	14.77	-	-	3	-	126	178	6	29.66	2-24	-	

CROSS, G. D. — Lancashire

Name: Gareth David Cross
Role: Right-hand bat, wicket-keeper
Born: 20 June 1984, Bury
Height: 5ft 9in **Weight:** 11st 9lbs
Nickname: Crossy
County debut: 2005
Place in batting averages: (2006 169th av. 27.00)
Parents: Duncan and Margaret
Marital status: Single
Family links with cricket: 'Dad played for Prestwich. Brother Matthew plays for Monton and Weaste'
Education: Moorside High School; Eccles College
Qualifications: 9 GCSEs, GNVQ Science
Overseas teams played for: St Kilda, Melbourne 2002-04

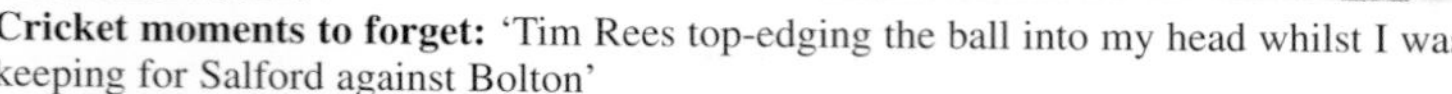

Cricket moments to forget: 'Tim Rees top-edging the ball into my head whilst I was keeping for Salford against Bolton'
Cricket superstitions: 'Just putting batting gear on in the same order'
Cricketers particularly admired: Ian Healy, Adam Gilchrist, Graeme Rummans

Young players to look out for: Steven Croft, Steven Crook
Other sports played: Football ('had a trial for Man United when I was 13')
Other sports followed: Football (Man United)
Favourite band: Eminem, Oasis
Relaxations: 'Watching football; five-a-side football'
Extras: Manchester Association Young Player of the Year. Bolton Association Young Player of the Year 2000. ECB Premier League Young Player of the Year. Liverpool Competition Player of the Year 2004. Played for Lancashire Board XI in the C&G 2003. Made five dismissals in first innings of Championship debut v Leicestershire at Old Trafford 2005
Best batting: 72 Lancashire v Kent, Canterbury 2006

2007 Season

	M	Inn	NO	Runs	HS	Avg	100	50	Ct	St	Balls	Runs	Wkts	Avg	BB	5I	10M
Test																	
FC	1	2	1	71	61 *	71.00	-	1	4	2	0	0	0		-	-	-
ODI																	
List A	7	7	1	178	76	29.66	-	1	3	-	0	0	0		-	-	
20/20 Int																	
20/20	6	6	1	113	62	22.60	-	1	4	3	0	0	0		-	-	

Career Performances

	M	Inn	NO	Runs	HS	Avg	100	50	Ct	St	Balls	Runs	Wkts	Avg	BB	5I	10M
Test																	
FC	7	11	1	271	72	27.10	-	3	26	8	0	0	0		-	-	-
ODI																	
List A	16	14	2	265	76	22.08	-	1	9	5	0	0	0		-	-	
20/20 Int																	
20/20	14	13	1	174	62	14.50	-	1	11	6	0	0	0		-	-	

18. Who became New Zealand's youngest Test captain when he took charge for the third Test v England at Christchurch in 1996-97, aged 23 years 319 days?

CUMMINS, R. A. G. Leicestershire

Name: Ryan Anthony Gilbert Cummins
Role: Right-hand bat, right-arm fast-medium bowler
Born: 14 April 1984, Sutton, Surrey
Height: 6ft 4in **Weight:** 13st 4lbs
Nickname: Rhino, Yummins
County debut: 2005
Place in batting averages: 233rd av. 17.33
Place in bowling averages: 109th av. 39.38 (2006 126th av. 44.53)
Parents: Tony and Sheila
Marital status: Single
Family links with cricket: 'Great-grandfather, Gilly Reay, played for Surrey. Father played county 2nd XI and sister plays county cricket for Northants'
Education: Wallington County Grammar School for Boys; Loughborough University
Qualifications: 11 GCSEs, 4 A-levels, BSc (Hons) Geography (2.2), Level 2 cricket coach, Level 1 hockey coach
Off-season: 'Tour to Australia; trek to Everest Base Camp [with PCA]; catching up with family and friends; coaching'
Career highlights to date: 'Playing in the winning Twenty20 side of 2006'
Cricket moments to forget: 'Bowling in the Twenty20 final 2006'
Cricketers particularly admired: Phil DeFreitas, Brian Lara, Adam Hollioake
Other sports played: Hockey, golf
Other sports followed: Rugby (Leicester Tigers), golf
Favourite band: Snow Patrol
Extras: Played for Loughborough UCCE 2003-05. Represented British Universities 2005
Opinions on cricket: 'Level of professionalism in the game must continue to improve, so as to improve both individuals and the standard of English cricket.'
Best batting: 34* Leicestershire v OUCCE, The Parks 2007
Best bowling: 5-60 Leicestershire v Northamptonshire, Leicester 2007

2007 Season

	M	Inn	NO	Runs	HS	Avg	100	50	Ct	St	Balls	Runs	Wkts	Avg	BB	5I	10M
Test																	
FC	5	9	3	104	34 *	17.33	-	-	2	-	890	512	13	39.38	5-60	1	-
ODI																	
List A	5	2	1	12	10	12.00	-	-	-	-	198	217	5	43.40	2-62	-	
20/20 Int																	
20/20																	

Career Performances

	M	Inn	NO	Runs	HS	Avg	100	50	Ct	St	Balls	Runs	Wkts	Avg	BB	5I	10M
Test																	
FC	20	25	11	177	34 *	12.64	-	-	5	-	3020	1916	42	45.61	5-60	1	-
ODI																	
List A	16	5	2	15	10	5.00	-	-	3	-	594	509	20	25.45	2-14	-	
20/20 Int																	
20/20	1	0	0	0	0		-	-	1	-	18	40	0		-	-	

CUSDEN, S. M. J. — Derbyshire

Name: Simon Mark James Cusden
Role: Right-hand bat, right-arm fast bowler
Born: 21 February 1985, Margate, Kent
Height: 6ft 6in **Weight:** 16st 10lbs
Nickname: Bungle, Stench, Alfred, Ronny Village, Boris
County debut: 2004 (Kent), 2007 (Derbyshire)
Parents: Mark and Karen
Marital status: Engaged
Family links with cricket: 'Dad Beltinge legend'
Education: Simon Langton GS for Boys, Canterbury
Qualifications: 3 A-levels, NVQ Level 3 plumbing, first aid
Off-season: 'Taxi driver; PCA trip to Everest; watching DVDs'
Overseas tours: England U19 to Australia 2002-03
Career highlights to date: 'My year with Derbyshire (keeping Elvaston in Derbyshire Premier League '07)'

Cricket moments to forget: 'Bowling a "32-ball over" in 2007 season for Derbyshire 2nd XI'
Cricketers particularly admired: Brett Crichton, Simon Katich
Players to look out for: Jake Needham, Wayne White, Ian Hunter
Other sports played: Squash, snooker
Injuries: Out for four weeks with an ankle impingement
Favourite band: The Zutons
Relaxations: 'Watching DVDs and listening to relaxation tapes'
Extras: Represented England U19 2004. Took wicket (Mal Loye) with his first ball for Kent, v Lancashire at Tunbridge Wells in the totesport League 2004. Kent Academy Scholar of the Year 2004. Released by Derbyshire at the end of the 2007 season
Opinions on cricket: 'Umpires should be more lenient on wides.'
Best batting: 14 Derbyshire v CUCCE, Fenner's 2007
Best bowling: 4-68 Kent v Northamptonshire, Canterbury 2004

2007 Season

	M	Inn	NO	Runs	HS	Avg	100	50	Ct	St	Balls	Runs	Wkts	Avg	BB	5I	10M
Test																	
FC	1	1	0	14	14	14.00	-	-	-	-	144	98	2	49.00	2-67	-	-
ODI																	
List A																	
20/20 Int																	
20/20																	

Career Performances

	M	Inn	NO	Runs	HS	Avg	100	50	Ct	St	Balls	Runs	Wkts	Avg	BB	5I	10M
Test																	
FC	7	8	5	42	14	14.00	-	-	2	-	1023	692	20	34.60	4-68	-	-
ODI																	
List A	6	3	1	5	3	2.50	-	-	-	-	192	193	4	48.25	1-29	-	
20/20 Int																	
20/20																	

19. England selected five county captains for the first Test v South Africa at Edgbaston in 1960 – Colin Cowdrey, Ted Dexter, Raman Subba Row, MJK Smith and Bob Barber. Which counties did they skipper at the time?

DAGGETT, L. M. — Warwickshire

Name: Lee Martin Daggett
Role: Right-hand bat, right-arm fast-medium bowler
Born: 1 October 1982, Bury, Lancashire
Height: 6ft **Weight:** 13st 6lbs
Nickname: Dags, Dagsy, Daggers, Len Dugout
County debut: 2006
Place in bowling averages: (2006 18th av. 25.31)
Parents: Peter and Kathleen
Marital status: Single
Family links with cricket: 'Father was captain of Ramsbottom CC in the Lancashire League. Also coached Ramsbottom CC and me'
Education: Woodhey High School, Bury; Holy Cross College, Bury; Durham University; Salford University
Qualifications: 10 GCSEs, 4 A-levels, BSc (Hons) Sport, Health and Exercise, ECB Level 2 coach, first aid
Career outside cricket: 'Studying physiotherapy at Salford Uni'
Off-season: 'Studying, coaching, training; possibly week in India at bowling academy'
Overseas tours: BUSA to South Africa 2004; Warwickshire to Grenada 2007
Overseas teams played for: Joondalup CC, Perth 2001, 2006, 2007
Career highlights to date: '8-94 v Durham for DUCCE in 2004; 6-30 v Durham for Warwickshire in 2006'
Cricket moments to forget: 'First game on Sky – getting swept out of the ground three times by Mal Loye'
Cricket superstitions: 'To run inside my mark'
Cricketers particularly admired: Allan Donald, Graeme Fowler, Brett Lee
Young players to look out for: Chris Woakes
Other sports played: Football ('played for Bury School of Excellence and North-West'), squash, tennis, golf
Other sports followed: Football (Manchester United; 'watch Bury's progress')
Injuries: Out for five weeks with an intercostal tear; for two weeks with a fractured eye socket
Favourite band: Oasis, Ocean Colour Scene, Arctic Monkeys
Relaxations: 'Cinema/movies'
Extras: Played for Durham UCCE 2003-05. Durham University Sportsman of the Year 2004. Represented British Universities 2004-05

Opinions on cricket: 'Need longer Twenty20 tournament. However, it completely ruins bowlers' rhythm for Championship cricket.'
Best batting: 33 Warwickshire v Durham, Riverside 2007
Best bowling: 8-94 DUCCE v Durham, Riverside 2004

2007 Season

	M	Inn	NO	Runs	HS	Avg	100	50	Ct	St	Balls	Runs	Wkts	Avg	BB	5I	10M
Test																	
FC	3	4	2	42	33	21.00	-	-	-	-	270	154	1	154.00	1-61	-	-
ODI																	
List A	7	1	1	1	1 *		-	-	1	-	320	233	8	29.12	2-38	-	
20/20 Int																	
20/20	3	0	0	0	0		-	-	2	-	36	62	1	62.00	1-13	-	

Career Performances

	M	Inn	NO	Runs	HS	Avg	100	50	Ct	St	Balls	Runs	Wkts	Avg	BB	5I	10M
Test																	
FC	17	24	12	100	33	8.33	-	-	1	-	2201	1366	34	40.17	8-94	2	-
ODI																	
List A	14	4	4	15	5 *		-	-	1	-	616	484	15	32.26	2-33	-	
20/20 Int																	
20/20	3	0	0	0	0		-	-	2	-	36	62	1	62.00	1-13	-	

DALRYMPLE, J. W. M. — Glamorgan

Name: James (Jamie) William Murray Dalrymple
Role: Right-hand bat, off-spin bowler
Born: 21 January 1981, Nairobi, Kenya
Height: 6ft **Weight:** 13st 7lbs
Nickname: JD, Pest
County debut: 2000 (one-day, Middlesex), 2001 (first-class, Middlesex)
County cap: 2004 (Middlesex)
ODI debut: 2006
Twenty20 Int debut: 2006
1st-Class 200s: 2
Place in batting averages: 216th av. 20.33 (2006 107th av. 34.42)
Place in bowling averages: 142nd av. 57.41 (2006 93rd av. 37.37)
Parents: Douglas and Patricia
Marital status: Single

Family links with cricket: 'Dad played lots of club cricket.' Brother Simon played for Oxford University in 2002 and 2004
Education: Radley College, Abingdon; St Peter's College, Oxford University
Qualifications: 10 GCSEs, 5 A-levels, degree in History
Overseas tours: Middlesex to South Africa 2000; England A to West Indies 2005-06; England to India (ICC Champions Trophy) 2006-07, to Australia 2006-07, to West Indies (World Cup) 2006-07
Cricket moments to forget: 'Middlesex v Warwickshire at Edgbaston 2003 – being part of the loss of eight wickets in a session, and the match'
Cricketers particularly admired: David Gower, Carl Hooper, Ian Botham, Mark Waugh
Other sports played: Rugby (college), hockey (university)
Other sports followed: Rugby (Northampton RUFC)
Favourite band: 'Don't have a favourite'
Relaxations: Reading, golf
Extras: Represented England U19 2000. Played for Oxford UCCE 2001 and (as captain) 2002. Represented British Universities 2001 and (as captain) 2002. Oxford Blue 2001, 2002 (captain) and 2003 (captain). Scored double century (236*) in the Varsity Match at Fenner's 2003 and took 5-49 in the Cambridge first innings. C&G Man of the Match awards v Wales Minor Counties at Lamphey (104*; second fifty in 14 balls) and v Glamorgan at Lord's (107) 2004. ECB National Academy 2005-06, 2006-07. Left Middlesex at the end of the 2007 season and has joined Glamorgan for 2008
Best batting: 244 Middlesex v Surrey, The Oval 2004
Best bowling: 5-49 Oxford University v Cambridge University, Fenner's 2003

2007 Season

	M	Inn	NO	Runs	HS	Avg	100	50	Ct	St	Balls	Runs	Wkts	Avg	BB	5I	10M
Test																	
FC	12	17	2	305	57	20.33	-	1	3	-	1191	689	12	57.41	3-86	-	-
ODI																	
List A	16	16	5	341	68 *	31.00	-	2	5	-	627	557	15	37.13	4-39	-	
20/20 Int																	
20/20	6	6	1	113	61	22.60	-	1	-	-	90	121	5	24.20	2-8	-	

Career Performances

	M	Inn	NO	Runs	HS	Avg	100	50	Ct	St	Balls	Runs	Wkts	Avg	BB	5I	10M
Test																	
FC	75	122	12	3727	244	33.88	5	19	38	-	9648	5370	120	44.75	5-49	1	-
ODI	27	26	1	487	67	19.48	-	2	12	-	840	666	14	47.57	2-5	-	
List A	127	116	24	2519	107	27.38	2	14	52	-	3999	3313	94	35.24	4-14	-	
20/20 Int	3	3	0	60	32	20.00	-	-	1	-	30	39	2	19.50	1-10	-	
20/20	25	23	4	420	61	22.10	-	1	5	-	294	417	15	27.80	2-8	-	

DANISH KANERIA Essex

Name: Danish Prabha Shanker Kaneria
Role: Right-hand bat, right-arm leg-spin and googly bowler
Born: 16 December 1980, Karachi, Pakistan
Height: 6ft 1in
Nickname: Danny Boy, Dani
County debut: 2004
County cap: 2004
Test debut: 2000-01
ODI debut: 2001-02
50 wickets in a season: 2
Place in batting averages: 247th av. 14.40
Place in bowling averages: 13th av. 22.20 (2006 106th av. 40.17)
Parents: Prabha Shanker Kaneria and Babita P. Kaneria
Wife and date of marriage: Dharmeta Danish Kaneria, 15 February 2004
Family links with cricket: Cousin, wicket-keeper Anil Dalpat, played nine Tests for Pakistan 1983-84
Education: St Patrick's High School, Karachi
Overseas tours: Pakistan U19 to Sri Lanka (U19 World Cup) 1999-2000; Pakistan A to Kenya 2000, to Sri Lanka 2001; Pakistan to Bangladesh 2001-02, to Sharjah (v West Indies) 2001-02, to Sharjah (v Australia) 2002-03, to New Zealand 2003-04, to Australia 2004-05, to India 2004-05, to West Indies 2004-05, to Sri Lanka 2005-06, to Scotland and England 2006, to South Africa 2006-07, to West Indies (World Cup) 2006-07, to India 2007-08, plus other one-day tournaments in Sharjah, Sri Lanka and England
Overseas teams played for: Several in Pakistan, including Karachi Whites 1998-99 – 2001-02; Habib Bank 1999-2000 –
Career highlights to date: 'Playing for Pakistan. English county cricket'
Cricket superstitions: 'I kiss the ground when taking the field'
Cricketers particularly admired: Abdul Qadir, Viv Richards, Joel Garner
Other sports played: Football, table tennis
Other sports followed: Football (Brazil)
Favourite band: 'I like Indian music'
Relaxations: 'Listening to music and being with family'
Extras: Represented Pakistan U19 1998-99. The second Hindu to play in Tests for Pakistan, after his cousin Anil Dalpat. Had match figures of 12-94 (6-42/6-52) v Bangladesh at Multan in the first match of the Asian Test Championship 2001-02, winning Man of the Match award. His other international awards include Man of the

[Test] Series v Bangladesh 2001-02 and Man of the Match in the second Test v Sri Lanka at Karachi 2004-05 (3-72/7-118). An overseas player with Essex 2004-05 and 2007; has returned for 2008

Best batting: 65 Essex v Nottinghamshire, Trent Bridge 2007

Best bowling: 7-39 Karachi Whites v Gujranwala, Karachi (C) 2000-01

Stop press: Became sixth Pakistan bowler to take 200 Test wickets when he dismissed Ashwell Prince in the first Test v South Africa in Karachi 2007-08

2007 Season

	M	Inn	NO	Runs	HS	Avg	100	50	Ct	St	Balls	Runs	Wkts	Avg	BB	5I	10M
Test																	
FC	13	16	1	216	65	14.40	-	1	1	-	3365	1643	74	22.20	7-95	7	1
ODI																	
List A	12	8	2	73	33 *	12.16	-	-	3	-	555	323	26	12.42	5-22	2	
20/20 Int																	
20/20	8	2	1	4	3	4.00	-	-	2	-	156	192	7	27.42	2-22	-	

Career Performances

	M	Inn	NO	Runs	HS	Avg	100	50	Ct	St	Balls	Runs	Wkts	Avg	BB	5I	10M
Test	46	62	29	230	29	6.96	-	-	15	-	13034	6408	198	32.36	7-77	12	2
FC	121	149	65	819	65	9.75	-	1	39	-	32336	15410	581	26.52	7-39	42	6
ODI	18	10	8	12	6 *	6.00	-	-	2	-	854	682	15	45.46	3-31	-	
List A	106	54	26	209	33 *	7.46	-	-	21	-	5364	3630	167	21.73	5-21	5	
20/20 Int																	
20/20	22	6	1	15	5	3.00	-	-	5	-	419	521	24	21.70	4-31	-	

20. Who was Allan Donald's new-ball partner in five out of six innings of the 1994 Test series against England?

DAVIES, A. P. Glamorgan

Name: Andrew Philip Davies
Role: Left-hand bat, right-arm medium-fast bowler
Born: 7 November 1976, Neath
Height: 6ft **Weight:** 12st 3lbs
Nickname: Diver
County debut: 1995
County cap: 2007
Place in batting averages: 97th av. 36.66
Place in bowling averages: 136th av. 49.27
Parents: Anne and Phil
Wife and date of marriage: Nerys, 1 February 2003
Children: Aaron and Joseph, 1 July 2005
Family links with cricket: 'Father and brother play local league cricket'
Education: Dwr-y-Felin, Neath; Christ College, Brecon
Qualifications: GCSEs, A-levels, Level 2 coach
Overseas tours: Wales MC to Barbados; Glamorgan to Pretoria, to Cape Town
Overseas teams played for: Marist CC, Whangarei, New Zealand 1995-96; Marist Old Boys, Napier, New Zealand
Career highlights: 'Winning two one-day championships'
Cricket moments to forget: 'Any hammering'
Cricket superstitions: 'None'
Cricketers particularly admired: Matthew Maynard, Steve Watkin
Young players to look out for: Ben Wright, Tom Maynard
Other sports followed: Football (Tottenham Hotspur)
Favourite band: Oasis
Relaxations: 'Music'
Extras: Wales U19 Player of the Year 1995. Wales Player of the Year 1996. 2nd XI cap 1998. 2nd XI Player of the Year 1998, 1999. 1st XI Player of the Month August-September 1998. Glamorgan's leading wicket-taker (21) in the NUL 2001. Fastest Glamorgan player to 100 one-day wickets. Retired at the end of the 2007 season
Best batting: 54 Glamorgan v Somerset, Taunton 2007
Best bowling: 5-79 Glamorgan v Worcestershire, Cardiff 2002

2007 Season

	M	Inn	NO	Runs	HS	Avg	100	50	Ct	St	Balls	Runs	Wkts	Avg	BB	5I	10M
Test																	
FC	7	12	6	220	54	36.66	-	1	3	-	804	542	11	49.27	4-46	-	-
ODI																	
List A	10	9	2	65	27	9.28	-	-	-	-	435	419	6	69.83	1-23	-	
20/20 Int																	
20/20	6	0	0	0	0		-	-	-	-	108	123	5	24.60	2-12	-	

Career Performances

	M	Inn	NO	Runs	HS	Avg	100	50	Ct	St	Balls	Runs	Wkts	Avg	BB	5I	10M
Test																	
FC	41	58	17	707	54	17.24	-	1	11	-	5496	3400	77	44.15	5-79	1	-
ODI																	
List A	108	54	28	330	27	12.69	-	-	13	-	4712	4122	147	28.04	5-19	2	
20/20 Int																	
20/20	24	7	2	23	11	4.60	-	-	5	-	516	702	27	26.00	3-17	-	

DAVIES, M. A. — Durham

Name: Mark Anthony Davies
Role: Right-hand bat, right-arm fast-medium bowler
Born: 4 October 1980, Stockton-on-Tees
Height: 6ft 3in **Weight:** 13st
Nickname: Davo
County debut: 1998 (one-day), 2002 (first-class) (*see **Extras***)
County cap: 2005
50 wickets in a season: 1
Place in batting averages: 263rd av. 12.75
Place in bowling averages: 25th av. 24.23
Parents: Howard and Mandy
Marital status: Single
Education: Northfield School, Billingham; Stockton Sixth Form College
Qualifications: 5 GCSEs, NVQ Level 3 Sport and Recreation
Overseas tours: Durham to South Africa 2002
Overseas teams played for: North Kalgoorlie CC, Western Australia
Cricketers particularly admired: Glenn McGrath
Other sports played: Football, golf, boxing

Other sports followed: Football (Middlesbrough)
Relaxations: Socialising, golf
Extras: Represented England U19 2000. Attended Durham Academy. Was the first bowler to reach 50 first-class wickets in 2004. Played one first-class match for Nottinghamshire on loan 2007, returning career-best innings figures of 7-59 v Northamptonshire at Trent Bridge
Best batting: 62 Durham v Somerset, Stockton 2005
Best bowling: 7-59 Nottinghamshire v Northamptonshire, Trent Bridge 2007

2007 Season

	M	Inn	NO	Runs	HS	Avg	100	50	Ct	St	Balls	Runs	Wkts	Avg	BB	5I	10M
Test																	
FC	11	13	5	102	35 *	12.75	-	-	5	-	1756	824	34	24.23	7-59	1	-
ODI																	
List A	2	0	0	0	0		-	-	1	-	96	60	2	30.00	2-27	-	
20/20 Int																	
20/20																	

Career Performances

	M	Inn	NO	Runs	HS	Avg	100	50	Ct	St	Balls	Runs	Wkts	Avg	BB	5I	10M
Test																	
FC	54	78	28	590	62	11.80	-	1	14	-	8595	4122	182	22.64	7-59	8	-
ODI																	
List A	65	34	12	164	31 *	7.45	-	-	10	-	2658	1832	62	29.54	4-13	-	
20/20 Int																	
20/20	9	4	3	11	6	11.00	-	-	2	-	204	241	8	30.12	2-14	-	

DAVIES, S. M. — Worcestershire

Name: Steven (Steve) Michael Davies
Role: Left-hand bat, wicket-keeper
Born: 17 June 1986, Bromsgrove
Height: 5ft 11in **Weight:** 11st 7lbs
Nickname: Davo
County debut: 2004 (one-day), 2005 (first-class)
County colours: 2005
1000 runs in a season: 1
50 dismissals in a season: 2
Place in batting averages: 133rd av. 31.37 (2006 85th av. 37.57)
Parents: Lin and Michael
Marital status: Single
Education: King Charles I School, Kidderminster
Qualifications: 9 GCSEs, 1 A-level, 2 AS-levels

Off-season: 'Selected as England Performance player – attending winter programme'
Overseas tours: England U17 to Netherlands 2003; England U19 to Bangladesh (U19 World Cup) 2003-04, to India 2004-05 (c); England A to West Indies 2005-06, to Bangladesh 2006-07; England Performance Programme to India 2007-08; England Lions to India 2007-08
Career highlights to date: 'Maiden first-class century against Somerset 2005. Pro40 champions 2007'
Cricket superstitions: 'None'
Cricketers particularly admired: Adam Gilchrist, Michael Hussey, Matthew Hayden
Young players to look out for: Moeen Ali
Other sports played: Basketball (trials for England), golf
Other sports followed: Football (Arsenal)
Favourite band: Air Traffic, Justin Nozuka
Relaxations: 'Playing golf and basketball; socialising with friends; listening to music'
Extras: Represented England U19 2004, 2005. Took six catches in Leicestershire's first innings at Worcester 2006, equalling Worcestershire record for wicket-keeping catches in a first-class innings. Achieved double of 1000 (1052) runs and 50 (68) dismissals in first-class cricket 2006. ECB National Academy 2004-05 (part-time), 2005-06 (including visit to World Cricket Academy, India), 2006-07
Opinions on cricket: 'Increase in amount of Twenty20 games good for cricket. Only one overseas player allowed should create more opportunities for young players.'
Best batting: 192 Worcestershire v Gloucestershire, Bristol 2006
Stop press: Forced to withdraw from England Lions tour to India 2007-08 with a knee injury

2007 Season

	M	Inn	NO	Runs	HS	Avg	100	50	Ct	St	Balls	Runs	Wkts	Avg	BB	5I	10M
Test																	
FC	16	27	3	753	87	31.37	-	4	47	4	0	0	0		-	-	-
ODI																	
List A	17	14	2	457	84	38.08	-	3	15	3	0	0	0		-	-	
20/20 Int																	
20/20	7	6	3	74	30	24.66	-	-	4	2	0	0	0		-	-	

Career Performances

	M	Inn	NO	Runs	HS	Avg	100	50	Ct	St	Balls	Runs	Wkts	Avg	BB	5I	10M
Test																	
FC	46	78	6	2510	192	34.86	4	9	125	12	0	0	0		-	-	-
ODI																	
List A	52	43	8	863	84	24.65	-	4	50	14	0	0	0		-	-	
20/20 Int																	
20/20	15	12	4	171	30	21.37	-	-	6	2	0	0	0		-	-	

DAVIS, M. J. G. Sussex

Name: Mark Jeffrey Gronow Davis
Role: Right-hand bat, right-arm off-spin bowler
Born: 10 October 1971, Port Elizabeth, South Africa
Height: 6ft 2in **Weight:** 12st 8lbs
Nickname: Davo, Doxy, Sparky
County debut: 2001
County cap: 2002
Parents: Jeremy and Marilyn
Wife and date of marriage: Candice, 8 April 2000
Family links with cricket: 'Father supports Sussex. My brothers, William and Patrick, play league cricket in Sussex'
Education: Grey High School; University of Pretoria
Qualifications: BA Psychology and English
Career outside cricket: Coach of UPE International Cricket Academy in Port Elizabeth
Overseas tours: South Africa U24 to Sri Lanka 1995; Northern Transvaal to Zimbabwe 1992-93, to Kenya 1994-95, 1995-96
Overseas teams played for: Northern Transvaal/Northerns 1990-91 – 1999-2000
Career highlights: 'Winning the County Championship [2003]. It was second to none, unbelievable! That and my 168 v Middlesex the same season'
Cricket superstitions: 'None'
Cricketers particularly admired: 'All my team-mates', Tim May, Shane Warne
Other sports played: Golf, tennis
Other sports followed: Rugby ('support the Springboks'), football (Middlesbrough)
Favourite band: 'Very eclectic tastes – no real favourite'
Relaxations: 'Golf, music, going out with friends, watching good movies'

Extras: Represented South Africa A 1995. Captain of Northern Transvaal/Northerns 1997-2000, during which time the province won the first two trophies in its history. Member of MCC. Scored maiden first-class century (111) v Somerset at Taunton 2002, in the process sharing with Robin Martin-Jenkins (205*) in a record eighth-wicket partnership for Sussex (291); the stand fell one run short of the record eighth-wicket partnership in English first-class cricket, set in 1896. Retired at the end of the 2005 season to become club coach but registration retained. Is not considered an overseas player

Best batting: 168 Sussex v Middlesex, Hove 2003

Best bowling: 8-37 Northerns B v North West, Potchefstroom 1994-95

2007 Season (did not make any first-class or one-day appearances)

Career Performances

	M	Inn	NO	Runs	HS	Avg	100	50	Ct	St	Balls	Runs	Wkts	Avg	BB	5I	10M
Test																	
FC	127	187	30	2941	168	18.73	2	8	69	-	18475	8368	232	36.06	8-37	5	1
ODI																	
List A	160	90	35	946	37	17.20	-	-	34	-	7306	5316	142	37.43	4-14	-	
20/20 Int																	
20/20	17	9	5	78	20 *	19.50	-	-	5	-	276	343	13	26.38	3-13	-	

DAWSON, L. A. Hampshire

Name: Liam Andrew Dawson

Role: Right-hand bat, slow left-arm bowler; all-rounder

Born: 1 March 1990, Swindon

Height: 5ft 8in **Weight:** 11st

Nickname: Daws, Lemmy

County debut: 2007

Parents: Andy and Bev

Marital status: Single

Family links with cricket: 'Dad played club cricket for Goatacre; brother also plays for them'

Education: The John Bentley School, Calne

Qualifications: GCSEs

Off-season: 'Playing in the U19 World Cup and training in Perth'

Overseas tours: West of England U15 to West Indies 2005; England U16 to South

Africa 2006; England U19 to Malaysia 2006-07, to Malaysia (U19 World Cup) 2007-08
Overseas teams played for: Melville, Perth 2006-07
Career highlights to date: 'Making my one-day and first-class debuts'
Cricket moments to forget: 'Being hit for 20-odd in an over'
Cricket superstitions: 'None'
Cricketers particularly admired: Shane Warne, Dan Vettori
Young players to look out for: Benny Howell, Alex Wakely
Other sports played: Football (Calne Town Youth)
Other sports followed: Football (Bury)
Favourite band: Coldplay
Relaxations: 'Rugby league'
Extras: Hampshire Academy Player of the Year 2005. Bunbury Festival All-rounder of the Tournament 2005. Represented England U19 2007. Made List A debut v Northamptonshire at Northampton in the Pro40 2007 aged 17, scoring a 31-ball 32
Opinions on cricket: 'Good to see young players getting their chance in the game, mainly because of Twenty20 competition.'

2007 Season

	M	Inn	NO	Runs	HS	Avg	100	50	Ct	St	Balls	Runs	Wkts	Avg	BB	5I	10M
Test																	
FC	1	0	0	0	0		-	-	-	-	0	0	0		-	-	-
ODI																	
List A	3	2	0	40	32	20.00	-	-	-	-	72	68	0		-	-	
20/20 Int																	
20/20																	

Career Performances

	M	Inn	NO	Runs	HS	Avg	100	50	Ct	St	Balls	Runs	Wkts	Avg	BB	5I	10M
Test																	
FC	1	0	0	0	0		-	-	-	-	0	0	0		-	-	-
ODI																	
List A	3	2	0	40	32	20.00	-	-	-	-	72	68	0		-	-	
20/20 Int																	
20/20																	

21. Who was Man of the Match on debut in the third Test between England and South Africa at Trent Bridge in 2003?

DAWSON, R. K. J. Northamptonshire

Name: Richard Kevin James Dawson
Role: Right-hand bat, right-arm off-spin bowler
Born: 4 August 1980, Doncaster
Height: 6ft 4in **Weight:** 11st 4lbs
Nickname: Billy Dog
County debut: 2001 (Yorkshire), 2007 (Northamptonshire)
County cap: 2004 (Yorkshire)
Test debut: 2001-02
Place in batting averages: (2006 269th av. 10.58)
Parents: Kevin and Pat
Marital status: Single
Family links with cricket: Brother Gareth plays for Doncaster Town CC
Education: Batley GS; Exeter University
Qualifications: 10 GCSEs, 4 A-levels, degree in Exercise and Sports Science
Overseas tours: England U18 to Bermuda 1997; England U19 to New Zealand 1998-99; England to India and New Zealand 2001-02, to Australia 2002-03; ECB National Academy to Sri Lanka 2002-03; England A to Sri Lanka 2004-05
Cricketers particularly admired: Steve Waugh, Graeme Swann
Other sports played: Football
Other sports followed: Football (Doncaster Rovers FC)
Relaxations: Sleeping, listening to music
Extras: Captained England U15. Sir John Hobbs Silver Jubilee Memorial Prize 1995. Represented England U19 1999. Captained British Universities 2000. NBC Denis Compton Award for the most promising young Yorkshire player 2001. Made Test debut in the first Test v India at Mohali 2001-02, taking 4-134 in India's first innings. Released by Northamptonshire at the end of the 2007 season
Best batting: 87 Yorkshire v Kent, Canterbury 2002
Best bowling: 6-82 Yorkshire v Glamorgan, Scarborough 2001

2007 Season

	M	Inn	NO	Runs	HS	Avg	100	50	Ct	St	Balls	Runs	Wkts	Avg	BB	5I	10M
Test																	
FC	3	4	1	45	26	15.00	-	-	2	-	282	168	5	33.60	3-25	-	-
ODI																	
List A	6	2	0	6	4	3.00	-	-	-	-	228	249	4	62.25	2-66	-	
20/20 Int																	
20/20	3	0	0	0	0		-	-	-	-	12	46	0		-	-	

Career Performances

	M	Inn	NO	Runs	HS	Avg	100	50	Ct	St	Balls	Runs	Wkts	Avg	BB	5I	10M
Test	7	13	3	114	19 *	11.40	-	-	3	-	1116	677	11	61.54	4-134	-	-
FC	91	136	16	2541	87	21.17	-	11	48	-	13993	7814	186	42.01	6-82	5	-
ODI																	
List A	106	65	14	484	41	9.49	-	-	35	-	4109	3287	109	30.15	4-13	-	
20/20 Int																	
20/20	25	8	3	71	22	14.20	-	-	7	-	461	604	24	25.16	3-24	-	

DEAN, K. J. — Derbyshire

Name: Kevin James Dean
Role: Left-hand bat, left-arm medium bowler
Born: 16 October 1975, Derby
Height: 6ft 5in **Weight:** 14st
Nickname: Deany, Red Face, George, Dada
County debut: 1996
County cap: 1998
Benefit: 2006
50 wickets in a season: 2
Place in bowling averages: 53rd av. 28.65
Parents: Ken and Dorothy
Wife and date of marriage: Sharon, 20 October 2007
Education: Leek High School; Leek College of Further Education
Qualifications: 8 GCSEs, 1 AS-level, 3 A-levels, ECB Level 2 coaching, FA Level 7 referee
Career outside cricket: 'Director of BaileyDean Properties. Tipster at Uttoxeter Racecourse. Betfair Trading'
Off-season: 'Refereeing. Tipping and working on Betfair'
Overseas tours: MCC to Australia 2002-03
Overseas teams played for: Sturt CC, Adelaide 1996-97
Career highlights to date: 'Can't split – 1) Hitting the winning runs against Australia for Derbyshire in 1997; 2) Getting either hat-trick'
Cricket moments to forget: 'Being hit on the head [whilst] batting by Andy Bichel whilst unable to bend due to a back injury'
Cricket superstitions: 'Last person out of changing room for first session of fielding'
Cricketers particularly admired: Dominic Cork, Wasim Akram, Michael Holding
Young players to look out for: Dan Redfern, James Harris
Other sports played: Football, indoor cricket, golf, snooker

Other sports followed: Horse racing, football (Derby County)
Injuries: Out for three weeks with a broken thumb
Favourite band: Stereophonics, Pink, The Killers, Oasis
Relaxations: 'Horse racing, football'
Extras: Took Championship hat-trick (E. Smith, Hooper, Llong) v Kent at Derby 1998. Took second Championship hat-trick (DeFreitas, Kumble, Ormond) v Leicestershire at Leicester 2000. Joint leading wicket-taker in English first-class cricket 2002 (with Martin Saggers) with 83 wickets (av. 23.50). Derbyshire Player of the Year 2002 (jointly with Michael DiVenuto)
Best batting: 54* Derbyshire v Worcestershire, Derby 2002
Best bowling: 8-52 Derbyshire v Kent, Canterbury 2000

2007 Season

	M	Inn	NO	Runs	HS	Avg	100	50	Ct	St	Balls	Runs	Wkts	Avg	BB	5I	10M
Test																	
FC	10	12	6	46	16	7.66	-	-	2	-	1602	659	23	28.65	5-24	1	-
ODI																	
List A	7	5	5	22	14 *		-	-	-	-	330	277	4	69.25	1-21	-	
20/20 Int																	
20/20	6	2	1	4	3	4.00	-	-	1	-	110	154	7	22.00	2-24	-	

Career Performances

	M	Inn	NO	Runs	HS	Avg	100	50	Ct	St	Balls	Runs	Wkts	Avg	BB	5I	10M
Test																	
FC	115	153	50	1176	54 *	11.41	-	2	22	-	18300	10208	387	26.37	8-52	16	4
ODI																	
List A	144	67	37	261	16 *	8.70	-	-	24	-	6377	4889	160	30.55	5-32	2	
20/20 Int																	
20/20	21	6	5	15	8 *	15.00	-	-	5	-	388	517	18	28.72	2-14	-	

22. Pieter van der Bijl made his Test debut in the first Test v England at Johannesburg in 1938-39. For which English county did his son play in 1980 and 1981?

DENLY, J. L. Kent

Name: Joseph (Joe) Liam Denly
Role: Right-hand bat, leg-spin bowler
Born: 16 March 1986, Canterbury
Height: 6ft **Weight:** 11st 9lbs
Nickname: No Pants
County debut: 2004
1000 runs in a season: 1
Place in batting averages: 63rd av. 41.79
Parents: Jayne and Nick
Marital status: Single
Family links with cricket: 'Dad and brother play local cricket'
Education: Chaucer Technology School
Qualifications: 10 GCSEs, Level 1 coach
Overseas tours: England U18 to Netherlands 2003; England U19 to India 2004-05; England Performance Programme to India 2007-08; England Lions to India 2007-08
Overseas teams played for: Hamersley Carine, Perth 2003; UTS Balmain Tigers, Sydney 2005-07
Career highlights to date: 'First first-class hundred'
Cricket moments to forget: 'Golden duck on first-class debut'
Cricket superstitions: 'Left pad on first'
Cricketers particularly admired: Steve Waugh
Young players to look out for: Sam Denly
Other sports played: Football (Charlton Athletic U14, U15)
Other sports followed: Football (Arsenal)
Favourite band: Westlife
Extras: Represented England U17, U18 and U19. Carried bat in scoring his first Championship century (115*) v Hampshire at Canterbury 2007. Represented England Lions 2007
Opinions on cricket: 'It's great.'
Best batting: 115* Kent v Hampshire, Canterbury 2007
Best bowling: 2-13 Kent v Surrey, Canterbury 2007

2007 Season

	M	Inn	NO	Runs	HS	Avg	100	50	Ct	St	Balls	Runs	Wkts	Avg	BB	5I	10M
Test																	
FC	16	27	3	1003	115 *	41.79	2	6	9	-	403	203	6	33.83	2-13	-	-
ODI																	
List A	15	13	1	255	102 *	21.25	1	1	5	-	6	6	0		-	-	
20/20 Int																	
20/20	11	10	1	279	63 *	31.00	-	1	6	-	0	0	0		-	-	

Career Performances

	M	Inn	NO	Runs	HS	Avg	100	50	Ct	St	Balls	Runs	Wkts	Avg	BB	5I	10M
Test																	
FC	21	35	4	1404	115 *	45.29	4	8	10	-	619	307	10	30.70	2-13	-	-
ODI																	
List A	26	24	3	448	102 *	21.33	1	2	7	-	6	6	0		-	-	
20/20 Int																	
20/20	15	12	1	285	63 *	25.90	-	1	8	-	0	0	0		-	-	

DERNBACH, J. W. — Surrey

Name: Jade Winston Dernbach
Role: Right-hand bat, right-arm fast bowler
Born: 3 March 1986, Johannesburg, South Africa
Height: 6ft 2in **Weight:** 13st
County debut: 2003
Parents: Carmen and Graeme
Marital status: Single
Education: St John the Baptist
Overseas tours: La Manga tournament, Spain 2003
Cricketers particularly admired: Jacques Kallis, Jonty Rhodes, James Anderson, Rikki Clarke
Other sports played: Rugby (Surrey U16)
Other sports followed: Football (Arsenal)
Favourite band: Usher
Relaxations: 'Going out with friends; swimming, playing football and rugby; listening to music'
Extras: Sir Jack Hobbs Fair Play Award. Surrey U19 Player of the Year. Made first-class debut v India A at The Oval 2003 aged 17, becoming the youngest player for 30 years to play first-class cricket for Surrey. Surrey Academy 2003, 2004

Best batting: 10 Surrey v Warwickshire, Edgbaston 2007
Best bowling: 3-67 Surrey v Gloucestershire, Bristol 2006

2007 Season

	M	Inn	NO	Runs	HS	Avg	100	50	Ct	St	Balls	Runs	Wkts	Avg	BB	5I	10M
Test																	
FC	4	4	1	16	10	5.33	-	-	1	-	469	335	9	37.22	3-85	-	-
ODI																	
List A	4	4	3	9	8 *	9.00	-	-	1	-	180	170	12	14.16	5-44	1	
20/20 Int																	
20/20	7	0	0	0	0		-	-	2	-	84	138	2	69.00	1-20	-	

Career Performances

	M	Inn	NO	Runs	HS	Avg	100	50	Ct	St	Balls	Runs	Wkts	Avg	BB	5I	10M
Test																	
FC	10	11	5	34	10	5.66	-	-	2	-	1103	835	18	46.38	3-67	-	-
ODI																	
List A	23	11	4	38	21	5.42	-	-	7	-	846	873	38	22.97	5-44	1	
20/20 Int																	
20/20	16	2	0	1	1	.50	-	-	5	-	239	405	7	57.85	1-19	-	

DE WET, F. Middlesex

Name: Friedel de Wet
Role: Right-hand bat, right-arm fast-medium bowler
Born: 26 June 1980, Durban, South Africa
County debut: No first-team appearance
Education: Grenswag HS; Tswane University of Technology, Pretoria
Overseas tours: South Africa Academy to Australia (International Academy Challenge) 2002; South Africa Emerging Players to Australia (Cricket Australia Emerging Players Tournament) 2007; South Africa A to India 2007-08
Overseas teams played for: Northerns 2001-02 – 2002-03; North West 2004-05 – ; Lions 2004-05 –
Extras: Represented Rest of South Africa v Indians 2006-07. Leading wicket-taker in South African first-class cricket 2006-07 (61 wickets; av. 20.21). His match awards include Man of the Match v Warriors at Johannesburg (5-53/3-76 plus 43*) and v

Dolphins at Potchefstroom (3-59/5-66), both in the SuperSport Series 2006-07. Is not considered an overseas player
Best batting: 43* Lions v Warriors, Johannesburg 2006-07
Best bowling: 7-61 Lions v Cape Cobras, Cape Town 2005-06
Stop press: Represented South Africa A v New Zealanders and West Indians 2007-08

2007 Season (did not make any first-class or one-day appearances)

Career Performances

	M	Inn	NO	Runs	HS	Avg	100	50	Ct	St	Balls	Runs	Wkts	Avg	BB	5I	10M
Test																	
FC	25	34	8	392	43 *	15.07	-	-	10	-	5039	2502	118	21.20	7-61	9	2
ODI																	
List A	36	15	10	158	56 *	31.60	-	1	8	-	1592	1290	38	33.94	5-59	1	
20/20 Int																	
20/20	8	3	1	6	6	3.00	-	-	2	-	156	220	9	24.44	2-18	-	

DEXTER, N. J. — Kent

Name: Neil John Dexter
Role: Right-hand bat, right-arm medium bowler; all-rounder
Born: 21 August 1984, Johannesburg, South Africa
Height: 6ft **Weight:** 11st 4lbs
Nickname: Ted, Dex, Sexy Dexy
County debut: 2005
Place in batting averages: 54th av. 43.75 (2006 26th av. 57.87)
Parents: John and Susan
Marital status: Single
Education: Northwood School, Durban; UNISA (University of South Africa)
Qualifications: Matriculation
Overseas teams played for: Crusaders CC 2000-06
Career highlights to date: 'Scoring first ton, against Glamorgan 2006'
Cricket moments to forget: 'Being hit for 25 in one over against Worcester'
Cricketers particularly admired: Steve Waugh, Brett Lee
Young players to look out for: Alex Blake, Sam Northeast, Joe Denly
Other sports played: Golf, tennis, 'most sports'
Other sports followed: Football (Man Utd)

Favourite band: Simple Plan, Goo Goo Dolls
Relaxations: 'Lying around doing nothing'
Extras: Played for Natal U13-19, Natal Academy and Natal A. Is not considered an overseas player
Opinions on cricket: 'Very professional with lots of opportunities.'
Best batting: 131* Kent v Nottinghamshire, Canterbury 2006
Best bowling: 2-40 Kent v Lancashire, Old Trafford 2006

2007 Season

	M	Inn	NO	Runs	HS	Avg	100	50	Ct	St	Balls	Runs	Wkts	Avg	BB	5I	10M
Test																	
FC	8	10	2	350	86	43.75	-	3	6	-	78	72	1	72.00	1-35	-	-
ODI																	
List A	8	5	1	38	14	9.50	-	-	-	-	198	160	4	40.00	3-27	-	
20/20 Int																	
20/20	6	2	1	45	31 *	45.00	-	-	3	-	12	27	0		-	-	

Career Performances

	M	Inn	NO	Runs	HS	Avg	100	50	Ct	St	Balls	Runs	Wkts	Avg	BB	5I	10M
Test																	
FC	19	28	7	989	131 *	47.09	2	6	13	-	804	514	9	57.11	2-40	-	-
ODI																	
List A	25	20	2	480	135 *	26.66	1	1	3	-	444	386	14	27.57	3-17	-	
20/20 Int																	
20/20	15	11	1	212	36	21.20	-	-	10	-	102	182	4	45.50	3-27	-	

DIGHTON, M. G. Derbyshire

Name: Michael Gray Dighton
Role: Right-hand bat, right-arm medium bowler, occasional wicket-keeper
Born: 24 April 1976, Toowoomba, Australia
Height: 6ft 4in **Weight:** 14st 2lbs
Nickname: Dighta
County debut: 2004 (one-day, Hampshire), 2007 (Derbyshire)
Place in batting averages: 127th av. 32.15
Overseas teams played for: Western Australia 1997-98 – 1999-2000; Tasmania 2001-02 –
Extras: Captained Western Australia U17 and U19. Australian Cricket Academy 1996. Played for ACB Chairman's XI v England XI 1998-99 and v Pakistanis 1999-2000. Played for Netherlands in the NatWest 2000. Tasmania's Pura Cup Player of the Year 2003-04 and a member of Tasmania's first Pura Cup winning side 2006-07. Returned a competition record 6-25 on KFC Twenty20 debut v Queensland at Toowoomba 2006-07. Has won several match awards, including Man of the Match v Queensland at

Hobart in the Pura Cup 2006-07 (126/65*) and v New South Wales at Sydney in the KFC Twenty20 2006-07 (56-ball 111, the competition's first century). Was a temporary overseas player with Hampshire during the 2004 season, striking a 64-ball 74 on debut v Gloucestershire at Bristol in the totesport League. Is a British passport-holder and played for Derbyshire as a non-overseas player during the 2007 season
Best batting: 182* Western Australia v Queensland, Perth 1999-2000
Best bowling: 2-47 Derbyshire v Essex, Derby 2007
Stop press: Set record for the highest individual score for Tasmania in a List A match with his 146* v New South Wales at Sydney in the Ford Ranger Cup 2007-08, winning Man of the Match award

2007 Season

	M	Inn	NO	Runs	HS	Avg	100	50	Ct	St	Balls	Runs	Wkts	Avg	BB	5I	10M
Test																	
FC	7	14	1	418	68	32.15	-	2	10	-	246	133	4	33.25	2-47	-	-
ODI																	
List A	6	6	0	175	67	29.16	-	2	4	-	132	103	3	34.33	2-46	-	
20/20 Int																	
20/20	6	6	1	94	27	18.80	-	-	1	-	72	74	3	24.66	1-9	-	

Career Performances

	M	Inn	NO	Runs	HS	Avg	100	50	Ct	St	Balls	Runs	Wkts	Avg	BB	5I	10M
Test																	
FC	62	112	6	3917	182 *	36.95	8	19	48	-	408	242	5	48.40	2-47	-	-
ODI																	
List A	55	54	1	1524	113	28.75	1	12	21	1	156	126	4	31.50	2-46	-	
20/20 Int																	
20/20	10	10	2	235	111	29.37	1	-	1	-	96	121	9	13.44	6-25	1	

DIPPENAAR, H. H. Leicestershire

Name: Hendrik Human (Boeta) Dippenaar
Role: Right-hand bat, right-arm off-break bowler
Born: 14 June 1977, Kimberley, South Africa
County debut: No first-team appearance
Test debut: 1999-2000
ODI debut: 1999-2000
Twenty20 Int debut: 2005-06
1st-Class 200s: 2
Education: Grey College, Bloemfontein
Overseas tours: South Africa U19 to England 1995, to India 1995-96; Free State to West Indies 1996-97; South Africa A to Zimbabwe 2004, to Zimbabwe 2007-08 (c), to India 2007-08 (c); South Africa to Kenya (LG Cup) 1999-2000, to Zimbabwe 1999-2000, to Kenya (ICC Knockout Trophy) 2000-01, to West Indies 2000-01, to Zimbabwe 2001-02, to Australia 2001-02, to Sri Lanka (ICC Champions Trophy) 2002-03, to Bangladesh 2003, to England 2003, to Pakistan 2003-04, to Sri Lanka 2004, to India 2004-05, to West Indies 2004-05, to Sri Lanka 2006, to India (ICC Champions Trophy) 2006-07, plus other one-day tournaments and series in Australia, Singapore, Morocco and New Zealand
Overseas teams played for: Free State 1995-96 – 2003-04; Eagles 2004-05 –
Extras: Represented South Africa in the 2002-03 World Cup. Scored 177* in the first Test v Bangladesh in Chittagong 2003, in the process sharing with Jacques Rudolph (222*) in the highest partnership for any wicket for South Africa in Tests (429*). One of *South African Cricket Annual*'s five Cricketers of the Year 2005. Played for an African XI in the Afro-Asian Cup 2005-06, 2007. His numerous match and series awards include Man of the [ODI] Series v Pakistan 2003-04 and v West Indies 2004-05 (317 runs; av. 105.66). Has joined Leicestershire as overseas player for 2008
Best batting: 250* Eagles v Warriors, Kimberley 2006-07

2007 Season (did not make any first-class or one-day appearances)

Career Performances

	M	Inn	NO	Runs	HS	Avg	100	50	Ct	St	Balls	Runs	Wkts	Avg	BB	5I	10M
Test	38	62	5	1718	177 *	30.14	3	7	27	-	12	1	0		-	-	-
FC	125	207	18	8151	250 *	43.12	25	32	98	-	19	13	0		-	-	-
ODI	107	95	14	3421	125 *	42.23	4	26	36	-	0	0	0		-	-	
List A	183	165	24	5728	125 *	40.62	7	40	60	-	6	2	0		-	-	
20/20 Int	1	1	0	1	1	1.00	-	-	-	-	0	0	0		-	-	
20/20	14	13	2	191	35 *	17.36	-	-	4	-	0	0	0		-	-	

DIVENUTO, M. J. Durham

Name: Michael James DiVenuto
Role: Left-hand bat, right-arm medium/ leg-break bowler
Born: 12 December 1973, Hobart, Tasmania
Height: 5ft 11in **Weight:** 12st 12lbs
Nickname: Diva
County debut: 1999 (Sussex), 2000 (Derbyshire), 2007 (Durham)
County cap: 1999 (Sussex), 2000 (Derbyshire)
ODI debut: 1996-97
1000 runs in a season: 7
1st-Class 200s: 3
Place in batting averages: 7th av. 66.45 (2006 31st av. 54.45)
Parents: Enrico and Elizabeth
Wife and date of marriage: Renae, 31 December 2003
Children: Sophia Lily, 21 March 2005; Luca Michael, 3 September 2007
Family links with cricket: 'Dad and older brother Peter both played grade cricket in Tasmania.' Brother Peter also played for Italy
Education: St Virgil's College, Hobart
Qualifications: HSC (5 x Level III subjects), Level 3 cricket coach
Career outside cricket: 'Own a cafe, "Say Cheese Salamanca", in Hobart'
Off-season: 'Playing for Tasmania and spending time in the cafe'
Overseas tours: Australian Cricket Academy to India and Sri Lanka 1993, to South Africa 1996; Australia A to Malaysia (Super 8s) 1997 (c), to Scotland and Ireland 1998 (c), to Los Angeles 1999; Australia to South Africa 1996-97 (one-day series), to Hong Kong (Super 6s) 1997, to Malaysia (Super 8s) 1998; Tasmania to Zimbabwe 1995-96

Overseas teams played for: North Hobart CC, Tasmania; Kingborough, Tasmania; Tasmania 1991-92 –
Career highlights to date: 'Playing for Australia. Man of the Match award v South Africa at Johannesburg 1997. Dismissing Jamie Cox at Taunton in 1999, my first wicket in first-class cricket. Winning Tasmania's first Pura Cup 2006-07. Winning Durham's first trophy and being part of the awesome 2007 season with Durham'
Cricket moments to forget: 'Being dismissed by Jamie Cox at Taunton in 1999, *his* first wicket in first-class cricket'
Cricketers particularly admired: David Boon, Dean Jones, Kepler Wessels, Mark and Steve Waugh
Young players to look out for: Kyle Coetzer, Mark Stoneman, Ben Harmison
Other sports played: Australian Rules (Tasmanian U15, U16 and Sandy Bay FC)
Other sports followed: Australian Rules football (Geelong Cats)
Favourite band: U2
Relaxations: Golf, sleeping and eating
Extras: Man of the Match in the fifth ODI v South Africa at Johannesburg 1997 (89). Was Sussex overseas player 1999; an overseas player with Derbyshire 2000-06; an overseas player with Durham 2007. Scored 173* v Derbyshire Board XI at Derby in NatWest 2000, a record for Derbyshire in one-day cricket. Carried bat for 192* v Middlesex at Lord's 2002; also scored 113 in the second innings. Derbyshire Player of the Year 2002 (jointly with Kevin Dean). First batsman to 1000 Championship runs 2003. Vice-captain of Derbyshire 2002-06 (was appointed captain for 2004 but was unable to take up post due to back surgery). Tasmania Pura Cup Player of the Year (David Boon Medal) 2006-07. Carried bat for 155* on Durham first-class debut v Worcestershire at Worcester 2007 and again for 204* v Kent at Riverside 2007. Holds an Italian passport and is no longer considered an overseas player
Opinions on cricket: 'The game is in great shape.'
Best batting: 230 Derbyshire v Northamptonshire, Derby 2002
Best bowling: 1-0 Tasmania v Queensland, Brisbane (AB) 1999-2000

2007 Season

	M	Inn	NO	Runs	HS	Avg	100	50	Ct	St	Balls	Runs	Wkts	Avg	BB	5I	10M
Test																	
FC	13	25	5	1329	204 *	66.45	3	9	21	-	0	0	0		-	-	-
ODI																	
List A	18	17	0	394	64	23.17	-	3	9	-	0	0	0		-	-	
20/20 Int																	
20/20	3	2	0	29	16	14.50	-	-	-	-	0	0	0		-	-	

Career Performances

	M	Inn	NO	Runs	HS	Avg	100	50	Ct	St	Balls	Runs	Wkts	Avg	BB	5I	10M
Test																	
FC	255	454	27	19035	230	44.57	42	115	302	-	807	484	5	96.80	1-0	-	-
ODI	9	9	0	241	89	26.77	-	2	1	-	0	0	0		-	-	
List A	271	265	16	8255	173 *	33.15	13	42	104	-	200	181	5	36.20	1-10	-	
20/20 Int																	
20/20	30	28	4	727	95 *	30.29	-	6	4	-	78	88	5	17.60	3-19	-	

DIXEY, P. G. Kent

Name: Paul Garrod Dixey
Role: Right-hand bat, wicket-keeper
Born: 2 November 1987, Canterbury
Height: 5ft 8in **Weight:** 10st 7lbs
Nickname: Dix
County debut: 2005
Place in batting averages: 275th av. 10.50
Parents: James and Lindsay
Marital status: Single
Family links with cricket: 'Dad used to play club cricket for St Lawrence and Highland Court'
Education: King's School, Canterbury; Durham University (Hatfield College)
Qualifications: 8 GCSEs, 4 AS-levels, 3 A-levels
Overseas tours: England U16 to South Africa
Career highlights to date: 'First-class debut against Bangladesh A at Canterbury'
Cricket moments to forget: 'Losing to Western Province U17 at Fairbairn College off the last ball of a closely fought two-day game'
Cricket superstitions: 'None'
Cricketers particularly admired: Adam Gilchrist, Ian Healy, Alan Knott
Young players to look out for: Alex Blake, Sam Northeast, James Iles
Other sports played: Hockey, rugby
Other sports followed: Rugby ('follow the Premiership')
Favourite band: Ne-Yo
Relaxations: 'Skiing, fly fishing, listening to music'
Extras: *Daily Telegraph* Bunbury ESCA Wicket-keeping Scholarship Award 2003; Magic Moment Award (Bunbury 2003). Represented England U19 2006. Played for Durham UCCE and MCC 2007

Opinions on cricket: 'As a young player hoping to make my way in the game, I am pleased to see the new ruling of limiting overseas players to one per county.'
Best batting: 25 DUCCE v Nottinghamshire, Durham 2007

2007 Season

	M	Inn	NO	Runs	HS	Avg	100	50	Ct	St	Balls	Runs	Wkts	Avg	BB	5I	10M
Test																	
FC	4	8	0	84	25	10.50	-	-	9	1	0	0	0		-	-	-
ODI																	
List A	1	0	0	0	0		-	-	3	-	0	0	0		-	-	
20/20 Int																	
20/20																	

Career Performances

	M	Inn	NO	Runs	HS	Avg	100	50	Ct	St	Balls	Runs	Wkts	Avg	BB	5I	10M
Test																	
FC	6	11	1	124	25	12.40	-	-	15	1	0	0	0		-	-	-
ODI																	
List A	1	0	0	0	0		-	-	3	-	0	0	0		-	-	
20/20 Int																	
20/20																	

DOSHI, N. D. — Derbyshire

Name: Nayan Dilip Doshi
Role: Right-hand bat, left-arm spin bowler
Born: 6 October 1978, Nottingham
Height: 6ft 4in
Nickname: Dosh, Troll, Turtlehead
County debut: 2004 (Surrey)
County cap: 2006 (Surrey)
50 wickets in a season: 1
Place in bowling averages: 140th av. 53.61 (2006 31st av. 28.11)
Parents: Dilip and Kalindi
Marital status: Married
Family links with cricket: Father is former India Test and ODI spin bowler Dilip Doshi, who also played for Nottinghamshire and Warwickshire
Education: King Alfred School, London
Career outside cricket: Family business
Overseas teams played for: Saurashtra, India 2001-02 – 2006-07

Career highlights to date: 'Twenty20 semi-final 2004'
Cricket moments to forget: 'Too many'
Cricketers particularly admired: Viv Richards, Sachin Tendulkar, Garfield Sobers
Favourite band: 'Like lots of them'
Relaxations: Wildlife photography
Extras: Made first-class debut for Saurashtra v Baroda at Rajkot 2001-02. Recorded maiden first-class ten-wicket match return (5-125/6-57) v Lancashire at Old Trafford 2004 and another (3-73/7-110) v Sussex at Hove in the following Championship match. Took 21 wickets in the Twenty20 Cup 2006, breaking the competition season record of 20 held by Adam Hollioake. Became first bowler to 50 Twenty20 wickets, v Hampshire at The Oval 2007. Is England-qualified. Left Surrey during the 2007 season and has joined Derbyshire for 2008
Best batting: 37 Saurashtra v Vidarbha, Rajkot (MS) 2005-06
Best bowling: 7-110 Surrey v Sussex, Hove 2004

2007 Season

	M	Inn	NO	Runs	HS	Avg	100	50	Ct	St	Balls	Runs	Wkts	Avg	BB	5I	10M
Test																	
FC	5	6	1	42	15	8.40	-	-	1	-	1046	697	13	53.61	6-111	1	-
ODI																	
List A	5	3	0	7	6	2.33	-	-	3	-	258	219	2	109.50	1-26	-	
20/20 Int																	
20/20	7	1	1	0	0 *		-	-	1	-	126	143	7	20.42	3-6	-	

Career Performances

	M	Inn	NO	Runs	HS	Avg	100	50	Ct	St	Balls	Runs	Wkts	Avg	BB	5I	10M
Test																	
FC	53	68	16	505	37	9.71	-	-	8	-	9324	5026	136	36.95	7-110	6	3
ODI																	
List A	60	28	6	197	38 *	8.95	-	-	16	-	2545	2355	54	43.61	5-30	1	
20/20 Int																	
20/20	34	7	5	4	1 *	2.00	-	-	10	-	666	777	53	14.66	4-22	-	

23. Who rang down the curtain on a 133-match Test career after the fifth Test between England and South Africa at The Oval in 2003?

DU PLESSIS, F. — Lancashire

Name: Francois du Plessis
Role: Right-hand bat, leg-break bowler
Born: 13 July 1984, Pretoria, South Africa
Nickname: Faf
County debut: No first-team appearance
Overseas tours: South Africa U19 to England 2003; South Africa Academy to Pakistan 2004-05; South Africa Emerging Players to Australia (Cricket Australia Emerging Players Tournament) 2007; South Africa VI to Hong Kong 2007
Overseas teams played for: Northerns 2003-04 – 2005-06; Titans 2005-06 –
Extras: Scored 177 v England U19 in the third 'Test' at Chelmsford 2003. Played for Nottinghamshire 2nd XI 2006, scoring 138-ball 203* v Minor Counties U25 at the Brian Wakefield Sports Ground, Nottingham, in the 2nd XI Trophy. Man of the Match v Warriors in East London in the MTN Domestic Championship 2006-07 (80). Played for Todmorden in the Lancashire League 2007. Is not considered an overseas player
Best batting: 156 Northerns v Gauteng, Johannesburg (WM) 2005-06
Best bowling: 4-39 Northerns v Free State, Pretoria (LCD) 2004-05

2007 Season (did not make any first-class or one-day appearances)

Career Performances

	M	Inn	NO	Runs	HS	Avg	100	50	Ct	St	Balls	Runs	Wkts	Avg	BB	5I	10M
Test																	
FC	18	33	4	1152	156	39.72	2	8	14	-	539	317	15	21.13	4-39	-	-
ODI																	
List A	27	24	4	805	114	40.25	1	5	11	-	585	482	14	34.42	4-47	-	
20/20 Int																	
20/20	6	6	0	150	76	25.00	-	1	1	-	78	120	5	24.00	2-26	-	

DURSTON, W. J. Somerset

Name: Wesley (Wes) John Durston
Role: Right-hand bat, right-arm off-spin bowler, 'very occasional' wicket-keeper
Born: 6 October 1980, Taunton
Height: 5ft 10in **Weight:** 12st 7lbs
Nickname: Bestie
County debut: 2002
Place in batting averages: (2006 81st av. 38.25)
Place in bowling averages: (2006 112th av. 41.60)
Parents: Gill and Steve
Wife and date of marriage: Christina, 4 October 2003
Children: Daisy, 4 July 2004; Joseph, 29 September 2006
Family links with cricket: 'Dad and my two brothers, Dan and Greg, all play. On occasions all four played in same local team (Compton Dundon)'
Education: Millfield School; University College Worcester
Qualifications: 3 A-levels, BSc Sport & Exercise Science, ECB Level II cricket coaching, Level 1 hockey coaching, Level 1 football coaching
Career outside cricket: 'Coaching at Millfield School'
Off-season: 'Working at my game and fitness in Taunton, whilst coaching hockey and cricket at Millfield School'
Overseas tours: West of England to West Indies 1996; Somerset to Cape Town 2006
Career highlights to date: 'Winning the Twenty20 trophy with Somerset CCC in 2005. County Championship 2007' (*Somerset were division two champions*)
Cricket moments to forget: 'Being out lbw for first-ball duck on Sky Sports (v Kent 2006)'
Cricket superstitions: 'Right foot on to and off field first. Saluting magpies'
Cricketers particularly admired: Ian Botham
Young players to look out for: Joseph Buttler, Joseph Durston
Other sports played: Hockey (Firebrands HC), golf (12 handicap)
Other sports followed: Football (Man Utd)
Injuries: Out for two weeks with a fractured thumb
Favourite band: Barenaked Ladies
Relaxations: 'Spending time with family and children'
Extras: Captained winning Lord's Taverners team v Shrewsbury School at Trent Bridge 1996. Wetherell Schools All-rounder Award 1999; scored 956 runs and took 35 wickets. Has captained Somerset 2nd XI on occasion. Scored 44-ball 55 on first-class

debut at Taunton 2002 as Somerset, chasing 454 to win, tied with West Indies A. Attended World Cricket Academy, Mumbai, 2005
Opinions on cricket: 'With the success of Twenty20 it may be very easy to lose sight of the importance of Championship cricket, which would be very detrimental to the game, as it provides English cricket with the only specific grooming for the Test arena.'
Best batting: 146* Somerset v Derbyshire, Derby 2005
Best bowling: 3-23 Somerset v Sri Lanka A, Taunton 2004

2007 Season

	M	Inn	NO	Runs	HS	Avg	100	50	Ct	St	Balls	Runs	Wkts	Avg	BB	5I	10M
Test																	
FC	3	4	1	140	58	46.66	-	2	-	-	144	117	0		-	-	-
ODI																	
List A	5	5	0	77	43	15.40	-	-	-	-	132	141	1	141.00	1-22	-	
20/20 Int																	
20/20	8	5	0	55	17	11.00	-	-	4	-	54	72	5	14.40	2-19	-	

Career Performances

	M	Inn	NO	Runs	HS	Avg	100	50	Ct	St	Balls	Runs	Wkts	Avg	BB	5I	10M
Test																	
FC	28	47	7	1443	146 *	36.07	1	10	33	-	1905	1287	24	53.62	3-23	-	-
ODI																	
List A	43	38	12	754	62 *	29.00	-	5	9	-	780	793	19	41.73	3-44	-	
20/20 Int																	
20/20	32	24	5	273	34	14.36	-	-	11	-	190	283	15	18.86	3-25	-	

EALHAM, M. A. — Nottinghamshire

Name: Mark Alan Ealham
Role: Right-hand bat, right-arm medium bowler; all-rounder
Born: 27 August 1969, Ashford, Kent
Height: 5ft 10in **Weight:** 14st
Nickname: Ealy, Border, Skater
County debut: 1989 (Kent), 2004 (Nottinghamshire)
County cap: 1992 (Kent), 2004 (Nottinghamshire)
Benefit: 2003 (Kent)
Test debut: 1996
ODI debut: 1996
1000 runs in a season: 1
50 wickets in a season: 1
Place in batting averages: 179th av. 25.00 (2006 129th av. 31.82)
Place in bowling averages: 49th av. 27.68 (2006 5th av. 20.78)

Parents: Alan and Sue
Wife and date of marriage: Kirsty, 24 February 1996
Children: George, 8 March 2002
Family links with cricket: Father played for Kent
Education: Stour Valley Secondary School
Qualifications: 9 CSEs
Career outside cricket: Plumber
Overseas tours: England A to Australia 1996-97, to Kenya and Sri Lanka 1997-98; England VI to Hong Kong 1997, 2001; England to Sharjah (Champions Trophy) 1997-98, to Bangladesh (Wills International Cup) 1998-99, to Australia 1998-99 (CUB Series), to Sharjah (Coca-Cola Cup) 1998-99, to South Africa and Zimbabwe 1999-2000 (one-day series), to Kenya (ICC Knockout Trophy) 2000-01, to Pakistan and Sri Lanka 2000-01 (one-day series)
Overseas teams played for: South Perth, Australia 1992-93; University, Perth 1993-94
Cricketers particularly admired: Ian Botham, Viv Richards, Robin Smith, Steve Waugh, Paul Blackmore and Albert 'for his F and G'
Other sports followed: Football (Manchester United), 'and most other sports'
Relaxations: Playing golf and snooker, watching films
Extras: Set then record for fastest Sunday League century (44 balls), v Derbyshire at Maidstone 1995. Represented England in the 1999 World Cup. Returned a then England record ODI bowling analysis with his 5-15 v Zimbabwe at Kimberley in 1999-2000; all five were lbw. Vice-captain of Kent 2001. Won the Walter Lawrence Trophy 2006 (fastest first-class century of the season) for his 45-ball hundred (finishing with 112*) v MCC at Lord's
Best batting: 153* Kent v Northamptonshire, Canterbury 2001
Best bowling: 8-36 Kent v Warwickshire, Edgbaston 1996

2007 Season

	M	Inn	NO	Runs	HS	Avg	100	50	Ct	St	Balls	Runs	Wkts	Avg	BB	5I	10M
Test																	
FC	13	16	4	300	74 *	25.00	-	2	16	-	1954	886	32	27.68	4-37	-	-
ODI																	
List A	9	6	4	60	28 *	30.00	-	-	4	-	410	278	18	15.44	3-13	-	
20/20 Int																	
20/20	6	3	0	18	10	6.00	-	-	2	-	123	143	6	23.83	3-26	-	

Career Performances

	M	Inn	NO	Runs	HS	Avg	100	50	Ct	St	Balls	Runs	Wkts	Avg	BB	5I	10M
Test	8	13	3	210	53 *	21.00	-	2	4	-	1060	488	17	28.70	4-21	-	-
FC	253	385	59	10527	153 *	32.29	12	65	143	-	33936	16092	585	27.50	8-36	22	1
ODI	64	45	4	716	45	17.46	-	-	9	-	3227	2197	67	32.79	5-15	2	
List A	394	323	73	6121	112	24.48	1	26	108	-	17551	11977	450	26.61	6-53	4	
20/20 Int																	
20/20	33	28	5	434	91	18.86	-	1	4	-	731	835	29	28.79	3-26	-	

EDMONDSON, B. M. Gloucestershire

Name: Ben Matthew Edmondson
Role: Left-hand bat, right-arm fast-medium bowler
Born: 28 September 1978, Southport, Queensland, Australia
Height: 6ft 1in
Nickname: Edo
County debut: 2007
County cap: 2007
Overseas tours: Australian Academy to South Africa and Zimbabwe 2006-07; Western Australia to India 2007-08
Overseas teams played for: Western Australia 2003-04 –
Extras: Played for Queensland Colts and Queensland Academy of Sport. Played for Denmark in the 2004 C&G. Played for the Prime Minister's XI v Pakistanis at Canberra 2004-05, taking 3-38. Represented Australia Centre of Excellence in the Cricket Australia Emerging Players Tournament 2006. Man of the Match v Tasmania at Hobart in the Pura Cup 2006-07 (6-28/4-169) and v South Australia at Perth in the Ford Ranger Cup 2006-07 (5-39). Leading wicket-taker for Western Australia in the Pura Cup 2003-04 (28 wickets; av. 31.60), 2004-05 (29; av. 36.41), 2006-07 (41; av. 29.95). Was a temporary overseas player with Gloucestershire during the 2007 season as a locum for Marcus North
Best batting: 18 Gloucestershire v Northamptonshire, Northampton 2007
Best bowling: 6-28 Western Australia v Tasmania, Hobart 2006-07

2007 Season

	M	Inn	NO	Runs	HS	Avg	100	50	Ct	St	Balls	Runs	Wkts	Avg	BB	5I	10M
Test																	
FC	5	6	2	28	18	7.00	-	-	2	-	618	446	9	49.55	4-50	-	-
ODI																	
List A	2	0	0	0	0		-	-	-	-	84	90	1	90.00	1-37	-	
20/20 Int																	
20/20	9	2	1	4	2 *	4.00	-	-	3	-	189	211	12	17.58	3-20	-	

Career Performances

	M	Inn	NO	Runs	HS	Avg	100	50	Ct	St	Balls	Runs	Wkts	Avg	BB	5I	10M
Test																	
FC	38	40	20	102	18	5.10	-	-	11	-	6927	4624	141	32.79	6-28	2	1
ODI																	
List A	19	10	5	18	4	3.60	-	-	1	-	990	828	29	28.55	5-39	1	
20/20 Int																	
20/20	15	3	2	6	2 *	6.00	-	-	3	-	328	389	19	20.47	3-16	-	

EDWARDS, N. J. — Somerset

Name: Neil James Edwards
Role: Left-hand bat, occasional right-arm medium bowler
Born: 14 October 1983, Truro, Cornwall
Height: 6ft 3in **Weight:** 14st
Nickname: Toastie, Shanksy
County debut: 2002
1000 runs in a season: 1
1st-Class 200s: 1
Place in batting averages: 41st av. 48.11 (2006 136th av. 30.90)
Parents: Lynn and John
Marital status: Single
Family links with cricket: 'Cousin played first-class cricket for Worcestershire'
Education: Cape Cornwall School; Richard Huish College
Qualifications: 11 GCSEs, 3 A-levels, Level 1 coach
Overseas tours: Cornwall U13 to South Africa 1997; West of England to West Indies 1999; Somerset Academy to Australia 2002; England U19 to Australia 2002-03
Cricket moments to forget: 'Duck on debut for Cornwall'

Cricket superstitions: 'Never change batting gloves when batting'
Cricketers particularly admired: Marcus Trescothick, Matthew Hayden
Other sports played: Football
Other sports followed: Football (Stoke City FC)
Favourite band: 'I listen to any music'
Extras: Scored 213 for Cornwall U19 v Dorset U19 at 16 years old. Scored a second innings 97 in England U19 victory over Australia U19 in the first 'Test' at Adelaide 2002-03. Represented England U19 2003. Somerset Wyverns Award for Best Performance by an Uncapped Player 2003 (160 v Hampshire)
Best batting: 212 Somerset v LUCCE, Taunton 2007
Best bowling: 1-16 Somerset v Derbyshire, Taunton 2004

2007 Season

	M	Inn	NO	Runs	HS	Avg	100	50	Ct	St	Balls	Runs	Wkts	Avg	BB	5I	10M
Test																	
FC	17	26	0	1251	212	48.11	2	8	10	-	0	0	0		-	-	-
ODI																	
List A																	
20/20 Int																	
20/20																	

Career Performances

	M	Inn	NO	Runs	HS	Avg	100	50	Ct	St	Balls	Runs	Wkts	Avg	BB	5I	10M
Test																	
FC	41	67	0	2557	212	38.16	3	13	27	-	281	193	2	96.50	1-16	-	-
ODI																	
List A	5	5	0	113	65	22.60	-	1	1	-	0	0	0		-	-	
20/20 Int																	
20/20	1	1	0	1	1	1.00	-	-	-	-	0	0	0		-	-	

ELLIOTT, M. T. G. — Glamorgan

Name: Matthew Thomas Gray Elliott
Role: Left-hand bat, left-arm orthodox bowler
Born: 28 September 1971, Chelsea, Victoria, Australia
Height: 6ft 3in **Weight:** 13st 8lbs
Nickname: Hoarse, Herb
County debut: 2000 (Glamorgan), 2002 (Yorkshire)
County cap: 2000 (Glamorgan)
Test debut: 1996-97
ODI debut: 1997
1000 runs in a season: 2
1st-Class 200s: 2

Place in batting averages: 62nd av. 41.83
Parents: John and Glenda
Wife and date of marriage: Megan, 11 December 1994
Children: Zachary, 22 November 1997; Samuel, 18 February 2000; William, June 2004
Education: Kyabram Secondary College
Qualifications: VCE
Overseas tours: Young Australia (Australia A) to England and Netherlands 1995; Australia to South Africa 1996-97, to England 1997, to West Indies 1998-99; FICA World XI to New Zealand 2004-05
Overseas teams played for: Victoria 1992-93 – 2004-05; South Australia 2005-06 –
Career highlights to date: 'Taking the 2002 C&G Trophy through Scarborough on an open-top bus with a police escort!'

Cricket moments to forget: 'Being dismissed by Dean Cosker at Sophia Gardens in '97!'
Cricket superstitions: 'Always put left shoe on first'
Cricketers particularly admired: Shane Warne, Allan Border, Steve Waugh
Other sports played: Australian Rules football
Other sports followed: Australian Rules football (Collingwood FC)
Relaxations: 'Fishing; reading biographies; drinking Corona'
Extras: Scored 556 runs (av. 55.60) in the 1997 Ashes series. One of *Wisden*'s Five Cricketers of the Year 1998. Sheffield Shield Player of the Year 1995-96 and 1998-99. Was an overseas player with Glamorgan 2000, 2004-05 and a temporary overseas player with the county during the 2007 season. Scored 177 v Sussex at Colwyn Bay 2000, sharing with Stephen James in a Glamorgan record first-wicket partnership of 374. Was Yorkshire's overseas player for the latter part of 2002. C&G Man of the Match award for his 128* in the final v Somerset at Lord's 2002. Pura Cup Player of the Year 2003-04 and Man of the Match in the final v Queensland at Melbourne (155/55*). *Wisden Australia*'s Pura Cup Cricketer of the Year 2004-05
Best batting: 203 Victoria v Tasmania, Melbourne 1995-96
Best bowling: 3-68 Victoria v Queensland, Melbourne 2004-05

2007 Season

	M	Inn	NO	Runs	HS	Avg	100	50	Ct	St	Balls	Runs	Wkts	Avg	BB	5I	10M
Test																	
FC	4	6	0	251	95	41.83	-	2	6	-	0	0	0		-	-	-
ODI																	
List A	3	2	0	100	87	50.00	-	1	1	-	0	0	0		-	-	
20/20 Int																	
20/20																	

Career Performances

	M	Inn	NO	Runs	HS	Avg	100	50	Ct	St	Balls	Runs	Wkts	Avg	BB	5I	10M
Test	21	36	1	1172	199	33.48	3	4	14	-	12	4	0		-	-	-
FC	206	379	27	16822	203	47.78	50	81	223	-	1242	754	13	58.00	3-68	-	-
ODI	1	1	0	1	1	1.00	-	-	-	-	0	0	0		-	-	
List A	153	148	20	5690	156	44.45	15	33	60	-	92	92	0		-	-	
20/20 Int																	
20/20	9	9	1	276	52 *	34.50	-	2	3	-	0	0	0		-	-	

ERVINE, S. M. — Hampshire

Name: Sean Michael Ervine
Role: Left-hand bat, right-arm medium-fast bowler; all-rounder
Born: 6 December 1982, Harare, Zimbabwe
Height: 6ft 2in **Weight:** 14st
Nickname: Slug
County debut: 2005
County cap: 2005
Test debut: 2003
ODI debut: 2001-02
Place in batting averages: 106th av. 34.50 (2006 180th av. 24.42)
Place in bowling averages: (2006 107th av. 40.76)
Parents: Rory and Judy
Marital status: Single
Family links with cricket: 'Grandfather played cricket for Rhodesia and father and uncle both played for Rhodesia'
Education: Lomagundi College, Zimbabwe
Qualifications: 5 O-levels, Levels 1 and 2 coaching
Overseas tours: Zimbabwe U19 to Sri Lanka (U19 World Cup) 1999-2000, to New

Zealand (U19 World Cup) 2001-02; Zimbabwe to Bangladesh 2001-02, to Sri Lanka 2001-02 (one-day series), to Sri Lanka (ICC Champions Trophy) 2002-03, to England 2003, to Australia 2003-04, plus one-day tournaments in Sharjah
Overseas teams played for: Midlands, Zimbabwe 2001-02 – 2003-04; Western Australia 2006-07 –
Cricket moments to forget: 'Fielding the ball off my own bowling and rupturing my knee, needing a total knee reconstruction'
Cricket superstitions: 'None'
Cricketers particularly admired: Andy Flower, Shane Warne
Young players to look out for: Shaun Marsh (Western Australia)
Other sports played: Golf, tennis, squash, fishing
Other sports followed: AFL (Kangaroos)
Favourite band: Snow Patrol
Relaxations: 'Music, art'
Extras: CFX [Zimbabwean] Academy 2000-01. Represented Zimbabwe in the World Cup 2002-03. Struck 99-ball century (100) at Adelaide in the VB Series 2003-04 as Zimbabwe fell just three runs short of India's 280-7. Man of the Match in the first Test v Bangladesh at Harare 2003-04 (86/74). C&G Man of the Match awards in the semi-final v Yorkshire at The Rose Bowl (100) and in the final v Warwickshire at Lord's (104) 2005. Holds an Irish passport and is not considered an overseas player
Opinions on cricket: 'No rest time for players in between games.'
Best batting: 126 Midlands v Manicaland, Mutare 2002-03
Best bowling: 6-82 Midlands v Mashonaland, Kwekwe 2002-03

2007 Season

	M	Inn	NO	Runs	HS	Avg	100	50	Ct	St	Balls	Runs	Wkts	Avg	BB	5I	10M
Test																	
FC	7	10	2	276	103 *	34.50	1	1	5	-	899	549	8	68.62	2-48	-	-
ODI																	
List A	15	15	3	480	80 *	40.00	-	6	7	-	509	550	14	39.28	2-13	-	
20/20 Int																	
20/20	6	6	1	134	50 *	26.80	-	1	4	-	60	81	1	81.00	1-42	-	

Career Performances

	M	Inn	NO	Runs	HS	Avg	100	50	Ct	St	Balls	Runs	Wkts	Avg	BB	5I	10M
Test	5	8	0	261	86	32.62	-	3	7	-	570	388	9	43.11	4-146	-	-
FC	70	110	12	3075	126	31.37	5	17	63	-	8602	5271	135	39.04	6-82	5	-
ODI	42	34	7	698	100	25.85	1	2	5	-	1649	1561	41	38.07	3-29	-	
List A	122	108	18	2646	104	29.40	3	13	30	-	4630	4178	129	32.38	5-50	2	
20/20 Int																	
20/20	16	13	1	252	50 *	21.00	-	1	6	-	210	299	12	24.91	3-18	-	

EVANS, D. Middlesex

Name: Daniel (Danny) Evans
Role: Right-hand bat, right-arm fast-medium bowler
Born: 24 July 1987, Hartlepool
Height: 6ft 6in **Weight:** 15st
Nickname: Hightower, Stella, Asbo
County debut: 2007
Parents: Richard and Barbara
Marital status: Single
Family links with cricket: 'Brother played for Durham; he now plays for Newcastle. My dad played a little bit, too; he said he was awesome'
Education: Brierton Comprehensive, Hartlepool
Qualifications: 9 GCSEs, GNVQ in IT
Off-season: 'Keeping fit; also attending England Skills Sets at Loughborough'
Overseas tours: England U17 to Netherlands 2003; MCC A to Papua New Guinea and New Zealand 2007
Overseas teams played for: Tea Tree Gully, Adelaide 2006
Career highlights to date: 'Making debut at Lord's, getting a wicket maiden first over'
Cricket moments to forget: 'Getting a run of ducks towards the end of the season in 2007'
Cricketers particularly admired: Brett Lee, Steve Harmison
Young players to look out for: Billy Godleman, Steve Finn, Eoin Morgan
Other sports played: Five-a-side football, rugby (West Hartlepool RUFC)
Other sports followed: Football (Newcastle)
Favourite band: Bloc Party, The Verve, Oasis
Relaxations: 'Poker, pool, films'
Extras: Attended Darren Lehmann Academy, Adelaide 2006. Dismissed Craig Spearman in wicket maiden first over on first-class debut v Gloucestershire at Lord's 2007
Opinions on cricket: 'Youngsters should be given more of a chance. I think we play too much as well, players not getting enough rest between games.'
Best batting: 7 Middlesex v Essex, Chelmsford 2007
Best bowling: 3-31 Middlesex v Gloucestershire, Bristol 2007

2007 Season

	M	Inn	NO	Runs	HS	Avg	100	50	Ct	St	Balls	Runs	Wkts	Avg	BB	5I	10M
Test																	
FC	4	5	1	7	7	1.75	-	-	1	-	324	169	5	33.80	3-31	-	-
ODI																	
List A																	
20/20 Int																	
20/20																	

Career Performances

	M	Inn	NO	Runs	HS	Avg	100	50	Ct	St	Balls	Runs	Wkts	Avg	BB	5I	10M
Test																	
FC	4	5	1	7	7	1.75	-	-	1	-	324	169	5	33.80	3-31	-	-
ODI																	
List A																	
20/20 Int																	
20/20																	

EVANS, L. — Durham

Name: Luke Evans
Role: Right-hand bat, right-arm fast bowler
Born: 26 April 1987, Sunderland
Height: 6ft 7in **Weight:** 13st 6lbs
Nickname: Daisy Duke, Longshanks, Lukey, Evo
County debut: 2007
Parents: Gayle and Stephen
Marital status: Single ('long-term girlfriend')
Family links with cricket: 'I feel obliged to mention my dad's role as an anchor batsman for Farringdon School in the 1970s…so he says'
Education: St Aidan's Comprehensive RC School
Qualifications: 10 GCSEs, 2 A-levels
Career outside cricket: 'Guitar and bass tuition'
Off-season: 'Resting well, then working on strength and conditioning; looking to do some bowling abroad in the New Year'
Overseas tours: Durham CCC to Dubai 2006, to Cape Town 2007

Career highlights to date: 'First-class debut against Sri Lanka A. Forty wickets in the 2nd XI Championship in 2007'
Cricket moments to forget: 'Any attempted slower balls that end up as beamers'
Cricket superstitions: 'None'
Cricketers particularly admired: Curtly Ambrose, Jason Gillespie, Stephen Harmison, Ottis Gibson
Young players to look out for: Andrew Smith, Scott Borthwick, Karl Turner, Ben Stokes
Other sports played: Basketball (school), darts ('casual player')
Other sports followed: Football (Sunderland AFC)
Favourite band: Black Label Society, Pantera, Van Halen, Extreme, Soundgarden, RATM ('anything with frightening guitar skill')
Relaxations: 'Fine art, playing guitar, learning piano, going to the driving range'
Extras: Represented ECB Development of Excellence XI v Bangladesh U19 2004. Represented England U17 v MCC YC. City of Sunderland Young Achievers Award for Sport 2004. Sue Wright Sporting Achievement Award (from school)
Opinions on cricket: 'I think a greater effort should be made to implement a universal ball to be used everywhere in the world.'
Best batting: 1 Durham v Sri Lanka A, Riverside 2007
Best bowling: 2-39 Durham v Sri Lanka A, Riverside 2007

2007 Season

	M	Inn	NO	Runs	HS	Avg	100	50	Ct	St	Balls	Runs	Wkts	Avg	BB	5I	10M
Test																	
FC	1	2	1	1	1	1.00	-	-	-	-	121	115	4	28.75	2-39	-	-
ODI																	
List A																	
20/20 Int																	
20/20																	

Career Performances

	M	Inn	NO	Runs	HS	Avg	100	50	Ct	St	Balls	Runs	Wkts	Avg	BB	5I	10M
Test																	
FC	1	2	1	1	1	1.00	-	-	-	-	121	115	4	28.75	2-39	-	-
ODI																	
List A																	
20/20 Int																	
20/20																	

EVANS, L. J. — Surrey

Name: Laurie John Evans
Role: Right-hand bat, right-arm fast-medium bowler; all-rounder
Born: 12 October 1987, Lambeth, London
Height: 6ft **Weight:** 13st 3lbs
Nickname: Lau, Evs, Augustus ('because I eat a lot')
County debut: No first-team appearance
Place in batting averages: 29th av. 52.14
Parents: Sue and Marcus
Marital status: Single
Education: John Fisher, Purley; Whitgift School, South Croydon; Durham University
Qualifications: BTEC Sport, 3 A-levels
Overseas tours: Surrey Academy to South Africa 2006
Cricket moments to forget: 'I only dropped three catches all season in 2005 and they were all in the U17 national final v Yorkshire'
Cricket superstitions: 'None'
Cricketers particularly admired: Mark Ramprakash
Young players to look out for: Simon King, Zafar Ansari
Other sports played: Rugby (Harlequins Academy; won U15 *Daily Mail* National Schools Cup with Whitgift v Millfield at Twickenham 2003)
Other sports followed: Football (Arsenal)
Favourite band: James Brown, 112, Usher, Arctic Monkeys
Relaxations: 'Love cooking, clothes'
Extras: Represented ECB Development of Excellence XI v India U19 2006. Played for Durham UCCE 2007, scoring 133* v Lancashire at Durham. Played for MCC v West Indians at Durham 2007, scoring 51
Opinions on cricket: 'The game today is more exciting than ever. It's got quicker and more interesting to spectators. However, I think that it shouldn't be changed too much, otherwise it will lose its history and essence.'
Best batting: 133* DUCCE v Lancashire, Durham 2007

2007 Season (did not make any first-class or one-day appearances for his county)

Career Performances

	M	Inn	NO	Runs	HS	Avg	100	50	Ct	St	Balls	Runs	Wkts	Avg	BB	5I	10M
Test																	
FC	4	8	1	365	133 *	52.14	1	2	4	-	0	0	0		-	-	-
ODI																	
List A																	
20/20 Int																	
20/20																	

FERLEY, R. S. — Nottinghamshire

Name: Robert Steven Ferley
Role: Right-hand bat, left-arm spin bowler
Born: 4 February 1982, Norwich
Height: 5ft 8in **Weight:** 12st 4lbs
Nickname: Mr Shaky Shake, Billy Bob, Bob Turkey
County debut: 2003 (Kent), 2007 (Nottinghamshire)
Parents: Pam and Tim (divorced)
Marital status: Single
Education: King Edward VII High School; Sutton Valence School (A-levels); Grey College, Durham University
Qualifications: 10 GCSEs, 3 A-levels
Overseas tours: England U19 to India 2000-01; British Universities to South Africa 2002
Cricketers particularly admired: Steve Waugh, Steve Marsh, Min Patel, Charles Clarke
Other sports played: Rugby, hockey, tennis, football
Other sports followed: Football (Liverpool)
Relaxations: 'Films, interior design, keeping fit'
Extras: Represented England U17 1999. Played for Durham UCCE 2001, 2002 and 2003. Represented British Universities 2001, 2002 and 2003. Represented England U19 2001. Took 4-76 on Championship debut v Surrey at The Oval 2003
Best batting: 78* DUCCE v Durham, Durham 2003
Best bowling: 6-136 Kent v Middlesex, Canterbury 2006

2007 Season

	M	Inn	NO	Runs	HS	Avg	100	50	Ct	St	Balls	Runs	Wkts	Avg	BB	5I	10M
Test																	
FC	3	3	2	85	43 *	85.00	-	-	-	-	378	283	1	283.00	1-151	-	-
ODI																	
List A	8	1	0	13	13	13.00	-	-	4	-	375	331	10	33.10	3-32	-	
20/20 Int																	
20/20	4	2	0	0	0	0.00	-	-	-	-	75	88	3	29.33	2-29	-	

Career Performances

	M	Inn	NO	Runs	HS	Avg	100	50	Ct	St	Balls	Runs	Wkts	Avg	BB	5I	10M
Test																	
FC	29	37	9	587	78 *	20.96	-	2	8	-	4146	2551	55	46.38	6-136	1	-
ODI																	
List A	40	19	5	239	42	17.07	-	-	16	-	1801	1445	51	28.33	4-33	-	
20/20 Int																	
20/20	10	4	2	17	16 *	8.50	-	-	2	-	165	228	5	45.60	2-29	-	

FERRABY, N. J. Leicestershire

Name: Nicholas (Nick) John Ferraby
Role: Right-hand bat, right-arm medium bowler
Born: 31 May 1983, Market Harborough, Leicestershire
Height: 6ft
Nickname: Furbs, Ferrers
County debut: 2007 (one-day)
Education: Oakham School; Loughborough University
Qualifications: 9 GCSEs, 2 A-levels, 2.1 in Sport and Leisure Management, Level 1 coaching
Overseas tours: Leicestershire U19 to Johannesburg 2000-01; Kibworth CC to Barbados (Fred Rumsey Cricket Festival) 2004
Overseas teams played for: Belville CC, Cape Town 2004-05
Other sports played: Hockey (England U16, U18 – 'gold medal in European competition' – and U21; Loughborough Students – 'National Prem')
Extras: Leicestershire Young Batsman of the Year 2000. Played for Leicestershire Board XI in the 2003 C&G. Played for Loughborough UCCE 2003, 2004. Played for

Cambridgeshire in Minor Counties competitions 2006, 2007. Formerly on the Leicestershire staff; played one Pro40 match for Leicestershire 2007

2007 Season

	M	Inn	NO	Runs	HS	Avg	100	50	Ct	St	Balls	Runs	Wkts	Avg	BB	5I	10M
Test																	
FC																	
ODI																	
List A	1	1	1	13	13 *		-	-	-	-	0	0	0		-	-	
20/20 Int																	
20/20																	

Career Performances

	M	Inn	NO	Runs	HS	Avg	100	50	Ct	St	Balls	Runs	Wkts	Avg	BB	5I	10M
Test																	
FC																	
ODI																	
List A	3	3	1	14	13 *	7.00	-	-	-	-	42	31	0		-	-	
20/20 Int																	
20/20																	

FINCH, J. M. — Yorkshire

Name: James Matthew Finch
Role: Right-hand lower-order bat, off-spin bowler
Born: 17 November 1988, Leeds
Height: 6ft 3in **Weight:** 15st
Nickname: Dog, Finchy
County debut: No first-team appearance
Parents: Paul and Mandy
Marital status: Single
Family links with cricket: 'Dad played local league cricket. Twin sister does a bit of scoring. Mum is a passionate fan'
Education: Guiseley School
Qualifications: 10 GCSEs, 2 A-levels, GNVQ in Cricket, Level 2 coach
Career outside cricket: 'Do a bit of coaching'
Off-season: 'Two months in South Africa, then back home to train hard'

Overseas teams played for: St Andrews, Bloemfontein 2006-07; Old Andreans CC, Bloemfontein 2007-08
Career highlights to date: 'Getting a professional contract with Yorkshire and my time spent playing in Bloemfontein'
Cricket moments to forget: 'My grandad passing away whilst I was playing in South Africa in January 2007'
Cricket superstitions: 'Try to come out of the changing room either second or last'
Cricketers particularly admired: Daniel Vettori, Marcus Trescothick, Gareth Batty
Young players to look out for: Chris Allinson, Simon Tennant, Ian Hartley
Other sports played: Golf, snooker, five-a-side football
Other sports followed: Football (Man Utd), rugby league (Leeds Rhinos), rugby union (Free State Cheetahs)
Favourite band: Plain White T's
Relaxations: 'Going out with friends; watching films'
Extras: Returned the best figures by a Yorkshire Schoolboy as an U14 (17-4-24-8) v Northamptonshire at Oundle School. Attended Yorkshire Academy
Opinions on cricket: 'I think the general opinion that you have to be a wrist spinner to succeed as a spin bowler in the modern game is wrong.'

FINN, S. T. — Middlesex

Name: Steven Thomas Finn
Role: Right-hand bat, right-arm fast-medium bowler
Born: 4 April 1989, Watford
Height: 6ft 7in **Weight:** 13st 9lbs
Nickname: Finny, Lurch, Streak
County debut: 2005
Place in bowling averages: 11th av. 21.72
Parents: Diana and Terry
Marital status: Single
Family links with cricket: 'Dad played top-level club cricket/Minor Counties. Grandad played club cricket'
Education: Parmiter's School, Watford, Herts
Qualifications: 10 GCSEs, 3 A-levels
Off-season: 'U19 World Cup in Malaysia; journalism'
Overseas tours: England U16 to South Africa 2004-05; England U19 to Malaysia 2006-07, to Malaysia (U19 World Cup) 2007-08; England Performance Programme to India 2007-08
Career highlights to date: 'First-class debut. Debut at Lord's'

Cricket moments to forget: 'Third man out in a hat-trick v India U19 2006'
Cricket superstitions: 'Too many to mention'
Cricketers particularly admired: Glenn McGrath
Young players to look out for: Billy Godleman, Dan Housego, Rhys Williams, Alex Wakely
Other sports played: Basketball (county), football (district)
Other sports followed: Football (Watford)
Favourite band: Coldplay, Arctic Monkeys
Relaxations: 'Music'
Extras: Has represented England U15, U16, U17 and U19. Youngest person to play first-class cricket for Middlesex since Fred Titmus in 1949
Opinions on cricket: 'Pleased to see countless opportunities for young players to show what they can do.'
Best batting: 3 Middlesex v Essex, Chelmsford 2007
Best bowling: 4-51 Middlesex v Gloucestershire, Bristol 2007
Stop press: Called up to the England Performance Programme in India 2007-08 as a replacement for the injured Luke Wright

2007 Season

	M	Inn	NO	Runs	HS	Avg	100	50	Ct	St	Balls	Runs	Wkts	Avg	BB	5I	10M
Test																	
FC	3	5	2	4	3	1.33	-	-	-	-	437	239	11	21.72	4-51	-	-
ODI																	
List A	5	1	0	2	2	2.00	-	-	-	-	186	152	8	19.00	3-23	-	
20/20 Int																	
20/20																	

Career Performances

	M	Inn	NO	Runs	HS	Avg	100	50	Ct	St	Balls	Runs	Wkts	Avg	BB	5I	10M
Test																	
FC	4	5	2	4	3	1.33	-	-	-	-	557	292	13	22.46	4-51	-	-
ODI																	
List A	5	1	0	2	2	2.00	-	-	-	-	186	152	8	19.00	3-23	-	
20/20 Int																	
20/20																	

24. Which Somerset player and future Test umpire was called up from his coaching job in Johannesburg to represent England in the fifth Test at Port Elizabeth in 1964-65?

FISHER, I. D. Gloucestershire

Name: Ian Douglas Fisher
Role: Left-hand bat, left-arm spin bowler
Born: 31 March 1976, Bradford
Height: 5ft 11in **Weight:** 13st 6lbs
Nickname: Fish, Flash, Fishy
County debut: 1995-96 (Yorkshire), 2002 (Gloucestershire)
County cap: 2004 (Gloucestershire)
Place in batting averages: 272nd av. 11.16 (2006 161st av. 28.00)
Place in bowling averages: (2006 147th av. 75.50)
Parents: Geoff and Linda
Marital status: Single
Family links with cricket: Father played club cricket
Education: Beckfoot Grammar School
Qualifications: 9 GCSEs, NCA coaching award, sports leader's award, lifesaver (bronze), YMCA gym instructor
Overseas tours: Yorkshire to Zimbabwe 1996, to South Africa 1998, 1999, 2001, to Perth 2000; MCC to Sri Lanka 2001
Overseas teams played for: Somerset West, Cape Town 1994-95; Petone Riverside, Wellington, New Zealand 1997-98
Career highlights to date: 'Winning the Championship with Yorkshire [2001]'
Cricket moments to forget: 'My pair'
Cricketers particularly admired: Darren Lehmann, Shane Warne
Other sports played: Football (Westbrook)
Other sports followed: Football (Leeds United)
Relaxations: Music, movies, catching up with friends, shopping, eating out
Extras: Played England U17 and Yorkshire Schools U15, U16 and Yorkshire U19. Bowled the last first-class ball delivered at Northlands Road, Southampton, September 2000. Recorded three Championship five-wicket returns in successive innings 2003, including his maiden ten-wicket match (5-30/5-93) v Durham at Bristol
Best batting: 103* Gloucestershire v Essex, Gloucester 2002
Best bowling: 5-30 Gloucestershire v Durham, Bristol 2003

2007 Season

	M	Inn	NO	Runs	HS	Avg	100	50	Ct	St	Balls	Runs	Wkts	Avg	BB	5I	10M
Test																	
FC	3	6	0	67	41	11.16	-	-	1	-	330	153	2	76.50	1-58	-	-
ODI																	
List A	12	8	2	94	37 *	15.66	-	-	3	-	473	474	9	52.66	3-40	-	
20/20 Int																	
20/20	9	4	1	11	6	3.66	-	-	7	-	125	134	8	16.75	3-7	-	

Career Performances

	M	Inn	NO	Runs	HS	Avg	100	50	Ct	St	Balls	Runs	Wkts	Avg	BB	5I	10M
Test																	
FC	78	118	19	2197	103 *	22.19	1	7	27	-	12390	6706	157	42.71	5-30	7	1
ODI																	
List A	66	40	13	288	37 *	10.66	-	-	20	-	2571	1997	67	29.80	3-18	-	
20/20 Int																	
20/20	25	9	4	41	9 *	8.20	-	-	14	-	329	439	22	19.95	4-22	-	

FLEMING, S. P. — Nottinghamshire

Name: Stephen Paul Fleming
Role: Left-hand bat, occasional right-arm slow-medium bowler
Born: 1 April 1973, Christchurch, New Zealand
Height: 6ft 3in
County debut: 2001 (Middlesex), 2003 (Yorkshire), 2005 (Nottinghamshire)
County cap: 2001 (Middlesex), 2005 (Notts)
Test debut: 1993-94
ODI debut: 1993-94
Twenty20 Int debut: 2004-05
1000 runs in a season: 1
1st-Class 200s: 5
Place in batting averages: 14th av. 58.12 (2006 45th av. 49.60)
Wife and date of marriage: Kelly, May 2007
Education: Cashmere High School; Christchurch College of Education
Overseas tours: New Zealand U19 to India 1991-92; New Zealand to England 1994, to South Africa 1994-95, to India 1995-96, to India and Pakistan (World Cup) 1995-96, to West Indies 1995-96, to Pakistan 1996-97, to Zimbabwe 1997-98 (c), to

Australia 1997-98 (c), to Sri Lanka 1997-98 (c), to Bangladesh (Wills International Cup) 1998-99 (c), to UK, Ireland and Netherlands (World Cup) 1999 (c), to England 1999 (c), to India 1999-2000 (c), to Zimbabwe 2000-01 (c), to Kenya (ICC Knockout Trophy) 2000-01 (c), to South Africa 2000-01 (c), to Australia 2001-02 (c), to Pakistan 2002 (c), to West Indies 2002 (c), to Sri Lanka (ICC Champions Trophy) 2002-03 (c), to Africa (World Cup) 2002-03 (c), to Sri Lanka 2003 (c), to India 2003-04 (c), to England 2004 (c), to England (ICC Champions Trophy) 2004 (c), to Bangladesh 2004-05 (c), to Australia 2004-05 (c), to Zimbabwe 2005-06 (c), to South Africa 2005-06 (c), to India (ICC Champions Trophy) 2006-07 (c), to West Indies (World Cup) 2006-07 (c), to South Africa 2007-08, plus other one-day tournaments in Sharjah, India, Singapore, Sri Lanka and Australia; ICC World XI to Australia (Tsunami Relief) 2004-05

Overseas teams played for: Canterbury 1991-92 – 1999-2000; Wellington 2000-01 –

Extras: Captain of New Zealand 1996-97 – 2007. Led his country to series victory in England in 1999, which included New Zealand's first wins at Lord's and The Oval. His Test awards include Man of the Match in the first Test v Pakistan at Hamilton 2003-04 (192) and in the second Test v South Africa at Cape Town 2005-06 (262). Has won numerous ODI awards, including Man of the Match for his 134* v South Africa at Johannesburg in the 2002-03 World Cup and Man of the NatWest Series in England 2004. One of *New Zealand Cricket Almanack*'s two Players of the Year 1998, 2003, 2004. Is New Zealand's most-capped Test player and highest Test run-scorer. Was Middlesex overseas player in 2001; was a Yorkshire overseas player in 2003; was an overseas player with Nottinghamshire and captain 2005-07. Retired from ODI cricket in September 2007

Best batting: 274* New Zealand v Sri Lanka, Colombo (PSS) 2002-03

2007 Season

	M	Inn	NO	Runs	HS	Avg	100	50	Ct	St	Balls	Runs	Wkts	Avg	BB	5I	10M
Test																	
FC	11	17	1	930	243	58.12	4	2	21	-	0	0	0		-	-	-
ODI																	
List A	10	10	0	384	107	38.40	1	3	7	-	0	0	0		-	-	
20/20 Int																	
20/20	6	6	0	117	49	19.50	-	-	3	-	0	0	0		-	-	

Career Performances

	M	Inn	NO	Runs	HS	Avg	100	50	Ct	St	Balls	Runs	Wkts	Avg	BB	5I	10M
Test	104	177	10	6620	274 *	39.64	9	41	159	-	0	0	0		-	-	-
FC	239	392	32	15819	274 *	43.94	35	88	327	-	102	129	0		-	-	-
ODI	280	269	21	8037	134 *	32.40	8	49	133	-	29	28	1	28.00	1-8	-	
List A	455	433	38	13667	139 *	34.60	22	82	223	-	35	31	2	15.50	1-3	-	
20/20 Int	5	5	0	110	38	22.00	-	-	2	-	0	0	0		-	-	
20/20	33	33	1	755	64 *	23.59	-	5	10	-	0	0	0		-	-	

FLINTOFF, A. — Lancashire

Name: Andrew Flintoff
Role: Right-hand bat, right-arm fast-medium bowler; all-rounder
Born: 6 December 1977, Preston
Height: 6ft 4in
Nickname: Freddie
County debut: 1995
County cap: 1998
Benefit: 2006
Test debut: 1998
ODI debut: 1998-99
Twenty20 Int debut: 2005
Place in bowling averages: (2006 41st av. 29.28)
Parents: Colin and Susan
Wife and date of marriage: Rachael, 5 March 2005
Children: Holly, 6 September 2004; Corey, 8 March 2006
Family links with cricket: Brother Chris and father both local league cricketers
Education: Ribbleton Hall High School, Preston
Qualifications: 9 GCSEs
Overseas tours: England Schools U15 to South Africa 1993; England U19 to West Indies 1994-95, to Zimbabwe 1995-96, to Pakistan 1996-97 (c); England A to Kenya and Sri Lanka 1997-98, to Zimbabwe and South Africa 1998-99; England to Sharjah (Coca-Cola Cup) 1998-99, to South Africa and Zimbabwe 1999-2000, to Kenya (ICC Knockout Trophy) 2000-01, to Pakistan and (one-day series) Sri Lanka 2000-01, to Zimbabwe (one-day series) 2001-02, to India and New Zealand 2001-02, to Australia 2002-03, to Africa (World Cup) 2002-03, to Bangladesh and Sri Lanka 2003-04, to West Indies 2003-04, to South Africa 2004-05, to Pakistan 2005-06, to India 2005-06, to India (ICC Champions Trophy) 2006-07 (c), to Australia 2006-07 (Test c), to West Indies (World Cup) 2006-07, to South Africa (World 20/20) 2007-08; ECB National Academy to Australia 2001-02; England VI to Hong Kong 2001; ICC World XI to Australia (Super Series) 2005-06
Other sports/games played: Represented Lancashire Schools at chess
Injuries: Out for much of the 2007 season with a recurrence of an ankle problem
Extras: Represented England U14 to U19. Cricket Writers' Club Young Player of the Year and PCA Young Player of the Year 1998. Scored first century before lunch by a Lancashire batsman in a Roses match, v Yorkshire at Old Trafford 1999. Won the EDS Walter Lawrence Trophy 1999 (for the fastest first-class century of the season). Lancashire Player of the Year 2000. Vice-captain of Lancashire 2002. BBC North West

Sports Personality of the Year 2003. One of *Wisden*'s Five Cricketers of the Year 2004. Vodafone England Cricketer of the Year 2003-04 and 2005-06. Shared with Andrew Strauss in a record stand for any wicket for England in ODIs (226), v West Indies at Lord's in the NatWest Series 2004. His Test awards include England's Man of the Series v West Indies 2004 and v Australia 2005 (plus the inaugural Compton-Miller Medal 2005 for Ashes Player of the Series), and Man of the Series v India 2005-06. His ODI awards include Man of the NatWest Series 2003 and Man of the Series v Bangladesh 2003-04. Winner of inaugural ICC One-Day Player of the Year award 2003-04. PCA Player of the Year award 2004, 2005. ICC Player of the Year award (jointly with Jacques Kallis) 2005. BBC Sports Personality of the Year 2005. Appointed MBE in 2006 New Year Honours as part of 2005 Ashes-winning England team. Has captained England in the absence of Michael Vaughan. England 12-month central contract 2007-08

Best batting: 167 England v West Indies, Edgbaston 2004

Best bowling: 5-24 Lancashire v Hampshire, Southampton 1999

2007 Season

	M	Inn	NO	Runs	HS	Avg	100	50	Ct	St	Balls	Runs	Wkts	Avg	BB	5I	10M
Test																	
FC	3	4	0	128	61	32.00	-	1	4	-	209	120	5	24.00	3-38	-	-
ODI	4	2	0	14	9	7.00	-	-	2	-	213	144	10	14.40	5-56	1	
List A	8	6	0	142	66	23.66	-	1	3	-	297	201	12	16.75	5-56	1	
20/20 Int																	
20/20	1	1	0	3	3	3.00	-	-	-	-	18	24	1	24.00	1-24	-	

Career Performances

	M	Inn	NO	Runs	HS	Avg	100	50	Ct	St	Balls	Runs	Wkts	Avg	BB	5I	10M
Test	67	110	6	3381	167	32.50	5	24	44	-	12562	6308	197	32.02	5-58	2	-
FC	163	257	18	8343	167	34.90	15	49	168	-	19183	9452	297	31.82	5-24	3	-
ODI	127	112	14	3090	123	31.53	3	16	41	-	5026	3665	146	25.10	5-56	1	
List A	265	238	25	6292	143	29.53	6	32	99	-	8692	6035	262	23.03	5-56	1	
20/20 Int	7	7	1	76	31	12.66	-	-	5	-	150	161	5	32.20	2-23	-	
20/20	15	15	1	318	85	22.71	-	1	7	-	281	309	14	22.07	3-4	-	

25. Which current Northamptonshire all-rounder scored a then ground Test record 174 at Port Elizabeth in the second Test between England and South Africa in 1999-2000?

FLOWER, G. W. Essex

Name: Grant William Flower
Role: Right-hand top-order bat, left-arm spin bowler; all-rounder
Born: 20 December 1970, Harare, Zimbabwe
Height: 5ft 10in **Weight:** 11st
Nickname: Gobby
County debut: 2002 (Leicestershire), 2005 (Essex)
County cap: 2005 (Essex)
Test debut: 1992-93
ODI debut: 1992-93
1st-Class 200s: 4
Place in batting averages: 66th av. 40.73 (2006 116th av. 33.09)
Parents: Bill and Jean
Marital status: Single
Family links with cricket: Younger brother of Andy Flower (formerly of Zimbabwe and Essex and now England assistant coach)
Education: St George's College, Harare
Qualifications: 8 O-levels, 1 A-level, Level 3 coaching
Career outside cricket: Coaching
Off-season: 'Coaching, training, travelling, drinking'
Overseas tours: Zimbabwe to India 1992-93, to Pakistan 1993-94, to Australia (one-day series) 1994-95, to New Zealand 1995-96, to India and Pakistan (World Cup) 1995-96, to Sri Lanka and Pakistan 1996-97, to Sri Lanka and New Zealand 1997-98, to Bangladesh (Wills International Cup) 1998-99, to Pakistan 1998-99, to UK, Ireland and Netherlands (World Cup) 1999, to South Africa 1999-2000, to West Indies 1999-2000, to England 2000, to Kenya (ICC Knockout Trophy) 2000-01, to India 2000-01, to New Zealand and Australia 2000-01, to Bangladesh, Sri Lanka and India 2001-02, to Sri Lanka (ICC Champions Trophy) 2002-03, to England 2003, to Australia 2003-04 (VB Series), plus other one-day tournaments in Sharjah, South Africa, Kenya, India, Bangladesh and Singapore
Overseas teams played for: Mashonaland 1994-95 – 2003-04
Career highlights to date: 'Scoring 201* v Pakistan in 1994-95 in our first Test match victory in Harare'
Cricket moments to forget: 'Losing to Kenya in the 2002-03 World Cup for Zimbabwe'
Cricket superstitions: 'None'
Cricketers particularly admired: Graeme Hick, Sachin Tendulkar
Young players to look out for: 'Many'

Other sports played: Squash, tennis
Other sports followed: Squash, tennis, football, rugby, golf
Relaxations: 'Reading, TV, films, fishing and drinking'
Extras: Appeared in Zimbabwe's inaugural Test, v India at Harare 1992-93. Scored 201* v Pakistan at Harare 1994-95 in Zimbabwe's first Test win, in the process sharing with Andy Flower (156) in a record fourth-wicket stand for Zimbabwe in Tests (269). Became the first player to score a hundred in each innings of a Test for Zimbabwe (104/151) in the first Test v New Zealand at Harare 1997-98. His Test awards include Man of the Series v New Zealand 1997-98. His ODI awards include Zimbabwe's Man of the Series v Pakistan 1996-97, as well as Man of the Match v England at Trent Bridge in the NatWest Series 2003 (96*) and v Australia at Adelaide in the VB Series 2003-04 (94). Was Leicestershire's overseas player during June 2002. Announced his retirement from international cricket in 2004. Is no longer considered an overseas player
Opinions on cricket: 'Still too much cricket and not enough quality time to prepare physically and mentally for the next game. Forty-over competition should be scrapped but because of financial implications for the counties, this will not happen. County committees are not interested in players' opinions.'
Best batting: 243* Mashonaland v Matabeleland, Harare (A) 1996-97
Best bowling: 7-31 Zimbabweans v Lahore City, Lahore 1998-99

2007 Season

	M	Inn	NO	Runs	HS	Avg	100	50	Ct	St	Balls	Runs	Wkts	Avg	BB	5I	10M
Test																	
FC	11	16	1	611	203	40.73	2	1	17	-	96	54	1	54.00	1-50	-	-
ODI																	
List A	10	9	0	203	55	22.55	-	3	2	-	114	108	0		-	-	
20/20 Int																	
20/20	7	6	0	140	40	23.33	-	-	1	-	0	0	0		-	-	

Career Performances

	M	Inn	NO	Runs	HS	Avg	100	50	Ct	St	Balls	Runs	Wkts	Avg	BB	5I	10M
Test	67	123	6	3457	201 *	29.54	6	15	43	-	3378	1537	25	61.48	4-41	-	-
FC	179	305	23	10679	243 *	37.86	23	58	168	-	12331	5504	163	33.76	7-31	3	-
ODI	219	212	18	6536	142 *	33.69	6	40	86	-	5420	4187	104	40.25	4-32	-	
List A	324	309	26	9516	148 *	33.62	11	62	127	-	8356	6190	176	35.17	4-32	-	
20/20 Int																	
20/20	16	9	2	147	40	21.00	-	-	4	-	142	194	10	19.40	3-20	-	

FOOTITT, M. H. A. Nottinghamshire

Name: Mark Harold Alan Footitt
Role: Right-hand bat, left-arm fast bowler
Born: 25 November 1985, Nottingham
Height: 6ft 2in **Weight:** 12st 7lbs
Nickname: Footy
County debut: 2005
Parents: Graham and Julie
Marital status: Engaged to Kerry Ann Pashley
Family links with cricket: 'Dad and grandad played local cricket'
Education: Carlton le Willows School
Qualifications: 3 GCSEs, Level 1 coaching
Overseas tours: Nottinghamshire to South Africa 2006
Career highlights to date: 'Playing my first game for Notts. Being picked for the National Academy 2006'

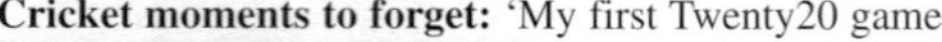

Cricket moments to forget: 'My first Twenty20 game'
Cricket superstitions: 'None'
Cricketers particularly admired: Brett Lee
Other sports played: Football
Other sports followed: Football (Man Utd)
Favourite band: The Killers
Relaxations: 'Playing on PS2 and PC; watching TV/DVDs'
Extras: Attended MRF Pace Foundation, India 2000, 2001, 2006. Played for Nottinghamshire Board XI in the 2002 C&G. Represented England U19 2005. ECB National Academy 2005-06
Best batting: 19* Nottinghamshire v Hampshire, Rose Bowl 2005
Best bowling: 5-45 Nottinghamshire v West Indies A, Trent Bridge 2006

2007 Season

	M	Inn	NO	Runs	HS	Avg	100	50	Ct	St	Balls	Runs	Wkts	Avg	BB	5I	10M
Test																	
FC	3	0	0	0	0		-	-	-	-	274	191	7	27.28	5-59	1	-
ODI																	
List A																	
20/20 Int																	
20/20																	

Career Performances

	M	Inn	NO	Runs	HS	Avg	100	50	Ct	St	Balls	Runs	Wkts	Avg	BB	5I	10M
Test																	
FC	8	6	4	40	19 *	20.00	-	-	1	-	835	671	20	33.55	5-45	2	-
ODI																	
List A	1	0	0	0	0		-	-	-	-	18	18	0			-	-
20/20 Int																	
20/20	1	0	0	0	0		-	-	-	-	12	34	0			-	-

FOSTER, J. S. — Essex

Name: James Savin Foster
Role: Right-hand bat, wicket-keeper, county vice-captain
Born: 15 April 1980, Whipps Cross, London
Height: 6ft **Weight:** 12st
Nickname: Fozzy, Chief
County debut: 2000
County cap: 2001
Test debut: 2001-02
ODI debut: 2001-02
1000 runs in a season: 1
50 dismissals in a season: 3
1st-Class 200s: 2
Place in batting averages: 89th av. 37.59 (2006 49th av. 48.35)
Parents: Martin and Diana
Marital status: Single
Family links with cricket: 'Dad played for Essex Amateurs'
Education: Forest School; Durham University
Qualifications: 10 GCSEs, 3 A-levels, hockey and cricket Level 1 coaching awards
Overseas tours: BUSA to South Africa 1999; Durham University to South Africa 1999, to Vienna (European Indoor Championships) 1999; England A to West Indies 2000-01; England to Zimbabwe (one-day series) 2001-02, to India and New Zealand 2001-02, to Australia 2002-03; England Lions to India 2007-08
Overseas teams played for: Claremont-Nedlands, Perth 2006-07
Career highlights to date: 'Playing for my country'
Cricketers particularly admired: Nasser Hussain, Stuart Law, Robert Rollins, Ian Healy, Jack Russell, Alec Stewart, Adam Gilchrist
Other sports played: Hockey (Essex U21), tennis (played for GB U14 v Sweden U14; national training squad)

Other sports followed: Football
Relaxations: 'Socialising'
Extras: Essex U17 Player of the Year 1997. Represented ECB U19 1998 and England U19 1999. Represented BUSA 1999, 2000 and 2001. Voted Essex Cricket Society 2nd XI Player of the Year 2000. Played for Durham UCCE 2001. NBC Denis Compton Award for the most promising young Essex player 2001. Achieved double (1037 first-class runs plus 51 dismissals) 2004. Vice-captain of Essex since part-way through the 2007 season
Best batting: 212 Essex v Leicestershire, Chelmsford 2004
Stop press: Called up to squad for England Lions tour to India 2007-08 as a replacement for the injured Steve Davies

2007 Season

	M	Inn	NO	Runs	HS	Avg	100	50	Ct	St	Balls	Runs	Wkts	Avg	BB	5I	10M
Test																	
FC	15	23	1	827	204	37.59	1	5	31	5	0	0	0		-	-	-
ODI																	
List A	15	14	3	281	69 *	25.54	-	2	17	5	0	0	0		-	-	
20/20 Int																	
20/20	8	7	1	135	52	22.50	-	1	3	1	0	0	0		-	-	

Career Performances

	M	Inn	NO	Runs	HS	Avg	100	50	Ct	St	Balls	Runs	Wkts	Avg	BB	5I	10M
Test	7	12	3	226	48	25.11	-	-	17	1	0	0	0		-	-	-
FC	121	177	22	5415	212	34.93	9	27	307	33	12	6	0		-	-	-
ODI	11	6	3	41	13	13.66	-	-	13	7	0	0	0		-	-	
List A	117	90	24	1522	69 *	23.06	-	5	144	32	0	0	0		-	-	
20/20 Int																	
20/20	34	27	5	374	62 *	17.00	-	2	13	11	0	0	0		-	-	

FRANCIS, J. D. — Somerset

Name: John Daniel Francis
Role: Left-hand bat, slow left-arm bowler
Born: 13 November 1980, Bromley, Kent
Height: 5ft 11in **Weight:** 13st
Nickname: Long John, Franky, Junior
County debut: 2001 (Hampshire), 2004 (Somerset)
1000 runs in a season: 1
Place in batting averages: (2006 248th av. 14.55)
Parents: Linda and Daniel
Marital status: Single

Family links with cricket: Brother Simon played for Hampshire, Somerset and Nottinghamshire. Father played club cricket. Grandfather played in the services
Education: King Edward VI, Southampton; Durham and Loughborough Universities
Qualifications: 10 GCSEs, 3 A-levels, BSc Sports Science, ECB Level 1 coaching award
Overseas tours: Twyford School to Barbados 1993; West of England U15 to West Indies 1995; King Edward VI, Southampton to South Africa 1998; Durham University to South Africa 2000; British Universities to South Africa 2002
Career highlights to date: 'Scoring maiden first-class century for Somerset v Yorkshire at Scarborough 2004, sharing in a partnership of 197 runs with Ricky Ponting'

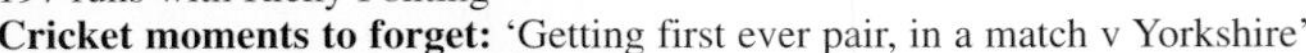

Cricket moments to forget: 'Getting first ever pair, in a match v Yorkshire'
Cricket superstitions: 'Too many to say'
Cricketers particularly admired: Graham Thorpe, Adam Hollioake, Mike Hussey, Simon Francis
Other sports played: Hockey (England U18), golf, squash
Favourite band: David Gray
Relaxations: Drawing and painting, socialising
Extras: Hampshire Young Sportsman of the Year 1995. Sir John Hobbs Silver Jubilee Memorial Prize for outstanding U16 player of the year 1996. Leading run-scorer in U15 World Cup 1996. Played for Loughborough UCCE 2001, 2002 and 2003. NBC Denis Compton Award for the most promising young Hampshire player 2002. Represented British Universities 2002 and 2003
Best batting: 125* Somerset v Yorkshire, Headingley 2005
Best bowling: 1-1 Hampshire v Leicestershire, Leicester 2002

2007 Season

	M	Inn	NO	Runs	HS	Avg	100	50	Ct	St	Balls	Runs	Wkts	Avg	BB	5I	10M
Test																	
FC	1	2	0	40	30	20.00	-	-	-	-	0	0	0		-	-	-
ODI																	
List A																	
20/20 Int																	
20/20	4	4	1	50	35 *	16.66	-	-	1	-	0	0	0		-	-	

Career Performances

	M	Inn	NO	Runs	HS	Avg	100	50	Ct	St	Balls	Runs	Wkts	Avg	BB	5I	10M
Test																	
FC	55	98	8	2678	125 *	29.75	6	14	32	-	273	164	4	41.00	1-1	-	-
ODI																	
List A	65	61	10	1745	103 *	34.21	1	12	15	-	0	0	0			-	-
20/20 Int																	
20/20	14	14	4	271	49	27.10	-	-	1	-	0	0	0			-	-

FRANCIS, S. R. G. Nottinghamshire

Name: Simon Richard George Francis
Role: Right-hand bat, right-arm medium-fast bowler
Born: 15 August 1978, Bromley, Kent
Height: 6ft 1in **Weight:** 14st
Nickname: Franco, Guru
County debut: 1997 (Hampshire), 2002 (Somerset), 2007 (Nottinghamshire)
Parents: Daniel and Linda
Marital status: Single
Family links with cricket: Brother John plays at Somerset. Father played club cricket. Grandfather played for the Navy
Education: King Edward VI, Southampton; Durham University
Qualifications: 9 GCSEs, 1 AS-Level, 3 A-levels, BA (Hons) Sport in the Community, Level 1 coaching in hockey, Level III coaching in cricket
Career outside cricket: Cricket and hockey coaching
Overseas tours: England U17 to Netherlands (International Youth Tournament) 1995; England U19 to Pakistan 1996-97; Durham University to Zimbabwe 1997-98; Hampshire to Boland 2001; England A to Malaysia and India 2003-04
Overseas teams played for: Maties (Stellenbosch University), South Africa 2000; Melville CC, Perth 2001
Cricket moments to forget: 'Whole of the B&H competition 2002'
Cricketers particularly admired: Malcolm Marshall, Richard Hadlee, Allan Donald, Graham Dilley
Other sports played: Golf, hockey (England U18 1995)
Relaxations: 'Films, sleeping, reading, listening to music'
Extras: Played in Durham University's BUSA Championship-winning side 1999.

Took hat-trick v Loughborough UCCE at Taunton 2003. ECB National Academy 2003-04. His 8-66 v Derbyshire at Derby in the C&G 2004 is the best return by a Somerset bowler in one-day cricket. Joined Nottinghamshire during the 2007 season to bolster the pace-bowling department; released by Nottinghamshire at the end of the 2007 season

Best batting: 44 Somerset v Yorkshire, Taunton 2003

Best bowling: 5-42 Somerset v Glamorgan, Taunton 2004

2007 Season

	M	Inn	NO	Runs	HS	Avg	100	50	Ct	St	Balls	Runs	Wkts	Avg	BB	5I	10M
Test																	
FC	2	0	0	0	0		-	-	1	-	72	74	1	74.00	1-43	-	-
ODI																	
List A																	
20/20 Int																	
20/20	2	1	1	8	8 *		-	-	-	-	24	30	1	30.00	1-19	-	

Career Performances

	M	Inn	NO	Runs	HS	Avg	100	50	Ct	St	Balls	Runs	Wkts	Avg	BB	5I	10M
Test																	
FC	60	77	33	509	44	11.56	-	-	19	-	8583	5595	136	41.13	5-42	3	-
ODI																	
List A	70	36	17	240	33 *	12.63	-	-	16	-	2929	2644	77	34.33	8-66	1	
20/20 Int																	
20/20	22	10	5	39	9 *	7.80	-	-	4	-	384	628	11	57.09	2-22	-	

26. Which Essex all-rounder's second innings during the fourth Test between England and South Africa at Headingley in 1955 included a period of 79 minutes without scoring ?

FRANKS, P. J. Nottinghamshire

Name: Paul John Franks
Role: Left-hand bat, right-arm fast-medium bowler; all-rounder
Born: 3 February 1979, Sutton-in-Ashfield
Height: 6ft 2in **Weight:** 14st
Nickname: Franksie, Pike
County debut: 1996
County cap: 1999
Benefit: 2007
ODI debut: 2000
50 wickets in a season: 2
Place in batting averages: 195th av. 22.91 (2006 199th av. 22.11)
Place in bowling averages: 92nd av. 34.06 (2006 146th av. 59.50)
Parents: Patricia and John
Wife and date of marriage: Helen, 1 October 2005
Family links with cricket: 'Dad was league legend for 25 years'
Education: Minster School, Southwell; West Notts College
Qualifications: 7 GCSEs, GNVQ (Advanced) Leisure Management, coaching Level 1
Overseas tours: England U19 to Pakistan 1996-97, to South Africa (including U19 World Cup) 1997-98; England A to Zimbabwe and South Africa 1998-99, to Bangladesh and New Zealand 1999-2000, to West Indies 2000-01, to Sri Lanka 2004-05; Notts CCC to South Africa 1998, 1999
Overseas teams played for: Bellville CC, Cape Town 2006
Career highlights to date: 'England debut. Notts Championship win 2005. Twenty20 finals day 2006'
Cricket moments to forget: 'Being injured'
Cricketers particularly admired: Ian Botham, Andrew Flintoff, Chris Cairns, Mark Ealham
Other sports played: Golf
Other sports followed: Football (Mansfield Town)
Favourite band: The Killers, Red Hot Chili Peppers
Relaxations: 'TV; temperature control of Guinness!'
Extras: Took Championship hat-trick (Penney, Brown, Welch) v Warwickshire at Trent Bridge 1997 (aged 18 years 163 days). Won U19 World Cup winner's medal in Johannesburg 1998. NBC Denis Compton Award 1999. Cricket Writers' Young Player of the Year 2000. Vice-captain of Nottinghamshire 2003-04. ECB National Academy 2004-05. 'Youngest Notts player to be awarded a benefit year, aged 28'
Best batting: 123* Nottinghamshire v Leicestershire, Leicester 2003
Best bowling: 7-56 Nottinghamshire v Middlesex, Lord's 2000

2007 Season

	M	Inn	NO	Runs	HS	Avg	100	50	Ct	St	Balls	Runs	Wkts	Avg	BB	5I	10M
Test																	
FC	11	13	1	275	92	22.91	-	1	5	-	1582	1090	32	34.06	3-28	-	-
ODI																	
List A	3	2	1	15	10	15.00	-	-	-	-	90	116	2	58.00	1-22	-	
20/20 Int																	
20/20	1	0	0	0	0		-	-	-	-	6	7	0		-	-	

Career Performances

	M	Inn	NO	Runs	HS	Avg	100	50	Ct	St	Balls	Runs	Wkts	Avg	BB	5I	10M
Test																	
FC	146	210	41	4432	123 *	26.22	3	21	49	-	22257	12496	395	31.63	7-56	11	-
ODI	1	1	0	4	4	4.00	-	-	1	-	54	48	0		-	-	
List A	138	103	30	1542	84 *	21.12	-	4	20	-	5429	4389	161	27.26	6-27	2	
20/20 Int																	
20/20	27	17	7	196	29 *	19.60	-	-	4	-	135	201	9	22.33	2-19	-	

FROST, T. Warwickshire

Name: Tony Frost
Role: Right-hand bat, wicket-keeper
Born: 17 November 1975, Stoke-on-Trent
Height: 5ft 10in **Weight:** 10st 6lbs
County debut: 1997
County cap: 1999
50 dismissals in a season: 1
Parents: Ivan and Christine
Marital status: Single
Family links with cricket: Father played for Staffordshire
Education: James Brinkley High School; Stoke-on-Trent College
Qualifications: 5 GCSEs
Overseas tours: Kidsgrove U18 to Australia 1990-91
Other sports followed: Football, golf
Extras: Represented Staffordshire at all levels from U11 to U19. Won Texaco U16 competition with Staffordshire in 1992. Played for Development of Excellence XI U17, U18, and U19. Scored century (135*) v Sussex at Horsham 2004, in the process setting with Ian Bell (262*) a new Warwickshire record partnership for the seventh wicket (289*). C&G Man of the

Match award in the semi-final v Lancashire at Edgbaston 2005. Retired at the end of the 2006 season; has rejoined Warwickshire staff for 2008
Best batting: 135* Warwickshire v Sussex, Horsham 2004

2007 Season (did not make any first-class or one-day appearances)

Career Performances

	M	Inn	NO	Runs	HS	Avg	100	50	Ct	St	Balls	Runs	Wkts	Avg	BB	5I	10M
Test																	
FC	92	134	21	3178	135 *	28.12	3	16	225	16	12	15	0		-	-	-
ODI																	
List A	79	43	16	485	47	17.96	-	-	76	19	0	0	0		-	-	
20/20 Int																	
20/20	13	7	2	92	33 *	18.40	-	-	10	8	0	0	0		-	-	

GALE, A. W. — Yorkshire

Name: Andrew William Gale
Role: Left-hand bat, right-arm off-spin bowler
Born: 28 November 1983, Dewsbury
Height: 6ft 2in **Weight:** 14st
Nickname: Galey, G-Dog, G-Unit
County debut: 2004
Place in batting averages: 156th av. 27.87 (2006 182nd av. 24.33)
Parents: Denise and Alan
Marital status: 'Attached'
Family links with cricket: 'Grandad played club cricket'
Education: Whitcliffe Mount; Heckmondwike Grammar
Qualifications: 9 GCSEs, 3 A-levels, Level 3 cricket coaching
Career outside cricket: 'Cricket coaching (www.procoachcricketacademy.co.uk)'

Off-season: 'Business, chilling, football'
Overseas tours: England U17 to Australia 2001; England U19 to Australia 2002-03; Yorkshire to Grenada 2001, to India 2005
Overseas teams played for: Blacktown, Sydney 2004-05
Career highlights to date: 'Scoring maiden first-class hundred'
Cricket moments to forget: 'Any ducks'
Cricket superstitions: 'Don't like odd numbers'

Cricketers particularly admired: Marcus Trescothick
Young players to look out for: Adam Lyth, Oliver Hannon-Dalby
Other sports played: Football ('played for district')
Other sports followed: Football (Huddersfield Town)
Favourite band: Oasis, Simply Red
Relaxations: 'PlayStation'
Extras: Played for England age groups from U15. Yorkshire League Young Batsman of the Year 2002. Yorkshire Player of the Year 2006
Opinions on cricket: 'Glad to see overseas players back down to one.'
Best batting: 149 Yorkshire v Warwickshire, Scarborough 2006
Best bowling: 1-33 Yorkshire v LUCCE, Headingley 2007

2007 Season

	M	Inn	NO	Runs	HS	Avg	100	50	Ct	St	Balls	Runs	Wkts	Avg	BB	5I	10M
Test																	
FC	6	8	0	223	68	27.87	-	2	5	-	12	33	1	33.00	1-33	-	-
ODI																	
List A	16	11	4	371	81	53.00	-	3	3	-	0	0	0		-	-	
20/20 Int																	
20/20	7	5	1	94	56	23.50	-	1	5	-	0	0	0		-	-	

Career Performances

	M	Inn	NO	Runs	HS	Avg	100	50	Ct	St	Balls	Runs	Wkts	Avg	BB	5I	10M
Test																	
FC	15	24	0	520	149	21.66	1	2	9	-	12	33	1	33.00	1-33	-	-
ODI																	
List A	42	35	6	886	81	30.55	-	5	10	-	0	0	0		-	-	
20/20 Int																	
20/20	19	15	2	259	56	19.92	-	2	12	-	0	0	0		-	-	

27. Who became the first batsman to score ten centuries for South Africa in Tests during the course of his 275 in the third Test v England at Durban in 1999-2000?

GALLIAN, J. E. R. Essex

Name: Jason Edward Riche Gallian
Role: Right-hand bat, right-arm medium bowler
Born: 25 June 1971, Manly, NSW, Australia
Height: 6ft **Weight:** 14st 7lbs
Nickname: Gal
County debut: 1990 (Lancashire), 1998 (Nottinghamshire)
County cap: 1994 (Lancashire), 1998 (Nottinghamshire)
Benefit: 2005 (Nottinghamshire)
Test debut: 1995
1000 runs in a season: 6
1st-Class 300s: 1
Place in batting averages: 88th av. 37.60 (2006 160th av. 28.29)
Parents: Ray and Marilyn
Wife and date of marriage: Charlotte, 2 October 1999
Children: Tom, 11 May 2001; Harry, 8 September 2003; Emily, 6 October 2006
Family links with cricket: Father played for Stockport
Education: The Pittwater House Schools, Australia; Oxford University
Qualifications: Higher School Certificate, Diploma in Social Studies (Keble College, Oxford)
Career outside cricket: 'Involved in a media training company'
Overseas tours: Australia U20 to West Indies 1989-90; England A to India 1994-95, to Pakistan 1995-96, to Australia 1996-97; England to South Africa 1995-96; Nottinghamshire to Johannesburg 2000, to South Africa 2001; MCC to UAE and Oman 2004
Overseas teams played for: NSW U19 1988-89; NSW Colts and NSW 2nd XI 1990-91; Manly 1993-94
Career highlights to date: 'First Test match'
Cricket moments to forget: 'Breaking a finger in my first Test match'
Cricket superstitions: 'None'
Cricketers particularly admired: Desmond Haynes, Mike Gatting
Young players to look out for: Charlie Shreck, Samit Patel
Other sports followed: Rugby league and union, football
Favourite band: Midnight Oil
Relaxations: 'Looking after the kids'
Extras: Represented Australia YC 1988-90 (captain v England YC 1989-90); also represented Australia U20 and U21 1991-92. Took wicket of D. A. Hagan of Oxford

University with his first ball in first-class cricket 1990. Played for Oxford University and Combined Universities 1992; captained Oxford University 1993. Qualified to play for England 1994. Recorded highest individual score in history of Old Trafford with his 312 v Derbyshire in 1996. Captain of Nottinghamshire from part-way through the 1998 season to 2002 and in 2004; Nottinghamshire club captain and captain in first-class cricket 2003. Left Nottinghamshire at the end of the 2007 season and has joined Essex for 2008

Opinions on cricket: 'More 50-over cricket to develop World Cup cricketers.'

Best batting: 312 Lancashire v Derbyshire, Old Trafford 1996

Best bowling: 6-115 Lancashire v Surrey, Southport 1996

2007 Season

	M	Inn	NO	Runs	HS	Avg	100	50	Ct	St	Balls	Runs	Wkts	Avg	BB	5I	10M
Test																	
FC	17	25	0	940	178	37.60	2	4	9	-	60	53	1	53.00	1-36	-	-
ODI																	
List A	4	4	0	215	97	53.75	-	2	1	-	0	0	0		-	-	
20/20 Int																	
20/20																	

Career Performances

	M	Inn	NO	Runs	HS	Avg	100	50	Ct	St	Balls	Runs	Wkts	Avg	BB	5I	10M
Test	3	6	0	74	28	12.33	-	-	1	-	84	62	0		-	-	-
FC	235	399	35	14173	312	38.93	36	67	200	-	7138	4152	96	43.25	6-115	1	-
ODI																	
List A	213	209	15	6070	134	31.28	8	38	72	-	2049	1808	55	32.87	5-15	1	
20/20 Int																	
20/20	8	8	0	152	62	19.00	-	1	1	-	0	0	0		-	-	

28. Which owner of a famous cricketing name became the first New Zealand bowler to take seven wickets (7-74) in a Test innings against England, in the second Test at Headingley in 1983?

GAZZARD, C. M. Somerset

Name: Carl Matthew Gazzard
Role: Right-hand bat, wicket-keeper
Born: 15 April 1982, Penzance
Height: 6ft **Weight:** 13st
Nickname: Gazza, Sling Boy, Coral
County debut: 2002
Place in batting averages: (2006 241st av. 15.25)
Parents: Paul and Alison
Marital status: Single
Family links with cricket: Father and brother both played for Cornwall Schools; mother's a keen follower
Education: Mounts Bay Comprehensive; Richard Huish College, Taunton
Qualifications: 10 GCSEs, 2 A-levels, Levels 1 and 2 coaching
Overseas tours: Cornwall Schools U13 to Johannesburg; West of England U15 to West Indies; Somerset Academy to Durban 1999
Overseas teams played for: Subiaco-Floreat, Perth 2000-01; Scarborough, Perth 2002-03
Career highlights to date: '157 v Derby in totesport game [2004]'
Cricket moments to forget: 'Dislocating my shoulder in Perth – kept me out for 2001 season'
Cricket superstitions: 'None'
Cricketers particularly admired: Marcus Trescothick, Graham Rose
Young players to look out for: James Hildreth
Other sports played: Football (played through the age groups for Cornwall)
Other sports followed: Football (West Ham United)
Favourite band: Red Hot Chili Peppers
Extras: Played for England U13, U14, U15, U19. Won the Graham Kersey Award for Best Wicket-keeper at Bunbury Festival. Played for Cornwall in Minor Counties aged 16. Scored 136-ball 157 (his maiden one-day century) v Derbyshire at Derby in the totesport League 2004. Man of the Match in Twenty20 Cup semi-final v Leicestershire at The Oval 2005
Best batting: 74 Somerset v Worcestershire, Worcester 2005

2007 Season

	M	Inn	NO	Runs	HS	Avg	100	50	Ct	St	Balls	Runs	Wkts	Avg	BB	5I	10M
Test																	
FC																	
ODI																	
List A																	
20/20 Int																	
20/20	2	0	0	0	0		-	-	1	1	0	0	0		-	-	

Career Performances

	M	Inn	NO	Runs	HS	Avg	100	50	Ct	St	Balls	Runs	Wkts	Avg	BB	5I	10M
Test																	
FC	27	42	6	732	74	20.33	-	1	58	1	0	0	0		-	-	-
ODI																	
List A	52	44	4	924	157	23.10	1	4	48	6	0	0	0		-	-	
20/20 Int																	
20/20	27	17	4	221	39	17.00	-	-	14	6	0	0	0		-	-	

GIBSON, O. D. — Durham

Name: Ottis Delroy Gibson
Role: Right-hand bat, 'right-arm gas' bowler; bowling all-rounder
Born: 16 March 1969, Barbados
Height: 6ft 2in **Weight:** 13st 7lbs
Nickname: Gibbo
County debut: 1994 (Glamorgan), 2004 (Leicestershire), 2006 (Durham)
County cap: 2004 (Leicestershire)
Test debut: 1995
ODI debut: 1995-96
50 wickets in a season: 3
Place in batting averages: 162nd av. 27.52 (2006 115th av. 33.11)
Place in bowling averages: 8th av. 20.75 (2006 44th av. 29.75)
Parents: Barry
Marital status: 'Girlfriend'
Children: Michael James
Education: Ellerslie Secondary School, Barbados
Qualifications: Level 4 coaching certificate
Career outside cricket: Coaching

Overseas tours: West Indies A to Sri Lanka 1996-97, to South Africa 1997-98; West Indies to England 1995, to Australia 1995-96, to India and Pakistan (World Cup) 1995-96, to Malaysia (Commonwealth Games) 1998-99, to South Africa 1998-99, plus one-day tournament in Sharjah
Overseas teams played for: Barbados 1990-91 – 1997-98; Border 1992-93 – 1994-95; Griqualand West 1998-99 – 1999-2000; Gauteng 2000-01
Career highlights: 'Making debut for West Indies'
Cricket moments to forget: 'My 14 overs for 101 v Hampshire [2006]'
Cricket superstitions: 'None'
Cricketers particularly admired: Malcolm Marshall, Courtney Walsh, Allan Donald
Other sports played: Basketball (district), football, golf
Other sports followed: 'All sports', football (Man United), basketball (Lakers)
Favourite band: Oasis, 'any reggae band'
Relaxations: 'Watching TV'
Extras: One of *South African Cricket Annual*'s five Cricketers of the Year 1993. Was Glamorgan overseas player 1994-96. Scored maiden first-class century (101*) from 69 balls for West Indians v Somerset at Taunton 1995, batting at No. 9. Has won numerous domestic match awards and was also Man of the Match v Australia at Brisbane in B&H World Series Cup 1995-96 (40-ball 52/2-38). Leicestershire Player of the Year 2004. Scored century (155) v Yorkshire at Headingley 2006, in the process sharing with Dale Benkenstein (151) in a new record seventh-wicket partnership for Durham (315). Returned figures of 10-47 v Hampshire at Riverside 2007 to become the first bowler to take all ten wickets in a Championship innings since Richard Johnson in 1994. Man of the Match in the Friends Provident final at Lord's 2007, taking a wicket with each of the first two deliveries of Hampshire's reply (finished with 3-24 to add to a 7-ball 15). Took a Durham season record 80 Championship wickets (as well as scoring 578 runs) in 2007. NatWest PCA Player of the Year 2007 and winner of the inaugural PCA Most Valuable Player award 2007. Is no longer considered an overseas player. Retired at the end of the 2007 season and has been appointed England bowling coach
Best batting: 155 Durham v Yorkshire, Headingley 2006
Best bowling: 10-47 Durham v Hampshire, Riverside 2007

2007 Season

	M	Inn	NO	Runs	HS	Avg	100	50	Ct	St	Balls	Runs	Wkts	Avg	BB	5I	10M
Test																	
FC	15	23	2	578	71	27.52	-	4	6	-	2879	1660	80	20.75	10-47	4	3
ODI																	
List A	18	11	6	120	41	24.00	-	-	4	-	785	681	34	20.02	3-21	-	
20/20 Int																	
20/20	6	2	0	25	22	12.50	-	-	1	-	90	137	2	68.50	1-24	-	

Career Performances

	M	Inn	NO	Runs	HS	Avg	100	50	Ct	St	Balls	Runs	Wkts	Avg	BB	5I	10M
Test	2	4	0	93	37	23.25	-	-	-	-	472	275	3	91.66	2-81	-	-
FC	177	267	36	5604	155	24.25	2	29	68	-	32441	18319	659	27.79	10-47	28	8
ODI	15	11	1	141	52	14.10	-	1	3	-	739	621	34	18.26	5-40	2	
List A	212	159	38	2548	102 *	21.05	1	5	59	-	9827	7533	310	24.30	5-19	5	
20/20 Int																	
20/20	25	16	2	166	22	11.85	-	-	7	-	475	617	18	34.27	2-20	-	

GIDMAN, A. P. R. — Gloucestershire

Name: Alexander (Alex) Peter Richard Gidman
Role: Right-hand bat, right-arm medium bowler, county vice-captain
Born: 22 June 1981, High Wycombe
Height: 6ft 2in **Weight:** 14st
Nickname: G, Giddo
County debut: 2001 (one-day), 2002 (first-class)
County cap: 2004
1000 runs in a season: 3
Place in batting averages: 72nd av. 40.12 (2006 44th av. 49.76)
Place in bowling averages: (2006 127th av. 44.82)
Parents: Alistair and Jane
Marital status: Single
Family links with cricket: Brother Will is at Durham CCC
Education: Wycliffe College, Stonehouse, Gloucestershire
Qualifications: 6 GCSEs, 1 A-level, GNVQ Level 2 in Leisure and Tourism
Overseas tours: MCC Young Cricketers to Cape Town 1999; Gloucestershire to South Africa; England A to Malaysia and India 2003-04 (c), to Sri Lanka 2004-05, to Bangladesh 2006-07
Overseas teams played for: Albion CC, New Zealand 2001; Otago, New Zealand 2007-08
Career highlights to date: 'Two C&G Trophy final victories. Academy captain'
Cricket moments to forget: 'C&G quarter-final loss to Kent 2002'
Cricket superstitions: 'None'
Cricketers particularly admired: Steve Waugh
Other sports played: Golf
Other sports followed: Football (Wolves), rugby (Gloucester)

Favourite band: Matchbox Twenty, Train
Relaxations: 'Just chilling out; movies, golf'
Extras: Gloucestershire Young Player of the Year 2002, 2003. NBC Denis Compton Award for the most promising young Gloucestershire player 2002, 2003. ECB National Academy 2003-04, 2004-05. Gloucestershire Players' Player of the Year 2006. Vice-captain of Gloucestershire since 2006. Scored century in each innings (130/105*) v Northamptonshire at Gloucester 2007. Represented England Lions 2007
Best batting: 142 Gloucestershire v Surrey, Bristol 2005
Best bowling: 4-47 Gloucestershire v Glamorgan, Cardiff 2005

2007 Season

	M	Inn	NO	Runs	HS	Avg	100	50	Ct	St	Balls	Runs	Wkts	Avg	BB	5I	10M
Test																	
FC	17	29	4	1003	130	40.12	3	5	10	-	978	581	9	64.55	1-4	-	-
ODI																	
List A	15	15	1	487	88 *	34.78	-	5	5	-	324	311	10	31.10	3-46	-	
20/20 Int																	
20/20	9	8	3	101	34 *	20.20	-	-	1	-	78	85	1	85.00	1-12	-	

Career Performances

	M	Inn	NO	Runs	HS	Avg	100	50	Ct	St	Balls	Runs	Wkts	Avg	BB	5I	10M
Test																	
FC	85	150	17	5114	142	38.45	11	31	52	-	5673	3606	74	48.72	4-47	-	-
ODI																	
List A	104	96	12	2178	88 *	25.92	-	13	38	-	1810	1587	44	36.06	5-42	1	
20/20 Int																	
20/20	31	25	7	446	61	24.77	-	2	8	-	126	169	4	42.25	1-2	-	

GIDMAN, W. R. S. Durham

Name: William (Will) Robert Simon Gidman
Role: Left-hand bat, right-arm medium bowler; all-rounder
Born: 14 February 1985, High Wycombe
Height: 6ft 2in **Weight:** 12st 7lbs
Nickname: Gidders, Giddo, Rev, PT
County debut: 2007
Parents: Alistair and Jane
Marital status: Single
Family links with cricket: Brother of Alex Gidman, vice-captain of Gloucestershire
Education: Wycliffe College, Stonehouse, Gloucestershire; Berkshire College of Agriculture
Qualifications: 7 GCSEs, Level 2 cricket coaching, Level 1 rugby and football coaching

Career outside cricket: 'Part-time teacher'
Overseas tours: Wycliffe College to South Africa 2000; MCC YC to Sri Lanka 2004, to India 2005, to Lanzarote 2006; Durham to Cape Town 2007
Overseas teams played for: Gold Coast Dolphins, Australia 2004-05
Career highlights to date: 'Signing for Durham CCC'
Cricket moments to forget: 'Giving away four overthrows off Freddie Flintoff's bowling whilst doing 12th man duties for England against Bangladesh'
Cricket superstitions: 'None'
Cricketers particularly admired: Garfield Sobers, Graham Thorpe, Mike Hussey, Alex Gidman
Young players to look out for: Garry Park
Other sports played: Football (Stroud and District), rugby, golf, table tennis
Other sports followed: Football (Wolves), rugby (Gloucester)
Favourite band: Embrace
Relaxations: 'Music, TV, walking the dog, Sudoku'
Extras: Was first Gloucestershire U10 to score a hundred. Played for Gloucestershire Board XI in the 2003 C&G. MCC YC cap
Opinions on cricket: 'I love the traditions of our game and the thought of things like drop-in pitches and taking too many decisions away from the umpires in the middle, I am not sure about.'
Best batting: 8 Durham v Sri Lanka A, Riverside 2007
Best bowling: 3-37 Durham v Sri Lanka A, Riverside 2007

2007 Season

	M	Inn	NO	Runs	HS	Avg	100	50	Ct	St	Balls	Runs	Wkts	Avg	BB	5I	10M
Test																	
FC	1	2	0	8	8	4.00	-	-	-	-	138	86	4	21.50	3-37	-	-
ODI																	
List A																	
20/20 Int																	
20/20																	

Career Performances

	M	Inn	NO	Runs	HS	Avg	100	50	Ct	St	Balls	Runs	Wkts	Avg	BB	5I	10M
Test																	
FC	1	2	0	8	8	4.00	-	-	-	-	138	86	4	21.50	3-37	-	-
ODI																	
List A	1	1	0	12	12	12.00	-	-	-	-	0	0	0		-	-	
20/20 Int																	
20/20																	

GILBERT, C. R. Yorkshire

Name: Christopher (Chris) Robert Gilbert
Role: Right-hand bat, right-arm medium bowler; all-rounder
Born: 16 April 1984, Scarborough
Height: 5ft 10in **Weight:** 12st 11lbs
Nickname: Gilly
County debut: 2006 (one-day), 2007 (first-class)
Parents: Roger and Vicky
Marital status: Single
Family links with cricket: 'Dad sports teacher and played some representative. Brother played Yorkshire senior schools'
Education: Scarborough College
Qualifications: Level 2 coaching
Career outside cricket: Coaching
Overseas tours: England U17 to Australia 2001; England U19 to Australia and (U19 World Cup) New Zealand 2001-02

Overseas teams played for: Scarborough, Perth; Upper Valley, New Zealand
Career highlights to date: 'Gaining a contract with Yorkshire'
Cricket moments to forget: 'Getting out to my brother in the league!'
Cricket superstitions: 'None'
Cricketers particularly admired: Craig White, Darren Gough
Young players to look out for: Greg Wood, Mark Lawson
Other sports played: Hockey (England U16, U18)
Other sports followed: Premiership football and rugby
Favourite band: Green Day, Arctic Monkeys, Kaiser Chiefs
Relaxations: 'Travelling'
Extras: Played for Yorkshire Board XI in the 2003 C&G. Released by Yorkshire at the end of the 2007 season

Opinions on cricket: 'Quick and energetic – good to play and watch.'
Best batting: 64 Yorkshire v LUCCE, Headingley 2007

2007 Season

	M	Inn	NO	Runs	HS	Avg	100	50	Ct	St	Balls	Runs	Wkts	Avg	BB	5I	10M
Test																	
FC	1	1	0	64	64	64.00	-	1	1	-	18	11	0		-	-	-
ODI																	
List A	2	1	0	37	37	37.00	-	-	2	-	66	69	2	34.50	2-44	-	
20/20 Int																	
20/20	7	5	1	43	22	10.75	-	-	3	-	0	0	0		-	-	

Career Performances

	M	Inn	NO	Runs	HS	Avg	100	50	Ct	St	Balls	Runs	Wkts	Avg	BB	5I	10M
Test																	
FC	1	1	0	64	64	64.00	-	1	1	-	18	11	0		-	-	-
ODI																	
List A	6	5	0	68	37	13.60	-	-	3	-	220	232	8	29.00	3-33	-	
20/20 Int																	
20/20	13	9	2	107	36 *	15.28	-	-	6	-	0	0	0		-	-	

GILES, A. F. — Warwickshire

Name: Ashley Fraser Giles
Role: Right-hand bat, slow left-arm bowler
Born: 19 March 1973, Chertsey, Surrey
Height: 6ft 4in **Weight:** 15st 7lbs
Nickname: Splash, Skinny, Gilo
County debut: 1993
County cap: 1996
Benefit: 2006
Test debut: 1998
ODI debut: 1997
50 wickets in a season: 2
Parents: Michael and Paula
Wife and date of marriage: Stine, 9 October 1999
Children: Anders Fraser, 29 May 2000; Matilde, February 2002
Family links with cricket: Father played and brother Andrew a club cricketer
Education: George Abbott County Secondary, Burpham, Guildford
Qualifications: 9 GCSEs, 2 A-levels, coaching certificate

Overseas tours: Surrey U19 to Barbados 1990-91; Warwickshire to Cape Town 1996, 1997, to Bloemfontein 1998; England A to Australia 1996-97, to Kenya and Sri Lanka 1997-98; England to Sharjah (Champions Trophy) 1997-98, to Bangladesh (Wills International Cup) 1998-99, to Australia 1998-99 (CUB Series), to South Africa and Zimbabwe 1999-2000 (one-day series), to Kenya (ICC Knockout Trophy) 2000-01, to Pakistan and Sri Lanka 2000-01, to India and New Zealand 2001-02, to Sri Lanka (ICC Champions Trophy) 2002-03, to Australia 2002-03, to Africa (World Cup) 2002-03, to Bangladesh and Sri Lanka 2003-04, to West Indies 2003-04, to Zimbabwe (one-day series) 2004-05, to South Africa 2004-05, to Pakistan 2005-06, to Australia 2006-07
Overseas teams played for: Vredenburg/Saldanha, Cape Town 1992-95; Avendale CC, Cape Town 1995-96
Cricketers particularly admired: Dermot Reeve, Tim Munton, Dougie Brown, Ian Botham
Other sports played: Golf (14 handicap), football
Other sports followed: Football (QPR)
Relaxations: 'Cinema, music, spending lots of time with my family'
Extras: Surrey Young Cricketer of the Year 1991. NBC Denis Compton Award for Warwickshire 1996. Warwickshire Player of the Year 1996 and 2000. Warwickshire Most Improved Player 1996. Cricket Society's Leading Young All-rounder 1996. Scored hundred (123*) and had five-wicket innings return (5-28) v Oxford University at The Parks 1999. Took 17 Test wickets v Pakistan 2000-01, the highest total by an England bowler in a series in Pakistan. Man of the Match in the fifth ODI v India at Delhi 2001-02 (5-57). Scored 71* v Essex at Edgbaston in the C&G 2003, sharing with Dougie Brown (108) in a competition record seventh-wicket partnership (170). Man of the Match in the first Test v West Indies at Lord's 2004 (4-129/5-81). One of *Wisden*'s Five Cricketers of the Year 2005. Appointed MBE in 2006 New Year Honours as part of 2005 Ashes-winning England team. Retired in August 2007 because of persistent hip problems and has taken up the post of Director of Cricket at Warwickshire
Best batting: 128* Warwickshire v Sussex, Hove 2000
Best bowling: 8-90 Warwickshire v Northamptonshire, Northampton 2000

2007 Season (did not make any first-class or one-day appearances)

Career Performances

	M	Inn	NO	Runs	HS	Avg	100	50	Ct	St	Balls	Runs	Wkts	Avg	BB	5I	10M
Test	54	81	13	1421	59	20.89	-	4	33	-	12180	5806	143	40.60	5-57	5	-
FC	178	249	46	5346	128 *	26.33	3	22	80	-	37304	15958	539	29.60	8-90	26	3
ODI	62	35	13	385	41	17.50	-	-	22	-	2856	2069	55	37.61	5-57	1	
List A	224	141	41	2089	107	20.89	1	5	73	-	9729	6961	272	25.59	5-21	3	
20/20 Int																	
20/20	2	1	1	0	0 *		-	-	-	-	42	34	2	17.00	2-21	-	

GILLESPIE, J. N. Glamorgan

Name: Jason Neil Gillespie
Role: Right-hand bat, right-arm fast bowler
Born: 19 April 1975, Darlinghurst, Australia
Height: 6ft 5in **Weight:** 14st 7lbs
Nickname: Dizzy
County debut: 2006 (Yorkshire)
County cap: 2007 (Yorkshire)
Test debut: 1996-97
ODI debut: 1996
Twenty20 Int debut: 2005
1st-Class 200s: 1
Place in batting averages: 111th av. 33.75 (2006 179th av. 24.66)
Place in bowling averages: 97th av. 34.91 (2006 72nd av. 33.61)
Parents: Neil and Vicki
Wife and date of marriage: Anna, 20 September 2003
Children: Sapphire, 2 March 1995; Jackson Anderson, 1 February 2006; Brandon Ryder, October 2007
Education: Cabra College, Adelaide
Career outside cricket: 'Property investments and developments; radio'
Off-season: 'Playing for the Southern Redbacks in Australia'
Overseas tours: Australia U19 to India 1993-94; Australia A to Scotland and Ireland 1998, to Pakistan 2007-08; Australia to Sri Lanka (Singer World Series) 1996, to South Africa 1996-97, to England 1997, to West Indies 1998-99, to Sri Lanka 1999, to Kenya (ICC Knockout Trophy) 2000-01, to India 2000-01, to England 2001, to South Africa 2001-02, to Sri Lanka (ICC Champions Trophy) 2002-03, to Sri Lanka and Sharjah (v Pakistan) 2002-03, to Africa (World Cup) 2002-03, to West Indies 2002-03, to Sri Lanka 2003-04, to England (ICC Champions Trophy) 2004, to India 2004-05, to New Zealand 2004-05, to England 2005, to Bangladesh 2005-06, plus other one-day series and tournaments in India, Kenya, Zimbabwe, Netherlands and England
Overseas teams played for: Adelaide CC 1986 – ; South Australia 1994-95 –
Career highlights to date: 'Winning cricket matches – that is what we play for'
Cricket moments to forget: 'Colliding with Steve Waugh in a Test match' (*During the first Test v Sri Lanka in Kandy 1999, Waugh and Gillespie collided while attempting to catch Mahela Jayawardene. Waugh's nose was broken; Gillespie suffered a broken leg and wrist*)
Cricket superstitions: 'Not any more'
Cricketers particularly admired: Michael Kasprowicz, Darren Lehmann

Young players to look out for: Adam Lyth, Peter George
Other sports played: 'Will play social basketball when I finish playing cricket'
Other sports followed: 'Can watch most sports except rugby union and hockey'
Favourite band: 'Whatever is on radio'
Relaxations: 'Time with family and friends'
Extras: Is the first known male cricketer of indigenous descent (great-grandson of a Kamilaroi warrior) to have played Test cricket for Australia. One of *Wisden*'s Five Cricketers of the Year 2002. Is sixth in the all-time list of Australia's Test wicket-takers. Scored 201* batting as nightwatchman in the second Test v Bangladesh at Chittagong 2005-06, reaching his double century on his 31st birthday. His match awards include Man of the Match v England in the fourth Test at Headingley 1997 (7-37/2-65) and v India at Centurion in the 2002-03 World Cup (3-13 from 10 overs). An overseas player with Yorkshire 2006-07. Scored century (123*) v Surrey at The Oval 2007, in the process sharing with Tim Bresnan (116) in a new record ninth-wicket partnership for Yorkshire (246). Has joined Glamorgan as an overseas player for 2008
Opinions on cricket: 'Cricket administrators are big on the "spirit of cricket" and even offer an award in various competitions around the world, which basically amounts to an "encouragement award". Yet there are no clear guidelines on what the "spirit of cricket" actually is. The problem is that different teams and different countries interpret the "spirit of cricket" very differently. This also includes umpires, match referees, fans and even the administrators themselves. I would like to see it abolished.'
Best batting: 201* Australia v Bangladesh, Chittagong (B) 2005-06
Best bowling: 8-50 South Australia v New South Wales, Sydney 2001-02

2007 Season

	M	Inn	NO	Runs	HS	Avg	100	50	Ct	St	Balls	Runs	Wkts	Avg	BB	5I	10M
Test																	
FC	12	13	5	270	123 *	33.75	1	-	3	-	1431	803	23	34.91	3-40	-	-
ODI																	
List A	10	2	1	15	15 *	15.00	-	-	3	-	498	301	11	27.36	3-35	-	
20/20 Int																	
20/20	8	3	2	11	8 *	11.00	-	-	4	-	156	194	8	24.25	2-19	-	

Career Performances

	M	Inn	NO	Runs	HS	Avg	100	50	Ct	St	Balls	Runs	Wkts	Avg	BB	5I	10M
Test	71	93	28	1218	201 *	18.73	1	2	27	-	14234	6770	259	26.13	7-37	8	-
FC	167	220	54	3015	201 *	18.16	2	7	62	-	31282	14680	564	26.02	8-50	21	2
ODI	97	39	16	289	44 *	12.56	-	-	10	-	5144	3611	142	25.42	5-22	3	
List A	170	75	33	539	44 *	12.83	-	-	26	-	9106	6295	231	27.25	5-22	3	
20/20 Int	1	1	0	24	24	24.00	-	-	-	-	24	49	1	49.00	1-49	-	
20/20	18	5	2	38	24	12.66	-	-	5	-	367	471	18	26.16	2-19	-	

GITSHAM, M. T. — Gloucestershire

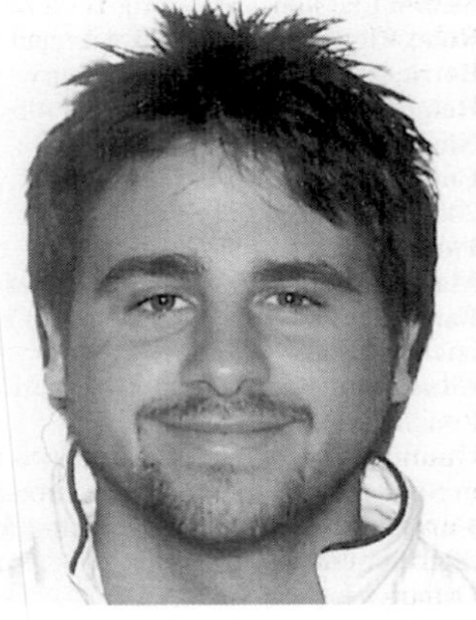

Name: Matthew Thomas Gitsham
Role: Right-hand bat, right-arm leg-spin bowler
Born: 1 February 1982, Truro, Cornwall
Height: 5ft 10in **Weight:** 14st
Nickname: Gitchie
Parents: Colin and Marilyn
Marital status: Single ('long-term girlfriend Tamsyn')
Family links with cricket: 'Brother Simon plays good club cricket for Wembdon CC'
Education: Queen's College, Taunton; College of St Mark and St John, Plymouth
Qualifications: GCSEs, 2 A-levels, BA (Hons) Sports Science and IT
Career outside cricket: Builder
Off-season: 'Working and practising'
Overseas tours: England U17 to Northern Ireland (ECC Colts Festival) 1999
Overseas teams played for: Wanneroo DCC, Perth 2000-01; Sturt Hill, Adelaide 2006-07
Career highlights to date: 'Gaining a professional contract'
Cricket moments to forget: 'Knee injury 2005-06'
Cricketers particularly admired: Shane Warne, Ricky Ponting
Young players to look out for: Alex Bailey
Other sports played: Hockey, surfing
Other sports followed: Football (Tottenham Hotspur FC)
Favourite band: Jack Johnson, Jason Mraz
Relaxations: 'Playing the guitar'
Extras: Brian Johnston Memorial Trust Scholarship to Adelaide (with Terry Jenner) 1999. Played for Somerset Board XI in the 2001 and 2002 C&G

2007 Season (did not make any first-class or one-day appearances)

Career Performances

	M	Inn	NO	Runs	HS	Avg	100	50	Ct	St	Balls	Runs	Wkts	Avg	BB	5I	10M
Test																	
FC																	
ODI																	
List A	2	1	0	15	15	15.00	-	-	-	-	0	0	0		-	-	
20/20 Int																	
20/20																	

GODDARD, L. J. Durham

Name: Lee James Goddard
Role: Right-hand bat, wicket-keeper
Born: 22 October 1982, Dewsbury
Height: 5ft 10½in **Weight:** 11st 4lbs
Nickname: Godders, Goddy
County debut: 2004 (Derbyshire), 2007 (Durham)
Parents: Steve and Lynda
Marital status: Engaged to Kelly Moore
Family links with cricket: 'Dad is a cricket badger!'
Education: Batley Grammar School; Loughborough University
Qualifications: GCSEs, Foundation degree in Sports Science, ECB Level 1 coaching
Career outside cricket: 'Relaxing; bit of this, bit of that'
Off-season: 'Pre-season tour'
Overseas teams played for: Parramatta DCC, Sydney 2001-02
Career highlights to date: 'Five catches in first innings on Championship debut for Derbyshire [v Hampshire 2004]. Fifty off 31 balls (fastest first-class fifty in Durham history) on first-class debut for Durham [v Sri Lanka A 2007]. Friends Provident win [2007] (Durham's first trophy)'
Cricket superstitions: 'Left pad on first'
Cricketers particularly admired: Adam Gilchrist, Damien Martyn, Paul Nixon
Young players to look out for: Scott Borthwick, Karl Turner, Rich Hopwood
Other sports played: Squash, golf, football (Huddersfield Town aged 9-15)
Other sports followed: Football (Leeds United), rugby league (Leeds Rhinos)
Favourite band: Jack Johnson
Relaxations: 'Gym; planning the wedding!'
Extras: Played in Yorkshire's U17 County Championship winning side. Played for Yorkshire Board XI in the 2003 C&G. Played for Loughborough UCCE in 2003. Was in British Universities squad for match v Zimbabweans 2003. Derbyshire CCC 2nd XI Player of the Year 2004. Shared with Graham Wagg in a new record seventh-wicket partnership for Derbyshire in matches v Surrey (181) at Derby 2006. Scored 31-ball fifty on first-class debut for Durham v Sri Lanka A at Riverside 2007, breaking record (jointly held by Ian Botham, Martin Speight and Phil Mustard) for fastest first-class fifty for the county
Opinions on cricket: 'Limit on Kolpaks [*see page 13*] per squad (there must be some way to limit the intrusion). More opportunities for youth! That's what academies are there for!'
Best batting: 91 Derbyshire v Surrey, Derby 2006

2007 Season

	M	Inn	NO	Runs	HS	Avg	100	50	Ct	St	Balls	Runs	Wkts	Avg	BB	5I	10M
Test																	
FC	1	2	0	59	52	29.50	-	1	5	-	0	0	0		-	-	-
ODI																	
List A																	
20/20 Int																	
20/20	1	0	0	0	0		-	-	-	-	0	0	0		-	-	

Career Performances

	M	Inn	NO	Runs	HS	Avg	100	50	Ct	St	Balls	Runs	Wkts	Avg	BB	5I	10M
Test																	
FC	10	14	4	324	91	32.40	-	2	22	-	0	0	0		-	-	-
ODI																	
List A	6	5	2	69	36	23.00	-	-	8	-	0	0	0		-	-	
20/20 Int																	
20/20	1	0	0	0	0		-	-	-	-	0	0	0		-	-	

GODLEMAN, B-A. Middlesex

Name: Billy-Ashley (Billy) Godleman
Role: Left-hand opening bat, right-arm leg-spin bowler
Born: 11 February 1989, Islington, London
Height: 6ft 2in **Weight:** 13st
Nickname: G
County debut: 2005
Place in batting averages: 84th av. 38.27
Parents: Ashley Fitzgerald and John Godleman
Marital status: Single
Family links with cricket: 'Dad played club cricket for Hampstead'
Education: Central Foundation School; Islington Green School
Qualifications: 7 GCSEs
Off-season: 'England U19 World Cup'
Overseas tours: England U16 to South Africa 2004-05; England U19 to Malaysia 2006-07, to Malaysia (U19 World Cup) 2007-08; England Performance Programme to India 2007-08
Career highlights to date: 'Maiden first-class century – 113* v Somerset'
Cricketers particularly admired: Graeme Smith, Andy Flower, Matthew Hayden

Young players to look out for: Steven Finn, Eoin Morgan, Tom Westley, Ben Brown, Alex Wakely
Other sports played: Football
Other sports followed: Football (Liverpool FC), cricket (Brondesbury)
Favourite band: Pink Floyd, Led Zeppelin, Fleetwood Mac
Relaxations: 'Spending time with my little brother Johnny and family; reading; watching Liverpool FC'
Extras: Named best player in country U13, U14 and U15 at regional tournaments; scored 168-ball 143 for South v West at Bunbury U15 Festival at Nottingham 2004. Made 2nd XI Trophy debut for Middlesex 2003. Scored 69* on first-class debut v Cambridge UCCE at Fenner's 2005. Represented England U19 2006, 2007. Scored maiden first-class century (113*) on Championship debut v Somerset at Taunton 2007
Opinions on cricket: 'You get out what you put in.'
Best batting: 113* Middlesex v Somerset, Taunton 2007
Stop press: Called up to the England Performance Programme in India 2007-08

2007 Season

	M	Inn	NO	Runs	HS	Avg	100	50	Ct	St	Balls	Runs	Wkts	Avg	BB	5I	10M
Test																	
FC	15	24	2	842	113 *	38.27	1	6	22	-	30	35	0		-	-	-
ODI																	
List A	2	2	0	33	18	16.50	-	-	-	-	0	0	0		-	-	
20/20 Int																	
20/20																	

Career Performances

	M	Inn	NO	Runs	HS	Avg	100	50	Ct	St	Balls	Runs	Wkts	Avg	BB	5I	10M
Test																	
FC	16	25	3	911	113 *	41.40	1	7	22	-	30	35	0		-	-	-
ODI																	
List A	2	2	0	33	18	16.50	-	-	-	-	0	0	0		-	-	
20/20 Int																	
20/20	4	3	0	71	41	23.66	-	-	-	-	0	0	0		-	-	

29. Whose 'frog-in-a-blender' bowling action was first seen at Test level in the fourth Test between England and South Africa at Port Elizabeth in 1995-96?

GOODMAN, J. E. — Kent

Name: James Elliot Goodman
Role: Right-hand bat, right-arm medium bowler; all-rounder
Born: 19 November 1990, Farnborough, Kent
Height: 5ft 10in **Weight:** 10st 12lbs
Nickname: Goody
County debut: 2007 (one-day)
Parents: Elizabeth and Trevor
Marital status: Single
Education: St Olave's Grammar School, Orpington
Career outside cricket: 'Student'
Off-season: 'At school; net sessions at Canterbury'
Overseas tours: England U19 to Malaysia (U19 World Cup) 2007-08
Career highlights to date: 'Being picked for England U19 World Cup squad'
Cricket moments to forget: 'Having Marvan Atapattu hit 24 off one of my overs in a game against Lashings'
Cricketers particularly admired: Sachin Tendulkar, Michael Bevan
Young players to look out for: Sam Northeast, Alex Blake, Paul Dixey
Other sports followed: Football (Chelsea)
Favourite band: Kanye West
Relaxations: 'Watching sport'
Extras: Youngest player to captain Kent 2nd XI, aged 16. Kent Academy Player of the Year 2007
Opinions on cricket: 'Too many cricket matches played in professional game. I think it detracts from the quality of the game from the county to the international arena.'

2007 Season

	M	Inn	NO	Runs	HS	Avg	100	50	Ct	St	Balls	Runs	Wkts	Avg	BB	5I	10M
Test																	
FC																	
ODI																	
List A	1	0	0	0	0		-	-	1	-	0	0	0		-	-	
20/20 Int																	
20/20																	

Career Performances

	M	Inn	NO	Runs	HS	Avg	100	50	Ct	St	Balls	Runs	Wkts	Avg	BB	5I	10M
Test																	
FC																	
ODI																	
List A	1	0	0	0	0		-	-	1	-	0	0	0		-	-	
20/20 Int																	
20/20																	

GOODWIN, M. W. — Sussex

Name: Murray William Goodwin
Role: Right-hand bat, right-arm medium/leg-spin bowler
Born: 11 December 1972, Harare, Zimbabwe
Height: 5ft 9in **Weight:** 11st 2lbs
Nickname: Muzza, Fuzz, Goodie
County debut: 2001
County cap: 2001
Test debut: 1997-98
ODI debut: 1997-98
1000 runs in a season: 6
1st-Class 200s: 6
1st-Class 300s: 1
Place in batting averages: 23rd av. 55.18 (2006 12th av. 63.42)
Parents: Penny and George
Wife and date of marriage: Tarsha, 13 December 1997
Children: Jayden William; Ashton George, 19 November 2006
Family links with cricket: 'Dad is a coach. Eldest brother played for Zimbabwe'
Education: St John's, Harare, Zimbabwe; Newtonmoore Senior High, Bunbury, Western Australia
Qualifications: Level II coach
Overseas tours: Australian Cricket Academy to South Africa 1992, to Sri Lanka and India 1993; Zimbabwe to Sri Lanka and New Zealand 1997-98, to Bangladesh (Wills International Cup) 1998-99, to Pakistan 1998-99, to UK, Ireland and Netherlands (World Cup) 1999, to South Africa 1999-2000, to West Indies 1999-2000, to England 2000
Overseas teams played for: Excelsior, Netherlands 1997; Mashonaland 1997-98 – 1998-99; Western Australia 1994-95 – 1996-97, 2000-01 – 2005-06; Warriors 2006-07

Career highlights to date: 'Becoming the highest individual scorer in Sussex's history – 335* v Leicestershire, September 2003 at Hove. Broke Duleepsinhji's record of 333 in 1930'
Cricketers particularly admired: Allan Border, Steve Waugh, Curtly Ambrose, Sachin Tendulkar
Other sports played: Hockey (WA Country), golf, tennis
Other sports followed: 'All'
Favourite band: 'No real favourites; I have a very eclectic collection'
Relaxations: 'Socialising with friends'
Extras: Attended Australian Cricket Academy. Scored 166* v Pakistan at Bulawayo 1997-98, in the process sharing with Andy Flower (100*) in the highest partnership for Zimbabwe for any wicket in Tests (277*). His international awards include Man of the Match in the second ODI v Sri Lanka at Colombo 1997-98 (111) and in the second Test v England at Trent Bridge 2000 (148*). Retired from international cricket in 2000. Scored double century (203*) and century (115) v Nottinghamshire at Trent Bridge 2001 and again (119/205*) v Surrey at Hove 2007. Joint Sussex Player of the Year (with Richard Montgomerie) 2001. Scored 335* v Leicestershire at Hove 2003, surpassing K. S. Duleepsinhji's 333 in 1930 to set a new record for the highest individual score for Sussex (and winning the Sussex Outstanding Performance of the Year Award 2003). Scored 214* v Warwickshire at Hove 2006, in the process sharing with Michael Yardy (159*) in a new Sussex record partnership for the third wicket (385*). Overseas player with Sussex 2001-04. Is no longer considered an overseas player
Best batting: 335* Sussex v Leicestershire, Hove 2003
Best bowling: 2-23 Zimbabweans v Lahore City, Lahore 1998-99

2007 Season

	M	Inn	NO	Runs	HS	Avg	100	50	Ct	St	Balls	Runs	Wkts	Avg	BB	5I	10M
Test																	
FC	15	27	5	1214	205 *	55.18	4	5	10	-	6	6	0		-	-	-
ODI																	
List A	14	13	2	455	111	41.36	1	3	2	-	0	0	0		-	-	
20/20 Int																	
20/20	9	9	1	302	102 *	37.75	1	1	1	-	0	0	0		-	-	

Career Performances

	M	Inn	NO	Runs	HS	Avg	100	50	Ct	St	Balls	Runs	Wkts	Avg	BB	5I	10M
Test	19	37	4	1414	166 *	42.84	3	8	10	-	119	69	0		-	-	-
FC	218	383	30	17037	335 *	48.26	52	72	130	-	701	363	7	51.85	2-23	-	-
ODI	71	70	3	1818	112 *	27.13	2	8	20	-	248	210	4	52.50	1-12	-	
List A	299	289	32	8961	167	34.86	12	56	94	-	351	306	7	43.71	1-9	-	
20/20 Int																	
20/20	36	31	3	648	102 *	23.14	1	2	5	-	0	0	0		-	-	

GOUGH, D. Yorkshire

Name: Darren Gough
Role: Right-hand bat, right-arm fast bowler, county captain
Born: 18 September 1970, Barnsley
Height: 5ft 11in **Weight:** 13st 9lbs
Nickname: Rhino, Dazzler
County debut: 1989 (Yorkshire), 2004 (Essex)
County cap: 1993 (Yorkshire), 2004 (Essex)
Benefit: 2001 (Yorkshire)
Test debut: 1994
ODI debut: 1994
Twenty20 Int debut: 2005
50 wickets in a season: 4
Place in batting averages: 242nd av. 15.64
Place in bowling averages: 20th av. 23.67 (2006 35th av. 28.96)
Parents: Trevor and Christine
Children: Liam James, 24 November 1994; Brennan Kyle, 9 December 1997
Education: Priory Comprehensive; Airedale and Wharfedale College (part-time)
Qualifications: 2 O-levels, 5 CSEs, BTEC Leisure, NCA coaching award
Overseas tours: England YC to Australia 1989-90; Yorkshire to Barbados 1989-90, to South Africa 1991-92, 1992-93; England A to South Africa 1993-94; England to Australia 1994-95, to South Africa 1995-96, to India and Pakistan (World Cup) 1995-96, to Zimbabwe and New Zealand 1996-97, to Australia 1998-99, to Sharjah (Coca-Cola Cup) 1998-99, to South Africa and Zimbabwe 1999-2000, to Kenya (ICC Knockout Trophy) 2000-01, to Pakistan and Sri Lanka 2000-01, to India and New Zealand 2001-02 (one-day series), to Australia 2002-03, to West Indies 2003-04 (one-day series), to Zimbabwe (one-day series) 2004-05, to South Africa 2004-05 (one-day series); ICC World XI to Australia (Tsunami Relief) 2004-05; England VI to Hong Kong 2006
Overseas teams played for: East Shirley, Christchurch, New Zealand 1991-92
Cricketers particularly admired: Shane Warne, Steve Waugh, Ian Botham, Michael Atherton, Malcolm Marshall
Other sports played: Golf, football
Other sports followed: Football (Barnsley and Tottenham Hotspur)
Relaxations: Golf, cinema
Extras: Yorkshire Sports Personality of the Year 1994. Cornhill England Player of the Year 1994-95, 1998-99. Whyte and Mackay Bowler of the Year 1996. Took hat-trick (Healy, MacGill, Miller) in the fifth Test v Australia at Sydney 1998-99. *Sheffield Star* Sports Personality of the Year. One of *Wisden*'s Five Cricketers of the Year 1999. Won Freeserve Fast Ball award 2000 for a delivery timed at 93.1 mph during the first Test v Zimbabwe at Lord's. Vodafone England Cricketer of the Year 2000-01. *GQ* Sportsman

of the Year 2001. Took 200th Test wicket (Rashid Latif) v Pakistan at Lord's 2001 in his 50th Test. His international awards include Man of the [Test] Series v Sri Lanka 2000-01 and England's Man of the [Test] Series v West Indies 2000. Retired from Test cricket during the 2003 season. Granted Freedom of the City of London in March 2004. Took 200th ODI wicket (Harbhajan Singh) v India at Lord's in the NatWest Challenge 2004, becoming the first England bowler to reach the milestone. Winner, with Lilia Kopylova, of *Strictly Come Dancing*, December 2005. Vice-captain of Essex 2005-06. Rejoined Yorkshire for 2007 as captain
Best batting: 121 Yorkshire v Warwickshire, Headingley 1996
Best bowling: 7-28 Yorkshire v Lancashire, Headingley 1995

2007 Season

	M	Inn	NO	Runs	HS	Avg	100	50	Ct	St	Balls	Runs	Wkts	Avg	BB	5I	10M
Test																	
FC	14	15	1	219	50	15.64	-	1	2	-	1726	876	37	23.67	6-47	3	-
ODI																	
List A	14	7	4	75	49 *	25.00	-	-	5	-	611	455	23	19.78	3-30	-	
20/20 Int																	
20/20	8	3	0	16	9	5.33	-	-	1	-	126	174	8	21.75	2-10	-	

Career Performances

	M	Inn	NO	Runs	HS	Avg	100	50	Ct	St	Balls	Runs	Wkts	Avg	BB	5I	10M
Test	58	86	18	855	65	12.57	-	2	13	-	11821	6503	229	28.39	6-42	9	-
FC	240	315	59	4459	121	17.41	1	20	47	-	43129	22689	846	26.81	7-28	33	3
ODI	159	87	38	609	46 *	12.42	-	-	25	-	8470	6209	235	26.42	5-44	2	
List A	404	222	74	2054	72 *	13.87	-	2	69	-	20033	13947	577	24.17	7-27	7	
20/20 Int	2	0	0	0	0		-	-	-	-	41	49	3	16.33	3-16	-	
20/20	23	14	2	179	37	14.91	-	-	1	-	461	588	25	23.52	3-16	-	

30. Who top-scored with 42 batting at No. 11 in England's second innings of the third Test v South Africa at Cape Town in 2004-05?

GRANT, R. N. Glamorgan

Name: Richard Neil Grant
Role: Right-hand bat, right-arm medium bowler; 'batter who bowls a little'
Born: 5 June 1984, Neath
Height: 5ft 10in **Weight:** 13st 8lbs
Nickname: Pingu, Wig
County debut: 2004 (one-day), 2005 (first-class)
Place in batting averages: 164th av. 26.92 (2006 222nd av. 17.81)
Parents: Kevin ('Sven-Göran Eriksson') and Moira
Marital status: Single ('long-term girlfriend Samantha')
Family links with cricket: 'Brother Glamorgan 2nd XI, MCC YC (groundstaff); Dad local cricket (not very good, though)'
Education: Cefn Saeson Comprehensive, Neath; Neath Port Talbot College
Qualifications: 6 GCSEs, NVQ Level II Carpentry, Level II coaching award
Career outside cricket: '12-month contract'
Overseas tours: South Wales Junior League to Australia 1998; Wales U16 to Jersey 2000; Neath Port Talbot College to Goa 2001, to Malta 2002, to South Africa 2003
Overseas teams played for: Havelock North, Napier, New Zealand 2003-04; Balmain Tigers, Sydney 2007-08
Cricket moments to forget: 'None, they have all been great'
Cricket superstitions: 'Left pad on first'
Young players to look out for: James Harris
Other sports played: Golf
Other sports followed: Football (Swansea City, Blackburn), rugby (Ospreys)
Favourite band: Coldplay
Relaxations: 'Spending time with girlfriend Samantha'
Extras: Neath Port Talbot College Sportsman of the Year 2002; Neath Port Talbot County Borough Council Sportsman of the Year 2002. Glamorgan 2nd XI Player of the Year 2005
Opinions on cricket: 'Ninety overs in the day plus longer tea break.'
Best batting: 79 Glamorgan v Northamptonshire, Colwyn Bay 2007
Best bowling: 1-7 Glamorgan v Somerset, Taunton 2007

2007 Season

	M	Inn	NO	Runs	HS	Avg	100	50	Ct	St	Balls	Runs	Wkts	Avg	BB	5I	10M
Test																	
FC	8	13	0	350	79	26.92	-	2	1	-	70	78	2	39.00	1-7	-	-
ODI																	
List A	9	9	0	146	44	16.22	-	-	3	-	24	42	1	42.00	1-14	-	
20/20 Int																	
20/20	6	5	0	91	45	18.20	-	-	3	-	0	0	0		-	-	

Career Performances

	M	Inn	NO	Runs	HS	Avg	100	50	Ct	St	Balls	Runs	Wkts	Avg	BB	5I	10M
Test																	
FC	19	31	1	649	79	21.63	-	2	5	-	243	224	5	44.80	1-7	-	-
ODI																	
List A	39	36	2	662	45	19.47	-	-	9	-	247	315	7	45.00	2-21	-	
20/20 Int																	
20/20	16	14	1	333	77	25.61	-	2	6	-	63	130	7	18.57	4-38	-	

GREEN, J. A. G. — Sussex

Name: Jeremy Arthur Graham Green
Role: Right-hand bat, right-arm medium-fast bowler
Born: 17 September 1984, Cuckfield
Height: 6ft 2in
Nickname: Jez
County debut: 2002 (one-day), 2007 (first-class)
Parents: David and Janis
Family links with cricket: Father is chairman of Sussex CCC
Education: Lancing College
Qualifications: 11 GCSEs
Overseas tours: Sussex Academy to Sri Lanka 2001
Other sports played: Golf, football, hockey, skiing
Extras: Attended Sussex Academy. Has played for Sussex 2nd XI since 2002. Played one first-class match for Sussex 2007
Best batting: 28 Sussex v Sri Lanka A, Hove 2007

2007 Season

	M	Inn	NO	Runs	HS	Avg	100	50	Ct	St	Balls	Runs	Wkts	Avg	BB	5I	10M
Test																	
FC	1	1	0	28	28	28.00	-	-	-	-	48	32	0		-	-	-
ODI																	
List A																	
20/20 Int																	
20/20																	

Career Performances

	M	Inn	NO	Runs	HS	Avg	100	50	Ct	St	Balls	Runs	Wkts	Avg	BB	5I	10M
Test																	
FC	1	1	0	28	28	28.00	-	-	-	-	48	32	0		-	-	-
ODI																	
List A	1	1	0	7	7	7.00	-	-	1	-	0	0	0		-	-	
20/20 Int																	
20/20																	

GREENIDGE, C. G. — Gloucestershire

Name: Carl Gary Greenidge
Role: Right-hand bat, right-arm fast-medium bowler
Born: 20 April 1978, Basingstoke
Height: 5ft 10in **Weight:** 12st 8lbs
Nickname: Carlos, Gs, Jackal
County debut: 1998 (one-day, Surrey), 1999 (first-class, Surrey), 2002 (Northamptonshire), 2005 (Gloucestershire)
County cap: 2005 (Gloucestershire)
50 wickets in a season: 1
Place in bowling averages: 44th av. 26.85
Parents: Gordon and Anita
Marital status: Single
Family links with cricket: Father Gordon played for Hampshire and West Indies, as did cousin (on mother's side) Andy Roberts
Education: St Michael's, Barbados; Heathcote School, Chingford; City of Westminster College
Qualifications: GNVQ Leisure and Tourism, NCA senior coaching award
Cricket moments to forget: 'Yorkshire v Northants, April 2003, first game of the season – easily my worst ever game' (*Northants conceded 673 runs and lost by an innings*)

Cricket superstitions: 'None'
Cricketers particularly admired: Malcolm Marshall, Michael Holding, Viv Richards
Other sports played: Football ('PlayStation!')
Other sports followed: Football (Arsenal), basketball (LA Lakers)
Favourite band: Bob Marley and the Wailers
Relaxations: 'PlayStation, movies, reading, music'
Extras: Spent a year on Lord's groundstaff. Took 5-60 (8-124 the match) on Championship debut for Surrey, v Yorkshire at The Oval 1999
Best batting: 46 Northamptonshire v Derbyshire, Derby 2002
Best bowling: 6-40 Northamptonshire v Durham, Riverside 2002

2007 Season

	M	Inn	NO	Runs	HS	Avg	100	50	Ct	St	Balls	Runs	Wkts	Avg	BB	5I	10M
Test																	
FC	8	11	1	95	27	9.50	-	-	3	-	1098	752	28	26.85	5-54	1	-
ODI																	
List A	11	5	2	39	29	13.00	-	-	1	-	442	454	14	32.42	4-15	-	
20/20 Int																	
20/20	9	4	2	25	20	12.50	-	-	3	-	165	235	7	33.57	3-20	-	

Career Performances

	M	Inn	NO	Runs	HS	Avg	100	50	Ct	St	Balls	Runs	Wkts	Avg	BB	5I	10M
Test																	
FC	49	60	8	443	46	8.51	-	-	18	-	7374	4972	140	35.51	6-40	5	-
ODI																	
List A	65	28	11	140	29	8.23	-	-	16	-	2789	2622	77	34.05	4-15	-	
20/20 Int																	
20/20	29	9	5	34	20	8.50	-	-	11	-	585	843	32	26.34	3-15	-	

31. Which Yorkshire opener made his Test debut v South Africa at Edgbaston in 1924 and played his 54th and final Test against the same opposition at Lord's in 1935?

GRIFFITHS, D. A. Hampshire

Name: David Andrew Griffiths
Role: Left-hand bat, right-arm fast-medium bowler
Born: 10 September 1985, Newport, Isle of Wight
Height: 6ft **Weight:** 12st 7lbs
Nickname: Griff
County debut: 2006
Place in bowling averages: 93rd av. 34.25
Parents: Adrian Griffiths and Lizbeth Porter; Dave Porter (stepfather); Sharon Griffiths (stepmother)
Marital status: Single ('girlfriend Sophie')
Family links with cricket: 'Father captained Wales. Stepfather captained Isle of Wight. Uncles play league cricket'
Education: Sandown High School, Isle of Wight
Qualifications: Levels 1 and 2 cricket coaching
Career outside cricket: 'Coaching and odd jobs'
Off-season: 'Perth, January to March'
Overseas tours: West of England U15 to West Indies 2001; England U19 to India 2004-05
Overseas teams played for: Melville, Perth 2007
Career highlights to date: 'Making Championship debut against Durham [2007]'
Cricket moments to forget: 'The first ball in Championship cricket – Ottis Gibson hitting me on the head'
Cricket superstitions: 'Turn right at end of run-up'
Cricketers particularly admired: Darren Gough, Brett Lee
Young players to look out for: Liam Dawson, Benny Howell
Other sports played: Football (Isle of Wight U11-U18), rugby (IOW)
Other sports followed: Football (Man Utd), rugby league (St Helens)
Favourite band: 'No band – R&B music'
Relaxations: Golf
Extras: Represented England U19 2004. Southern League Young Player of the Year 2004. Took 3-13 on Twenty20 debut v Essex at The Rose Bowl 2007
Best batting: 31* Hampshire v Surrey, Rose Bowl 2007
Best bowling: 4-46 Hampshire v Durham, Riverside 2007

2007 Season

	M	Inn	NO	Runs	HS	Avg	100	50	Ct	St	Balls	Runs	Wkts	Avg	BB	5I	10M
Test																	
FC	5	8	3	42	31 *	8.40	-	-	1	-	603	411	12	34.25	4-46	-	-
ODI																	
List A																	
20/20 Int																	
20/20	3	1	1	4	4 *		-	-	-	-	42	55	3	18.33	3-13	-	

Career Performances

	M	Inn	NO	Runs	HS	Avg	100	50	Ct	St	Balls	Runs	Wkts	Avg	BB	5I	10M
Test																	
FC	6	9	4	58	31 *	11.60	-	-	1	-	639	440	12	36.66	4-46	-	-
ODI																	
List A																	
20/20 Int																	
20/20	3	1	1	4	4 *		-	-	-	-	42	55	3	18.33	3-13	-	

GROENEWALD, T. D. Warwickshire

Name: Timothy (Tim) Duncan Groenewald
Role: Right-hand bat, right-arm fast-medium bowler; bowling all-rounder
Born: 10 January 1984, Pietermaritzburg, South Africa
Height: 6ft 2in **Weight:** 13st
Nickname: Groeners
County debut: 2006
Place in batting averages: 223rd av. 19.00 (2006 192nd av. 22.42)
Parents: Neil and Tessa
Wife and date of marriage: Michelle, 5 January 2008
Education: Maritzburg College, Natal; University of South Africa
Qualifications: Matric, marketing degree
Career outside cricket: Part-time student
Off-season: 'Three months in South Africa; getting married on 5 January'
Overseas tours: Natal U15 to UK 1999
Overseas teams played for: Zingari CC, Natal 1999-2005; Natal Dolphins 2002-03; KZN Inland 2004-05; Rovers CC 2006

Career highlights to date: 'Getting Kevin Pietersen out in the Friends Provident semi-final [2007]'
Cricket moments to forget: 'Double relegation in 2007'
Cricketers particularly admired: Allan Donald, Steve Waugh, Hansie Cronje
Young players to look out for: James Ord
Other sports played: Hockey (Midlands U21 A 2003), tennis and golf ('socially')
Other sports followed: Super 14 rugby (Sharks)
Injuries: Out for two weeks in August with a hip injury
Favourite band: Snow Patrol
Relaxations: 'Listening to music, watching sport, sleeping, spending time with friends'
Extras: Leading wicket-taker at National U19 Week and represented South African Schools Colts U19. Seventh in the Sky Sports Sixes League 2007 with 20
Opinions on cricket: 'Don't get rid of the Pro40. New ball back to 90 overs in County Championship – get spinners more involved.'
Best batting: 76 Warwickshire v Durham, Riverside 2006
Best bowling: 3-26 Warwickshire v Hampshire, Edgbaston 2007

2007 Season

	M	Inn	NO	Runs	HS	Avg	100	50	Ct	St	Balls	Runs	Wkts	Avg	BB	5I	10M
Test																	
FC	8	9	2	133	41 *	19.00	-	-	8	-	795	430	9	47.77	3-26	-	-
ODI																	
List A	13	10	1	123	36	13.66	-	-	3	-	434	415	12	34.58	3-25	-	
20/20 Int																	
20/20	8	7	2	140	41	28.00	-	-	4	-	114	165	6	27.50	2-10	-	

Career Performances

	M	Inn	NO	Runs	HS	Avg	100	50	Ct	St	Balls	Runs	Wkts	Avg	BB	5I	10M
Test																	
FC	14	18	4	290	76	20.71	-	1	9	-	1497	826	15	55.06	3-26	-	-
ODI																	
List A	18	13	2	132	36	12.00	-	-	4	-	554	553	14	39.50	3-25	-	
20/20 Int																	
20/20	10	7	2	140	41	28.00	-	-	5	-	138	208	6	34.66	2-10	-	

GURNEY, H. F. — Leicestershire

Name: Harry Frederick Gurney
Role: Right-hand bat, left-arm seam bowler
Born: 25 October 1986, Nottingham
Height: 6ft 2in **Weight:** 12st
Nickname: Gurns
County debut: 2007
Parents: Jane and John
Marital status: Single
Education: Garendon High School; Loughborough Grammar School; University of Leeds
Qualifications: 9 GCSEs, 4 A-levels
Career outside cricket: 'Student'
Off-season: 'Training, then playing cricket in Australia'
Overseas tours: Loughborough GS to Cape Town 2004; Leicestershire Academy/U19 to India 2005-06
Career highlights to date: 'First-class debut'
Cricket moments to forget: 'My performance in first game against first-class opposition – Yorkshire at Headingley'
Cricket superstitions: 'None'
Cricketers particularly admired: Glenn McGrath, Courtney Walsh
Young players to look out for: Sam Reddish, Johnny and Alfie Gurney
Other sports played: 'Recreational football'
Other sports followed: Football (West Ham United)
Injuries: Out for most of the 2007 season (until late August) with an ankle injury
Favourite band: ELO, Queen
Relaxations: 'Poker'
Extras: Played for Bradford/Leeds UCCE 2006, 2007
Best batting: 1 Leicestershire v Northamptonshire, Leicester 2007
Best bowling: 1-84 Leicestershire v Northamptonshire, Leicester 2007

2007 Season

	M	Inn	NO	Runs	HS	Avg	100	50	Ct	St	Balls	Runs	Wkts	Avg	BB	5I	10M
Test																	
FC	1	2	1	1	1	1.00	-	-	-	-	216	173	2	86.50	1-84	-	-
ODI																	
List A																	
20/20 Int																	
20/20																	

Career Performances

	M	Inn	NO	Runs	HS	Avg	100	50	Ct	St	Balls	Runs	Wkts	Avg	BB	5I	10M
Test																	
FC	1	2	1	1	1	1.00	-	-	-	-	216	173	2	86.50	1-84	-	-
ODI																	
List A																	
20/20 Int																	
20/20																	

GUY, S. M. Yorkshire

Name: Simon Mark Guy
Role: Right-hand bat, wicket-keeper
Born: 17 November 1978, Rotherham
Height: 5ft 7in **Weight:** 10st 7lbs
Nickname: Rat
County debut: 2000
Place in batting averages: (2006 176th av. 25.00)
Parents: Darrell and Denise
Wife and date of marriage: Suzanne, 13 October 2001
Children: Isaac Simon, 15 January 2004; Rowan Joseph
Family links with cricket: 'Father played for Nottinghamshire and Worcestershire 2nd XI and for Rotherham Town CC. Brothers play local cricket for Treeton CC'
Education: Wickersley Comprehensive School
Qualifications: GNVQ in Leisure and Recreation, Level 3 coaching award
Off-season: 'I will be starting my Level 4 coaching in October [2007]; I will also be training and looking to spend time with my family; I will also be an assistant coach for the Northern Skill Sets'
Overseas tours: Yorkshire to South Africa 1999, 2001, to Grenada 2002
Overseas teams played for: Orange CYMS, NSW 1999-2000
Career highlights to date: 'Playing the last ever County Championship game at Southampton [Northlands Road in 2000] and winning off the last ball with 13 Yorkshire and past Yorkshire men on the pitch at the same time'
Cricket moments to forget: 'On my debut against the Zimbabweans, smashing a door after getting out – but I still say it was an accident'
Cricket superstitions: 'Just a lot of routines'

Cricketers particularly admired: Jack Russell, Darren Lehmann
Young players to look out for: Oliver Hannon-Dalby
Other sports played: 'I like to play all sports', rugby (played for South Yorkshire and Yorkshire)
Other sports followed: Rugby (Rotherham RUFC), 'Treeton Welfare CC, where all my family play'
Favourite band: My Chemical Romance
Relaxations: 'Playing all sports, socialising with friends, watching cartoons, and eating a lot'
Extras: Topped Yorkshire 2nd XI batting averages 1998 (106.00). Awarded 2nd XI cap 2000. Took five catches in an innings for first time for Yorkshire 1st XI v Surrey at Scarborough 2000
Opinions on cricket: 'I think the Twenty20 has revitalised the game and helped bring in younger and new supporters which can only be a good thing for the survival of the game.'
Best batting: 52* Yorkshire v Durham, Headingley 2006

2007 Season

	M	Inn	NO	Runs	HS	Avg	100	50	Ct	St	Balls	Runs	Wkts	Avg	BB	5I	10M
Test																	
FC	4	5	0	115	37	23.00	-	-	11	-	0	0	0		-	-	-
ODI																	
List A	6	4	0	59	36	14.75	-	-	5	-	0	0	0		-	-	
20/20 Int																	
20/20																	

Career Performances

	M	Inn	NO	Runs	HS	Avg	100	50	Ct	St	Balls	Runs	Wkts	Avg	BB	5I	10M
Test																	
FC	36	50	6	727	52 *	16.52	-	1	97	12	24	8	0		-	-	-
ODI																	
List A	25	18	3	254	40	16.93	-	-	23	7	0	0	0		-	-	
20/20 Int																	
20/20																	

HALES, A. D. Nottinghamshire

Name: Alexander (Alex) Daniel Hales
Role: Right-hand bat, off-spin bowler, part-time wicket-keeper
Born: 3 January 1989, Hillingdon, Middlesex
Height: 6ft 5in **Weight:** 13st 6lbs
Nickname: Halesy, Trigg
County debut: No first-team appearance
Parents: Gary and Lisa
Marital status: Single
Education: Chesham High School, Chesham, Buckinghamshire
Qualifications: 10 GCSEs, 3 AS-levels
Off-season: 'Planning to go to Melbourne and play grade cricket'
Overseas tours: London County CC to Cape Town 2006; MCC YC to St Kitts and Nevis 2007
Overseas teams played for: Pennant Hills District CC, Sydney 2007

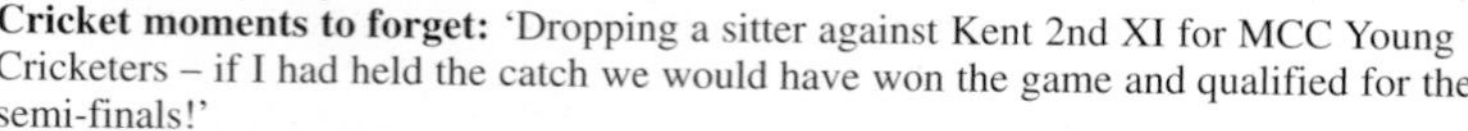

Cricket moments to forget: 'Dropping a sitter against Kent 2nd XI for MCC Young Cricketers – if I had held the catch we would have won the game and qualified for the semi-finals!'
Cricket superstitions: 'Always put my left pad on before my right one'
Cricketers particularly admired: Ian Bell, Nick Lines, Vinnie Fazio
Young players to look out for: Lee Hodgson, Luke Fletcher, Dave Cranfield-Thompson
Other sports played: 'Play a bit of football in the winter for my local team. Used to play county tennis and table tennis'
Other sports followed: Football (Arsenal)
Injuries: 'Pulled my groin pre-season last year and was out for a couple of weeks'
Favourite band: Oasis
Relaxations: 'Enjoy playing poker and socialising with mates'
Extras: Once scored 52 in one over on the Lord's Nursery ground – over included eight sixes and a four plus three no-balls for an overall total of 55. Played for Buckinghamshire in Minor Counties competitions 2006, 2007. Played for MCC YC 2006, 2007. 'Grandfather once took Rod Laver to five sets at Wimbledon'
Opinions on cricket: 'The tempo of cricket has become a lot higher with the introduction of Twenty20 and Pro40 and this is changing the overall image of the game.'

HALL, A. J. Northamptonshire

Name: Andrew James Hall
Role: Right-hand bat, right-arm fast-medium bowler; all-rounder
Born: 31 July 1975, Johannesburg, South Africa
County debut: 2003 (Worcestershire), 2005 (Kent)
County cap: 2003 (Worcestershire colours), 2005 (Kent)
Test debut: 2001-02
ODI debut: 1998-99
Twenty20 Int debut: 2005-06
Place in batting averages: 145th av. 29.33
Place in bowling averages: 118th av. 40.66 (2006 10th av. 23.85)
Wife: Leanie
Education: Hoërskool Alberton
Overseas tours: South Africa to Sri Lanka (Singer Triangular Series) 2000, to Australia (Super Challenge) 2000, to Singapore (Godrej Singapore Challenge) 2000-01, to Kenya (ICC Knockout Trophy) 2000-01, to Bangladesh (TVS Cup) 2003, to England 2003, to Pakistan 2003-04, to India 2004-05, to West Indies 2004-05, to India (one-day series) 2005-06, to Australia 2005-06 (VB Series), to Sri Lanka 2006, to India (ICC Champions Trophy) 2006-07, to West Indies (World Cup) 2006-07, to Ireland (one-day series v India) 2007; South Africa A to Zimbabwe 2007-08
Overseas teams played for: Transvaal/Gauteng 1994-95 – 2000-01; Easterns 2001-02 – 2003-04; Lions 2004-05 – 2005-06; Dolphins 2006-07
Extras: Played for South Africa Academy 1997. Was shot in the hand and face by a mugger in Johannesburg in 1999 and was car-jacked in 2002. Man of the Match in the tied second indoor ODI v Australia at Melbourne 2000 (37/2-8). His other international awards include Man of the Match in the first Test v India at Kanpur 2004-05 (163), in the fifth ODI v New Zealand at Centurion 2005-06 (4-23) and v England at Bridgetown in the 2006-07 World Cup (5-18). One of *South African Cricket Annual*'s five Cricketers of the Year 2002. His South African domestic awards include Man of the SuperSport Series 2002-03 and Man of the Match in the final (6-77/5-22). An overseas player with Worcestershire 2003-04. Man of the Match v Lancashire in the C&G semi-final at Worcester 2003. An overseas player with Kent 2005-07. Retired from international cricket in late summer 2007. Left Kent at the end of the 2007 season and has joined Northamptonshire for 2008. Is no longer considered an overseas player
Best batting: 163 South Africa v India, Kanpur 2004-05
Best bowling: 6-77 Easterns v Western Province, Benoni 2002-03

2007 Season

	M	Inn	NO	Runs	HS	Avg	100	50	Ct	St	Balls	Runs	Wkts	Avg	BB	5I	10M
Test																	
FC	7	10	1	264	77	29.33	-	2	6	-	978	610	15	40.66	5-59	1	-
ODI																	
List A	7	7	1	269	123	44.83	1	1	3	-	317	240	9	26.66	2-12	-	
20/20 Int																	
20/20	1	0	0	0	0		-	-	-	-	18	25	2	12.50	2-25	-	

Career Performances

	M	Inn	NO	Runs	HS	Avg	100	50	Ct	St	Balls	Runs	Wkts	Avg	BB	5I	10M
Test	21	33	4	760	163	26.20	1	3	16	-	3001	1617	45	35.93	3-1	-	-
FC	126	184	25	5353	163	33.66	5	36	91	-	21210	9993	382	26.15	6-77	13	1
ODI	88	56	13	905	81	21.04	-	3	29	-	3341	2515	95	26.47	5-18	1	
List A	242	189	34	4686	129 *	30.23	5	25	70	-	9912	7424	277	26.80	5-18	1	
20/20 Int	2	1	0	11	11	11.00	-	-	-	-	48	60	3	20.00	3-22	-	
20/20	31	29	2	596	59	22.07	-	1	10	-	624	815	37	22.02	3-15	-	

HAMILTON-BROWN, R. J. Sussex

Name: Rory James Hamilton-Brown
Role: Right-hand bat, right-arm off-spin bowler
Born: 3 September 1987, London
Height: 6ft **Weight:** 13st 7lbs
Nickname: Bear, Stewi, RHB
County debut: 2005 (Surrey)
Parents: Roger and Holly
Marital status: Single
Family links with cricket: 'Dad played for Warwickshire'
Education: Millfield School
Qualifications: 9 GCSEs, 3 A-levels
Overseas tours: England U16 to South Africa; England U19 to Bangladesh 2005-06, to Sri Lanka (U19 World Cup) 2005-06
Career highlights to date: 'Facing Mushtaq Ahmed on debut against Sussex in the totesport League'
Cricket moments to forget: 'Dropping a very simple catch which single-handedly meant Surrey U19 were knocked out of national competition'
Cricket superstitions: 'None'

Cricketers particularly admired: Damien Martyn, Mark Ramprakash, Alec Stewart
Young players to look out for: Billy Godleman, Ben Wright
Other sports played: Rugby (England U16, England Junior National Academy)
Other sports followed: Football (Birmingham City)
Favourite band: Donell Jones, Trey Songz
Relaxations: 'Relaxing with friends'
Extras: Captained England U15. *Daily Telegraph* Bunbury Scholar (Batsman) 2003. Broke Millfield batting record 2004 at 16. Made 2nd XI Championship debut 2004, scoring 43 and 84 v Sussex 2nd XI at Hove. Represented England U19 2006 and (as captain) 2007. Left Surrey at the end of the 2007 season and has joined Sussex for 2008
Best batting: 9 Surrey v Bangladesh A, The Oval 2005

2007 Season

	M	Inn	NO	Runs	HS	Avg	100	50	Ct	St	Balls	Runs	Wkts	Avg	BB	5I	10M
Test																	
FC																	
ODI																	
List A	5	5	1	28	17	7.00	-	-	3	-	168	159	6	26.50	3-28	-	
20/20 Int																	
20/20																	

Career Performances

	M	Inn	NO	Runs	HS	Avg	100	50	Ct	St	Balls	Runs	Wkts	Avg	BB	5I	10M
Test																	
FC	1	2	0	14	9	7.00	-	-	1	-	0	0	0		-	-	-
ODI																	
List A	9	8	1	71	20	10.14	-	-	3	-	168	159	6	26.50	3-28	-	
20/20 Int																	
20/20																	

32. Which pair of New Zealand brothers appeared in a Test together for the first time in the first Test v England at The Oval in 1983: a) Hedley and Geoff Howarth; b) Dayle and Richard Hadlee; c) Jeff and Martin Crowe?

HANNON-DALBY, O. J. Yorkshire

Name: Oliver James Hannon-Dalby
Role: Left-hand bat, right-arm medium-fast bowler
Born: 20 June 1989, Halifax
Height: 6ft 7in **Weight:** 13st 8lbs
Nickname: Bunse, Dave, Shaggy
County debut: No first-team appearance
Parents: Sally Hannon and Stephen Dalby
Marital status: Single
Family links with cricket: 'Whole family on both sides play and support cricket'
Education: The Brooksbank School Sports College and Sixth Form
Qualifications: 13 GCSEs, 3 A-levels, 1 NVQ, Community Sports Leader Award and Higher Sports Leader Award
Off-season: 'Tour of Bloemfontein; tour of Dubai'
Overseas tours: Yorkshire Schools Cricket Association to Cape Town 2007
Career highlights to date: 'Taking 6-32 v Scotland for Yorkshire 2nd XI 2007'
Cricket moments to forget: 'Jersey Cricket Festival final 2005'
Cricket superstitions: 'None'
Cricketers particularly admired: Fred Hemmingway, Peter Blake, Brett Lee
Young players to look out for: Chris Allinson, James Finch
Other sports played: Football (Hebden Bridge Saints, Copley United)
Other sports followed: Football (Leeds United), 'all England teams'
Injuries: Out for one month at the end of the 2007 season with an Achilles impingement
Favourite band: Stone Roses, Arctic Monkeys, Oasis, The Verve
Relaxations: 'Snooker, guitar playing'
Extras: Ian Steen Memorial Award 2004 for Most Improved U15 Player. YCB Alec Holdsworth U17 Bowling Award 2006. YCCSA Young Player of the Year 2007
Opinions on cricket: 'With the development of much larger bats and with shorter boundaries being used in recent years, it's definitely a batsman's game.'

HARBHAJAN SINGH Surrey

Name: Harbhajan Singh
Role: Right-hand bat, right-arm off-spin bowler
Born: 3 July 1980, Jalandhar, India
Nickname: Bhaji
County debut: 2005
Test debut: 1997-98
ODI debut: 1997-98
Twenty20 Int debut: 2006-07
Place in batting averages: 253rd av. 13.66
Place in bowling averages: 4th av. 18.54
Overseas tours: India U19 to South Africa (U19 World Cup) 1997-98; India to Sharjah (Coca-Cola Cup) 1997-98, to Zimbabwe 1998-99, to New Zealand 1998-99, to Sri Lanka (Asian Test Championship) 1998-99, to Australia 1999-2000, to Zimbabwe 2001, to Sri Lanka 2001, to South Africa 2001-02, to West Indies 2001-02, to England 2002, to Sri Lanka (ICC Champions Trophy) 2002-03, to New Zealand 2002-03, to Africa (World Cup) 2002-03, to Australia 2003-04, to England (ICC Champions Trophy) 2004, to Bangladesh 2004-05, to Zimbabwe 2005-06, to Pakistan 2005-06, to West Indies 2006, to South Africa 2006-07, to West Indies (World Cup) 2006-07, to South Africa (World 20/20) 2007-08, to Australia 2007-08, plus other one-day tournaments in Sri Lanka, Malaysia, Bangladesh, England and Abu Dhabi
Overseas teams played for: Punjab (India) 1997-98 –
Extras: Popularly nicknamed the 'Turbanator'. Became the first Indian to take a Test hat-trick (Ponting, Gilchrist, Warne), in the second Test v Australia in Kolkata 2000-01, taking 32 wickets (av. 17.03) overall in the three-Test rubber and winning the Man of the Series award. His other series and match awards include Man of the [Test] Series v West Indies 2002-03 (20 wickets; av. 16.75), Man of the Match in the second Test v South Africa in Kolkata 2004-05 (2-54/7-87) and Man of the Match in the first ODI v England in Delhi 2005-06 (5-31/37). One of *Indian Cricket*'s five Cricketers of the Year 2001. Represented India in the ICC Champions Trophy 2006-07 and Asian Cricket Council XI in the Afro-Asia Cup 2007. Was an overseas player with Surrey 2005 and during July and August 2007
Best batting: 84 Punjab v Haryana, Amritsar 2000-01
84 Surrey v Gloucestershire, Bristol 2005
Best bowling: 8-84 India v Australia, Chennai (Madras) 2000-01

2007 Season

	M	Inn	NO	Runs	HS	Avg	100	50	Ct	St	Balls	Runs	Wkts	Avg	BB	5I	10M
Test																	
FC	6	7	1	82	29	13.66	-	-	3	-	1705	686	37	18.54	6-57	3	1
ODI																	
List A	5	2	2	27	25 *		-	-	-	-	228	177	6	29.50	2-34	-	
20/20 Int																	
20/20																	

Career Performances

	M	Inn	NO	Runs	HS	Avg	100	50	Ct	St	Balls	Runs	Wkts	Avg	BB	5I	10M
Test	57	79	18	985	66	16.14	-	2	30	-	15162	7108	238	29.86	8-84	19	4
FC	120	158	34	2367	84	19.08	-	6	63	-	28934	13566	509	26.65	8-84	33	6
ODI	151	79	22	728	46	12.77	-	-	41	-	8131	5619	174	32.29	5-31	2	
List A	197	108	30	1026	46	13.15	-	-	60	-	10415	7190	233	30.85	5-31	2	
20/20 Int	8	2	0	8	7	4.00	-	-	3	-	156	203	8	25.37	2-24	-	
20/20	21	9	2	91	31 *	13.00	-	-	6	-	390	446	16	27.87	2-22	-	

HARDINGES, M. A. Gloucestershire

Name: Mark Andrew Hardinges
Role: Right-hand bat, right-arm medium-fast bowler
Born: 5 February 1978, Gloucester
Height: 6ft 1in **Weight:** 13st 7lbs
Nickname: Dinges
County debut: 1999
County cap: 2004
Place in batting averages: 187th av. 23.92 (2006 110th av. 34.15)
Place in bowling averages: 138th av. 51.37 (2006 123rd av. 43.95)
Parents: David and Jean
Marital status: Single
Family links with cricket: Brother and father played club cricket
Education: Malvern College; Bath University
Qualifications: 10 GCSEs, 3 A-levels, BSc (Hons) Economics and Politics
Overseas tours: Malvern College to South Africa 1996; Gloucestershire to South Africa 1999, 2000
Overseas teams played for: Newtown and Chilwell, Geelong, Australia 1997

Career highlights to date: 'Norwich Union debut v Notts 2001 – scored 65 and set [then] domestic one-day seventh-wicket partnership record (164) with J. Snape. Also Lord's final v Surrey'
Cricket moments to forget: 'Glos v Somerset [Norwich Union 2001] – bowled three overs for 30 and was run out for 0 on Sky TV'
Cricketers particularly admired: Kim Barnett, Steve Waugh, Mark Alleyne
Other sports played: Golf, tennis (Gloucester U14), football (university first team)
Other sports followed: Football (Tottenham)
Relaxations: Golf
Extras: Represented British Universities 2000. C&G Man of the Match award for his 4-19 v Shropshire at Shrewsbury School 2002. Scored maiden one-day century (111*) v Lancashire at Old Trafford in the totesport League 2005, in the process sharing with Ramnaresh Sarwan (118*) in a new competition record fifth-wicket partnership (221*)
Best batting: 172 Gloucestershire v OUCCE, The Parks 2002
Best bowling: 5-51 Gloucestershire v Kent, Maidstone 2005

2007 Season

	M	Inn	NO	Runs	HS	Avg	100	50	Ct	St	Balls	Runs	Wkts	Avg	BB	5I	10M
Test																	
FC	9	15	1	335	104	23.92	1	1	6	-	1290	822	16	51.37	3-59	-	-
ODI																	
List A	14	14	3	328	70	29.81	-	3	5	-	499	544	15	36.26	3-35	-	
20/20 Int																	
20/20	9	5	2	81	39 *	27.00	-	-	2	-	174	187	11	17.00	2-16	-	

Career Performances

	M	Inn	NO	Runs	HS	Avg	100	50	Ct	St	Balls	Runs	Wkts	Avg	BB	5I	10M
Test																	
FC	44	67	7	1510	172	25.16	4	4	22	-	5799	3485	85	41.00	5-51	1	-
ODI																	
List A	73	66	10	1100	111 *	19.64	1	6	28	-	2546	2328	65	35.81	4-19	-	
20/20 Int																	
20/20	36	25	5	435	94 *	21.75	-	2	9	-	497	738	26	28.38	3-18	-	

33. Who became the first Test batsman to be given out obstructing the field in the fifth Test between England and South Africa at The Oval in 1951?

HARINATH, A. Surrey

Name: Arun Harinath
Role: Left-hand bat, off-spin bowler
Born: 26 March 1987, Carshalton, Surrey
Height: 5ft 11in **Weight:** 11st 10lbs
Nickname: The Baron
County debut: No first-team appearance
Parents: Mala and Suppiah
Marital status: Single
Family links with cricket: Brother Muhunthan played for Surrey 2nd XI 2006
Education: Tiffin Boys Grammar School; Loughborough University
Overseas tours: Surrey U19 to Sri Lanka 2002, to Cape Town 2005; Surrey Academy to Perth 2004; England U17 to Netherlands 2004
Overseas teams played for: Randwick Petersham, Sydney 2005-06
Cricket moments to forget: 'Dropping Samit Patel against Nottinghamshire 2nds at Sutton'
Cricketers particularly admired: Steve Waugh, Michael Hussey, Justin Langer, Brian Lara, Rahul Dravid, Mohammad Yousuf
Young players to look out for: Muhunthan Harinath
Other sports played: Rugby, badminton
Other sports followed: Rugby (Bath), NFL (Atlanta Falcons)
Relaxations: 'Films and music mainly'
Extras: Made 2nd XI Championship debut 2003. Played for Loughborough UCCE 2007
Opinions on cricket: 'The harder you work, the more you will get out of the game.'
Best batting: 69 LUCCE v Worcestershire, Worcester 2007

2007 Season (did not make any first-class or one-day appearances for his county)

Career Performances

	M	Inn	NO	Runs	HS	Avg	100	50	Ct	St	Balls	Runs	Wkts	Avg	BB	5I	10M
Test																	
FC	3	5	0	128	69	25.60	-	2	3	-	0	0	0		-	-	-
ODI																	
List A																	
20/20 Int																	
20/20																	

HARMISON, B. W. Durham

Name: Ben William Harmison
Role: Left-hand bat, right-arm fast-medium bowler; all-rounder
Born: 9 January 1986, Ashington, Northumberland
Height: 6ft 5in **Weight:** 14st
Nickname: Harmy
County debut: 2005 (one-day), 2006 (first-class)
Place in batting averages: 174th av. 25.57 (2006 86th av. 37.53)
Parents: Margaret and Jim
Marital status: Single
Family links with cricket: Brother Stephen plays for Durham and England. Father Jim and brother James play league cricket for Ashington CC
Education: Ashington High School
Overseas tours: England U19 to Bangladesh (U19 World Cup) 2003-04, to India 2004-05; Durham to India 2005
Career highlights to date: 'Two hundreds in my first two [first-class] games for Durham'
Cricket moments to forget: 'Getting a first-baller v Bangladesh A in a one-dayer'
Cricket superstitions: 'Left pad first'
Cricketers particularly admired: Andrew Flintoff
Young players to look out for: Moeen Ali 'and Durham Academy lads'
Other sports played: Golf, fishing, football
Other sports followed: Football (Newcastle United)
Relaxations: 'Fishing, listening to music'
Extras: Represented England U19 2005. Scored century (110) on first-class debut v Oxford UCCE at The Parks 2006 and another (105) in his next first-class match v West Indies A at Riverside 2006
Opinions on cricket: 'More time for rest and preparation for the next game!'
Best batting: 110 Durham v OUCCE, The Parks 2006
Best bowling: 2-29 Durham v Warwickshire, Riverside 2007

2007 Season

	M	Inn	NO	Runs	HS	Avg	100	50	Ct	St	Balls	Runs	Wkts	Avg	BB	5I	10M
Test																	
FC	9	16	2	358	101	25.57	1	2	7	-	320	286	3	95.33	2-29	-	-
ODI																	
List A	5	3	1	33	18	16.50	-	-	3	-	60	28	1	28.00	1-8	-	
20/20 Int																	
20/20	3	2	0	12	10	6.00	-	-	1	-	0	0	0		-	-	

Career Performances

	M	Inn	NO	Runs	HS	Avg	100	50	Ct	St	Balls	Runs	Wkts	Avg	BB	5I	10M
Test																	
FC	18	33	4	921	110	31.75	3	5	12	-	320	286	3	95.33	2-29	-	-
ODI																	
List A	13	11	1	175	57	17.50	-	1	8	-	90	79	2	39.50	1-8	-	
20/20 Int																	
20/20	5	4	0	20	10	5.00	-	-	2	-	0	0	0		-	-	

HARMISON, S. J. Durham

Name: Stephen James Harmison
Role: Right-hand bat, right-arm fast bowler
Born: 23 October 1978, Ashington, Northumberland
Height: 6ft 4in **Weight:** 14st
Nickname: Harmy
County debut: 1996
County cap: 1999
Test debut: 2002
ODI debut: 2002-03
Twenty20 Int debut: 2005
50 wickets in a season: 4
Place in batting averages: 246th av. 14.72 (2006 224th av. 17.50)
Place in bowling averages: 15th av. 22.33 (2006 24th av. 26.54)
Parents: Jimmy and Margaret
Wife and date of marriage: Hayley, 8 October 1999
Children: Emily Alice, 1 June 1999; Abbie Meg; Isabel Grace, May 2006
Family links with cricket: Brother James has played for Northumberland; brother Ben played for England U19 and is now at Durham

Education: Ashington High School
Overseas tours: England U19 to Pakistan 1996-97; England A to Zimbabwe and South Africa 1998-99; ECB National Academy to Australia 2001-02; England to Australia 2002-03, to Africa (World Cup) 2002-03, to Bangladesh 2003-04, to West Indies 2003-04, to South Africa 2004-05, to Pakistan 2005-06, to India 2005-06, to India (ICC Champions Trophy) 2006-07, to Australia 2006-07, to Sri Lanka 2007-08, to New Zealand 2007-08; ICC World XI to Australia (Super Series) 2005-06
Overseas teams played for: Highveld Lions, South Africa 2007-08
Cricketers particularly admired: David Boon, Courtney Walsh
Other sports played: Football (played for Ashington in Northern League), golf, snooker
Other sports followed: Football (Newcastle United)
Relaxations: Spending time with family
Extras: Man of the [Test] Series v West Indies 2003-04 (23 wickets at 14.86, including 7-12 at Kingston) and England's Man of the [Test] Series v New Zealand 2004 (21 wickets at 22.09). Had match figures of 9-121 (6-46/3-75) in the fourth Test v West Indies at The Oval 2004 to go to the top of the PricewaterhouseCoopers ratings for Test bowlers. His other international awards include Man of the Match in the second Test v Pakistan at Old Trafford 2006 (6-19/5-57). Became second England bowler (after James Anderson) to take an ODI hat-trick (Kaif, Balaji, Nehra), v India at Trent Bridge in the NatWest Challenge 2004. One of *Wisden*'s Five Cricketers of the Year 2005. Became first bowler to take a first-class hat-trick for Durham (Pipe, Mason, Wigley) v Worcestershire at Riverside 2005. Appointed MBE in 2006 New Year Honours as part of 2005 Ashes-winning England team. Retired from ODI cricket in December 2006. England 12-month central contract 2007-08
Best batting: 42 England v South Africa, Cape Town 2004-05
Best bowling: 7-12 England v West Indies, Kingston 2003-04

2007 Season

	M	Inn	NO	Runs	HS	Avg	100	50	Ct	St	Balls	Runs	Wkts	Avg	BB	5I	10M
Test	4	4	1	54	18	18.00	-	-	-	-	901	548	16	34.25	4-95	-	-
FC	12	16	5	162	30	14.72	-	-	1	-	2180	1184	53	22.33	6-87	3	-
ODI																	
List A	6	3	3	26	14 *		-	-	3	-	264	197	5	39.40	2-31	-	
20/20 Int																	
20/20	3	2	0	5	5	2.50	-	-	1	-	54	89	3	29.66	2-27	-	

Career Performances

	M	Inn	NO	Runs	HS	Avg	100	50	Ct	St	Balls	Runs	Wkts	Avg	BB	5I	10M
Test	54	73	18	632	42	11.49	-	-	7	-	11788	6319	205	30.82	7-12	8	1
FC	147	204	55	1493	42	10.02	-	-	24	-	28644	14960	516	28.99	7-12	18	1
ODI	46	22	13	67	13 *	7.44	-	-	8	-	2443	2057	67	30.70	5-33	1	
List A	109	51	27	168	17	7.00	-	-	18	-	5381	4387	139	31.56	5-33	1	
20/20 Int	2	0	0	0	0		-	-	1	-	39	42	1	42.00	1-13	-	
20/20	6	2	0	5	5	2.50	-	-	2	-	117	150	5	30.00	2-27	-	

HARRIS, A. J. — Nottinghamshire

Name: Andrew James Harris
Role: Right-hand bat, right-arm fast-medium bowler
Born: 26 June 1973, Ashton-under-Lyne, Lancashire
Height: 6ft **Weight:** 11st 9lbs
Nickname: AJ, Honest
County debut: 1994 (Derbyshire), 2000 (Nottinghamshire)
County cap: 1996 (Derbyshire), 2000 (Nottinghamshire)
Benefit: 2008 (Nottinghamshire)
50 wickets in a season: 1
Place in bowling averages: 113th av. 40.10 (2006 46th av. 30.28)
Parents: Norman (deceased) and Joyce
Wife and date of marriage: Kate, 7 October 2000
Children: Jacob Alexander, 28 August 2002
Education: Hadfield Comprehensive School; Glossopdale Community College
Qualifications: 6 GCSEs, 1 A-level
Overseas tours: England A to Australia 1996-97
Overseas teams played for: Ginninderra West Belconnen, Australian Capital Territory 1992-93; Victoria University of Wellington CC, New Zealand 1997-98
Cricket superstitions: 'None'
Cricketers particularly admired: Merv Hughes, Allan Donald
Other sports played: Golf, snooker, football
Other sports followed: Football (Man City)
Relaxations: 'Good food, good wine and the odd game of golf'
Extras: Nottinghamshire Player of the Year 2002. Had the misfortune to be 'timed out' v Durham UCCE at Trent Bridge 2003 (was suffering from groin injury)
Best batting: 41* Nottinghamshire v Northamptonshire, Northampton 2002
Best bowling: 7-54 Nottinghamshire v Northamptonshire, Trent Bridge 2002

2007 Season

	M	Inn	NO	Runs	HS	Avg	100	50	Ct	St	Balls	Runs	Wkts	Avg	BB	5I	10M
Test																	
FC	6	9	2	39	15 *	5.57	-	-	2	-	1182	762	19	40.10	4-69	-	-
ODI																	
List A	7	3	3	5	2 *		-	-	-	-	348	299	7	42.71	2-33	-	
20/20 Int																	
20/20	2	1	1	0	0 *		-	-	-	-	47	66	2	33.00	2-29	-	

Career Performances

	M	Inn	NO	Runs	HS	Avg	100	50	Ct	St	Balls	Runs	Wkts	Avg	BB	5I	10M
Test																	
FC	123	167	41	1069	41 *	8.48	-	-	36	-	21167	12717	406	31.32	7-54	16	3
ODI																	
List A	140	53	22	216	34	6.96	-	-	27	-	6250	5239	182	28.78	5-35	1	
20/20 Int																	
20/20	20	5	3	6	6	3.00	-	-	4	-	345	521	16	32.56	2-13	-	

HARRIS, J. A. R. — Glamorgan

Name: James Alexander Russell Harris
Role: Right-hand bat, right-arm fast-medium bowler; bowling all-rounder
Born: 16 May 1990, Morriston, Swansea
Height: 6ft **Weight:** 10st 7lbs
Nickname: Bones, Lloyd Christmas
County debut: 2007
Place in batting averages: 239th av. 16.33
Place in bowling averages: 30th av. 24.57
Parents: Helen and Russ
Marital status: Single
Family links with cricket: 'Dad played for British Universities'
Education: Pontarddulais Comprehensive; Gorseinon College
Qualifications: 9 GCSEs, 3 AS-levels
Career outside cricket: 'Entrepreneur'
Off-season: 'Touring Malaysia with England U19 for the U19 World Cup'
Overseas tours: West of England U15 to West Indies 2004-05 (c); England U16 to South Africa 2005-06 (c); England Performance Programme to India 2007-08; England U19 to Malaysia (U19 World Cup) 2007-08
Career highlights to date: 'Taking 12 wickets in a match May 2007, becoming the youngest player in Championship history to do so'
Cricket moments to forget: 'None, they've all been brilliant'
Cricket superstitions: 'Put left pad on first, then right before batting'
Cricketers particularly admired: Glenn McGrath, Ricky Ponting
Young players to look out for: Billy Godleman, Steven Finn, Ben Wright, Tom Maynard
Injuries: Out for two weeks with a sore back
Favourite band: Lighthouse Family, The Killers

Relaxations: 'Shopping for clothes; music'
Extras: ESCA Bunbury Scholarship 2005. Signed professional contract aged 16 years 9 days. Youngest Glamorgan player to take a Championship wicket, v Nottinghamshire at Trent Bridge 2007 aged 16 years 351 days. Youngest player in Championship history to take ten wickets in a match – 7-66/5-52 v Gloucestershire at Bristol 2007 on only his second first-class appearance, aged 17 years 3 days. Youngest Glamorgan player to score a Championship fifty – 87* v Nottinghamshire at Swansea 2007. Represented England U19 2007. Glamorgan Young Player of the Year 2007
Best batting: 87* Glamorgan v Nottinghamshire, Swansea 2007
Best bowling: 7-66 Glamorgan v Gloucestershire, Bristol 2007
Stop press: Called up to the England Performance Programme in India 2007-08

2007 Season

	M	Inn	NO	Runs	HS	Avg	100	50	Ct	St	Balls	Runs	Wkts	Avg	BB	5I	10M
Test																	
FC	9	14	2	196	87 *	16.33	-	1	4	-	1487	811	33	24.57	7-66	2	1
ODI																	
List A	3	3	0	15	5	5.00	-	-	1	-	114	120	4	30.00	2-57	-	
20/20 Int																	
20/20																	

Career Performances

	M	Inn	NO	Runs	HS	Avg	100	50	Ct	St	Balls	Runs	Wkts	Avg	BB	5I	10M
Test																	
FC	9	14	2	196	87 *	16.33	-	1	4	-	1487	811	33	24.57	7-66	2	1
ODI																	
List A	3	3	0	15	5	5.00	-	-	1	-	114	120	4	30.00	2-57	-	
20/20 Int																	
20/20																	

34. Who scored his maiden Test double century (219) and took the Man of the Match award as England won the fifth Test at The Oval and squared the series against South Africa in 2003?

HARRIS, P. L. — Warwickshire

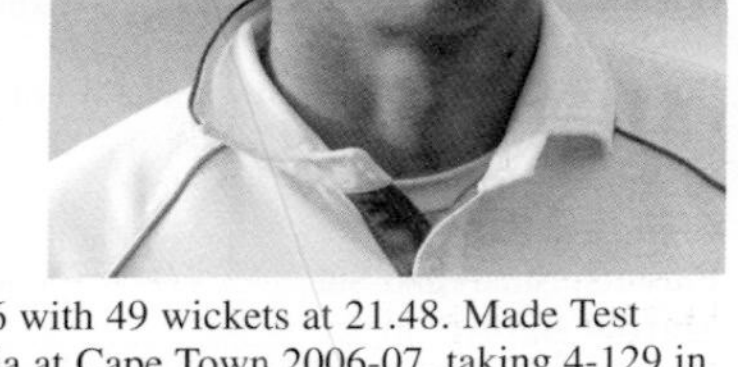

Name: Paul Lee Harris
Role: Right-hand bat, slow left-arm bowler
Born: 2 November 1978, Harare, Zimbabwe
County debut: 2006
Test debut: 2006-07
Place in batting averages: (2006 254th av. 14.00)
Place in bowling averages: (2006 40th av. 29.19)
Overseas tours: South Africa A to Zimbabwe 2007-08; South Africa to Pakistan 2007-08
Overseas teams played for: Western Province 1998-99 – 2001-02; Northerns 2002-03 – 2005-06; Titans 2004-05 –
Extras: Man of the Match v Dolphins at Durban in the SuperSport Series 2005-06 (5-32/3-58). Joint leading wicket-taker (with Dale Steyn) in the SuperSport Series 2005-06 with 49 wickets at 21.48. Made Test debut for South Africa in the third Test v India at Cape Town 2006-07, taking 4-129 in India's first innings (but losing his Kolpak status – *see page 13* – and returned to Warwickshire as an overseas player for part of the 2007 season)
Best batting: 55 Warwickshire v Durham, Riverside 2007
Best bowling: 6-54 Titans v Cape Cobras, Benoni 2005-06
Stop press: One of *South African Cricket Annual*'s five Cricketers of the Year 2007

2007 Season

	M	Inn	NO	Runs	HS	Avg	100	50	Ct	St	Balls	Runs	Wkts	Avg	BB	5I	10M
Test																	
FC	4	3	0	59	55	19.66	-	1	-	-	725	341	4	85.25	2-50	-	-
ODI																	
List A	2	1	0	5	5	5.00	-	-	-	-	78	69	1	69.00	1-33	-	
20/20 Int																	
20/20	8	1	1	1	1 *		-	-	3	-	156	163	9	18.11	3-18	-	

Career Performances

	M	Inn	NO	Runs	HS	Avg	100	50	Ct	St	Balls	Runs	Wkts	Avg	BB	5I	10M
Test	4	7	1	26	11 *	4.33	-	-	2	-	703	314	11	28.54	4-46	-	-
FC	57	69	10	834	55	14.13	-	1	21	-	12538	5701	198	28.79	6-54	11	-
ODI																	
List A	30	8	2	30	10	5.00	-	-	12	-	1266	962	30	32.06	3-33	-	
20/20 Int																	
20/20	14	4	3	5	3	5.00	-	-	3	-	276	336	14	24.00	3-18	-	

HARRISON, A. J. Glamorgan

Name: Adam James Harrison
Role: Right-hand bat, right-arm fast-medium bowler; all-rounder
Born: 30 October 1985, Newport, Gwent
Height: 6ft **Weight:** 13st 12lbs
Nickname: Worm, Crafty, Ceedo
County debut: 2005
Parents: Stuart and Sue
Marital status: Single
Family links with cricket: 'Father played in 1970s for Glamorgan. Brother [David] currently on staff'
Education: West Monmouth School; St Albans High School
Qualifications: 10 GCSEs, 3 A-levels, Level 1 coaching award
Off-season: 'Having third and final operation on left ankle'
Overseas tours: West of England U15 to West Indies 2001; England U18 to Netherlands 2003; England U19 to Qatar 2003, to Bangladesh (U19 World Cup) 2003-04, to India 2004-05
Career highlights to date: 'First-class debut at Lord's 2004 [for MCC]. Glamorgan debut. U19 World Cup 2004'
Cricketers particularly admired: Jacques Kallis, Andrew Flintoff, Alex Wharf
Other sports played: Golf, squash (Wales age groups), football (Football Association of Wales)
Other sports followed: Football (Manchester United)
Injuries: Out for most of the season with an ankle impingement
Relaxations: 'Playing golf, watching Sky'
Extras: BBC *Test Match Special* U15 Cricketer of the Year 2001. Sir John Hobbs Memorial Award 2001. Royal Variety Club Outstanding Newcomer Award 2002. NBC

Denis Compton Award for the most promising young Glamorgan player 2003. Represented England U19 2003, 2004, 2005. Made first-class debut for MCC v Sussex at Lord's 2004. ECB National Academy 2004-05 (part-time). Released by Glamorgan at the end of the 2007 season

Opinions on cricket: 'One too many competitions – extend Twenty20; finish Pro40.'

Best batting: 34* MCC v Sussex, Lord's 2004

Best bowling: 2-65 MCC v Sussex, Lord's 2004

2007 Season

	M	Inn	NO	Runs	HS	Avg	100	50	Ct	St	Balls	Runs	Wkts	Avg	BB	5I	10M
Test																	
FC																	
ODI																	
List A	2	2	0	7	7	3.50	-	-	-	-	48	82	1	82.00	1-45	-	
20/20 Int																	
20/20																	

Career Performances

	M	Inn	NO	Runs	HS	Avg	100	50	Ct	St	Balls	Runs	Wkts	Avg	BB	5I	10M
Test																	
FC	3	3	1	37	34 *	18.50	-	-	-	-	370	243	5	48.60	2-65	-	-
ODI																	
List A	3	3	0	13	7	4.33	-	-	1	-	102	141	2	70.50	1-45	-	
20/20 Int																	
20/20	3	1	1	1	1 *		-	-	2	-	67	92	5	18.40	2-12	-	

35. Who had match figures of 10-87 as South Africa beat England in the second Test at Trent Bridge in 1965: a) Hugh Tayfield; b) Peter Pollock; c) Mike Procter?

HARRISON, D. S. — Glamorgan

Name: David Stuart Harrison
Role: Right-hand bat, right-arm fast-medium bowler
Born: 31 July 1981, Newport, Gwent
Height: 6ft 4in **Weight:** 16st
Nickname: Harry, Hazza, Des, Moorehead, Butter, Pass Me, Get Off My Train, Your Eyes, Gangster
County debut: 1999
County cap: 2006
50 wickets in a season: 1
Place in batting averages: (2006 201st av. 21.61)
Place in bowling averages: (2006 103rd av. 39.62)
Parents: Stuart and Susan
Marital status: Single
Family links with cricket: Father played for Glamorgan in the 1970s. Brother Adam also played for Glamorgan. 'Mum tea lady for local club'
Education: West Monmouth School; Pontypool College; UWIC
Qualifications: 8 GCSEs, 2 A-levels, Levels 1 and 2 cricket coaching, 'qualified school caretaker'
Career outside cricket: 'Coaching/developing CV'
Off-season: 'Getting back to fitness after missing season with back injury; coaching; studying for master's in Sports Development and Coaching at UWIC'
Overseas tours: Wales U15 to Ireland; Gwent YC to South Africa 1996; Wales U16 to Jersey 1997, 1998; England U19 to Malaysia and (U19 World Cup) Sri Lanka 1999-2000; Glamorgan to Cape Town 2002; England A to Sri Lanka 2004-05; MCC to Bahrain 2005-06, to Papua New Guinea and New Zealand 2007
Overseas teams played for: Claremont, Cape Town 2002 (one game during Glamorgan tour)
Career highlights to date: 'Glamorgan debut 1999. Winning National League 2002 at Canterbury with friends and family. England A selection'
Cricket superstitions: 'Always wear a cap so don't burn my head!'
Cricketers particularly admired: Matthew Maynard, Mike Kasprowicz
Other sports played: Squash (Wales junior squads), rugby (East Wales U11 caps), boxing (Welsh champion at U14; 'still have odd spar')
Other sports followed: 'All sports (i.e. Sky Sports)', rugby (Pontypool), football (Man Utd), darts (Terry Jenkins)
Injuries: Out for the 2007 season with a slipped disc

Extras: Has played for Glamorgan from U12. Represented England at U17, U18 and U19. Glamorgan Young Player of the Year 2003, 2004. ECB National Academy 2004-05
Best batting: 88 Glamorgan v Essex, Chelmsford 2004
Best bowling: 5-48 Glamorgan v Somerset, Swansea 2004

2007 Season (did not make any first-class or one-day appearances)

Career Performances

	M	Inn	NO	Runs	HS	Avg	100	50	Ct	St	Balls	Runs	Wkts	Avg	BB	5I	10M
Test																	
FC	68	98	14	1341	88	15.96	-	4	24	-	10633	6200	170	36.47	5-48	6	-
ODI																	
List A	58	37	12	357	37 *	14.28	-	-	6	-	2446	1850	68	27.20	5-26	2	
20/20 Int																	
20/20	10	3	0	5	4	1.66	-	-	3	-	177	252	9	28.00	2-17	-	

HARRISON, P. W. Leicestershire

Name: Paul William Harrison
Role: Right-hand bat, wicket-keeper
Born: 22 May 1984, Cuckfield, West Sussex
Height: 6ft 2in **Weight:** 12st 12lbs
Nickname: Harry, Potter
County debut: 2005 (Warwickshire), 2005 (one-day, Leicestershire), 2006 (first-class, Leicestershire)
Parents: Angela and Brian
Marital status: Single
Family links with cricket: 'Dad and uncle played league cricket in Sussex. Brother Leigh played YCs and 2nd XI at Sussex'
Education: The Forest School; College of Richard Collyer, Horsham; Loughborough University
Qualifications: 3 A-levels, Level 1 coaching
Overseas tours: Sussex Young Cricketers to Sri Lanka 2001, to South Africa 2003
Overseas teams played for: Tuart Hill, Perth 2002
Career highlights to date: 'Beating Worcestershire first team with Loughborough UCCE 2005'
Cricket moments to forget: 'Dropping a catch on the boundary for my club that would have got us promoted to the premier division'

Cricketers particularly admired: Mark Waugh, Alec Stewart, Adam Gilchrist
Young players to look out for: David Wainwright, Ryan Cummins
Other sports played: Football (county U18), golf (Mannings Heath; 7 handicap)
Other sports followed: Football (Arsenal, Brighton & Hove Albion)
Favourite band: Red Hot Chili Peppers
Extras: Sussex U19 Player of the Year. Played for Loughborough UCCE 2004-06. Played one first-class game for Warwickshire 2005 and played for Leicestershire in the International Twenty20 Club Championship 2005. Represented British Universities 2006. Released by Leicestershire at the end of the 2007 season
Best batting: 54 LUCCE v Nottinghamshire, Trent Bridge 2005

2007 Season

	M	Inn	NO	Runs	HS	Avg	100	50	Ct	St	Balls	Runs	Wkts	Avg	BB	5I	10M
Test																	
FC	1	1	0	1	1	1.00	-	-	1	-	0	0	0		-	-	-
ODI																	
List A	4	4	0	41	19	10.25	-	-	2	-	0	0	0		-	-	
20/20 Int																	
20/20	5	5	0	70	26	14.00	-	-	1	-	0	0	0		-	-	

Career Performances

	M	Inn	NO	Runs	HS	Avg	100	50	Ct	St	Balls	Runs	Wkts	Avg	BB	5I	10M
Test																	
FC	11	17	4	298	54	22.92	-	1	16	-	0	0	0		-	-	-
ODI																	
List A	7	7	0	139	61	19.85	-	1	5	-	0	0	0		-	-	
20/20 Int																	
20/20	12	11	1	119	26	11.90	-	-	2	-	0	0	0		-	-	

36. Who were the captains of England and South Africa throughout the 1994 Test series?

HARVEY, I. J. Derbyshire

Name: Ian Joseph Harvey
Role: Right-hand bat, right-arm fast-medium bowler
Born: 10 April 1972, Wonthaggi, Victoria, Australia
Height: 5ft 9in **Weight:** 12st 8lbs
Nickname: Freak
County debut: 1999 (Gloucestershire), 2004 (Yorkshire), 2007 (Derbyshire)
County cap: 1999 (Gloucestershire), 2005 (Yorkshire)
ODI debut: 1997-98
1st-Class 200s: 1
Place in batting averages: (2006 28th av. 56.10)
Place in bowling averages: (2006 37th av. 29.07)
Marital status: Married
Family links with cricket: Brothers club cricketers in Australia
Education: Wonthaggi Technical College

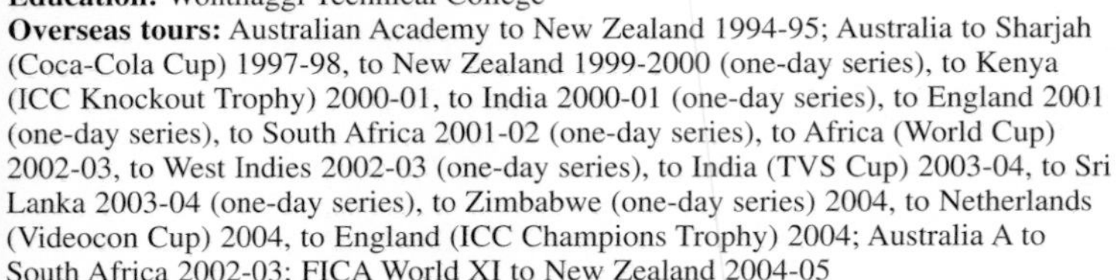

Overseas tours: Australian Academy to New Zealand 1994-95; Australia to Sharjah (Coca-Cola Cup) 1997-98, to New Zealand 1999-2000 (one-day series), to Kenya (ICC Knockout Trophy) 2000-01, to India 2000-01 (one-day series), to England 2001 (one-day series), to South Africa 2001-02 (one-day series), to Africa (World Cup) 2002-03, to West Indies 2002-03 (one-day series), to India (TVS Cup) 2003-04, to Sri Lanka 2003-04 (one-day series), to Zimbabwe (one-day series) 2004, to Netherlands (Videocon Cup) 2004, to England (ICC Champions Trophy) 2004; Australia A to South Africa 2002-03; FICA World XI to New Zealand 2004-05
Overseas teams played for: Victoria 1993-94 – 2004-05; Cape Cobras 2005-06 –
Extras: The nickname 'Freak' is a reference to his brilliant fielding and was reportedly coined by Shane Warne. Attended Commonwealth Bank [Australian] Cricket Academy 1994. An overseas player with Gloucestershire 1999-2003 and in 2006; an overseas player with Yorkshire 2004-05. Man of the Match in the Carlton Series first final v West Indies at Sydney 2000-01 (47*/2-5). Won the Walter Lawrence Trophy 2001 for the season's fastest first-class hundred with his 61-ball century v Derbyshire at Bristol; also took 5-89 in Derbyshire's second innings. Has won numerous Australian and English domestic awards, including C&G Man of the Match in the final v Worcestershire at Lord's 2003 (2-37/36-ball 61). Scored the first ever century in the Twenty20 Cup (100* from 50 balls), v Warwickshire at Edgbaston 2003. One of *Wisden*'s Five Cricketers of the Year 2004. Appeared as an overseas player for Derbyshire 2007; left Derbyshire at the end of the 2007 season

Best batting: 209* Yorkshire v Somerset, Headingley 2005
Best bowling: 8-101 Australia A v South Africa A, Adelaide 2002-03

2007 Season

	M	Inn	NO	Runs	HS	Avg	100	50	Ct	St	Balls	Runs	Wkts	Avg	BB	5I	10M
Test																	
FC	2	3	1	289	153	144.50	2	-	4	-	180	116	2	58.00	1-14	-	-
ODI																	
List A	2	2	1	67	60 *	67.00	-	1	2	-	108	77	0		-	-	
20/20 Int																	
20/20																	

Career Performances

	M	Inn	NO	Runs	HS	Avg	100	50	Ct	St	Balls	Runs	Wkts	Avg	BB	5I	10M
Test																	
FC	165	272	29	8409	209 *	34.60	15	46	114	-	24274	11693	425	27.51	8-101	15	2
ODI	73	51	11	715	48 *	17.87	-	-	17	-	3279	2577	85	30.31	4-16	-	
List A	304	267	27	5973	112	24.88	2	28	83	-	13601	9949	445	22.35	5-19	9	
20/20 Int																	
20/20	32	31	3	993	109	35.46	3	4	8	-	629	844	33	25.57	3-28	-	

37. Who scored 99* as nightwatchman to carry England to victory in the first Test v New Zealand at Edgbaston in 1999?

HASSAN ADNAN — Derbyshire

Name: Mohammad Hassan Adnan Syed
Role: Right-hand bat, right-arm off-spin bowler
Born: 15 May 1975, Lahore, Pakistan
Height: 5ft 8½in **Weight:** 11st 8lbs
Nickname: Hassy
County debut: 2003
County cap: 2004
1000 runs in a season: 1
Place in batting averages: 206th av. 21.00 (2006 117th av. 33.07)
Parents: Syed Inam Ali and Methab Bano
Wife and date of marriage: Naila, 18 January 2006
Education: MAO College, Lahore
Overseas teams played for: Islamabad 1994-95, 2000-01; Gujranwala 1997-98 – 1998-99; Water and Power Development Authority (WAPDA) 1997-98 – 2004-05
Career highlights to date: 'Being a capped player'
Cricket superstitions: 'None'
Cricketers particularly admired: Steve Waugh
Young players to look out for: Gary Ballance, Jake Needham
Other sports played: Badminton
Other sports followed: Football
Relaxations: 'Playing computer games; listening to music'
Extras: Won two Man of the Match awards in the Tissot Cup domestic competition in Pakistan. Scored century (113*) as Derbyshire beat New Zealanders in 50-over match at Derby 2004. Scored 1247 County Championship runs in his first full season 2004. Derbyshire Supporters' Club Player of the Year 2004. Is England-qualified. Released by Derbyshire at the end of the 2007 season
Opinions on cricket: 'Twenty20 cricket has brought a lot of excitement to the game. It has attracted a lot of new fans.'
Best batting: 191 Derbyshire v Somerset, Taunton 2005
Best bowling: 1-4 Derbyshire v Yorkshire, Derby 2004
1-4 WAPDA v Allied Bank, Karachi 2004-05
1-4 Derbyshire v Gloucestershire, Derby 2006

2007 Season

	M	Inn	NO	Runs	HS	Avg	100	50	Ct	St	Balls	Runs	Wkts	Avg	BB	5I	10M
Test																	
FC	11	21	2	399	63	21.00	-	2	5	-	0	0	0		-	-	-
ODI																	
List A	4	4	0	86	51	21.50	-	1	-	-	0	0	0		-	-	
20/20 Int																	
20/20																	

Career Performances

	M	Inn	NO	Runs	HS	Avg	100	50	Ct	St	Balls	Runs	Wkts	Avg	BB	5I	10M
Test																	
FC	127	213	24	7211	191	38.15	10	48	67	-	453	318	4	79.50	1-4	-	-
ODI																	
List A	73	70	9	1875	113 *	30.73	2	14	26	-	187	162	6	27.00	2-13	-	
20/20 Int																	
20/20	11	9	2	167	54 *	23.85	-	1	4	-	54	68	2	34.00	1-18	-	

HEMP, D. L. — Glamorgan

Name: David Lloyd Hemp
Role: Left-hand bat, right-arm medium bowler, county captain
Born: 15 November 1970, Hamilton, Bermuda
Height: 6ft 1in **Weight:** 12st 7lbs
Nickname: Hempy, Gramps, Mad Dog
County debut: 1991 (Glamorgan), 1997 (Warwickshire)
County cap: 1994 (Glamorgan), 1997 (Warwickshire)
Benefit: 2008 (Glamorgan)
ODI debut: 2006-07
1000 runs in a season: 6
1st-Class 200s: 1
Place in batting averages: 107th av. 34.45 (2006 97th av. 35.82)
Parents: Clive and Elisabeth
Wife and date of marriage: Angela, 16 March 1996
Children: Cameron, January 2002; Kendal Noa, 6 September 2007
Family links with cricket: Father and brother both played for Swansea CC
Education: Olchfa Comprehensive School; Millfield School; Birmingham University

Qualifications: 5 O-levels, 2 A-levels, MBA, Level 3 coaching award
Career outside cricket: PR/marketing; coaching
Off-season: 'Bermuda tour to Kenya and Dubai; Level 4 coaching award'
Overseas tours: Welsh Cricket Association U18 to Barbados 1986; Welsh Schools U19 to Australia 1987-88; Glamorgan to Trinidad 1990; South Wales Cricket Association to New Zealand and Australia 1991-92; England A to India 1994-95; Bermuda to Kenya 2006-07, to South Africa (ICC Associates Tri-Series) 2006-07, to West Indies (World Cup) 2006-07, to Kenya and UAE 2007-08
Overseas teams played for: Crusaders, Durban 1992-98
Career highlights to date: '99* England A v India A, Calcutta "Test" match 1994-95. World Cup 2007 – playing for Bermuda'
Cricket moments to forget: 'None'
Cricket superstitions: 'None'
Cricketers particularly admired: Brian Lara, Graeme Hick, Mark Ramprakash
Young players to look out for: Moeen Ali, James Harris
Other sports played: Football, golf
Other sports followed: Football (Swansea City, West Ham United)
Favourite band: Manic Street Preachers, Stereophonics
Relaxations: Golf, reading
Extras: In 1989 scored 104* and 101* for Welsh Schools U19 v Scottish Schools U19 and 120 and 102* v Irish Schools U19. Scored 258* for Wales v MCC 1991. Scored two centuries (138/114*) v Hampshire at Southampton 1997. Vice-captain of Warwickshire 2001. Left Warwickshire in the 2001-02 off-season and rejoined Glamorgan for 2002. Scored 88-ball 102 v Surrey at The Oval in the C&G 2002 as Glamorgan made 429 in reply to Surrey's 438-5. Won Glamorgan's Byron Denning Award 2004. Glamorgan Player of the Year 2005. Has played first-class and ODI cricket for Bermuda. Recorded highest score by a Bermuda player at the 2006-07 World Cup – 76* v India at Port of Spain. Glamorgan captain since mid-September 2006
Opinions on cricket: 'Slightly reduce amount of cricket played, which would allow for more quality practices. Practice facilities, although improving, still need to get better. No overseas players as the best are not available, which would therefore hopefully give more opportunities to home-grown players. Larger fines for clubs for playing more than one Kolpak player [*see page 13*] per team, therefore placing more emphasis on developing home-grown talent.'
Best batting: 247* Bermuda v Netherlands, Pretoria (LCD) 2006
Best bowling: 3-23 Glamorgan v South Africa A, Cardiff 1996

2007 Season

	M	Inn	NO	Runs	HS	Avg	100	50	Ct	St	Balls	Runs	Wkts	Avg	BB	5I	10M
Test																	
FC	15	25	1	827	152 *	34.45	1	5	8	-	24	8	0		-	-	-
ODI																	
List A	14	13	0	278	59	21.38	-	2	6	-	0	0	0		-	-	
20/20 Int																	
20/20	6	5	1	105	68 *	26.25	-	1	3	-	0	0	0		-	-	

Career Performances

	M	Inn	NO	Runs	HS	Avg	100	50	Ct	St	Balls	Runs	Wkts	Avg	BB	5I	10M
Test																	
FC	251	427	38	14146	247 *	36.36	27	76	170	-	1134	821	17	48.29	3-23	-	-
ODI	17	17	2	438	76 *	29.20	-	3	5	-	114	119	1	119.00	1-25	-	
List A	274	243	29	5713	121	26.69	5	30	99	-	303	297	12	24.75	4-32	-	
20/20 Int																	
20/20	33	30	6	716	74	29.83	-	4	19	-	0	0	0		-	-	

HENDERSON, C. W. Leicestershire

Name: Claude William Henderson
Role: Right-hand bat, left-arm spin bowler
Born: 14 June 1972, Worcester, South Africa
Height: 6ft 2in **Weight:** 14st 2lbs
Nickname: Hendy, Hendo
County debut: 2004
County cap: 2004
Test debut: 2001-02
ODI debut: 2001-02
Place in batting averages: 178th av. 25.07 (2006 144th av. 30.27)
Place in bowling averages: 111th av. 39.80 (2006 114th av. 41.91)
Parents: Henry and Susan
Wife and date of marriage: Nicci, 29 March 2003
Children: Mia, 2007
Family links with cricket: Brother James played first-class cricket
Education: Worcester High School
Qualifications: Level 2 coaching, basic computer skills, basic bookkeeping skills
Career outside cricket: 'Family business'

Overseas tours: South Africa A to Sri Lanka 1998; South Africa to Zimbabwe 2001-02, to Australia 2001-02
Overseas teams played for: Boland 1990-91 – 1997-98; Western Province 1998-99- 2003-04; Highveld Lions 2006-07
Career highlights to date: 'Playing for South Africa'
Cricket moments to forget: 'Losing to Devon in C&G 2004'
Cricket superstitions: 'None'
Cricketers particularly admired: Shane Warne, Jacques Kallis
Other sports played: Golf, tennis, fishing
Other sports followed: Rugby (Leicester Tigers)
Favourite band: U2
Relaxations: 'Cinema, travelling, spending time with family'
Extras: Has won several match awards in South African domestic cricket. Scored fifty (63) and recorded five-wicket innings return (5-28) on Championship debut for Leicestershire v Glamorgan at Leicester 2004; recorded a further five-wicket return (5-24) on one-day debut v Yorkshire at Headingley in the totesport League 2004. Appointed player/coach at Leicestershire for 2008 with responsibility for spin bowling. Is not considered an overseas player
Best batting: 81 Leicestershire v Gloucestershire, Leicester 2007
Best bowling: 7-57 Boland v Eastern Province, Paarl (PCC) 1994-95

2007 Season

	M	Inn	NO	Runs	HS	Avg	100	50	Ct	St	Balls	Runs	Wkts	Avg	BB	5I	10M
Test																	
FC	10	13	0	326	81	25.07	-	1	3	-	2115	1035	26	39.80	5-56	2	-
ODI																	
List A	12	8	2	57	20 *	9.50	-	-	1	-	428	367	12	30.58	3-34	-	
20/20 Int																	
20/20	5	0	0	0	0		-	-	-	-	48	54	1	54.00	1-16	-	

Career Performances

	M	Inn	NO	Runs	HS	Avg	100	50	Ct	St	Balls	Runs	Wkts	Avg	BB	5I	10M
Test	7	7	0	65	30	9.28	-	-	2	-	1962	928	22	42.18	4-116	-	-
FC	180	245	55	3590	81	18.89	-	10	68	-	44720	19352	616	31.41	7-57	22	1
ODI	4	0	0	0	0		-	-	-	-	217	132	7	18.85	4-17	-	
List A	198	110	55	928	45	16.87	-	-	47	-	8878	6212	242	25.66	6-29	2	
20/20 Int																	
20/20	25	8	2	20	9 *	3.33	-	-	7	-	337	404	16	25.25	3-26	-	

HENDERSON, T. — Middlesex

Name: Tyron Henderson
Role: Right-hand bat, right-arm fast-medium bowler; all-rounder
Born: 1 August 1974, Durban, South Africa
Nickname: The Blacksmith
County debut: 2006 (Kent), 2007 (one-day, Middlesex)
Twenty20 Int debut: 2006-07
Place in batting averages: (2006 218th av. 18.25)
Family links with cricket: Grandfather (J. K. Henderson) and great-uncle (W. A. Henderson) played first-class cricket for North Eastern Transvaal
Overseas tours: South Africa Academy to Ireland and Scotland 1999; South Africa A to Sri Lanka 2005-06
Overseas teams played for: Border 1998-99 – 2003-04; Eastern Cape 2003-04; Warriors 2004-05 – 2005-06; Lions 2006-07; Cape Cobras 2007-08 – ; Boland 2007-08 –
Extras: Played for Berkshire in the 2003 C&G. Has represented South Africa A. His awards include Man of the Match v Griqualand West at Kimberley in the Standard Bank Cup 2003-04 (3-45/126*) and v Dolphins at Port Elizabeth in the Standard Bank Pro20 Series 2004-05 (3-24/44). An overseas player with Kent from June to September 2006; was a temporary overseas player with Middlesex during the 2007 season as a locum for Chaminda Vaas
Best batting: 81 Border v Gauteng, Johannesburg 1999-2000
Best bowling: 6-56 Border v Free State, Bloemfontein 2000-01

2007 Season

	M	Inn	NO	Runs	HS	Avg	100	50	Ct	St	Balls	Runs	Wkts	Avg	BB	5I	10M
Test																	
FC																	
ODI																	
List A																	
20/20 Int																	
20/20	6	5	0	56	22	11.20	-	-	1	-	108	106	6	17.66	2-11	-	

Career Performances

	M	Inn	NO	Runs	HS	Avg	100	50	Ct	St	Balls	Runs	Wkts	Avg	BB	5I	10M
Test																	
FC	81	129	17	1867	81	16.66	-	6	29	-	14883	6627	242	27.38	6-56	9	-
ODI																	
List A	90	71	16	1287	126 *	23.40	1	7	21	-	3996	2809	107	26.25	5-5	3	
20/20 Int	1	1	0	0	0	0.00	-	-	-	-	24	31	0		-	-	
20/20	42	37	2	707	85	20.20	-	5	3	-	884	1040	44	23.63	3-11	-	

HICK, G. A. — Worcestershire

Name: Graeme Ashley Hick
Role: Right-hand bat, off-spin bowler
Born: 23 May 1966, Harare, Zimbabwe
Height: 6ft 3in **Weight:** 14st 4lbs
Nickname: Hicky, Ash
County debut: 1984
County cap: 1986; colours 2002
Benefit: 1999; testimonial 2006
Test debut: 1991
ODI debut: 1991
1000 runs in a season: 19
1st-Class 200s: 13
1st-Class 300s: 2
1st-Class 400s: 1
Place in batting averages: 60th av. 41.86 (2006 47th av. 48.71)
Parents: John and Eve
Wife and date of marriage: Jackie, 5 October 1991
Children: Lauren Amy, 12 September 1992; Jordan Ashley, 5 September 1995
Family links with cricket: Father has served on Zimbabwe Cricket Union Board of Control and played representative cricket in Zimbabwe
Education: Prince Edward Boys' High School, Zimbabwe
Qualifications: 4 O-levels, NCA coaching award
Overseas tours: Zimbabwe to England (World Cup) 1983, to Sri Lanka 1983-84, to England 1985; England to Australia and New Zealand (World Cup) 1991-92, to India and Sri Lanka 1992-93, to West Indies 1993-94, to Australia 1994-95, to South Africa 1995-96, to India and Pakistan (World Cup) 1995-96, to Sharjah (Champions Trophy) 1997-98, to West Indies 1997-98 (one-day series), to Bangladesh (Wills International Cup) 1998-99, to Australia 1998-99, to Sharjah (Coca-Cola Cup) 1998-99, to South Africa and Zimbabwe 1999-2000 (one-day series), to Kenya (ICC Knockout Trophy) 2000-01, to Pakistan and Sri Lanka 2000-01; FICA World XI to New Zealand 2004-05

Overseas teams played for: Old Hararians, Zimbabwe 1982-90; Northern Districts, New Zealand 1987-89; Queensland 1990-91; Auckland 1997-98
Cricketers particularly admired: Steve Waugh, Glenn McGrath
Other sports played: Golf ('relaxation'), hockey (played for Zimbabwe)
Other sports followed: Football (Liverpool FC), golf, tennis, squash, hockey
Extras: One of *Wisden*'s Five Cricketers of the Year 1987. In 1988 he made 405* v Somerset at Taunton and scored 1000 first-class runs by the end of May. PCA Player of the Year 1988. Qualified to play for England 1991. Scored 100th first-class century (132) v Sussex at Worcester 1998; at the age of 32, he became the second youngest player after Wally Hammond to score 100 centuries. Scored 200* v Durham at Riverside 2001, in the process achieving the feat of having recorded centuries against each of the other 17 counties, both home and away. Became leading run-scorer in the history of the one-day league, v Middlesex at Lord's 2005. Took eight catches in match v Essex at Chelmsford 2005, equalling the Worcestershire record. Scored 130th career first-class century (139) v Northamptonshire at Worcester 2006 to move into eighth spot on the all-time first-class century-makers' list and become the eighth batsman (the first for Worcestershire) to register 100 first-class centuries for a single county. Became fifth quickest batsman to reach 40,000 runs in first-class cricket (in terms of innings played) v Warwickshire at Edgbaston 2007. His series and match awards include England's Man of the CUB Series 1998-99 and Man of the Match v Zimbabwe, the country of his birth, for his match-winning 87* at Bulawayo and his 80 and 5-33 at Harare 1999-2000. Captain of Worcestershire 2000-02. Winner of Sky Sports Sixes Award 2007
Best batting: 405* Worcestershire v Somerset, Taunton 1988
Best bowling: 5-18 Worcestershire v Leicestershire, Worcester 1995

2007 Season

	M	Inn	NO	Runs	HS	Avg	100	50	Ct	St	Balls	Runs	Wkts	Avg	BB	5I	10M
Test																	
FC	15	24	1	963	110	41.86	2	6	16	-	0	0	0		-	-	-
ODI																	
List A	16	15	5	701	120	70.10	1	5	4	-	0	0	0		-	-	
20/20 Int																	
20/20	7	6	0	193	110	32.16	1	-	1	-	0	0	0		-	-	

Career Performances

	M	Inn	NO	Runs	HS	Avg	100	50	Ct	St	Balls	Runs	Wkts	Avg	BB	5I	10M
Test	65	114	6	3383	178	31.32	6	18	90	-	3057	1306	23	56.78	4-126	-	-
FC	515	853	81	40423	405 *	52.36	134	156	684	-	20889	10308	232	44.43	5-18	5	1
ODI	120	118	15	3846	126 *	37.33	5	27	64	-	1236	1026	30	34.20	5-33	1	
List A	641	620	95	21881	172 *	41.67	40	139	281	-	8603	6649	225	29.55	5-19	4	
20/20 Int																	
20/20	28	27	2	929	116 *	37.16	2	7	8	-	0	0	0		-	-	

HILDRETH, J. C. Somerset

Name: James Charles Hildreth
Role: Right-hand bat, right-arm medium bowler; all-rounder
Born: 9 September 1984, Milton Keynes
Height: 5ft 10in **Weight:** 12st
Nickname: Hildy, Hildz
County debut: 2003
County cap: 2007
1000 runs in a season: 1
1st-Class 200s: 1
Place in batting averages: 26th av. 52.91 (2006 103rd av. 34.69)
Parents: David and Judy
Marital status: Single
Family links with cricket: 'Dad played county league cricket in Kent and Northants'
Education: Millfield School
Qualifications: 10 GCSEs, 3 A-levels, ECB Level 1 coaching
Overseas tours: 'West' to West Indies 1999, 2000; Millfield to Sri Lanka 2001; England U19 to Bangladesh (U19 World Cup) 2003-04; England Performance Programme to India 2007-08; England Lions to India 2007-08
Cricket moments to forget: 'Being bowled first ball by Shoaib Akhtar'
Cricket superstitions: 'Left pad before right when getting padded up'
Other sports played: Hockey (West of England), squash (South of England), tennis (South of England), football (England Independent Schools, Luton Town), rugby (Millfield)
Other sports followed: Football (Charlton Athletic)
Favourite band: Jack Johnson
Relaxations: Travelling, snowboarding, music
Extras: NBC Denis Compton Award for the most promising young Somerset player 2003. Scored maiden first-class century (101) plus 72 in the second innings v Durham at Taunton 2004 in his second Championship match. Represented England U19 v Bangladesh U19 2004, scoring 210 in second 'Test' at Taunton. Cricket Society's Most Promising Young Cricketer of the Year 2004. Scored maiden first-class double century (227*) at Taunton 2006, setting a new record for the highest score by a Somerset batsman v Northamptonshire. ECB National Academy 2004-05 (part-time)
Best batting: 227* Somerset v Northamptonshire, Taunton 2006
Best bowling: 2-39 Somerset v Hampshire, Taunton 2004

2007 Season

	M	Inn	NO	Runs	HS	Avg	100	50	Ct	St	Balls	Runs	Wkts	Avg	BB	5I	10M
Test																	
FC	17	26	2	1270	163	52.91	4	6	15	-	126	102	2	51.00	1-13	-	-
ODI																	
List A	15	15	2	415	56	31.92	-	1	4	-	24	21	1	21.00	1-8	-	
20/20 Int																	
20/20	8	7	1	128	40	21.33	-	-	4	-	33	57	0		-	-	

Career Performances

	M	Inn	NO	Runs	HS	Avg	100	50	Ct	St	Balls	Runs	Wkts	Avg	BB	5I	10M
Test																	
FC	61	101	9	3774	227 *	41.02	9	20	53	-	348	278	4	69.50	2-39	-	-
ODI																	
List A	77	74	12	1884	122	30.38	1	7	22	-	114	138	3	46.00	1-8	-	
20/20 Int																	
20/20	34	33	4	565	71	19.48	-	3	13	-	169	247	10	24.70	3-24	-	

HINDS, W. W. — Derbyshire

Name: Wavell Wayne Hinds
Role: Left-hand bat, right-arm medium bowler
Born: 7 September 1976, Kingston, Jamaica
County debut: No first-team appearance
Test debut: 1999-2000
ODI debut: 1999
Twenty20 Int debut: 2005-06
1st-Class 200s: 1
Overseas tours: West Indies U19 to Pakistan 1995-96; West Indies A to South Africa 1997-98, to Bangladesh and India 1998-99; West Indies to Singapore (Coca-Cola Singapore Challenge) 1999, to Bangladesh 1999-2000, to New Zealand 1999-2000, to England 2000, to Kenya (ICC Knockout Trophy) 2000-01, to Australia 2000-01, to Zimbabwe and Kenya 2001, to Sharjah (v Pakistan) 2001-02, to Sri Lanka (ICC Champions Trophy) 2002-03, to India and Bangladesh 2002-03, to Africa (World Cup) 2002-03, to Zimbabwe and South Africa 2003-04, to England (ICC Champions Trophy) 2004, to Australia 2005-06, to India (ICC Champions Trophy) 2006-07, plus other one-day tournaments and series in Toronto, Sharjah, Australia, New Zealand and Malaysia

Overseas teams played for: Jamaica 1995-96 –
Extras: Scored 213 in the first Test at Georgetown 2004-05, in the process sharing with Shivnarine Chanderpaul (203*) in a record fourth-wicket partnership for West Indies in Tests against South Africa (284). His match and series awards include Man of the [Test] Series v Pakistan 1999-2000 and of the [ODI] Series v Australia 2002-03. Is not considered an overseas player
Best batting: 213 West Indies v South Africa, Georgetown 2004-05
Best bowling: 3-9 Jamaica v West Indies B, Montego Bay 2000-01

2007 Season (did not make any first-class or one-day appearances)

Career Performances

	M	Inn	NO	Runs	HS	Avg	100	50	Ct	St	Balls	Runs	Wkts	Avg	BB	5I	10M
Test	45	80	1	2608	213	33.01	5	14	32	-	1123	590	16	36.87	3-79	-	-
FC	124	214	8	7119	213	34.55	18	32	62	-	2398	1127	29	38.86	3-9	-	-
ODI	114	107	9	2835	127 *	28.92	5	14	28	-	945	837	28	29.89	3-24	-	
List A	186	175	14	4551	127 *	28.26	6	24	44	-	1298	1146	44	26.04	4-35	-	
20/20 Int	1	1	0	14	14	14.00	-	-	-	-	0	0	0		-	-	
20/20	3	2	1	58	44 *	58.00	-	-	-	-	12	13	0		-	-	

HODD, A. J. Sussex

Name: Andrew John Hodd
Role: Right-hand bat, wicket-keeper
Born: 12 January 1984, Chichester
Height: 5ft 9½in **Weight:** 11st 8lbs
Nickname: Hoddy
County debut: 2002 (one-day, Sussex), 2003 (first-class, Sussex), 2005 (Surrey)
Place in batting averages: 76th av. 39.25
Parents: Karen and Adrian
Marital status: Single
Family links with cricket: 'Long line of enthusiastic club cricketers'
Education: Bexhill High School; Bexhill College; 'short stint at Loughborough Uni'
Qualifications: 9 GCSEs, 4 A-levels, Level 1 coach
Career outside cricket: Coaching
Overseas tours: South of England U14 to West Indies 1998; Sussex Academy to Cape Town 1999, to Sri Lanka 2001; England U17 to Australia 2000-01; England U19 to Australia 2002-03
Cricket superstitions: 'Too many! Must drink coffee the morning of a game'

Cricketers particularly admired: David Hussey, Matt Prior
Young players to look out for: Luke Wright, Ollie Rayner, Ben Brown
Other sports played: Golf, football, boxing
Other sports followed: Football (Brighton & Hove Albion)
Favourite band: Hard-Fi
Relaxations: 'Cinema, DVDs, gym, going out'
Extras: Played for England U14, U15, U17 and U19. Graham Kersey Trophy, Bunbury 1999. Several junior Player of the Year awards at Sussex. Sussex County League Young Player of the Year 2002. Sussex 2nd XI Player of the Year 2003. Joined Surrey for 2004, leaving at the end of the 2005 season to rejoin Sussex for 2006
Best batting: 123 Sussex v Yorkshire, Hove 2007

2007 Season

	M	Inn	NO	Runs	HS	Avg	100	50	Ct	St	Balls	Runs	Wkts	Avg	BB	5I	10M
Test																	
FC	14	21	5	628	123	39.25	2	2	21	7	0	0	0		-	-	-
ODI																	
List A	11	9	2	179	42	25.57	-	-	5	-	0	0	0		-	-	
20/20 Int																	
20/20	8	2	0	16	14	8.00	-	-	3	3	0	0	0		-	-	

Career Performances

	M	Inn	NO	Runs	HS	Avg	100	50	Ct	St	Balls	Runs	Wkts	Avg	BB	5I	10M
Test																	
FC	19	27	7	769	123	38.45	2	4	32	7	0	0	0		-	-	-
ODI																	
List A	14	12	2	192	42	19.20	-	-	8	-	0	0	0		-	-	
20/20 Int																	
20/20	9	2	0	16	14	8.00	-	-	3	3	0	0	0		-	-	

HODGE, B. J. — Lancashire

Name: Bradley (Brad) John Hodge
Role: Right-hand bat, right-arm off-spin bowler
Born: 29 December 1974, Sandringham, Melbourne, Australia
Height: 5ft 7½in **Weight:** 12st 8lbs
Nickname: Bunk
County debut: 2002 (Durham), 2003 (Leicestershire), 2005 (Lancashire)
County cap: 2003 (Leicestershire), 2006 (Lancashire)
Test debut: 2005-06
ODI debut: 2005-06
Twenty20 Int debut: 2007-08
1000 runs in a season: 2

1st-Class 200s: 7
1st-Class 300s: 1
Place in batting averages: 126th av. 32.18
Parents: John and Val
Wife: Megan
Children: Jesse
Education: St Bede's College, Mentone; Deakin University
Overseas tours: Australia U19 to New Zealand 1992-93; Commonwealth Bank [Australian] Cricket Academy to Zimbabwe 1998-99; Australia A to Los Angeles (Moov America Challenge) 1999, to Pakistan 2005-06; Australia to India 2004-05, to New Zealand 2004-05, to England 2005, to New Zealand (one-day series) 2005-06, 2006-07, to West Indies (World Cup) 2006-07, to South Africa (World 20/20) 2007-08, to India (one-day series) 2007-08
Overseas teams played for: Victoria 1993-94 –
Cricketers particularly admired: Allan Border, Dennis Lillee, Dean Jones, Sachin Tendulkar
Other sports played/followed: Australian Rules football (Melbourne), golf, tennis, soccer, skiing
Extras: Attended Commonwealth Bank [Australian] Cricket Academy 1993. Leading run-scorer for Victoria in the Sheffield Shield in his first season (1993-94) with 903 runs (av. 50.16). Victoria's Pura Cup Player of the Year 2000-01 and 2001-02; winner of the national Pura Cup Player of the Season Award 2001-02 (jointly with Jimmy Maher of Queensland). Was Durham's overseas player 2002 from late July; an overseas player with Leicestershire 2003-04 (appointed vice-captain for 2004; assumed the captaincy in July on the resignation of Phillip DeFreitas). Scored 202* v Loughborough UCCE at Leicester 2003, in the process sharing with Darren Maddy (229*) in a record partnership for any wicket for Leicestershire (436*). His 302* v Nottinghamshire at Trent Bridge 2003 was the then highest individual first-class score by a Leicestershire player. ING Cup Player of the Year 2003-04. Has won numerous Australian and English domestic awards, including Man of the Match in the Twenty20 Cup final at Edgbaston 2004 for his 53-ball 77*. Man of the Match in the first Test v South Africa at Perth 2005-06 (41/203*) and v Netherlands in St Kitts in the 2006-07 World Cup (123). An overseas player with Lancashire since 2005
Best batting: 302* Leicestershire v Nottinghamshire, Trent Bridge 2003
Best bowling: 4-17 Australia A v West Indians, Hobart 2000-01

2007 Season

	M	Inn	NO	Runs	HS	Avg	100	50	Ct	St	Balls	Runs	Wkts	Avg	BB	5I	10M
Test																	
FC	8	13	2	354	156 *	32.18	1	-	4	-	12	5	0		-	-	-
ODI																	
List A	8	8	3	439	141 *	87.80	3	-	3	-	96	80	4	20.00	2-16	-	
20/20 Int																	
20/20	6	6	0	172	57	28.66	-	1	5	-	66	97	2	48.50	1-22	-	

Career Performances

	M	Inn	NO	Runs	HS	Avg	100	50	Ct	St	Balls	Runs	Wkts	Avg	BB	5I	10M
Test	5	9	2	409	203 *	58.42	1	1	9	-	12	8	0		-	-	-
FC	198	348	35	15089	302 *	48.20	46	55	113	-	4881	2751	68	40.45	4-17	-	-
ODI	18	15	2	516	123	39.69	1	3	12	-	54	33	1	33.00	1-17	-	
List A	199	190	24	6911	164	41.63	17	34	80	-	1446	1264	37	34.16	5-28	1	
20/20 Int	6	3	1	82	36	41.00	-	-	2	-	12	20	0		-	-	
20/20	39	36	4	1465	106	45.78	1	11	22	-	342	441	23	19.17	4-17	-	

HODGKINSON, R. Derbyshire

Name: Richard Hodgkinson
Role: Right-hand bat, right-arm fast bowler
Born: 9 December 1983, Sutton-in-Ashfield
Height: 6ft 4in **Weight:** 14st
Nickname: Hodgy
County debut: 2005 (one-day, Nottinghamshire), 2007 (Derbyshire)
Education: Kirkby Centre; West Notts College
Qualifications: 9 GCSEs, BTEC First Diploma in Sports Science, Level 1 coach
Overseas tours: Nottinghamshire to Johannesburg 2003
Overseas teams played for: Mildura Settlers and Claremont-Nedlands (both Australia) 2000
Other sports played: Football (had trials for Nottingham Forest and Mansfield Town), golf
Other sports followed: Football (Mansfield Town)
Extras: Played for Nottinghamshire Board XI in the ECB 38-County Cup 2001 and 2002 and in the 2002 C&G. Attended Dennis Lillee's fast-bowling clinic in Chennai

(Madras) 2004, 2005. Has also played for Surrey 2nd XI. Joined Derbyshire in 2007 as pace-bowling cover; released by Derbyshire at the end of the 2007 season
Best batting: 6 Derbyshire v Nottinghamshire, Trent Bridge 2007

2007 Season

	M	Inn	NO	Runs	HS	Avg	100	50	Ct	St	Balls	Runs	Wkts	Avg	BB	5I	10M
Test																	
FC	1	1	0	6	6	6.00	-	-	-	-	60	75	0		-	-	-
ODI																	
List A																	
20/20 Int																	
20/20																	

Career Performances

	M	Inn	NO	Runs	HS	Avg	100	50	Ct	St	Balls	Runs	Wkts	Avg	BB	5I	10M
Test																	
FC	1	1	0	6	6	6.00	-	-	-	-	60	75	0		-	-	-
ODI																	
List A	2	1	0	0	0	0.00	-	-	1	-	96	78	3	26.00	2-36	-	
20/20 Int																	
20/20																	

HODNETT, G. P. — Gloucestershire

Name: Grant Phillip Hodnett
Role: Right-hand top-order bat, right-arm leg-spin bowler, occasional wicket-keeper
Born: 17 August 1982, Johannesburg, South Africa
Height: 6ft 4in **Weight:** 14st
Nickname: Hodders, Hoddy
County debut: 2005
County cap: 2005
Place in batting averages: 93rd av. 36.91
Parents: Phillip and Julia
Marital status: Single
Family links with cricket: Brother Kyle an MCC Young Cricketer
Education: Northwood High School, Durban
Qualifications: Matriculation, ECB Level 1 coach, GFA Fitness Instructor

Overseas tours: Gloucestershire to South Africa 2006
Overseas teams played for: Durban Collegians 2005-06
Cricket superstitions: 'None'
Cricketers particularly admired: Hansie Cronje, Jonty Rhodes, Steve Waugh, Andrew Flintoff, Michael Atherton
Other sports played: Golf, squash, bodyboarding, football, rugby
Other sports followed: Rugby union (England), football (Newcastle United)
Favourite band: Blink-182
Relaxations: 'Going to gym; swimming; reading sports magazines'
Extras: Represented KwaZulu-Natal Schools. West of England Premier League Batsman of the Year 2004. Is not considered an overseas player
Best batting: 168 Gloucestershire v Derbyshire, Bristol 2007

2007 Season

	M	Inn	NO	Runs	HS	Avg	100	50	Ct	St	Balls	Runs	Wkts	Avg	BB	5I	10M
Test																	
FC	15	25	1	886	168	36.91	2	6	8	-	15	10	0		-	-	-
ODI																	
List A	3	3	0	107	50	35.66	-	1	2	-	0	0	0		-	-	
20/20 Int																	
20/20																	

Career Performances

	M	Inn	NO	Runs	HS	Avg	100	50	Ct	St	Balls	Runs	Wkts	Avg	BB	5I	10M
Test																	
FC	16	27	1	945	168	36.34	2	6	9	-	15	10	0		-	-	-
ODI																	
List A	4	4	0	114	50	28.50	-	1	2	-	0	0	0		-	-	
20/20 Int																	
20/20																	

HOGG, K. W. — Lancashire

Name: Kyle William Hogg
Role: Left-hand bat, right-arm fast-medium bowler; all-rounder
Born: 2 July 1983, Birmingham
Height: 6ft 4in **Weight:** 13st
Nickname: Boss, Hoggy
County debut: 2001 (*see* ***Extras***)
Place in batting averages: (2006 92nd av. 36.28)
Place in bowling averages: (2006 81st av. 35.20)
Parents: Sharon and William

Marital status: Single
Family links with cricket: Father played for Lancashire and Warwickshire; grandfather Sonny Ramadhin played for Lancashire and West Indies
Education: Saddleworth High School, Oldham
Qualifications: GCSEs
Overseas tours: England U19 to India 2000-01, to Australia and (U19 World Cup) New Zealand 2001-02; Lancashire to South Africa, to Grenada; ECB National Academy to Australia and Sri Lanka 2002-03
Overseas teams played for: Otago 2006-07
Cricket moments to forget: '[B&H 2002] semi-final v Warwickshire'
Cricket superstitions: 'None'
Cricketers particularly admired: Andrew Flintoff, David Byas, Stuart Law, Carl Hooper
Other sports played: Football
Other sports followed: Football (Man Utd)
Favourite band: Stone Roses, Red Hot Chili Peppers, Bob Marley
Relaxations: 'Relaxing with friends'
Extras: Represented England U19 2001, 2002. NBC Denis Compton Award for the most promising young Lancashire player 2001. Recorded maiden first-class five-wicket return (5-48) on Championship debut v Leicestershire at Old Trafford 2002. Included in provisional England squad of 30 for the 2002-03 World Cup. Played two first-class and four List A matches for Worcestershire on loan 2007 and two first-class and three List A matches for Nottinghamshire on loan 2007
Best batting: 71 Otago v Central Districts, Napier 2006-07
Best bowling: 5-48 Lancashire v Leicestershire, Old Trafford 2002

2007 Season

	M	Inn	NO	Runs	HS	Avg	100	50	Ct	St	Balls	Runs	Wkts	Avg	BB	5I	10M
Test																	
FC	6	6	2	110	30	27.50	-	-	-	-	750	346	7	49.42	3-44	-	-
ODI																	
List A	9	6	1	42	25	8.40	-	-	1	-	378	338	8	42.25	3-43	-	
20/20 Int																	
20/20	4	3	1	36	27	18.00	-	-	-	-	48	71	3	23.66	2-23	-	

Career Performances

	M	Inn	NO	Runs	HS	Avg	100	50	Ct	St	Balls	Runs	Wkts	Avg	BB	5I	10M
Test																	
FC	39	48	5	982	71	22.83	-	7	11	-	5090	2696	66	40.84	5-48	1	-
ODI																	
List A	87	53	16	586	41 *	15.83	-	-	15	-	3161	2507	86	29.15	4-20	-	
20/20 Int																	
20/20	10	8	1	102	27	14.57	-	-	-	-	109	169	8	21.12	2-10	-	

HOGGARD, M. J. — Yorkshire

Name: Matthew James Hoggard
Role: Right-hand bat, right-arm fast-medium bowler
Born: 31 December 1976, Leeds
Height: 6ft 2in **Weight:** 14st
Nickname: Oggie
County debut: 1996
County cap: 2000
Benefit: 2008
Test debut: 2000
ODI debut: 2001-02
50 wickets in a season: 2
Place in batting averages: 257th av. 13.44
Place in bowling averages: 9th av. 21.40 (2006 79th av. 34.72)
Parents: Margaret and John
Wife and date of marriage: Sarah, 2 October 2004
Children: Ernie, May 2007
Family links with cricket: 'Dad is a cricket badger'
Education: Pudsey Grangefield School, West Yorkshire
Qualifications: GCSEs and A-levels
Overseas tours: Yorkshire CCC to South Africa; England U19 to Zimbabwe 1995-96; England to Kenya (ICC Knockout Trophy) 2000-01, to Pakistan and Sri Lanka 2000-01, to Zimbabwe (one-day series) 2001-02, to India and New Zealand 2001-02, to Sri Lanka (ICC Champions Trophy) 2002-03, to Australia 2002-03, to Africa (World Cup) 2002-03, to Bangladesh and Sri Lanka 2003-04, to West Indies 2003-04, to South Africa 2004-05, to Pakistan 2005-06, to India 2005-06, to Australia 2006-07, to Sri Lanka 2007-08, to New Zealand 2007-08
Overseas teams played for: Pirates, Johannesburg 1995-97; Free State 1998-2000
Cricketers particularly admired: Allan Donald, Courtney Walsh

Other sports played: Rugby
Other sports followed: Rugby league (Leeds Rhinos)
Relaxations: Dog walking
Extras: Was top wicket-taker in the 2000 National League competition with 37 wickets at 12.37. PCA Young Player of the Year 2000. Took 7-63 v New Zealand in the first Test at Christchurch 2001-02, the best innings return by an England pace bowler in Tests v New Zealand. Took hat-trick (Sarwan, Chanderpaul, Ryan Hinds) in the third Test v West Indies at Bridgetown 2003-04. His international awards include Man of the [Test] Series v Bangladesh 2003-04 and Man of the Match in the fourth Test v South Africa at Johannesburg 2004-05 (5-144/7-61) and in the first Test v India at Nagpur 2005-06 (6-57). Appointed MBE in 2006 New Year Honours as part of 2005 Ashes-winning England team. One of *Wisden*'s Five Cricketers of the Year 2006. Took 200th Test wicket (Farveez Maharoof) in the first Test v Sri Lanka at Lord's 2006. Took 237th Test wicket (Dwayne Bravo) in the fourth Test v West Indies at Riverside 2007 to move into sixth place in the England list of Test wicket-takers. England 12-month central contract 2007-08
Best batting: 89* Yorkshire v Glamorgan, Headingley 2004
Best bowling: 7-49 Yorkshire v Somerset, Headingley 2003

2007 Season

	M	Inn	NO	Runs	HS	Avg	100	50	Ct	St	Balls	Runs	Wkts	Avg	BB	5I	10M
Test	2	1	0	0	0	0.00	-	-	-	-	283	115	5	23.00	3-28	-	-
FC	13	11	2	121	61	13.44	-	1	2	-	1667	856	40	21.40	5-32	2	-
ODI																	
List A	5	2	1	5	4	5.00	-	-	-	-	228	217	2	108.50	1-46	-	
20/20 Int																	
20/20																	

Career Performances

	M	Inn	NO	Runs	HS	Avg	100	50	Ct	St	Balls	Runs	Wkts	Avg	BB	5I	10M
Test	64	87	27	444	38	7.40	-	-	23	-	13291	7208	240	30.03	7-61	7	1
FC	160	203	61	1273	89 *	8.96	-	3	45	-	29554	15217	560	27.17	7-49	18	1
ODI	26	6	2	17	7	4.25	-	-	5	-	1306	1152	32	36.00	5-49	1	
List A	125	38	20	66	7 *	3.66	-	-	15	-	5905	4385	174	25.20	5-28	4	
20/20 Int																	
20/20	6	2	1	19	18	19.00	-	-	1	-	132	221	7	31.57	3-23	-	

HOLE, S. M. — Warwickshire

Name: Stuart Mark Hole
Role: Right-hand bat, right-arm seam bowler
Born: 17 July 1985, Oxford
Height: 6ft 1in **Weight:** 12st 7lbs
Nickname: Holey
County debut: 2007
Parents: Les and Sally
Marital status: Single
Education: Bartholomew School, Eynsham
Qualifications: Premier Training personal trainer, gym instructor and sports masseur
Career outside cricket: Personal trainer
Off-season: 'Training hard at Edgbaston'
Career highlights to date: 'First-class debut against Yorkshire [2007]'
Cricket moments to forget: 'None as yet'
Cricketers particularly admired: Matthew Hoggard
Young players to look out for: Chris Woakes
Other sports played: Football ('played at Wycombe Wanderers FC for four years'), golf
Other sports followed: Football (Liverpool, Wycombe Wanderers)
Injuries: Out for six weeks with a bruised bone in the right knee
Favourite band: 112
Relaxations: 'Music, PlayStation 3'
Extras: Played for Oxfordshire in Minor Counties competitions 2005-06
Best batting: 24 Warwickshire v Yorkshire, Scarborough 2007

2007 Season

	M	Inn	NO	Runs	HS	Avg	100	50	Ct	St	Balls	Runs	Wkts	Avg	BB	5I	10M
Test																	
FC	1	2	1	24	24	24.00	-	-	-	-	90	65	0		-	-	-
ODI																	
List A	2	0	0	0	0		-	-	-	-	18	16	1	16.00	1-16	-	
20/20 Int																	
20/20																	

Career Performances

	M	Inn	NO	Runs	HS	Avg	100	50	Ct	St	Balls	Runs	Wkts	Avg	BB	5I	10M
Test																	
FC	1	2	1	24	24	24.00	-	-	-	-	90	65	0		-	-	-
ODI																	
List A	2	0	0	0	0		-	-	-	-	18	16	1	16.00	1-16	-	
20/20 Int																	
20/20																	

HOLLIOAKE, A. J. — Essex

Name: Adam John Hollioake
Role: Right-hand bat, right-arm medium bowler
Born: 5 September 1971, Melbourne, Australia
Height: 5ft 11in
Nickname: Smokey
County debut: 1992 (one-day, Surrey), 1993 (first-class, Surrey), 2007 (one-day, Essex)
County cap: 1995 (Surrey)
Benefit: 2004 (Surrey)
Test debut: 1997
ODI debut: 1996
1000 runs in a season: 2
1st-Class 200s: 1
Parents: John and Daria
Wife: Sherryn
Children: Bennaya, 25 May 2002; Addison, June 2006
Education: St Joseph's College, Sydney; St Patrick's College, Ballarat (Australia); St George's College, Weybridge; Surrey Tutorial College, Guildford
Qualifications: GCSEs, A-levels
Career outside cricket: Property developer
Overseas tours: Surrey YC to Australia; England YC to New Zealand 1990-91; England A to Australia 1996-97 (c); England VI to Hong Kong 1997 (c), 2002; England to Sharjah (Champions Trophy) 1997-98 (c), to West Indies 1997-98 (ODI c), to Bangladesh (Wills International Cup) 1998-99 (c), to Australia 1998-99 (CUB Series), to Sharjah (Coca-Cola Cup) 1998-99, to Australia 2002-03 (VB Series)
Overseas teams played for: Fremantle, Western Australia 1990-91; North Shore, Sydney 1992-93; Geelong, Victoria; North Perth, Western Australia 1995-97
Other sports played: Rugby (played for London Counties, Middlesex and South of England; England U18 trialist)

Extras: Scored a century (123) on first-class debut v Derbyshire at Ilkeston 1993. Surrey Young Player of the Year 1993. Surrey Supporters' Player of the Year and Surrey Players' Player of the Year 1996. England's Man of the [ODI] Series v Australia 1997. Captained England in the Texaco Trophy one-day series v South Africa 1998. Represented England in the 1999 World Cup. Coached Hong Kong in the Asian Cricket Council Trophy in Sharjah 2000. C&G Man of the Match award for his 59-ball 117* (century from 52 balls) in the quarter-final v Sussex at Hove 2002. One of *Wisden*'s Five Cricketers of the Year 2003. Captain of Surrey 1997-2003. Leading wicket-taker in the Twenty20 Cup 2003 and 2004. Retired from county cricket at the end of the 2004 season. Took hat-trick (Dravid, Vaas, Kumble) for International XI v Asian XI in Tsunami Relief Fund match at The Oval 2005. Completed a 2000-mile walk/cycle/sail from Edinburgh to Tangier during autumn 2003 to raise money for the Ben Hollioake Memorial Fund; ran London Marathon 2007 to raise money for the CHASE Ben Hollioake Fund; took part in boxing bout against former All Black Eric Rush in aid of Sparks charity 2007. Came out of county cricket retirement to play for Essex in the Twenty20 2007

Best batting: 208 Surrey v Leicestershire, The Oval 2002

Best bowling: 5-62 Surrey v Glamorgan, Swansea 1998

2007 Season

	M	Inn	NO	Runs	HS	Avg	100	50	Ct	St	Balls	Runs	Wkts	Avg	BB	5I	10M
Test																	
FC																	
ODI																	
List A																	
20/20 Int																	
20/20	8	6	2	49	21	12.25	-	-	3	-	84	110	4	27.50	1-4	-	

Career Performances

	M	Inn	NO	Runs	HS	Avg	100	50	Ct	St	Balls	Runs	Wkts	Avg	BB	5I	10M
Test	4	6	0	65	45	10.83	-	-	4	-	144	67	2	33.50	2-31	-	-
FC	173	263	21	9376	208	38.74	18	55	157	-	8808	4927	120	41.05	5-62	1	-
ODI	35	30	6	606	83 *	25.25	-	3	13	-	1208	1019	32	31.84	4-23	-	
List A	284	249	36	5984	117 *	28.09	2	30	87	-	9074	8186	352	23.25	6-17	7	
20/20 Int																	
20/20	22	19	6	306	65 *	23.53	-	1	5	-	385	515	40	12.87	5-21	2	

HOPKINSON, C. D. — Sussex

Name: <u>Carl</u> Daniel Hopkinson
Role: Right-hand bat, right-arm medium-fast bowler; 'batter that bowls'
Born: 14 September 1981, Brighton
Height: 5ft 11in
Nickname: Hoppo
County debut: 2001 (one-day), 2002 (first-class)
Place in batting averages: 214th av. 20.41 (2006 173rd av. 25.82)
Parents: Jane and Jerry
Marital status: Single
Family links with cricket: 'Dad played in the local team, which got me interested, and coached me from a young age'
Education: Chailey; Brighton College
Qualifications: 7 GCSEs, 3 A-levels, Level 1 coaching
Overseas tours: Tours to India 1997-98, to South Africa 1999
Overseas teams played for: Rockingham-Mandurah, Western Australia 2000-01
Cricketers particularly admired: Dennis Lillee, Ian Botham, Viv Richards, Graham Thorpe
Other sports played: Rugby ('won Rosslyn Park National Sevens'), squash, football
Other sports followed: Football (West Ham)
Favourite band: 50 Cent
Extras: South of England and England squads until U17. Sussex Young Player of the Year 2000. Sussex 2nd XI Fielder of the Year 2001, 2003. Took wicket (John Wood) with his third ball on county debut, in the Norwich Union League v Lancashire at Hove 2001. C&G Man of the Match award v Nottinghamshire at Hove 2005 (51 plus run-out of Stephen Fleming)
Best batting: 83 Sussex v Worcestershire, Worcester 2007
Best bowling: 1-20 Sussex v LUCCE, Hove 2004

2007 Season

	M	Inn	NO	Runs	HS	Avg	100	50	Ct	St	Balls	Runs	Wkts	Avg	BB	5I	10M
Test																	
FC	10	17	0	347	83	20.41	-	2	10	-	84	79	0		-	-	-
ODI																	
List A	13	11	2	238	123 *	26.44	1	-	4	-	36	33	1	33.00	1-33	-	
20/20 Int																	
20/20	7	4	1	50	26 *	16.66	-	-	2	-	0	0	0		-	-	

Career Performances

	M	Inn	NO	Runs	HS	Avg	100	50	Ct	St	Balls	Runs	Wkts	Avg	BB	5I	10M
Test																	
FC	38	63	1	1473	83	23.75	-	11	25	-	328	246	2	123.00	1-20	-	-
ODI																	
List A	78	62	8	1225	123 *	22.68	1	6	36	-	548	539	15	35.93	3-19	-	
20/20 Int																	
20/20	22	14	4	124	26 *	12.40	-	-	5	-	0	0	0		-	-	

HORTON, P. J. Lancashire

Name: Paul James Horton
Role: Right-hand bat, right-arm medium/off-spin bowler
Born: 20 September 1982, Sydney, Australia
Height: 5ft 10in **Weight:** 11st 3lbs
Nickname: Horts, Ozzy
County debut: 2003
County cap: 2007
1000 runs in a season: 1
Place in batting averages: 37th av. 48.52
Parents: Donald William and Norma
Marital status: Single
Education: Colo High School, Sydney/Broadgreen Comprehensive, Liverpool; St Margaret's High School, Liverpool
Qualifications: 11 GCSEs, 3 A-levels, Level 2 ECB coach
Overseas tours: Hawkesbury U15 to New Zealand 1997; Lancashire to Cape Town 2002-03, to Grenada 2003
Overseas teams played for: Hawkesbury, Sydney 1992-93 – 1997-98; Penrith, NSW 2002-03
Cricket moments to forget: 'First 2nd XI game for Lancashire at Old Trafford – out for 0'
Cricket superstitions: 'None'
Cricketers particularly admired: Dean Jones, Sachin Tendulkar, Mark Waugh
Other sports played: Football, golf, squash, tennis, badminton
Other sports followed: Football (Liverpool)
Favourite band: Red Hot Chili Peppers
Relaxations: 'Golf, socialising with friends, watching sport'
Extras: Captained Lancashire U17 and U19. Captained Lancashire Board XI in the

C&G 2003. Lancashire Young Player of the Year Award 2001, 2002. Leading run-scorer for Lancashire 2nd XI in the 2nd XI Championship 2003 (861 runs; av. 50.65)
Best batting: 152 Lancashire v Hampshire, Old Trafford 2007

2007 Season

	M	Inn	NO	Runs	HS	Avg	100	50	Ct	St	Balls	Runs	Wkts	Avg	BB	5I	10M
Test																	
FC	14	25	2	1116	152	48.52	3	5	17	-	0	0	0		-	-	-
ODI																	
List A	8	8	0	153	47	19.12	-	-	1	-	0	0	0		-	-	
20/20 Int																	
20/20																	

Career Performances

	M	Inn	NO	Runs	HS	Avg	100	50	Ct	St	Balls	Runs	Wkts	Avg	BB	5I	10M
Test																	
FC	26	43	5	1717	152	45.18	3	9	23	1	0	0	0		-	-	-
ODI																	
List A	18	15	0	296	47	19.73	-	-	1	-	0	0	0		-	-	
20/20 Int																	
20/20	5	4	1	28	11	9.33	-	-	2	-	0	0	0		-	-	

HOUSEGO, D. M. — Middlesex

Name: Daniel (<u>Dan</u>) Mark Housego
Role: Right-hand top-order bat, right-arm off-spin bowler
Born: 12 October 1988, Windsor
Height: 5ft 9in **Weight:** 11st 2lbs
Nickname: Harry Housego
County debut: No first-team appearance
Parents: Beryl and Jim
Marital status: Single
Education: The Oratory School, Reading
Qualifications: 8 GCSEs, 3 A-levels, Level 1 coaching
Off-season: 'Australia (Darren Lehmann Academy) for six months'
Overseas tours: England U15 to South Africa; England U16 to South Africa
Overseas teams played for: Adelaide CC, 2007-08
Career highlights to date: '138* v Somerset 2nd XI; 161 v Derbyshire 2nd XI'

Cricket moments to forget: 'None. Don't regret anything'
Cricket superstitions: 'None'
Cricketers particularly admired: Ian Bell
Young players to look out for: Billy Godleman, Steve Finn, Eoin Morgan
Other sports played: Football (Oxford United Academy 1998-2003), athletics (age-group 200m national champion 2002)
Other sports followed: Football (Chelsea), golf (Tiger Woods)
Favourite band: Timbaland
Relaxations: 'Fishing, golf'
Extras: Neil Lloyd Trophy (Bunbury Festival). Represented England U15, U16, U17. Played for Berkshire in the Minor Counties Championship 2006
Opinions on cricket: 'Absolutely love it!'

HOWELL, B. A. C. — Hampshire

Name: Benjamin (Benny) Alexander Cameron Howell
Role: Right-hand opening bat, right-arm medium bowler
Born: 5 October 1988, Bordeaux, France
Height: 5ft 11in **Weight:** 12st
Nickname: Growler, Howly, Schofield
County debut: No first-team appearance
Parents: Jonathan and Julie
Marital status: Single
Family links with cricket: 'Dad played one game for Warwickshire first team; made a half-century. Brother Nick played county age-group cricket for Berkshire'
Education: The Oratory School, Reading
Qualifications: 9 GCSEs, 3 A-levels
Overseas tours: Oratory School to Barbados 2003, 2004
Overseas teams played for: Melville, Perth 2007-08
Career highlights to date: '172 not out in a 50-over game for Hampshire Cricket Academy, August 2007'
Cricket moments to forget: 'Every time I bowl!'
Cricketers particularly admired: Shane Warne, Nic Pothas, Brett Lee, Steve Waugh, Sachin Tendulkar, Brian Lara
Young players to look out for: Liam Dawson, Hamza Riazuddin, James Vince, Dan Housego
Other sports played: Football, rugby, golf, tennis, squash, basketball, real tennis, snooker, darts

Other sports followed: Football (Everton FC), AFL (Melbourne Demons)
Favourite band: Justin Timberlake, 50 Cent, Timbaland, Chris Brown, Akon, Eminem, Kanye West
Relaxations: 'Movies, music, sports (playing and watching), sleeping'
Extras: Hampshire Academy Player of the Year 2006. Southern Electric Premier League Player of the Month, August 2007
Opinions on cricket: 'At the end of the day, cricket is all about enjoying playing and watching and entertaining the spectators. Twenty20 does that; it is exciting, explosive and highly skilful. This brings in the crowds and money to develop the game. It has to be played more often.'

HOWGEGO, B. H. — Northamptonshire

Name: Benjamin Henry Howgego
Role: Left-hand bat, right-arm medium-fast bowler
Born: 3 March 1988, Norfolk
County debut: No first-team appearance
Education: The King's School, Ely; Stowe School
Extras: Made 2nd XI Championship debut 2005. Represented both ECB Development of Excellence XI and ECB Schools v India U19 2006

38. Who took ten wickets or more in Tests between England and South Africa an astonishing six times during 1912 and 1913-14?

HUGHES, L. D. — Derbyshire

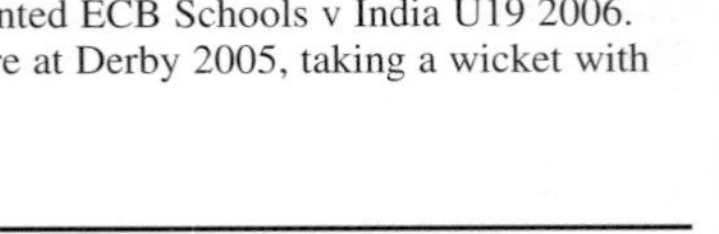

Name: Liam Daniel Hughes
Role: Right-hand bat, right-arm medium-fast bowler
Born: 21 March 1988, Wordsley, West Midlands
Height: 6ft 1in
Nickname: Yozza
County debut: No first-team appearance
Parents: Angela and Malcolm
Marital status: Single
Education: Ounsdale High School; Wolverhampton University
Qualifications: 2 A-levels
Career highlights to date: 'Taking a wicket with my first ball in second-team cricket for Derbyshire v Lancashire'
Cricket moments to forget: 'A pair v Yorkshire'
Cricketers particularly admired: Glenn McGrath
Other sports followed: Football (Wolves), American football (St Louis Rams)
Favourite band: Pussycat Dolls
Extras: Played for Staffordshire U15. Represented ECB Schools v India U19 2006. Made 2nd XI Championship debut v Lancashire at Derby 2005, taking a wicket with his first ball

HUNTER, I. D. — Derbyshire

Name: Ian David Hunter
Role: Right-hand bat, right-arm fast-medium bowler
Born: 11 September 1979, Durham City
Height: 6ft 2in **Weight:** 13st
Nickname: Sticks, Hunts, Kingsley
County debut: 1999 (one-day, Durham), 2000 (first-class, Durham), 2004 (Derbys)
Place in batting averages: (2006 247th av. 14.57)
Place in bowling averages: (2006 90th av. 36.88)
Parents: Ken and Linda
Marital status: Single
Family links with cricket: Brother local village cricketer
Education: Fyndoune Community College, Sacriston; New College, Durham
Qualifications: 9 GCSEs, 1 A-level (PE), BTEC National Diploma in Sports Science,

Level I and II cricket coaching awards
Overseas tours: Durham U21 to Sri Lanka 1996; Durham to Cape Town 2002
Career highlights to date: 'Taking 5-63 against Durham at Riverside [2005]'
Cricket moments to forget: 'All of 2007 season – out through knee injuries'
Cricket superstitions: 'Always put my left pad on first'
Cricketers particularly admired: Allan Donald, Graeme Welch, Steve Waugh
Young players to look out for: Dan Redfern, Gary Ballance
Other sports played: Football, golf
Other sports followed: Football (Newcastle United FC), rugby league (St Helens)
Injuries: Out for most of the 2007 season with torn cartilage and patellar tendonopathy of the right knee
Favourite band: Arctic Monkeys
Relaxations: 'Golf, gym, socialising with friends'
Extras: Set a then Durham best analysis for the 2nd XI Championship with his 11-155 v Lancashire 2nd XI at Great Crosby 1999. Represented England U19 1999
Opinions on cricket: 'Too much one-day cricket played; not enough time to recover between games.'
Best batting: 65 Durham v Northamptonshire, Northampton 2002
Best bowling: 5-63 Derbyshire v Durham, Riverside 2005

2007 Season

	M	Inn	NO	Runs	HS	Avg	100	50	Ct	St	Balls	Runs	Wkts	Avg	BB	5I	10M
Test																	
FC	1	1	1	1	1 *		-	-	-	-	276	130	3	43.33	2-63	-	-
ODI																	
List A	4	1	1	3	3 *		-	-	-	-	162	149	5	29.80	3-38	-	
20/20 Int																	
20/20	3	2	0	2	2	1.00	-	-	-	-	66	90	3	30.00	2-38	-	

Career Performances

	M	Inn	NO	Runs	HS	Avg	100	50	Ct	St	Balls	Runs	Wkts	Avg	BB	5I	10M
Test																	
FC	50	68	17	898	65	17.60	-	2	15	-	7920	4910	121	40.57	5-63	1	-
ODI																	
List A	76	46	11	277	39	7.91	-	-	14	-	3299	2707	81	33.41	4-29	-	
20/20 Int																	
20/20	15	6	2	41	25 *	10.25	-	-	3	-	318	453	17	26.64	3-26	-	

HUSSEY, D. J. Nottinghamshire

Name: David (Dave) John Hussey
Role: Right-hand bat, right-arm off-spin bowler, occasional wicket-keeper
Born: 15 July 1977, Perth, Western Australia
Height: 5ft 11in **Weight:** 13st 3lbs
Nickname: Huss, Hussa, Husscat
County debut: 2004
County cap: 2004
1000 runs in a season: 4
1st-Class 200s: 3
Place in batting averages: 2nd av. 83.93 (2006 51st av. 47.62)
Parents: Helen and Ted
Marital status: Single
Family links with cricket: Brother Mike plays for Australia and Western Australia and has played for Northamptonshire, Gloucestershire and Durham
Education: Prendiville Catholic College; Edith Cowan University
Qualifications: Bachelor of Business (Sports Management and Sports Science)
Overseas tours: Commonwealth Bank [Australian] Cricket Academy to Sri Lanka 1997-98; Australia A to Pakistan 2007-08
Overseas teams played for: Wanneroo DCC, Perth 1992-2001; Prahran CC, Victoria; Victoria 2002-03 –
Career highlights to date: 'Winning Pura Cup with Victoria 2004. Winning Championship with Notts 2005'
Cricket moments to forget: 'Debut for Victoria – dropped S. Waugh on 4; he went on to make 211'
Cricket superstitions: 'Left shoe on first'
Cricketers particularly admired: Brendon Julian, Mark Waugh, Damien Martyn
Young players to look out for: Andrew Hodd
Other sports played: Australian Rules football, squash, tennis, football
Other sports followed: AFL (St Kilda FC), football (Brighton & Hove Albion)
Favourite band: Keane, Foo Fighters
Relaxations: 'Reading'
Extras: Played for Western Australia U19 and 2nd XI. Represented Australia U19 1995-96. Has represented Australia A. Scored 212* and won Man of the Match award as Victoria scored 455-7 to beat New South Wales at Newcastle in the Pura Cup 2003-04. His other awards include Man of the Match v New South Wales at Melbourne in the Pura Cup 2003-04 (120/50) and v South Australia at Adelaide in the ING Cup 2003-04 (113). Scored 275 v Essex at Trent Bridge 2007, in the process sharing with

Chris Read (165*) in a new record fifth-wicket partnership for Nottinghamshire (359). An overseas player with Nottinghamshire since 2004
Best batting: 275 Nottinghamshire v Essex, Trent Bridge 2007
Best bowling: 4-105 Nottinghamshire v Hampshire, Trent Bridge 2005
Stop press: Man of the Match v South Australia at Adelaide (104/74*) and v Tasmania at Hobart (103/31*), both in the Pura Cup 2007-08; also won three match awards in five days in the KFC Twenty20 Big Bash 2007-08

2007 Season

	M	Inn	NO	Runs	HS	Avg	100	50	Ct	St	Balls	Runs	Wkts	Avg	BB	5I	10M
Test																	
FC	13	17	2	1259	275	83.93	4	5	16	-	29	23	0		-	-	-
ODI																	
List A	12	12	2	465	88	46.50	-	5	4	-	94	83	5	16.60	3-26	-	
20/20 Int																	
20/20	6	6	1	114	36	22.80	-	-	3	-	36	57	3	19.00	2-11	-	

Career Performances

	M	Inn	NO	Runs	HS	Avg	100	50	Ct	St	Balls	Runs	Wkts	Avg	BB	5I	10M
Test																	
FC	108	164	18	8111	275	55.55	30	31	124	-	1635	1120	20	56.00	4-105	-	-
ODI																	
List A	115	106	17	3580	130	40.22	5	21	54	-	713	672	18	37.33	3-26	-	
20/20 Int																	
20/20	38	36	4	907	86	28.34	-	4	21	-	106	129	5	25.80	2-11	-	

39. Sir Richard Hadlee's knighthood was announced during an England v New Zealand Test series. But in which year: a) 1988; b) 1990; c) 1992?

HUTTON, B. L. — Middlesex

Name: Benjamin (Ben) Leonard Hutton
Role: Left-hand bat, right-arm medium bowler
Born: 29 January 1977, Johannesburg, South Africa
Height: 6ft 1½in **Weight:** 12st
Nickname: Gibbo
County debut: 1999
County cap: 2003
1000 runs in a season: 2
Place in batting averages: 83rd av. 38.33 (2006 139th av. 30.68)
Parents: Charmaine and Richard
Marital status: Single
Family links with cricket: Sir Leonard Hutton (grandfather) Yorkshire and England; Richard Hutton (father) Yorkshire and England; Ben Brocklehurst (grandfather) Somerset; Oliver Hutton (brother) Oxford University
Education: Radley College; Durham University
Qualifications: 10 GCSEs, 3 A-levels, BA (Hons) Social Sciences, NCA coaching award
Overseas tours: Durham University to Zimbabwe 1997-98; Middlesex to Portugal 1996, 1997, 1998, to South Africa 1999, to Malta 2001, to Mumbai 2003; MCC to Italy
Overseas teams played for: Pirates CC, Johannesburg 1996; Wanderers CC, Johannesburg 1997; Gosnells, Perth 2001-02
Cricket moments to forget: 'Breaking my hand v Gloucestershire 2001. Two Championship pairs'
Cricket superstitions: 'None'
Cricketers particularly admired: Sir Leonard Hutton, Justin Langer, Mark Ramprakash, Andy Flower
Young players to look out for: Nick Compton, Eoin Morgan
Other sports played: Golf (12 handicap)
Other sports followed: 'All sport, except motor racing'
Favourite band: 'Too many to mention'
Relaxations: 'Reading and listening to music'
Extras: Played in Durham University's BUSA Championship winning side 1997, 1998 (shared) and 1999. Opened for Middlesex v Essex at Southend 1999 with Andrew Strauss, his former opening partner at Radley. Scored century in each innings (100/107) v Kent at Southgate 2004. Captain of Middlesex 2005-06. Retired at the end of the 2007 season

Best batting: 152 Middlesex v Kent, Lord's 2005
Best bowling: 4-37 Middlesex v Sri Lankans, Shenley 2002

2007 Season

	M	Inn	NO	Runs	HS	Avg	100	50	Ct	St	Balls	Runs	Wkts	Avg	BB	5I	10M
Test																	
FC	4	7	1	230	118	38.33	1	-	4	-	48	28	0		-	-	-
ODI																	
List A	2	2	1	26	23 *	26.00	-	-	1	-	38	44	1	44.00	1-44	-	
20/20 Int																	
20/20	4	3	2	6	3 *	6.00	-	-	-	-	6	13	1	13.00	1-13	-	

Career Performances

	M	Inn	NO	Runs	HS	Avg	100	50	Ct	St	Balls	Runs	Wkts	Avg	BB	5I	10M
Test																	
FC	110	189	16	5746	152	33.21	18	18	136	-	3558	2239	35	63.97	4-37	-	-
ODI																	
List A	120	98	18	1603	77	20.03	-	7	60	-	1765	1635	52	31.44	5-45	1	
20/20 Int																	
20/20	22	17	5	120	27 *	10.00	-	-	8	-	90	142	5	28.40	2-21	-	

ILES, J. A. — Kent

Name: James Alexander Iles
Role: Right-hand bat, right-arm fast-medium bowler
Born: 11 February 1990, Chatham, Kent
Height: 6ft 4in **Weight:** 14st 7lbs
Nickname: Ilo
County debut: 2006
Parents: Diane and Peter
Marital status: Single
Education: Maidstone Grammar School for Boys
Qualifications: 10 GCSEs
Overseas tours: England U16 to South Africa 2005-06
Career highlights to date: 'First-class debut, 17 May 2006 v Cambridge UCCE'
Cricket moments to forget: 'Whilst playing for my club as a colt, I chased a ball to the boundary with no bearing as to where the sightscreen was – I slid straight into it, cutting my shin open'

Cricket superstitions: 'I have to put my left pad on before my right'
Cricketers particularly admired: Andrew Flintoff
Other sports played: Rugby ('Kent, three years')
Other sports followed: Football (Arsenal), rugby (Wasps)
Favourite band: Brian McKnight
Relaxations: 'Watching my local rugby team; listening to music'
Extras: Kent Academy scholar. Youngest player to make first-class debut for Kent, aged 16 years 92 days
Opinions on cricket: 'I believe that teams should only be allowed one overseas or Kolpak player [*see page 13*] per season. This will allow younger, home-grown players to be given the opportunity to play first-class cricket.'
Best bowling: 1-27 Kent v CUCCE, Fenner's 2006

2007 Season

	M	Inn	NO	Runs	HS	Avg	100	50	Ct	St	Balls	Runs	Wkts	Avg	BB	5I	10M
Test																	
FC																	
ODI																	
List A	1	0	0	0	0		-	-	1	-	36	27	1	27.00	1-27	-	
20/20 Int																	
20/20																	

Career Performances

	M	Inn	NO	Runs	HS	Avg	100	50	Ct	St	Balls	Runs	Wkts	Avg	BB	5I	10M
Test																	
FC	1	0	0	0	0		-	-	-	-	78	37	1	37.00	1-27	-	-
ODI																	
List A	1	0	0	0	0		-	-	1	-	36	27	1	27.00	1-27	-	
20/20 Int																	
20/20																	

40. Which pair of double internationals opened the batting for England v New Zealand in the third Test at Headingley in 1958?

IMRAN TAHIR — Yorkshire

Name: Mohammad Imran Tahir
Role: Right-hand bat, right-arm leg-spin bowler
Born: 27 March 1979, Lahore, Pakistan
County debut: 2003 (Middlesex), 2007 (Yorkshire)
Overseas tours: Pakistan U19 to South Africa 1996-97, to Australia 1997-98, to South Africa (U19 World Cup) 1997-98; Pakistan A to Sri Lanka 2004-05
Overseas teams played for: Several in Pakistan, including Lahore City 1996-97 – 1997-98, Pakistan International Airlines 2004-05 – 2006-07; Titans, South Africa 2007-08 –
Extras: Played for Staffordshire in the C&G 2004 and 2005, winning Man of the Match award v Lancashire at Stone 2004 (3-31/18-ball 41*). Represented both Pakistan A and a PCB Patron's XI v England XI 2005-06. Was a temporary overseas player with Middlesex 2003; was a temporary overseas player with Yorkshire during the 2007 season as a replacement for Jason Gillespie
Best batting: 48 REDCO v KRL, Rawalpindi (KRL) 1999-2000
Best bowling: 8-76 REDCO v Karachi Blues, Lahore (C) 1999-2000

2007 Season

	M	Inn	NO	Runs	HS	Avg	100	50	Ct	St	Balls	Runs	Wkts	Avg	BB	5I	10M
Test																	
FC	1	2	0	5	5	2.50	-	-	-	-	222	141	0		-	-	-
ODI																	
List A																	
20/20 Int																	
20/20																	

Career Performances

	M	Inn	NO	Runs	HS	Avg	100	50	Ct	St	Balls	Runs	Wkts	Avg	BB	5I	10M
Test																	
FC	60	73	13	614	48	10.23	-	-	32	-	10662	5583	209	26.71	8-76	11	2
ODI																	
List A	33	14	6	147	41 *	18.37	-	-	11	-	1622	1133	48	23.60	5-30	1	
20/20 Int																	
20/20	6	3	1	25	13	12.50	-	-	3	-	126	120	5	24.00	3-25	-	

INZAMAM-UL-HAQ Yorkshire

Name: Inzamam-ul-Haq
Role: Right-hand bat, slow left-arm bowler
Born: 3 March 1970, Multan, Pakistan
County debut: 2007
Test debut: 1992
ODI debut: 1991-92
Twenty20 Int debut: 2006
1st-Class 200s: 3
1st-Class 300s: 1

Overseas tours: Pakistan U19 to Australia (U19 World Cup) 1987-88, to India 1988-89; Pakistan A to Sri Lanka 1991; Pakistan to Australia and New Zealand (World Cup) 1991-92, to England 1992, to Australia and New Zealand 1992-93, to West Indies 1992-93, to New Zealand 1993-94, to Sri Lanka 1994, to South Africa and Zimbabwe 1994-95, to Australia and New Zealand 1995-96, to England 1996, to Sri Lanka 1996-97, to South Africa and Zimbabwe 1997-98, to India 1998-99, to UK, Ireland and Netherlands (World Cup) 1999, to Australia 1999-2000, to West Indies 1999-2000, to Sri Lanka 2000, to Kenya (ICC Knockout Trophy) 2000-01, to New Zealand 2000-01, to England 2001, to Bangladesh 2001-02, to Sharjah (v West Indies) 2001-02, to Zimbabwe and South Africa 2002-03, to Africa (World Cup) 2002-03, to New Zealand 2003-04 (c), to England (ICC Champions Trophy) 2004 (c), to Australia 2004-05 (c), to India 2004-05 (c), to West Indies 2004-05 (c), to Sri Lanka 2005-06 (c), to Scotland and England 2006 (c), to South Africa 2006-07 (c), to West Indies (World Cup) 2006-07 (c), plus other one-day series and tournaments in Sharjah, South Africa, Singapore, Toronto, Australia, India, Sri Lanka, Bangladesh, Morocco, Kenya, Netherlands and Abu Dhabi; ICC World XI to Australia (Super Series) 2005-06; Asian Cricket Council XI to South Africa (Afro-Asia Cup) 2005-06

Overseas teams played for: Several in Pakistan, including Multan 1985-86 – 2003-04, United Bank 1988-89 – 1996-97, WAPDA 2006-07

Extras: Popularly nicknamed 'Inzy'. Was a member of Pakistan's World Cup winning team 1991-92. Scored 329 (the second highest score in Tests by a Pakistan batsman) in the first Test v New Zealand in Lahore 2002, winning the Man of the Match award. His other series and match awards include Man of the [ODI] Series v India 2003-04, Man of the [Test] Series v England 2005-06 (431 runs; av. 107.75, including twin centuries – 109/100* – in the second Test in Faisalabad) and Man of the Match in the third Test v Bangladesh in Multan 2003-04 (138*). Scored century (184) in his 100th Test, v India in Bangalore 2004-05. Captain of Pakistan from September 2003 to March 2007. Retired from ODI cricket in March 2007, having scored more ODI runs than any other Pakistan batsman (11,701 for Pakistan; 11,739 overall). Was a temporary overseas player with Yorkshire during the 2007 season as a replacement for Younus Khan

Best batting: 329 Pakistan v New Zealand, Lahore 2001-02

Best bowling: 5-80 Multan v Bahawalpur, Sahiwal 1989-90

Stop press: Retired from Test cricket after the second Test v South Africa in Lahore 2007-08, having scored more Test centuries than any other Pakistan batsman (25) and lying second in the list of all-time Pakistan Test run-scorers (8829 runs) behind Javed Miandad (8832)

2007 Season

	M	Inn	NO	Runs	HS	Avg	100	50	Ct	St	Balls	Runs	Wkts	Avg	BB	5I	10M
Test																	
FC	3	4	0	89	51	22.25	-	1	5	-	0	0	0		-	-	-
ODI																	
List A	3	3	0	69	53	23.00	-	1	-	-	0	0	0		-	-	
20/20 Int																	
20/20																	

Career Performances

	M	Inn	NO	Runs	HS	Avg	100	50	Ct	St	Balls	Runs	Wkts	Avg	BB	5I	10M
Test	119	198	22	8813	329	50.07	25	46	81	-	9	8	0		-	-	-
FC	244	391	58	16768	329	50.35	45	87	172	-	2704	1295	39	33.20	5-80	2	-
ODI	378	350	53	11739	137 *	39.52	10	83	113	-	58	64	3	21.33	1-0	-	
List A	458	430	69	13746	157 *	38.07	12	97	128	-	896	740	30	24.66	3-18	-	
20/20 Int	1	1	1	11	11 *		-	-	-	-	0	0	0		-	-	
20/20	2	2	1	32	21	32.00	-	-	-	-	0	0	0		-	-	

41. Which all-rounder scored a century and recorded a five-wicket innings return in a Test for the fifth time in the first Test between England and New Zealand at Wellington in 1983-84?

IQBAL, M. M. Durham

Name: Moneeb Mohammed Iqbal
Role: Right-hand bat, leg-break bowler
Born: 28 February 1986, Glasgow, Scotland
County debut: 2006
Family links with cricket: Brother-in-law Mohammad Ramzan played Test cricket for Pakistan
Overseas tours: Scotland U19 to New Zealand (U19 World Cup) 2001-02, to Bangladesh (U19 World Cup) 2003-04, to Sri Lanka (U19 World Cup) 2005-06, plus various Scotland age-group tours to Europe
Extras: Man of the Match v Kenya U19 at Carisbrook in the U19 World Cup 2001-02 (2-16/40) and v Nepal U19 at Chittagong in the U19 World Cup 2003-04 (2-34/67). Played for Scotland in the C&G 2002, aged 16. Attended Durham Academy
Best batting: 20 Durham v Kent, Stockton 2006
Best bowling: 4-36 Durham v OUCCE, The Parks 2006

2007 Season (did not make any first-class or one-day appearances)

Career Performances

	M	Inn	NO	Runs	HS	Avg	100	50	Ct	St	Balls	Runs	Wkts	Avg	BB	5I	10M
Test																	
FC	4	8	3	53	20	10.60	-	-	2	-	487	417	9	46.33	4-36	-	-
ODI																	
List A	1	0	0	0	0		-	-	-	-	18	24	0		-	-	
20/20 Int																	
20/20																	

IRANI, R. C. — Essex

Name: Ronald (Ronnie) Charles Irani
Role: Right-hand bat
Born: 26 October 1971, Leigh, Lancashire
Height: 6ft 4in **Weight:** 14st 8lbs
Nickname: Reggie
County debut: 1990 (Lancashire), 1994 (Essex)
County cap: 1994 (Essex)
Benefit: 2003 (Essex)
Test debut: 1996
ODI debut: 1996
1000 runs in a season: 7
50 wickets in a season: 1
1st-Class 200s: 2
Place in batting averages: (2006 19th av. 59.72)
Parents: Jimmy and Anne
Wife: Lorraine
Children: Simone, 25 September 2000; Maria, 6 January 2002
Family links with cricket: 'Father played league cricket for over 30 years. Mum did teas for years as well'
Education: Smithills School, Bolton
Qualifications: 9 GCSEs
Overseas tours: England YC to Australia 1989-90; England A to Pakistan 1995-96, to Bangladesh and New Zealand 1999-2000; England to Zimbabwe and New Zealand 1996-97, to Sri Lanka (ICC Champions Trophy) 2002-03, to Australia 2002-03 (VB Series), to Africa (World Cup) 2002-03; England VI to Hong Kong 2002
Overseas teams played for: Technicol Natal, Durban 1992-93; Eden-Roskill, Auckland 1993-94
Career highlights: 'Playing for England. Winning one-day trophies with Essex'
Cricket moments to forget: 'Admiring lady streaker and getting caught on TV cameras doing it!'
Cricketers particularly admired: Graham Gooch, Javed Miandad, Viv Richards, Wasim Akram
Other sports played: Golf, pool
Other sports followed: Football (Manchester United), Muay Thai (Thai boxing)
Favourite band: Manic Street Preachers, Travis, Joyce Simms, Alexander O'Neal
Relaxations: Fly fishing
Extras: Bull Man of the Series, England YC v Australia YC 1991. Appointed vice-captain of Essex 1999. Achieved double of 1000 first-class runs and 50 first-class wickets 1999. Took over 1st XI captaincy of Essex at the start of the 2000 season,

Nasser Hussain remaining as club captain until his retirement in 2004. Recorded a five-wicket innings return (5-58) and scored a century (119) for Essex v Surrey at Ilford 2001. Man of the Match v India at The Oval in the NatWest Series 2002 (53/5-26); also named 'Fans' Player of the Series'. Captained England XI v Sir Donald Bradman XI at Bowral 2002-03. Granted Freedom of the City of London in April 2003. Forced by knee injury to give up bowling 2003. Scored century (100* from 61 balls) v Sussex at Hove in the Twenty20 2006. Scored career-best 218 v Glamorgan at Chelmsford 2007, in the process taking part in a fifth-wicket partnership of 313 with Ryan ten Doeschate (148). Retired in June 2007 because of further knee problems
Best batting: 218 Essex v Glamorgan, Chelmsford 2007
Best bowling: 6-71 Essex v Nottinghamshire, Trent Bridge 2002

2007 Season

	M	Inn	NO	Runs	HS	Avg	100	50	Ct	St	Balls	Runs	Wkts	Avg	BB	5I	10M
Test																	
FC	4	6	2	465	218	116.25	2	-	4	-	0	0	0		-	-	-
ODI																	
List A	5	5	1	235	90 *	58.75	-	3	2	-	0	0	0		-	-	
20/20 Int																	
20/20																	

Career Performances

	M	Inn	NO	Runs	HS	Avg	100	50	Ct	St	Balls	Runs	Wkts	Avg	BB	5I	10M
Test	3	5	0	86	41	17.20	-	-	2	-	192	112	3	37.33	1-22	-	-
FC	232	373	49	13472	218	41.58	28	72	79	-	20387	10007	339	29.51	6-71	9	-
ODI	31	30	5	360	53	14.40	-	1	6	-	1283	989	24	41.20	5-26	1	
List A	315	293	43	7733	158 *	30.93	7	46	83	-	10452	7796	309	25.22	5-26	4	
20/20 Int																	
20/20	27	26	3	651	100 *	28.30	1	4	12	-	0	0	0		-	-	

42. Who took his 200th Test wicket, against the country of his birth, in the third Test between England and New Zealand at Auckland in 2001-02?

IRELAND, A. J. — Gloucestershire

Name: Anthony John Ireland
Role: Right-hand bat, right-arm medium bowler
Born: 30 August 1984, Masvingo, Zimbabwe
County debut: 2007
County cap: 2007
ODI debut: 2005-06
Twenty20 Int debut: 2006-07
Overseas tours: ZCU President's XI to India (Duleep Trophy) 2005-06; Zimbabwe A to Bangladesh 2006-07; Zimbabwe to West Indies (one-day series) 2006, to South Africa (one-day series) 2006-07, to India (ICC Champions Trophy) 2006-07, to Bangladesh (one-day series) 2006-07, to West Indies (World Cup) 2006-07
Overseas teams played for: Midlands 2002-03 – 2005-06
Extras: Retired from international cricket in April 2007. Is not considered an overseas player
Best batting: 15 Midlands v Matabeleland, Kwekwe 2002-03
Best bowling: 7-36 Zimbabwe A v Bangladesh A, Mirpur 2006-07

2007 Season

	M	Inn	NO	Runs	HS	Avg	100	50	Ct	St	Balls	Runs	Wkts	Avg	BB	5I	10M
Test																	
FC	3	5	3	21	10 *	10.50	-	-	2	-	540	332	7	47.42	3-39	-	-
ODI																	
List A	7	4	4	14	5 *		-	-	5	-	278	289	8	36.12	2-23	-	
20/20 Int																	
20/20	6	2	1	10	8 *	10.00	-	-	1	-	122	157	12	13.08	3-10	-	

Career Performances

	M	Inn	NO	Runs	HS	Avg	100	50	Ct	St	Balls	Runs	Wkts	Avg	BB	5I	10M
Test																	
FC	12	21	6	63	15	4.20	-	-	4	-	1665	977	33	29.60	7-36	1	1
ODI	26	13	5	30	8 *	3.75	-	-	2	-	1326	1115	38	29.34	3-41	-	
List A	42	22	12	69	17	6.90	-	-	8	-	1994	1683	63	26.71	4-16	-	
20/20 Int	1	1	1	2	2 *		-	-	-	-	18	33	1	33.00	1-33	-	
20/20	8	4	2	20	8 *	10.00	-	-	2	-	146	203	13	15.61	3-10	-	

JACOBS, A. — Leicestershire

Name: Arno Jacobs
Role: Left-hand bat, right-arm off-break bowler, occasional wicket-keeper
Born: 13 March 1977, Potchefstroom, South Africa
County debut: 2007
Place in batting averages: 169th av. 26.28
Family links with cricket: Brother Stefan played for Transvaal and Gauteng
Education: Hoër Volkskool, Potchefstroom; Potchefstroom University
Overseas tours: South Africa Academy to Ireland and Scotland 1999
Overseas teams played for: Western Transvaal 1995-96; North West 1997-98 – 2002-03; Eastern Province 2003-04; Eastern Cape 2003-04; Warriors 2004-05 –
Extras: Represented South Africa A v Sri Lanka A 1999-2000, SA Board President's XI v India A 2001-02 and Rest of South Africa v South Africa A 2002-03. His match awards include Man of the Match v Easterns (118/2-22 plus a catch and a run-out) and v Northerns (75*), both in the Standard Bank Cup 2002-03 at Potchefstroom. Has played for Rishton in the Lancashire League and Middleton in the Central Lancashire League. Played for Scotland in the Friends Provident 2007. Joined Leicestershire as a non-overseas player 2007; released by Leicestershire at the end of the 2007 season
Best batting: 197 North West v Border, Potchefstroom 2001-02
Best bowling: 1-2 FSGWNW Combined XI v Sri Lanka A, Potchefstroom 1999-2000

2007 Season

	M	Inn	NO	Runs	HS	Avg	100	50	Ct	St	Balls	Runs	Wkts	Avg	BB	5I	10M
Test																	
FC	6	9	2	184	55	26.28	-	1	5	-	12	13	0		-	-	-
ODI																	
List A	3	3	0	86	49	28.66	-	-	-	-	12	11	0		-	-	
20/20 Int																	
20/20																	

Career Performances	M	Inn	NO	Runs	HS	Avg	100	50	Ct	St	Balls	Runs	Wkts	Avg	BB	5I	10M
Test																	
FC	76	133	19	4295	197	37.67	9	22	89	-	600	375	3	125.00	1-2	-	-
ODI																	
List A	102	98	8	3018	118	33.53	6	12	53	2	220	208	8	26.00	2-22	-	
20/20 Int																	
20/20	24	22	3	343	45	18.05	-	-	7	-	103	125	11	11.36	5-26	1	

JACOBS, D. J. Northamptonshire

Name: David (Davey) Johan Jacobs
Role: Right-hand bat, right-arm medium bowler, wicket-keeper
Born: 4 November 1982, Klerksdorp, South Africa
County debut: 2007
1st-Class 200s: 1
Place in batting averages: 230th av. 17.87
Overseas tours: South Africa U19 to New Zealand (U19 World Cup) 2001-02; South Africa Academy to Australia 2002; South Africa Emerging Players to Australia (Cricket Australia Emerging Players Tournament) 2006
Overseas teams played for: North West 2001-02 – 2003-04; Eagles 2004-05 – 2006-07; Warriors 2007-08 –

Extras: Represented Rest of South Africa v Sri Lankans 2002-03 and v New Zealanders 2005-06. Represented South Africa A v New Zealanders at Potchefstroom 2005-06. His awards include Man of the Match v India U19 in the semi-final of the U19 World Cup 2001-02 at Lincoln (45-ball 69*) and v Cape Cobras in the final of the Standard Bank Pro20 2005-06 at Bloemfontein. Was a temporary overseas player with Northamptonshire 2007 as a locum for Chris Rogers
Best batting: 218 Eagles v Dolphins, Bloemfontein 2004-05

2007 Season

	M	Inn	NO	Runs	HS	Avg	100	50	Ct	St	Balls	Runs	Wkts	Avg	BB	5I	10M
Test																	
FC	4	8	0	143	56	17.87	-	1	2	-	0	0	0		-	-	-
ODI																	
List A	2	2	0	157	88	78.50	-	2	-	-	0	0	0		-	-	
20/20 Int																	
20/20																	

Career Performances

	M	Inn	NO	Runs	HS	Avg	100	50	Ct	St	Balls	Runs	Wkts	Avg	BB	5I	10M
Test																	
FC	48	90	4	3372	218	39.20	11	13	48	1	34	20	0		-	-	-
ODI																	
List A	54	52	5	1275	101 *	27.12	1	7	39	5	0	0	0		-	-	
20/20 Int																	
20/20	18	18	4	400	53 *	28.57	-	1	9	-	6	14	0		-	-	

JAMES, N. A. — Warwickshire

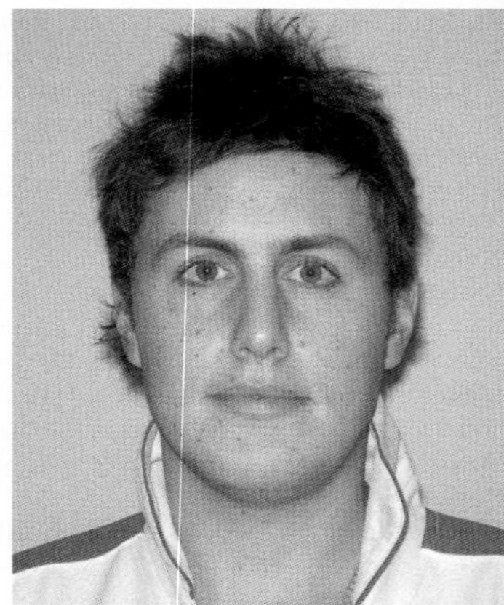

Name: Nicholas (Nick) Alexander James
Role: Left-hand bat, slow left-arm bowler; all-rounder
Born: 17 September 1986, Sandwell, West Midlands
Height: 5ft 10in **Weight:** 12st 7lbs
Nickname: Jaymo
County debut: 2006 (one-day)
Parents: Ann and Mike
Marital status: Single
Family links with cricket: 'Dad and brother Chris play at Aldridge CC. Dad also coaches'
Education: King Edward VI Aston School, Birmingham
Qualifications: 10 GCSEs, 3 A-levels
Off-season: 'Training and playing overseas – Club Cricket Conference to Australia; pre-season away with county'
Overseas tours: England U19 to Bangladesh 2005-06, to Sri Lanka (U19 World Cup) 2005-06; CCC to Australia 2007-08
Career highlights to date: 'Representing England U19. Reaching semi-final of 2006 U19 World Cup. Playing for Warwickshire first team in C&G, Pro40 and Twenty20'

Cricket moments to forget: 'Fracturing hand diving to stop ball (against Lancashire) 2006 – unavailable for six weeks. Watching ball I had just hit for six bounce and smash through rear window of my car (while bringing my 150 up) v Hampshire 2nd XI at Basingstoke 2007'
Cricketers particularly admired: Brian Lara, Ashley Giles, Nick Knight
Young players to look out for: Andrew Miller, Chris Woakes
Other sports played: 'Recreational football, golf'
Other sports followed: Football (Aston Villa)
Favourite band: Daughtry ('although enjoy most types of music')
Relaxations: 'Relaxing with friends'
Extras: Captain of Warwickshire U17 County Championship winning side 2004. Member of ECB U18 Development Squad 2004. Represented England U19 and captained ECB Development of Excellence XI v Sri Lanka U19 2005. Has won eight Warwickshire youth awards, including Tiger Smith Memorial Award for the most promising young player 2005. Acted as 12th man (one day only) for England A v Sri Lankans at Worcester 2006. Attended ECB Elite Skills Set Spin Programme at Loughborough 2006-07. Birmingham Premier League Young Player of the Year 2007. ECB Scholarship for Club Cricket Conference tour to Australia 2007-08
Opinions on cricket: 'Great game. Can't forget to enjoy yourself!'

2007 Season

	M	Inn	NO	Runs	HS	Avg	100	50	Ct	St	Balls	Runs	Wkts	Avg	BB	5I	10M
Test																	
FC																	
ODI																	
List A	5	3	2	55	25	55.00	-	-	1	-	54	45	2	22.50	1-22	-	
20/20 Int																	
20/20	2	2	1	13	12 *	13.00	-	-	2	-	0	0	0		-	-	

Career Performances

	M	Inn	NO	Runs	HS	Avg	100	50	Ct	St	Balls	Runs	Wkts	Avg	BB	5I	10M
Test																	
FC																	
ODI																	
List A	8	5	2	99	30	33.00	-	-	2	-	210	141	6	23.50	2-34	-	
20/20 Int																	
20/20	2	2	1	13	12 *	13.00	-	-	2	-	0	0	0		-	-	

JAQUES, P. A. — Worcestershire

Name: Philip (Phil) Anthony Jaques
Role: Left-hand bat
Born: 3 May 1979, Wollongong, Australia
Height: 6ft 1in **Weight:** 14st 11lbs
Nickname: Pro, PJ
County debut: 2003 (Northamptonshire), 2004 (Yorkshire), 2006 (Worcestershire)
County cap: 2003 (Northamptonshire), 2005 (Yorkshire), 2006 (Worcestershire colours)
Test debut: 2005-06
ODI debut: 2005-06
1000 runs in a season: 4
1st-Class 200s: 8
Place in batting averages: 130th av. 31.82 (2006 2nd av. 88.30)
Parents: Mary and Stuart
Wife and date of marriage: Danielle, 5 May 2006
Family links with cricket: 'Dad played league cricket in Sheffield, England'
Education: Figtree High School, Wollongong; Australian College of Physical Education
Qualifications: Fitness certificate, Level II coach
Overseas tours: New South Wales to New Zealand 2000-01; Australia A to Pakistan 2005-06, 2007-08; Australia to South Africa 2005-06 (one-day series), to Bangladesh 2005-06, to New Zealand (one-day series) 2006-07, plus one-day tournament in Malaysia
Overseas teams played for: Sutherland DCC, Sydney; New South Wales Blues 2000-01 – 2001-02, 2003-04 –
Career highlights to date: 'Playing cricket for Australia'
Cricket moments to forget: 'Dropping an outfield catch on my first-class one-day debut and not getting a hand on it'
Cricket superstitions: 'Always put gear on same way in same order every time I bat'
Cricketers particularly admired: Steve Waugh, Mark Taylor
Young players to look out for: Moises Henriques (NSW)
Other sports played: Tennis, rugby league, golf, basketball
Other sports followed: Rugby league (St George Illawarra), football (Liverpool)
Favourite band: Coldplay, Bon Jovi
Relaxations: 'Golf, beach, watching movies'
Extras: Attended Australian Cricket Academy 2000. Scored maiden first-class century (149*) v Worcestershire at Worcester 2003 and maiden first-class double century (222)

in his next Championship innings v Yorkshire at Northampton 2003. Scored 1409 first-class runs in his first season of county cricket 2003. Holds a British passport and was not considered an overseas player with Northamptonshire in 2003. An overseas player with Yorkshire 2004 (having played for New South Wales 2003-04), deputising for Ian Harvey and Darren Lehmann, and in 2005. Named Australia's State Player of the Year at the 2006 Allan Border Medal awards; also won the Steve Waugh Medal (NSW Player of the Year) 2005-06. His match awards include Man of the Match v Tasmania at Sydney in the Pura Cup 2006-07 (192). His wife, Danielle Small, is an Australia soccer international. Was an overseas player with Worcestershire 2006-07. Scored century (107) on first-class debut for Worcestershire v Surrey at The Oval 2006 and another (112) on one-day debut for the county v Northamptonshire at Worcester in the C&G 2006

Best batting: 244 Worcestershire v Essex, Chelmsford 2006

2007 Season

	M	Inn	NO	Runs	HS	Avg	100	50	Ct	St	Balls	Runs	Wkts	Avg	BB	5I	10M
Test																	
FC	10	17	0	541	124	31.82	2	1	6	-	0	0	0		-	-	-
ODI																	
List A	12	12	0	529	113	44.08	3	1	2	-	0	0	0		-	-	
20/20 Int																	
20/20	4	4	0	115	59	28.75	-	1	4	-	0	0	0		-	-	

Career Performances

	M	Inn	NO	Runs	HS	Avg	100	50	Ct	St	Balls	Runs	Wkts	Avg	BB	5I	10M
Test	2	3	0	96	66	32.00	-	1	1	-	0	0	0		-	-	-
FC	109	192	8	10255	244	55.73	31	47	85	-	68	87	0		-	-	-
ODI	6	6	0	125	94	20.83	-	1	3	-	0	0	0		-	-	
List A	118	116	7	4606	158 *	42.25	12	25	30	-	18	19	0		-	-	
20/20 Int																	
20/20	30	30	1	903	92	31.13	-	6	8	-	6	15	0		-	-	

JAYASURIYA, S. T. Warwickshire

Name: Sanath Teran Jayasuriya
Role: Left-hand bat, slow left-arm bowler
Born: 30 June 1969, Matara, Sri Lanka
Height: 5ft 6in
County debut: 2005 (Somerset), 2007 (Lancashire)
Test debut: 1990-91
ODI debut: 1989-90
Twenty20 Int debut: 2006
1st-Class 200s: 4
1st-Class 300s: 1
Place in batting averages: (2006 179th av. 25.15)
Overseas tours: Sri Lankan Young Cricketers to Australia (U19 World Cup) 1987-88; Sri Lanka B to Pakistan 1988-89; Sri Lanka U24 to South Africa 1992-93; Sri Lanka to Australia 1989-90, to England 1990, to New Zealand 1990-91, to England 1991, to Pakistan 1991-92, to Australia and New Zealand (World Cup) 1991-92, to India 1993-94, to Zimbabwe and South Africa 1994-95, to New Zealand 1994-95, to Pakistan 1995-96, to Australia 1995-96, to India and Pakistan (World Cup) 1995-96, to New Zealand 1996-97, to West Indies 1996-97, to India 1997-98, to South Africa 1997-98, to England 1998, to Bangladesh (Wills International Cup) 1998-99, to UK, Ireland and Netherlands (World Cup) 1999, to Zimbabwe 1999-2000 (c), to Pakistan 1999-2000 (c), to Kenya (ICC Knockout Trophy) 2000-01 (c), to South Africa 2000-01 (c), to England 2002 (c), to South Africa 2002-03 (c), to Africa (World Cup) 2002-03 (c), to West Indies 2003, to Zimbabwe 2004, to Australia 2004, to England (ICC Champions Trophy) 2004, to Pakistan 2004-05, to New Zealand 2004-05, to England 2006, to India (ICC Champions Trophy) 2006-07, to New Zealand 2006-07, to West Indies (World Cup) 2006-07, to South Africa (World 20/20) 2007-08, to Australia 2007-08, plus other one-day series and tournaments in Sharjah, India, Singapore, West Indies, Kenya, Pakistan, Australia, Bangladesh, New Zealand, Morocco, Netherlands and Abu Dhabi; Asian Cricket Council XI to Australia (Tsunami Relief Fund) 2004-05, to India (Afro-Asia Cup) 2007; FICA World XI to New Zealand 2004-05
Overseas teams played for: Colombo 1988-89 – 1992; Bloomfield C&AC 1994 –
Extras: One of *Indian Cricket*'s five Cricketers of the Year 1996. One of *Wisden*'s Five Cricketers of the Year 1997. Holds the record for the highest individual score for Sri Lanka in ODIs (189 v India in the Coca-Cola Champions Trophy in Sharjah 2000-01) and also held the corresponding record in Tests (340 v India in the first Test in Colombo 1997) until surpassed by Mahela Jayawardene (374) in 2006. Captain of Sri

Lanka 1999-2003. Became the fourth batsman to reach 10,000 runs in ODIs v India in Colombo in the Indian Oil Cup 2005. Has won many, many international series and match awards, including Man of the Series at the 1995-96 World Cup and Man of the [ODI] Series v England 2006. Made his 100th Test appearance in the second Test v Bangladesh at Colombo 2005-06. Retired briefly from Test cricket in 2006. Was a temporary overseas player with Somerset during the 2005 season; was a temporary overseas player with Lancashire during the 2007 season as a locum for Muttiah Muralitharan; has joined Warwickshire as a temporary overseas player for 2008
Best batting: 340 Sri Lanka v India, Colombo (RPS) 1997-98
Best bowling: 5-34 Sri Lanka v South Africa, Colombo (SSC) 2004
Stop press: Became the first player to make 400 ODI appearances when he took the field in the second ODI v England in Dambulla 2007-08. Retired from Test cricket after the first Test v England at Kandy 2007-08, bowing out with a 106-ball 78

2007 Season

	M	Inn	NO	Runs	HS	Avg	100	50	Ct	St	Balls	Runs	Wkts	Avg	BB	5I	10M
Test																	
FC	2	2	0	56	38	28.00	-	-	-	-	60	15	1	15.00	1-10	-	-
ODI																	
List A																	
20/20 Int																	
20/20	4	4	0	60	32	15.00	-	-	1	-	89	108	9	12.00	4-24	-	

Career Performances

	M	Inn	NO	Runs	HS	Avg	100	50	Ct	St	Balls	Runs	Wkts	Avg	BB	5I	10M
Test	107	182	14	6791	340	40.42	14	30	78	-	8002	3281	96	34.17	5-34	2	-
FC	252	397	33	14295	340	39.27	29	67	158	-	14450	6352	192	33.08	5-34	2	-
ODI	398	387	18	12116	189	32.83	25	64	114	-	13963	11093	304	36.49	6-29	4	
List A	473	459	24	13978	189	32.13	28	72	135	-	16027	12749	363	35.12	6-29	5	
20/20 Int	7	7	1	246	88	41.00	-	3	-	-	125	155	9	17.22	3-21	-	
20/20	14	14	2	343	88	28.58	-	3	2	-	262	319	23	13.86	4-24	-	

43. Who became the first England bowler to be called for throwing in a Test in England when he deliberately threw his first (and last) 'ball' at the end of the second Test between England and New Zealand at Trent Bridge in 1986?

JAYAWARDENE, D. P. M. D. Derbyshire

Name: Denagamage Proboth Mahela de Silva Jayawardene
Role: Right-hand bat, right-arm medium bowler
Born: 27 May 1977, Colombo, Sri Lanka
County debut: No first-team appearance
Test debut: 1997
ODI debut: 1997-98
Twenty20 Int debut: 2006
1st-Class 200s: 5
1st-Class 300s: 1
Wife and date of marriage: Christina, November 2005
Overseas tours: Sri Lanka to India 1997-98, to South Africa 1997-98, to England 1998, to UK, Ireland and Netherlands (World Cup) 1999, to Zimbabwe 1999-2000, to Pakistan 1999-2000, to Kenya (ICC Knockout Trophy) 2000-01, to South Africa 2000-01, to England 2002, to South Africa 2002-03, to Africa (World Cup) 2002-03, to West Indies 2003, to Zimbabwe 2004, to Australia 2004, to England (ICC Champions Trophy) 2004, to Pakistan 2004-05, to New Zealand 2004-05, to India 2005-06, to Bangladesh 2005-06 (c), to England 2006 (c), to India (ICC Champions Trophy) 2006-07 (c), to New Zealand 2006-07 (c), to West Indies (World Cup) 2006-07 (c), to South Africa (World 20/20) 2007-08 (c), to Australia 2007-08 (c), plus other one-day tournaments and series in Malaysia, Australia, India, Sharjah, Bangladesh, New Zealand, Morocco, Netherlands and Abu Dhabi
Overseas teams played for: Sinhalese Sports Club 1996-97 – 2006-07
Extras: Represented Sri Lanka U19. Played for an Asian Cricket Council XI in the Afro-Asia Cup 2005-06, 2007. Scored Sri Lanka record 374 in the first Test v South Africa at Colombo 2006, in the process sharing with Kumar Sangakkara (287) in the highest partnership for any wicket in first-class cricket history (624) and winning Man of the Match award. His numerous other match and series awards include Sri Lanka's Man of the [Test] Series v England 2002 and Man of the Match in the first Test v England at Lord's 2006 (61/119) and v New Zealand in Kingston in the semi-final of the 2006-07 World Cup (115*). One of *Wisden*'s Five Cricketers of the Year 2007. Captain of Sri Lanka since 2006. Has joined Derbyshire as an overseas player for 2008
Best batting: 374 Sri Lanka v South Africa, Colombo (SSC) 2006
Best bowling: 5-72 Sinhalese Sports Club v Colts, Colombo (CCC) 1996-97
Stop press: Man of the [Test] Series v England 2007-08 (474 runs; av. 158.00)

2007 Season (did not make any first-class or one-day appearances)

Career Performances

	M	Inn	NO	Runs	HS	Avg	100	50	Ct	St	Balls	Runs	Wkts	Avg	BB	5I	10M
Test	88	143	10	6630	374	49.84	18	29	123	-	458	228	4	57.00	2-32	-	-
FC	166	260	19	12219	374	50.70	35	56	209	-	2858	1531	50	30.62	5-72	1	-
ODI	256	239	26	7141	128	33.52	10	41	128	-	582	558	7	79.71	2-56	-	
List A	314	291	35	8652	128	33.79	10	52	154	-	1179	1042	22	47.36	3-25	-	
20/20 Int	8	8	2	170	65	28.33	-	1	3	-	6	8	0		-	-	
20/20	10	10	2	184	65	23.00	-	1	5	-	51	61	2	30.50	2-22	-	

JEFFERSON, W. I. Nottinghamshire

Name: William (Will) Ingleby Jefferson
Role: Right-hand opening bat
Born: 25 October 1979, Derby ('but native of Norfolk')
Height: 6ft 10½in **Weight:** 15st 2lbs
Nickname: Santa, Lemar, Jeffo
County debut: 2000 (Essex), 2007 (Nottinghamshire)
County cap: 2002 (Essex)
1000 runs in a season: 1
1st-Class 200s: 1
Place in batting averages: 102nd av. 35.11
Parents: Richard
Marital status: Single
Family links with cricket: Grandfather Jefferson played for the Army and Combined Services in the 1920s. Father, R. I. Jefferson, played for Cambridge University 1961 and Surrey 1961-66
Education: Oundle School, Northants; Durham University
Qualifications: 9 GCSEs, 3 A-levels, BA (Hons) Sport in the Community, Level 3 cricket coach
Overseas tours: Oundle School to South Africa 1995; England A to Bangladesh 2006-07
Overseas teams played for: Young People's Club, Paarl, South Africa 1998-99; South Perth, Western Australia 2002-03
Career highlights to date: 'Being awarded [Essex] county cap on final day of the 2002 season. Scoring 165* to help beat Notts and secure 2002 second division Championship. 222 v Hampshire at Rose Bowl [2004]'

Cricket moments to forget: 'Any dropped catch; any time bowled playing across the line'
Cricket superstitions: 'Put batting gear on in the same order'
Cricketers particularly admired: Andy Flower, Nasser Hussain
Other sports played: Golf (12 handicap), tennis ('occasionally')
Other sports followed: Rugby (British & Irish Lions, England), golf (Ryder Cup)
Favourite band: U2
Relaxations: 'Escaping to Norfolk, Pilates, spending time with family'
Extras: Holmwoods School Cricketer of the Year 1998. Represented British Universities 2000, 2001 and 2002. Played for Durham UCCE 2001 and 2002. NBC Denis Compton Award for the most promising young Essex player 2002. Scored century before lunch on the opening day for Essex v Cambridge UCCE at Fenner's 2003. C&G Man of the Match awards for his 97 v Scotland at Edinburgh 2004 and for his 126 v Nottinghamshire at Trent Bridge in the next round. Essex Player of the Year 2004. Essex Boundary Club Trophy for scoring most runs for Essex 1st XI 2004. Represented England Lions 2007
Opinions on cricket: 'Agree with the two up/two down system – gives teams something to play for right up until final day of the season. One-day tournament structure not right – one too many. International cricket 50 overs and 20 overs so county cricket should mirror. One overseas player good. Need to be producing more English county captains and coaches so they are the best around.'
Best batting: 222 Essex v Hampshire, Rose Bowl 2004
Best bowling: 1-16 Essex v Yorkshire, Headingley 2005

2007 Season

	M	Inn	NO	Runs	HS	Avg	100	50	Ct	St	Balls	Runs	Wkts	Avg	BB	5I	10M
Test																	
FC	5	9	0	316	73	35.11	-	1	3	-	0	0	0		-	-	-
ODI																	
List A	6	6	1	182	60 *	36.40	-	2	2	-	0	0	0		-	-	
20/20 Int																	
20/20	4	4	1	57	31	19.00	-	-	1	-	0	0	0		-	-	

Career Performances

	M	Inn	NO	Runs	HS	Avg	100	50	Ct	St	Balls	Runs	Wkts	Avg	BB	5I	10M
Test																	
FC	74	132	11	4669	222	38.58	11	18	62	-	120	60	1	60.00	1-16	-	-
ODI																	
List A	74	73	5	2487	132	36.57	4	14	34	-	24	9	2	4.50	2-9	-	
20/20 Int																	
20/20	16	16	2	208	51	14.85	-	1	4	-	0	0	0		-	-	

JOHNSON, R. L. Middlesex

Name: Richard Leonard Johnson
Role: Right-hand bat, right-arm fast-medium bowler
Born: 29 December 1974, Chertsey, Surrey
Height: 6ft 2in **Weight:** 14st 3lbs
Nickname: Jono, Lenny, The Greek
County debut: 1992 (Middlesex), 2001 (Somerset)
County cap: 1995 (Middlesex), 2001 (Somerset)
Benefit: 2006 (Somerset)
Test debut: 2003
ODI debut: 2003
50 wickets in a season: 4
Place in batting averages: (2006 214th av. 19.18)
Place in bowling averages: (2006 62nd av. 32.59)
Parents: Roger and Mary Anne
Wife and date of marriage: Nikki, 4 October 2003
Family links with cricket: Father and grandfather played club cricket
Education: Sunbury Manor School; Spelthorne College
Qualifications: 9 GCSEs, A-level in Physical Education, NCA senior coaching award
Overseas tours: England U18 to South Africa 1992-93; England U19 to Sri Lanka 1993-94; England A to India 1994-95; MCC to Bangladesh 1999-2000, to Canada 2000-01; England to India 2001-02, to Bangladesh and Sri Lanka 2003-04
Career highlights: 'Playing in a domestic final for Somerset. Making England debut'
Cricket moments to forget: 'Losing C&G final [2002]'
Cricketers particularly admired: Ian Botham, Richard Hadlee, Angus Fraser
Young players to look out for: James Hildreth
Other sports followed: Football (Tottenham), rugby (London Irish)
Extras: Represented Middlesex at all levels from U11. Took 10 for 45 v Derbyshire at Derby 1994, becoming the first person to take ten wickets in an English first-class innings since 1964. Won Man of the Match awards in his first two Tests: for his 6-33 on debut in the second Test v Zimbabwe at Riverside 2003 and 5-49/4-44 in the second Test v Bangladesh at Chittagong 2003-04. Won Walter Lawrence Trophy 2004 (for the season's fastest hundred) for his 63-ball century v Durham at Riverside. Left Somerset at the end of the 2006 season and rejoined Middlesex for 2007. Retired at the end of the 2007 season
Opinions on cricket: 'Twenty20 cricket has been fantastic for the game, bringing in a new generation of cricket followers. We still need to look at the amount of cricket being played, though!'

Best batting: 118 Somerset v Gloucestershire, Bristol 2003
Best bowling: 10-45 Middlesex v Derbyshire, Derby 1994

2007 Season

	M	Inn	NO	Runs	HS	Avg	100	50	Ct	St	Balls	Runs	Wkts	Avg	BB	5I	10M
Test																	
FC	4	4	0	48	39	12.00	-	-	1	-	577	384	6	64.00	2-69	-	-
ODI																	
List A	4	3	0	1	1	.33	-	-	-	-	192	187	6	31.16	2-36	-	
20/20 Int																	
20/20																	

Career Performances

	M	Inn	NO	Runs	HS	Avg	100	50	Ct	St	Balls	Runs	Wkts	Avg	BB	5I	10M
Test	3	4	0	59	26	14.75	-	-	-	-	547	275	16	17.18	6-33	2	-
FC	166	227	28	3545	118	17.81	2	8	63	-	27846	15094	528	28.58	10-45	20	3
ODI	10	4	1	16	10	5.33	-	-	-	-	402	239	11	21.72	3-22	-	
List A	194	127	30	1108	53	11.42	-	1	23	-	8607	6995	213	32.84	5-50	1	
20/20 Int																	
20/20	9	5	1	24	10	6.00	-	-	1	-	198	279	14	19.92	3-21	-	

JOHNSON, R. M. — Warwickshire

Name: Richard Matthew Johnson
Role: Right-hand bat, wicket-keeper
Born: 1 September 1988, Solihull
Height: 5ft 10in **Weight:** 10st 7lbs
Nickname: Johnno
County debut: No first-team appearance (*see below*)
Parents: Barry and Lorraine
Marital status: Single
Family links with cricket: 'Dad played club cricket'
Education: Solihull School
Qualifications: 3 A-levels, ECB Level 2 coaching award
Off-season: 'Darren Lehmann Cricket Academy, Adelaide (1 January to 27 February)'
Overseas tours: England U16 to Cape Town 2005; Warwickshire Academy to Cape Town 2005; Solihull School to Barbados 2007

Career highlights to date: 'Warwickshire first-team debut – top-scored with 71' (*Note: this three-day match was against Bradford/Leeds UCCE in 2007 and was not considered first-class*)
Cricket moments to forget: 'Breaking a bone in my thumb before playing for England U15'
Cricket superstitions: 'Pack playing kit in same position'
Cricketers particularly admired: Keith Piper
Young players to look out for: Chris Woakes, Tom Lewis
Other sports played: Football (Wolverhampton Wanderers U10, U11, U12), rugby (Solihull School 1st XV)
Other sports followed: Football (Aston Villa)
Favourite band: Oasis
Relaxations: 'Music, TV, computer, friends, watching Aston Villa'
Extras: Best Wicket-keeper Award at Bunbury Festival 2005
Opinions on cricket: 'Twenty20 cricket influences bigger and new audiences. More technology should be brought into the game.'

JONES, G. O. — Kent

Name: Geraint Owen Jones
Role: Right-hand bat, wicket-keeper
Born: 14 July 1976, Kundiawa, Papua New Guinea
Height: 5ft 10in **Weight:** 11st
Nickname: Jonesy
County debut: 2001
County cap: 2003
Test debut: 2003-04
ODI debut: 2004
Twenty20 Int debut: 2005
50 dismissals in a season: 1
Place in batting averages: 104th av. 34.61 (2006 194th av. 22.40)
Parents: Emrys, Carol (deceased), Maureen (stepmother)
Marital status: Single
Family links with cricket: 'Father was star off-spinner in local school side'
Education: Harristown State High School, Toowoomba, Queensland; MacGregor SHS, Brisbane
Qualifications: Level 1 coach
Overseas tours: Beenleigh-Logan U19 to New Zealand 1995; Kent to Port Elizabeth 2001-02; England to Bangladesh and Sri Lanka 2003-04, to West Indies 2003-04, to

Zimbabwe (one-day series) 2004-05, to South Africa 2004-05, to Pakistan 2005-06, to India 2005-06, to Australia 2006-07
Overseas teams played for: Beenleigh-Logan, Brisbane 1995-98, 2006-07; Valleys, Brisbane 2001-02
Cricket superstitions: 'Left pad first'
Cricketers particularly admired: Jack Russell, Alec Stewart
Other sports played: Golf
Other sports followed: Rugby (Crickhowell RFC)
Favourite band: Matchbox Twenty
Extras: Set new competition record for a season's tally of wicket-keeping dismissals in the one-day league (33; 27/6) 2003; also equalled record for number of wicket-keeping catches in one match, six v Leicestershire at Canterbury 2003. Made 59 first-class dismissals plus 985 first-class runs in his first full season of county cricket 2003. Man of the Match in the second Test v New Zealand at Headingley 2004, in which he scored his maiden Test century (100). His other international awards include Man of the Match v Australia in the tied final of the NatWest Series 2005 (71 plus five catches). Appointed MBE in 2006 New Year Honours as part of 2005 Ashes-winning England team. Made 100th Test dismissal (Mahela Jayawardene, caught) in the first Test v Sri Lanka at Lord's 2006, becoming the fastest England wicket-keeper to the milestone (27 matches)
Best batting: 108* Kent v Essex, Chelmsford 2003

2007 Season

	M	Inn	NO	Runs	HS	Avg	100	50	Ct	St	Balls	Runs	Wkts	Avg	BB	5I	10M
Test																	
FC	15	21	3	623	106 *	34.61	2	3	42	4	12	14	0		-	-	-
ODI																	
List A	17	14	2	235	45	19.58	-	-	18	2	0	0	0		-	-	
20/20 Int																	
20/20	11	7	2	62	24 *	12.40	-	-	2	4	0	0	0		-	-	

Career Performances

	M	Inn	NO	Runs	HS	Avg	100	50	Ct	St	Balls	Runs	Wkts	Avg	BB	5I	10M
Test	34	53	4	1172	100	23.91	1	6	128	5	0	0	0		-	-	-
FC	92	135	16	3683	108 *	30.94	6	21	277	19	18	18	0		-	-	-
ODI	49	41	8	815	80	24.69	-	4	68	4	0	0	0		-	-	
List A	120	103	18	1996	80	23.48	-	7	140	20	0	0	0		-	-	
20/20 Int	2	2	1	33	19	33.00	-	-	2	-	0	0	0		-	-	
20/20	20	15	4	166	24 *	15.09	-	-	11	4	0	0	0		-	-	

JONES, P. S. Somerset

Name: Philip Steffan Jones
Role: Right-hand bat, right-arm fast-medium bowler
Born: 9 February 1974, Llanelli
Height: 6ft 1in **Weight:** 15st 2lbs
Nickname: Jona
County debut: 1997 (Somerset), 2004 (Northamptonshire), 2006 (Derbyshire)
50 wickets in a season: 2
Place in batting averages: 128th av. 31.87 (2006 243rd av. 15.13)
Place in bowling averages: 115th av. 40.57 (2006 57th av. 31.71)
Parents: Lyndon and Ann
Wife and date of marriage: Alex, 12 October 2002
Children: Seren, 2006
Family links with cricket: 'Father played locally in South Wales'
Education: Ysgol Gyfun y Strade, Llanelli; Loughborough University; Homerton College, Cambridge University
Qualifications: BSc Sports Science, PGCE in Physical Education
Career outside cricket: 'Sports conditioner'
Overseas tours: Wales Minor Counties to Barbados 1996; Somerset CCC to South Africa 1999, 2000, 2001
Overseas teams played for: Clarence CC, Tasmania 2005
Career highlights to date: 'C&G final 2001 with Somerset. 6-25 v Glamorgan for Derbyshire [at Cardiff 2006]' (*His full second innings figures were 20-14-25-6*)
Cricket moments to forget: '2003-04'
Cricket superstitions: 'Getting early to the ground'
Cricketers particularly admired: 'Pop' Welch, Brett Lee
Other sports played: Rugby union ('professionally for Bristol and Moseley 1997-99')
Other sports followed: Rugby union
Favourite band: Pussycat Dolls, Black Eyed Peas
Relaxations: 'Going to the cinema'
Extras: Took nine wickets (6-67/3-81) in the Varsity Match at Lord's 1997. Derbyshire's Championship Player of the Year 2006. Left Derbyshire at the end of the 2006 season and rejoined Somerset for 2007
Opinions on cricket: 'Overkill on Twenty20! Moderation is the key to bringing the crowds in and keeping them interested. Wickets have also become too flat!'
Best batting: 114 Somerset v Leicestershire, Leicester 2007
Best bowling: 6-25 Derbyshire v Glamorgan, Cardiff 2006

2007 Season

	M	Inn	NO	Runs	HS	Avg	100	50	Ct	St	Balls	Runs	Wkts	Avg	BB	5I	10M
Test																	
FC	13	12	4	255	114	31.87	1	1	3	-	1527	1055	26	40.57	6-61	1	-
ODI																	
List A	15	11	6	102	26	20.40	-	-	1	-	660	646	15	43.06	2-30	-	
20/20 Int																	
20/20	5	2	1	19	13 *	19.00	-	-	-	-	104	144	4	36.00	3-27	-	

Career Performances

	M	Inn	NO	Runs	HS	Avg	100	50	Ct	St	Balls	Runs	Wkts	Avg	BB	5I	10M
Test																	
FC	113	132	34	1804	114	18.40	2	5	24	-	18529	11105	292	38.03	6-25	7	1
ODI																	
List A	166	90	44	574	27	12.47	-	-	29	-	7490	6551	221	29.64	6-56	3	
20/20 Int																	
20/20	24	10	4	60	24 *	10.00	-	-	3	-	490	701	27	25.96	3-26	-	

JONES, R. A. Worcestershire

Name: Richard Alan Jones
Role: Right-hand bat, right-arm medium-fast bowler
Born: 6 November 1986, Wordsley, West Midlands
Height: 6ft 2in **Weight:** 13st
Nickname: Jonesy, Jonah
County debut: 2007
County colours: 2007
Parents: Bob and Julie
Marital status: Single
Education: The Grange School, Stourbridge; King Edward VI College, Stourbridge
Qualifications: 13 GCSEs, 3 A-levels
Off-season: 'Going to play club cricket in Perth, Australia, for six months'
Overseas tours: England U19 to Bangladesh 2005-06
Career highlights to date: 'Making first-class debut for Worcestershire against Warwickshire 2007'
Cricket moments to forget: 'Opening over against Sussex in last game of 2007 season – it went for plenty!'

Cricket superstitions: 'None'
Cricketers particularly admired: Ian Botham, Andrew Flintoff, Brett Lee
Young players to look out for: Chris Bending, Adam Bending, Keith Bradley
Other sports played: Football (district schools), golf
Other sports followed: Football (West Bromwich Albion)
Injuries: Out for four/five weeks with a recurrence of a back injury
Favourite band: Arctic Monkeys
Relaxations: 'Football, listening to music, staying fit, chatting with friends'
Extras: Scored first league hundred aged 17 for local side Old Hill (Birmingham & District Premier League)
Opinions on cricket: 'Going back to one overseas per team will give more younger players a chance to shine in county cricket, which can only be a good thing. The emergence and success of Twenty20 cricket at international level will eventually see it becoming the leading form of cricket in the future.'
Best batting: 24 Worcestershire v LUCCE, Worcester 2007
Best bowling: 3-37 Worcestershire v LUCCE, Worcester 2007

2007 Season

	M	Inn	NO	Runs	HS	Avg	100	50	Ct	St	Balls	Runs	Wkts	Avg	BB	5I	10M
Test																	
FC	3	5	1	38	24	9.50	-	-	1	-	378	295	7	42.14	3-37	-	-
ODI																	
List A																	
20/20 Int																	
20/20																	

Career Performances

	M	Inn	NO	Runs	HS	Avg	100	50	Ct	St	Balls	Runs	Wkts	Avg	BB	5I	10M
Test																	
FC	3	5	1	38	24	9.50	-	-	1	-	378	295	7	42.14	3-37	-	-
ODI																	
List A																	
20/20 Int																	
20/20																	

JONES, S. P. Worcestershire

Name: Simon Philip Jones
Role: Left-hand bat, right-arm fast bowler
Born: 25 December 1978, Morriston, Swansea
Height: 6ft 3in **Weight:** 15st
Nickname: Horse
County debut: 1998 (Glamorgan)
County cap: 2002 (Glamorgan)
Test debut: 2002
ODI debut: 2004-05
Place in batting averages: 249th av. 14.33
Parents: Irene and Jeff
Marital status: Single
Family links with cricket: 'Father played for England [1963-64 – 1967-68]'
Education: Coedcae Comprehensive School; Millfield School
Qualifications: 12 GCSEs, 1 A-level, basic and senior coaching awards
Overseas tours: Dyfed Schools to Zimbabwe 1994; Glamorgan to South Africa 1998; ECB National Academy to Australia 2001-02; England to Australia 2002-03, to West Indies 2003-04, to Zimbabwe (one-day series) 2004-05, to South Africa 2004-05, to India 2005-06; England A to Malaysia and India 2003-04
Career highlights to date: 'Winning Ashes series 2005'
Cricket moments to forget: 'Every injury'
Cricket superstitions: 'Right boot on first'
Cricketers particularly admired: Allan Donald
Young players to look out for: Ben Wright
Other sports played: Football (trials with Leeds United)
Favourite band: Eminem
Extras: NBC Denis Compton Award for the most promising young Glamorgan player 2001. Made Test debut in the first Test v India at Lord's 2002, striking a 43-ball 44 (more runs than his father scored in his 15-Test career); the Joneses are the eleventh father and son to have played in Tests for England. ECB National Academy 2003-04. Recorded maiden Test five-wicket return (5-57) in the second Test v West Indies at Port-of-Spain 2003-04; the Joneses thus became the first father and son to have taken five-wicket hauls for England. Had best strike rate among Test bowlers taking 20 or more wickets in the calendar year 2005 (38.50 balls/wicket). Appointed MBE in 2006 New Year Honours as part of 2005 Ashes-winning England team. One of *Wisden*'s Five Cricketers of the Year 2006. Left Glamorgan at the end of the 2007 season and has joined Worcestershire for 2008

Best batting: 46 Glamorgan v Yorkshire, Scarborough 2001
Best bowling: 6-45 Glamorgan v Derbyshire, Cardiff 2002

2007 Season

	M	Inn	NO	Runs	HS	Avg	100	50	Ct	St	Balls	Runs	Wkts	Avg	BB	5I	10M
Test																	
FC	4	7	1	86	39	14.33	-	-	-	-	534	290	1	290.00	1-39	-	-
ODI																	
List A	7	4	2	44	26	22.00	-	-	-	-	262	255	4	63.75	3-56	-	
20/20 Int																	
20/20																	

Career Performances

	M	Inn	NO	Runs	HS	Avg	100	50	Ct	St	Balls	Runs	Wkts	Avg	BB	5I	10M
Test	18	18	5	205	44	15.76	-	-	4	-	2821	1666	59	28.23	6-53	3	-
FC	79	97	31	802	46	12.15	-	-	17	-	11733	7190	218	32.98	6-45	11	1
ODI	8	1	0	1	1	1.00	-	-	-	-	348	275	7	39.28	2-43	-	
List A	30	13	8	76	26	15.20	-	-	2	-	1262	1099	22	49.95	3-19	-	
20/20 Int																	
20/20																	

JORDAN, C. J. — Surrey

Name: Christopher (Chris) James Jordan
Role: Right-hand bat, right-arm fast bowler; all-rounder
Born: 4 October 1988, Barbados
Height: 6ft 2in
Nickname: CJ
County debut: 2007
Place in bowling averages: 28th av. 24.50
Parents: Robert and Rosie
Marital status: Single
Education: Dulwich College
Qualifications: 2 A-levels
Overseas tours: Barbados U15 to St Vincent 2004
Cricket superstitions: 'Have to touch my box, my thigh pad and my pads before I settle down to bat'
Cricketers particularly admired: Dwayne Bravo, Brian Lara, Brett Lee
Young players to look out for: Dwayne Smith

Other sports played: Football (Dulwich College 1st XI)
Other sports followed: Football (Manchester United)
Favourite band: Sizzla Kolongi
Extras: Scored 208 in a semi-final for school. Played for Surrey 2nd XI 2006
Opinions on cricket: 'It has become more exciting since Twenty20 has been introduced.'
Best batting: 34 Surrey v Lancashire, The Oval 2007
Best bowling: 3-42 Surrey v Durham, Riverside 2007

2007 Season

	M	Inn	NO	Runs	HS	Avg	100	50	Ct	St	Balls	Runs	Wkts	Avg	BB	5I	10M
Test																	
FC	5	6	2	97	34	24.25	-	-	1	-	835	490	20	24.50	3-42	-	-
ODI																	
List A	7	4	0	13	8	3.25	-	-	2	-	312	270	13	20.76	3-28	-	
20/20 Int																	
20/20																	

Career Performances

	M	Inn	NO	Runs	HS	Avg	100	50	Ct	St	Balls	Runs	Wkts	Avg	BB	5I	10M
Test																	
FC	5	6	2	97	34	24.25	-	-	1	-	835	490	20	24.50	3-42	-	-
ODI																	
List A	7	4	0	13	8	3.25	-	-	2	-	312	270	13	20.76	3-28	-	
20/20 Int																	
20/20																	

44. Who made his Test debut for England in the third Test v New Zealand at Old Trafford in 1949, aged 18 years 149 days?

JOSEPH, R. H. Kent

Name: Robert Hartman Joseph Jnr
Role: Right-hand bat, right-arm fast-medium bowler
Born: 20 January 1982, Antigua
Height: 6ft 1in **Weight:** 13st 7lbs
Nickname: RJ, Blueie
County debut: 2004
Place in bowling averages: (2006 92nd av. 37.37)
Education: Sutton Valence School; St Mary's University College
Overseas tours: Antigua Young Lions to England 1997; Antigua and Leeward Islands U15 to Trinidad and St Lucia
Cricket moments to forget: 'Local school final – getting out on 47 needing one to win with four wickets in hand and losing'
Cricketers particularly admired: Sir Vivian Richards, Andy Roberts
Other sports played: Golf
Other sports followed: Football (Arsenal)
Favourite band: Maroon 5
Relaxations: Listening to music
Extras: Made first-class debut for First-Class Counties XI v New Zealand A at Milton Keynes 2000
Best batting: 36* Kent v Sussex, Hove 2007
Best bowling: 5-19 Kent v Bangladesh A, Canterbury 2005

2007 Season

	M	Inn	NO	Runs	HS	Avg	100	50	Ct	St	Balls	Runs	Wkts	Avg	BB	5I	10M
Test																	
FC	3	5	4	60	36 *	60.00	-	-	2	-	342	233	3	77.66	3-78	-	-
ODI																	
List A	2	0	0	0	0		-	-	1	-	120	100	3	33.33	3-50	-	
20/20 Int																	
20/20																	

Career Performances

	M	Inn	NO	Runs	HS	Avg	100	50	Ct	St	Balls	Runs	Wkts	Avg	BB	5I	10M
Test																	
FC	22	30	13	212	36 *	12.47	-	-	7	-	3203	2013	56	35.94	5-19	2	-
ODI																	
List A	16	7	5	23	15	11.50	-	-	3	-	648	516	18	28.66	3-50	-	
20/20 Int																	
20/20																	

JOYCE, E. C. Middlesex

Name: Edmund (Ed) Christopher Joyce
Role: Left-hand bat, occasional right-arm medium bowler, county vice-captain
Born: 22 September 1978, Dublin
Height: 5ft 10in **Weight:** 12st 7lbs
Nickname: Joycey, Spud, Piece
County debut: 1999
County cap: 2002
ODI debut: 2006
Twenty20 Int debut: 2006
1st-Class 200s: 1
1000 runs in a season: 5
Place in batting averages: 78th av. 39.11 (2006 35th av. 52.82)
Parents: Maureen and Jimmy
Marital status: Single
Family links with cricket: Two brothers and two sisters have represented Ireland
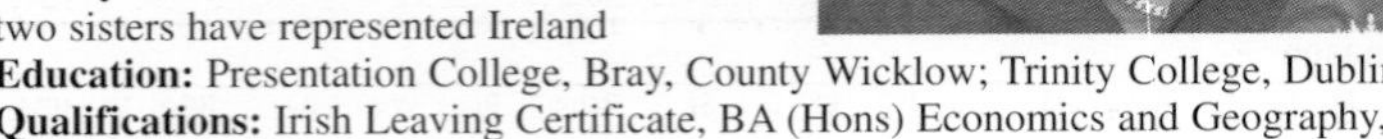
Education: Presentation College, Bray, County Wicklow; Trinity College, Dublin
Qualifications: Irish Leaving Certificate, BA (Hons) Economics and Geography, Level II coach
Overseas tours: Ireland U19 to Bermuda (International Youth Tournament) 1997, to South Africa (U19 World Cup) 1997-98; Ireland to Zimbabwe (ICC Emerging Nations Tournament) 1999-2000, to Canada (ICC Trophy) 2001; MCC to Namibia and Uganda 2004-05; England A to West Indies 2005-06; England to India (ICC Champions Trophy) 2006-07, to Australia 2006-07, to West Indies (World Cup) 2006-07; England Lions to India 2007-08
Overseas teams played for: Coburg CC, Melbourne 1996-97; University CC, Perth 2001-02
Cricket superstitions: 'None'
Cricketers particularly admired: Larry Gomes, Brian Lara

Young players to look out for: Eoin Morgan, Nick Compton
Other sports played: Golf, rugby, soccer, snooker
Other sports followed: Rugby (Leinster), football (Manchester United)
Favourite band: The Mars Volta
Relaxations: Cinema, eating out, listening to music
Extras: NBC Denis Compton Award for the most promising young Middlesex player 2000. Became the first Irish-born-and-bred player to record a century in the County Championship with his 104 v Warwickshire at Lord's 2001. C&G Man of the Match award for his 72 v Northamptonshire at Northampton 2003. Vice-captain of Middlesex June 2004 to end of 2004 season (captaining the county in the absence of Andrew Strauss on international duty) and since 2007. First batsman to 1000 first-class runs in 2005 (18 June). Has represented Ireland in first-class and one-day cricket. Made England ODI debut in Belfast 2006 v Ireland, for whom his brother Dominick was also making his ODI debut. Has also represented England in Twenty20 International cricket. ECB National Academy 2005-06. Scored maiden ODI century (107) v Australia at Sydney in the Commonwealth Bank Series 2006-07, winning Man of the Match award. Man of the Match v Kenya in St Lucia in the World Cup 2006-07 (75)
Best batting: 211 Middlesex v Warwickshire, Edgbaston 2006
Best bowling: 2-34 Middlesex v CUCCE, Fenner's 2004

2007 Season

	M	Inn	NO	Runs	HS	Avg	100	50	Ct	St	Balls	Runs	Wkts	Avg	BB	5I	10M
Test																	
FC	14	20	2	704	106	39.11	1	4	5	-	120	103	0		-	-	-
ODI																	
List A	17	17	0	517	77	30.41	-	4	8	-	78	89	4	22.25	1-14	-	
20/20 Int																	
20/20	6	6	1	69	22	13.80	-	-	2	-	0	0	0		-	-	

Career Performances

	M	Inn	NO	Runs	HS	Avg	100	50	Ct	St	Balls	Runs	Wkts	Avg	BB	5I	10M
Test																	
FC	108	178	16	7519	211	46.41	18	41	84	-	1275	1016	10	101.60	2-34	-	-
ODI	17	17	0	471	107	27.70	1	3	6	-	0	0	0		-	-	
List A	151	143	17	4364	115 *	34.63	4	30	56	-	240	270	6	45.00	2-10	-	
20/20 Int	2	1	0	1	1	1.00	-	-	-	-	0	0	0		-	-	
20/20	18	17	2	180	31	12.00	-	-	4	-	6	12	0		-	-	

KARTIK, M. — Middlesex

Name: Murali Kartik
Role: Left-hand bat, orthodox left-arm spin bowler
Born: 11 September 1976, Chennai (Madras), India
Height: 6ft **Weight:** 12st
Nickname: Pirate, Gary, Karts, Trickster, Special K
County debut: 2005 (Lancashire), 2007 (Middlesex)
County cap: 2007 (Middlesex)
Test debut: 1999-2000
ODI debut: 2001-02
50 wickets in a season: 1
Place in batting averages: 222nd av. 19.00
Place in bowling averages: 34th av. 24.96
Parents: Mr R. Murali and the late Mrs Shanta Murali
Wife and date of marriage: Shweta Kartik, 11 September 2002
Education: Sardar Patel Vidyalaya, New Delhi; Hindu College, Delhi University
Qualifications: BCom (Hons)
Career outside cricket: Broadcasting
Off-season: 'Playing for my first-class side, Railways in India'
Overseas tours: India A to Pakistan 1997-98, to West Indies 1999-2000, to South Africa 2001-02, to Sri Lanka 2002, to England 2003; India to Bangladesh 2000-01, to Australia 2003-04, to Pakistan 2003-04, to Bangladesh 2004-05, to Zimbabwe 2005-06 (Videocon Tri-Series), to Pakistan 2005-06 (one-day series)
Overseas teams played for: Railways, India 1996-97 –
Career highlights to date: 'My Test debut in 1999 v South Africa. Our Test victories in Australia and Pakistan in 2003-04. 9-70 v Bombay in the Irani Trophy'
Cricket moments to forget: 'Losing to Essex this year [2007] in a Twenty20 game at Lord's'
Cricket superstitions: 'None'
Cricketers particularly admired: Sir Garfield Sobers, Steve Waugh
Young players to look out for: Steven Finn, Eoin Morgan, Tom Westley
Other sports played: Golf, table tennis
Other sports followed: Formula One, tennis, golf
Injuries: Out for a month with a hamstring injury to the right leg
Favourite band: UB40
Relaxations: 'Listening to music, photography, reading, sleeping'
Extras: Represented India U19. Spinner of the Year award in India 2001. Man of the Match in the fourth Test v Australia at Mumbai (Bombay) 2004-05 (4-44/3-32). Was a

temporary overseas player with Lancashire during the 2005 and 2006 seasons, taking 10-168 (5-93/5-75) on Championship debut v Essex at Chelmsford 2005; an overseas player with Middlesex since 2007
Opinions on cricket: 'Too much cricket played in too little time.'
Best batting: 96 Railways v Rest of India, Delhi (KS) 2005-06
Best bowling: 9-70 Rest of India v Mumbai, Mumbai (Bombay) 2000-01
Stop press: Man of the Match in the seventh ODI v Australia at Mumbai 2007-08 (6-27). Made Twenty20 Int debut v Australia at Mumbai 2007-08

2007 Season

	M	Inn	NO	Runs	HS	Avg	100	50	Ct	St	Balls	Runs	Wkts	Avg	BB	5I	10M
Test																	
FC	12	15	4	209	35 *	19.00	-	-	12	-	2787	1273	51	24.96	6-21	3	-
ODI																	
List A	15	5	2	29	12	9.66	-	-	3	-	714	494	21	23.52	3-15	-	
20/20 Int																	
20/20	6	2	1	1	1 *	1.00	-	-	4	-	102	97	9	10.77	5-13	1	

Career Performances

	M	Inn	NO	Runs	HS	Avg	100	50	Ct	St	Balls	Runs	Wkts	Avg	BB	5I	10M
Test	8	10	1	88	43	9.77	-	-	2	-	1932	820	24	34.16	4-44	-	-
FC	115	136	19	2182	96	18.64	-	11	74	-	25076	10110	399	25.33	9-70	23	3
ODI	30	11	4	89	32 *	12.71	-	-	10	-	1530	1312	27	48.59	3-36	-	
List A	139	62	22	444	37 *	11.10	-	-	46	-	7140	5213	172	30.30	5-29	1	
20/20 Int																	
20/20	6	2	1	1	1 *	1.00	-	-	4	-	102	97	9	10.77	5-13	1	

45. Who resigned as England captain after
the first Test v South Africa at Edgbaston in 2003?

KATICH, S. M. Derbyshire

Name: Simon Mathew Katich
Role: Left-hand bat, left-arm wrist-spin bowler
Born: 21 August 1975, Midland, Western Australia
Height: 6ft **Weight:** 12st 8lbs
Nickname: Kat
County debut: 2000 (Durham), 2002 (Yorkshire), 2003 (Hampshire), 2007 (Derbyshire)
County cap: 2000 (Durham), 2003 (Hampshire), 2007 (Derbyshire)
Test debut: 2001
ODI debut: 2000-01
Twenty20 Int debut: 2004-05
1000 runs in a season: 3
1st-Class 200s: 3
Place in batting averages: 3rd av. 75.52
Parents: Vince and Kerry
Wife and date of marriage: Georgie, May 2006
Education: Trinity College, Perth; University of Western Australia
Qualifications: Bachelor of Commerce degree
Career outside cricket: Entrepreneur
Overseas tours: Australian Cricket Academy to South Africa 1996; Australia to Sri Lanka and Zimbabwe 1999-2000, to England 2001, to Sri Lanka 2003-04, to India 2004-05, to New Zealand 2004-05, to England 2005, to New Zealand (one-day series) 2005-06, to South Africa 2005-06 (one-day series), to Bangladesh 2005-06 (one-day series), to Malaysia (DLF Cup) 2006-07; Australia A to South Africa 2002-03 (vc)
Overseas teams played for: Western Australia 1996-97 – 2001-02; New South Wales 2002-03 – ; Randwick Petersham, Sydney
Career highlights to date: 'Making my maiden Test century v India at the SCG [2003-04]'
Cricket moments to forget: 'Any time I drop a catch'
Cricket superstitions: 'Like to wear old gear'
Cricketers particularly admired: Viv Richards
Other sports played: Australian Rules, hockey
Other sports followed: Australian Rules (Richmond), football (Newcastle United)
Favourite band: U2
Relaxations: 'Golf, watching movies and going to the beach in Sydney'
Extras: Attended Commonwealth Bank [Australian] Cricket Academy 1996. *Wisden Australia*'s Sheffield Shield Cricketer of the Year 1999. Became the first WA batsman to score a century against each of the other states in a single season 2000-01. His

awards include Man of the Match in the Pura Cup final v Queensland at Brisbane 2002-03. Was Durham's overseas player in 2000. Was Yorkshire's overseas player during June 2002. Was an overseas player with Hampshire in 2003, from August to September 2004 and in 2005. Hampshire Cricket Society Player of the Year 2003. Named State Player of the Year at the 2004 Allan Border Medal awards. Captain of New South Wales since 2004-05. Was an overseas player with Derbyshire and captain 2007

Best batting: 228* Western Australia v South Australia, Perth 2000-01
Best bowling: 7-130 New South Wales v Victoria, Melbourne 2002-03

2007 Season

	M	Inn	NO	Runs	HS	Avg	100	50	Ct	St	Balls	Runs	Wkts	Avg	BB	5I	10M
Test																	
FC	13	23	6	1284	221	75.52	3	8	9	-	228	144	2	72.00	1-17	-	-
ODI																	
List A	13	13	1	303	81	25.25	-	1	5	-	0	0	0		-	-	
20/20 Int																	
20/20	6	6	2	159	39 *	39.75	-	-	2	-	0	0	0		-	-	

Career Performances

	M	Inn	NO	Runs	HS	Avg	100	50	Ct	St	Balls	Runs	Wkts	Avg	BB	5I	10M
Test	23	38	3	1260	125	36.00	2	8	15	-	659	406	12	33.83	6-65	1	-
FC	168	288	41	12841	228 *	51.98	34	68	153	-	5201	3130	80	39.12	7-130	3	-
ODI	45	42	5	1324	107 *	35.78	1	9	13	-	0	0	0		-	-	
List A	202	195	22	6483	136 *	37.47	7	49	92	-	823	766	24	31.91	3-21	-	
20/20 Int	3	2	0	69	39	34.50	-	-	2	-	0	0	0		-	-	
20/20	18	17	5	533	59 *	44.41	-	2	7	-	0	0	0		-	-	

46. Which South African created a sensation when he brilliantly ran out Ken Barrington and Jim Parks with direct hits in the first Test at Lord's in 1965?

KEEDY, G. Lancashire

Name: Gary Keedy
Role: Left-hand bat, left-arm spin bowler
Born: 27 November 1974, Wakefield
Height: 5ft 11in **Weight:** 13st
Nickname: Keeds, Phil Mitchell, Minty
County debut: 1994 (Yorkshire), 1995 (Lancashire)
County cap: 2000 (Lancashire)
50 wickets in a season: 3
Place in bowling averages: 89th av. 33.87 (2006 27th av. 27.21)
Parents: Roy and Pat
Wife and date of marriage: Andrea, 12 October 2002
Children: Erin Grace, 8 September 2006
Education: Garforth Comprehensive; Open University
Qualifications: 8 GCSEs, Level 2 cricket coach, Certificate in Natural Sciences
Overseas tours: England U18 to South Africa 1992-93, to Denmark 1993; England U19 to Sri Lanka 1993-94; Lancashire to Portugal 1995, to Jamaica 1996, to South Africa 1997; MCC to UAE and Oman 2004
Overseas teams played for: Frankston, Melbourne 1995-96
Career highlights to date: 'County cap; playing for Lancashire. Fourteen wickets in match v Glos at Old Trafford 2004. Five wickets v Yorks at Headingley'
Cricket superstitions: 'None'
Cricketers particularly admired: Graham Gooch, Shane Warne
Other sports followed: Rugby league (Leeds Rhinos), football (Leeds United)
Relaxations: 'Wine tasting; looking after family'
Extras: Player of the Series for England U19 v West Indies U19 1993; also played v India U19 1994. Had match figures of 14-227 (7-95/7-132) v Gloucestershire at Old Trafford 2004, the best return by an English spinner since Martyn Ball's 14-169 in 1993. Leading English wicket-taker (second overall) in the Championship 2004 (72 at 25.68). Lancashire Player of the Year 2004
Opinions on cricket: 'Congratulations to all the counties who have academies in place and are hell-bent on producing the next generation of England stars. I'm all for quality overseas players coming over. I certainly have benefited by playing with and against world-class players. I won't mention Kolpak [*see page 13*] this year!'
Best batting: 57 Lancashire v Yorkshire, Headingley 2002
Best bowling: 7-95 Lancashire v Gloucestershire, Old Trafford 2004

2007 Season

	M	Inn	NO	Runs	HS	Avg	100	50	Ct	St	Balls	Runs	Wkts	Avg	BB	5I	10M
Test																	
FC	10	9	5	34	9	8.50	-	-	3	-	1635	813	24	33.87	5-159	1	-
ODI																	
List A	9	4	2	31	22	15.50	-	-	-	-	377	271	15	18.06	3-42	-	
20/20 Int																	
20/20	6	0	0	0	0		-	-	-	-	137	129	4	32.25	2-11	-	

Career Performances

	M	Inn	NO	Runs	HS	Avg	100	50	Ct	St	Balls	Runs	Wkts	Avg	BB	5I	10M
Test																	
FC	157	176	93	895	57	10.78	-	1	44	-	32145	15113	481	31.42	7-95	23	5
ODI																	
List A	43	12	6	52	22	8.66	-	-	2	-	1716	1368	47	29.10	5-30	1	
20/20 Int																	
20/20	29	5	2	15	9 *	5.00	-	-	2	-	593	619	27	22.92	3-25	-	

KEEGAN, C. B. — Middlesex

Name: Chad Blake Keegan
Role: Right-hand bat, right-arm fast-medium bowler
Born: 30 July 1979, Sandton, Johannesburg, South Africa
Height: 6ft 1in **Weight:** 12st
Nickname: Wick
County debut: 2001
County cap: 2003
50 wickets in a season: 1
Place in batting averages: (2006 260th av. 12.33)
Place in bowling averages: (2006 97th av. 38.73)
Parents: Sharon and Blake
Marital status: Single
Education: Durban High School
Qualifications: YMCA fitness instructor
Overseas tours: MCC to Argentina and Chile 2001
Overseas teams played for: Durban High School Old Boys 1994-97; Crusaders, Durban 1998-99
Career highlights to date: 'Being awarded Player of the Year for Middlesex 2003'

Cricket moments to forget: 'Losing my pants diving for a ball at Lord's'
Cricket superstitions: 'Tapping the bat either side of the crease three times'
Cricketers particularly admired: Malcolm Marshall, Neil Johnson
Other sports played: 'Any extreme sports, golf'
Other sports followed: Football (Liverpool)
Favourite band: Jack Johnson
Relaxations: 'Making and listening to music (guitar); sketching'
Extras: Represented KwaZulu-Natal U13, KwaZulu-Natal Schools, KwaZulu-Natal U19, KwaZulu-Natal Academy. MCC Young Cricketer. Middlesex Player of the Year 2003. Is not considered an overseas player. Released by Middlesex at the end of the 2007 season
Best batting: 44 Middlesex v Surrey, The Oval 2004
Best bowling: 6-114 Middlesex v Leicestershire, Southgate 2003

2007 Season

	M	Inn	NO	Runs	HS	Avg	100	50	Ct	St	Balls	Runs	Wkts	Avg	BB	5I	10M
Test																	
FC																	
ODI																	
List A	5	4	2	16	9 *	8.00	-	-	1	-	153	164	4	41.00	3-13	-	
20/20 Int																	
20/20	6	5	2	77	24	25.66	-	-	2	-	108	107	5	21.40	3-14	-	

Career Performances

	M	Inn	NO	Runs	HS	Avg	100	50	Ct	St	Balls	Runs	Wkts	Avg	BB	5I	10M
Test																	
FC	47	57	6	607	44	11.90	-	-	14	-	8395	4887	140	34.90	6-114	6	-
ODI																	
List A	87	56	19	610	50	16.48	-	1	20	-	4007	3174	133	23.86	6-33	3	
20/20 Int																	
20/20	18	16	4	228	42	19.00	-	-	5	-	354	473	12	39.41	3-14	-	

47. Who led South Africa to their first Test series win in England in 1935?

KERVEZEE, A. N. Worcestershire

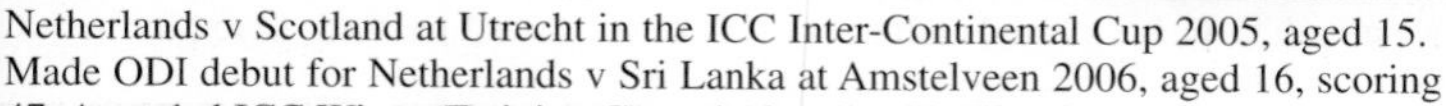

Name: Alexei Nicolaas Kervezee
Role: Right-hand bat, right-arm medium bowler
Born: 11 September 1989, Walvis Bay, Namibia
County debut: No first-team appearance
ODI debut: 2006
Overseas tours: Netherlands to UAE (EurAsia Series) 2006, to Scotland (European Championship) 2006, to South Africa (ICC Associates Tri-Series) 2006-07, to Kenya (ICC World Cricket League) 2006-07, to West Indies (World Cup) 2006-07, to Canada 2007, to Ireland (Quadrangular Series) 2007, plus various Netherlands age-group tours
Overseas teams played for: HBS, Netherlands
Extras: Made first-class debut for Netherlands v Scotland at Utrecht in the ICC Inter-Continental Cup 2005, aged 15. Made ODI debut for Netherlands v Sri Lanka at Amstelveen 2006, aged 16, scoring 47. Attended ICC Winter Training Camp in South Africa 2006-07
Best batting: 98 Netherlands v Canada, Toronto (MSE) 2007
Best bowling: 1-33 Netherlands v Scotland, Aberdeen 2007

2007 Season (did not make any first-class or one-day appearances for his county)

Career Performances

	M	Inn	NO	Runs	HS	Avg	100	50	Ct	St	Balls	Runs	Wkts	Avg	BB	5I	10M
Test																	
FC	8	11	2	304	98	33.77	-	2	2	-	90	44	1	44.00	1-33	-	-
ODI	18	15	2	341	62	26.23	-	1	6	-	6	8	0		-	-	
List A	20	17	2	392	62	26.13	-	1	7	-	30	47	0		-	-	
20/20 Int																	
20/20																	

KEY, R. W. T. Kent

Name: Robert William Trevor Key
Role: Right-hand bat, off-spin bowler, county captain
Born: 12 May 1979, Dulwich, London
Height: 6ft 1in **Weight:** 12st 7lbs
Nickname: Keysy
County debut: 1998
County cap: 2001
Test debut: 2002
ODI debut: 2003
1000 runs in a season: 5
1st-Class 200s: 1
Place in batting averages: 17th av. 56.81 (2006 90th av. 36.76)
Parents: Trevor and Lynn
Wife and date of marriage: Fleur, 2006
Children: Aaliyah, September 2006
Family links with cricket: Mother played for Kent Ladies. Father played club cricket in Derby. Sister Elizabeth played for her junior school side
Education: Langley Park Boys' School
Qualifications: 10 GCSEs, NCA coaching award, GNVQ Business Studies
Overseas tours: Kent U13 to Netherlands; England U17 to Bermuda (International Youth Tournament) 1997 (c); England U19 to South Africa (including U19 World Cup) 1997-98; England A to Zimbabwe and South Africa 1998-99; ECB National Academy to Australia 2001-02, to Sri Lanka 2002-03; England to Australia 2002-03, to South Africa 2004-05
Overseas teams played for: Greenpoint CC, Cape Town 1996-97
Cricketers particularly admired: Min Patel, Neil Taylor, Alan Wells, Mark Ealham
Other sports played: Hockey, football, snooker, tennis (played for county)
Other sports followed: Football (Chelsea), basketball (Chicago Bulls)
Extras: Represented England U19 1997 and was England U19 Man of the Series v Pakistan U19 1998 (award shared with Graeme Swann). NBC Denis Compton Award for the most promising young Kent player 2001. Scored 221 in the first Test v West Indies 2004, in the process sharing with Andrew Strauss (137) in a record second-wicket stand for Test cricket at Lord's (291). Leading run-scorer in English first-class cricket 2004 with 1896 runs at 79.00, including nine centuries. One of *Wisden*'s Five Cricketers of the Year 2005. Scored twin centuries (112/189) v Surrey at Tunbridge Wells 2005, in the second innings sharing with Martin van Jaarsveld (168) in a new Kent record third-wicket partnership (323). Carried bat for 75* v Surrey at Canterbury 2007. ECB National Academy 2005-06, 2006-07. Captain of Kent since 2006
Best batting: 221 England v West Indies, Lord's 2004

2007 Season

	M	Inn	NO	Runs	HS	Avg	100	50	Ct	St	Balls	Runs	Wkts	Avg	BB	5I	10M
Test																	
FC	15	25	3	1250	182	56.81	5	4	4	-	42	33	0		-	-	-
ODI																	
List A	16	15	1	695	108	49.64	3	2	8	-	0	0	0		-	-	
20/20 Int																	
20/20	6	6	2	282	68 *	70.50	-	4	-	-	0	0	0		-	-	

Career Performances

	M	Inn	NO	Runs	HS	Avg	100	50	Ct	St	Balls	Runs	Wkts	Avg	BB	5I	10M
Test	15	26	1	775	221	31.00	1	3	11	-	0	0	0		-	-	-
FC	175	303	18	11900	221	41.75	35	46	104	-	152	92	0		-	-	-
ODI	5	5	0	54	19	10.80	-	-	-	-	0	0	0		-	-	
List A	156	149	11	4333	114	31.39	4	28	29	-	0	0	0		-	-	
20/20 Int																	
20/20	22	22	5	544	68 *	32.00	-	5	4	-	0	0	0		-	-	

KHAN, A. — Kent

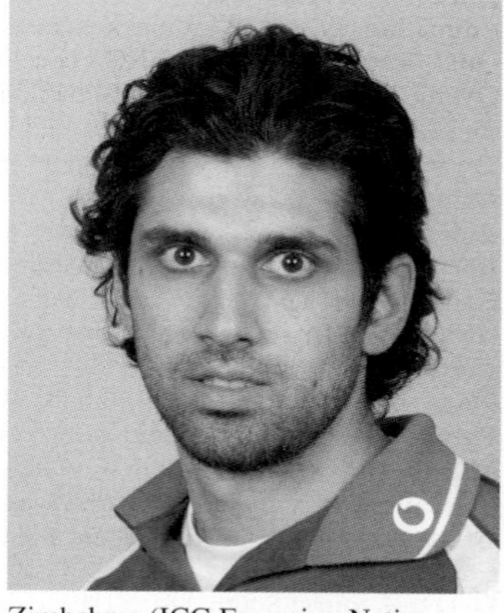

Name: Amjad Khan
Role: Right-hand bat, right-arm fast bowler
Born: 14 October 1980, Copenhagen, Denmark
Height: 6ft **Weight:** 11st 6lbs
Nickname: Ammy
County debut: 2001
County cap: 2005
50 wickets in a season: 2
Place in bowling averages: (2006 48th av. 30.41)
Parents: Aslam and Raisa
Marital status: Single
Education: Skolen på Duevej, Denmark; Falkonĕrgårdens Gymnasium
Overseas tours: Denmark U19 to Canada 1996, to Bermuda 1997, to South Africa (U19 World Cup) 1997-98, to Wales 1998, to Ireland 1999; Denmark to Netherlands 1998, to Zimbabwe (ICC Emerging Nations Tournament) 1999-2000, to Canada (ICC Trophy) 2001; England A to Bangladesh 2006-07
Overseas teams played for: Kjøbenhavns Boldklub, Denmark

Cricket moments to forget: 'I try to forget most of the games where I didn't perform as well as I would like'
Cricketers particularly admired: Wasim Akram, Dennis Lillee
Other sports followed: Football (Denmark)
Favourite band: Marvin Gaye, George Michael, Nerd (Neptunes)
Injuries: Out for the whole of the 2007 season with a knee injury
Relaxations: 'Music, sleeping, reading'
Extras: Made debut for Denmark at the age of 17. Took 50 (63) first-class wickets in his first full season 2002. NBC Denis Compton Award for the most promising young Kent player 2002. Is England-qualified
Best batting: 78 Kent v Middlesex, Lord's 2003
Best bowling: 6-52 Kent v Yorkshire, Canterbury 2002

2007 Season (did not make any first-class or one-day appearances)

Career Performances

	M	Inn	NO	Runs	HS	Avg	100	50	Ct	St	Balls	Runs	Wkts	Avg	BB	5I	10M
Test																	
FC	57	65	23	824	78	19.61	-	3	9	-	9338	6192	190	32.58	6-52	6	-
ODI																	
List A	51	28	6	265	65 *	12.04	-	1	13	-	2107	1818	56	32.46	4-26	-	
20/20 Int																	
20/20	17	7	2	30	15	6.00	-	-	1	-	313	466	22	21.18	3-11	-	

KIESWETTER, C. — Somerset

Name: Craig Kieswetter
Role: Right-hand bat, wicket-keeper
Born: 28 November 1987, Johannesburg, South Africa
Height: 5ft 11in **Weight:** 13st 5lbs
Nickname: Bangle, Hobnob, Shnitz, Kitchen Utensil
County debut: 2007
Place in batting averages: 146th av. 29.00
Parents: Wayne and Belinda
Marital status: Single
Education: Diocesan College (Bishops), Cape Town; Millfield School
Off-season: 'Fifteen days in India and two months in Johannesburg – cricket training. Christmas in Cape Town'
Overseas tours: South Africa U19 to Sri Lanka (U19 World Cup) 2005-06
Overseas teams played for: Alma Marist CC, Cape Town 2005-06
Career highlights to date: 'Making first-class and List A debuts in first year aged 19'
Cricket superstitions: 'Routine to put gear on; mark guard after every ball; certain amount of taps when bowler running in'

Cricketers particularly admired: Marcus Trescothick, Andrew Caddick, Ian Blackwell, Justin Langer, Neil McKenzie, Damien Martyn, Adam Gilchrist
Other sports played: Hockey (provincial)
Other sports followed: Football (Aston Villa)
Favourite band: Justin Timberlake, Ne-Yo, R&B, NDubz, Plan B
Relaxations: 'PlayStation B, Pro Evolution Soccer, music, girlfriend'
Extras: Represented South Africa Schools 2005. Man of the Match v USA U19 at Colombo in the U19 World Cup 2005-06 (80). Struck 58-ball 69* on List A debut v Glamorgan at Taunton in the Friends Provident 2007. Magic Moment v Warwickshire at Edgbaston in the Twenty20 2007

Best batting: 93 Somerset v Glamorgan, Taunton 2007

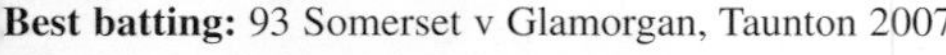

2007 Season

	M	Inn	NO	Runs	HS	Avg	100	50	Ct	St	Balls	Runs	Wkts	Avg	BB	5I	10M
Test																	
FC	14	16	3	377	93	29.00	-	3	46	-	0	0	0		-	-	-
ODI																	
List A	15	15	3	329	69 *	27.41	-	2	18	2	0	0	0		-	-	
20/20 Int																	
20/20	6	6	2	81	48	20.25	-	-	1	-	0	0	0		-	-	

Career Performances

	M	Inn	NO	Runs	HS	Avg	100	50	Ct	St	Balls	Runs	Wkts	Avg	BB	5I	10M
Test																	
FC	14	16	3	377	93	29.00	-	3	46	-	0	0	0		-	-	-
ODI																	
List A	15	15	3	329	69 *	27.41	-	2	18	2	0	0	0		-	-	
20/20 Int																	
20/20	6	6	2	81	48	20.25	-	-	1	-	0	0	0		-	-	

KILLEEN, N. Durham

Name: Neil Killeen
Role: Right-hand bat, right-arm medium-fast bowler
Born: 17 October 1975, Shotley Bridge
Height: 6ft 1in **Weight:** 15st
Nickname: Killer, Bully, Quinny, Squeaky, Bull
County debut: 1995
County cap: 1999
Benefit: 2006
50 wickets in a season: 1
Place in bowling averages: (2006 82nd av. 35.31)
Parents: Glen and Thora
Wife and date of marriage: Clare Louise, 5 February 2000
Children: Jonathan David
Family links with cricket: 'Dad best armchair player in the game'
Education: Greencroft Comprehensive School; Derwentside College, University of Teesside
Qualifications: 8 GCSEs, 2 A-levels, first year Sports Science, Level III coaching award, Level I staff coach
Career outside cricket: Cricket coaching
Overseas tours: Durham CCC to Zimbabwe 1992; England U19 to West Indies 1994-95; MCC to Bangladesh 1999-2000
Career highlights to date: 'My county cap and first-class debut'
Cricket moments to forget: 'Injury causing me to miss most of 2001 season'
Cricketers particularly admired: Ian Botham, Curtly Ambrose, Courtney Walsh, David Boon
Other sports played: Athletics (English Schools javelin)
Sports followed: Football (Sunderland AFC), cricket (Anfield Plain CC)
Relaxations: 'Good food, good wine; golf; spending time with wife and family'
Extras: Was first Durham bowler to take five wickets in a Sunday League game (5-26 v Northamptonshire at Northampton 1995). Scored 35 batting at No. 10 as Durham made 453-9 to beat Somerset at Taunton 2004. Had figures of 8.3-7-5-2 v Derbyshire at Riverside in the totesport League 2004
Best batting: 48 Durham v Somerset, Riverside 1995
Best bowling: 7-70 Durham v Hampshire, Riverside 2003

2007 Season

	M	Inn	NO	Runs	HS	Avg	100	50	Ct	St	Balls	Runs	Wkts	Avg	BB	5I	10M
Test																	
FC	2	0	0	0	0		-	-	-	-	255	117	6	19.50	4-22	-	-
ODI																	
List A	18	5	3	9	3 *	4.50	-	-	2	-	843	527	19	27.73	3-9	-	
20/20 Int																	
20/20	6	2	2	2	1 *		-	-	1	-	93	132	2	66.00	1-19	-	

Career Performances

	M	Inn	NO	Runs	HS	Avg	100	50	Ct	St	Balls	Runs	Wkts	Avg	BB	5I	10M
Test																	
FC	100	143	30	1297	48	11.47	-	-	25	-	16271	8150	254	32.08	7-70	8	-
ODI																	
List A	214	112	43	644	32	9.33	-	-	38	-	10126	6992	288	24.27	6-31	4	
20/20 Int																	
20/20	30	14	10	85	17 *	21.25	-	-	6	-	603	742	32	23.18	4-7	-	

KING, S. J. Surrey

Name: Simon James King
Role: Right-hand bat, right-arm off-spin bowler
Born: 4 September 1987, Lambeth, London
Height: 6ft 1in **Weight:** 11st
Nickname: Kingy
County debut: No first-team appearance
Parents: Angela Pocock and David King
Marital status: Single
Family links with cricket: 'Brother plays'
Education: Warlingham Secondary School; John Fisher Sixth Form College
Qualifications: GCSEs, BTEC National Diploma in Sport, ECB Level 2 coaching
Overseas tours: Surrey Academy to South Africa 2005; Surrey CCC to India 2006
Overseas teams played for: Mildura West CC, Victoria; Millewa CC, Victoria (both Australia)
Career highlights to date: 'Receiving first contract at the end of the 2006 season. First five-wicket haul, v Sussex 2nd XI 2005'

Cricket moments to forget: 'Dropping a skyer into my face in an England regional match'
Cricketers particularly admired: Alec Stewart, Shane Warne, Mark Ramprakash, Phil Matthews
Young players to look out for: Zafar Ansari, Daryl King, Harry Allen
Other sports played: Football (Warlingham FC, Hamsey Rangers FC)
Other sports followed: Football (Fulham)
Favourite band: Goo Goo Dolls, Oasis, U2, Lifehouse
Relaxations: 'Sleeping'
Extras: Surrey U15 Player of the Year 2003. Surrey Academy Player of the Year 2006

KIRBY, S. P. — Gloucestershire

Name: Steven Paul Kirby
Role: Right-hand bat, right-arm fast bowler
Born: 4 October 1977, Bury, Lancashire
Height: 6ft 3in **Weight:** 13st 5lbs
Nickname: Tango
County debut: 2001 (Yorkshire), 2005 (Gloucestershire)
County cap: 2003 (Yorkshire), 2005 (Gloucestershire)
50 wickets in a season: 1
Place in bowling averages: 18th av. 23.43 (2006 104th av. 39.67)
Parents: Paul and Alison
Wife and date of marriage: Sasha, 11 October 2003
Children: Joel, 2005; Aleisha, 2007
Education: Elton High School, Walshaw, Bury, Lancs; Bury College
Qualifications: 10 GCSEs, BTEC/GNVQ Advanced Leisure and Tourism
Overseas tours: Yorkshire to Grenada 2001; ECB National Academy to Australia 2001-02; England A to India 2003-04; England Lions to India 2007-08
Overseas teams played for: Egmont Plains, New Zealand 1997-98
Cricket moments to forget: 'Being knocked out by Nixon McLean trying to take a return catch'
Cricketers particularly admired: Steve Waugh, Richard Hadlee, Glenn McGrath, Michael Atherton, Curtly Ambrose, Sachin Tendulkar
Other sports played: Basketball, table tennis, squash, golf – 'anything sporty and competitive'
Other sports followed: Football (Manchester United), rugby (Leicester Tigers)

Extras: Formerly with Leicestershire but did not appear for first team. Took 14 wickets (41-18-47-14) in one day for Egmont Plains v Hawera in a New Zealand club match 1997-98. Took 7-50 in Kent's second innings at Headingley 2001, the best bowling figures by a Yorkshire player on first-class debut; Kirby had replaced Matthew Hoggard (called up by England) halfway through the match. Took 13-154 (5-74/8-80) v Somerset at Taunton 2003, the best match return by a Yorkshire bowler for 36 years

Best batting: 57 Yorkshire v Hampshire, Headingley 2002

Best bowling: 8-80 Yorkshire v Somerset, Taunton 2003

Stop press: Called up to squad for England Lions tour to India 2007-08

2007 Season

	M	Inn	NO	Runs	HS	Avg	100	50	Ct	St	Balls	Runs	Wkts	Avg	BB	5I	10M
Test																	
FC	11	13	1	119	37	9.91	-	-	1	-	1876	961	41	23.43	5-41	3	1
ODI																	
List A	7	5	1	21	13	5.25	-	-	1	-	328	338	14	24.14	5-36	1	
20/20 Int																	
20/20																	

Career Performances

	M	Inn	NO	Runs	HS	Avg	100	50	Ct	St	Balls	Runs	Wkts	Avg	BB	5I	10M
Test																	
FC	87	119	37	672	57	8.19	-	1	17	-	15678	9306	319	29.17	8-80	13	4
ODI																	
List A	44	21	7	64	15	4.57	-	-	8	-	1795	1742	45	38.71	5-36	1	
20/20 Int																	
20/20	11	3	1	1	1 *	.50	-	-	1	-	216	289	13	22.23	2-15	-	

48. Which current Hampshire batsman made his Test debut at Lord's in 1994 in England's first official Test against South Africa after the latter's isolation ended?

KIRTLEY, R. J. Sussex

Name: Robert James Kirtley
Role: Right-hand bat, right-arm fast-medium bowler
Born: 10 January 1975, Eastbourne
Height: 6ft **Weight:** 12st
Nickname: Ambi
County debut: 1995
County cap: 1998
Benefit: 2006
Test debut: 2003
ODI debut: 2001-02
Twenty20 Int debut: 2007-08
50 wickets in a season: 7
Place in batting averages: 240th av. 16.33
Place in bowling averages: 134th av. 47.25 (2006 111th av. 41.55)
Parents: Bob and Pip
Wife and date of marriage: Jenny, 26 October 2002
Family links with cricket: Brother plays league cricket
Education: St Andrew's School, Eastbourne; Clifton College, Bristol
Qualifications: 9 GCSEs, 2 A-levels, NCA coaching first level
Overseas tours: Sussex YC to Barbados 1993, to Sri Lanka 1995; Sussex to Grenada 2001; England A to Bangladesh and New Zealand 1999-2000, to Bangladesh 2006-07; England to Zimbabwe (one-day series) 2001-02, to Sri Lanka (ICC Champions Trophy) 2002-03, to Australia 2002-03 (VB Series), to Bangladesh and Sri Lanka 2003-04, to West Indies 2003-04 (one-day series), to South Africa (World 20/20) 2007-08
Overseas teams played for: Mashonaland, Zimbabwe 1996-97; Namibian Cricket Board/Wanderers, Windhoek, Namibia 1998-99
Career highlights to date: 'My Test debut at Trent Bridge'
Cricket moments to forget: 'The three times I've bagged a pair'
Cricket superstitions: 'Put my left boot on first!'
Cricketers particularly admired: Curtly Ambrose, Jim Andrew, Darren Gough
Other sports followed: Rugby (England), football (Brighton & Hove Albion)
Relaxations: 'Inviting friends round for a braai (barbeque) and enjoying a cold beer with them'
Extras: Played in the Mashonaland side which defeated England on their 1996-97 tour of Zimbabwe, taking seven wickets in the match. NBC Denis Compton Award for the most promising young Sussex player 1997. Leading wicket-taker in English first-class cricket 2001 with 75 wickets (av. 23.32). Sussex Player of the Year 2002. Made Test debut in the third Test v South Africa at Trent Bridge 2003, taking 6-34 in South

Africa's second innings and winning Man of the Match award. C&G Man of the Match award for his 5-27 in the final v Lancashire at Lord's 2006. Took 600th first-class wicket (Yuvraj Singh) v Indians at Hove 2007. Vice-captain of Sussex 2001-05
Best batting: 59 Sussex v Durham, Eastbourne 1998
Best bowling: 7-21 Sussex v Hampshire, Southampton 1999

2007 Season

	M	Inn	NO	Runs	HS	Avg	100	50	Ct	St	Balls	Runs	Wkts	Avg	BB	5I	10M
Test																	
FC	7	8	2	98	51	16.33	-	1	6	-	1110	567	12	47.25	4-44	-	-
ODI																	
List A	15	7	4	40	19 *	13.33	-	-	3	-	545	501	28	17.89	5-36	2	
20/20 Int																	
20/20	9	2	1	2	2	2.00	-	-	4	-	173	214	13	16.46	4-22	-	

Career Performances

	M	Inn	NO	Runs	HS	Avg	100	50	Ct	St	Balls	Runs	Wkts	Avg	BB	5I	10M
Test	4	7	1	32	12	5.33	-	-	3	-	1079	561	19	29.52	6-34	1	-
FC	165	226	75	1976	59	13.08	-	4	58	-	31293	16292	606	26.88	7-21	29	4
ODI	11	2	0	2	1	1.00	-	-	5	-	549	481	9	53.44	2-33	-	
List A	218	82	40	396	30 *	9.42	-	-	60	-	9630	7393	328	22.53	5-27	7	
20/20 Int	1	1	1	2	2 *		-	-	-	-	6	17	0		-	-	
20/20	31	10	4	9	2 *	1.50	-	-	7	-	573	733	29	25.27	4-22	-	

49. Which former county director of cricket scored a hundred (107*) on his Test debut in the second Test between England and New Zealand at Auckland in 1987-88?

KLOKKER, F. A. Derbyshire

Name: Frederik Andreas Klokker
Role: Left-hand bat, wicket-keeper
Born: 13 March 1983, Odense, Denmark
Height: 5ft 11in **Weight:** 14st 2lbs
Nickname: Kloks, J-Lo, The Great Dane
County debut: 2006 (Warwickshire), 2007 (Derbyshire)
Parents: Peter Palle and Ingermarie
Marital status: Single
Family links with cricket: 'Dad played for Denmark for many years and is now head coach of Danish cricket. My two sisters played a bit when they were younger'
Education: Hindsholmskolen, Denmark
Qualifications: Levels 1 and 2 coaching. Levels 1 and 2 fitness instructor
Career outside cricket: Philatelist
Off-season: 'I'm going to Kenya and Namibia with Denmark in October and November'
Overseas tours: Denmark U19 to South Africa (U19 World Cup) 1997-98; Denmark to Zimbabwe (ICC Emerging Nations Tournament) 1999-2000, to Canada (ICC Trophy) 2001, to Ireland (ICC Trophy) 2005, to Kenya 2007, to Namibia (ICC World Cricket League) 2007-08, plus various other tours and tournaments with Denmark and Denmark age groups; MCC YC to Sri Lanka 2003-04
Overseas teams played for: Kerteminde CC, Denmark 1989-99; Skanderborg CC, Denmark 2000-01; South Perth CC 2001-02 – 2003-04; Prospect CC, Adelaide 2006-07
Career highlights to date: 'Playing in the 1997 U19 World Cup in South Africa. Debut for Denmark. Debut for Warwickshire. Breaking record for most runs by an MCC Young Cricketer. Hundred for Derbyshire on my first-class debut for them'
Cricket moments to forget: 'The game against the West Indies in the 1997 U19 World Cup'
Cricket superstitions: 'Not really'
Cricketers particularly admired: Waugh twins, Dominic Ostler
Young players to look out for: Michael Pedersen (MCC YC)
Other sports played: 'Played handball in the winter before I started going to Australia'
Other sports followed: Handball (GOG)
Favourite band: Live
Relaxations: 'Can't beat a good movie'
Extras: MCC Young Cricketer 2002-05, acting as substitute fielder for England in the

first Test v New Zealand at Lord's 2004. Has represented Denmark in one-day cricket, including NatWest/C&G. Man of the Match v USA at Armagh in the ICC Trophy 2005 (149-ball 138*). Played for European XI v MCC at Rotterdam 2006. Played one first-class match and one C&G match for Warwickshire 2006 as injury cover in the wicket-keeping department, scoring 40 as nightwatchman v Sussex at Hove. Played two first-class matches for Derbyshire 2007, scoring century (100*) on debut for the county v Cambridge UCCE at Fenner's

Best batting: 100* Derbyshire v CUCCE, Fenner's 2007

2007 Season

	M	Inn	NO	Runs	HS	Avg	100	50	Ct	St	Balls	Runs	Wkts	Avg	BB	5I	10M
Test																	
FC	2	3	1	171	100 *	85.50	1	-	3	-	0	0	0		-	-	-
ODI																	
List A																	
20/20 Int																	
20/20																	

Career Performances

	M	Inn	NO	Runs	HS	Avg	100	50	Ct	St	Balls	Runs	Wkts	Avg	BB	5I	10M
Test																	
FC	3	4	1	211	100 *	70.33	1	-	6	-	0	0	0		-	-	-
ODI																	
List A	12	10	1	241	138 *	26.77	1	1	14	3	0	0	0		-	-	
20/20 Int																	
20/20																	

50. Geraint Jones stumped Andrew Hall off the last ball of the second ODI between England and South Africa in Bloemfontein in 2004-05 to bring about a tie. But who bowled that final delivery?

KLUSENER, L. Northamptonshire

Name: Lance Klusener
Role: Left-hand bat, right-arm fast-medium bowler; all-rounder
Born: 4 September 1971, Durban, South Africa
Height: 5ft 10in **Weight:** 12st 4lbs
Nickname: Zulu
County debut: 2002 (Nottinghamshire), 2004 (Middlesex), 2006 (Northamptonshire)
County cap: 2006 (Northamptonshire)
Test debut: 1996-97
ODI debut: 1995-96
1000 runs in a season: 2
Place in batting averages: 40th av. 48.23 (2006 8th av. 65.84)
Place in bowling averages: 105th av. 38.78 (2006 89th av. 36.78)
Parents: Peter and Dawn
Wife and date of marriage: Isabelle, 13 May 2000
Children: Matthew, 23 January 2002; Thomas, 1 July 2006
Education: Durban High School; Technikon Natal
Career outside cricket: 'Farming – sugar'
Overseas tours: South Africa U24 to Sri Lanka 1995; South Africa A to England 1996; South Africa to India 1996-97, to Pakistan 1997-98, to Australia 1997-98, to England 1998, to New Zealand 1998-99, to UK, Ireland and Netherlands (World Cup) 1999, to Zimbabwe 1999-2000, to India 1999-2000, to Sri Lanka 2000, to Kenya (ICC Knockout Trophy) 2000-01, to West Indies 2000-01, to Zimbabwe 2001-02, to Australia 2001-02, to Sri Lanka (ICC Champions Trophy) 2002-03, to New Zealand 2003-04 (one-day series), to Sri Lanka 2004, to England (ICC Champions Trophy) 2004, plus other one-day tournaments in Kenya, Sharjah, Australia, Singapore and Morocco; FICA World XI to New Zealand 2004-05
Overseas teams played for: Natal/KwaZulu-Natal 1993-94 – 2003-04; Dolphins 2004-05 – 2006-07
Career highlights to date: 'World Cup Man of the Tournament [1999]'
Cricketers particularly admired: Malcolm Marshall, Shaun Pollock
Young players to look out for: Hashim Amla
Other sports played: Golf
Other sports followed: Rugby (Natal Sharks, Springboks)
Relaxations: 'Fishing, hunting'
Extras: Returned the best innings analysis by a South African on Test debut – 8-64 in the second Test v India at Kolkata 1996-97. One of *South African Cricket Annual*'s

five Cricketers of the Year 1997, 1999. Scored 174 in the second Test v England at Port Elizabeth 1999-2000, winning Man of the Match award. His other Test awards include Man of the Series v Sri Lanka 2000. One of *Wisden*'s Five Cricketers of the Year 2000. Has won numerous ODI awards, including Player of the Tournament in the World Cup 1999. His domestic awards include Man of the Match in the SuperSport Series final v Western Province at Cape Town 2003-04 (7-70/5-90). An overseas player with Nottinghamshire at the start of the 2002 season; an overseas player with Middlesex 2004. Is no longer considered an overseas player. Scored 126* and 62 and had first innings figures of 4-50 on Championship debut for Northamptonshire v Essex at Chelmsford 2006; scored century (122) and followed up with first innings figures of 5-62 v Leicestershire at Oakham School 2006
Best batting: 174 South Africa v England, Port Elizabeth 1999-2000
Best bowling: 8-34 Natal v Western Province, Durban 1995-96

2007 Season

	M	Inn	NO	Runs	HS	Avg	100	50	Ct	St	Balls	Runs	Wkts	Avg	BB	5I	10M
Test																	
FC	16	26	5	1013	122	48.23	2	5	6	-	2595	1280	33	38.78	5-40	2	-
ODI																	
List A	14	13	6	239	36 *	34.14	-	-	1	-	552	475	9	52.77	4-40	-	
20/20 Int																	
20/20	7	5	2	204	111 *	68.00	1	-	1	-	108	149	4	37.25	2-30	-	

Career Performances

	M	Inn	NO	Runs	HS	Avg	100	50	Ct	St	Balls	Runs	Wkts	Avg	BB	5I	10M
Test	49	69	11	1906	174	32.86	4	8	34	-	6887	3033	80	37.91	8-64	1	-
FC	183	263	55	8426	174	40.50	19	39	96	-	30635	14809	502	29.50	8-34	20	4
ODI	171	137	50	3576	103 *	41.10	2	19	35	-	7336	5751	192	29.95	6-49	6	
List A	313	258	97	6424	142 *	39.90	3	33	81	-	13127	10219	328	31.15	6-49	8	
20/20 Int																	
20/20	38	34	14	814	111 *	40.70	1	3	12	-	642	936	23	40.69	2-13	-	

KNAPPETT, J. P. T. Worcestershire

Name: Joshua (Josh) Philip Thomas Knappett
Role: Right-hand bat, wicket-keeper
Born: 15 April 1985, Westminster, London
Height: 6ft **Weight:** 12st 4lbs
Nickname: Badger, Edwin (van der Sar)
County debut: 2007
County colours: 2007
Place in batting averages: (2006 120th av. 32.85)
Parents: Phil and Janie
Marital status: Single
Family links with cricket: Father is Youth and Coaching Manager at Middlesex and has played club cricket. 'Brother, Jon, plays socially'
Education: East Barnet School; Oxford Brookes University
Qualifications: 10 GCSEs, 3 A-levels, Level 3 ECB tutor-trained and assessor-trained cricket coach, swimming, football and rugby Level 1 coaching qualifications
Career outside cricket: Coaching and coach education
Overseas tours: MCC A to Canada 2005
Cricket moments to forget: 'Being hit on the head by Jimmy Ormond on first-class debut for OUCCE'
Cricketers particularly admired: Jack Russell, Adam Gilchrist
Young players to look out for: Eoin Morgan, Billy Godleman, Richard Jones
Other sports played: Squash, trampolining
Other sports followed: Football (Tottenham Hotspur)
Favourite band: 'Led Zeppelin, Jack Johnson, DJ Shadow, Montana, Hendrix, Gomez etc.'
Relaxations: 'Listening to music, eating and sleeping (as well as training)'
Extras: Played for Oxford UCCE 2004-06. Represented British Universities 2005, 2006. Attended training camp in Mumbai, India 2005 (World Cricket Academy)
Best batting: 100* OUCCE v Durham, The Parks 2006

2007 Season

	M	Inn	NO	Runs	HS	Avg	100	50	Ct	St	Balls	Runs	Wkts	Avg	BB	5I	10M
Test																	
FC	1	2	0	11	7	5.50	-	-	-	-	0	0	0		-	-	-
ODI																	
List A																	
20/20 Int																	
20/20																	

Career Performances

	M	Inn	NO	Runs	HS	Avg	100	50	Ct	St	Balls	Runs	Wkts	Avg	BB	5I	10M
Test																	
FC	11	18	2	518	100 *	32.37	1	3	21	3	0	0	0		-	-	-
ODI																	
List A																	
20/20 Int																	
20/20																	

KRUGER, G. J-P. Leicestershire

Name: Garnett John-Peter Kruger
Role: Right-hand bat, right-arm medium-fast bowler
Born: 5 January 1977, Port Elizabeth, South Africa
Height: 6ft 3in
County debut: 2007
ODI debut: 2005-06
Twenty20 Int debut: 2005-06
Place in bowling averages: 33rd av. 24.92
Family links with cricket: Father played cricket in Eastern Province
Education: Gelvan High School; Russell Road College
Qualifications: Fitting and machinery; architecture
Overseas tours: South Africa A to West Indies 2000-01, to Zimbabwe 2004, to Sri Lanka 2005-06; South Africa VI to Hong Kong 2003; South Africa to Australia 2005-06; South Africa Emerging Players to Australia (Cricket Australia Emerging Players Tournament) 2006

Overseas teams played for: Eastern Province 1997-98 – 2002-03; Gauteng 2003-04; Lions 2003-04 –
Cricketers particularly admired: Glenn McGrath
Other sports played: Basketball
Extras: Has represented South Africa A against various touring teams. His match awards include Man of the Match v North West at Port Elizabeth in the Standard Bank Cup 1999-2000 (6-23), v Dolphins at Durban in the SuperSport Series 2005-06 (8-112) and v Warriors at Johannesburg in the SuperSport Series 2005-06 (7-44/4-46). Was due to join Leicestershire as an overseas player in 2004 but was forced to pull out through injury; is no longer considered an overseas player
Best batting: 58 South Africa A v Windward Islands, Arnos Vale 2000-01
Best bowling: 8-112 Lions v Dolphins, Durban 2005-06
Stop press: Man of the Match v Dolphins at Durban in the SuperSport Series 2007-08 (6-49)

2007 Season

	M	Inn	NO	Runs	HS	Avg	100	50	Ct	St	Balls	Runs	Wkts	Avg	BB	5I	10M
Test																	
FC	4	4	0	28	15	7.00	-	-	1	-	510	324	13	24.92	5-62	1	-
ODI																	
List A	4	2	2	6	6 *		-	-	1	-	114	118	2	59.00	2-40	-	
20/20 Int																	
20/20	5	0	0	0	0		-	-	1	-	66	101	2	50.50	2-25	-	

Career Performances

	M	Inn	NO	Runs	HS	Avg	100	50	Ct	St	Balls	Runs	Wkts	Avg	BB	5I	10M
Test																	
FC	73	89	26	795	58	12.61	-	2	18	-	12731	7204	238	30.26	8-112	10	2
ODI	3	2	1	0	0 *	0.00	-	-	1	-	138	139	2	69.50	1-43	-	
List A	96	27	16	93	20 *	8.45	-	-	14	-	4213	3355	135	24.85	6-23	4	
20/20 Int	1	1	0	3	3	3.00	-	-	-	-	24	29	0		-	-	
20/20	18	4	3	18	12 *	18.00	-	-	3	-	364	507	14	36.21	3-32	-	

51. Which veteran of two first-class matches made his Test debut in the second Test between England and New Zealand at Wellington in 1996-97, aged 18 years 10 days?

KRUIS, G. J. Yorkshire

Name: Gideon (Deon) Jacobus Kruis
Role: Right-hand bat, right-arm fast-medium bowler
Born: 9 May 1974, Pretoria, South Africa
Height: 6ft 3in **Weight:** 14st 7lbs
Nickname: Kruisie, Chicken Head
County debut: 2005
County cap: 2006
50 wickets in a season: 1
Place in batting averages: (2006 268th av. 10.62)
Place in bowling averages: (2006 83rd av. 35.31)
Parents: Fanie and Hester
Wife and date of marriage: Marna, 29 June 2002
Children: Elé, 5 October 2006
Family links with cricket: Brother-in-law P. J. Koortzen plays first-class cricket in South Africa
Education: St Alban's College, Pretoria; University of Pretoria
Qualifications: BCom (Hotel and Catering Management)
Off-season: 'Got a sports clothing manufacturing business in Kimberley. Doing commentary on SuperSport in South Africa. Coaching at St Andrew's School in Bloemfontein'
Overseas tours: MCC to Bermuda, to Denmark; South African Invitation XI to Malawi
Overseas teams played for: Northern Transvaal 1993-97; Griqualand West 1997-2004; Goodyear Eagles 2004-05
Career highlights to date: 'Playing for Yorkshire and being Player of the Year in 2005'
Cricket moments to forget: 'This season [2007]! Too many injuries!'
Cricket superstitions: 'Left boot on first; four knots when batting, five when bowling on left boot'
Cricketers particularly admired: Allan Donald, Clive Rice, Richard Hadlee, Dennis Lillee, Glenn McGrath, Steve Waugh
Young players to look out for: Adam Lyth, Adil Rashid, Joe Denly
Other sports played: Golf, squash
Other sports followed: Golf, football (Liverpool)
Injuries: Out for four weeks with an injury to the left hamstring; for two weeks with an oblique injury; for five weeks with an injury to the right hamstring
Favourite band: The Killers

Relaxations: Golf, falconry
Extras: Yorkshire Player of the Year 2005. Is not considered an overseas player
Opinions on cricket: 'First-division cricket is very strong. I think we can have less one-day games so we can prepare better for them. Players can work on more specific areas and this could improve the standard of one-day cricket in general. Maybe do away with the Pro40 and expand the Twenty20 competition. I think the schedule of games can be better so games are spread out more evenly. Counties will have to adapt with only one overseas player in 2008 and this will hopefully give some of the younger players a chance to play more often.'
Best batting: 59 Griqualand West v Bangladeshis, Kimberley 2000-01
Best bowling: 7-58 Griqualand West v Northerns, Centurion 1997-98

2007 Season

	M	Inn	NO	Runs	HS	Avg	100	50	Ct	St	Balls	Runs	Wkts	Avg	BB	5I	10M
Test																	
FC	6	6	3	44	20	14.66	-	-	1	-	662	409	8	51.12	2-39	-	-
ODI																	
List A	4	1	1	0	0 *		-	-	1	-	172	142	10	14.20	4-17	-	
20/20 Int																	
20/20	1	1	1	5	5 *		-	-	-	-	18	31	1	31.00	1-31	-	

Career Performances

	M	Inn	NO	Runs	HS	Avg	100	50	Ct	St	Balls	Runs	Wkts	Avg	BB	5I	10M
Test																	
FC	111	157	48	1535	59	14.08	-	2	42	-	22378	11085	362	30.62	7-58	18	1
ODI																	
List A	107	51	18	404	31 *	12.24	-	-	27	-	5009	3935	131	30.03	4-17	-	
20/20 Int																	
20/20	14	2	1	6	5 *	6.00	-	-	3	-	289	317	13	24.38	2-15	-	

LAMB, G. A. — Hampshire

Name: Gregory (Greg) Arthur Lamb
Role: Right-hand bat, right-arm off-spin or medium bowler; all-rounder
Born: 4 March 1981, Harare, Zimbabwe
Height: 6ft **Weight:** 12st
Nickname: Lamby
County debut: 2004
Parents: Terry and Jackie
Marital status: Single
Children: Isabella Grace Saskia Lamb
Education: Lomagundi College; Guildford College (both Zimbabwe)
Qualifications: School and coaching qualifications

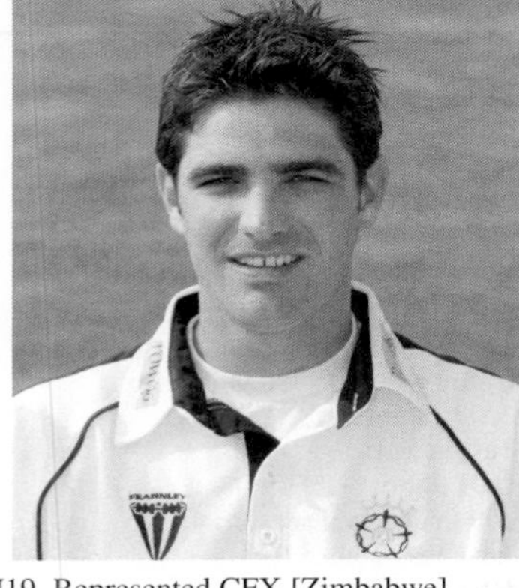

Overseas tours: Zimbabwe U19 to South Africa (U19 World Cup) 1997-98, to Sri Lanka (U19 World Cup) 1999-2000; Zimbabwe A to Sri Lanka 1999-2000
Overseas teams played for: CFX [Zimbabwe] Academy 1999-2000; Mashonaland A 2000-01
Career highlights to date: 'Playing against Australia. Making my first first-class hundred'
Cricket superstitions: 'Every time I hit a four I have to touch the other side of the pitch'
Cricketers particularly admired: Aravinda de Silva
Other sports played: 'All sports'
Favourite band: Matchbox Twenty
Relaxations: 'Fishing, playing sport'
Extras: Played for Zimbabwe U12, U15 and U19. Represented CFX [Zimbabwe] Academy, ZCU President's XI and Zimbabwe A against various touring sides. Scored 94 on Championship debut for Hampshire v Derbyshire at Derby 2004
Best batting: 100* CFX Academy v Manicaland, Mutare 1999-2000
Best bowling: 7-73 CFX Academy v Midlands, Kwekwe 1999-2000

2007 Season

	M	Inn	NO	Runs	HS	Avg	100	50	Ct	St	Balls	Runs	Wkts	Avg	BB	5I	10M
Test																	
FC																	
ODI																	
List A	2	2	1	12	11 *	12.00	-	-	1	-	54	47	1	47.00	1-29	-	
20/20 Int																	
20/20	7	5	0	28	16	5.60	-	-	1	-	60	97	3	32.33	2-17	-	

Career Performances

	M	Inn	NO	Runs	HS	Avg	100	50	Ct	St	Balls	Runs	Wkts	Avg	BB	5I	10M
Test																	
FC	29	44	5	903	100 *	23.15	1	5	24	-	1460	854	31	27.54	7-73	1	-
ODI																	
List A	46	40	5	826	100 *	23.60	1	4	27	-	548	487	18	27.05	4-38	-	
20/20 Int																	
20/20	28	23	2	400	67	19.04	-	2	8	-	166	258	11	23.45	4-28	-	

LANGER, J. L. Somerset

Name: Justin Lee Langer
Role: Left-hand bat, right-arm medium bowler, county captain
Born: 21 November 1970, Subiaco, Western Australia
Height: 5ft 8in **Weight:** 12st 4lbs
Nickname: JL, Alfie
County debut: 1998 (Middlesex), 2006 (Somerset)
County cap: 1998 (Middlesex), 2007 (Somerset)
Test debut: 1992-93
ODI debut: 1993-94
1000 runs in a season: 4
1st-Class 200s: 10
1st-Class 300s: 2
Place in batting averages: 20th av. 55.95
Parents: Colin and Joy-Anne
Wife and date of marriage: Sue, 13 April 1996
Children: Jessica, 28 March 1997; Ali-Rose, November 1998; Sophie, April 2001; Grace, November 2005
Family links with cricket: Uncle, Robbie Langer, played Sheffield Shield cricket for Western Australia and World Series for Australia
Education: Liwara Catholic School; Aquinas College, Perth; University of Western Australia
Career outside cricket: Writing and public speaking
Overseas tours: Young Australia to England 1995; Australia A to South Africa 2002-03 (c); Australia to New Zealand 1992-93, to Pakistan 1994-95, to West Indies 1994-95, to South Africa 1996-97, to England 1997, to Pakistan 1998-99, to West Indies 1998-99, to Sri Lanka and Zimbabwe 1999-2000, to New Zealand 1999-2000, to India 2000-01, to England 2001, to South Africa 2001-02, to Sri Lanka and Sharjah (v Pakistan) 2002-03, to West Indies 2002-03, to Sri Lanka 2003-04, to India 2004-05, to New Zealand 2004-05, to England 2005, to South Africa 2005-06, plus other one-day tournaments in Sharjah, Sri Lanka and Pakistan
Overseas teams played for: Scarborough CC, Perth; Western Australia 1991-92 –
Career highlights to date: 'Winning back the Ashes 2006-07'
Cricket moments to forget: 'Losing the Ashes 2005'
Cricketers particularly admired: Allan Border, Steve Waugh, Ricky Ponting, Mark Ramprakash
Young players to look out for: James Hildreth, Neil Edwards, Shaun Marsh, Craig Kieswetter

Other sports played: Tennis, golf, Australian Rules, martial arts (has black belt in zen do kai)
Other sports followed: Australian Rules (West Coast Eagles)
Favourite band: U2, The Wurzels
Relaxations: Family, writing
Extras: Scored 54 (Australia's only fifty of the match) in the second innings of his debut Test v West Indies at Adelaide 1992-93. Overseas player with Middlesex 1998-2000; county vice-captain 1999 and captain 2000. Scored 166 for Middlesex v Essex at Southgate 1998, in the process sharing with Mike Gatting (241) in a new Middlesex record partnership for the first wicket (372). Put on 238 for the sixth wicket with Adam Gilchrist as Australia successfully chased 369 to beat Pakistan in the second Test at Hobart 1999-2000; his 127 (coupled with 59 in the first innings) won him the Man of the Match award. His numerous other awards include Man of the [Test] Series v New Zealand 2001-02, and Man of the Match in the fourth Test v England at Melbourne 2002-03 (250) and in the first Test v West Indies at Georgetown 2002-03 (146/78*). One of *Wisden*'s Five Cricketers of the Year 2001. Became first Western Australian to make 100 Test appearances, in the third Test v South Africa at Johannesburg 2005-06. A temporary overseas player with Somerset during the 2006 season and an overseas player with the county and captain since 2007. Scored 342 v Surrey at Guildford 2006, setting a new record for the highest individual first-class score by a Somerset player. Retired from international cricket after the fifth Test v England at Sydney 2006-07. Latest book, *See the Sunrise*, published in February 2008
Opinions on cricket: 'I believe Twenty20 and Pro40 cricket are the way of the future and provide a perfect blend to the four-day and Test match arenas. I also feel the shorter versions of the game will produce more athletic and professional county cricket players, which will be great for the game.'
Best batting: 342 Somerset v Surrey, Guildford 2006
Best bowling: 2-17 Australia A v South Africans, Brisbane 1997-98

2007 Season

	M	Inn	NO	Runs	HS	Avg	100	50	Ct	St	Balls	Runs	Wkts	Avg	BB	5I	10M
Test																	
FC	16	23	1	1231	315	55.95	3	3	14	-	0	0	0		-	-	-
ODI																	
List A	15	15	1	764	145	54.57	2	5	8	-	0	0	0		-	-	
20/20 Int																	
20/20	8	8	0	119	45	14.87	-	-	2	-	0	0	0		-	-	

Career Performances

	M	Inn	NO	Runs	HS	Avg	100	50	Ct	St	Balls	Runs	Wkts	Avg	BB	5I	10M
Test	105	182	12	7696	250	45.27	23	30	73	-	6	3	0		-	-	-
FC	320	556	52	25698	342	50.98	78	97	277	-	374	204	5	40.80	2-17	-	-
ODI	8	7	2	160	36	32.00	-	-	2	1	0	0	0		-	-	
List A	204	197	19	6994	146	39.29	11	49	97	2	193	215	7	30.71	3-51	-	
20/20 Int																	
20/20	16	16	1	583	97	38.86	-	4	5	-	0	0	0		-	-	

LANGEVELDT, C. K. Leicestershire

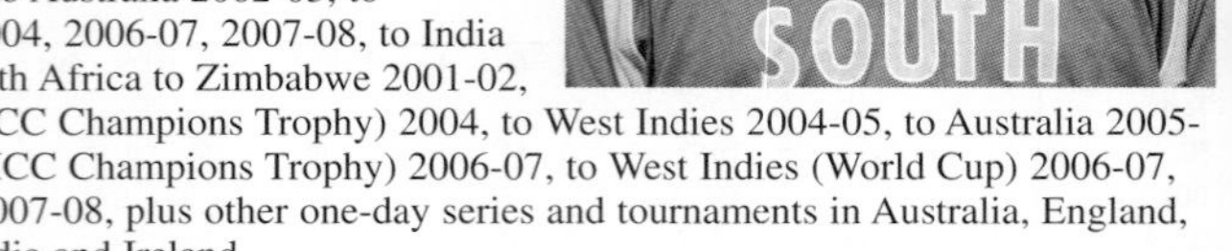

Name: Charl Kenneth Langeveldt
Role: Right-hand bat, right-arm fast-medium bowler
Born: 17 December 1974, Stellenbosch, South Africa
County debut: 2005 (Somerset), 2007 (Leicestershire)
County cap: 2005 (Somerset)
Test debut: 2004-05
ODI debut: 2001-02
Twenty20 Int debut: 2005-06
Career outside cricket: Formerly a prison officer
Overseas tours: South Africa Academy to Zimbabwe 1998-99; South Africa A to West Indies 2000, to Australia 2002-03, to Zimbabwe 2004, 2006-07, 2007-08, to India 2007-08; South Africa to Zimbabwe 2001-02, to England (ICC Champions Trophy) 2004, to West Indies 2004-05, to Australia 2005-06, to India (ICC Champions Trophy) 2006-07, to West Indies (World Cup) 2006-07, to Pakistan 2007-08, plus other one-day series and tournaments in Australia, England, Sri Lanka, India and Ireland
Overseas teams played for: Boland 1997-98 – 2002-03; Border 2003-04; Lions 2003-04 – 2006-07; Cape Cobras 2007-08 –
Extras: Represented South Africa in the 2002-03 World Cup. Took 5-46 on Test debut in the third Test v England at Cape Town 2004-05. Took 5-62 in the third ODI v West Indies at Bridgetown 2004-05, including a hat-trick (Bradshaw, Powell, Collymore) to secure a one-run win and series victory, winning the Man of the Match award. His other match awards include Man of the Match v Bangladesh at Edgbaston in the ICC Champions Trophy 2004 (3-17) and (shared with Lasith Malinga) v Sri Lanka at Providence Stadium, Guyana, in the 2006-07 World Cup (5-39). Was joint leading

wicket-taker (with Andrew Hall) for South Africa in the 2006-07 World Cup (14; av. 25.78). Was a temporary overseas player with Somerset during the 2005 season; was a temporary overseas player with Leicestershire during the 2007 season, as a replacement for RP Singh

Best batting: 56 Boland v Eastern Province, Port Elizabeth 1999-2000

Best bowling: 6-48 Lions v Titans, Potchefstroom 2006-07

Stop press: One of *South African Cricket Annual*'s five Cricketers of the Year 2007

2007 Season

	M	Inn	NO	Runs	HS	Avg	100	50	Ct	St	Balls	Runs	Wkts	Avg	BB	5I	10M
Test																	
FC	3	4	3	25	10 *	25.00	-	-	-	-	610	295	8	36.87	4-41	-	-
ODI																	
List A	3	1	0	9	9	9.00	-	-	-	-	180	142	3	47.33	2-53	-	
20/20 Int																	
20/20																	

Career Performances

	M	Inn	NO	Runs	HS	Avg	100	50	Ct	St	Balls	Runs	Wkts	Avg	BB	5I	10M
Test	6	4	2	16	10	8.00	-	-	2	-	999	593	16	37.06	5-46	1	-
FC	69	87	33	781	56	14.46	-	1	19	-	12465	6131	212	28.91	6-48	6	1
ODI	48	10	3	23	9	3.28	-	-	7	-	2251	1885	63	29.92	5-39	2	
List A	139	51	16	250	33 *	7.14	-	-	25	-	6567	4968	203	24.47	5-7	6	
20/20 Int	2	2	1	2	2	2.00	-	-	1	-	36	34	4	8.50	2-14	-	
20/20	8	3	2	2	2	2.00	-	-	5	-	168	193	6	32.16	2-14	-	

52. Whose 210 in the first Test between England and New Zealand at Trent Bridge in 1994 was the last of his 20 Test hundreds?

LATOUF, K. J. — Hampshire

Name: Kevin John Latouf
Role: Right-hand bat, right-arm medium bowler
Born: 7 September 1985, Pretoria, South Africa
Height: 5ft 10in **Weight:** 12st
Nickname: Poindexter, Mushy, Latsy, Kev
County debut: 2005 (one-day), 2006 (first-class)
Parents: Colin and Josephine
Marital status: Single
Education: Millfield School; Barton Peveril Sixth Form College
Qualifications: 11 GCSEs, 4 AS-Levels
Overseas tours: West of England U15 to West Indies 2000, 2001
Overseas teams played for: Melville CC, Perth ('briefly')
Cricket moments to forget: 'Golden duck in England U15 trial match'
Cricket superstitions: 'Don't believe in superstition'
Cricketers particularly admired: Ricky Ponting, Jonty Rhodes, Allan Donald
Other sports played: Tennis (county trials), rugby (Bristol and Somerset trials), golf ('fun'), surfing, snowboarding
Other sports followed: Rugby (Natal Sharks), football (Arsenal), AFL (Collingwood)
Favourite band: Coldplay
Extras: Played for West of England U13, U14 and U15. Played for ECB U17 and ECB U19. Played in Hampshire's 2nd XI Trophy winning side 2003. Represented England U19 2005
Best batting: 29 Hampshire v LUCCE, Rose Bowl 2006

2007 Season (did not make any first-class or one-day appearances)

Career Performances

	M	Inn	NO	Runs	HS	Avg	100	50	Ct	St	Balls	Runs	Wkts	Avg	BB	5I	10M
Test																	
FC	1	1	0	29	29	29.00	-	-	-	-	0	0	0		-	-	-
ODI																	
List A	10	9	2	76	25	10.85	-	-	6	-	0	0	0		-	-	
20/20 Int																	
20/20																	

LAW, S. G. Lancashire

Name: Stuart Grant Law
Role: Right-hand bat, county captain
Born: 18 October 1968, Brisbane, Australia
Height: 6ft 1in **Weight:** 13st 7lbs
Nickname: Lawman, Judge
County debut: 1996 (Essex), 2002 (Lancashire)
County cap: 1996 (Essex), 2002 (Lancashire)
Benefit: 2007 (Lancashire)
Test debut: 1995-96
ODI debut: 1994-95
1000 runs in a season: 10
1st-Class 200s: 6
Place in batting averages: 8th av. 63.85 (2006 29th av. 55.15)
Parents: Grant and Pam
Wife and date of marriage: Debbie-Lee, 31 December 1998
Children: Max, 9 January 2002
Family links with cricket: 'Dad, grandad and uncles played'
Education: Craigslea State High School, Brisbane
Qualifications: Level 2 cricket coach
Off-season: 'Getting as much sun as possible'
Overseas tours: Australia B to Zimbabwe 1991-92; Young Australia (Australia A) to England and Netherlands 1995 (c); Australia to India and Pakistan (World Cup) 1995-96, to Sri Lanka (Singer World Series) 1996, to India (Titan World Series) 1996-97, to South Africa 1996-97 (one-day series), to New Zealand (one-day series) 1997-98
Overseas teams played for: Queensland Bulls 1988-89 – 2003-04
Career highlights to date: 'Playing for Australia. Winning first ever Sheffield Shield trophy with Queensland as captain [1994-95]'
Cricket superstitions: 'None'
Cricketers particularly admired: Greg Chappell, Viv Richards
Young players to look out for: Steve Croft, Gareth Cross, 'Max Law'
Other sports played: Golf ('very socially')
Other sports followed: Rugby league
Favourite band: Red Hot Chili Peppers, Foo Fighters
Relaxations: 'Beach'
Extras: Sheffield Shield Player of the Year 1990-91. Captain of Queensland 1994-95 – 1996-97 and 1999-2000 – 2001-02; is the most successful captain in modern-day Australian domestic cricket, having captained his state to five Sheffield Shield/Pura

Cup titles and to three one-day titles, and has a stand named after him at Queensland's Allan Border Field in Brisbane. One of *Wisden*'s Five Cricketers of the Year 1998. PCA Player of the Year 1999. Scored century (168) v Warwickshire at Edgbaston 2003, sharing with Carl Hooper (177) in a Lancashire record fifth-wicket partnership of 360 as the county scored 781. Lancashire Player of the Year 2003. Retired from Australian cricket at the end of 2003-04. Vice-captain of Lancashire 2005-07; appointed captain of Lancashire for 2008. Awarded Medal of the Order of Australia (OAM) in Australia Day Honours list 2007 for service to cricket as a state, national and international player. Is a UK citizen and not considered an overseas player
Opinions on cricket: 'Very lucky to do what I do.'
Best batting: 263 Essex v Somerset, Chelmsford 1999
Best bowling: 5-39 Queensland v Tasmania, Brisbane 1995-96

2007 Season

	M	Inn	NO	Runs	HS	Avg	100	50	Ct	St	Balls	Runs	Wkts	Avg	BB	5I	10M
Test																	
FC	14	22	2	1277	206	63.85	3	9	17	-	24	21	0		-	-	-
ODI																	
List A	2	2	0	118	89	59.00	-	1	1	-	0	0	0		-	-	
20/20 Int																	
20/20	5	5	0	87	44	17.40	-	-	2	-	0	0	0		-	-	

Career Performances

	M	Inn	NO	Runs	HS	Avg	100	50	Ct	St	Balls	Runs	Wkts	Avg	BB	5I	10M
Test	1	1	1	54	54 *		-	1	1	-	18	9	0		-	-	-
FC	352	576	63	26337	263	51.33	78	124	395	-	8433	4236	83	51.03	5-39	1	-
ODI	54	51	5	1237	110	26.89	1	7	12	-	807	635	12	52.91	2-22	-	
List A	375	354	26	11419	163	34.81	20	61	150	-	3855	3166	90	35.17	5-26	1	
20/20 Int																	
20/20	30	30	2	821	101	29.32	1	5	10	-	6	10	0		-	-	

LAWSON, M. A. K. Yorkshire

Name: Mark Anthony Kenneth Lawson
Role: Right-hand bat, right-arm leg-spin bowler
Born: 24 November 1985, Leeds
Height: 5ft 8in **Weight:** 12st ('approx')
Nickname: Sauce
County debut: 2004
Place in batting averages: (2006 238th av. 15.50)
Place in bowling averages: (2006 78th av. 34.50)
Parents: Anthony and Dawn
Marital status: Single

Family links with cricket: 'Father played local league cricket and encouraged me to take up the game'
Education: Castle Hall Language College, Mirfield, West Yorkshire
Qualifications: 11 GCSEs
Overseas tours: England U19 to Australia 2002-03, to Bangladesh (U19 World Cup) 2003-04, to India 2004-05
Cricketers particularly admired: Shane Warne, Gareth Batty
Other sports played: Football (school), rugby union (school, Cleckheaton 'in early teens'), rugby league (Dewsbury Moor ARLFC 'in early teens')
Other sports followed: Rugby league (Bradford Bulls)
Relaxations: Music, dining out, cinema

Extras: Played for Yorkshire Schools U11-U16 (captain U13-U15); ESCA North of England U14 and U15; North of England Development of Excellence U17 and U19. Represented England U15, U17 and U19. Awarded Brian Johnston Scholarship. Voted Yorkshire Supporters' Young Player of the Year 2003. 2nd XI cap 2006
Best batting: 44 Yorkshire v Hampshire, Rose Bowl 2006
Best bowling: 6-88 Yorkshire v Middlesex, Scarborough 2006

2007 Season

	M	Inn	NO	Runs	HS	Avg	100	50	Ct	St	Balls	Runs	Wkts	Avg	BB	5I	10M
Test																	
FC	2	2	1	9	5	9.00	-	-	1	-	144	122	0		-	-	-
ODI																	
List A																	
20/20 Int																	
20/20																	

Career Performances

	M	Inn	NO	Runs	HS	Avg	100	50	Ct	St	Balls	Runs	Wkts	Avg	BB	5I	10M
Test																	
FC	15	21	5	197	44	12.31	-	-	7	-	2331	1699	42	40.45	6-88	4	-
ODI																	
List A	4	4	0	30	20	7.50	-	-	1	-	118	141	3	47.00	2-50	-	
20/20 Int																	
20/20	2	1	1	4	4 *		-	-	1	-	48	87	3	29.00	2-34	-	

LAXMAN, V. V. S. Lancashire

Name: Vangipurappu Venkata Sai (VVS) Laxman
Role: Right-hand bat, right-arm off-break bowler
Born: 1 November 1974, Hyderabad, India
County debut: 2007
Test debut: 1996-97
ODI debut: 1997-98
1st-Class 200s: 4
1st-Class 300s: 2
Place in batting averages: 49th av. 44.56
Overseas tours: India U19 to England 1994; India to South Africa 1996-97, to West Indies 1996-97, to New Zealand 1998-99; to Australia 1999-2000, to Zimbabwe 2001, to South Africa 2001-02, to West Indies 2001-02, to England 2002, to Sri Lanka (ICC Champions Trophy) 2002-03, to New Zealand 2002-03, to Australia 2003-04, to Pakistan 2003-04, to England (ICC Champions Trophy) 2004, to Bangladesh 2004-05, to Zimbabwe 2005-06, to Pakistan 2005-06, to West Indies 2006, to South Africa 2006-07, to England 2007, to Australia 2007-08, plus other one-day tournaments in Sharjah, Malaysia, Sri Lanka, Netherlands and England
Overseas teams played for: Hyderabad, India 1992-93 –
Extras: Popularly nicknamed 'Very Very Special'. One of *Wisden*'s Five Cricketers of the Year 2002. Scored 281 in the second Test v Australia in Kolkata 2000-01 (following a first-innings 59), in the process sharing with Rahul Dravid (180) in a record fifth-wicket partnership for India in Tests (376) and winning Man of the Match award. Scored 178 in the fourth Test v Australia in Sydney 2003-04, in the process sharing with Sachin Tendulkar (241) in a record fourth-wicket partnership for India in Tests (353). His other series and match awards include Man of the [Test] Series v New Zealand 2003-04 and Man of the Match v Australia in Brisbane in the VB Series 2003-04 (103*) and v Pakistan in the fifth ODI in Lahore 2003-04 (107). Was a temporary overseas player with Lancashire during the 2007 season as a replacement for Brad Hodge
Best batting: 353 Hyderabad v Karnataka, Bangalore 1999-2000
Best bowling: 3-11 Hyderabad v Railways, Delhi (KS) 1999-2000

2007 Season

	M	Inn	NO	Runs	HS	Avg	100	50	Ct	St	Balls	Runs	Wkts	Avg	BB	5I	10M
Test	3	5	1	205	54	51.25	-	2	4	-	6	5	0		-	-	-
FC	11	18	2	713	103	44.56	2	5	15	-	54	36	1	36.00	1-16	-	-
ODI																	
List A	3	3	1	161	85 *	80.50	-	2	-	-	24	28	0		-	-	
20/20 Int																	
20/20																	

Career Performances

	M	Inn	NO	Runs	HS	Avg	100	50	Ct	St	Balls	Runs	Wkts	Avg	BB	5I	10M
Test	83	135	16	5083	281	42.71	10	29	90	-	258	105	1	105.00	1-32	-	-
FC	193	312	33	14450	353	51.79	42	65	211	-	1688	707	20	35.35	3-11	-	-
ODI	86	83	7	2338	131	30.76	6	10	39	-	42	40	0		-	-	
List A	166	161	18	4944	131	34.57	9	27	72	-	698	548	8	68.50	2-42	-	
20/20 Int																	
20/20																	

LEE, J. E. — Yorkshire

Name: James Edward Lee
Role: Left-hand bat, right-arm medium-fast bowler
Born: 23 December 1988, Sheffield
Height: 6ft 1in **Weight:** 12st
Nickname: Binga
County debut: 2006
Parents: Diane and Steven
Marital status: Single
Family links with cricket: Father played Yorkshire Colts
Education: Immanuel College, Bradford
Qualifications: 8 GCSEs, 2 AS-levels
Off-season: 'England U19 – World Cup in Malaysia'
Overseas tours: England U19 to Malaysia (U19 World Cup) 2007-08
Career highlights to date: 'First-class debut v Lancashire in Roses match 2006'
Cricket superstitions: 'Tap three times'
Cricketers particularly admired: Brett Lee
Young players to look out for: Joe Root

Other sports followed: Football (Arsenal FC)
Favourite band: Reverend And The Makers
Relaxations: 'TV'
Opinions on cricket: 'Twenty20 cricket and internationals sell out all over the country, highlighting cricket's improving popularity and also showing that it is yet to reach its peak.'
Best batting: 21* Yorkshire v Lancashire, Old Trafford 2006

2007 Season (did not make any first-class or one-day appearances)

Career Performances

	M	Inn	NO	Runs	HS	Avg	100	50	Ct	St	Balls	Runs	Wkts	Avg	BB	5I	10M
Test																	
FC	1	2	1	22	21 *	22.00	-	-	-	-	54	36	0		-	-	-
ODI																	
List A																	
20/20 Int																	
20/20																	

LETT, R. J. H. — Somerset

Name: Robin Jonathan Hugh Lett
Role: Right-hand top/middle-order bat, right-arm medium bowler
Born: 23 December 1986, Westminster, London
Height: 6ft 2in **Weight:** 13st 5lbs
Nickname: Letty
County debut: 2006
Parents: Angela and Brian
Marital status: Single
Family links with cricket: 'Grandfather, Peter Jaques, Leicestershire CCC'
Education: Millfield School; Oxford Brookes University
Qualifications: 3 A-levels
Overseas tours: Millfield School to South Africa 2000, 2002; West of England to West Indies 2002

Career highlights to date: 'Championship fifty on debut v Glamorgan, August 2006'
Cricket moments to forget: 'Any time I have bowled'
Cricket superstitions: 'None'
Cricketers particularly admired: Nasser Hussain, Michael Atherton

Young players to look out for: Craig Kieswetter, Rory Hamilton-Brown
Other sports played: 'Any ball games'
Other sports followed: Football (Manchester United), rugby (Harlequins)
Favourite band: Oasis
Relaxations: 'Cards, swimming'
Extras: Scored 57-ball 50 on first-class debut v Glamorgan at Taunton 2006. Somerset 2nd XI Player of the Year 2006. Played for Oxford UCCE 2007
Opinions on cricket: 'The game is moving so fast it is difficult to know where to start. I think it's important that we keep the traditional values of the game going – for example, more Test cricket and no technology for lbw decisions.'
Best batting: 57 OUCCE v Glamorgan, The Parks 2007

2007 Season (did not make any first-class or one-day appearances for his county)

Career Performances

	M	Inn	NO	Runs	HS	Avg	100	50	Ct	St	Balls	Runs	Wkts	Avg	BB	5I	10M
Test																	
FC	6	10	1	208	57	23.11	-	3	2	-	0	0	0		-	-	-
ODI																	
List A																	
20/20 Int																	
20/20																	

53. Who in 1960 became the first South Africa bowler to take a Test hat-trick when he also became the first ever bowler to take a Test hat-trick at Lord's?

LEVY, S. A. M. — Middlesex

Name: Shaun Anthony Matthew Levy
Role: Left-hand bat, right-arm medium-fast bowler
Born: 13 May 1988, Edmonton, Middlesex
Height: 5ft 7in **Weight:** 10st 7lbs
County debut: No first-team appearance
Parents: Bing and Delores
Marital status: Single
Education: Enfield Grammar School; University of Kent
Qualifications: 10 GCSEs, 2 AS-levels, ACVE Double Award Advanced Business
Career outside cricket: Student
Off-season: 'I am currently playing in the Kent Indoor League for the university and training hard for the coming season'
Career highlights to date: 'Getting 114 on my Middlesex 2nd XI debut in 2005 against Surrey'

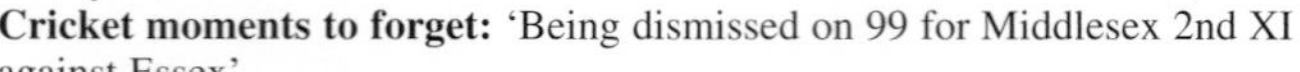

Cricket moments to forget: 'Being dismissed on 99 for Middlesex 2nd XI against Essex'
Cricket superstitions: 'None'
Cricketers particularly admired: Brian Lara, Matthew Hayden
Young players to look out for: Steven Finn
Other sports played: Football
Other sports followed: Football (Arsenal), basketball (LA Lakers)
Injuries: Out for four weeks with a broken hand
Favourite band: Jadakiss
Relaxations: 'Reading, music, designing'
Extras: His Middlesex CCC age-group awards include Ron Gerard batting awards in 2001 and 2002. Winchmore Hill U15 Player of the Year 2002 and 1st XI Player of the Year 2005, 2006, scoring club record 987 runs (av. 75.92) in the Middlesex League 2006; scored 11 hundreds and 13 fifties in all cricket 2006. Middlesex CCC Young Player of the Year 2006
Opinions on cricket: 'The game is evolving more and more into a batsman's game and also batsmen are becoming increasingly aggressive.'

LEWIS, J. Gloucestershire

Name: Jonathan (Jon) Lewis
Role: Right-hand bat, right-arm fast-medium bowler, county captain
Born: 26 August 1975, Aylesbury
Height: 6ft 3in **Weight:** 14st
Nickname: Lewy, JJ, King Black
County debut: 1995
County cap: 1998
Benefit: 2007
Test debut: 2006
ODI debut: 2005
Twenty20 Int debut: 2005
50 wickets in a season: 6
Place in batting averages: 262nd av. 13.00 (2006 221st av. 17.93)
Place in bowling averages: 108th av. 39.33 (2006 6th av. 21.70)
Parents: John and Jane
Marital status: Married
Children: Jacob, 2007
Education: Churchfields School, Swindon; Swindon College
Qualifications: 9 GCSEs, BTEC in Leisure and Hospitality, Level III coach
Overseas tours: Bath Schools to New South Wales 1993; England A to West Indies 2000-01, to Sri Lanka 2004-05; England to South Africa 2004-05, to India (ICC Champions Trophy) 2006-07, to Australia 2006-07 (C'wealth Bank Series), to West Indies (World Cup) 2006-07
Overseas teams played for: Marist, Christchurch, New Zealand 1994-95; Richmond City, Melbourne 1995-96; Wanderers, Johannesburg 1996-98; Techs CC, Cape Town 1998-99; Randwick-Petersham, Sydney 2003-04
Cricket moments to forget: 'Any injury'
Cricket superstitions: 'I always get a haircut if I go for a gallon'
Cricketers particularly admired: Courtney Walsh, Jack Russell, Jonty Rhodes
Other sports played: Golf (7 handicap), football (Bristol North West FC)
Other sports followed: Football (Swindon Town FC)
Favourite band: Brand New Heavies
Relaxations: Movies
Extras: Was on Northamptonshire staff in 1994 but made no first-team appearance. Took Championship hat-trick (Gallian, Afzaal, Morris) v Nottinghamshire at Trent Bridge 2000. Leading first-class wicket-taker among English bowlers in 2000 with 72 wickets (av. 20.91). Gloucestershire Player of the Year 2000. C&G Man of the Match award for his 4-39 v Hampshire at Bristol 2004. ECB National Academy 2004-05,

2006-07. Took 4-24 v Australia at The Rose Bowl in Twenty20 International 2005. Captain of Gloucestershire since 2006

Best batting: 62 Gloucestershire v Worcestershire, Cheltenham 1999

Best bowling: 8-95 Gloucestershire v Zimbabweans, Gloucester 2000

2007 Season

	M	Inn	NO	Runs	HS	Avg	100	50	Ct	St	Balls	Runs	Wkts	Avg	BB	5I	10M
Test																	
FC	8	8	1	91	42 *	13.00	-	-	2	-	901	472	12	39.33	5-41	1	-
ODI	1	1	0	17	17	17.00	-	-	-	-	60	63	1	63.00	1-63	-	
List A	6	5	3	19	17	9.50	-	-	-	-	257	280	9	31.11	4-45	-	
20/20 Int																	
20/20	3	1	0	17	17	17.00	-	-	1	-	66	59	3	19.66	2-28	-	

Career Performances

	M	Inn	NO	Runs	HS	Avg	100	50	Ct	St	Balls	Runs	Wkts	Avg	BB	5I	10M
Test	1	2	0	27	20	13.50	-	-	-	-	246	122	3	40.66	3-68	-	-
FC	166	230	48	2604	62	14.30	-	5	40	-	30668	15672	586	26.74	8-95	31	5
ODI	13	8	2	50	17	8.33	-	-	-	-	716	500	18	27.77	4-36	-	
List A	172	100	39	635	40	10.40	-	-	30	-	8098	6058	225	26.92	5-19	2	
20/20 Int	2	2	1	1	1	1.00	-	-	1	-	42	55	4	13.75	4-24	-	
20/20	23	10	4	134	43	22.33	-	-	4	-	475	633	29	21.82	4-24	-	

LEWRY, J. D. — Sussex

Name: Jason David Lewry

Role: Left-hand bat, left-arm fast-medium bowler

Born: 2 April 1971, Worthing

Height: 6ft 3in **Weight:** 'Going up'

Nickname: Lew, Lewie

County debut: 1994

County cap: 1996

Benefit: 2002

50 wickets in a season: 5

Place in batting averages: (2006 265th av. 11.12)

Place in bowling averages: 70th av. 30.81 (2006 9th av. 23.17)

Parents: David and Veronica

Wife and date of marriage: Naomi Madeleine, 18 August 1997

Children: William, 14 February 1998; Louis, 20 November 2000
Family links with cricket: Father coaches
Education: Durrington High School, Worthing; Worthing Sixth Form College
Qualifications: 6 O-levels, 3 GCSEs, City and Guilds, NCA Award
Career outside cricket: 'Still looking, but with more urgency with each passing year!'
Overseas tours: Goring CC to Isle of Wight 1992, 1993; England A to Zimbabwe and South Africa 1998-99
Cricket moments to forget: 'King pair, Eastbourne 1995'
Cricketers particularly admired: David Gower, Martin Andrews, Darren Lehmann
Other sports played: Golf, squash; darts, pool ('anything you can do in a pub')
Other sports followed: Football (West Ham United)
Favourite band: REM
Relaxations: Golf, pub games, films
Extras: Took seven wickets in 14 balls v Hampshire at Hove 2001, the second most (most by a seamer) outstanding spell of wicket-taking in first-class cricket (after Pat Pocock's seven in 11 for Surrey v Sussex at Eastbourne in 1972). His 5-75 v Lancashire at Liverpool 2006 included his 500th first-class wicket (Glen Chapple)
Opinions on cricket: 'More points should be awarded for a four-day win – 14 not enough.'
Best batting: 72 Sussex v Surrey, The Oval 2004
Best bowling: 8-106 Sussex v Leicestershire, Hove 2003

2007 Season

	M	Inn	NO	Runs	HS	Avg	100	50	Ct	St	Balls	Runs	Wkts	Avg	BB	5I	10M
Test																	
FC	14	14	6	73	13 *	9.12	-	-	4	-	2089	1017	33	30.81	4-81	-	-
ODI																	
List A	2	0	0	0	0		-	-	-	-	0	0	0		-	-	
20/20 Int																	
20/20																	

Career Performances

	M	Inn	NO	Runs	HS	Avg	100	50	Ct	St	Balls	Runs	Wkts	Avg	BB	5I	10M
Test																	
FC	166	219	59	1682	72	10.51	-	2	45	-	28613	15065	570	26.42	8-106	31	4
ODI																	
List A	78	44	15	217	16 *	7.48	-	-	13	-	3531	2712	100	27.12	4-29	-	
20/20 Int																	
20/20	11	4	1	10	8 *	3.33	-	-	4	-	197	239	14	17.07	3-34	-	

LIDDLE, C. J. Sussex

Name: Christopher (Chris) John Liddle
Role: Right-hand bat, left-arm fast-medium bowler
Born: 1 February 1984, Middlesbrough
Height: 6ft 4in **Weight:** 13st
Nickname: Lids, Chuck, Ice Man, Dolce
County debut: 2005 (Leicestershire), 2007 (Sussex)
Place in bowling averages: (2006 120th av. 43.45)
Parents: Pat and John
Marital status: Single
Family links with cricket: 'Brother plays cricket'
Education: Nunthorpe Comprehensive School, Middlesbrough; TTE Modern Apprenticeship
Qualifications: 9 GCSEs, fully qualified instrument artificer, Level 1 coaching
Off-season: 'On the Skills Set at Loughborough and training in Brighton'
Overseas teams played for: Balcatta CC, Perth
Cricket superstitions: 'Too many to list'
Cricketers particularly admired: Mushtaq Ahmed, Naved-ul-Hasan, Jason Lewry
Young players to look out for: Ben Brown, Mike Thornely, Tom Smith, Mike Gould
Other sports played: Football
Other sports followed: Football (Middlesbrough)
Injuries: Hamstring strain
Favourite band: The Killers
Extras: Yorkshire Area Bowler of the Year 2001-02. Has attended Paul Terry Academy, Perth
Best batting: 53 Sussex v Worcestershire, Hove 2007
Best bowling: 3-42 Leicestershire v Somerset, Leicester 2006

2007 Season

	M	Inn	NO	Runs	HS	Avg	100	50	Ct	St	Balls	Runs	Wkts	Avg	BB	5I	10M
Test																	
FC	5	5	1	99	53	24.75	-	1	3	-	670	365	5	73.00	2-43	-	-
ODI																	
List A	5	1	0	11	11	11.00	-	-	1	-	228	239	5	47.80	3-60	-	
20/20 Int																	
20/20																	

Career Performances

	M	Inn	NO	Runs	HS	Avg	100	50	Ct	St	Balls	Runs	Wkts	Avg	BB	5I	10M
Test																	
FC	12	11	4	105	53	15.00	-	1	5	-	1514	888	16	55.50	3-42	-	-
ODI																	
List A	6	2	0	12	11	6.00	-	-	2	-	276	289	5	57.80	3-60	-	
20/20 Int																	
20/20																	

LOGAN, R. J. Northamptonshire

Name: Richard James Logan
Role: Right-hand bat, right-arm fast bowler
Born: 28 January 1980, Cannock, Staffordshire
Height: 6ft 1in **Weight:** 14st
Nickname: Bungle
County debut: 1999 (Northants), 2001 (Notts), 2005 (Hants)
Place in bowling averages: 127th av. 43.73
Parents: Margaret and Robert
Marital status: Single
Family links with cricket: 'Dad played local cricket for Cannock'
Education: Wolverhampton Grammar School
Qualifications: 11 GCSEs, 1 A-level
Overseas tours: England U17 to Bermuda (International Youth Tournament) 1997; England U19 to South Africa (including U19 World Cup) 1997-98, to New Zealand 1998-99
Overseas teams played for: St George, Sydney 1999-2000; Lancaster Park, New Zealand; Rovers, Durban; Northerns Goodwood, Cape Town
Career highlights to date: 'Winning junior World Cup'
Cricketers particularly admired: Malcolm Marshall, Dennis Lillee
Other sports played: Hockey
Other sports followed: Football (Wolverhampton Wanderers)
Relaxations: 'Spending time with my mates. Training'
Extras: Played for Staffordshire U11-U19 (captain U13-U17); Midlands U14 and U15 (both as captain); HMC Schools U15. 1995 *Daily Telegraph*/Lombard U15 Midlands Bowler and Batsman of the Year. Played for Northamptonshire U17 and U19 national champions 1997. Played for England U15, U17 and U19. C&G Man of the Match award for his 5-24 v Suffolk at Mildenhall 2001. Took 5-26 v Lancashire at Trent Bridge 2003, the best return by a Nottinghamshire bowler in the Twenty20 Cup

Best batting: 37* Nottinghamshire v Hampshire, Trent Bridge 2001
Best bowling: 6-93 Nottinghamshire v Derbyshire, Trent Bridge 2001

2007 Season

	M	Inn	NO	Runs	HS	Avg	100	50	Ct	St	Balls	Runs	Wkts	Avg	BB	5I	10M
Test																	
FC	7	8	3	32	10	6.40	-	-	1	-	1134	656	15	43.73	3-38	-	-
ODI																	
List A	9	2	1	13	8 *	13.00	-	-	2	-	288	344	9	38.22	4-47	-	
20/20 Int																	
20/20																	

Career Performances

	M	Inn	NO	Runs	HS	Avg	100	50	Ct	St	Balls	Runs	Wkts	Avg	BB	5I	10M
Test																	
FC	53	72	16	526	37 *	9.39	-	-	16	-	7822	5129	132	38.85	6-93	4	-
ODI																	
List A	65	30	11	215	28 *	11.31	-	-	21	-	2548	2464	70	35.20	5-24	1	
20/20 Int																	
20/20	17	8	4	39	11 *	9.75	-	-	-	-	244	315	17	18.52	5-26	1	

LOUDON, A. G. R. — Warwickshire

Name: Alexander (Alex) Guy Rushworth Loudon
Role: Right-hand bat, right-arm off-spin bowler
Born: 6 September 1980, London
Height: 6ft 3in **Weight:** 14st 8lbs
Nickname: Noisy, The Minotaur, Dolf, A-Lo, Minor
County debut: 2002 (one-day, Kent), 2003 (first-class, Kent), 2005 (Warwickshire)
County cap: 2006 (Warwickshire)
ODI debut: 2006
Place in batting averages: 109th av. 34.00 (2006 170th av. 26.19)
Place in bowling averages: (2006 74th av. 34.28)
Parents: Jane and James
Marital status: Single
Family links with cricket: 'Father and brother played at Hampshire CCC. Grandmother played for Hindleap Harriers CC'

Education: Eton College; Durham University
Qualifications: 9 GCSEs, 1 AO-level, 3 A-levels, 2.1 degree, ECB Level 1 coaching
Overseas tours: England U19 to Malaysia and (U19 World Cup) Sri Lanka 1999-2000 (c); Kent to South Africa 2002; England to Pakistan 2005-06; England A to West Indies 2005-06, to Bangladesh 2006-07
Overseas teams played for: University, Western Australia 2005
Cricket superstitions: 'Not to have any!'
Cricketers particularly admired: Nick Knight
Other sports played: American football, golf, rackets, tennis
Other sports followed: Football (Man Utd, Brazil)
Favourite band: U2, The Levellers
Relaxations: 'Reading, studying, learning the guitar, TV, eating, travelling, photography, sleeping'
Extras: Captained England U15 in U15 World Cup 1996. Len Newbery Award for Best Schools Cricketer 1999. NBC Denis Compton Award for the most promising young Kent player 1999. Silk Trophy batting award 1999. Played for Durham UCCE 2001, 2002 and 2003, and was captain of Durham's BUSA winning side 2003. Represented British Universities 2003. Retired at the end of the 2007 season
Opinions on cricket: 'It is an exciting time for the game in England. Clever balancing is required to ensure its continued ascendancy in the public domain.'
Best batting: 172 DUCCE v Durham, Durham 2003
Best bowling: 6-47 Kent v Middlesex, Canterbury 2004

2007 Season

	M	Inn	NO	Runs	HS	Avg	100	50	Ct	St	Balls	Runs	Wkts	Avg	BB	5I	10M
Test																	
FC	16	24	1	782	105	34.00	3	2	9	-	1341	726	8	90.75	4-123	-	-
ODI																	
List A	16	14	5	281	53 *	31.22	-	1	6	-	468	374	7	53.42	2-27	-	
20/20 Int																	
20/20	8	7	0	73	24	10.42	-	-	6	-	78	114	4	28.50	2-18	-	

Career Performances

	M	Inn	NO	Runs	HS	Avg	100	50	Ct	St	Balls	Runs	Wkts	Avg	BB	5I	10M
Test																	
FC	76	122	7	3594	172	31.25	5	20	52	-	8381	4611	116	39.75	6-47	7	-
ODI	1	1	0	0	0	0.00	-	-	-	-	36	36	0		-	-	
List A	77	67	11	1312	73 *	23.42	-	8	29	-	2199	1779	44	40.43	4-48	-	
20/20 Int																	
20/20	25	21	0	222	27	10.57	-	-	12	-	270	327	20	16.35	5-33	1	

LOYE, M. B. Lancashire

Name: Malachy (Mal) Bernard Loye
Role: Right-hand bat, occasional wicket-keeper
Born: 27 September 1972, Northampton
Height: 6ft 2in **Weight:** 13st 12lbs
Nickname: Malcolm
County debut: 1991 (Northamptonshire), 2003 (Lancashire)
County cap: 1994 (Northamptonshire), 2003 (Lancashire)
Benefit: 2008 (Lancashire)
ODI debut: 2006-07
1000 runs in a season: 5
1st-Class 200s: 2
1st-Class 300s: 1
Place in batting averages: 100th av. 35.58 (2006 24th av. 58.90)
Parents: Patrick and Anne
Marital status: Single
Family links with cricket: 'Brother and Dad played for Cogenhoe CC in Northampton'
Education: Moulton Comprehensive, Northampton
Qualifications: GCSEs, coaching Levels 1-3
Off-season: 'Getting my body right; benefit'
Overseas tours: England U18 to Canada (International Youth Tournament) 1991; England U19 to Pakistan 1991-92; England A to South Africa 1993-94, to Zimbabwe and South Africa 1998-99; Northamptonshire to Cape Town 1993, to Zimbabwe 1995, 1998, to Johannesburg 1996, to Grenada 2001, 2002; England VI to Hong Kong 2006; England to Australia 2006-07 (C'wealth Bank Series)
Overseas teams played for: Riccarton, Christchurch 1992-93 – 1994-95; Canterbury B 1993; Onslow, Wellington 1995-96; North Perth 1997-98, 1999-2000; Claremont, Western Australia 2000-01; Auckland 2006-07
Career highlights to date: 'PCA Player of the Year 1998'
Cricket moments to forget: '[C&G] semi-final against Worcester 2003'
Cricketers particularly admired: Gordon Greenidge, Wayne Larkins, Peter Carlstein, Graeme Hick, John Crawley
Young players to look out for: Gareth Cross, Steven Croft
Other sports played: 'Muck about at anything'
Other sports followed: Football (Northampton Town, Liverpool), rugby union
Injuries: Out for six weeks with a back (disc) injury
Favourite band: U2

Player website: www.malloyebenefit.com
Extras: Played for England YC and for England U19. PCA Young Player of the Year and Whittingdale Young Player of the Year 1993. Scored 322* v Glamorgan at Northampton 1998 (the then highest individual first-class score for the county), in the process sharing with David Ripley in a new record partnership for any wicket for Northamptonshire (401). PCA Player of the Year 1998. Scored century (126) on Championship debut for Lancashire v Surrey at The Oval 2003 and another (113) in the next match v Nottinghamshire at Old Trafford to become the first batsman to score centuries in his first two matches for the county
Best batting: 322* Northamptonshire v Glamorgan, Northampton 1998
Best bowling: 1-8 Lancashire v Kent, Blackpool 2003

2007 Season

	M	Inn	NO	Runs	HS	Avg	100	50	Ct	St	Balls	Runs	Wkts	Avg	BB	5I	10M
Test																	
FC	8	14	2	427	105 *	35.58	1	1	5	-	0	0	0		-	-	-
ODI																	
List A	8	8	0	213	55	26.62	-	1	2	-	0	0	0		-	-	
20/20 Int																	
20/20	5	5	1	231	89	57.75	-	2	1	-	0	0	0		-	-	

Career Performances

	M	Inn	NO	Runs	HS	Avg	100	50	Ct	St	Balls	Runs	Wkts	Avg	BB	5I	10M
Test																	
FC	222	354	32	13317	322 *	41.35	39	53	109	-	55	61	1	61.00	1-8	-	-
ODI	7	7	0	142	45	20.28	-	-	-	-	0	0	0		-	-	
List A	278	272	31	8383	127	34.78	10	54	63	-	0	0	0		-	-	
20/20 Int																	
20/20	28	28	2	856	100	32.92	1	5	9	-	0	0	0		-	-	

54. Who is reputed to have uttered 'You guys are history' before turning in 9-57 at The Oval in 1994?

LUCAS, D. S. Northamptonshire

Name: David Scott Lucas
Role: Right-hand bat, left-arm medium-fast bowler
Born: 19 August 1978, Nottingham
Height: 6ft 3in **Weight:** 13st 3lbs
Nickname: Muke, Lukey
County debut: 1999 (Nottinghamshire), 2005 (Yorkshire), 2007 (Northamptonshire)
Place in batting averages: 188th av. 23.88
Place in bowling averages: 110th av. 39.52
Parents: Mary and Terry
Marital status: Married
Education: Djanogly City Technology College, Nottingham
Qualifications: 6 GCSEs, pass in Computer-Aided Design
Overseas tours: England (Indoor) to Australia (Indoor Cricket World Cup) 1998

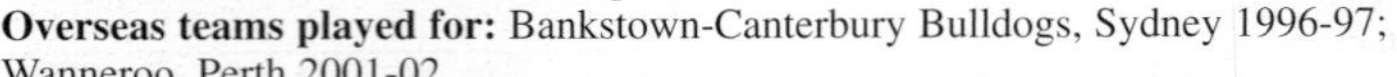

Overseas teams played for: Bankstown-Canterbury Bulldogs, Sydney 1996-97; Wanneroo, Perth 2001-02
Career highlights to date: 'Getting Man of the Match against Derbyshire in a close fixture' (*4-27 v Derbyshire at Derby in the NUL 2000*)
Cricket superstitions: 'Always walk back to the left of my mark when bowling. Always put left pad on first'
Cricketers particularly admired: Wasim Akram, Glenn McGrath, Steve Waugh, Damien Martyn
Other sports played: Indoor cricket, football
Other sports followed: Football (Arsenal FC)
Relaxations: 'Food, cars, PS2, movies'
Extras: Won Yorkshire League with Rotherham in 1996. NBC Denis Compton Award for the most promising young Nottinghamshire player 2000
Best batting: 49 Nottinghamshire v DUCCE, Trent Bridge 2002
Best bowling: 5-49 Yorkshire v Bangladesh A, Headingley 2005

2007 Season

	M	Inn	NO	Runs	HS	Avg	100	50	Ct	St	Balls	Runs	Wkts	Avg	BB	5I	10M
Test																	
FC	9	13	4	215	37	23.88	-	-	2	-	1212	751	19	39.52	5-49	1	-
ODI																	
List A	9	3	1	21	13 *	10.50	-	-	1	-	309	317	9	35.22	3-43	-	
20/20 Int																	
20/20	7	2	2	7	5 *		-	-	-	-	90	142	5	28.40	2-37	-	

Career Performances

	M	Inn	NO	Runs	HS	Avg	100	50	Ct	St	Balls	Runs	Wkts	Avg	BB	5I	10M
Test																	
FC	32	41	12	651	49	22.44	-	-	5	-	4526	2744	79	34.73	5-49	3	-
ODI																	
List A	44	16	4	130	32	10.83	-	-	5	-	1740	1703	53	32.13	4-27	-	
20/20 Int																	
20/20	7	2	2	7	5 *		-	-	-	-	90	142	5	28.40	2-37	-	

LUMB, M. J. — Hampshire

Name: Michael John Lumb
Role: Left-hand bat, right-arm medium bowler
Born: 12 February 1980, Johannesburg, South Africa
Height: 6ft **Weight:** 13st
Nickname: China, Joe
County debut: 2000 (Yorkshire), 2007 (Hampshire)
County cap: 2003 (Yorkshire)
1000 runs in a season: 1
Place in batting averages: 139th av. 31.00 (2006 69th av. 41.86)
Parents: Richard and Sue
Marital status: Single
Family links with cricket: Father played for Yorkshire. Uncle played for Natal
Education: St Stithians College
Qualifications: Matriculation
Overseas tours: Transvaal U19 to Barbados; Yorkshire to Cape Town 2001, to Grenada 2002; England A to Malaysia and India 2003-04
Overseas teams played for: Pirates CC, Johannesburg; Wanderers CC, Johannesburg
Cricket moments to forget: 'Relegation in 2002 [with Yorkshire]'
Cricket superstitions: 'None'
Cricketers particularly admired: Graham Thorpe, Darren Lehmann, Craig White, Stephen Fleming
Other sports played: Golf
Other sports followed: Rugby union (Sharks in Super 14, Leeds Tykes)
Favourite band: Oasis
Relaxations: 'Golf, socialising with friends'
Extras: Scored maiden first-class century (122) v Leicestershire at Headingley 2001; the Lumbs thus became only the fourth father and son to have scored centuries for

Yorkshire. Yorkshire Young Player of the Year 2002, 2003. ECB National Academy 2003-04. C&G Man of the Match award in the quarter-final v Northamptonshire at Headingley 2005 (89). Scored 98 v Durham at Headingley 2006, in the process sharing with Darren Lehmann (339) in a new record fourth-wicket partnership for Yorkshire (358)

Best batting: 144 Yorkshire v Middlesex, Southgate 2006
Best bowling: 2-10 Yorkshire v Kent, Canterbury 2001

2007 Season

	M	Inn	NO	Runs	HS	Avg	100	50	Ct	St	Balls	Runs	Wkts	Avg	BB	5I	10M
Test																	
FC	16	25	0	775	89	31.00	-	8	13	-	24	30	0		-	-	-
ODI																	
List A	17	17	0	654	108	38.47	1	6	6	-	0	0	0		-	-	
20/20 Int																	
20/20	7	7	0	71	22	10.14	-	-	-	-	0	0	0		-	-	

Career Performances

	M	Inn	NO	Runs	HS	Avg	100	50	Ct	St	Balls	Runs	Wkts	Avg	BB	5I	10M
Test																	
FC	97	166	12	5061	144	32.86	8	33	61	-	318	242	6	40.33	2-10	-	-
ODI																	
List A	125	119	8	3303	108	29.75	1	24	38	-	12	28	0		-	-	
20/20 Int																	
20/20	33	33	3	513	84 *	17.10	-	4	8	-	36	65	3	21.66	3-32	-	

LUNGLEY, T. Derbyshire

Name: Tom Lungley
Role: Left-hand bat, right-arm medium bowler
Born: 25 July 1979, Derby
Height: 6ft 2in **Weight:** 13st
Nickname: Lungfish, Monkfish, Sweaty, Full Moon, Half Moon, Lungo
County debut: 2000
County cap: 2007
50 wickets in a season: 1
Place in batting averages: 270th av. 11.26
Place in bowling averages: 42nd av. 26.35
Parents: Richard and Christina
Marital status: 'Taken'
Family links with cricket: 'Dad was captain of Derby Road CC. Grandad was bat maker in younger days'
Education: Saint John Houghton School, Kirk Hallam; South East Derbyshire College

Qualifications: 9 GCSEs, Sport and Recreation Levels 1 and 2, pool lifeguard qualification, coaching qualifications in cricket, tennis, basketball, football and volleyball
Career outside cricket: Painter and decorator
Overseas teams played for: Delacombe Park, Melbourne 1999-2000
Cricket moments to forget: 'Unable to speak when interviewed by Sybil Ruscoe on *Channel 4 Cricket Roadshow* (live)'
Cricketers particularly admired: Ian Botham, Dennis Lillee, Courtney Walsh, Curtly Ambrose, Brian Lara, Richard Hadlee, Glenn McGrath
Other sports played: 'Enjoy playing most sports, mainly football and basketball'
Other sports followed: Football (Derby County), basketball
Extras: First home-grown cricketer to become professional from Ockbrook and Borrowash CC (for whom he struck the Derbyshire Premier League 2006 season's best, 213 v Marehay). NBC Denis Compton Award for the most promising young Derbyshire player 2003
Best batting: 47 Derbyshire v Warwickshire, Derby 2001
Best bowling: 5-20 Derbyshire v Leicestershire, Derby 2007

2007 Season

	M	Inn	NO	Runs	HS	Avg	100	50	Ct	St	Balls	Runs	Wkts	Avg	BB	5I	10M
Test																	
FC	15	21	6	169	30 *	11.26	-	-	5	-	2615	1555	59	26.35	5-20	3	-
ODI																	
List A	10	5	2	13	6 *	4.33	-	-	2	-	408	356	13	27.38	3-11	-	
20/20 Int																	
20/20	6	2	1	8	8 *	8.00	-	-	1	-	100	130	6	21.66	4-11	-	

Career Performances

	M	Inn	NO	Runs	HS	Avg	100	50	Ct	St	Balls	Runs	Wkts	Avg	BB	5I	10M
Test																	
FC	38	57	12	593	47	13.17	-	-	13	-	5123	3297	108	30.52	5-20	3	-
ODI																	
List A	67	40	11	366	45	12.62	-	-	17	-	2529	2168	74	29.29	4-28	-	
20/20 Int																	
20/20	22	12	4	105	25	13.12	-	-	6	-	364	454	21	21.61	4-11	-	

LYTH, A. Yorkshire

Name: Adam Lyth
Role: Left-hand bat, right-arm medium bowler
Born: 25 September 1987, Whitby, North Yorkshire
Height: 5ft 9in **Weight:** 10st
Nickname: Peanut
County debut: 2006 (one-day), 2007 (first-class)
Parents: Alistair and Christine
Marital status: Single
Family links with cricket: 'Grandfather – wicket-keeper; father and brother played cricket'
Education: Caedmon School; Whitby Community College
Qualifications: GCSEs
Off-season: 'Training and playing cricket abroad'
Overseas tours: England U16 to South Africa 2004; England U19 to Malaysia 2006-07
Career highlights to date: 'Getting hundred [122] for England U19 on home ground at Scarborough in the first "Test" against Pakistan [2007]'
Cricket moments to forget: 'Getting caught by my brother when we played against each other'
Cricket superstitions: 'None'
Cricketers particularly admired: Craig White, Darren Lehmann, Graham Thorpe
Young players to look out for: Adil Rashid
Other sports played: Football (represented district and North Yorkshire; had trials with Man City and Sunderland); golf
Other sports followed: Football (Arsenal), 'follow all sports – sports mad'
Favourite band: Jay-Z
Relaxations: 'Socialising'
Extras: North Player of Tournament at Taunton at U13. Played in Bunbury Festival 2003. Led Yorkshire to U17 County Championship 2005. Represented England at U15, U16, U17 and U19 levels, scoring 64 and 113 on U19 "Test" debut v India U19 at Canterbury 2006. Scarborough and District Best Male Achiever award. Promising Yorkshire Young Cricketer award
Best batting: 31 Yorkshire v LUCCE, Headingley 2007
Best bowling: 1-12 Yorkshire v LUCCE, Headingley 2007

2007 Season

	M	Inn	NO	Runs	HS	Avg	100	50	Ct	St	Balls	Runs	Wkts	Avg	BB	5I	10M
Test																	
FC	1	1	0	31	31	31.00	-	-	-	-	6	12	1	12.00	1-12	-	-
ODI																	
List A	2	2	1	11	10	11.00	-	-	2	-	0	0	0		-	-	
20/20 Int																	
20/20																	

Career Performances

	M	Inn	NO	Runs	HS	Avg	100	50	Ct	St	Balls	Runs	Wkts	Avg	BB	5I	10M
Test																	
FC	1	1	0	31	31	31.00	-	-	-	-	6	12	1	12.00	1-12	-	-
ODI																	
List A	3	3	1	34	23	17.00	-	-	3	-	0	0	0		-	-	
20/20 Int																	
20/20																	

MacLEOD, C. S. — Warwickshire

Name: Calum Scott MacLeod
Role: Right-hand bat, right-arm medium-fast bowler
Born: 15 November 1988, Rutherglen, Glasgow
Height: 6ft 1in **Weight:** 13st 2lbs
Nickname: Cloudy, Highlander, Scot
County debut: No first-team appearance
Parents: Donald and Morag
Marital status: Single
Family links with cricket: 'Brother Allan (21) represented West District U15 and U18 and brother Niall (15) represented West District U13 and U15 and Scotland U12 and U13. Our mother Morag managed Scotland U12 for four years'
Education: Hillpark Secondary School, Glasgow
Qualifications: 8 Standard Grades, 2 Higher Grades
Off-season: 'On Cricket Scotland Scholarship to Sydney, Australia, playing grade cricket for Penrith CC'

Overseas tours: West District to Australia 2004-05; Warwickshire Academy to South Africa 2005-06; Scotland U19 to Sri Lanka (U19 World Cup) 2005-06, plus other Scotland age-group tours
Overseas teams played for: Penrith CC, Sydney 2007-08
Career highlights to date: 'Making first-class Scotland debut against UAE on 27 June 2007 at Ayr as youngest ever player for Scotland at full international level. Signing a two-year contract with Warwickshire CCC'
Cricket moments to forget: 'Being sacked as district U12 captain after only one game!'
Cricket superstitions: 'Scratch my guard mark on the crease nine times before batting'
Cricketers particularly admired: Glenn McGrath, Mohammad Ramzan ('Pakistan Test batsman who was local club professional and helped develop my game at a young age')
Young players to look out for: Richard Johnson (Warwickshire)
Other sports played: Hockey (Stepps HC Glasgow; represented West District and Scotland Select)
Other sports followed: Football (Celtic FC)
Injuries: Out for two weeks with a slight strain in left knee
Favourite band: Dire Straits
Relaxations: 'Like to go shopping, spend time with friends and listen to music'
Extras: City of Glasgow Young Sportsperson of the Year 2005 and North Lanarkshire Male Youth Sportsperson of the Year 2005. Has twice been European U19 Championship Player of the Year. Cricket Scotland National Young Player of the Year 2006, 2007. Warwickshire Most Improved 2nd XI Player 2007. Made first-class debut for Scotland v UAE in the ICC Inter-Continental Cup 2007 at Ayr
Opinions on cricket: 'To add interest and excitement to the one-day game, "power-play" regulations should be changed to mirror current Australian State cricket, where the mandatory ten-over period is followed by both the batting and fielding teams being able to choose another five-over period each.'

2007 Season (did not make any first-class or one-day appearances for his county)

Career Performances

	M	Inn	NO	Runs	HS	Avg	100	50	Ct	St	Balls	Runs	Wkts	Avg	BB	5I	10M
Test																	
FC	1	0	0	0	0		-	-	-	-	48	30	0		-	-	-
ODI																	
List A																	
20/20 Int																	
20/20																	

MADDY, D. L. Warwickshire

Name: Darren Lee Maddy
Role: Right-hand bat, right-arm medium bowler, county captain
Born: 23 May 1974, Leicester
Height: 5ft 9in **Weight:** 12st 7lbs
Nickname: Madds
County debut: 1993 (one-day, Leicestershire), 1994 (first-class, Leicestershire), 2007 (Warwickshire)
County cap: 1996 (Leicestershire), 2007 (Warwickshire)
Benefit: 2006 (Leicestershire)
Test debut: 1999
ODI debut: 1998
Twenty20 Int debut: 2007-08
1000 runs in a season: 4
1st-Class 200s: 2
Place in batting averages: 43rd av. 46.82 (2006 146th av. 29.88)
Place in bowling averages: 46th av. 27.26 (2006 141st av. 51.27)
Parents: William Arthur and Hilary Jean
Wife and date of marriage: Justine Marie, 7 October 2000
Children: George William, 13 October 2005
Family links with cricket: Father and younger brother, Greg, play club cricket
Education: Roundhill, Thurmaston; Wreake Valley, Syston
Qualifications: 8 GCSEs, Level 1 coach
Career outside cricket: Fitness advisor
Off-season: 'Spending time with my family; playing in the ICL'
Overseas tours: Leicestershire to Bloemfontein 1995, to Western Transvaal 1996, to Durban 1997, to Barbados 1998, to Anguilla 2000, to Potchefstroom 2001; England A to Kenya and Sri Lanka 1997-98, to Zimbabwe and South Africa 1998-99; England to South Africa and Zimbabwe 1999-2000, to South Africa (World 20/20) 2007-08; England VI to Hong Kong 2003, 2004, 2005, 2006; Lord's Taverners to Dubai 2006, 2007, 2008; Warwickshire to Grenada 2007
Overseas teams played for: Wanderers, Johannesburg 1992-93; Northern Free State, South Africa 1993-95; Rhodes University, South Africa 1995-97; Sunshine CC, Grenada 2002; Perth CC, 2002-04
Career highlights to date: 'Winning two Championship medals. Playing for England. Winning Twenty20 final 2004 and 2006. Being awarded the Warwickshire captaincy 2007'
Cricket moments to forget: 'Being relegated in two competitions 2007'

Cricket superstitions: 'Always put my left pad on first'
Cricketers particularly admired: 'Anyone who has made a success of their career'
Young players to look out for: Ian Westwood, Vaughn van Jaarsveld
Other sports played: Touch rugby, golf, squash, five-a-side football
Other sports followed: Rugby (Leicester Tigers), football (Leicester City), baseball, golf, boxing – 'most sports really except for horse racing and motor racing'
Injuries: Out for a week with a sprained ankle
Favourite band: 'Too many to mention – Two Tone Deaf, Bon Jovi, Def Leppard, Stereophonics, Aerosmith, Red Hot Chili Peppers'
Relaxations: 'Going to the gym, playing sport, spending time with my wife, Justine; listening to music, watching TV, going on holiday, scuba diving, bungee jumping, playing the drums'
Extras: Rapid Cricketline 2nd XI Championship Player of the Year 1994. Was leading run-scorer on England A's 1997-98 tour (687; av. 68.7). In 1998, broke the season record for runs scored in the B&H (629; av. 125.80), winning five Gold Awards. Scored 229* v Loughborough UCCE at Leicester 2003, in the process sharing with Brad Hodge (202*) in a record partnership for any wicket for Leicestershire (436*). Struck 60-ball 111 v Yorkshire at Headingley in the Twenty20 2004, in the process sharing with Brad Hodge (78) in a then competition record partnership for any wicket (167). Scored 86* (also took a wicket and two catches) in the final of the Twenty20 Cup at Trent Bridge 2006, becoming the first player to pass 1000 career runs in the competition and winning the Man of the Match award. President of the Leicestershire School Sports Federation. Vice-captain of Leicestershire July 2004-2005. Captain of Warwickshire since 2007
Opinions on cricket: 'Regional cricket against touring sides. Two one-day competitions – Twenty20 and 50-over cricket.'
Best batting: 229* Leicestershire v LUCCE, Leicester 2003
Best bowling: 5-37 Leicestershire v Hampshire, Rose Bowl 2002

2007 Season

	M	Inn	NO	Runs	HS	Avg	100	50	Ct	St	Balls	Runs	Wkts	Avg	BB	5I	10M
Test																	
FC	14	20	3	796	148 *	46.82	4	2	14	-	996	409	15	27.26	5-63	1	-
ODI																	
List A	15	14	0	541	117	38.64	2	3	10	-	282	237	4	59.25	2-28	-	
20/20 Int																	
20/20	8	8	1	167	51	23.85	-	1	6	-	72	104	3	34.66	2-30	-	

Career Performances

	M	Inn	NO	Runs	HS	Avg	100	50	Ct	St	Balls	Runs	Wkts	Avg	BB	5I	10M
Test	3	4	0	46	24	11.50	-	-	4	-	84	40	0		-	-	-
FC	228	370	24	11469	229 *	33.14	23	55	242	-	11448	6143	188	32.67	5-37	5	-
ODI	8	6	0	113	53	18.83	-	1	1	-	0	0	0		-	-	
List A	310	286	29	7929	167 *	30.85	11	47	121	-	6242	5264	180	29.24	4-16	-	
20/20 Int	4	4	0	113	50	28.25	-	1	1	-	18	26	3	8.66	2-6	-	
20/20	47	47	5	1391	111	33.11	1	11	28	-	560	728	25	29.12	2-6	-	

MAGOFFIN, S. J. — Surrey

Name: Steven (Steve) James Magoffin
Role: Left-hand bat, right-arm fast-medium bowler
Born: 17 December 1979, Corinda, Queensland, Australia
Height: 6ft 4in
Nickname: Mal
County debut: 2007
Education: Indooroopilly HS, Brisbane; Curtin University, Western Australia
Overseas tours: Australian Cricket Academy to India 2003-04; University of Western Australia to India 2006-07
Overseas teams played for: Western Australia 2004-05 –
Extras: Played for Queensland Colts, Queensland Academy of Sport and Australian Cricket Academy. Man of the Match v South Australia at Perth in the Pura Cup 2006-07 (3-18/4-13). Was a temporary overseas player with Surrey during the 2007 season as a locum for Matthew Nicholson
Best batting: 30 Western Australia v Victoria, Melbourne (SK) 2005-06
Best bowling: 8-47 Western Australia v South Australia, Perth 2005-06

2007 Season

	M	Inn	NO	Runs	HS	Avg	100	50	Ct	St	Balls	Runs	Wkts	Avg	BB	5I	10M
Test																	
FC	1	2	1	15	9 *	15.00	-	-	-	-	180	94	2	47.00	2-73	-	-
ODI																	
List A	2	1	1	5	5 *		-	-	-	-	92	115	4	28.75	4-58	-	
20/20 Int																	
20/20																	

Career Performances

	M	Inn	NO	Runs	HS	Avg	100	50	Ct	St	Balls	Runs	Wkts	Avg	BB	5I	10M
Test																	
FC	30	41	13	348	30	12.42	-	-	11	-	5815	2813	95	29.61	8-47	2	-
ODI																	
List A	23	12	8	38	9 *	9.50	-	-	9	-	1187	971	31	31.32	4-58	-	
20/20 Int																	
20/20	1	0	0	0	0		-	-	-	-	18	15	2	7.50	2-15	-	

MAHER, J. P. — Glamorgan

Name: James (Jimmy) Patrick Maher
Role: Left-hand bat, right-arm medium bowler, occasional wicket-keeper
Born: 27 February 1974, Innisfail, Queensland, Australia
Height: 6ft **Weight:** 13st 5lbs
Nickname: Rock, Mahbo
County debut: 2001 (Glamorgan), 2005 (Durham)
County cap: 2001 (Glamorgan)
ODI debut: 1997-98
1000 runs in a season: 1
1st-Class 200s: 4
Place in batting averages: 235th av. 16.80 (2006 101st av. 34.92)
Parents: Marie Ann and Warren George
Wife and date of marriage: Debbie, 6 April 2001
Children: Lily Matilda, 2002
Family links with cricket: Father and uncle played for Queensland Country
Education: St Augustine's College, Cairns; Nudgee College, Brisbane
Overseas tours: Australia U19 to New Zealand 1992-93; Queensland Academy to South Africa 1993; Australia to South Africa 2001-02 (one-day series), to Kenya (PSO Tri-Nation Tournament) 2002, to Sri Lanka (ICC Champions Trophy) 2002-03, to Africa (World Cup) 2002-03, to West Indies 2002-03 (one-day series), to India (TVS Cup) 2003-04
Overseas teams played for: Queensland 1993-94 –
Career highlights to date: 'Playing for Australia. Being part of Queensland's first ever Sheffield Shield title win at The Gabba [1994-95]'
Cricket moments to forget: 'Running out Allan Border on my debut'

Cricketers particularly admired: Allan Border, Matt Hayden, Shane Warne, Glenn McGrath
Other sports played: Squash ('played State titles U12-U16'), tennis ('ranked in top ten in Queensland at U14')
Other sports followed: Rugby union (Queensland Reds), rugby league (Canterbury Bulldogs)
Relaxations: 'Golf, dinner with friends, couple of lagers with mates'
Extras: Represented Australia U17 and U19. Attended Australian Cricket Academy 1993. Pura Cup Player of the Year 2001-02 (jointly with Brad Hodge of Victoria) and *Wisden Australia*'s Pura Cup Cricketer of the Year 2002-03. Recalled to Australia's one-day squad for tour of South Africa 2001-02 and was Man of the Match in his first two ODIs since 1997-98 (95 and 43*). His other match awards include Man of the Match in the ING Cup final 2004-05 v Tasmania at The Gabba (104) and in the Pura Cup final 2005-06 at The Gabba (223 out of Queensland's 900-6 dec). Captain of Queensland since 2002-03 and has captained Australia A. Was Glamorgan's overseas player in 2001, returning in 2003 and 2007; was a temporary overseas player with Durham during the 2005 season, returning in 2006
Best batting: 223 Queensland v Victoria, Brisbane 2005-06
Best bowling: 3-11 Queensland v Western Australia, Perth 1995-96

2007 Season

	M	Inn	NO	Runs	HS	Avg	100	50	Ct	St	Balls	Runs	Wkts	Avg	BB	5I	10M
Test																	
FC	8	15	0	252	55	16.80	-	1	9	-	0	0	0		-	-	-
ODI																	
List A	8	8	0	164	76	20.50	-	1	3	-	2	0	0		-	-	
20/20 Int																	
20/20	2	2	0	31	26	15.50	-	-	1	-	0	0	0		-	-	

Career Performances

	M	Inn	NO	Runs	HS	Avg	100	50	Ct	St	Balls	Runs	Wkts	Avg	BB	5I	10M
Test																	
FC	196	352	31	12803	223	39.88	26	61	199	3	852	504	10	50.40	3-11	-	-
ODI	26	20	3	438	95	25.76	-	1	18	-	0	0	0		-	-	
List A	207	201	18	7265	187	39.69	15	36	101	1	165	168	6	28.00	3-29	-	
20/20 Int																	
20/20	13	13	2	285	59	25.90	-	3	3	-	0	0	0		-	-	

MAHMOOD, S. I. Lancashire

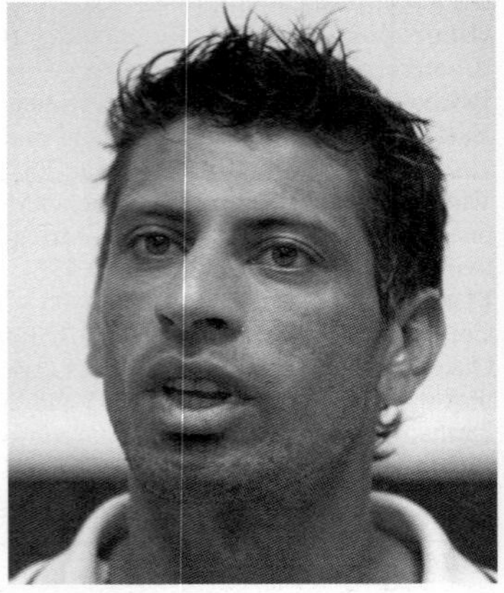

Name: Sajid Iqbal Mahmood
Role: Right-hand bat, right-arm fast-medium bowler
Born: 21 December 1981, Bolton
Height: 6ft 4in **Weight:** 12st 7lbs
Nickname: Saj, King
County debut: 2002
County cap: 2007
Test debut: 2006
ODI debut: 2004
Twenty20 Int debut: 2006
Place in batting averages: 256th av. 13.45 (2006 266th av. 11.00)
Place in bowling averages: 71st av. 31.83 (2006 21st av. 25.69)
Parents: Shahid and Femida
Marital status: Single
Family links with cricket: Father played in Bolton League; younger brother plays in Bolton League
Education: Smithills School; North College, Bolton (sixth form)
Qualifications: 9 GCSEs, 3 A-levels
Overseas tours: Lancashire to South Africa 2003; England A to Malaysia and India 2003-04, to Sri Lanka 2004-05, to West Indies 2005-06; England to India 2005-06 (one-day series), to India (ICC Champions Trophy) 2006-07, to Australia 2006-07, to West Indies (World Cup) 2006-07
Overseas teams played for: Napier, New Zealand 2002-03
Cricket moments to forget: 'None'
Cricket superstitions: 'None'
Cricketers particularly admired: Brett Lee, Shoaib Akhtar
Favourite band: Nelly, Eminem
Relaxations: 'Music and chillin' with mates'
Extras: NBC Denis Compton Award for the most promising young Lancashire player 2003. Man of the Match in the fifth ODI v Pakistan at Edgbaston 2006 (10-2-24-2) and v Bangladesh in Bridgetown in the World Cup 2006-07 (3-27). ECB National Academy 2003-04, 2004-05, 2005-06. Is cousin of boxer Amir Khan
Best batting: 94 Lancashire v Sussex, Old Trafford 2004
Best bowling: 5-37 Lancashire v DUCCE, Durham 2003

2007 Season

	M	Inn	NO	Runs	HS	Avg	100	50	Ct	St	Balls	Runs	Wkts	Avg	BB	5I	10M
Test																	
FC	10	14	3	148	41	13.45	-	-	3	-	1623	955	30	31.83	4-21	-	-
ODI																	
List A	9	3	0	25	24	8.33	-	-	3	-	346	353	20	17.65	5-16	1	
20/20 Int																	
20/20																	

Career Performances

	M	Inn	NO	Runs	HS	Avg	100	50	Ct	St	Balls	Runs	Wkts	Avg	BB	5I	10M
Test	8	11	1	81	34	8.10	-	-	-	-	1130	762	20	38.10	4-22	-	-
FC	54	71	10	862	94	14.13	-	2	10	-	7665	4755	150	31.70	5-37	3	-
ODI	25	15	4	85	22 *	7.72	-	-	1	-	1155	1128	29	38.89	4-50	-	
List A	95	54	15	332	29	8.51	-	-	11	-	4122	3570	142	25.14	5-16	1	
20/20 Int	2	1	1	0	0 *		-	-	-	-	42	63	1	63.00	1-34	-	
20/20	12	6	2	38	21	9.50	-	-	-	-	252	332	6	55.33	1-17	-	

MAHOMED, U. Durham

Name: Uzair Mahomed
Role: Right-hand bat, right-arm off-spin bowler; batting all-rounder
Born: 20 August 1987, Johannesburg, South Africa
Height: 5ft 9in **Weight:** 11st 6lbs
Nickname: Uzi
County debut: No first-team appearance
Parents: Ishtiyak and Faghmida
Marital status: Single
Family links with cricket: Father captained Transvaal Schools and represented South Africa Schools. Brother played for Yorkshire Schools and Yorkshire Academy
Education: Woodhouse Grove; Bradford Grammar School
Qualifications: 10 GCSEs, 3 A-levels
Off-season: 'Training hard, working on my fitness'
Overseas tours: Two school tours to West Indies; Durham to Mumbai (World Cricket Academy), to Cape Town
Overseas teams played for: Delfos CC, Johannesburg 2005, 2006, 2007

Career highlights to date: '118 off 114 balls for Durham 2nd XI v Lancashire 2nd XI [2006]; 144 for Durham 2nd XI v MCC YC [2007]'
Cricket moments to forget: 'None. Every moment is an experience you can learn from'
Cricket superstitions: 'None'
Cricketers particularly admired: Jonty Rhodes, Hansie Cronje, Shaun Pollock
Young players to look out for: Paul Hindmarch
Other sports played: Golf
Other sports followed: Football (Liverpool)
Favourite band: Dr. Dre, Eminem, Gwen Stefani
Relaxations: 'Watching sport on TV; gym'
Extras: Youngest centurion for Bradford Grammar School (record previously held by Ashley Metcalfe). National U15 championship winner (Yorkshire Schools). Played for Northumberland in the Minor Counties Championship 2005
Opinions on cricket: '[Cricket is] becoming more aggressive and attacking with the success of Twenty20.'

MALAN, D. J. — Middlesex

Name: Dawid Johannes Malan
Role: Left-hand bat, right-arm leg-spin bowler
Born: 3 September 1987, Roehampton, London
Height: 6ft **Weight:** 13st
Nickname: AC ('as in AC Milan')
County debut: 2006 (one-day)
Parents: Dawid and Janet
Family links with cricket: Father played for the University of Stellenbosch and for Western Province B. Brother (Charl) an MCC Young Cricketer
Education: Paarl Boys' High, South Africa; UNISA
Overseas teams played for: Wellington CC 2005-06 – 2006-07; Boland 2005-06; Western Province/Boland Cricket Academy 2006
Career highlights to date: 'Playing for Middlesex in a Twenty20 game against Surrey at The Oval in front of a packed house'
Cricket moments to forget: 'Getting a first-ball in my school's yearly interschool match in my final year at school'
Cricket superstitions: 'The way I pack my cricket bag'

Cricketers particularly admired: Gary Kirsten
Young players to look out for: Eoin Morgan
Other sports played: Rugby, golf
Other sports followed: Rugby (Blue Bulls)
Favourite band: The Killers
Extras: Boland U19 Provincial Player of the Year 2005. Wellington CC Player of the Year 2005-06. Western Province/Boland Academy Player of the Year 2006. Is not considered an overseas player
Opinions on cricket: 'In my opinion the game has changed dramatically in the past few years. The introduction of Twenty20 has changed the mindset of batsmen and caused them to become more attacking in all forms of the game, which in turn has made cricket more exciting.'
Best batting: 64 Boland v Border, Paarl 2005-06
Best bowling: 1-22 Boland v Eastern Province, Port Elizabeth 2005-06

2007 Season (did not make any first-class or one-day appearances)

Career Performances

	M	Inn	NO	Runs	HS	Avg	100	50	Ct	St	Balls	Runs	Wkts	Avg	BB	5I	10M
Test																	
FC	4	7	0	158	64	22.57	-	1	2	-	159	152	3	50.66	1-22	-	-
ODI																	
List A	5	5	0	90	42	18.00	-	-	-	-	6	13	0		-	-	
20/20 Int																	
20/20	1	1	0	11	11	11.00	-	-	-	-	0	0	0		-	-	

55. Who claimed a second innings 6-54 for South Africa to doom England to defeat in the fourth Test at Headingley in 2003?

MALIK, M. N. Leicestershire

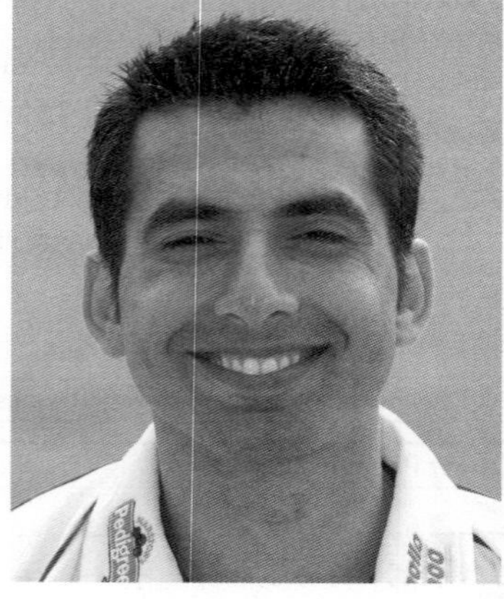

Name: Muhammad Nadeem Malik
Role: Right-hand bat, right-arm fast-medium bowler
Born: 6 October 1982, Nottingham
Height: 6ft 5in **Weight:** 14st 7lbs
Nickname: Nad, Busta, Nigel, Gerz
County debut: 2001 (Nottinghamshire), 2004 (Worcestershire)
County colours: 2004 (Worcestershire)
Place in batting averages: (2006 264th av. 11.33)
Place in bowling averages: 143rd av. 58.80 (2006 54th av. 31.52)
Parents: Abdul and Arshad
Marital status: Single
Family links with cricket: Brother plays club cricket for Carrington
Education: Wilford Meadows Secondary School; Bilborough College
Qualifications: 9 GCSEs
Career outside cricket: Personal trainer
Off-season: 'Rest; fitness work'
Overseas tours: ZRK to Pakistan 2000; Nottinghamshire to South Africa 2001; England U19 to India 2000-01, to Australia and (U19 World Cup) New Zealand 2001-02
Career highlights to date: '5-57 against Derbyshire 2001. Pro40 winners 2007 [Worcestershire]'
Cricket moments to forget: 'Norwich Union match v Yorkshire at Scarborough 2001 – Lehmann 191'
Cricketers particularly admired: Glenn McGrath, Wasim Akram, Curtly Ambrose
Young players to look out for: Mehraj Ahmed, James Taylor
Other sports played: Football
Other sports followed: 'Most major sports'
Relaxations: Music, games consoles
Extras: Made Nottinghamshire 2nd XI debut in 1999, aged 16, and took 15 wickets at an average of 19.40 for the 2nd XI 2000. Represented England U19 2001 and 2002. Played one first-class and one List A match for Nottinghamshire on loan 2007. Left Worcestershire at the end of the 2007 season and has joined Leicestershire for 2008
Best batting: 39* Worcestershire v New Zealanders, Worcester 2004
Best bowling: 5-57 Nottinghamshire v Derbyshire, Trent Bridge 2001

2007 Season

	M	Inn	NO	Runs	HS	Avg	100	50	Ct	St	Balls	Runs	Wkts	Avg	BB	5I	10M
Test																	
FC	14	19	8	104	24 *	9.45	-	-	5	-	2254	1470	25	58.80	3-94	-	-
ODI																	
List A	11	2	2	11	10 *		-	-	1	-	352	331	9	36.77	4-60	-	
20/20 Int																	
20/20	3	0	0	0	0		-	-	1	-	18	43	1	43.00	1-22	-	

Career Performances

	M	Inn	NO	Runs	HS	Avg	100	50	Ct	St	Balls	Runs	Wkts	Avg	BB	5I	10M
Test																	
FC	51	67	25	380	39 *	9.04	-	-	8	-	7769	4992	137	36.43	5-57	4	-
ODI																	
List A	58	24	17	94	11	13.42	-	-	8	-	2219	1971	54	36.50	4-42	-	
20/20 Int																	
20/20	15	4	2	4	3 *	2.00	-	-	2	-	282	434	17	25.52	3-23	-	

MALINGA, S. L. — Kent

Name: Separamadu Lasith Malinga Swarnajith
Role: Right-hand bat, right-arm fast bowler
Born: 28 August 1983, Galle, Sri Lanka
County debut: 2007
Test debut: 2004
ODI debut: 2004
Twenty20 Int debut: 2006
Overseas tours: Sri Lanka A to India 2003-04, to New Zealand 2003-04; Sri Lanka to Australia 2004, to Pakistan 2004-05, to New Zealand 2004-05, to India 2005-06, to Bangladesh 2005-06, to England 2006, to India (ICC Champions Trophy) 2006-07, to New Zealand 2006-07, to West Indies (World Cup) 2006-07, to South Africa (World 20/20) 2007-08, to Australia 2007-08, plus other one-day tournaments and series in Netherlands, India and Abu Dhabi
Overseas teams played for: Galle CC 2001-02 – 2003-04; Nondescripts CC 2004-05 – 2006-07

Extras: Became first bowler to take four wickets in four balls in an ODI (Pollock, Hall, Kallis, Ntini) v South Africa in Guyana in the World Cup 2006-07, sharing the Man of the Match award with Charl Langeveldt. Man of the Match in the first Test v New Zealand at Napier 2004-05 (4-130/5-80). Was a temporary overseas player with Kent during the 2007 season as a replacement for Andrew Hall
Best batting: 30 Nondescripts v Saracens Sports Club, Colombo (Bur) 2005-06
Best bowling: 6-17 Galle v Police Sports Club, Colombo (PP) 2003-04

2007 Season

	M	Inn	NO	Runs	HS	Avg	100	50	Ct	St	Balls	Runs	Wkts	Avg	BB	5I	10M
Test																	
FC	4	3	1	13	12	6.50	-	-	-	-	240	197	2	98.50	1-40	-	-
ODI																	
List A	3	1	1	1	1 *		-	-	-	-	142	145	2	72.50	1-44	-	
20/20 Int																	
20/20	2	0	0	0	0		-	-	-	-	46	74	4	18.50	3-30	-	

Career Performances

	M	Inn	NO	Runs	HS	Avg	100	50	Ct	St	Balls	Runs	Wkts	Avg	BB	5I	10M
Test	24	28	11	132	26	7.76	-	-	7	-	3925	2551	83	30.73	5-68	2	-
FC	75	90	38	426	30	8.19	-	-	22	-	10301	6792	230	29.53	6-17	6	-
ODI	40	17	8	70	15	7.77	-	-	5	-	1867	1461	61	23.95	4-44	-	
List A	65	31	13	125	23 *	6.94	-	-	8	-	2971	2372	101	23.48	4-16	-	
20/20 Int	7	4	1	53	27	17.66	-	-	5	-	120	140	7	20.00	3-43	-	
20/20	14	5	2	53	27	17.66	-	-	5	-	250	297	13	22.84	3-30	-	

56. Which Somerset player appeared v South Africa at Old Trafford in 1924 in his one and only Test in a match abandoned to rain after 165 minutes' play?

MANSOOR AMJAD Leicestershire

Name: Mansoor Amjad
Role: Right-hand bat, leg-spin bowler; all-rounder
Born: 14 December 1987, Sialkot, Punjab, Pakistan
County debut: 2006
Place in batting averages: 148th av. 29.00
Place in bowling averages: 141st av. 53.75
Overseas tours: Pakistan U19 to Bangladesh (U19 World Cup) 2003-04; Pakistan A to India (Kenstar Tournament) 2003-04, to Kenya 2004, to Zimbabwe 2004-05, to UAE (EurAsia Cricket Series) 2006, to Australia (Top End Series) 2006
Overseas teams played for: Sialkot/Sialkot Stallions 2001-02 – 2006-07; Zarai Taraqiati Bank 2003-04 – 2004-05; National Bank of Pakistan 2005-06 –
Extras: Represented Pakistan U19, winning Man of the Match award v Ireland U19 at Khulna in the U19 World Cup 2003-04 (4-28). Scored 81-ball 99 and had second innings figures of 6-19 for Pakistan A v Zimbabwe A at Harare 2004-05. Took 5-97 for Pakistan A v England XI at Lahore 2005-06. Was an overseas player with Leicestershire during the 2006 season (as a locum for Dinesh Mongia) and in 2007
Best batting: 122* National Bank v Sialkot, Multan 2005-06
Best bowling: 6-19 Pakistan A v Zimbabwe A, Harare 2004-05

2007 Season

	M	Inn	NO	Runs	HS	Avg	100	50	Ct	St	Balls	Runs	Wkts	Avg	BB	5I	10M
Test																	
FC	9	13	2	319	105 *	29.00	1	1	6	-	968	645	12	53.75	3-16	-	-
ODI																	
List A	5	4	1	58	34 *	19.33	-	-	-	-	216	189	3	63.00	2-34	-	
20/20 Int																	
20/20																	

Career Performances

	M	Inn	NO	Runs	HS	Avg	100	50	Ct	St	Balls	Runs	Wkts	Avg	BB	5I	10M
Test																	
FC	50	75	7	1880	122 *	27.64	3	8	26	-	7446	4319	133	32.47	6-19	6	-
ODI																	
List A	74	55	12	866	56	20.13	-	2	20	-	3513	2865	97	29.53	5-37	2	
20/20 Int																	
20/20	13	9	1	81	23	10.12	-	-	7	-	72	98	4	24.50	2-28	-	

MARSHALL, H. J. H. Gloucestershire

Name: Hamish John Hamilton Marshall
Role: Right-hand bat, right-arm medium bowler
Born: 15 February 1979, Warkworth, Auckland, New Zealand
County debut: 2006
County cap: 2006
Test debut: 2000-01
ODI debut: 2003-04
Twenty20 Int debut: 2004-05
1000 runs in a season: 1
Place in batting averages: 65th av. 40.85 (2006 18th av. 60.90)
Family links with cricket: Twin brother James Marshall also plays for Northern Districts and has represented New Zealand
Overseas tours: New Zealand U19 to South Africa (U19 World Cup) 1997-98; New Zealand to South Africa 2000-01, to Pakistan (one-day series) 2003-04, to England 2004 (NatWest Series), to England (ICC Champions Trophy) 2004, to Bangladesh 2004-05, to Australia 2004-05, to Zimbabwe 2005-06, to South Africa 2005-06, to India (ICC Champions Trophy) 2006-07, to Australia (C'wealth Bank Series) 2006-07, to West Indies (World Cup) 2006-07
Overseas teams played for: Northern Districts 1998-99 – 2006-07
Extras: MCC Young Cricketer 1998. Attended New Zealand Cricket Academy 1999. Played for Buckinghamshire in the 2004 C&G competition. Represented New Zealand v FICA World XI 2004-05. One of *New Zealand Cricket Almanack*'s two Players of the Year 2005. His match awards include Man of the Match v West Indies at Cardiff in the NatWest Series 2004 (75*) and v Australia in the first ODI at Melbourne 2004-05 (50*). An overseas player with Gloucestershire 2006-07; is no longer considered an overseas player

Best batting: 168 Gloucestershire v Leicestershire, Cheltenham 2006
Best bowling: 1-6 Northern Districts v Central Districts, Gisborne 2006-07

2007 Season

	M	Inn	NO	Runs	HS	Avg	100	50	Ct	St	Balls	Runs	Wkts	Avg	BB	5I	10M
Test																	
FC	13	21	1	817	123	40.85	3	3	9	-	114	81	2	40.50	1-9	-	-
ODI																	
List A	9	9	0	340	122	37.77	1	2	4	-	24	29	0		-	-	
20/20 Int																	
20/20	7	7	1	281	100	46.83	1	1	8	-	0	0	0		-	-	

Career Performances

	M	Inn	NO	Runs	HS	Avg	100	50	Ct	St	Balls	Runs	Wkts	Avg	BB	5I	10M
Test	13	19	2	652	160	38.35	2	2	1	-	6	4	0		-	-	-
FC	97	163	12	5496	168	36.39	13	25	49	-	972	493	10	49.30	1-6	-	-
ODI	66	62	9	1454	101 *	27.43	1	12	18	-	0	0	0		-	-	
List A	181	173	21	4204	122	27.65	4	28	73	-	84	101	1	101.00	1-14	-	
20/20 Int	3	3	0	12	8	4.00	-	-	1	-	0	0	0		-	-	
20/20	13	13	1	329	100	27.41	1	1	11	-	0	0	0		-	-	

MARSHALL, S. J. — Lancashire

Name: Simon James Marshall
Role: Right-hand bat, right-arm leg-spin bowler; all-rounder
Born: 20 September 1982, Arrowe Park, Wirral
Height: 6ft 3in **Weight:** 13st 2lbs
Nickname: Tron, David Dickinson
County debut: 2005
Parents: Jim and Dinah
Marital status: Single
Family links with cricket: Father captained Radley School and Liverpool University
Education: Birkenhead School; Cambridge University
Qualifications: 9 GCSEs, 4 A-levels, BA (Cantab) Land Economy
Overseas tours: ESCA and ECB age-group tours 1996-2001; British Universities to South Africa 2004

Overseas teams played for: Adelaide Buffalos CC, Adelaide 2004-05; West Torrens Eagles, Adelaide 2005-06
Career highlights to date: 'First-class debut for Lancashire CCC'
Cricket moments to forget: 'Losing the C&G final to Sussex 2006'
Cricket superstitions: 'Like to give the bat a few spins before facing up'
Cricketers particularly admired: Carl Hooper, Brad Hodge, Mal Loye, Gary Keedy
Other sports played: Hockey (Cambridge Blue)
Other sports followed: Football (Everton FC), hockey (Cambridge University HC)
Favourite band: Dire Straits, Man From Michael
Extras: Played for Cheshire in the C&G 2002, 2003. Played for Cambridge UCCE 2002, (as captain) 2003, and 2004; took 6-128 then followed up with 99 in CUCCE's second innings v Essex at Fenner's 2002. Cambridge Blue 2002-04. Represented British Universities 2004. Cambridge University Sportsman of the Year 2004
Opinions on cricket: 'Heavy scheduling makes it very difficult to achieve and maintain an intensity of performance in all competitions throughout the season. A straight knockout format in one of the limited-over competitions would be preferable.'
Best batting: 126* Cambridge University v Oxford University, Fenner's 2003
Best bowling: 6-128 CUCCE v Essex, Fenner's 2002

2007 Season

	M	Inn	NO	Runs	HS	Avg	100	50	Ct	St	Balls	Runs	Wkts	Avg	BB	5I	10M
Test																	
FC	1	1	0	7	7	7.00	-	-	1	-	168	84	2	42.00	1-32	-	-
ODI																	
List A	5	4	0	29	22	7.25	-	-	-	-	181	107	5	21.40	3-36	-	
20/20 Int																	
20/20																	

Career Performances

	M	Inn	NO	Runs	HS	Avg	100	50	Ct	St	Balls	Runs	Wkts	Avg	BB	5I	10M
Test																	
FC	19	30	6	780	126 *	32.50	1	3	5	-	3734	1976	30	65.86	6-128	1	-
ODI																	
List A	21	10	0	54	22	5.40	-	-	7	-	843	671	15	44.73	3-36	-	
20/20 Int																	
20/20	8	6	2	97	47	24.25	-	-	5	-	184	186	12	15.50	4-20	-	

MARTIN-JENKINS, R. S. C. — Sussex

Name: Robin Simon Christopher Martin-Jenkins
Role: Right-hand bat, right-arm medium-fast bowler; all-rounder
Born: 28 October 1975, Guildford
Height: 6ft 5in **Weight:** 14st
Nickname: Tucker
County debut: 1995
County cap: 2000
Benefit: 2008
1000 runs in a season: 1
1st-Class 200s: 1
Place in batting averages: 120th av. 32.56 (2006 118th av. 32.88)
Place in bowling averages: 10th av. 21.41 (2006 80th av. 34.92)
Parents: Christopher and Judy
Wife and date of marriage: Flora, 19 February 2000
Family links with cricket: Father is *The Times* senior cricket columnist and BBC *TMS* commentator. Brother plays for the Radley Rangers
Education: Radley College, Oxon; Durham University
Qualifications: 10 GCSEs, 3 A-levels, 1 AS-level, Grade 3 bassoon (with merit), BA (Hons) Social Sciences, Don MacKenzie School of Professional Photography Certificate, SWPP (Society of Wedding and Portrait Photographers), BPPA (British Professional Photographers Associates), Wine and Spirit Education Trust Intermediate and Advanced Certificates
Career outside cricket: Land agent
Off-season: 'Organising my benefit'
Overseas tours: Radley College to Barbados 1992; Sussex U19 to Sri Lanka 1995; Durham University to Vienna 1995; MCC to Kenya 1999; Sussex to Grenada 2001, 2002
Overseas teams played for: Lima CC, Peru 1994; Bellville CC, Cape Town 2000-01
Career highlights to date: 'Maiden first-class ton and double ton; three Championship titles; C&G Trophy final 2006 – the last six or seven years at Sussex in general'
Cricket superstitions: 'Never bowl first at Colwyn Bay'
Young players to look out for: Matt Machan, Will Beer
Other sports played: Golf, tennis, Rugby fives
Other sports followed: Rugby, football (Liverpool)
Favourite band: Keane

Relaxations: 'Wine, food, guitar'
Extras: Played for ESCA U15-U19. European Player of the Year, Vienna 1995. Best Performance Award for Sussex 1998. NBC Denis Compton Award for the most promising young Sussex player 1998, 1999, 2000. Scored 205* v Somerset at Taunton 2002, in the process sharing with Mark Davis (111) in a record eighth-wicket stand for Sussex (291); the stand fell one run short of the record eighth-wicket partnership in English first-class cricket, set in 1896. BBC South Cricketer of the Year 2002
Opinions on cricket: 'Scrap all 50-over cricket and replace with 40-over. Forty-over cricket produces more exciting finishes and reduces the workload on bowlers and players generally. Twenty 40-over international matches a year would mean 400 fewer overs for the players (equivalent of eight 50-over innings).'
Best batting: 205* Sussex v Somerset, Taunton 2002
Best bowling: 7-51 Sussex v Leicestershire, Horsham 2002

2007 Season

	M	Inn	NO	Runs	HS	Avg	100	50	Ct	St	Balls	Runs	Wkts	Avg	BB	5I	10M
Test																	
FC	15	22	6	521	99	32.56	-	2	8	-	1794	771	36	21.41	5-67	1	-
ODI																	
List A	14	11	3	135	44	16.87	-	-	1	-	516	431	15	28.73	4-50	-	
20/20 Int																	
20/20	9	3	1	10	5 *	5.00	-	-	1	-	138	205	6	34.16	2-21	-	

Career Performances

	M	Inn	NO	Runs	HS	Avg	100	50	Ct	St	Balls	Runs	Wkts	Avg	BB	5I	10M
Test																	
FC	145	223	31	5878	205 *	30.61	3	29	42	-	19561	9815	299	32.82	7-51	6	-
ODI																	
List A	195	147	26	1778	68 *	14.69	-	3	42	-	8570	6002	206	29.13	4-22	-	
20/20 Int																	
20/20	23	14	4	163	56 *	16.30	-	1	7	-	445	582	20	29.10	4-20	-	

57. Which future Hollywood actor captained England v South Africa at Port Elizabeth in the first ever Test between the countries in 1888-89?

MASCARENHAS, D. A. Hampshire

Name: Dimitri Adrian Mascarenhas
Role: Right-hand bat, right-arm medium bowler
Born: 30 October 1977, Chiswick, London
Height: 6ft 1in **Weight:** 12st 2lbs
Nickname: Dimi, D-Train
County debut: 1996
County cap: 1998
Benefit: 2007
ODI debut: 2007
Twenty20 Int debut: 2007
50 wickets in a season: 1
Place in batting averages: 103rd av. 34.92 (2006 210th av. 19.75)
Place in bowling averages: 73rd av. 32.06 (2006 15th av. 24.97)
Parents: Malik and Pauline
Marital status: Single
Family links with cricket: Uncle played in Sri Lanka and brothers both play for Melville CC in Perth, Western Australia
Education: Trinity College, Perth
Qualifications: Level 2 coaching
Career outside cricket: Personal trainer
Overseas tours: England VI to Hong Kong 2004, 2005; England to South Africa (World 20/20) 2007-08, to Sri Lanka 2007-08 (one-day series), to New Zealand 2007-08 (one-day series)
Overseas teams played for: Melville CC, Perth 1991 –
Cricketers particularly admired: Sir Viv Richards, Malcolm Marshall, Shane Warne
Other sports followed: Australian Rules (Collingwood)
Favourite band: Red Hot Chili Peppers
Relaxations: Tennis, golf, Australian Rules
Extras: Played for Western Australia at U17 and U19 level as captain. Took 6-88 on first-class debut, for Hampshire v Glamorgan at Southampton 1996. Won NatWest Man of the Match awards in semi-final v Lancashire at Southampton 1998 (3-28/73) and in quarter-final v Middlesex at Lord's 2000 (4-25). Scorer of the first Championship century at The Rose Bowl (104) v Worcestershire 2001. Took Hampshire competition best 5-14 v Sussex at Hove in the Twenty20 2004, including the competition's first hat-trick (Davis, Mushtaq Ahmed, Lewry). Struck 15-ball 36* in the sixth ODI v India at The Oval 2007, including a six off each of the last five balls of the England innings

Best batting: 131 Hampshire v Kent, Canterbury 2006
Best bowling: 6-25 Hampshire v Derbyshire, Rose Bowl 2004

2007 Season

	M	Inn	NO	Runs	HS	Avg	100	50	Ct	St	Balls	Runs	Wkts	Avg	BB	5I	10M
Test																	
FC	10	16	2	489	90	34.92	-	3	2	-	1140	481	15	32.06	4-33	-	-
ODI	7	5	1	98	52	24.50	-	1	1	-	336	214	6	35.66	3-23	-	
List A	18	14	2	325	74	27.08	-	3	5	-	780	511	15	34.06	3-23	-	
20/20 Int	2	2	1	20	18 *	20.00	-	-	3	-	42	71	2	35.50	2-39	-	
20/20	4	4	1	54	31	18.00	-	-	3	-	78	101	6	16.83	3-17	-	

Career Performances

	M	Inn	NO	Runs	HS	Avg	100	50	Ct	St	Balls	Runs	Wkts	Avg	BB	5I	10M
Test																	
FC	156	236	26	5258	131	25.03	7	19	60	-	22367	10223	364	28.08	6-25	14	-
ODI	7	5	1	98	52	24.50	-	1	1	-	336	214	6	35.66	3-23	-	
List A	199	175	33	3316	79	23.35	-	21	51	-	8385	5872	237	24.77	5-27	1	
20/20 Int	7	7	3	39	18 *	9.75	-	-	5	-	126	193	6	32.16	3-18	-	
20/20	29	29	11	423	52	23.50	-	1	14	-	527	672	34	19.76	5-14	1	

MASON, M. S. — Worcestershire

Name: Matthew (Matt) Sean Mason
Role: Right-hand bat, right-arm fast-medium bowler
Born: 20 March 1974, Claremont, Perth, Western Australia
Height: 6ft 5in **Weight:** 16st
Nickname: Mase, Moose
County debut: 2002
County colours: 2002
50 wickets in a season: 3
Place in batting averages: (2006 250th av. 14.16)
Place in bowling averages: (2006 8th av. 22.19)
Parents: Bill and Sue
Wife and date of marriage: Kellie, 8 October 2005
Children: Evie, 27 March 2007

Family links with cricket: Brother plays first-grade for Claremont-Nedlands in Western Australia

Education: Mazenod College, Perth; Edith Cowan University, Perth
Qualifications: Level 1 ACB coach
Career outside cricket: 'Would love to become a fast-bowling coach'
Off-season: Player-coach of Claremont-Nedlands CC in Perth
Overseas tours: Worcestershire to South Africa 2003
Overseas teams played for: Western Australia 1996-97 – 1997-98; Wanneroo District CC 1999-2001; Claremont-Nedlands CC, Perth 2007-08
Career highlights to date: 'Back-to-back Lord's finals 2003 and 2004'
Cricket moments to forget: 'Losing back-to-back Lord's finals 2003 and 2004'
Cricketers particularly admired: Dennis Lillee, Darren Gough, Justin Langer
Young players to look out for: Moeen Ali
Other sports played: Golf ('badly'), tennis, Australian Rules football
Other sports followed: Australian Rules football (West Coast Eagles), rugby union (Worcester Warriors)
Injuries: Out for the whole of the 2007 season with a shoulder injury
Favourite band: Snow Patrol
Relaxations: 'Love being at home with my family'
Extras: Scored maiden first-class fifty (50) from 27 balls v Derbyshire at Worcester 2002. Dick Lygon Award for the [Worcestershire] Clubman of the Year 2003. Is England-qualified
Opinions on cricket: 'I do not believe that we play too many matches. We need to return to the old C&G format. Would not like Twenty20 to take over cricket.'
Best batting: 63 Worcestershire v Warwickshire, Worcester 2004
Best bowling: 8-45 Worcestershire v Gloucestershire, Worcester 2006

2007 Season

	M	Inn	NO	Runs	HS	Avg	100	50	Ct	St	Balls	Runs	Wkts	Avg	BB	5I	10M
Test																	
FC	1	2	0	15	15	7.50	-	-	-	-	144	62	1	62.00	1-51	-	-
ODI																	
List A																	
20/20 Int																	
20/20																	

Career Performances

	M	Inn	NO	Runs	HS	Avg	100	50	Ct	St	Balls	Runs	Wkts	Avg	BB	5I	10M
Test																	
FC	69	89	23	939	63	14.22	-	3	13	-	13003	6046	226	26.75	8-45	8	1
ODI																	
List A	70	32	12	153	25	7.65	-	-	14	-	3254	2311	84	27.51	4-34	-	
20/20 Int																	
20/20	10	4	2	18	8 *	9.00	-	-	2	-	220	290	9	32.22	3-42	-	

MASTERS, D. D. — Essex

Name: David Daniel Masters
Role: Right-hand bat, right-arm medium-fast bowler
Born: 22 April 1978, Chatham, Kent
Height: 6ft 4ins **Weight:** 12st 5lbs
Nickname: Hod, Race Horse, Hoddy
County debut: 2000 (Kent), 2003 (Leicestershire)
County cap: 2007 (Leicestershire)
Place in batting averages: 234th av. 17.28 (2006 246th av. 14.60)
Place in bowling averages: 16th av. 22.53 (2006 96th av. 38.50)
Parents: Kevin and Tracey
Marital status: Single
Family links with cricket: 'Dad was on staff at Kent 1983-86'
Education: Fort Luton High School, Chatham; Mid-Kent College
Qualifications: 8 GCSEs, GNVQ in Leisure and Tourism, qualified coach in cricket, football and athletics, bricklayer and plasterer
Career outside cricket: Builder
Overseas teams played for: Doubleview, Perth 1998-99
Cricketers particularly admired: Ian Botham
Other sports played: Football, boxing 'and most other sports'
Other sports followed: Football (Manchester United)
Relaxations: 'Going out with mates'
Extras: Joint Kent Player of the Year 2000 (with Martin Saggers). NBC Denis Compton Award for the most promising young Kent player 2000. Leicestershire Player of the Year 2005. Left Leicestershire at the end of the 2007 season and has joined Essex for 2008
Best batting: 119 Leicestershire v Sussex, Hove 2003
Best bowling: 6-27 Kent v Durham, Tunbridge Wells 2000

2007 Season

	M	Inn	NO	Runs	HS	Avg	100	50	Ct	St	Balls	Runs	Wkts	Avg	BB	5I	10M
Test																	
FC	11	16	2	242	46	17.28	-	-	1	-	1966	924	41	22.53	6-60	3	-
ODI																	
List A	12	6	0	43	16	7.16	-	-	3	-	444	349	11	31.72	2-32	-	
20/20 Int																	
20/20	5	0	0	0	0		-	-	1	-	57	80	3	26.66	2-23	-	

Career Performances

	M	Inn	NO	Runs	HS	Avg	100	50	Ct	St	Balls	Runs	Wkts	Avg	BB	5I	10M
Test																	
FC	89	110	22	1195	119	13.57	1	2	27	-	14639	7477	236	31.68	6-27	8	-
ODI																	
List A	91	52	20	383	39	11.96	-	-	11	-	3631	2841	76	37.38	5-20	1	
20/20 Int																	
20/20	32	7	4	16	7	5.33	-	-	10	-	561	712	30	23.73	3-7	-	

MAUNDERS, J. K. — Leicestershire

Name: John Kenneth Maunders
Role: Left-hand opening bat, right-arm medium bowler
Born: 4 April 1981, Ashford, Middlesex
Height: 5ft 10in **Weight:** 13st
Nickname: Rod, Weaz
County debut: 1999 (Middlesex), 2003 (Leicestershire)
Place in batting averages: 170th av. 26.13 (2006 109th av. 34.25)
Parents: Lynn and Kenneth
Marital status: Single
Family links with cricket: Grandfather and two uncles club cricketers for Thames Valley Ramblers
Education: Ashford High School; Spelthorne College
Qualifications: 10 GCSEs, coaching certificates
Career outside cricket: Cricket coach
Overseas tours: England U19 to New Zealand 1998-99, to Malaysia and (U19 World Cup) Sri Lanka 1999-2000
Overseas teams played for: University CC, Perth 2001-02
Career highlights to date: 'Scoring maiden first-class hundred v Surrey at Grace Road'
Cricket moments to forget: 'Not any one in particular; getting 0 and dropping catches are not great moments!'
Cricket superstitions: 'Just a few small ones'
Cricketers particularly admired: Brad Hodge, Justin Langer
Other sports played: Football, hockey, squash
Other sports followed: Horse racing

Extras: Has been Seaxe Player of Year. Represented England U17 and U19. NBC Denis Compton Award 1999. Released by Leicestershire at the end of the 2007 season
Best batting: 180 Leicestershire v Gloucestershire, Cheltenham 2006
Best bowling: 4-15 Leicestershire v Worcestershire, Worcester 2006

2007 Season

	M	Inn	NO	Runs	HS	Avg	100	50	Ct	St	Balls	Runs	Wkts	Avg	BB	5I	10M
Test																	
FC	13	22	0	575	97	26.13	-	4	12	-	299	203	2	101.50	1-8	-	-
ODI																	
List A	8	8	2	315	109 *	52.50	1	1	3	-	30	21	0		-	-	
20/20 Int																	
20/20	5	1	1	6	6 *		-	-	1	-	12	14	2	7.00	2-14	-	

Career Performances

	M	Inn	NO	Runs	HS	Avg	100	50	Ct	St	Balls	Runs	Wkts	Avg	BB	5I	10M
Test																	
FC	69	124	3	3544	180	29.28	5	18	38	-	1525	928	24	38.66	4-15	-	-
ODI																	
List A	30	30	3	629	109 *	23.29	1	1	9	-	139	103	4	25.75	2-16	-	
20/20 Int																	
20/20	14	7	3	24	10	6.00	-	-	2	-	12	14	2	7.00	2-14	-	

MAYNARD, T. L. — Glamorgan

Name: Thomas (Tom) Lloyd Maynard
Role: Right-hand bat, right-arm medium bowler
Born: 25 March 1989, Cardiff
Height: 6ft 2in **Weight:** 15st
Nickname: George, Squirrel
County debut: 2007
Parents: Matthew and Sue
Marital status: Single
Family links with cricket: 'Dad used to play [for Glamorgan and England]. Uncle plays'
Education: Millfield School; Whitchurch High
Qualifications: 11 GCSEs, 3 A-levels
Off-season: 'Working the nightlife in the 'Diff and other European cities'
Overseas tours: England U15 to South Africa 2003-04

Career highlights to date: 'Debut for Glamorgan'
Cricket moments to forget: 'None'
Cricket superstitions: 'None'
Cricketers particularly admired: Brian Lara, Kevin Pietersen
Young players to look out for: Ed Jackson, Richard Davies, Alex Nielsen
Other sports played: Rugby (Bath Youth/Cardiff Youth)
Other sports followed: Football (Man City)
Injuries: Out for three weeks with a broken thumb
Favourite band: Oasis
Relaxations: 'Golf'
Extras: Played for Wales Minor Counties 2006-07. Scored 75-ball 71 on List A debut v Gloucestershire at Colwyn Bay in the Friends Provident 2007
Opinions on cricket: 'Twenty20 is a good form of the game and is good for cricket on the whole.'
Best batting: 18 Glamorgan v Derbyshire, Cardiff 2007

2007 Season

	M	Inn	NO	Runs	HS	Avg	100	50	Ct	St	Balls	Runs	Wkts	Avg	BB	5I	10M
Test																	
FC	2	3	0	35	18	11.66	-	-	-	-	12	18	0		-	-	-
ODI																	
List A	2	2	0	72	71	36.00	-	1	-	-	0	0	0		-	-	
20/20 Int																	
20/20	4	3	0	26	11	8.66	-	-	2	-	0	0	0		-	-	

Career Performances

	M	Inn	NO	Runs	HS	Avg	100	50	Ct	St	Balls	Runs	Wkts	Avg	BB	5I	10M
Test																	
FC	2	3	0	35	18	11.66	-	-	-	-	12	18	0		-	-	-
ODI																	
List A	2	2	0	72	71	36.00	-	1	-	-	0	0	0		-	-	
20/20 Int																	
20/20	4	3	0	26	11	8.66	-	-	2	-	0	0	0		-	-	

McGARRY, A. C. Essex

Name: Andrew Charles McGarry
Role: Right-hand bat, right-arm fast-medium bowler
Born: 8 November 1981, Basildon
Height: 6ft 5in
Nickname: Rodders
County debut: 1999
Education: King Edward VI GS, Chelmsford; South East Essex College of Arts and Technology, Southend
Qualifications: 9 GCSEs, Level 1 and 2 ECB coaching awards
Overseas tours: England U19 to India 2000-01
Cricketers particularly admired: Ian Botham, Allan Donald
Other sports played: Basketball, volleyball, football
Other sports followed: Football (Aston Villa)
Injuries: Out from May 2007 with a fractured metacarpal

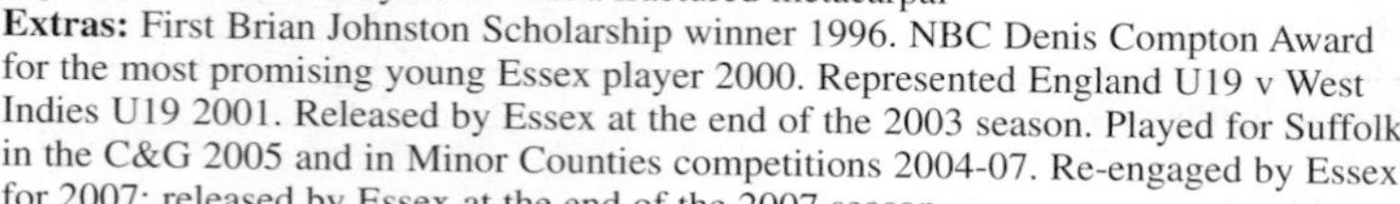

Extras: First Brian Johnston Scholarship winner 1996. NBC Denis Compton Award for the most promising young Essex player 2000. Represented England U19 v West Indies U19 2001. Released by Essex at the end of the 2003 season. Played for Suffolk in the C&G 2005 and in Minor Counties competitions 2004-07. Re-engaged by Essex for 2007; released by Essex at the end of the 2007 season
Best batting: 11* Essex v CUCCE, Fenner's 2002
Best bowling: 5-27 Essex v CUCCE, Fenner's 2003

2007 Season

	M	Inn	NO	Runs	HS	Avg	100	50	Ct	St	Balls	Runs	Wkts	Avg	BB	5I	10M
Test																	
FC	4	2	1	15	10	15.00	-	-	1	-	271	160	2	80.00	2-62	-	-
ODI																	
List A																	
20/20 Int																	
20/20																	

Career Performances

	M	Inn	NO	Runs	HS	Avg	100	50	Ct	St	Balls	Runs	Wkts	Avg	BB	5I	10M
Test																	
FC	19	20	14	43	11 *	7.16	-	-	4	-	2403	1546	29	53.31	5-27	1	-
ODI																	
List A	16	4	2	2	1	1.00	-	-	2	-	489	420	11	38.18	2-20	-	
20/20 Int																	
20/20																	

McGRATH, A. Yorkshire

Name: Anthony McGrath
Role: Right-hand bat, right-arm medium bowler, county vice-captain
Born: 6 October 1975, Bradford
Height: 6ft 2in **Weight:** 14st 7lbs
Nickname: Gripper, Mags, Terry
County debut: 1995
County cap: 1999
Test debut: 2003
ODI debut: 2003
1000 runs in a season: 2
Place in batting averages: 45th av. 46.55 (2006 15th av. 61.57)
Place in bowling averages: (2006 108th av. 40.77)
Parents: Terry and Kath
Marital status: Single
Education: Yorkshire Martyrs Collegiate School
Qualifications: 9 GCSEs, BTEC National Diploma in Leisure Studies, senior coaching award
Overseas tours: England U19 to West Indies 1994-95; England A to Pakistan 1995-96, to Australia 1996-97; MCC to Bangladesh 1999-2000; England to Bangladesh and Sri Lanka 2003-04 (one-day series), to West Indies 2003-04 (one-day series)
Overseas teams played for: Deep Dene, Melbourne 1998-99; Wanneroo, Perth 1999-2001
Cricket moments to forget: 'Losing semi-final to Lancashire 1996. Relegation to Division Two 2002'
Cricketers particularly admired: Darren Lehmann, Robin Smith
Other sports followed: 'Most sports', football (Manchester United)
Relaxations: 'Music; spending time with friends; eating out'

Extras: Captained Yorkshire Schools U13, U14, U15, U16; captained English Schools U17. Bradford League Young Cricketer of the Year 1992 and 1993. Played for England U17 and U19. Captain of Yorkshire 2003; vice-captain of Yorkshire since 2007
Best batting: 188* Yorkshire v Warwickshire, Edgbaston 2007
Best bowling: 5-39 Yorkshire v Derbyshire, Derby 2004

2007 Season

	M	Inn	NO	Runs	HS	Avg	100	50	Ct	St	Balls	Runs	Wkts	Avg	BB	5I	10M
Test																	
FC	14	22	2	931	188 *	46.55	3	6	11	-	456	223	5	44.60	2-12	-	-
ODI																	
List A	15	13	3	567	135 *	56.70	2	3	5	-	174	156	4	39.00	2-19	-	
20/20 Int																	
20/20	8	8	2	152	55	25.33	-	1	2	-	72	104	2	52.00	1-18	-	

Career Performances

	M	Inn	NO	Runs	HS	Avg	100	50	Ct	St	Balls	Runs	Wkts	Avg	BB	5I	10M
Test	4	5	0	201	81	40.20	-	2	3	-	102	56	4	14.00	3-16	-	-
FC	184	312	25	10747	188 *	37.44	25	52	133	-	6731	3446	100	34.46	5-39	1	-
ODI	14	12	2	166	52	16.60	-	1	4	-	228	175	4	43.75	1-13	-	
List A	245	226	31	6271	148	32.15	6	35	78	-	2702	2265	65	34.84	4-41	-	
20/20 Int																	
20/20	29	28	5	536	58 *	23.30	-	3	8	-	281	418	12	34.83	3-27	-	

58. Who became Mark Boucher's 100th Test catch in the fourth Test between England and South Africa at Cape Town in 1999-2000 after batting for 1032 minutes since his previous Test dismissal?

McKENZIE, N. D. Durham

Name: Neil Douglas McKenzie
Role: Right-hand bat, right-arm medium bowler
Born: 24 November 1975, Johannesburg, South Africa
Nickname: Bertie
County debut: 2007 (Somerset)
Test debut: 2000
ODI debut: 1999-2000
Twenty20 Int debut: 2005-06
Family links with cricket: Father Kevin played for North Eastern Transvaal and Transvaal
Education: King Edward VII School, Johannesburg; RAU, Johannesburg
Overseas tours: South Africa U19 to England 1995 (c); Transvaal to Australia 1997-98; South Africa to India 1999-2000 (one-day series), to Sri Lanka 2000, to West Indies 2000-01, to Zimbabwe 2001-02, to Australia 2001-02, to Bangladesh 2003, to England 2003, to Pakistan 2003-04, to New Zealand 2003-04, plus other one-day tournaments in Sharjah, Australia and Singapore; South Africa A to Zimbabwe 2002-03, 2004; South Africa Emerging Players to Australia (Cricket Australia Emerging Players Tournament) 2006 (c)
Overseas teams played for: Transvaal 1994-95 – 1996-97; Gauteng 1997-98 – 1998-99; Northerns 1999-2000 – 2003-04; Lions 2003-04 –
Extras: Captained South Africa Schools. One of *South African Cricket Annual*'s five Cricketers of the Year 2001. His match awards include Man of the Match in the second Test v New Zealand in Port Elizabeth 2000-01 (120) and in the second ODI v Sri Lanka in East London 2000-01 (120*). Captain of Highveld Lions. Was a temporary overseas player with Somerset during the 2007 season as a replacement for Cameron White; has joined Durham as an overseas player for 2008 as a locum for Shivnarine Chanderpaul
Best batting: 175 Northerns v Gauteng, Centurion 1999-2000
Best bowling: 1-6 Gauteng v Border, East London 1998-99
Stop press: Man of the Match v Dolphins at Potchefstroom in the SuperSport Series 2007-08 (164). Recalled to South Africa Test side for the second Test v West Indies at Cape Town 2007-08

2007 Season

	M	Inn	NO	Runs	HS	Avg	100	50	Ct	St	Balls	Runs	Wkts	Avg	BB	5I	10M
Test																	
FC	3	5	1	271	84	67.75	-	3	2	-	0	0	0		-	-	-
ODI																	
List A	5	5	0	233	86	46.60	-	2	-	-	0	0	0		-	-	
20/20 Int																	
20/20																	

Career Performances

	M	Inn	NO	Runs	HS	Avg	100	50	Ct	St	Balls	Runs	Wkts	Avg	BB	5I	10M
Test	41	65	4	2028	120	33.24	2	13	37	-	72	63	0		-	-	-
FC	145	244	29	9201	175	42.79	23	50	110	-	552	322	5	64.40	1-6	-	-
ODI	59	51	10	1580	131 *	38.53	2	9	19	-	46	27	0		-	-	
List A	190	169	28	5124	131 *	36.34	7	34	56	-	255	248	4	62.00	2-19	-	
20/20 Int	1	0	0	0	0		-	-	-	-	0	0	0		-	-	
20/20	24	23	7	591	85 *	36.93	-	4	9	-	12	19	0		-	-	

McLAREN, R. — Kent

Name: Ryan McLaren
Role: Left-hand bat, right-arm medium-fast bowler
Born: 9 February 1983, Kimberley, South Africa
County debut: 2007
County cap: 2007
Place in batting averages: 208th av. 20.92
Place in bowling averages: 29th av. 24.52
Family links with cricket: Father (Paul McLaren) and uncle (Keith McLaren) played for Griqualand West. Cousin (Adrian McLaren) plays for Griqualand West
Overseas tours: South Africa U19 to New Zealand (U19 World Cup) 2001-02
Overseas teams played for: Free State 2003-04 – 2004-05; Eagles 2004-05 –
Extras: SuperSport Series Cricketer of the Year 2007. Took hat-trick (H. Marshall, Adshead, Fisher) v Gloucestershire in the final of the Twenty20 Cup at Edgbaston 2007, winning Man of the Match award. His other awards include Man of the Match v Canada U19 at Auckland in the U19 World Cup 2001-02 (4-9; full figures 10-4-9-4), v Warriors at Bloemfontein in the Supersport

Series 2005-06 (140; 3-31/4-50) and v Dolphins at Bloemfontein in the SuperSport Series 2006-07 (53*; 5-57/4-59). Is not considered an overseas player
Best batting: 140 Eagles v Warriors, Bloemfontein 2005-06
Best bowling: 8-38 Eagles v Cape Cobras, Stellenbosch (US) 2006-07

2007 Season

	M	Inn	NO	Runs	HS	Avg	100	50	Ct	St	Balls	Runs	Wkts	Avg	BB	5I	10M
Test																	
FC	15	18	5	272	54 *	20.92	-	1	7	-	1896	1079	44	24.52	5-24	1	-
ODI																	
List A	13	11	3	202	78 *	25.25	-	1	4	-	546	457	17	26.88	4-29	-	
20/20 Int																	
20/20	11	8	5	128	46 *	42.66	-	-	9	-	191	250	11	22.72	3-22	-	

Career Performances

	M	Inn	NO	Runs	HS	Avg	100	50	Ct	St	Balls	Runs	Wkts	Avg	BB	5I	10M
Test																	
FC	48	69	13	1613	140	28.80	1	9	28	-	7760	3876	158	24.53	8-38	7	1
ODI																	
List A	49	34	11	713	78 *	31.00	-	4	18	-	1599	1291	42	30.73	4-29	-	
20/20 Int																	
20/20	28	19	9	225	46 *	22.50	-	-	12	-	455	551	19	29.00	3-22	-	

MEAKER, S. C. Surrey

Name: Stuart Christopher Meaker
Role: Right-hand bat, right-arm fast bowler
Born: 21 January 1989, Durban, South Africa
Height: 5ft 11in **Weight:** 13st
Nickname: Meaksy, Herc
County debut: No first-team appearance
Parents: Vivien White
Marital status: Single
Education: Cranleigh School
Qualifications: GCSEs, 4 A-levels
Career outside cricket: 'Barman'
Off-season: 'Touring with England U19'
Overseas tours: England U16 to South Africa; England U19 to Malaysia (U19 World Cup) 2007-08
Career highlights to date: 'Being given a contract by Surrey CCC'

Cricket moments to forget: 'Playing against Kent CCC for Surrey in a pre-season friendly and going for an astonishing amount of runs'
Cricket superstitions: 'Wearing my helmet way before I go in to bat'
Cricketers particularly admired: Allan Donald, Mark Ramprakash
Young players to look out for: Zafar Ansari
Other sports played: Rugby, hockey, water polo, athletics, swimming, golf
Other sports followed: Rugby (Natal Sharks, Sale Sharks)
Injuries: Out for six weeks with a stress fracture of the lower back and a chip fracture of the middle bowling finger
Favourite band: Lifehouse
Relaxations: 'Playing guitar, bodyboarding'
Extras: Lord's fielding award. Represented England U19 2007

MICKLEBURGH, J. C. — Essex

Name: Jaik Charles Mickleburgh
Role: Right-hand bat, right-arm medium-fast bowler
Born: 30 March 1990, Norwich, Norfolk
County debut: No first-team appearance
Extras: Made 2nd XI Championship debut 2006. Attended World Cricket Academy, Mumbai 2007. Played for Norfolk in Minor Counties competitions 2007. Played for Essex in the Twenty20 Floodlit Cup 2007 but has yet to appear for the county in first-class cricket or a major domestic one-day competition

59. Which batsman ended his 42-Test career after the fifth Test v England at Port Elizabeth in 1948-49 with a total of 3471 runs, which remained a South African record until the post-isolation era?

MIDDLEBROOK, J. D. Essex

Name: James Daniel Middlebrook
Role: Right-hand bat, off-spin bowler
Born: 13 May 1977, Leeds
Height: 6ft 1in **Weight:** 13st
Nickname: Midhouse, Midi, Midders
County debut: 1998 (Yorkshire), 2002 (Essex)
County cap: 2003 (Essex)
50 wickets in a season: 1
Place in batting averages: 123rd av. 32.38 (2006 137th av. 30.87)
Place in bowling averages: 123rd av. 42.50 (2006 113th av. 41.60)
Parents: Ralph and Mavis
Marital status: Single
Family links with cricket: 'Dad is a senior staff coach'
Education: Crawshaw, Pudsey
Qualifications: NVQ Level 2 in Coaching Sport and Recreation, ECB senior coach
Overseas tours: Yorkshire CCC to Guernsey
Overseas teams played for: Stokes Valley CC, New Zealand; Gold Coast Dolphins, Brisbane; Surfers Paradise CC, Brisbane; Upper Valley CC, Wellington, New Zealand 2006-07
Cricket superstitions: 'Always put my batting gear on the same way'
Cricketers particularly admired: John Emburey, Ian Botham
Young players to look out for: Tom Westley
Other sports played: Golf, tennis, squash, badminton
Other sports followed: Football (Leeds United), athletics
Relaxations: 'Any music – MTV – sleeping, socialising, catching up with old friends'
Extras: Played for Yorkshire from U11 to 1st XI. His 6-82 v Hampshire at Southampton 2000 included a spell of four wickets in five balls. Took Championship hat-trick (Saggers, Muralitharan, Sheriyar) v Kent at Canterbury 2003
Opinions on cricket: 'Too much cricket without rest in between games so you can practise at your skill level.'
Best batting: 127 Essex v Middlesex, Lord's 2007
Best bowling: 6-82 Yorkshire v Hampshire, Southampton 2000

2007 Season

	M	Inn	NO	Runs	HS	Avg	100	50	Ct	St	Balls	Runs	Wkts	Avg	BB	5I	10M
Test																	
FC	17	24	6	583	127	32.38	1	3	15	-	2051	1020	24	42.50	4-53	-	-
ODI																	
List A	15	12	1	198	40	18.00	-	-	2	-	547	434	7	62.00	2-43	-	
20/20 Int																	
20/20	5	4	2	17	7 *	8.50	-	-	1	-	12	22	0		-	-	

Career Performances

	M	Inn	NO	Runs	HS	Avg	100	50	Ct	St	Balls	Runs	Wkts	Avg	BB	5I	10M
Test																	
FC	121	172	22	3795	127	25.30	4	15	62	-	20658	10775	274	39.32	6-82	7	1
ODI																	
List A	123	81	21	1109	47	18.48	-	-	34	-	4465	3413	101	33.79	4-27	-	
20/20 Int																	
20/20	27	22	5	238	43	14.00	-	-	6	-	300	412	9	45.77	3-25	-	

MILLER, A. S. — Warwickshire

Name: Andrew Stephen Miller
Role: Right-hand bat, right-arm medium-fast bowler
Born: 27 September 1987, Preston
Height: 6ft 4in **Weight:** 13st 3lbs
Nickname: Millsy, Donk
County debut: No first-team appearance
Parents: Steve and Sharon
Family links with cricket: 'Dad and brother played club cricket at Longridge CC'
Education: St Cecilia's RC High School; Preston College
Qualifications: 10 GCSEs, BTEC National Diploma in Sport Fitness and Development, coaching Levels 1 and 2
Off-season: 'Going to Melbourne, Australia, from October to January'
Overseas tours: England U16 to South Africa 2004; England U19 to India 2004-05, to Bangladesh 2005-06, to Sri Lanka (U19 World Cup) 2005-06, to Malaysia 2006-07
Overseas teams played for: Yarroweyah United CC, Victoria 2007-08

Career highlights to date: 'Playing in an U19 Cricket World Cup and getting a full-time contract at Warwickshire CCC'
Cricket moments to forget: 'Being super-subbed for England U19 in the semi-final of the U19 World Cup on TV after seven overs of the first innings of the match'
Cricket superstitions: 'Always step over the boundary rope; never split it'
Cricketers particularly admired: Glenn McGrath, Curtly Ambrose
Young players to look out for: Nick James
Other sports played: Golf, football, swimming
Other sports followed: Football (Blackburn Rovers)
Favourite band: Arctic Monkeys
Relaxations: 'Watching TV, music, eating and sleeping'
Extras: Represented England U19 2005, 2006, 2007. NBC Denis Compton Award for the most promising young Warwickshire player 2006

MITCHELL, D. K. H. — Worcestershire

Name: Daryl Keith Henry Mitchell
Role: Right-hand bat, right-arm medium bowler; batting all-rounder
Born: 25 November 1983, Evesham
Height: 5ft 10in **Weight:** 11st 10lbs
Nickname: Mitch, Peggy, Toucan
County debut: 2005
County colours: 2005
Place in batting averages: 56th av. 43.33 (2006 52nd av. 47.00)
Parents: Keith and Jane
Marital status: Single
Family links with cricket: 'Dad played club cricket and coaches WYC (Worcestershire Young Cricketers) U13'
Education: Prince Henry's High, Evesham; University of Worcester
Qualifications: 10 GCSEs, 4 A-levels, BSc (Hons) Sports Studies and Geography (2.2), ECB Level 1 coaching
Career outside cricket: 'None as yet. Hoping to become a teacher'
Off-season: 'Midland-Guildford CC (Perth, WA)'
Overseas tours: Worcestershire to Guernsey 2007
Overseas teams played for: Midland-Guildford, Perth 2005-08
Career highlights to date: '134* v Glamorgan – maiden first-class century 2006. Winning Pro40 2007'
Cricket moments to forget: 'Run out first ball by a Monty direct hit v Northants, Twenty20 2006'

Cricket superstitions: 'Put gloves on before helmet'
Cricketers particularly admired: Michael Atherton, Graeme Hick
Young players to look out for: Steve Davies, Moeen Ali
Other sports played: Football, golf ('badly'), pool, darts, skittles
Other sports followed: Football (Aston Villa), rugby (Worcester), AFL (West Coast Eagles)
Favourite band: Oasis
Relaxations: 'Music, movies, PlayStation'
Extras: Scored 210* for Worcestershire v Bradford/Leeds UCCE at Harrogate 2006. Carried bat for 70* v Sussex at Hove 2007
Opinions on cricket: 'Game in this country is in good shape. Standard is high in all forms. Move to one overseas in 2008 is a good one, as it will allow the abundance of young English talent to break through.'
Best batting: 134* Worcestershire v Glamorgan, Colwyn Bay 2006
Best bowling: 3-50 Worcestershire v Sussex, Hove 2007

2007 Season

	M	Inn	NO	Runs	HS	Avg	100	50	Ct	St	Balls	Runs	Wkts	Avg	BB	5I	10M
Test																	
FC	5	8	2	260	112	43.33	1	1	7	-	249	116	6	19.33	3-50	-	-
ODI																	
List A	6	4	1	101	53	33.66	-	1	3	-	138	141	2	70.50	1-26	-	
20/20 Int																	
20/20	3	1	1	1	1 *		-	-	1	-	66	69	5	13.80	3-18	-	

Career Performances

	M	Inn	NO	Runs	HS	Avg	100	50	Ct	St	Balls	Runs	Wkts	Avg	BB	5I	10M
Test																	
FC	15	26	6	738	134 *	36.90	2	5	16	-	339	215	7	30.71	3-50	-	-
ODI																	
List A	10	8	1	114	53	16.28	-	1	5	-	198	208	6	34.66	4-42	-	
20/20 Int																	
20/20	17	6	3	10	4	3.33	-	-	4	-	294	419	11	38.09	3-18	-	

MOHAMMAD AKRAM Surrey

Name: Mohammad Akram Awan
Role: Right-hand bat, right-arm fast bowler
Born: 10 September 1974, Islamabad, Pakistan
Height: 6ft 2in **Weight:** 13st 7lbs
Nickname: Haji, Akee
County debut: 1997 (Northamptonshire), 2003 (Essex), 2004 (Sussex), 2005 (Surrey)
County cap: 2006 (Surrey)
Test debut: 1995-96
ODI debut: 1995-96
Place in bowling averages: (2006 51st av. 30.80)
Parents: Mohammad Akbar
Wife and date of marriage: Hamera Akram, May 1999
Children: Imaan Akram; Amaar Akram
Education: Modern Secondary School; Gordon College, Rawalpindi
Career outside cricket: Business
Overseas tours: Pakistan to Australia 1995-96, to England 1996, to South Africa and Zimbabwe 1997-98, to Australia 1999-2000, to West Indies 1999-2000, to New Zealand 2000-01, plus one-day tournaments in Sharjah, Singapore, Toronto, Bangladesh and Sri Lanka
Overseas teams played for: Rawalpindi Cricket Association 1992-93 – 2002-03; Allied Bank 1996-97 – 2000-01
Career highlights to date: 'When I played Test cricket'
Cricket moments to forget: 'All good'
Cricket superstitions: 'None'
Cricketers particularly admired: Wasim, Waqar, Michael Holding
Other sports played: Football, gulee danda (traditional Pakistani game)
Other sports followed: Football, boxing
Favourite band: 'Not into music'
Relaxations: 'Meeting friends, swimming, eating out'
Extras: Was Northamptonshire's overseas player in 1997. Took 5-98 on Championship debut for Essex v Sussex at Colchester 2003. Took career best 8-49 v Surrey at The Oval 2003, including the first four wickets without conceding a run. Is no longer classed as an overseas player. Released by Surrey at the end of the 2007 season
Best batting: 35* Sussex v Warwickshire, Edgbaston 2004
Best bowling: 8-49 Essex v Surrey, The Oval 2003

2007 Season

	M	Inn	NO	Runs	HS	Avg	100	50	Ct	St	Balls	Runs	Wkts	Avg	BB	5I	10M
Test																	
FC	3	6	2	17	8 *	4.25	-	-	-	-	438	236	6	39.33	2-22	-	-
ODI																	
List A	10	2	1	2	1 *	2.00	-	-	1	-	441	322	17	18.94	4-36	-	
20/20 Int																	
20/20																	

Career Performances

	M	Inn	NO	Runs	HS	Avg	100	50	Ct	St	Balls	Runs	Wkts	Avg	BB	5I	10M
Test	9	15	6	24	10 *	2.66	-	-	4	-	1477	859	17	50.52	5-138	1	-
FC	125	155	45	944	35 *	8.58	-	-	31	-	20169	11963	416	28.75	8-49	18	1
ODI	23	9	7	14	7 *	7.00	-	-	8	-	989	790	19	41.57	2-28	-	
List A	129	57	26	233	33	7.51	-	-	24	-	5891	4521	148	30.54	4-19	-	
20/20 Int																	
20/20	3	1	1	7	7 *		-	-	2	-	66	96	3	32.00	2-22	-	

MOHAMMAD ASIF — Surrey

Name: Mohammad Asif
Role: Left-hand bat, right-arm fast-medium bowler
Born: 20 December 1982, Sheikhupura, Pakistan
County debut: 2006 (Leicestershire)
Test debut: 2004-05
ODI debut: 2005-06
Twenty20 Int debut: 2006
Place in bowling averages: (2006 67th av. 33.20)
Overseas tours: Pakistan A to Sri Lanka 2004-05, to Namibia and Zimbabwe 2004-05; Pakistan to Australia 2004-05, to Sri Lanka 2005-06, to UAE (DLF Cup) 2006, to England 2006, to South Africa 2006-07, to Abu Dhabi (Warid Cricket Series) 2007, to South Africa (World 20/20) 2007-08; Asian Cricket Council XI to India (Afro-Asia Cup) 2007
Overseas teams played for: Lahore Division 1999-2000; Sheikhupura 2000-01 – 2001-02; Khan Research Laboratories 2001-02 – 2003-04; Quetta 2003-04; National Bank of Pakistan 2004-05 – 2005-06; Sialkot/Sialkot Stallions 2004-05 – 2006-07

Extras: Returned match figures of 10-106 (7-62/3-44) for Pakistan A v England XI at Lahore 2005-06. Man of the Match in the second Test v Sri Lanka at Kandy 2005-06 (6-44/5-27); also Man of the [Test] Series v Sri Lanka 2005-06. An overseas player with Leicestershire 2006; has joined Surrey as an overseas player for 2008
Best batting: 42 KRL v Allied Bank, Karachi 2002-03
Best bowling: 7-35 Sialkot v Multan, Multan 2004-05

2007 Season (did not make any first-class or one-day appearances)

Career Performances

	M	Inn	NO	Runs	HS	Avg	100	50	Ct	St	Balls	Runs	Wkts	Avg	BB	5I	10M
Test	9	13	6	40	12 *	5.71	-	-	2	-	1914	986	49	20.12	6-44	4	1
FC	68	91	37	448	42	8.29	-	-	26	-	12169	6713	280	23.97	7-35	17	5
ODI	28	9	3	28	6	4.66	-	-	4	-	1383	1064	31	34.32	3-28	-	
List A	55	21	13	90	12 *	11.25	-	-	16	-	2688	2111	63	33.50	4-30	-	
20/20 Int	9	1	1	4	4 *		-	-	3	-	209	269	12	22.41	4-18	-	
20/20	21	3	2	5	4 *	5.00	-	-	8	-	496	571	34	16.79	5-11	1	

MONTGOMERIE, R. R. Sussex

Name: Richard Robert Montgomerie
Role: Right-hand opening bat, occasional right-arm slow bowler
Born: 3 July 1971, Rugby
Height: 5ft 10in **Weight:** 13st
Nickname: Monty
County debut: 1991 (Northamptonshire), 1999 (Sussex)
County cap: 1995 (Northamptonshire), 1999 (Sussex)
Benefit: 2007 (Sussex)
1000 runs in a season: 6
Place in batting averages: 71st av. 40.32 (2006 124th av. 32.32)
Parents: Robert and Gillian
Wife and date of marriage: Frances Elizabeth, 23 October 2004
Family links with cricket: Father captained Oxfordshire
Education: Rugby School; Worcester College, Oxford University
Qualifications: 12 O-levels, 4 A-levels, BA (Hons) Chemistry, Level II coaching
Career outside cricket: Teacher

Overseas tours: Oxford University to Namibia 1991; Northamptonshire to Zimbabwe and Johannesburg; Christians in Sport to South Africa 2000; Sussex to Grenada 2001, 2002
Overseas teams played for: Sydney University CC 1995-96
Cricket moments to forget: 'Running [Northants] captain Allan Lamb out on my Championship debut … as his runner'
Other sports followed: Golf, rackets, real tennis 'and many others'
Favourite band: The Police
Relaxations: Any sport, good television, reading and 'occasionally testing my brain'
Extras: Oxford rackets Blue 1990. Faced first ball delivered by Durham in first-class cricket, for Oxford University at The Parks 1992. Captained Oxford University and Combined Universities 1994. Man of the Match award for his 157 in the Vodafone Challenge match against the Australians at Hove 2001. Joint Sussex Player of the Year (with Murray Goodwin) 2001. Sussex 1st XI Fielder of the Year 2003. 'Two first-class wickets!' Retired at the end of the 2007 season, having contributed 1000 runs and 27 catches to Sussex's third Championship success
Best batting: 196 Sussex v Hampshire, Hove 2002
Best bowling: 1-0 Sussex v Middlesex, Lord's 2001

2007 Season

	M	Inn	NO	Runs	HS	Avg	100	50	Ct	St	Balls	Runs	Wkts	Avg	BB	5I	10M
Test																	
FC	17	29	1	1129	195	40.32	2	7	31	-	0	0	0		-	-	-
ODI																	
List A	10	10	0	574	125	57.40	2	4	3	-	0	0	0		-	-	
20/20 Int																	
20/20																	

Career Performances

	M	Inn	NO	Runs	HS	Avg	100	50	Ct	St	Balls	Runs	Wkts	Avg	BB	5I	10M
Test																	
FC	251	433	33	14337	196	35.84	29	80	248	-	282	147	2	73.50	1-0	-	-
ODI																	
List A	199	195	21	6513	132 *	37.43	9	44	52	-	6	0	0		-	-	
20/20 Int																	
20/20	4	3	0	45	20	15.00	-	-	3	-	0	0	0		-	-	

MOORE, S. C. Worcestershire

Name: Stephen Colin Moore
Role: Right-hand opening bat, right-arm medium bowler
Born: 4 November 1980, Johannesburg, South Africa
Height: 6ft 1in **Weight:** 13st
Nickname: Mandy, Circles, Mork
County debut: 2003
County colours: 2003
1000 runs in a season: 2
1st-Class 200s: 1
Place in batting averages: 95th av. 36.75 (2006 108th av. 34.28)
Parents: Shane and Carrol
Marital status: Single
Education: St Stithians College, South Africa; Exeter University
Qualifications: MEng (Hons) Electronic Engineering
Off-season: 'Training and working in and around Worcester'
Overseas teams played for: Midland-Guildford, Perth 2002-04; Northern Districts, Adelaide
Career highlights to date: 'First-class debut and Lord's final 2004'
Cricket moments to forget: 'Losing Lord's final 2004 and getting a duck!'
Cricket superstitions: 'Left pad first!'
Other sports played: Hockey, tennis (both Exeter University 1st team), golf, squash
Other sports followed: Tennis
Favourite band: Soul Jazz Collective
Relaxations: 'My music (guitar and saxophone); watersports and wildlife'
Extras: Scored 1000 first-class runs in his first full season 2004. Is not considered an overseas player
Opinions on cricket: 'Twenty20 looks like it might be taking cricket to another level worldwide. Question for me is whether it is a novelty or a serious product with a long-term extensive future.'
Best batting: 246 Worcestershire v Derbyshire, Worcester 2005
Best bowling: 1-13 Worcestershire v Lancashire, Worcester 2004

2007 Season

	M	Inn	NO	Runs	HS	Avg	100	50	Ct	St	Balls	Runs	Wkts	Avg	BB	5I	10M
Test																	
FC	15	25	1	882	143	36.75	2	3	7	-	54	42	0		-	-	-
ODI																	
List A	9	9	1	192	66	24.00	-	1	3	-	0	0	0		-	-	
20/20 Int																	
20/20																	

Career Performances

	M	Inn	NO	Runs	HS	Avg	100	50	Ct	St	Balls	Runs	Wkts	Avg	BB	5I	10M
Test																	
FC	68	121	11	4342	246	39.47	7	22	33	-	342	321	5	64.20	1-13	-	-
ODI																	
List A	64	63	6	1746	105 *	30.63	2	10	15	-	35	42	1	42.00	1-1	-	
20/20 Int																	
20/20	26	22	4	370	53	20.55	-	1	11	-	0	0	0		-	-	

MORGAN, E. J. G. Middlesex

Name: Eoin Joseph Gerard Morgan
Role: Left-hand bat, right-arm medium bowler
Born: 10 September 1986, Dublin
Height: 5ft 10in **Weight:** 11st 11lbs
Nickname: Moggie
County debut: 2005 (one-day), 2006 (first-class)
ODI debut: 2006
1st-Class 200s: 1
Place in batting averages: 122nd av. 32.42 (2006 257th av. 13.09)
Parents: Joseph and Olivia
Marital status: Single
Family links with cricket: 'My father, three brothers, two sisters, grandfather and great-grandfather all played'
Education: Catholic University School, Dublin
Overseas tours: Ireland U19 to Bangladesh (U19 World Cup) 2003-04, to Sri Lanka (U19 World Cup) 2005-06; Ireland to Namibia (ICC Inter-Continental Cup) 2005, to Scotland (European Championship) 2006, to Kenya (ICC World Cricket League) 2006-07, to West Indies (World Cup) 2006-07, plus various Ireland age-group tours

Overseas teams played for: St Henry's Marist School U19, Durban 2003
Career highlights to date: 'Winning the Inter-Continental Cup with Ireland in Namibia [2005]'
Cricketers particularly admired: Ricky Ponting, Brian Lara
Young players to look out for: Billy Godleman
Other sports played: Rugby (Schools), Gaelic football
Other sports followed: Gaelic football (Dublin GAA – 'The Dubs'), rugby, snooker, darts
Favourite band: Aslan
Relaxations: 'Watching sports and listening to music'
Extras: Player of the Tournament at European U15 Championships 2000, 2002 and at European U17 Championships 2002. Became then youngest player to represent Ireland 2003. NBC Denis Compton Award for the most promising young Middlesex player 2003. C&G Man of the Match award for Ireland v Yorkshire in Belfast 2005 (59). Made ODI debut for Ireland v Scotland at Ayr in the European Championship 2006, winning Man of the Match award (99). Scored maiden first-class double century (209*) v UAE in Abu Dhabi in the 2006 ICC Inter-Continental Cup, winning Man of the Match award
Best batting: 209* Ireland v United Arab Emirates, Abu Dhabi (SZ) 2006-07
Best bowling: 2-24 Middlesex v Nottinghamshire, Lord's 2007

2007 Season

	M	Inn	NO	Runs	HS	Avg	100	50	Ct	St	Balls	Runs	Wkts	Avg	BB	5I	10M
Test																	
FC	5	7	0	227	76	32.42	-	3	4	-	67	32	2	16.00	2-24	-	-
ODI																	
List A	15	15	3	493	100	41.08	1	3	4	-	0	0	0		-	-	
20/20 Int																	
20/20	6	6	1	119	34	23.80	-	-	1	-	0	0	0		-	-	

Career Performances

	M	Inn	NO	Runs	HS	Avg	100	50	Ct	St	Balls	Runs	Wkts	Avg	BB	5I	10M
Test																	
FC	18	29	1	959	209 *	34.25	2	5	9	1	79	46	2	23.00	2-24	-	-
ODI	18	18	1	549	115	32.29	1	3	8	-	0	0	0		-	-	
List A	59	55	7	1596	115	33.25	2	10	19	-	30	44	0		-	-	
20/20 Int																	
20/20	14	13	1	293	66	24.41	-	1	5	-	0	0	0		-	-	

MORKEL, J. A. — Durham

Name: Johannes Albertus (Albie) Morkel
Role: Left-hand bat, right-arm medium-fast bowler; all-rounder
Born: 10 June 1981, Vereeniging, South Africa
County debut: No first-team appearance
ODI debut: 2003-04
Twenty20 Int debut: 2005-06
1st-Class 200s: 1
Family links with cricket: Father Albert played for Southern Transvaal Country Districts; brother Morne plays for Titans and South Africa
Overseas tours: South Africa U19 to Sri Lanka (U19 World Cup) 1999-2000; South Africa A to Zimbabwe 2002-03, to Australia 2002-03, to Zimbabwe 2004, to Sri Lanka (Triangular A Team Tournament) 2005-06, to Zimbabwe 2006-07; South Africa to New Zealand 2003-04, to India (one-day series) 2005-06, to Zimbabwe (one-day series) 2007-08, to Pakistan 2007-08 (one-day series); African XI to India (Afro-Asia Cup) 2007
Overseas teams played for: Easterns 1999-2000 – 2005-06; Titans 2003-04 –
Extras: Represented South Africa in the Twenty20 World Championship 2007-08. His match awards include Man of the Match for South Africa A v New Zealand A at Johannesburg 2004-05 (67*). Has joined Durham as an overseas player for 2008 as a locum for Shivnarine Chanderpaul
Best batting: 204* Titans v Western Province Boland, Paarl 2004-05
Best bowling: 6-36 Easterns v Griqualand West, Kimberley 1999-2000
Stop press: Man of the Match for Titans v Eagles at Benoni in the SuperSport Series 2007-08 (44/151)

2007 Season (did not make any first-class or one-day appearances)

Career Performances

	M	Inn	NO	Runs	HS	Avg	100	50	Ct	St	Balls	Runs	Wkts	Avg	BB	5I	10M
Test																	
FC	50	70	12	2347	204 *	40.46	3	16	18	-	8165	4172	140	29.80	6-36	3	-
ODI	12	9	1	182	97	22.75	-	1	1	-	408	376	11	34.18	2-23	-	
List A	98	74	20	1437	97	26.61	-	6	14	-	4241	3279	112	29.27	4-23	-	
20/20 Int	8	5	0	158	43	31.60	-	-	3	-	108	118	4	29.50	2-12	-	
20/20	31	24	4	440	56	22.00	-	1	3	-	485	623	20	31.15	2-12	-	

MORKEL, M. Kent

Name: Morne Morkel
Role: Left-hand bat, right-arm fast bowler
Born: 6 October 1984, Vereeniging, South Africa
County debut: 2007 (one-day)
Test debut: 2006-07
ODI debut: 2007
Twenty20 Int debut: 2007-08
Family links with cricket: Father Albert played for Southern Transvaal Country Districts; brother Albie plays for Titans and South Africa
Overseas tours: South Africa Academy to Pakistan 2005-06; African XI to India (Afro-Asia Cup) 2007; South Africa Emerging Players to Australia (Cricket Australia Emerging Players Tournament) 2007; South Africa to Zimbabwe (one-day series) 2007-08
Overseas teams played for: Easterns 2003-04 – 2006-07; Titans 2004-05 –
Extras: His match awards include Man of the Match v Eagles at Centurion in the SuperSport Series 2006-07 (22/57; 4-76/2-58). Made ODI debut for African XI v Asian Cricket Council XI in Bangalore 2007; has also played in ODIs for South Africa. Was a temporary overseas player with Kent during the 2007 season as a replacement for Andrew Hall. Represented South Africa in the Twenty20 World Championship 2007-08
Best batting: 57 Titans v Eagles, Centurion 2006-07
Best bowling: 6-66 Easterns/Northerns XI v Zimbabweans, Benoni 2004-05

2007 Season

	M	Inn	NO	Runs	HS	Avg	100	50	Ct	St	Balls	Runs	Wkts	Avg	BB	5I	10M
Test																	
FC																	
ODI																	
List A																	
20/20 Int																	
20/20	8	0	0	0	0		-	-	3	-	174	184	11	16.72	3-24	-	

Career Performances																
	M	Inn	NO	Runs	HS	Avg	100	50	Ct	St	Balls	Runs	Wkts	Avg	BB	5I	10M
Test	1	2	1	58	31 *	58.00	-	-	-	-	144	111	3	37.00	3-86	-	-
FC	19	26	6	379	57	18.95	-	1	13	-	3329	1948	66	29.51	6-66	3	-
ODI	6	3	2	52	25	52.00	-	-	2	-	360	282	12	23.50	3-50	-	
List A	21	9	5	102	35	25.50	-	-	5	-	1019	769	32	24.03	4-41	-	
20/20 Int	5	1	1	1	1 *		-	-	-	-	120	120	9	13.33	4-17	-	
20/20	25	4	3	11	6 *	11.00	-	-	4	-	509	587	28	20.96	4-17	-	

MORRIS, R. K. Hampshire

Name: Richard Kyle Morris
Role: Right-hand bat, right-arm fast bowler; all-rounder
Born: 26 September 1987, Newbury
Height: 6ft 1in **Weight:** 12st
Nickname: Mossa, Torres
County debut: No first-team appearance
Parents: David and Debbie
Marital status: Single
Family links with cricket: 'Brother Jimmy captained Durham UCCE and is currently playing grade cricket in Perth'
Education: Bradfield College; Loughborough University
Qualifications: GCSEs, A-levels, Level 1 coaching, 'hopefully a degree'
Career outside cricket: Student
Off-season: 'Final year at Loughborough. Perth pre-Christmas'
Overseas tours: Bradfield College to Cape Town 2001, to Sri Lanka 2004; British Universities to Pretoria 2007
Career highlights to date: 'Signing for Hampshire. Representing England. First-class debut v Essex 2006'
Cricket moments to forget: 'Any injury!'
Cricket superstitions: 'Touch my guard three times before I move into my stance'
Cricketers particularly admired: Andy Bichel, Robin Smith, Michael Brown, Ottis Gibson
Young players to look out for: James Vince, David Balcombe, Benny Howell
Other sports played: Football (Reading Academy 1998-2000)
Other sports followed: Football (Reading FC)
Injuries: Out for four months with an ankle fracture

Favourite band: The Libertines, Kings of Leon
Relaxations: 'Cooking, live music, travelling, squash, the beach'
Extras: Represented England U17. Made Hampshire 2nd XI debut aged 16 v Bangladesh U19 2004, taking 3-38 from 9.3 overs. *Cricketer* Cup winner with Bradfield Waifs 2005. Is a sports scholar at Loughborough University. Played for Loughborough UCCE 2006, 2007
Opinions on cricket: 'Reduction to only one overseas player [will be], long term, a benefit to the production of good young English players, providing they're willing to listen and seek advice from senior members of the dressing room.'
Best batting: 7 LUCCE v Essex, Chelmsford 2006
Best bowling: 2-58 LUCCE v Hampshire, Rose Bowl 2006

2007 Season (did not make any first-class or one-day appearances)

Career Performances

	M	Inn	NO	Runs	HS	Avg	100	50	Ct	St	Balls	Runs	Wkts	Avg	BB	5I	10M
Test																	
FC	2	2	0	8	7	4.00	-	-	1	-	186	166	3	55.33	2-58	-	-
ODI																	
List A																	
20/20 Int																	
20/20																	

MUCHALL, G. J. — Durham

Name: Gordon James Muchall
Role: Right-hand bat, right-arm medium bowler
Born: 2 November 1982, Newcastle upon Tyne
Height: 6ft **Weight:** 13st
Nickname: Much, Muchy, Hank, Melon
County debut: 2002
County cap: 2005
1st-Class 200s: 1
Place in batting averages: 183rd av. 24.76 (2006 162nd av. 27.78)
Parents: Mary and Arthur
Marital status: Single
Family links with cricket: 'Dad and brother Matthew play for South Shields CC; brother Paul for Tynemouth and Durham Academy'
Education: Durham School

Qualifications: 7 GCSEs, 2 A-levels, Level 2 cricket coach
Career outside cricket: Coaching
Overseas tours: England U19 to India 2000-01, to Australia and (U19 World Cup) New Zealand 2001-02; ECB National Academy to Australia and Sri Lanka 2002-03
Overseas teams played for: Fremantle 2001-02; Claremont-Nedlands, Perth 2005-06
Career highlights to date: '100 at Lord's. 200 against Kent. 250 for England U19. Winning Friends Provident Trophy [2007]'
Cricket moments to forget: 'With the opposition needing four off the last ball to win, going into the long barrier position and the ball bouncing over my head for four'
Cricketers particularly admired: Dale Benkenstein, Mike Hussey, Jimmy Maher, Paul Collingwood, Jon Lewis
Young players to look out for: Luke Evans, Paul Muchall, Scott Borthwick
Other sports played: Rugby (Durham School – played in *Daily Mail* Cup final at Twickenham)
Other sports followed: Rugby (Newcastle Falcons)
Favourite band: Green Day
Relaxations: Listening to music, socialising with friends
Extras: Represented England U19, scoring 254 in the first 'Test' v India U19 at Cardiff 2002. Cricket Society's Most Promising Young Cricketer of the Year Award 2002. NBC Denis Compton Award for the most promising young Durham player 2002. Durham Batsman of the Year 2004. Scored maiden first-class double century (219) v Kent at Canterbury 2006, in the process sharing with Phil Mustard (130) in a new Durham record partnership for the sixth wicket (249)
Opinions on cricket: 'Too many games; not enough time to prepare.'
Best batting: 219 Durham v Kent, Canterbury 2006
Best bowling: 3-26 Durham v Yorkshire, Headingley 2003

2007 Season

	M	Inn	NO	Runs	HS	Avg	100	50	Ct	St	Balls	Runs	Wkts	Avg	BB	5I	10M
Test																	
FC	12	22	1	520	66	24.76	-	4	9	-	0	0	0		-	-	-
ODI																	
List A	7	5	2	82	41 *	27.33	-	-	7	-	0	0	0		-	-	
20/20 Int																	
20/20	6	4	3	104	44 *	104.00	-	-	1	-	0	0	0		-	-	

Career Performances

	M	Inn	NO	Runs	HS	Avg	100	50	Ct	St	Balls	Runs	Wkts	Avg	BB	5I	10M
Test																	
FC	91	165	7	4529	219	28.66	7	23	60	-	890	615	15	41.00	3-26	-	-
ODI																	
List A	72	63	11	1554	101 *	29.88	1	7	19	-	162	137	1	137.00	1-15	-	
20/20 Int																	
20/20	29	25	6	567	64 *	29.84	-	1	10	-	12	8	1	8.00	1-8	-	

MUCHALL, P. B. Durham

Name: Paul Bernard Muchall
Role: Right-hand bat, right-arm medium-fast bowler; all-rounder
Born: 17 March 1987, Newcastle upon Tyne
Height: 6ft 2in **Weight:** 13st
Nickname: Much
County debut: No first-team appearance
Parents: Arthur and Mary
Marital status: Single
Family links with cricket: 'Grandad played for Northumberland in the Minor Counties Championship, Dad plays for Durham Over-50s and brother Gordon currently plays for Durham'
Education: Durham School
Qualifications: 10 GCSEs, 3 AS-levels, 2 A-levels, Level 2 personal trainer
Career outside cricket: Personal trainer
Off-season: 'Playing cricket in Australia for Fremantle'
Overseas teams played for: Fremantle DCC 2005-06, 2007-08
Career highlights to date: 'Scoring a century [107*] on debut for Durham 2nd XI, and receiving a contract for the coming 2008 season with Durham'
Cricket moments to forget: 'Getting a pair for Northumberland'
Cricket superstitions: 'Always put left pad on first'
Cricketers particularly admired: Steve Waugh, Gordon Muchall, Malcolm Marshall
Young players to look out for: Patrick Molinari (Fremantle), Theo Doropoulos (Western Australia), Michael Turns, Ben Stokes
Other sports played: Checkers, golf, football, rugby
Other sports followed: Football (Newcastle United), rugby (Newcastle Falcons, Westoe)
Favourite band: U2, Sneaky Sound System
Relaxations: 'Golf, beach'
Extras: Played for Northumberland in the Minor Counties Championship 2006, 2007
Opinions on cricket: 'Free hits in four-day games.'

MULLANEY, S. J. — Lancashire

Name: Steven John Mullaney
Role: Right-hand bat, right-arm medium bowler; all-rounder
Born: 19 November 1986, Warrington
Height: 5ft 10in **Weight:** 12st 5lbs
Nickname: Mull, Cadet Mahoney
County debut: 2006
Parents: Andrew and Elaine
Marital status: Single
Family links with cricket: 'Dad was club professional in 1980s and 1990s'
Education: St Mary's RC High School, Astley
Qualifications: 7 GCSEs
Off-season: 'In Australia with McKinnon CC (Victoria)'
Overseas tours: England U19 to India 2004-05, to Sri Lanka (U19 World Cup) 2005-06
Overseas teams played for: McKinnon, Melbourne 2006-08
Career highlights to date: '165* for Lancashire v Durham UCCE 2007 (maiden first-class hundred)' (*Scored in his only first-class innings of 2007*)
Cricket moments to forget: 'None'
Cricket superstitions: 'Put left pad on first'
Cricketers particularly admired: Andrew Flintoff
Young players to look out for: Karl Brown, Tom Smith, Moeen Ali, Gareth Cross
Other sports played: Rugby league (formerly; 'toured France with England U15')
Other sports followed: Football (Manchester City FC), rugby league (St Helens)
Favourite band: Westlife
Relaxations: 'Watching TV and other sports'
Extras: Scored 208 for Lancashire U17. Represented England U19 2005, 2006
Opinions on cricket: 'The standard is getting higher and higher so you have got to work harder and harder.'
Best batting: 165* Lancashire v DUCCE, Durham 2007

2007 Season

	M	Inn	NO	Runs	HS	Avg	100	50	Ct	St	Balls	Runs	Wkts	Avg	BB	5I	10M
Test																	
FC	1	1	1	165	165 *		1	-	2	-	42	13	0		-	-	-
ODI																	
List A	4	2	0	22	12	11.00	-	-	1	-	78	56	5	11.20	3-13	-	
20/20 Int																	
20/20	1	0	0	0	0		-	-	1	-	0	0	0		-	-	

Career Performances

	M	Inn	NO	Runs	HS	Avg	100	50	Ct	St	Balls	Runs	Wkts	Avg	BB	5I	10M
Test																	
FC	2	2	1	209	165 *	209.00	1	-	3	-	102	49	0		-	-	-
ODI																	
List A	5	2	0	22	12	11.00	-	-	1	-	104	79	6	13.16	3-13	-	
20/20 Int																	
20/20	2	1	0	5	5	5.00	-	-	1	-	0	0	0		-	-	

MUNDAY, M. K. — Somerset

Name: Michael Kenneth Munday
Role: Right-hand bat, leg-spin bowler
Born: 22 October 1984, Nottingham
Height: 5ft 8in **Weight:** 12st
County debut: 2005
Place in bowling averages: 1st av. 13.71 (2006 65th av. 32.90)
Parents: John and Maureen
Marital status: Single
Family links with cricket: 'Dad, brother and sister have played league cricket in Cornwall'
Education: Truro School; Corpus Christi College, Oxford University
Qualifications: 10 GCSEs, 3 A-levels, MChem (Oxon)
Off-season: 'Playing for Glenelg District CC (Adelaide) until Christmas'
Overseas tours: Cornwall Schools U13 to South Africa 1998; ESCA West U15 to West Indies 2000
Overseas teams played for: Glenelg DCC, Adelaide 2006-08
Career highlights to date: 'Taking 8-55 on the last day of the 2007 season'
Cricket moments to forget: 'Being hit on the point of the elbow by Steffan Jones's "skiddy" bouncer, OUCCE v Derbyshire 2006'
Cricket superstitions: 'Always wear an arm guard'
Cricketers particularly admired: Shane Warne, Marcus Trescothick
Young players to look out for: Joe Sayers, Luke Parker, Mark Turner, Jos Buttler
Other sports played: Chess ('Yes, it is a sport')
Other sports followed: Football (Liverpool)
Favourite band: Coldplay, The Killers
Relaxations: 'Swimming, reading, baby-sitting Kieswetter'
Extras: Played for Cornwall in the C&G 2001. Played for Oxford UCCE 2003-06.

Oxford Blue 2003-06, returning match figures of 11-143 v Cambridge University in the Varsity Match at The Parks 2006. Represented England U19 2004. Returned match figures of 10-65 (2-10/8-55) v Nottinghamshire at Taunton 2007
Best batting: 17* Oxford University v Cambridge University, The Parks 2006
Best bowling: 8-55 Somerset v Nottinghamshire, Taunton 2007

2007 Season

	M	Inn	NO	Runs	HS	Avg	100	50	Ct	St	Balls	Runs	Wkts	Avg	BB	5I	10M
Test																	
FC	3	3	1	13	9	6.50	-	-	2	-	264	192	14	13.71	8-55	1	1
ODI																	
List A																	
20/20 Int																	
20/20																	

Career Performances

	M	Inn	NO	Runs	HS	Avg	100	50	Ct	St	Balls	Runs	Wkts	Avg	BB	5I	10M
Test																	
FC	22	19	9	71	17 *	7.10	-	-	10	-	2717	1772	66	26.84	8-55	4	2
ODI																	
List A	1	0	0	0	0		-	-	-	-	30	39	1	39.00	1-39	-	
20/20 Int																	
20/20																	

MURALITHARAN, M. Lancashire

Name: Muttiah Muralitharan
Role: Right-hand bat, off-spin bowler
Born: 17 April 1972, Kandy, Sri Lanka
Height: 5ft 7in **Weight:** 9st 6lbs
Nickname: Murali
County debut: 1999 (Lancashire), 2003 (Kent)
County cap: 1999 (Lancashire), 2003 (Kent)
Test debut: 1992
ODI debut: 1993
Twenty20 Int debut: 2006-07
50 wickets in a season: 3
Place in bowling averages: 5th av. 18.66 (2006 3rd av. 18.10)
Parents: Sinnasamy and Lakshmi
Wife and date of marriage: Madhi Malar, 21 March 2005
Children: Naren
Education: St Anthony's College, Kandy
Overseas tours: Sri Lanka U24 to South Africa 1992-93; Sri Lanka to England 1991,

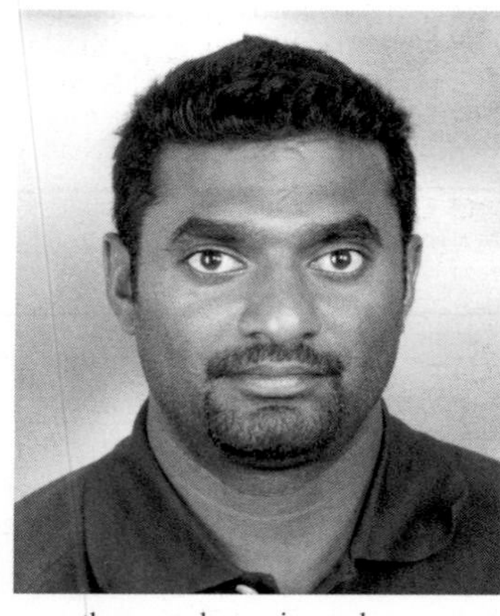

to India 1993-94, to Zimbabwe 1994-95, to South Africa 1994-95, to New Zealand 1994-95, to Pakistan 1995-96, to Australia 1995-96, to India and Pakistan (World Cup) 1995-96, to New Zealand 1996-97, to West Indies 1996-97, to India 1997-98, to South Africa 1997-98, to England 1998, to Bangladesh (Wills International Cup) 1998-99, to UK, Ireland and Netherlands (World Cup) 1999, to Zimbabwe 1999-2000, to Pakistan 1999-2000, to Kenya (ICC Knockout Trophy) 2000-01, to South Africa 2000-01, to England 2002, to South Africa 2002-03, to Africa (World Cup) 2002-03, to West Indies 2003, to Zimbabwe 2004, to India 2005-06, to Bangladesh 2005-06, to England 2006, to India (ICC Champions Trophy) 2006-07, to New Zealand 2006-07, to West Indies (World Cup) 2006-07, to Australia 2007-08, plus numerous other one-day series and tournaments in Sharjah, India, Singapore, West Indies, Kenya, Pakistan, Australia, Bangladesh, New Zealand and Morocco; Asian Cricket Council XI to Australia (Tsunami Relief) 2004-05, to South Africa (Afro-Asia Cup) 2005-06; FICA World XI to New Zealand 2004-05; ICC World XI to Australia (Super Series) 2005-06
Overseas teams played for: Tamil Union Cricket and Athletic Club; Kandurata
Extras: One of *Wisden*'s Five Cricketers of the Year 1999. Was an overseas player with Lancashire 1999 (taking 66 wickets in the 12 Championship innings in which he bowled), 2001, 2005 and 2007. Lancashire Player of the Year 1999. Took 7-30 v India in the Champions Trophy in Sharjah 2000, at the time the best return in ODI history. Has won numerous international series and match awards, including Man of the Match v England at The Oval 1998 (7-155/9-65 from 113.5 overs), in the first Test at Galle 2000 in Sri Lanka's first Test win over South Africa (6-87/7-84) and in the third Test v England at Trent Bridge 2006 (3-62/8-70). Was an overseas player with Kent July to September 2003. In the first Test v Bangladesh at Chittagong 2005-06 (his 100th Test), he became the first bowler to reach 1000 international wickets (589 Test/411 ODI) when he dismissed Khaled Mashud. Highest wicket-taker in Test cricket for the calendar year 2006 with 90 wickets in 11 matches. Took 700th Test wicket (Syed Rasel) in the third Test v Bangladesh on his home ground at Kandy 2007, becoming the second bowler to reach the milestone after Shane Warne. Took his 200th wicket for Lancashire v Hampshire at Old Trafford 2007 in his 27th match, reaching the milestone quicker than any other bowler for the county
Best batting: 67 Sri Lanka v India, Kandy 2001
Best bowling: 9-51 Sri Lanka v Zimbabwe, Kandy 2001-02
Stop press: His 6-55 in the first Test v England 2007-08 on his home ground at Kandy included his 709th Test wicket (Paul Collingwood), taking him to the top of the all-time list of Test wicket-takers

2007 Season

	M	Inn	NO	Runs	HS	Avg	100	50	Ct	St	Balls	Runs	Wkts	Avg	BB	5I	10M
Test																	
FC	8	7	5	58	28	29.00	-	-	1	-	2355	952	51	18.66	6-72	5	-
ODI																	
List A	4	1	0	27	27	27.00	-	-	1	-	180	138	5	27.60	3-38	-	
20/20 Int																	
20/20	2	0	0	0	0		-	-	-	-	48	39	5	7.80	4-18	-	

Career Performances

	M	Inn	NO	Runs	HS	Avg	100	50	Ct	St	Balls	Runs	Wkts	Avg	BB	5I	10M
Test	113	144	49	1117	67	11.75	-	1	64	-	37382	14931	700	21.33	9-51	60	20
FC	212	256	76	2048	67	11.37	-	1	115	-	60276	23748	1274	18.64	9-51	112	32
ODI	297	135	50	491	27	5.77	-	-	117	-	16094	10321	455	22.68	7-30	8	
List A	378	170	62	693	27	6.41	-	-	138	-	20095	12636	575	21.97	7-30	10	
20/20 Int	1	0	0	0	0		-	-	-	-	24	27	2	13.50	2-27	-	
20/20	8	2	1	16	9	16.00	-	-	2	-	174	156	17	9.17	4-18	-	

MURTAGH, C. P. — Surrey

Name: Christopher (Chris) Paul Murtagh
Role: Right-hand bat
Born: 14 October 1984, Lambeth, London
Height: 5ft 11in **Weight:** 11st 9lbs
Nickname: Murts, Baby, Brow
County debut: 2005 (one-day)
Place in batting averages: 165th av. 26.83
Parents: Dominic and Elizabeth
Marital status: Single
Family links with cricket: Elder brother Tim played for Surrey and is now with Middlesex; Uncle Andy (A. J. Murtagh) played for Hampshire
Education: John Fisher, Purley, Surrey; Loughborough University
Qualifications: 10 GCSEs, 2 A-levels
Overseas tours: Surrey U19 to Sri Lanka 2002, to Perth 2004

Overseas teams played for: Parramatta, Sydney 2004
Cricket moments to forget: 'Dislocating finger in first training session in Australia – unable to play for two weeks'
Cricket superstitions: 'Left pad on first'

Cricketers particularly admired: Sachin Tendulkar, Andrew Flintoff, Curtly Ambrose
Other sports played: Rugby, football, golf
Other sports followed: Football (Liverpool FC)
Relaxations: 'Playing golf; watching sport'
Extras: Played for Surrey age groups and attended Surrey Academy. Made 2nd XI Championship debut 2002. Played for Loughborough UCCE 2005, 2006, 2007, scoring century (107) v Yorkshire at Headingley 2007
Best batting: 107 LUCCE v Yorkshire, Headingley 2007

2007 Season (did not make any first-class or one-day appearances for his county)

Career Performances

	M	Inn	NO	Runs	HS	Avg	100	50	Ct	St	Balls	Runs	Wkts	Avg	BB	5I	10M
Test																	
FC	8	13	2	259	107	23.54	1	-	5	-	6	8	0		-	-	-
ODI																	
List A	2	2	2	34	30 *		-	-	2	-	0	0	0		-	-	
20/20 Int																	
20/20																	

MURTAGH, T. J. — Middlesex

Name: Timothy (Tim) James Murtagh
Role: Left-hand bat, right-arm fast-medium bowler
Born: 2 August 1981, Lambeth, London
Height: 6ft 2in **Weight:** 12st
County debut: 2000 (one-day, Surrey), 2001 (first-class, Surrey), 2007 (Middlesex)
Place in batting averages: 231st av. 17.80
Place in bowling averages: 32nd av. 24.85
Parents: Dominic and Elizabeth
Marital status: Single
Family links with cricket: Younger brother Chris plays for Surrey; Uncle Andy (A. J. Murtagh) played for Hampshire
Education: John Fisher, Purley, Surrey; St Mary's University, Twickenham
Qualifications: 10 GCSEs, 2 A-levels
Overseas tours: Surrey U17 to South Africa 1997; England U19 to Malaysia and (U19 World Cup) Sri Lanka 1999-2000; British Universities to South Africa 2002

Overseas teams played for: Eastern Suburbs, Sydney 2006-07
Cricketers particularly admired: Darren Gough, Glenn McGrath
Other sports played: Rugby (was captain of John Fisher 2nd XV), skiing ('in the past')
Other sports followed: Football (Liverpool FC), rugby
Relaxations: Playing golf, watching sport, films, reading
Extras: Represented British Universities 2000, 2001, 2002 and 2003. Represented England U19 2000. NBC Denis Compton Award for the most promising young Surrey player 2001. Took 6-24 v Middlesex at Lord's 2005, the best return in the history of the Twenty20 Cup
Best batting: 74* Surrey v Middlesex, The Oval 2004
74* Surrey v Warwickshire, Croydon 2005
Best bowling: 6-86 British Universities v Pakistanis, Trent Bridge 2001

2007 Season

	M	Inn	NO	Runs	HS	Avg	100	50	Ct	St	Balls	Runs	Wkts	Avg	BB	5I	10M
Test																	
FC	14	16	1	267	40	17.80	-	-	2	-	1778	1044	42	24.85	6-87	1	-
ODI																	
List A	16	9	2	78	23	11.14	-	-	6	-	732	589	39	15.10	4-21	-	
20/20 Int																	
20/20	6	2	1	47	40 *	47.00	-	-	1	-	94	139	2	69.50	1-24	-	

Career Performances

	M	Inn	NO	Runs	HS	Avg	100	50	Ct	St	Balls	Runs	Wkts	Avg	BB	5I	10M
Test																	
FC	52	69	23	1200	74 *	26.08	-	6	19	-	6450	3862	118	32.72	6-86	4	-
ODI																	
List A	82	54	19	428	31 *	12.22	-	-	24	-	3737	3207	119	26.94	4-14	-	
20/20 Int																	
20/20	35	18	6	137	40 *	11.41	-	-	5	-	673	987	39	25.30	6-24	1	

60. Which former wicket-keeper and current county director of cricket made his Test debut in the first Test v New Zealand at Trent Bridge in 1994?

MURTAZA HUSSAIN — Surrey

Name: Murtaza Hussain
Role: Right-hand bat, right-arm off-break bowler
Born: 20 December 1974, Bahawalpur, Pakistan
County debut: 2007
Place in bowling averages: 38th av. 25.63
Overseas teams played for: Several in Pakistan, including Bahawalpur 1990-91 – 1997-98, 2001-02, Khan Research Laboratories 1997-98 – 1999-2000, Pakistan Customs 2004-05 – , Multan Tigers 2005-06
Extras: Represented Pakistan U19 1991-92. Played for Combined XI v New Zealanders 1996-97, Dr Abdul Qadeer Khan's XI v West Indians 1997-98 and Pakistan A v India A at Karachi 1997-98. Has played for Derbyshire 2nd XI and Middlesex 2nd XI. Holds a British passport and is not considered an overseas player
Best batting: 117 Pakistan Customs v Attock, Karachi (UBL) 2006-07
Best bowling: 9-54 Bahawalpur v Islamabad, Bahawalpur 1995-96

2007 Season

	M	Inn	NO	Runs	HS	Avg	100	50	Ct	St	Balls	Runs	Wkts	Avg	BB	5I	10M
Test																	
FC	2	2	1	15	9 *	15.00	-	-	1	-	568	282	11	25.63	4-126	-	-
ODI																	
List A	2	2	1	1	1 *	1.00	-	-	1	-	96	90	1	90.00	1-49	-	
20/20 Int																	
20/20																	

Career Performances

	M	Inn	NO	Runs	HS	Avg	100	50	Ct	St	Balls	Runs	Wkts	Avg	BB	5I	10M
Test																	
FC	131	187	37	3231	117	21.54	1	10	68	-	30319	12580	535	23.51	9-54	36	7
ODI																	
List A	104	69	16	771	85	14.54	-	1	34	-	4719	3248	131	24.79	5-18	1	
20/20 Int																	
20/20																	

MUSHTAQ AHMED Sussex

Name: Mushtaq Ahmed
Role: Right-hand bat, leg-spin bowler
Born: 28 June 1970, Sahiwal, Pakistan
Height: 5ft 4in
Nickname: Mushie
County debut: 1993 (Somerset), 2002 (Surrey), 2003 (Sussex)
County cap: 1993 (Somerset), 2003 (Sussex)
Test debut: 1989-90
ODI debut: 1988-89
50 wickets in a season: 6
100 wickets in a season: 2
Place in batting averages: 267th av. 12.14 (2006 234th av. 15.85)
Place in bowling averages: 39th av. 25.66 (2006 4th av. 19.91)
Wife and date of marriage: Uzma, 18 December 1994
Children: Bazal, Nawal, Habiba, Sumea
Overseas tours: Pakistan YC to Australia (U19 World Cup) 1987-88; Pakistan to Sharjah (Sharjah Cup) 1988-89, to Australia 1989-90, to New Zealand and Australia (World Cup) 1991-92, to England 1992, to New Zealand 1992-93, to West Indies 1992-93, to New Zealand 1993-94, to Sri Lanka 1994-95, to Australia 1995-96, to New Zealand 1995-96, to England 1996, to Sri Lanka 1996-97, to South Africa 1997-98, to Zimbabwe 1997-98, to India 1998-99, to UK, Ireland and Netherlands (World Cup) 1999, to Australia 1999-2000, to West Indies 1999-2000, to Sri Lanka 2000, to New Zealand 2000-01, to England 2001, plus numerous other one-day tournaments in India, Sharjah, Australia, South Africa, Zimbabwe, Singapore, Toronto and Bangladesh
Overseas teams played for: Numerous in Pakistan, including Multan, United Bank, National Bank of Pakistan, WAPDA
Career highlights to date: 'Winning the 1992 cricket World Cup final'
Cricket moments to forget: 'Losing the 1996 World Cup quarter-final to India at Bangalore'
Cricket superstitions: 'None'
Other sports followed: Hockey, football (Brazil)
Relaxations: 'Spending time with family, prayer'
Extras: Somerset's overseas player 1993-95 and 1997-98; Player of the Year 1993. Had match figures of 9-198 and 9-186 in successive Tests (Man of the Match in the latter) v Australia 1995-96, following up with 10-171 in next Test v New Zealand eight days later, winning Man of the Match award. His other international awards include Man of the [Test] Series v England 1996 and v South Africa 1997-98. One of *Wisden*'s

Five Cricketers of the Year 1997. Was Surrey's overseas player during August 2002; an overseas player with Sussex since 2003. Took 103 Championship wickets (av. 24.65) 2003. Sussex Player of the Year 2003, 2006. PCA Player of the Year 2003. Took 1000th first-class wicket (Martin Bicknell) v Surrey at The Oval 2004. Took 9-48 (13-108 in the match) v Nottinghamshire at Trent Bridge 2006 to finish the season with 102 Championship wickets (av. 19.91). Took 7-132 (13-225 in the match) v Worcestershire at Hove 2007 to finish the season with 90 Championship wickets (av. 25.66) and as the competition's leading wicket-taker for the fifth consecutive season

Best batting: 90* Sussex v Kent, Hove 2005

Best bowling: 9-48 Sussex v Nottinghamshire, Trent Bridge 2006

2007 Season

	M	Inn	NO	Runs	HS	Avg	100	50	Ct	St	Balls	Runs	Wkts	Avg	BB	5I	10M
Test																	
FC	15	17	3	170	54	12.14	-	1	3	-	4013	2310	90	25.66	7-72	8	3
ODI																	
List A	9	5	1	27	10	6.75	-	-	1	-	414	274	8	34.25	2-22	-	
20/20 Int																	
20/20	9	3	2	26	20 *	26.00	-	-	1	-	192	204	9	22.66	2-8	-	

Career Performances

	M	Inn	NO	Runs	HS	Avg	100	50	Ct	St	Balls	Runs	Wkts	Avg	BB	5I	10M
Test	52	72	16	656	59	11.71	-	2	23	-	12532	6100	185	32.97	7-56	10	3
FC	303	379	56	5059	90 *	15.66	-	20	118	-	69502	35350	1388	25.46	9-48	103	32
ODI	144	76	34	399	34 *	9.50	-	-	30	-	7543	5361	161	33.29	5-36	1	
List A	380	219	75	1624	41	11.27	-	-	59	-	18913	13127	461	28.47	7-24	4	
20/20 Int																	
20/20	29	10	2	55	20 *	6.87	-	-	3	-	591	580	42	13.80	5-11	1	

61. Which Warwickshire player became the first batsman to score a double hundred (206) for New Zealand in Tests against England, at Lord's in 1949?

MUSTARD, P. Durham

Name: Philip (Phil) Mustard
Role: Left-hand bat, wicket-keeper
Born: 8 October 1982, Sunderland
Height: 5ft 11in **Weight:** 13st 3lbs
Nickname: Colonel
County debut: 2002
50 dismissals in a season: 2
Place in batting averages: 173rd av. 25.62 (2006 123rd av. 32.64)
Parents: Maureen
Marital status: Single
Children: Haydon Samuel, 12 July 2006
Education: Usworth Comprehensive, Washington, Tyne and Wear
Overseas tours: England to Sri Lanka 2007-08, to New Zealand 2007-08
Overseas teams played for: Bulleen, Melbourne 2002; Glenorchy, Tasmania 2003; Bankstown, Sydney 2004; Tea Tree Gully, South Australia
Career highlights to date: 'First century 2006. Playing for England U19'
Cricket moments to forget: 'First ball against Jimmy Anderson on debut in C&G' *(Caught Flintoff, bowled Anderson)*
Cricketers particularly admired: Alec Stewart
Young players to look out for: Ben Harmison
Other sports played: Golf, football
Other sports followed: Football (Newcastle)
Favourite band: Bee Gees
Relaxations: 'Socialising'
Extras: Scored 77-ball 75 on first-class debut v Sri Lankans at Riverside 2002. Represented England U19 2002. Scored maiden first-class century (130) v Kent at Canterbury 2006, in the process sharing with Gordon Muchall (219) in a new Durham record partnership for the sixth wicket (249). Made 50 (54) dismissals in a season for the first time and also scored 816 runs in first-class cricket 2006. Scored 21-ball fifty (ending with 40-ball 78) v Leicestershire at Riverside in the Pro40 2007, setting a new Durham record for fastest one-day fifty
Best batting: 130 Durham v Kent, Canterbury 2006
Stop press: Made ODI debut in the first ODI v Sri Lanka in Dambulla 2007-08

2007 Season

	M	Inn	NO	Runs	HS	Avg	100	50	Ct	St	Balls	Runs	Wkts	Avg	BB	5I	10M
Test																	
FC	17	31	2	743	76	25.62	-	4	70	3	0	0	0		-	-	-
ODI																	
List A	19	19	1	893	108	49.61	1	7	21	3	0	0	0		-	-	
20/20 Int																	
20/20	5	5	1	154	52 *	38.50	-	1	2	2	0	0	0		-	-	

Career Performances

	M	Inn	NO	Runs	HS	Avg	100	50	Ct	St	Balls	Runs	Wkts	Avg	BB	5I	10M
Test																	
FC	67	110	6	2846	130	27.36	2	13	221	10	0	0	0		-	-	-
ODI																	
List A	76	62	6	1556	108	27.78	1	9	81	14	0	0	0		-	-	
20/20 Int																	
20/20	29	29	2	601	67 *	22.25	-	4	7	11	0	0	0		-	-	

NAIK, J. K. H. — Leicestershire

Name: Jigar Kumar Hakumatrai Naik
Role: Right-hand bat, right-arm off-break bowler
Born: 10 August 1984, Leicester
Height: 6ft 2in **Weight:** 14st
Nickname: Jigs, Jiggy, Jigsy
County debut: 2006
Parents: Hakumatrai and Daxa
Marital status: Single
Education: Rushey Mead; Gateway College; Nottingham Trent University; Loughborough University
Qualifications: BSc (Hons) Multimedia Technology, MSc Computer Science
Career outside cricket: Technical systems engineer
Off-season: 'Season in South Africa – six months'
Overseas tours: Leicestershire to India and Sri Lanka 2007
Career highlights to date: 'Making my Championship and Pro40 debuts'
Cricketers particularly admired: Sachin Tendulkar, Erapalli Prasanna

Young players to look out for: Tom Parsons, Adil Rashid, Stuart Broad, Matt Boyce, Nathan Buck
Other sports played: Golf, tennis, football
Other sports followed: Tennis, football (Liverpool FC)
Favourite band: Nickelback
Relaxations: 'Music, movies, going to the gym'
Extras: Played for Leicestershire Board XI in the 2003 C&G. Attended World Cricket Academy 2007. Played for Loughborough UCCE 2007. First Leicester-born player of Asian origin to represent the county
Opinions on cricket: 'The new ruling of having only one overseas player can only be better for English cricket, so long as the overseas player has enough experience and talent at the highest level to provide input to the club and be helpful to the younger members of the squad.'
Best batting: 15 LUCCE v Yorkshire, Headingley 2007
Best bowling: 1-55 Leicestershire v West Indies A, Leicester 2006

2007 Season

	M	Inn	NO	Runs	HS	Avg	100	50	Ct	St	Balls	Runs	Wkts	Avg	BB	5I	10M
Test																	
FC	3	5	3	46	15	23.00	-	-	2	-	348	263	3	87.66	1-58	-	-
ODI																	
List A	2	0	0	0	0		-	-	1	-	86	77	6	12.83	3-24	-	
20/20 Int																	
20/20																	

Career Performances

	M	Inn	NO	Runs	HS	Avg	100	50	Ct	St	Balls	Runs	Wkts	Avg	BB	5I	10M
Test																	
FC	6	7	3	60	15	15.00	-	-	4	-	582	444	4	111.00	1-55	-	-
ODI																	
List A	4	1	0	1	1	1.00	-	-	1	-	200	152	6	25.33	3-24	-	
20/20 Int																	
20/20																	

62. Who carried his bat for 94* in the first innings and then scored a match-winning 118 in the second in the third Test between England and New Zealand at Christchurch in 1996-97?

NAPIER, G. R. — Essex

Name: Graham Richard Napier
Role: Right-hand bat, right-arm fast-medium bowler; all-rounder
Born: 6 January 1980, Colchester
Height: 5ft 9in **Weight:** 14st 2lbs
Nickname: George, Napes
County debut: 1997
Place in batting averages: 47th av. 45.28
Place in bowling averages: 144th av. 58.90
Parents: Roger and Carol
Marital status: Single
Family links with cricket: Father played for Palmers Boys School 1st XI (1965-68), Essex Police divisional teams, and Harwich Immigration CC
Education: Gilberd School, Colchester
Qualifications: City & Guilds Digital Imaging, NCA coaching award
Career outside cricket: Sports photography
Off-season: 'PCA Base Camp Challenge. Playing for Upper Valley CC, Wellington'
Overseas tours: England U17 to Bermuda (International Youth Tournament) 1997; England U19 to South Africa (including U19 World Cup) 1997-98; England A to Malaysia and India 2003-04; England VI to Hong Kong 2004; MCC to Namibia and Uganda 2004-05
Overseas teams played for: Campbelltown CC, Sydney 2000-01; North Perth, Western Australia 2001-02; Upper Valley CC, Wellington, New Zealand 2007-08
Career highlights to date: 'Testing myself against the world's best and scoring some runs'
Cricket moments to forget: 'Being run out in a Lord's final'
Young players to look out for: Tom Westley, Adam Wheater
Other sports followed: Golf
Favourite band: The Killers
Relaxations: 'Odd spot of fishing'
Extras: Represented England U19 1999. Man of the Match award for Essex Board XI v Lancashire Board XI in the NatWest 2000. ECB National Academy 2003-04. Included in preliminary England one-day squad of 30 for ICC Champions Trophy 2004
Opinions on cricket: 'Would like to play against some other teams in one-day cricket, rather than Kent, Sussex, Surrey, Hampshire and Middlesex.'
Best batting: 125 Essex v Nottinghamshire, Chelmsford 2007
Best bowling: 5-56 Essex v Derbyshire, Derby 2004

2007 Season

	M	Inn	NO	Runs	HS	Avg	100	50	Ct	St	Balls	Runs	Wkts	Avg	BB	5I	10M
Test																	
FC	10	10	3	317	125	45.28	1	1	4	-	901	589	10	58.90	3-55	-	-
ODI																	
List A	15	11	1	85	25 *	8.50	-	-	1	-	582	530	16	33.12	3-16	-	
20/20 Int																	
20/20	7	4	1	19	8 *	6.33	-	-	2	-	109	113	5	22.60	2-14	-	

Career Performances

	M	Inn	NO	Runs	HS	Avg	100	50	Ct	St	Balls	Runs	Wkts	Avg	BB	5I	10M
Test																	
FC	78	108	21	2746	125	31.56	3	17	34	-	9199	5988	142	42.16	5-56	2	-
ODI																	
List A	139	105	16	1469	79	16.50	-	7	32	-	3878	3310	130	25.46	6-29	1	
20/20 Int																	
20/20	24	14	1	141	38	10.84	-	-	3	-	501	590	28	21.07	3-13	-	

NASH, C. D. — Sussex

Name: Christopher (Chris) David Nash
Role: Right-hand bat, right-arm off-spin bowler
Born: 19 May 1983, Cuckfield
Height: 5ft 11½in **Weight:** 13st
Nickname: Knocker, Nashy, Nashdog, Hero, Tiny Ears, Pure
County debut: 2002
Place in batting averages: 157th av. 27.83 (2006 140th av. 30.66)
Parents: Nick and Jane
Marital status: Single
Family links with cricket: 'Brother played for Sussex 2nd XI'
Education: Tanbridge House; Collyers Sixth Form College; Loughborough University
Qualifications: 10 GCSEs, 4 A-levels, degree in Sports Science, Level II squash and cricket coaching
Off-season: 'Playing for Cornwall CC in Auckland, New Zealand'
Overseas tours: England U17 to Northern Ireland (ECC Colts Festival) 1999; Sussex U19 to Cape Town 1999; Horsham CC to Barbados 2005

Overseas teams played for: Subiaco Marist, Perth 2004-05, 2005-06; Cornwall CC, Auckland 2007-08
Career highlights to date: 'Winning the Championship 2006'
Cricket moments to forget: 'Every time I come on to bowl, I get a barrage of abuse from my team-mates (Lewry, Yardy, Hodd, Jenkins and everyone else)'
Cricketers particularly admired: Jason Lewry, Richard Hawkes, Dr John Dew, Phil Hudson, David Hussey
Other sports played: Squash (county and national U11-15), football (Sussex CCC FC, PureTown FC)
Other sports followed: Football (Brighton & Hove Albion, Horsham, PureTown)
Favourite band: Razorlight
Extras: 'Smallest ears in Sussex squad.' Represented England U15, U17, U18, U19, captaining at U17 and U18 levels. Sussex League Young Player of the Year 2001. Played for Loughborough UCCE 2002, 2003, 2004. Represented British Universities 2004. Man of the Match in the 2nd XI Trophy final v Nottinghamshire at Horsham 2005 (2-21/72*). Scored 82 v Warwickshire in the Pro40 at Hove 2006, winning Man of the Match award. Sussex Most Improved Player (Umer Rashid Memorial Award) 2006
Opinions on cricket: 'Pro40 has a place in domestic cricket. Keep raising the profile of the game and getting people in to watch.'
Best batting: 89 Sussex v Worcestershire, Hove 2007
Best bowling: 2-1 Sussex v Lancashire, Hove 2007

2007 Season

	M	Inn	NO	Runs	HS	Avg	100	50	Ct	St	Balls	Runs	Wkts	Avg	BB	5I	10M
Test																	
FC	17	30	0	835	89	27.83	-	7	10	-	61	40	3	13.33	2-1	-	-
ODI																	
List A	13	12	0	257	59	21.41	-	2	2	-	108	87	2	43.50	1-26	-	
20/20 Int																	
20/20	7	7	1	126	37	21.00	-	-	1	-	0	0	0		-	-	

Career Performances

	M	Inn	NO	Runs	HS	Avg	100	50	Ct	St	Balls	Runs	Wkts	Avg	BB	5I	10M
Test																	
FC	30	49	2	1382	89	29.40	-	12	15	-	773	584	9	64.88	2-1	-	-
ODI																	
List A	20	19	0	462	82	24.31	-	3	3	-	150	151	2	75.50	1-26	-	
20/20 Int																	
20/20	12	12	2	187	37	18.70	-	-	5	-	0	0	0		-	-	

NASH, D. C. Middlesex

Name: David Charles Nash
Role: Right-hand bat, wicket-keeper
Born: 19 January 1978, Chertsey, Surrey
Height: 5ft 7in **Weight:** 11st 5lbs
Nickname: Nashy, Knocker
County debut: 1995 (one-day), 1997 (first-class)
County cap: 1999
Benefit: 2007
50 dismissals in a season: 1
Place in batting averages: 11th av. 60.85 (2006 60th av. 46.00)
Parents: David and Christine
Marital status: Single
Family links with cricket: 'Father played club cricket; brother plays now and again for Ashford CC; mother is avid watcher and tea lady'
Education: Sunbury Manor; Malvern College
Qualifications: 9 O-levels, 1 A-level, Levels 1 and 2 cricket coaching, qualified football referee
Career outside cricket: Qualified cricket coach
Overseas tours: England U15 to South Africa 1993; British Airways Youth Team to West Indies 1993-94; England U19 to Zimbabwe 1995-96, to Pakistan 1996-97; England A to Kenya and Sri Lanka 1997-98
Overseas teams played for: Fremantle, Perth 2000-01, 2002-03
Career highlights to date: 'Touring with England A and scoring first hundred for Middlesex at Lord's v Somerset'
Cricket moments to forget: 'All golden ducks'
Cricket superstitions: 'Too many to mention'
Cricketers particularly admired: Angus Fraser
Other sports played: Rugby, football ('played for Millwall U15 and my district side'), 'and most other sports'
Other sports followed: Rugby (London Irish), football (Chelsea)
Relaxations: 'Listening to music, watching sport and socialising with friends'
Extras: Represented Middlesex at all ages. Played for England U14, U15, U17 and U19. Once took six wickets in six balls, aged 11 – 'when I could bowl!' Seaxe Young Player of the Year 1993
Best batting: 114 Middlesex v Somerset, Lord's 1998
Best bowling: 1-8 Middlesex v Essex, Chelmsford 1997

2007 Season

	M	Inn	NO	Runs	HS	Avg	100	50	Ct	St	Balls	Runs	Wkts	Avg	BB	5I	10M
Test																	
FC	7	10	3	426	103 *	60.85	3	-	20	2	0	0	0		-	-	-
ODI																	
List A	8	7	0	159	51	22.71	-	1	3	3	0	0	0		-	-	
20/20 Int																	
20/20																	

Career Performances

	M	Inn	NO	Runs	HS	Avg	100	50	Ct	St	Balls	Runs	Wkts	Avg	BB	5I	10M
Test																	
FC	131	188	40	5181	114	35.00	10	24	272	23	90	105	2	52.50	1-8	-	-
ODI																	
List A	120	89	18	1480	67	20.84	-	6	91	18	0	0	0		-	-	
20/20 Int																	
20/20																	

NAVED-UL-HASAN Yorkshire

Name: Rana Naved-ul-Hasan
Role: Right-hand bat, right-arm fast bowler
Born: 28 February 1978, Sheikhupura City, Pakistan
Height: 5ft 11in **Weight:** 12st 12lbs
County debut: 2005 (Sussex)
County cap: 2005 (Sussex)
Test debut: 2004-05
ODI debut: 2002-03
Twenty20 Int debut: 2006
50 wickets in a season: 2
Place in batting averages: 245th av. 14.76 (2006 232nd av. 16.75)
Place in bowling averages: 56th av. 29.08 (2006 2nd av. 16.71)
Parents: Rana Mehdi Hassan Khan
Wife and date of marriage: Najma Naveed, 29 April 1997
Children: Aqsa, Rimsha, Naima, Maha
Education: Government High School, Sheikhupura
Qualifications: School qualifications

Career outside cricket: 'With family'
Off-season: Holiday
Overseas tours: Pakistan U19 to New Zealand 1994-95; Pakistan to Sharjah (Cherry Blossom Sharjah Cup) 2002-03, to England (ICC Champions Trophy) 2004, to Australia 2004-05, to India 2004-05, to West Indies 2004-05, to Sri Lanka 2005-06, to UAE (DLF Cup) 2006, to England 2006, to India (ICC Champions Trophy) 2006-07, to South Africa 2006-07, to West Indies (World Cup) 2006-07, plus other one-day matches in England and India
Overseas teams played for: Lahore Division 1999-2000; Pakistan Customs 2000-01; Sheikhupura 2000-01 – 2001-02; Allied Bank 2001-02; WAPDA 2002-03 – 2003-04, 2006-07; Sialkot/Sialkot Stallions 2003-04 – 2006-07
Cricket moments to forget: 'When we lost the World Cup match against Ireland'
Cricketers particularly admired: Brian Lara
Young players to look out for: Adil Rashid
Other sports played: Hockey
Other sports followed: Football (Manchester United)
Injuries: Out for four weeks with a shoulder injury
Favourite band: 'Any music'
Relaxations: 'Music'
Extras: Played for Herefordshire in the 2003 C&G competition. Was selected in the World One-Day Team of the Year at the ICC Awards 2005. Has won several match and series awards, including Player of the [ODI] Series v India 2004-05 and Player of the [ODI] Series v West Indies 2006-07. An overseas player with Sussex 2005-07; has joined Yorkshire as an overseas player for 2008
Best batting: 139 Sussex v Middlesex, Lord's 2005
Best bowling: 7-49 Sheikhupura v Sialkot, Muridke 2001-02

2007 Season

	M	Inn	NO	Runs	HS	Avg	100	50	Ct	St	Balls	Runs	Wkts	Avg	BB	5I	10M
Test																	
FC	14	18	1	251	75	14.76	-	1	5	-	2265	1454	50	29.08	5-106	2	-
ODI																	
List A	9	9	2	120	51	17.14	-	1	1	-	439	401	13	30.84	3-33	-	
20/20 Int																	
20/20	9	8	3	85	25	17.00	-	-	5	-	188	229	5	45.80	3-26	-	

Career Performances

	M	Inn	NO	Runs	HS	Avg	100	50	Ct	St	Balls	Runs	Wkts	Avg	BB	5I	10M
Test	9	15	3	239	42 *	19.91	-	-	3	-	1565	1044	18	58.00	3-30	-	-
FC	101	143	15	2944	139	23.00	3	9	51	-	19123	10751	454	23.68	7-49	26	4
ODI	62	41	14	359	29	13.29	-	-	13	-	2854	2630	95	27.68	6-27	1	
List A	132	97	29	1339	70 *	19.69	-	5	37	-	6222	5355	207	25.86	6-27	3	
20/20 Int	2	1	1	17	17 *		-	-	1	-	42	55	1	55.00	1-26	-	
20/20	28	18	10	258	40 *	32.25	-	-	16	-	572	661	24	27.54	3-9	-	

NEEDHAM, J. Derbyshire

Name: Jake Needham
Role: Right-hand bat, right-arm off-spin bowler; all-rounder
Born: 30 September 1986, Portsmouth, Hampshire
Height: 6ft 1in **Weight:** 11st 7lbs
County debut: 2005
Extras: Man of the Match playing for Ockbrook & Borrowash v Kibworth in the Cockspur Cup final at Lord's 2004 (51/4-27). Derbyshire Academy Player of the Year 2005. Represented England U19 2006
Best batting: 48 Derbyshire v Nottinghamshire, Chesterfield 2007
Best bowling: 3-92 Derbyshire v Essex, Derby 2007

2007 Season

	M	Inn	NO	Runs	HS	Avg	100	50	Ct	St	Balls	Runs	Wkts	Avg	BB	5I	10M
Test																	
FC	4	6	2	125	48	31.25	-	-	2	-	500	256	7	36.57	3-92	-	-
ODI																	
List A	11	10	3	117	42	16.71	-	-	4	-	264	243	2	121.50	2-36	-	
20/20 Int																	
20/20	3	1	1	0	0 *		-	-	-	-	9	19	0		-	-	

Career Performances

	M	Inn	NO	Runs	HS	Avg	100	50	Ct	St	Balls	Runs	Wkts	Avg	BB	5I	10M
Test																	
FC	6	10	3	161	48	23.00	-	-	2	-	680	412	9	45.77	3-92	-	-
ODI																	
List A	22	17	7	177	42	17.70	-	-	6	-	644	580	8	72.50	2-36	-	
20/20 Int																	
20/20	3	1	1	0	0 *		-	-	-	-	9	19	0		-	-	

NEL, A. Essex

Name: Andre Nel
Role: Right-hand bat, right-arm fast-medium bowler
Born: 15 July 1977, Germiston, Gauteng, South Africa
County debut: 2003 (Northants), 2005 (Essex)
County cap: 2003 (Northants)
Test debut: 2001-02
ODI debut: 2000-01
Twenty20 Int debut: 2005-06
Place in bowling averages: 106th av. 39.10
Education: Hoërskool Dr E.G. Jansen, Boksburg
Overseas tours: South Africa Academy to Ireland and Scotland 1999; South Africa A to Zimbabwe 2002-03, to Australia 2002-03, to Zimbabwe 2007-08; South Africa to West Indies 2000-01, to Zimbabwe 2001-02, to England 2003 (NatWest Series), to Pakistan 2003-04, to New Zealand 2003-04, to West Indies 2004-05, to India (one-day series) 2005-06, to Australia 2005-06, to Sri Lanka 2006, to India (ICC Champions Trophy) 2006-07, to West Indies (World Cup) 2006-07, to Ireland (one-day series v India) 2007, to Pakistan 2007-08
Overseas teams played for: Easterns 1996-97 – 2005-06; Titans 2003-04 –
Extras: Was an overseas player with Northamptonshire 2003. One of *South African Cricket Annual*'s five Cricketers of the Year 2004, 2005. His match awards include Man of the Match in the fourth ODI v Pakistan at Rawalpindi 2003-04 (4-39) and in the third Test v West Indies in Barbados 2004-05 (4-56/6-32). Was an overseas player with Essex during the 2005 season as a locum for André Adams, taking a wicket (Matthew Wood) with his first ball for the county, v Somerset at Colchester; returned for part of the 2007 season. Represented South Africa in the Twenty20 World Championship 2007-08
Best batting: 44 Easterns v Free State, Benoni 2000-01
Best bowling: 6-25 Easterns v Gauteng, Johannesburg 2001-02

2007 Season

	M	Inn	NO	Runs	HS	Avg	100	50	Ct	St	Balls	Runs	Wkts	Avg	BB	5I	10M
Test																	
FC	4	5	1	19	10	4.75	-	-	-	-	734	391	10	39.10	3-62	-	-
ODI																	
List A	6	4	2	15	7	7.50	-	-	1	-	318	245	6	40.83	3-15	-	
20/20 Int																	
20/20																	

Career Performances

	M	Inn	NO	Runs	HS	Avg	100	50	Ct	St	Balls	Runs	Wkts	Avg	BB	5I	10M
Test	27	31	7	200	23 *	8.33	-	-	12	-	5935	3023	97	31.16	6-32	3	1
FC	93	105	34	929	44	13.08	-	-	34	-	18560	8611	327	26.33	6-25	12	1
ODI	65	17	9	61	22	7.62	-	-	17	-	3190	2459	89	27.62	5-45	1	
List A	171	67	37	298	22	9.93	-	-	41	-	8497	5968	243	24.55	6-27	4	
20/20 Int	2	1	1	0	0 *		-	-	1	-	48	42	2	21.00	2-19	-	
20/20	12	4	1	23	12	7.66	-	-	3	-	276	260	12	21.66	2-19	-	

NEL, J. D. — Worcestershire

Name: Johann Dewald Nel
Role: Right-hand bat, right-arm medium-fast bowler
Born: 6 June 1980, Klerksdorp, South Africa
County debut: 2007
ODI debut: 2006
Twenty20 Int debut: 2007-08
Overseas tours: Scotland to Ireland (ICC Trophy) 2005, to Kenya (ICC Associates Kenya Tri-Series) 2006-07, to Kenya (ICC World Cricket League) 2006-07, to West Indies (World Cup) 2006-07, to Ireland (Quadrangular Series) 2007, to South Africa (World 20/20) 2007-08, plus other tours and tournaments with Scotland and Scotland A
Extras: Has played first-class and one-day cricket for Scotland, including ODI, Twenty20 Int, totesport League and C&G/FP. Played for European XI v MCC in Rotterdam 2006. Joined Worcestershire 2007, initially as short-term cover, taking 4-74 on Championship debut v Yorkshire at Headingley; released by Worcestershire at the end of the 2007 season. Is not considered an overseas player

Best batting: 25 Scotland v Namibia, Aberdeen 2006
Best bowling: 4-74 Worcestershire v Yorkshire, Headingley 2007

2007 Season

	M	Inn	NO	Runs	HS	Avg	100	50	Ct	St	Balls	Runs	Wkts	Avg	BB	5I	10M
Test																	
FC	5	8	6	30	8	15.00	-	-	-	-	577	345	7	49.28	4-74	-	-
ODI																	
List A	8	5	0	26	15	5.20	-	-	1	-	396	308	11	28.00	3-23	-	
20/20 Int																	
20/20	3	0	0	0	0		-	-	-	-	60	76	2	38.00	1-25	-	

Career Performances

	M	Inn	NO	Runs	HS	Avg	100	50	Ct	St	Balls	Runs	Wkts	Avg	BB	5I	10M
Test																	
FC	11	15	9	82	25	13.66	-	-	2	-	1307	765	18	42.50	4-74	-	-
ODI	8	3	3	5	3 *		-	-	2	-	304	280	3	93.33	1-34	-	
List A	47	28	15	130	36 *	10.00	-	-	10	-	1738	1564	40	39.10	3-22	-	
20/20 Int	2	1	1	13	13 *		-	-	-	-	24	25	2	12.50	2-25	-	
20/20	5	1	1	13	13 *		-	-	-	-	84	101	4	25.25	2-25	-	

NELSON, M. A. G. — Northamptonshire

Name: Mark Anthony George Nelson
Role: Left-hand bat, right-arm medium-fast bowler
Born: 24 September 1986, Milton Keynes
Height: 5ft 11in **Weight:** 11st 7lbs
Nickname: Nelo, Nelly
County debut: 2006 (one-day), 2007 (first-class)
Parents: George and Janet
Marital status: Single
Education: Lord Grey School, Milton Keynes; Stowe School
Qualifications: 3 A-levels
Overseas tours: England U19 to Sri Lanka (U19 World Cup) 2005-06
Cricket moments to forget: 'Batting for U19, the ball hit my bat and a piece of bat broke off, knocked on to a stump and I was declared out'
Cricket superstitions: 'Nobody can touch my bat before I go in'

Cricketers particularly admired: Brian Lara 'for his skill'
Young players to look out for: Alex Wakely, Ben Howgego
Other sports played: Football 'for recreational purposes only'
Other sports followed: Football (Manchester United)
Favourite band: Tupac, Notorious B.I.G.
Relaxations: 'Music and dancing'
Extras: NBC Denis Compton Award for the most promising young Northamptonshire player 2006. Represented England U19 2006
Best batting: 13 Northamptonshire v Middlesex, Northampton 2007
Best bowling: 2-62 Northamptonshire v Middlesex, Northampton 2007

2007 Season

	M	Inn	NO	Runs	HS	Avg	100	50	Ct	St	Balls	Runs	Wkts	Avg	BB	5I	10M
Test																	
FC	1	1	0	13	13	13.00	-	-	1	-	48	62	2	31.00	2-62	-	-
ODI																	
List A	5	4	1	57	26	19.00	-	-	-	-	72	64	1	64.00	1-37	-	
20/20 Int																	
20/20																	

Career Performances

	M	Inn	NO	Runs	HS	Avg	100	50	Ct	St	Balls	Runs	Wkts	Avg	BB	5I	10M
Test																	
FC	1	1	0	13	13	13.00	-	-	1	-	48	62	2	31.00	2-62	-	-
ODI																	
List A	7	5	2	70	26	23.33	-	-	-	-	78	74	1	74.00	1-37	-	
20/20 Int																	
20/20																	

63. Whose 2-9 from seven overs brought him the Man of the Match award in the final of the NatWest Series between England and South Africa in 2003?

NEW, T. J. — Leicestershire

Name: Thomas (Tom) James New
Role: Left-hand bat, wicket-keeper, right-arm slow-medium bowler
Born: 18 January 1985, Sutton-in-Ashfield
Height: 5ft 9in **Weight:** 10st
Nickname: Newy, P
County debut: 2003 (one-day), 2004 (first-class)
Place in batting averages: 94th av. 36.80 (2006 106th av. 34.50)
Parents: Martin and Louise
Marital status: Engaged
Family links with cricket: 'Dad played local cricket'
Education: Quarrydale Comprehensive
Qualifications: GCSEs
Overseas tours: England U19 to Bangladesh (U19 World Cup) 2003-04
Overseas teams played for: Geelong Cement, Victoria 2001-02
Cricket moments to forget: 'Losing semi-final of Costcutter World Challenge 2000 to Pakistan'
Cricket superstitions: 'None'
Cricketers particularly admired: Ian Healy, Jack Russell
Other sports played: Golf, football
Other sports followed: Football (Mansfield Town)
Relaxations: 'Golf, music'
Extras: Played for Nottinghamshire U12, U13, U15, U16 and Midlands U13, U14, U15. Captained England U15 in Costcutter World Challenge [U15 World Cup] 2000. Sir John Hobbs Silver Jubilee Memorial Prize 2000. Represented England U19 2003 and 2004. NBC Denis Compton Award for the most promising young Leicestershire player 2003
Best batting: 125 Leicestershire v OUCCE, The Parks 2007
Best bowling: 2-18 Leicestershire v Gloucestershire, Leicester 2007

2007 Season

	M	Inn	NO	Runs	HS	Avg	100	50	Ct	St	Balls	Runs	Wkts	Avg	BB	5I	10M
Test																	
FC	16	29	3	957	125	36.80	1	8	20	1	169	168	4	42.00	2-18	-	-
ODI																	
List A	7	6	0	124	51	20.66	-	1	-	1	0	0	0		-	-	
20/20 Int																	
20/20																	

Career Performances

	M	Inn	NO	Runs	HS	Avg	100	50	Ct	St	Balls	Runs	Wkts	Avg	BB	5I	10M
Test																	
FC	34	59	7	1794	125	34.50	1	16	40	3	169	168	4	42.00	2-18	-	-
ODI																	
List A	24	22	0	549	68	24.95	-	3	1	1	0	0	0		-	-	
20/20 Int																	
20/20																	

NEWBY, O. J. Lancashire

Name: Oliver James Newby
Role: Right-hand bat, right-arm fast-medium bowler
Born: 26 August 1984, Blackburn
Height: 6ft 5in **Weight:** 13st
Nickname: Newbz, Uncle, Flipper
County debut: 2003 (*see* ***Extras***)
Place in bowling averages: 67th av. 30.45 (2006 29th av. 27.52)
Parents: Frank and Carol
Marital status: Single
Family links with cricket: 'Dad played league cricket for Read CC'
Education: Ribblesdale High School; Myerscough College
Qualifications: 10 GCSEs, ND Sports Science, Level 1 coaching
Career highlights to date: 'First-class debut'
Other sports played: Golf
Favourite band: Eminem, Counting Crows
Relaxations: Music
Extras: Took a wicket in each of his first two overs on one-day debut for Lancashire v India A at Blackpool 2003. Played two Championship matches for Nottinghamshire on loan 2005
Best batting: 38* Nottinghamshire v Kent, Trent Bridge 2005
Best bowling: 4-58 Lancashire v Nottinghamshire, Old Trafford 2006

2007 Season

	M	Inn	NO	Runs	HS	Avg	100	50	Ct	St	Balls	Runs	Wkts	Avg	BB	5I	10M
Test																	
FC	9	8	1	48	26	6.85	-	-	2	-	1066	670	22	30.45	3-44	-	-
ODI																	
List A	5	3	1	3	3	1.50	-	-	-	-	186	160	3	53.33	1-28	-	
20/20 Int																	
20/20	3	1	1	6	6 *		-	-	1	-	54	80	2	40.00	1-28	-	

Career Performances

	M	Inn	NO	Runs	HS	Avg	100	50	Ct	St	Balls	Runs	Wkts	Avg	BB	5I	10M
Test																	
FC	20	19	5	148	38 *	10.57	-	-	3	-	2563	1605	49	32.75	4-58	-	-
ODI																	
List A	12	8	5	19	7 *	6.33	-	-	2	-	476	468	9	52.00	2-37	-	
20/20 Int																	
20/20	10	4	2	14	6 *	7.00	-	-	3	-	162	216	6	36.00	2-34	-	

NEWMAN, S. A. — Surrey

Name: Scott Alexander Newman
Role: Left-hand bat
Born: 3 November 1979, Epsom
Height: 6ft 1in **Weight:** 13st 7lbs
Nickname: Ronaldo
County debut: 2001 (one-day), 2002 (first-class)
County cap: 2005
1000 runs in a season: 3
1st-Class 200s: 1
Place in batting averages: 121st av. 32.48 (2006 43rd av. 50.14)
Parents: Ken and Sandy
Marital status: Married
Children: Lemoy, 1985; Brandon, 8 September 2002
Family links with cricket: 'Dad and brother both played'
Education: Trinity School, Croydon; Brighton University
Qualifications: 10 GCSEs, GNVQ (Advanced) Business Studies
Overseas tours: SCB to Barbados; England A to Malaysia and India 2003-04
Overseas teams played for: Mount Lawley CC, Perth

Cricket moments to forget: 'Any time I fail'
Cricket superstitions: 'None'
Cricketers particularly admired: 'All of Surrey CCC'
Other sports played: 'Most sports'
Other sports followed: Football (Man Utd)
Favourite band: Nas
Relaxations: 'Music, relaxing with family'
Extras: Scored 99 on first-class debut v Hampshire at The Oval 2002. Scored 284 v Derbyshire 2nd XI at The Oval 2003, in the process sharing with Nadeem Shahid (266) in an opening partnership of 552, just three runs short of the English all-cricket record first-wicket stand of 555 set in 1932. Scored 117 and 219 v Glamorgan at The Oval 2005, becoming the first Surrey batsman to score a double hundred and a hundred in the same Championship match. ECB National Academy 2003-04
Best batting: 219 Surrey v Glamorgan, The Oval 2005

2007 Season

	M	Inn	NO	Runs	HS	Avg	100	50	Ct	St	Balls	Runs	Wkts	Avg	BB	5I	10M
Test																	
FC	15	25	0	812	124	32.48	1	5	17	-	0	0	0		-	-	-
ODI																	
List A	12	12	1	466	92 *	42.36	-	5	4	-	0	0	0		-	-	
20/20 Int																	
20/20																	

Career Performances

	M	Inn	NO	Runs	HS	Avg	100	50	Ct	St	Balls	Runs	Wkts	Avg	BB	5I	10M
Test																	
FC	73	126	3	5261	219	42.77	11	30	62	-	24	22	0		-	-	-
ODI																	
List A	59	58	3	1395	106	25.36	1	8	14	-	0	0	0		-	-	
20/20 Int																	
20/20	21	19	3	352	59	22.00	-	2	8	-	0	0	0		-	-	

64. Who scored a century (104*) in his first Test match as captain of South Africa, at Old Trafford in 1955?

NICHOLSON, M. J. Surrey

Name: Matthew James Nicholson
Role: Right-hand bat, right-arm fast-medium bowler
Born: 2 October 1974, Sydney, Australia
Height: 6ft 6in
Nickname: Nicho
County debut: 2006 (Northamptonshire), 2007 (Surrey)
County cap: 2007 (Surrey)
Test debut: 1998-99
Place in batting averages: 142nd av. 30.00 (2006 157th av. 28.37)
Place in bowling averages: 59th av. 29.29 (2006 59th av. 31.97)
Wife: Natalie
Children: 2 (twin boys)
Overseas tours: Australia U19 to New Zealand 1992-93, to India 1993-94; Australia to Zimbabwe 1999-2000
Overseas teams played for: Western Australia 1996-97 – 2002-03; New South Wales 2003-04 –
Extras: Australia U19 Player of the Year 1992-93. Attended Commonwealth Bank [Australian] Cricket Academy 1994-95. Had first innings figures of 7-77 (and scored 58*) for Western Australia v England XI at Perth 1998-99; it was his first first-class match after 18 months out with glandular fever and chronic fatigue syndrome (CFS). Man of the Match v South Australia at Adelaide in the Pura Cup 2001-02 (4-58/4-60). Had second innings figures of 5-60 v Queensland at Brisbane in the final of the Pura Cup 2004-05. Has played for Australia A against touring sides. An overseas player with Northamptonshire 2006; was an overseas player with Surrey 2007
Best batting: 106* Northamptonshire v Derbyshire, Northampton 2006
Best bowling: 7-62 Northamptonshire v Gloucestershire, Northampton 2006
Stop press: Man of the Match v Queensland at Brisbane in the Pura Cup 2007-08 (2-46/3-25 plus 80)

2007 Season

	M	Inn	NO	Runs	HS	Avg	100	50	Ct	St	Balls	Runs	Wkts	Avg	BB	5I	10M
Test																	
FC	12	12	4	240	48 *	30.00	-	-	6	-	2268	1289	44	29.29	5-89	1	-
ODI																	
List A	10	8	5	137	57 *	45.66	-	1	1	-	433	360	11	32.72	2-23	-	
20/20 Int																	
20/20	8	3	2	25	16 *	25.00	-	-	-	-	136	144	11	13.09	3-23	-	

Career Performances

	M	Inn	NO	Runs	HS	Avg	100	50	Ct	St	Balls	Runs	Wkts	Avg	BB	5I	10M
Test	1	2	0	14	9	7.00	-	-	-	-	150	115	4	28.75	3-56	-	-
FC	107	150	29	2504	106 *	20.69	2	4	59	-	21096	10992	377	29.15	7-62	11	-
ODI																	
List A	63	39	13	381	57 *	14.65	-	1	16	-	2792	2471	65	38.01	3-23	-	
20/20 Int																	
20/20	20	6	3	37	16 *	12.33	-	-	4	-	385	503	25	20.12	3-12	-	

NIXON, P. A. Leicestershire

Name: Paul Andrew Nixon
Role: Left-hand bat, wicket-keeper, county captain
Born: 21 October 1970, Carlisle
Height: 6ft **Weight:** 12st 10lbs
Nickname: Badger, Nico, Nobby
County debut: 1989 (Leicestershire), 2000 (Kent)
County cap: 1994 (Leicestershire), 2000 (Kent)
Benefit: 2007 (Leicestershire)
ODI debut: 2006-07
Twenty20 Int debut: 2006-07
1000 runs in a season: 1
50 dismissals in a season: 7
Place in batting averages: 36th av. 48.83 (2006 20th av. 59.66)
Parents: Brian and Sylvia
Wife and date of marriage: Jen, 9 October 1999
Family links with cricket: 'Grandad and father played local league cricket. Mum made the teas for Edenhall CC, Penrith'
Education: Ullswater High
Qualifications: 2 O-levels, 6 GCSEs, coaching certificates
Overseas tours: Cumbria Schools U15 to Denmark 1985; Leicestershire to Barbados, to Jamaica, to Netherlands, to Johannesburg, to Bloemfontein; MCC to Bangladesh 1999-2000; England A to India and Bangladesh 1994-95; England to Pakistan and Sri Lanka 2000-01, to Australia 2006-07 (C'wealth Bank Series), to West Indies (World Cup) 2006-07
Overseas teams played for: Melville, Western Australia; North Fremantle, Western Australia; Mitchells Plain, Cape Town 1993; Primrose CC, Cape Town 1995-96

Career highlights to date: 'Winning the Championship in 1996 with Leicestershire. Receiving phone call from David Graveney advising me of England [tour] selection'
Cricket moments to forget: 'Losing Lord's one-day finals'
Cricketers particularly admired: David Gower, Ian Botham, Ian Healy, Viv Richards
Other sports played: Golf, football (played for Carlisle United)
Other sports followed: Football (Leicester City, Carlisle United, Liverpool), rugby (Leicester Tigers)
Relaxations: Watching England rugby
Extras: Played for England U15. Played in Minor Counties Championship for Cumberland at 16. MCC Young Pro 1988. Took eight catches in debut match v Warwickshire at Hinckley 1989. Leicestershire Young Player of the Year two years running. In 1994 became only second Leicestershire wicket-keeper to score 1000 (1046) first-class runs in a season; also made 62 first-class dismissals to achieve double. Voted Cumbria Sports Personality of the Year 1994-95. Captained First-Class Counties Select XI v New Zealand A at Milton Keynes 2000. Released by Kent at the end of the 2002 season and rejoined Leicestershire for 2003. Took over as captain of county in the Championship in July 2007, scoring century (126) and taking eight catches in his first match in charge; appointed captain of Leicestershire at the end of August 2007
Best batting: 144* Leicestershire v Northamptonshire, Northampton 2006

2007 Season

	M	Inn	NO	Runs	HS	Avg	100	50	Ct	St	Balls	Runs	Wkts	Avg	BB	5I	10M
Test																	
FC	13	21	3	879	126	48.83	2	5	36	1	12	9	0		-	-	-
ODI																	
List A	16	14	3	559	61	50.81	-	5	13	4	0	0	0		-	-	
20/20 Int																	
20/20	5	5	1	107	65	26.75	-	1	1	1	0	0	0		-	-	

Career Performances

	M	Inn	NO	Runs	HS	Avg	100	50	Ct	St	Balls	Runs	Wkts	Avg	BB	5I	10M
Test																	
FC	310	458	102	12001	144 *	33.71	18	57	822	66	75	100	0		-	-	-
ODI	19	18	4	297	49	21.21	-	-	20	3	0	0	0		-	-	
List A	376	322	68	6578	101	25.89	1	29	392	92	3	1	0		-	-	
20/20 Int	1	1	1	31	31 *		-	-	-	1	0	0	0		-	-	
20/20	41	38	10	724	65	25.85	-	3	20	10	0	0	0		-	-	

NOFFKE, A. A. Middlesex

Name: Ashley Allan Noffke
Role: Right-hand bat, right-arm fast bowler; all-rounder
Born: 30 April 1977, Sunshine Coast, Queensland, Australia
Height: 6ft 3in **Weight:** 14st
Nickname: Noffers, Wombat
County debut: 2002 (Middlesex), 2005 (Durham), 2007 (Gloucestershire)
County cap: 2003 (Middlesex), 2007 (Gloucestershire)
Place in bowling averages: 14th av. 22.33
Parents: Rob and Lesley Simpson, and Allan Noffke
Wife and date of marriage: Michelle, 8 April 2000
Family links with cricket: Father played club cricket
Education: Immanuel Lutheran College; Sunshine Coast University
Qualifications: Bachelor of Business, ACB Level 2 coaching certificate
Overseas tours: Commonwealth Bank [Australian] Cricket Academy to Zimbabwe 1998-99; Australia to England 2001, to West Indies 2002-03; Australia A to Pakistan 2007-08
Overseas teams played for: Queensland 1999-2000 –
Career highlights to date: 'Man of the Match in a winning Pura Cup final for Queensland. Being selected for Australia for 2001 Ashes tour'
Cricket moments to forget: 'Rolling my ankle playing for Australia v Sussex, forcing me home from the [2001] Ashes tour'
Cricket superstitions: 'None'
Cricketers particularly admired: Steve Waugh
Other sports played: Golf
Other sports followed: Rugby league, rugby union, 'enjoy all sports'
Favourite band: Powderfinger
Relaxations: Fishing
Extras: Queensland Academy of Sport Player of the Year 1998-99. Awarded an ACB contract 2001-02 after just six first-class matches. Has represented Australia A. Sunshine Coast Sportstar of the Year 2001. His awards include Man of the Match in the Pura Cup final v Victoria 2000-01 for his 7-120 match return and 43 runs batting as nightwatchman and v South Australia at Brisbane in the Pura Cup 2003-04 (4-48/2-37; 114*). Was Middlesex overseas player for two periods during the 2002 season; returned as an overseas player for 2003. Was an overseas player with Durham

in 2005 but was ruled out with a back injury from late July. Was a temporary overseas player with Gloucestershire during the 2007 season. Has rejoined Middlesex as an overseas player for 2008 as early-season cover for Murali Kartik
Best batting: 114* Queensland v South Australia, Brisbane 2003-04
Best bowling: 8-24 Middlesex v Derbyshire, Derby 2002
Stop press: Made Twenty20 Int debut v New Zealand at Perth 2007-08. Man of the Match v Tasmania at Brisbane in the Pura Cup 2007-08 (5-33/2-114 plus 100*)

2007 Season

	M	Inn	NO	Runs	HS	Avg	100	50	Ct	St	Balls	Runs	Wkts	Avg	BB	5I	10M
Test																	
FC	3	5	0	109	61	21.80	-	1	1	-	748	335	15	22.33	6-68	1	-
ODI																	
List A	3	3	1	55	33	27.50	-	-	-	-	162	150	4	37.50	3-24	-	
20/20 Int																	
20/20																	

Career Performances

	M	Inn	NO	Runs	HS	Avg	100	50	Ct	St	Balls	Runs	Wkts	Avg	BB	5I	10M
Test																	
FC	88	115	20	2314	114 *	24.35	1	9	36	-	17080	8788	294	29.89	8-24	12	1
ODI																	
List A	91	47	17	447	58	14.90	-	1	23	-	4511	3478	101	34.43	4-32	-	
20/20 Int																	
20/20	8	5	2	29	11 *	9.66	-	-	2	-	175	201	14	14.35	3-22	-	

65. Which pair of Lancashire fast bowlers shared the new ball in the two-match Test series between England and New Zealand in 1970-71?

NORTH, M. J. — Gloucestershire

Name: Marcus James North
Role: Left-hand bat, right-arm off-spin bowler
Born: 28 July 1979, Pakenham, Melbourne, Australia
Height: 6ft 1in **Weight:** 12st 10lbs
County debut: 2004 (Durham), 2005 (Lancashire), 2006 (Derbyshire), 2007 (Gloucestershire)
County cap: 2007 (Gloucestershire)
1st-Class 200s: 3
Place in batting averages: 19th av. 56.50
Wife: Joanne
Overseas tours: Australia U19 to Pakistan 1996-97, to South Africa (U19 World Cup) 1997-98; Commonwealth Bank [Australian] Cricket Academy to Zimbabwe 1998-99; Australia A to Pakistan 2005-06
Overseas teams played for: Western Australia 1999-2000 –
Extras: Commonwealth Bank [Australian] Cricket Academy 1998. Won President's Silver Trophy (season's best individual performance for Western Australia) for his 200* v Victoria at Melbourne in the Pura Cup 2001-02. Scored 200* and 132 in the second 'Test' v Pakistan U19 at Sheikhupura 1996-97, winning Man of the Match award (also Australia's Man of the 'Test' Series). Other awards include Man of the Match for Australia A v Zimbabweans at Adelaide 2003-04 (115). An overseas player with Durham 2004; a temporary overseas player with Lancashire during the 2005 season; a temporary overseas player with Derbyshire during the 2006 season; was a temporary overseas player with Gloucestershire during the 2007 season and has returned as overseas player for 2008. Won the Walter Lawrence Trophy 2007 for the season's fastest first-class century for his 73-ball hundred (finishing with 106) v Leicestershire at Bristol. Captain of Western Australia
Best batting: 239* Western Australia v Victoria, Perth 2006-07
Best bowling: 4-16 Durham v DUCCE, Riverside 2004

2007 Season

	M	Inn	NO	Runs	HS	Avg	100	50	Ct	St	Balls	Runs	Wkts	Avg	BB	5I	10M
Test																	
FC	5	10	0	565	109	56.50	3	2	4	-	780	359	9	39.88	3-53	-	-
ODI																	
List A	6	6	0	211	77	35.16	-	2	-	-	144	119	6	19.83	3-22	-	
20/20 Int																	
20/20																	

Career Performances

	M	Inn	NO	Runs	HS	Avg	100	50	Ct	St	Balls	Runs	Wkts	Avg	BB	5I	10M
Test																	
FC	100	177	17	7045	239 *	44.03	19	37	70	-	5356	2850	60	47.50	4-16	-	-
ODI																	
List A	102	98	11	2914	134 *	33.49	5	20	29	-	1525	1293	48	26.93	4-26	-	
20/20 Int																	
20/20	17	16	1	277	59	18.46	-	1	6	-	144	161	4	40.25	2-19	-	

NORTHEAST, S. A. Kent

Name: Sam Alexander Northeast
Role Right-hand top-order bat, off-spin bowler
Born: 16 October 1989, Ashford, Kent
Height: 5ft 11in **Weight:** 11st
Nickname: North, Bam, Nick Knight
County debut: 2007
Parents: Allan and Diane
Marital status: Single
Family links with cricket: 'My brother played Kent age-group as a kid'
Education: Harrow School
Qualifications: 10 GCSEs
Overseas tours: Harrow School to Sri Lanka 2004; England U16 to South Africa; England U19 to Malaysia 2006-07, to Malaysia (U19 World Cup) 2007-08
Cricket moments to forget: 'Not scoring many runs in first two appearances at Lord's in the Eton v Harrow match'
Cricket superstitions: 'Right pad on first'
Cricketers particularly admired: Graham Thorpe, Steve Waugh
Young players to look out for: Alex Blake, Paul Dixey, Glen Querl
Other sports played: Football, squash and rackets
Other sports followed: Football (Spurs), rugby (Bath)
Favourite band: Starsailor, Snow Patrol
Relaxations: 'Fishing, gardening; playing rackets releases stress'
Extras: Broke Graham Cowdrey's run record at Wellesley House (prep school). Captained England U15. *Daily Telegraph* Bunbury Scholarship 2005. BBC *Test Match Special* Young Cricketer of the Year 2005. Sir John Hobbs Silver Jubilee Memorial Prize for the outstanding U16 schoolboy cricketer 2005. Scored 96 on debut for Kent 2nd XI v Derbyshire 2nd XI at Beckenham 2005. Scored 62* for Sir JP Getty's XI v

Sri Lankans in a 50-over game at Wormsley 2006. Top ten nominee for BBC Young Sports Personality of the Year 2006. Attended Kent Academy
Opinions on cricket: 'Young players are getting more of a chance to shine in the game. Hopefully that will help me.'
Best batting: 5 Kent v Durham, Canterbury 2007

2007 Season

	M	Inn	NO	Runs	HS	Avg	100	50	Ct	St	Balls	Runs	Wkts	Avg	BB	5I	10M
Test																	
FC	1	2	0	5	5	2.50	-	-	-	-	0	0	0		-	-	-
ODI																	
List A	1	0	0	0	0		-	-	-	-	0	0	0		-	-	
20/20 Int																	
20/20																	

Career Performances

	M	Inn	NO	Runs	HS	Avg	100	50	Ct	St	Balls	Runs	Wkts	Avg	BB	5I	10M
Test																	
FC	1	2	0	5	5	2.50	-	-	-	-	0	0	0		-	-	-
ODI																	
List A	1	0	0	0	0		-	-	-	-	0	0	0		-	-	
20/20 Int																	
20/20																	

66. Whose 310* in the third Test v New Zealand in 1965 remains the highest Test score by an England batsman at Headingley?

O'BRIEN, N. J. P. Northamptonshire

Name: Niall John Peter O'Brien
Role: Left-hand bat, slow bowler, wicket-keeper
Born: 8 November 1981, Dublin
Height: 5ft 9in **Weight:** 12st
Nickname: Nobby
County debut: 2004 (Kent), 2007 (Northamptonshire)
ODI debut: 2006
50 dismissals in a season: 1
Place in batting averages: 196th av. 22.63 (2006 209th av. 20.08)
Parents: Brendan and Camilla
Marital status: Single
Family links with cricket: 'Dad ex-captain of Ireland. My brother Kevin a current Irish international'
Education: Marian College, Ballsbridge, Dublin
Qualifications: 6 Leaving Certificates, Level 2 coaching
Career outside cricket: 'Property developer'
Off-season: 'Hopefully playing in the ICL in India'
Overseas tours: Ireland U19 to Sri Lanka (U19 World Cup) 1999-2000; Ireland to Namibia (ICC Inter-Continental Cup) 2005, to Scotland (European Championship) 2006, to Kenya (ICC World Cricket League) 2006-07, to West Indies (World Cup) 2006-07, plus various Ireland age-group and A tours; Kent to Spain, France and Guernsey
Overseas teams played for: Railway Union CC, Dublin; Mosman DCC, Sydney 2000-02; University of Port Elizabeth Academy, South Africa 2002; North Sydney DCC 2003-05
Career highlights to date: 'Playing in the Cricket World Cup. Getting Man of the Match v Pakistan in World Cup [2006-07]'
Cricket moments to forget: 'Getting stumped v Pakistan in World Cup'
Cricket superstitions: 'None'
Cricketers particularly admired: Steve Waugh
Young players to look out for: Andrew Balbirnie
Other sports played: Hockey (Railway Union, Dublin), football
Other sports followed: Football (Everton), rugby (Ireland)
Favourite band: Oasis
Relaxations: 'Music; walking my dog; socialising'
Extras: Made Ireland senior debut v Denmark 2002 and has played first-class and one-day cricket for Ireland, including ODI (debut v Scotland at Ayr 2006) and C&G.

Ireland Cricketer of the Year 2002. Scored 58* as Ireland defeated West Indians in 50-over game in Belfast 2004, winning Man of the Match award. Man of the Match v Pakistan in Kingston in the World Cup 2006-07 (72 plus two catches)
Best batting: 176 Ireland v United Arab Emirates, Windhoek 2005-06
Best bowling: 1-4 Kent v CUCCE, Fenner's 2006

2007 Season

	M	Inn	NO	Runs	HS	Avg	100	50	Ct	St	Balls	Runs	Wkts	Avg	BB	5I	10M
Test																	
FC	8	13	2	249	109	22.63	1	-	23	2	0	0	0		-	-	-
ODI																	
List A	9	6	1	95	43	19.00	-	-	8	2	0	0	0		-	-	
20/20 Int																	
20/20																	

Career Performances

	M	Inn	NO	Runs	HS	Avg	100	50	Ct	St	Balls	Runs	Wkts	Avg	BB	5I	10M
Test																	
FC	51	74	12	1833	176	29.56	3	8	138	21	3	4	1	4.00	1-4	-	-
ODI	21	21	0	503	72	23.95	-	5	16	3	0	0	0		-	-	
List A	66	45	4	831	72	20.26	-	5	50	17	0	0	0		-	-	
20/20 Int																	
20/20	20	11	6	59	12	11.80	-	-	5	5	0	0	0		-	-	

67. Who returned match figures of 12-205 to bowl England to victory in the fourth Test v South Africa at Johannesburg in 2004-05?

O'SHEA, M. P. — Glamorgan

Name: Michael Peter O'Shea
Role: Right-hand top-order bat, 'part-time' off-spin bowler
Born: 4 September 1987, Cardiff
Height: 5ft 11in **Weight:** 12st
Nickname: Chewey
County debut: 2005
Parents: Paul and June
Marital status: Single
Education: Barry Comprehensive School; Millfield School
Qualifications: 13 GCSEs
Off-season: 'Training and Glamorgan trip to India'
Overseas tours: England U19 to India 2004-05, to Bangladesh 2005-06; Glamorgan to India 2007-08
Career highlights to date: 'Championship debut v Kent'
Cricket moments to forget: 'Getting 0 on Championship debut'
Cricket superstitions: 'Put left pad on first'
Cricketers particularly admired: Damien Martyn, Andrew Flintoff
Young players to look out for: Chris Thompson, Rory Hamilton-Brown, Karl Brown, Andy Miller, Ben Wright, Greg Wood
Other sports played: Rugby (Millfield 1st XV – won national XVs competition)
Other sports followed: Rugby (Cardiff Blues, Wales)
Favourite band: Oasis, Westlife
Extras: Has represented England U15, U16, U17, U19. Played for Wales Minor Counties in the C&G 2005 and in Minor Counties competitions 2005-07
Best batting: 24 Glamorgan v Kent, Canterbury 2005

2007 Season

	M	Inn	NO	Runs	HS	Avg	100	50	Ct	St	Balls	Runs	Wkts	Avg	BB	5I	10M
Test																	
FC	2	2	0	10	10	5.00	-	-	-	-	0	0	0		-	-	-
ODI																	
List A	5	5	0	83	49	16.60	-	-	1	-	168	180	3	60.00	2-37	-	
20/20 Int																	
20/20																	

Career Performances

	M	Inn	NO	Runs	HS	Avg	100	50	Ct	St	Balls	Runs	Wkts	Avg	BB	5I	10M
Test																	
FC	5	7	0	62	24	8.85	-	-	1	-	0	0	0		-	-	-
ODI																	
List A	7	7	1	90	49	15.00	-	-	3	-	180	194	3	64.66	2-37	-	
20/20 Int																	
20/20																	

ONIONS, G. Durham

Name: Graham Onions
Role: Right-hand bat, right-arm medium-fast bowler
Born: 9 September 1982, Gateshead
Height: 6ft 2in **Weight:** 11st 2lbs
Nickname: Wills
County debut: 2004
50 wickets in a season: 1
Place in batting averages: 232nd av. 17.75 (2006 263rd av. 11.60)
Place in bowling averages: 80th av. 33.11 (2006 55th av. 31.55)
Parents: Maureen and Richard
Marital status: Single
Education: St Thomas More RC Comprehensive School, Blaydon
Qualifications: 10 GCSEs, GNVQ Advanced Science (Distinction), Level 2 coach
Career outside cricket: Mortgage advisor
Overseas tours: Durham to Dubai 2005, 2006; England A to Bangladesh 2006-07; England Performance Programme to India 2007-08; England Lions to India 2007-08
Overseas teams played for: South Perth CC 2004
Career highlights to date: 'Being selected in squad for England's NatWest Series against Pakistan [2006]. National Academy'
Cricket moments to forget: 'Getting out to my dad in a charity game!'
Cricket superstitions: 'Lick my fingers before I run in to bowl'
Cricketers particularly admired: Darren Gough, Paul Collingwood
Young players to look out for: Ben Harmison, Mark Turner
Other sports played: Badminton (England U17; plays for Durham County)
Other sports followed: Football (Newcastle United)
Favourite band: 'No favourite – prefer R&B'

Relaxations: 'Sleep, music, the pub with mates'
Extras: Attended UPE International Cricket Academy, Port Elizabeth 2005. Durham Young Player of the Year and Bowler of the Year 2006. ECB National Academy 2006-07. Represented England Lions 2007
Best batting: 41 Durham v Yorkshire, Headingley 2007
Best bowling: 8-101 Durham v Warwickshire, Edgbaston 2007

2007 Season

	M	Inn	NO	Runs	HS	Avg	100	50	Ct	St	Balls	Runs	Wkts	Avg	BB	5I	10M
Test																	
FC	14	17	5	213	41	17.75	-	-	3	-	2377	1490	45	33.11	8-101	2	-
ODI																	
List A	11	3	0	10	6	3.33	-	-	3	-	486	448	14	32.00	3-41	-	
20/20 Int																	
20/20	2	0	0	0	0		-	-	1	-	24	37	0		-	-	

Career Performances

	M	Inn	NO	Runs	HS	Avg	100	50	Ct	St	Balls	Runs	Wkts	Avg	BB	5I	10M
Test																	
FC	44	60	19	544	41	13.26	-	-	9	-	6715	4284	120	35.70	8-101	3	-
ODI																	
List A	34	12	3	46	11	5.11	-	-	4	-	1334	1172	34	34.47	3-39	-	
20/20 Int																	
20/20	13	4	0	37	31	9.25	-	-	4	-	282	291	11	26.45	3-25	-	

ORD, J. E. — Warwickshire

Name: James Edward Ord
Role: Right-hand middle-order bat, occasional right-arm medium/off-spin bowler
Born: 9 November 1987, Birmingham
Height: 5ft 10in **Weight:** 12st 8lbs
Nickname: Ordy, Johnny Bravo, Starters
County debut: No first-team appearance
Parents: Malcolm and Jennifer
Marital status: Single
Family links with cricket: 'Grandad, James Simpson Ord, played for Warwickshire and was a member of the Championship winning side of 1951'
Education: Solihull School; Loughborough University
Qualifications: 10 GCSEs, 3 A-levels
Career outside cricket: 'Student'
Off-season: 'Studying at Loughborough University and training with LUCCE'
Overseas tours: Warwickshire Academy to Cape Town 2005-06
Career highlights to date: 'Signing for Warwickshire'

Cricket moments to forget: 'Being relegated with my former club Dorridge CC from Birmingham League division one'
Cricket superstitions: 'None. I'm still searching for one that works!'
Cricketers particularly admired: Mark Waugh, Brian Lara, Damien Martyn, Darren Lehmann
Young players to look out for: Arun Harinath, Richard Johnson, Dan Redfern, Chris Woakes, 'Jonny Teepson'
Other sports played: Tennis (Warwickshire Youth county cup squads; school national runners-up in HSBC tournament), rugby (school 1st XV and VII)
Other sports followed: 'Follow most sports, especially at the highest level, but unusually I don't have a team. I watch tennis, rugby (both codes), athletics and football, of course'

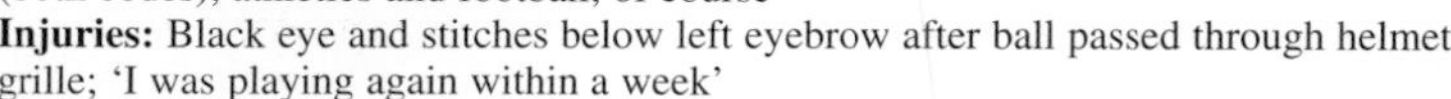

Injuries: Black eye and stitches below left eyebrow after ball passed through helmet grille; 'I was playing again within a week'
Favourite band: Kings of Leon
Relaxations: 'Gym, watching films, eating, wildlife documentaries, TV (*The Simpsons*, *Lost*)'
Extras: Played for ECB Schools v India U19 2006. Scored 188* for Warwickshire Academy v Glamorgan and Wales Academy at St Fagans 2006. Played for LUCCE 2007
Opinions on the game: 'Umpires should stand up against throwers/chuckers rather than turn a blind eye.'

68. Who stood in as England captain for the injured Nasser Hussain in the third Test v New Zealand at Old Trafford in 1999?

ORMOND, J. Surrey

Name: James Ormond
Role: Right-hand bat, right-arm fast'ish' bowler, can also bowl off-spin
Born: 20 August 1977, Walsgrave, Coventry
Height: 6ft 3in **Weight:** 15st
Nickname: Jimmy, Horse
County debut: 1995 (Leicestershire), 2002 (Surrey)
County cap: 1999 (Leicestershire), 2003 (Surrey)
Test debut: 2001
50 wickets in a season: 4
Place in batting averages: 276th av. 10.37
Place in bowling averages: 139th av. 53.33
Parents: Richard and Margaret
Marital status: Married
Family links with cricket: 'Dad played years of cricket in Warwickshire'
Education: St Thomas More, Nuneaton; North Warwickshire College of Further Education
Qualifications: 6 GCSEs
Overseas tours: England U19 to Zimbabwe 1995-96; England A to Kenya and Sri Lanka 1997-98; England to India and New Zealand 2001-02
Overseas teams played for: Sydney University CC 1996, 1998, 1999
Cricketers particularly admired: Curtly Ambrose, Courtney Walsh, Allan Donald, Sachin Tendulkar, Brian Lara, Steve Griffin
Other sports played: Football, mountain biking, 'anything'
Other sports followed: Football (Coventry City)
Relaxations: Spending time with friends and family
Extras: Played for the Development of Excellence side and England U19. NBC Denis Compton Award for the most promising young Leicestershire player 1998, 1999, 2000. Took 5-26 v Middlesex at The Oval in the Twenty20 2003 and was Man of the Match (4-11) at Trent Bridge in the inaugural final. Took four wickets in an over, all left-handers and including hat-trick (Hutton, Joyce, Weekes), in the Championship v Middlesex at Guildford 2003
Best batting: 57 Surrey v Gloucestershire, Bristol 2004
Best bowling: 7-63 Surrey v Glamorgan, Cardiff 2005

2007 Season

	M	Inn	NO	Runs	HS	Avg	100	50	Ct	St	Balls	Runs	Wkts	Avg	BB	5I	10M
Test																	
FC	7	10	2	83	25 *	10.37	-	-	1	-	1134	640	12	53.33	2-42	-	-
ODI																	
List A	2	0	0	0	0		-	-	-	-	90	87	2	43.50	1-43	-	
20/20 Int																	
20/20																	

Career Performances

	M	Inn	NO	Runs	HS	Avg	100	50	Ct	St	Balls	Runs	Wkts	Avg	BB	5I	10M
Test	2	4	1	38	18	12.66	-	-	-	-	372	185	2	92.50	1-70	-	-
FC	130	158	38	1827	57	15.22	-	2	27	-	24090	12918	435	29.69	7-63	20	1
ODI																	
List A	117	71	32	356	32	9.12	-	-	23	-	5292	3912	144	27.16	4-12	-	
20/20 Int																	
20/20	12	5	3	17	6	8.50	-	-	2	-	264	259	16	16.18	5-26	1	

OWEN, W. T. — Glamorgan

Name: William (Will) Thomas Owen
Role: Right-hand bat, right-arm fast-medium bowler
Born: 2 September 1988, St Asaph, North Wales
Height: 6ft **Weight:** 13st
Nickname: Willo
County debut: 2007
Parents: Haydn and Stephanie
Marital status: Single
Education: Prestatyn High School; UWIC
Qualifications: GCSEs and A-levels
Career outside cricket: Student (Sports Coaching course)
Off-season: 'Studying at university'
Career highlights to date: 'My first-class debut for Glamorgan against Gloucestershire 2007'
Cricketers particularly admired: Simon Jones
Young players to look out for: David Lloyd (Glamorgan Academy)
Other sports played: Rugby (represented North Wales at U12-U15)
Other sports followed: Football (Blackburn Rovers), rugby (Llanelli Scarlets)
Favourite band: Oasis

Relaxations: 'Going out with friends, playing Pro Evo and training'
Extras: Played for Wales Minor Counties in Minor Counties competitions 2007
Opinions on cricket: 'Cricket is changing rapidly, with the different formats of the game encouraging players to improvise new techniques and strategies, making the game more exciting for the spectators.'

2007 Season

	M	Inn	NO	Runs	HS	Avg	100	50	Ct	St	Balls	Runs	Wkts	Avg	BB	5I	10M
Test																	
FC	1	0	0	0	0		-	-	-	-	48	37	0		-	-	-
ODI																	
List A																	
20/20 Int																	
20/20																	

Career Performances

	M	Inn	NO	Runs	HS	Avg	100	50	Ct	St	Balls	Runs	Wkts	Avg	BB	5I	10M
Test																	
FC	1	0	0	0	0		-	-	-	-	48	37	0		-	-	-
ODI																	
List A																	
20/20 Int																	
20/20																	

PAGET, C. D. — Derbyshire

Name: Christopher (Chris) David Paget
Role: Right-hand bat, right-arm off-spin bowler
Born: 2 November 1987, Stafford
Height: 6ft **Weight:** 11st 8lbs
Nickname: Padge, Pooch, Noodles, Sheephead
County debut: 2004
Parents: Anne and Andy
Marital status: Single
Family links with cricket: 'Brother (Alex) plays for Milford Hall CC and the Old Man has played in several Lads v Dads games'
Education: Repton School; Durham University
Qualifications: 9 GCSEs, 3 A-levels
Overseas tours: Staffordshire to Barbados 2003; Repton School to Goa 2004, to Sri Lanka 2005-06; Derbyshire Academy to South Africa 2006-07
Career highlights to date: 'First-class debut'
Cricket moments to forget: 'Bagging my first pair v Durham 2nd XI 2006 – first duck being caught at deep fine leg; second, run out'

Cricket superstitions: 'Always run on to pitch when going out to bat'
Cricketers particularly admired: Damien Martyn
Other sports played: Tennis ('used to represent Staffs'); rugby, hockey, football (school); golf
Other sports followed: Football (Everton)
Favourite band: Snow Patrol, David Gray, Jack Johnson, The Rolling Stones
Relaxations: 'Spending time with mates; having fun'
Extras: Played Staffordshire age-group cricket for six years. Took 3-63 (Joseph, Bravo, Dwayne Smith) on first-class debut v West Indians at Derby 2004. Became youngest player to represent Derbyshire in the Championship, v Yorkshire at Headingley 2004, aged 16 years 283 days. Played for Durham UCCE 2007
Opinions on cricket: 'The diversification of the game, which is bringing a greater appeal to all ages, has to be a good thing.'
Best batting: 46 DUCCE v Lancashire, Durham 2007
Best bowling: 3-63 Derbyshire v West Indians, Derby 2004

2007 Season

	M	Inn	NO	Runs	HS	Avg	100	50	Ct	St	Balls	Runs	Wkts	Avg	BB	5I	10M
Test																	
FC	2	4	0	66	46	16.50	-	-	3	-	174	131	1	131.00	1-19	-	-
ODI																	
List A	1	1	0	3	3	3.00	-	-	-	-	36	48	1	48.00	1-48	-	
20/20 Int																	
20/20																	

Career Performances

	M	Inn	NO	Runs	HS	Avg	100	50	Ct	St	Balls	Runs	Wkts	Avg	BB	5I	10M
Test																	
FC	6	8	2	73	46	12.16	-	-	3	-	510	337	4	84.25	3-63	-	-
ODI																	
List A	2	1	0	3	3	3.00	-	-	-	-	96	109	2	54.50	1-48	-	
20/20 Int																	
20/20																	

PALLADINO, A. P. Essex

Name: Antonio (Tony) Paul Palladino
Role: Right-hand bat, right-arm medium-fast bowler; all-rounder
Born: 29 June 1983, Whitechapel, London
Height: 6ft **Weight:** 12st 8lbs
Nickname: Dino, TP, Freddie, Italian Stallion
County debut: 2003
Place in bowling averages: 57th av. 29.16 (2006 115th av. 42.07)
Parents: Antonio and Kathleen
Marital status: 'Attached'
Family links with cricket: 'Dad played cricket in the Kent League'
Education: Cardinal Pole Secondary School; Anglia Polytechnic University
Qualifications: 9 GCSEs, Advanced GNVQ Leisure and Tourism
Overseas teams played for: Mount Lawley CC, Perth 2005-06
Career highlights to date: '6-41 v Kent 2003; 6-68 v Leics 2006; 111 v Hampshire 2nd XI 2006'
Cricket moments to forget: 'Losing to Sussex 2006 in the C&G Trophy when defending nearly 300 and they were 30-4. Felt sick for about a week' (*Just for the record, the fourth Sussex wicket fell at 56 at Chelmsford 2006, but … – Ed*)
Cricket superstitions: 'Try and get a corner spot in changing room'
Cricketers particularly admired: Ian Botham, Andy and Grant Flower, Kevin Brooks
Other sports played: Football, golf, snooker
Other sports followed: Football (Chelsea), baseball (Boston Red Sox)
Favourite band: 'Various artists'
Relaxations: 'Computer games, cinema, going out with the lads'
Extras: Represented England U17. Represented ECB U19 2000 and 2001. Played for Cambridge UCCE 2003, 2004, 2005. Recorded maiden first-class five-wicket return (6-41) v Kent at Canterbury 2003 in only his second Championship match. Represented British Universities 2005. His 6-68 v Leicestershire at Chelmsford 2006 included a spell of 5-9 in seven overs
Best batting: 41 Essex v Nottinghamshire, Trent Bridge 2004
Best bowling: 6-41 Essex v Kent, Canterbury 2003

2007 Season

	M	Inn	NO	Runs	HS	Avg	100	50	Ct	St	Balls	Runs	Wkts	Avg	BB	5I	10M
Test																	
FC	7	8	2	51	18	8.50	-	-	1	-	641	350	12	29.16	4-44	-	-
ODI																	
List A	6	6	0	26	11	4.33	-	-	1	-	174	175	4	43.75	1-19	-	
20/20 Int																	
20/20	3	1	1	1	1 *		-	-	-	-	60	79	4	19.75	2-26	-	

Career Performances

	M	Inn	NO	Runs	HS	Avg	100	50	Ct	St	Balls	Runs	Wkts	Avg	BB	5I	10M
Test																	
FC	30	32	12	229	41	11.45	-	-	11	-	3951	2342	52	45.03	6-41	2	-
ODI																	
List A	20	10	1	43	16	4.77	-	-	2	-	756	639	22	29.04	3-32	-	
20/20 Int																	
20/20	9	1	1	1	1 *		-	-	-	-	162	202	10	20.20	2-3	-	

PANESAR, M. S. — Northamptonshire

Name: Mudhsuden Singh Panesar
Role: Left-hand bat, slow left-arm bowler
Born: 25 April 1982, Luton
Height: 6ft 1in **Weight:** 12st 7lbs
Nickname: Monty
County debut: 2001
County cap: 2006
Test debut: 2005-06
ODI debut: 2006-07
Twenty20 Int debut: 2006-07
50 wickets in a season: 3
Place in batting averages: (2006 270th av. 10.46)
Place in bowling averages: 43rd av. 26.66 (2006 33rd av. 28.57)
Parents: Paramjit and Gursharan
Marital status: Single
Family links with cricket: 'Father used to play cricket'
Education: Stopsley High School, Luton; Bedford Modern School; Loughborough University
Qualifications: 10 GCSEs, 3 A-levels, Computer Science degree

Overseas tours: Bedford Modern School to Barbados 1999; England U19 to India 2000-01; Northamptonshire to Grenada 2001-02; British Universities to South Africa 2002; ECB National Academy to Australia and Sri Lanka 2002-03; England to India 2005-06, to Australia 2006-07, to West Indies (World Cup) 2006-07, to Sri Lanka 2007-08, to New Zealand 2007-08; England Lions to India 2007-08
Career highlights to date: 'Playing for England'
Cricketers particularly admired: Sachin Tendulkar
Other sports followed: Football (Luton, Arsenal)
Relaxations: 'Reading'
Player website: www.monty-panesar.com
Extras: Represented England U19. Had match figures of 8-131 on first-class debut v Leicestershire at Northampton 2001, including 4-11 in the second innings. NBC Denis Compton Award for the most promising young Northamptonshire player 2001. Played for Loughborough UCCE 2002, 2004. Represented British Universities 2002, 2004, 2005. Had first innings figures of 5-92 in the third Test v Australia 2006-07, becoming the first England spinner to record a five-wicket innings return in a Test at Perth. One of *Wisden*'s Five Cricketers of the Year 2007. Had match figures of 10-187 (4-50/6-137) in the third Test v West Indies at Old Trafford 2007, winning Man of the Match award. England's Man of the [Test] Series v West Indies 2007. England 12-month central contract 2007-08
Best batting: 39* Northamptonshire v Worcestershire, Northampton 2005
Best bowling: 7-181 Northamptonshire v Essex, Chelmsford 2005

2007 Season

	M	Inn	NO	Runs	HS	Avg	100	50	Ct	St	Balls	Runs	Wkts	Avg	BB	5I	10M
Test	7	9	2	38	14 *	5.42	-	-	1	-	1648	833	31	26.87	6-129	3	1
FC	12	15	2	121	33	9.30	-	-	3	-	2785	1413	53	26.66	6-65	4	1
ODI	8	2	0	14	13	7.00	-	-	1	-	420	325	7	46.42	1-28	-	
List A	9	2	0	14	13	7.00	-	-	2	-	468	357	9	39.66	2-32	-	
20/20 Int																	
20/20																	

Career Performances

	M	Inn	NO	Runs	HS	Avg	100	50	Ct	St	Balls	Runs	Wkts	Avg	BB	5I	10M
Test	20	28	11	124	26	7.29	-	-	3	-	4593	2249	73	30.80	6-129	6	1
FC	65	84	30	460	39 *	8.51	-	-	16	-	15199	7308	250	29.23	7-181	16	3
ODI	25	7	3	23	13	5.75	-	-	3	-	1248	949	23	41.26	3-25	-	
List A	37	14	7	73	16 *	10.42	-	-	7	-	1782	1318	36	36.61	5-20	1	
20/20 Int	1	1	0	1	1	1.00	-	-	-	-	24	40	2	20.00	2-40	-	
20/20	7	2	0	3	2	1.50	-	-	-	-	168	235	10	23.50	2-22	-	

PARK, G. T. Durham

Name: Garry Terence Park
Role: Right-hand bat, wicket-keeper
Born: 19 April 1983, Empangeni, South Africa
Height: 5ft 7in **Weight:** 10st 10lbs
Nickname: Parkie
County debut: 2005 (one-day), 2006 (first-class)
Place in batting averages: 176th av. 25.28
Parents: Mike Park and Kirsty Reeves
Marital status: Single
Education: Eshowe High School, South Africa; Anglia Ruskin University, Cambridge
Qualifications: Matric Exemption (South Africa), ECB Levels 1 and 2 coaching
Off-season: 'Travelling abroad to work and play cricket'
Overseas tours: Cambridge UCCE to Grenada 2003
Overseas teams played for: Crusaders CC, Durban 2005; Zululand 2006-07
Career highlights to date: 'Hitting Tino Best for 20 off the over'
Cricket superstitions: 'None'
Cricketers particularly admired: Jonty Rhodes, Dale Benkenstein
Other sports played: Hockey (KwaZulu-Natal U15, U19), rugby (Natal U14), golf
Other sports followed: Rugby (The Sharks)
Relaxations: 'Deep-sea fishing, golf'
Extras: Played for Cambridge UCCE 2003-05. Is England-qualified
Best batting: 100* Durham v Yorkshire, Headingley 2006

2007 Season

	M	Inn	NO	Runs	HS	Avg	100	50	Ct	St	Balls	Runs	Wkts	Avg	BB	5I	10M
Test																	
FC	4	7	0	177	61	25.28	-	2	1	-	42	39	0		-	-	-
ODI																	
List A	7	6	1	86	33	17.20	-	-	2	-	0	0	0		-	-	
20/20 Int																	
20/20	6	4	1	63	25 *	21.00	-	-	1	-	6	7	0		-	-	

Career Performances

	M	Inn	NO	Runs	HS	Avg	100	50	Ct	St	Balls	Runs	Wkts	Avg	BB	5I	10M
Test																	
FC	17	28	6	824	100 *	37.45	1	4	20	-	342	300	0		-	-	-
ODI																	
List A	10	8	1	125	33	17.85	-	-	5	-	0	0	0		-	-	
20/20 Int																	
20/20	6	4	1	63	25 *	21.00	-	-	1	-	6	7	0		-	-	

PARKER, L. C. — Warwickshire

Name: Luke Charles Parker
Role: Right-hand bat, right-arm medium bowler
Born: 27 September 1983, Coventry
Height: 6ft **Weight:** 13st
Nickname: Parks
County debut: 2005
Place in batting averages: 254th av. 13.50 (2006 154th av. 28.73)
Parents: Linda and Neil
Marital status: Single
Family links with cricket: 'Dad played for Lincolnshire'
Education: Finham Park; Oxford Brookes University
Qualifications: 8 GCSEs, 3 A-levels, ECB Level 1 coach
Overseas teams played for: United, Cape Town 2002-03
Cricket moments to forget: 'Dropping Matt Windows three times in an innings of 200-plus'
Cricket superstitions: 'Not really'
Cricketers particularly admired: Nick Knight, Damien Martyn
Other sports played: Football (Coventry City Academy U10-15)
Other sports followed: Football (Coventry City)
Favourite band: Mylo
Extras: Played for Warwickshire Board XI in the 2002 C&G. Played for Oxford UCCE 2004-06 (captain 2005). Represented British Universities 2005 and as captain v Sri Lankans at Fenner's 2006
Best batting: 140 OUCCE v Durham, The Parks 2006
Best bowling: 2-37 OUCCE v Gloucestershire, The Parks 2005

2007 Season

	M	Inn	NO	Runs	HS	Avg	100	50	Ct	St	Balls	Runs	Wkts	Avg	BB	5I	10M
Test																	
FC	5	6	0	81	49	13.50	-	-	3	-	12	16	0		-	-	-
ODI																	
List A																	
20/20 Int																	
20/20	3	2	1	5	3 *	5.00	-	-	-	-	0	0	0		-	-	

Career Performances

	M	Inn	NO	Runs	HS	Avg	100	50	Ct	St	Balls	Runs	Wkts	Avg	BB	5I	10M
Test																	
FC	25	39	3	984	140	27.33	1	4	13	-	436	274	6	45.66	2-37	-	-
ODI																	
List A	4	4	1	40	17	13.33	-	-	2	-	12	11	0		-	-	
20/20 Int																	
20/20	3	2	1	5	3 *	5.00	-	-	-	-	0	0	0		-	-	

PARRY, S. D. Lancashire

Name: Stephen David Parry
Role: Right-hand bat, slow left-arm bowler
Born: 12 January 1986, Manchester
Height: 6ft **Weight:** 11st 7lbs
Nickname: Pazza
County debut: 2007
Parents: David and Ann-Marie
Marital status: Single
Education: Audenshaw High School, Greater Manchester
Qualifications: 9 GCSEs, 4 A-levels
Off-season: 'Playing cricket in Australia'
Overseas teams played for: Eastern Suburbs, Sydney 2005; Bundalaguah, Melbourne 2006, 2007; Gosnells, Perth 2008
Career highlights to date: 'Getting first full-time contract with Lancashire'
Cricket superstitions: 'None'
Cricketers particularly admired: Shane Warne
Other sports played: Football, table tennis
Other sports followed: Football (Man City), Australian Rules (St Kilda)
Favourite band: The Kooks

Extras: Lancashire Young Player of the Year. Played for Cumberland in Minor Counties competitions 2005, 2006. Recorded maiden first-class five-wicket return (5-23) on debut v DUCCE at Durham 2007
Best bowling: 5-23 Lancashire v DUCCE, Durham 2007

2007 Season

	M	Inn	NO	Runs	HS	Avg	100	50	Ct	St	Balls	Runs	Wkts	Avg	BB	5I	10M
Test																	
FC	1	0	0	0	0		-	-	-	-	115	46	5	9.20	5-23	1	-
ODI																	
List A																	
20/20 Int																	
20/20																	

Career Performances

	M	Inn	NO	Runs	HS	Avg	100	50	Ct	St	Balls	Runs	Wkts	Avg	BB	5I	10M
Test																	
FC	1	0	0	0	0		-	-	-	-	115	46	5	9.20	5-23	1	-
ODI																	
List A																	
20/20 Int																	
20/20																	

PARSONS, K. A. Somerset

Name: Keith Alan Parsons
Role: Right-hand bat, right-arm medium bowler; all-rounder
Born: 2 May 1973, Taunton
Height: 6ft 1in **Weight:** 14st 7lbs
Nickname: Pilot, Pars, Orv
County debut: 1992
County cap: 1999
Benefit: 2004
Place in batting averages: (2006 77th av. 39.30)
Place in bowling averages: (2006 64th av. 32.72)
Parents: Alan and Lynne
Wife and date of marriage: Sharon, 12 January 2002
Children: Joseph Luke, 17 October 2002; Alex Matthew, 23 March 2005

Family links with cricket: Identical twin brother, Kevin, was on the Somerset staff 1992-94 and then captained the Somerset Board XI. Father played six seasons for Somerset 2nd XI and captained National Civil Service XI
Education: The Castle School, Taunton; Richard Huish Sixth Form College, Taunton
Qualifications: 8 GCSEs, 3 A-levels, NCA senior coach
Career outside cricket: 'Working for Sporting Spectrum Ltd, a corporate hospitality company [based in Taunton] specialising in sporting events throughout England'
Off-season: 'Working for my company, Sporting Spectrum Ltd'
Overseas tours: Castle School to Barbados 1989; Somerset CCC to Cape Town 1999, 2000, 2001
Overseas teams played for: Kapiti Old Boys, Horowhenua, New Zealand 1992-93; Taita District, Wellington, New Zealand 1993-96; Wembley Downs CC, Perth 1998
Career highlights to date: 'C&G final 2001 v Leicestershire – great to win a trophy, and Man of the Match capped a dream day'
Cricket moments to forget: 'Any bad days at Taunton'
Cricket superstitions: 'None'
Cricketers particularly admired: Andy Caddick, Marcus Trescothick, Glenn McGrath, Saqlain Mushtaq
Other sports followed: Rugby union (Bath), football (Nottingham Forest), golf, horse racing
Injuries: Out for two weeks in April 2007 with a back injury
Relaxations: Playing golf, watching movies, listening to music 'and the odd social pint of beer'
Extras: Captained two National Cup winning sides – Taunton St Andrews in National U15 Club Championship and Richard Huish College in National U17 School Championship. Represented English Schools at U15 and U19 level. Somerset Young Player of the Year 1993. C&G Man of the Match award for his 52-ball 60* (including sixes from the last two balls of the innings) and 2-40 in the final v Leicestershire at Lord's 2001
Best batting: 193* Somerset v West Indians, Taunton 2000
Best bowling: 5-13 Somerset v Lancashire, Taunton 2000

2007 Season

	M	Inn	NO	Runs	HS	Avg	100	50	Ct	St	Balls	Runs	Wkts	Avg	BB	5I	10M
Test																	
FC																	
ODI																	
List A	8	7	0	126	37	18.00	-	-	-	-	252	203	3	67.66	2-49	-	
20/20 Int																	
20/20	1	1	0	9	9	9.00	-	-	-	-	0	0	0		-	-	

Career Performances

	M	Inn	NO	Runs	HS	Avg	100	50	Ct	St	Balls	Runs	Wkts	Avg	BB	5I	10M
Test																	
FC	130	209	23	5324	193 *	28.62	6	28	115	-	8004	4646	106	43.83	5-13	2	-
ODI																	
List A	247	216	40	5225	121	29.68	2	28	98	-	6333	5290	146	36.23	5-39	1	
20/20 Int																	
20/20	31	30	7	464	57 *	20.17	-	1	9	-	338	467	18	25.94	3-12	-	

PARSONS, T. W. Kent

Name: Thomas (Tom) William Parsons
Role: Right-hand lower-order bat, right-arm fast-medium bowler
Born: 2 May 1987, Melbourne, Australia
Height: 6ft 3in **Weight:** 13st 5lbs
Nickname: Teeps, TP, Jonny Teepson
County debut: 2007 (one-day)
Parents: Richard and Christine
Marital status: Single
Family links with cricket: 'Dad played Middlesex 2nd XI. Grandfathers, uncles and cousins all have played or play'
Education: Maidstone Grammar School; Loughborough University
Qualifications: 11 GCSEs, 3 A-levels, Level 2 cricket coach
Off-season: 'Studying for a Geography and Sport degree at Loughborough University; getting fit and working hard in the gym'
Career highlights to date: 'First-class debut for Loughborough UCCE against Worcestershire. First-team debut for Kent v Sri Lanka A. Getting Vikram Solanki out for my first first-class wicket. Taking two wickets on debut for Kent – two players who have played Test match cricket for Sri Lanka'
Cricket moments to forget: 'Getting hit on the head without a helmet in a school game, meaning I missed all my A-levels and was hospitalised for a while. Getting out needing two to win off the last ball for Loughborough UCCE against Yorkshire'
Cricket superstitions: 'Sliding my bat over the crease after every boundary'
Cricketers particularly admired: Glenn McGrath, Matthew Hoggard, Nick Knight, Ian Bell
Young players to look out for: Johan Malcolm, Arun Harinath, Jigar Naik, James Day, John Bowden, Dom O'Connell, Jonty Parsons, Robert Hulme

Other sports played: Hockey (Loughborough Town), rugby (Rutherford Hall 1st XV), squash, golf
Other sports followed: Football (Arsenal, Gillingham), rugby (Harlequins)
Injuries: Out from the end of July with a stress fracture in a foot
Favourite band: Bloc Party
Relaxations: 'Films, going out with friends, watching sport'
Extras: Kent Academy 2005. Played for Loughborough UCCE 2007
Opinions on cricket: 'Enjoy every minute of it!'
Best batting: 10 LUCCE v Worcestershire, Worcester 2007
Best bowling: 3-70 LUCCE v Worcestershire, Worcester 2007

2007 Season

	M	Inn	NO	Runs	HS	Avg	100	50	Ct	St	Balls	Runs	Wkts	Avg	BB	5I	10M
Test																	
FC	2	3	0	10	10	3.33	-	-	-	-	246	116	4	29.00	3-70	-	-
ODI																	
List A	1	0	0	0	0		-	-	-	-	36	41	2	20.50	2-41	-	
20/20 Int																	
20/20																	

Career Performances

	M	Inn	NO	Runs	HS	Avg	100	50	Ct	St	Balls	Runs	Wkts	Avg	BB	5I	10M
Test																	
FC	2	3	0	10	10	3.33	-	-	-	-	246	116	4	29.00	3-70	-	-
ODI																	
List A	1	0	0	0	0		-	-	-	-	36	41	2	20.50	2-41	-	
20/20 Int																	
20/20																	

69. Who was England's Man of the Test Series v South Africa in 2003?

PATEL, A. Derbyshire

Name: Akhil Patel
Role: Left-hand bat, left-arm wrist-spin bowler; all-rounder
Born: 18 June 1990, Nottingham
Height: 5ft 11in **Weight:** 12st 7lbs
County debut: 2007
Family links with cricket: 'Dad used to play club cricket in local Derbyshire league and Nottinghamshire League; played good standard of cricket. Brother Samit plays first-class cricket for Notts and has represented England at various stages U15-19'
Education: Trent College; Kimberley Comprehensive
Qualifications: 7 GCSEs, GNVQ in Leisure and Tourism
Career outside cricket: 'Want to be a coach after cricket'
Off-season: 'Training with Derbyshire Academy in the winter'
Overseas tours: Derbyshire Academy to South Africa 2006
Career highlights to date: 'Making my second-team debut last season against Lancashire, and also in the same year making my first-class debut against Cambridge UCCE'
Cricket moments to forget: 'Dropping three catches against Dunstall CC in the Derbyshire Premier League last season'
Cricket superstitions: 'Put right pad on first, and also run on to the pitch'
Cricketers particularly admired: Sachin Tendulkar, Shane Warne, Stephen Fleming, Brian Lara, Andrew Jackman
Young players to look out for: Samit Patel, Daniel Redfern, Liam Dawson, Chris Jordan, Luke Fletcher
Other sports played: 'Used to play rugby at a good standard at my old school; try to play football'
Other sports followed: Football (Arsenal), American football (San Francisco 49ers)
Favourite band: Pretty Ricky, Oasis
Relaxations: 'Going to the cinema, watching TV, going shopping'
Extras: Broke Trent College U13 record for the most runs in a season. Youngest player to appear for Trent College 1st XI. Third-youngest player to appear in first-class cricket for Derbyshire
Opinions on cricket: 'Fast bowlers shouldn't be able to swing the ball. Shouldn't be able to bring too many Kolpak players [*see page 13*] on to the county circuit.'
Best batting: 31 Derbyshire v CUCCE, Fenner's 2007

2007 Season

	M	Inn	NO	Runs	HS	Avg	100	50	Ct	St	Balls	Runs	Wkts	Avg	BB	5I	10M
Test																	
FC	1	2	1	43	31	43.00	-	-	-	-	54	30	0		-	-	-
ODI																	
List A																	
20/20 Int																	
20/20																	

Career Performances

	M	Inn	NO	Runs	HS	Avg	100	50	Ct	St	Balls	Runs	Wkts	Avg	BB	5I	10M
Test																	
FC	1	2	1	43	31	43.00	-	-	-	-	54	30	0		-	-	-
ODI																	
List A																	
20/20 Int																	
20/20																	

PATEL, M. M. — Kent

Name: Minal (Min) Mahesh Patel
Role: Right-hand bat, slow left-arm orthodox bowler
Born: 7 July 1970, Mumbai, India
Height: 5ft 7in **Weight:** 10st
Nickname: Ho Chi, Diamond, Geez
County debut: 1989
County cap: 1994
Benefit: 2004
Test debut: 1996
50 wickets in a season: 4
Place in batting averages: (2006 259th av. 12.78)
Place in bowling averages: (2006 88th av. 36.59)
Parents: Mahesh and Aruna
Wife and date of marriage: Karuna, 8 October 1995
Family links with cricket: Father played good club cricket in India, Africa and England
Education: Dartford Grammar School; Manchester Polytechnic
Qualifications: 6 O-levels, 3 A-levels, BA (Hons) Economics

Overseas tours: Dartford GS to Barbados 1988; England A to India and Bangladesh 1994-95; MCC to Malta 1997, 1999, to Fiji, Sydney and Hong Kong 1998, to East and Central Africa 1999, to Bangladesh 1999-2000 (c), to Argentina and Chile 2001, to Namibia and Uganda 2004-05 (c); Kent to Port Elizabeth 2001; Club Cricket Conference to Australia 2002
Overseas teams played for: St Augustine's, Cape Town 1993-94; Alberton, Johannesburg 1997-98
Career highlights to date: 'Winning 2001 Norwich Union League at Edgbaston. First Test cap. Any match-winning performance for Kent'
Cricket moments to forget: 'Being left out of the final XI for the Lord's Test v India 1996'
Cricketers particularly admired: Derek Underwood, Aravinda de Silva
Other sports played: Golf, snooker
Other sports followed: Football (Tottenham Hotspur), 'most sports that you can name'
Favourite band: 'A lot of 1970s/80s soul – Phyllis Hyman, Loose Ends, Keni Burke etc.'
Extras: Played for English Schools 1988, 1989 and NCA England South 1989. Was voted Kent League Young Player of the Year 1987 while playing for Blackheath. Whittingdale Young Player of the Year 1994. Vice-captain of Kent 2006-07
Best batting: 87 Kent v Glamorgan, Cardiff 2005
Best bowling: 8-96 Kent v Lancashire, Canterbury 1994

2007 Season

	M	Inn	NO	Runs	HS	Avg	100	50	Ct	St	Balls	Runs	Wkts	Avg	BB	5I	10M
Test																	
FC	1	2	0	67	52	33.50	-	1	1	-	186	107	1	107.00	1-17	-	-
ODI																	
List A	1	0	0	0	0		-	-	-	-	0	0	0		-	-	
20/20 Int																	
20/20																	

Career Performances

	M	Inn	NO	Runs	HS	Avg	100	50	Ct	St	Balls	Runs	Wkts	Avg	BB	5I	10M
Test	2	2	0	45	27	22.50	-	-	2	-	276	180	1	180.00	1-101	-	-
FC	208	278	51	3945	87	17.37	-	17	102	-	44787	19309	630	30.64	8-96	30	9
ODI																	
List A	85	43	16	269	27 *	9.96	-	-	24	-	3648	2701	88	30.69	3-20	-	
20/20 Int																	
20/20	9	4	1	18	8	6.00	-	-	-	-	196	257	15	17.13	4-26	-	

PATEL, S. R. — Nottinghamshire

Name: Samit Rohit Patel
Role: Right-hand bat, left-arm orthodox spin bowler; all-rounder
Born: 30 November 1984, Leicester
Height: 5ft 8in **Weight:** 12st
Nickname: Pilchy Patel
County debut: 2002
Place in batting averages: 32nd av. 50.68 (2006 17th av. 61.20)
Place in bowling averages: 19th av. 23.50
Parents: Rohit and Sejal
Marital status: Single
Family links with cricket: Father local league cricketer and brother Akhil is with Derbyshire
Education: Worksop College
Qualifications: 7 GCSEs, 2 A-levels
Career outside cricket: 'Want to be a coach'
Overseas tours: England U17 to Australia 2001; England U19 to Australia and (U19 World Cup) New Zealand 2001-02, to Australia 2002-03, to Bangladesh (U19 World Cup) 2003-04
Cricket moments to forget: 'Playing at Headingley in the Twenty20 Cup against Yorkshire, where I got hit for 28 in an over by Michael Lumb'
Cricket superstitions: 'Put my right pad on first'
Cricketers particularly admired: Sachin Tendulkar, Brian Lara
Young players to look out for: Akhil Patel
Other sports played: Rugby, hockey (both for Worksop College)
Other sports followed: Football (Nottingham Forest)
Favourite band: G-Unit
Relaxations: 'Listening to music; playing snooker; just generally relaxing'
Extras: Made Nottinghamshire 2nd XI debut in 1999, aged 14. Winner of inaugural BBC *Test Match Special* U15 Young Cricketer of the Year Award 2000. Represented England U19 2002, 2003 (captain in one-day series 2003) and 2004. Scored maiden Championship hundred (156) v Middlesex at Lord's 2006, progressing from century to 150 in 17 balls
Best batting: 176 Nottinghamshire v Gloucestershire, Bristol 2007
Best bowling: 4-68 Nottinghamshire v DUCCE, Durham 2007

2007 Season

	M	Inn	NO	Runs	HS	Avg	100	50	Ct	St	Balls	Runs	Wkts	Avg	BB	5I	10M
Test																	
FC	14	20	1	963	176	50.68	4	5	8	-	624	329	14	23.50	4-68	-	-
ODI																	
List A	14	13	3	308	72	30.80	-	1	5	-	162	158	4	39.50	2-42	-	
20/20 Int																	
20/20	6	6	2	178	84 *	44.50	-	2	5	-	0	0	0		-	-	

Career Performances

	M	Inn	NO	Runs	HS	Avg	100	50	Ct	St	Balls	Runs	Wkts	Avg	BB	5I	10M
Test																	
FC	27	39	3	1701	176	47.25	6	8	12	-	1430	715	22	32.50	4-68	-	-
ODI																	
List A	56	47	11	1142	93 *	31.72	-	5	9	-	1040	887	29	30.58	3-40	-	
20/20 Int																	
20/20	31	30	7	609	84 *	26.47	-	4	14	-	325	433	18	24.05	3-11	-	

PATTERSON, S. A. — Yorkshire

Name: Steven Andrew Patterson
Role: Right-hand bat, right-arm medium-fast bowler
Born: 3 October 1983, Hull
Height: 6ft 4in **Weight:** 14st
Nickname: Dead
County debut: 2005
Place in batting averages: (2006 251st av. 14.16)
Parents: Sue and Alan
Marital status: Single
Education: Malet Lambert School; St Mary's Sixth Form College; Leeds University
Qualifications: 11 GCSEs, 3 A-levels, BSc Maths, Level 2 cricket coach
Overseas tours: MCC A to UAE and Oman 2004
Overseas teams played for: Suburbs New Lynn CC, Auckland 2005-06

Career highlights to date: 'Making my first-class debut for Yorkshire'
Cricket moments to forget: 'Going in as nightwatchman and getting a first-ball duck!'

Cricket superstitions: 'Not really'
Cricketers particularly admired: Glenn McGrath, Allan Donald
Young players to look out for: Adam Lyth, James Lee
Other sports played: Football, golf, badminton, skiing, scuba diving
Favourite band: Coldplay
Relaxations: 'Playing guitar, travelling, reading'
Extras: Played for Yorkshire Board XI in the 2003 C&G. 2nd XI cap 2006
Best batting: 46 Yorkshire v Lancashire, Old Trafford 2006
Best bowling: 2-30 Yorkshire v LUCCE, Headingley 2007

2007 Season

	M	Inn	NO	Runs	HS	Avg	100	50	Ct	St	Balls	Runs	Wkts	Avg	BB	5I	10M
Test																	
FC	1	0	0	0	0		-	-	-	-	78	39	2	19.50	2-30	-	-
ODI																	
List A	3	0	0	0	0		-	-	-	-	140	127	1	127.00	1-54	-	
20/20 Int																	
20/20																	

Career Performances

	M	Inn	NO	Runs	HS	Avg	100	50	Ct	St	Balls	Runs	Wkts	Avg	BB	5I	10M
Test																	
FC	7	7	1	85	46	14.16	-	-	2	-	562	295	4	73.75	2-30	-	-
ODI																	
List A	17	11	10	69	25 *	69.00	-	-	3	-	760	670	14	47.85	3-11	-	
20/20 Int																	
20/20																	

70. Who scored a 145-ball 125 (plus a second innings 59) as South Africa beat England at Trent Bridge in 1965: a) Graeme Pollock; b) Barry Richards; c) Mike Procter?

PENG, N. Glamorgan

Name: Nicky Peng
Role: Right-hand bat
Born: 18 September 1982, Newcastle upon Tyne
Height: 6ft 3in **Weight:** 14st 5lbs
Nickname: Pengy
County debut: 2000 (Durham), 2006 (Glamorgan)
County cap: 2001 (Durham)
Place in batting averages: 226th av. 18.50 (2006 187th av. 23.80)
Parents: Linda and Wilf
Marital status: Single
Education: Royal Grammar School, Newcastle upon Tyne
Qualifications: 10 GCSEs
Overseas tours: England U19 to India 2000-01, to Australia and (U19 World Cup) New Zealand 2001-02 (c); ECB National Academy to Australia 2001-02; Durham to South Africa 2002
Overseas teams played for: Subiaco-Floreat, Perth
Career highlights: 'Double promotion at Durham. Signing for Glamorgan. PCA Young Player of the Year 2001'
Cricketers particularly admired: Steve Waugh, Jacques Kallis, Paul Collingwood
Other sports followed: Football (Newcastle United), rugby (Newcastle Falcons)
Extras: Full name Nicky Peng Gillender. Represented England at U14, U15, U17 and U19 levels. Represented Minor Counties at age 15. Sir John Hobbs Silver Jubilee Memorial Prize 1998. Scored 98 on Championship debut, v Surrey at Riverside 2000. NBC Denis Compton Award for the most promising young Durham player 2000, 2001. Durham CCC Young Player of the Year 2001. PCA Young Player of the Year 2001. Retired in July 2007
Best batting: 158 Durham v DUCCE, Durham 2003

2007 Season

	M	Inn	NO	Runs	HS	Avg	100	50	Ct	St	Balls	Runs	Wkts	Avg	BB	5I	10M
Test																	
FC	3	6	0	111	65	18.50	-	1	2	-	0	0	0		-	-	-
ODI																	
List A	7	6	0	55	20	9.16	-	-	-	-	0	0	0		-	-	
20/20 Int																	
20/20	1	1	0	16	16	16.00	-	-	-	-	0	0	0		-	-	

Career Performances

	M	Inn	NO	Runs	HS	Avg	100	50	Ct	St	Balls	Runs	Wkts	Avg	BB	5I	10M
Test																	
FC	79	137	2	3200	158	23.70	4	15	47	-	6	2	0		-	-	-
ODI																	
List A	106	104	5	2395	121	24.19	3	12	20	-	0	0	0		-	-	
20/20 Int																	
20/20	20	18	1	312	49	18.35	-	-	10	-	0	0	0		-	-	

PEPLOE, C. T. — Middlesex

Name: Christopher (Chris) Thomas Peploe
Role: Left-hand lower-order bat, slow left-arm bowler
Born: 26 April 1981, Hammersmith, London
Height: 6ft 4in **Weight:** 13st 7lbs
Nickname: Peps, Pepsy
County debut: 2003
Place in batting averages: (2006 235th av. 15.69)
Place in bowling averages: (2006 148th av. 78.66)
Parents: Trevor and Margaret
Marital status: Single
Education: Twyford C of E High School; University of Surrey, Roehampton
Qualifications: 9 GCSEs, 3 A-levels, Sports Science degree, ECB Level 2 coach, YMCA gym instructor
Career outside cricket: Cricket coach
Overseas tours: MCC Young Cricketers to South Africa 2002, to Sri Lanka 2003; Middlesex to India 2004
Overseas teams played for: Northern Districts CC, Sydney
Cricket moments to forget: 'Bowling at Nick Knight and Craig Spearman when they both scored 300-plus in 2004'
Cricket superstitions: 'None'
Cricketers particularly admired: Daniel Vettori, Andrew Strauss, Phil Tufnell
Other sports played: Golf
Other sports followed: English rugby
Favourite band: Linkin Park
Relaxations: 'Music, movies, golf'
Extras: MCC Young Cricketer 2002-03

Best batting: 46 Middlesex v Lancashire, Lord's 2006
Best bowling: 4-31 Middlesex v Yorkshire, Southgate 2006

2007 Season

	M	Inn	NO	Runs	HS	Avg	100	50	Ct	St	Balls	Runs	Wkts	Avg	BB	5I	10M
Test																	
FC	2	2	0	20	13	10.00	-	-	2	-	198	95	5	19.00	3-58	-	-
ODI																	
List A	2	1	1	6	6 *		-	-	1	-	84	77	0		-	-	
20/20 Int																	
20/20																	

Career Performances

	M	Inn	NO	Runs	HS	Avg	100	50	Ct	St	Balls	Runs	Wkts	Avg	BB	5I	10M
Test																	
FC	29	40	6	524	46	15.41	-	-	11	-	5230	2824	54	52.29	4-31	-	-
ODI																	
List A	18	10	3	36	14 *	5.14	-	-	7	-	816	596	26	22.92	4-38	-	
20/20 Int																	
20/20	15	6	4	12	7	6.00	-	-	4	-	221	378	10	37.80	3-35	-	

PETERS, S. D. — Northamptonshire

Name: Stephen David Peters
Role: Right-hand bat, leg-break bowler
Born: 10 December 1978, Harold Wood, Essex
Height: 5ft 11in **Weight:** 12st
Nickname: Pedro, Geezer
County debut: 1996 (Essex), 2002 (Worcestershire), 2006 (Northamptonshire)
County cap: 2002 (Worcestershire colours), 2007 (Northamptonshire)
1000 runs in a season: 2
Place in batting averages: 105th av. 34.50 (2006 74th av. 40.07)
Parents: Lesley and Brian
Marital status: Single
Family links with cricket: 'All family is linked with Upminster CC'
Education: Coopers Company and Coborn School
Qualifications: 9 GCSEs, Level 2 coaching

Off-season: 'Resting my back!'
Overseas tours: Essex U14 to Barbados; Essex U15 to Hong Kong; England U19 to Pakistan 1996-97, to South Africa (including U19 World Cup) 1997-98
Overseas teams played for: Cornwall CC, Auckland 2001-02; Willetton CC, Perth 2002-03
Career highlights to date: 'Winning B&H Cup in 1998 with Essex. Northants cap 2007'
Cricket moments to forget: 'Running myself out for a pair against Durham in 2003'
Cricketers particularly admired: 'Anyone who has played at the top level'
Young players to look out for: Alex Wakely
Other sports played: Golf, football
Other sports followed: Football (West Ham United)
Injuries: Out for the final game of the 2007 season with a broken thumb
Favourite band: Rooster
Relaxations: 'My sofa'
Extras: Sir John Hobbs Silver Jubilee Memorial Prize 1994. Represented England at U14, U15, U17 and U19. Scored century (110) on Essex first-class debut v Cambridge University at Fenner's 1996, aged 17 years 194 days. Essex Young Player of the Year 1996. Man of the Match in the U19 World Cup final in South Africa 1997-98 (107)
Best batting: 178 Northamptonshire v Essex, Northampton 2006
Best bowling: 1-19 Essex v Oxford University, Chelmsford 1999

2007 Season

	M	Inn	NO	Runs	HS	Avg	100	50	Ct	St	Balls	Runs	Wkts	Avg	BB	5I	10M
Test																	
FC	16	30	2	966	112	34.50	3	4	14	-	0	0	0		-	-	-
ODI																	
List A	10	9	0	284	107	31.55	1	2	4	-	0	0	0		-	-	
20/20 Int																	
20/20	1	0	0	0	0		-	-	-	-	0	0	0		-	-	

Career Performances

	M	Inn	NO	Runs	HS	Avg	100	50	Ct	St	Balls	Runs	Wkts	Avg	BB	5I	10M
Test																	
FC	148	253	21	7366	178	31.75	15	36	111	-	35	31	1	31.00	1-19	-	-
ODI																	
List A	132	120	6	2310	107	20.26	1	12	37	-	0	0	0		-	-	
20/20 Int																	
20/20	12	10	1	82	26 *	9.11	-	-	3	-	0	0	0		-	-	

PETTINI, M. L. Essex

Name: Mark Lewis Pettini
Role: Right-hand bat, occasional wicket-keeper, county captain
Born: 7 August 1983, Brighton
Height: 5ft 10in **Weight:** 11st 6lbs
Nickname: Swampy
County debut: 2001
County cap: 2006
1000 runs in a season: 1
1st-Class 200s: 1
Place in batting averages: 191st av. 23.23 (2006 56th av. 46.84)
Parents: Pauline and Max
Marital status: Single
Family links with cricket: 'Brother plays'
Education: Comberton Village College and Hills Road Sixth Form College, Cambridge; Cardiff University
Qualifications: 10 GCSEs, 3 A-levels, Level 1 cricket coaching award
Off-season: 'Fishing, then cricket in Perth and Adelaide – Darren Lehmann Academy'
Overseas tours: England U19 to Australia and (U19 World Cup) New Zealand 2001-02; MCC to Sierra Leone and Nigeria; Essex to Cape Town
Overseas teams played for: Rockingham-Mandurah CC, Perth 2005-07
Career highlights to date: 'Winning two Pro40 titles with Essex. Being made Essex captain [2007]'
Cricket moments to forget: 'Relegation to division two of Pro40 2007'
Cricket superstitions: 'Hundreds'
Cricketers particularly admired: Graham Gooch, Andy Flower, Ronnie Irani
Young players to look out for: Tom Westley, Adam Wheater
Other sports played: Tennis
Other sports followed: Football (Liverpool)
Favourite band: White Stripes, Foo Fighters, Editors
Relaxations: 'Fishing, surfing, travelling, music'
Extras: Captained Cambridgeshire U11-U16. Played for Development of Excellence XI (South) 2001. Represented England U19 2002. Essex 2nd XI Player of the Year 2002. Represented British Universities 2003 and 2004. Took over as captain of Essex during the 2007 season following the retirement of Ronnie Irani. Included in initial England squad of 30 for the Twenty20 World Championship 2007-08
Opinions on cricket: 'Great game but too much cricket in the season – 12 Championship games instead of 16. Twenty20 is great.'
Best batting: 208* Essex v Derbyshire, Chelmsford 2006

2007 Season

	M	Inn	NO	Runs	HS	Avg	100	50	Ct	St	Balls	Runs	Wkts	Avg	BB	5I	10M
Test																	
FC	17	27	1	604	86 *	23.23	-	6	17	-	0	0	0		-	-	-
ODI																	
List A	15	15	1	312	103 *	22.28	1	1	8	-	0	0	0		-	-	
20/20 Int																	
20/20	8	7	0	72	22	10.28	-	-	1	-	0	0	0		-	-	

Career Performances

	M	Inn	NO	Runs	HS	Avg	100	50	Ct	St	Balls	Runs	Wkts	Avg	BB	5I	10M
Test																	
FC	45	75	6	2338	208 *	33.88	3	14	41	-	0	0	0		-	-	-
ODI																	
List A	68	60	5	1335	103 *	24.27	1	10	24	-	0	0	0		-	-	
20/20 Int																	
20/20	30	27	3	543	60	22.62	-	2	8	-	0	0	0		-	-	

PHILLIPS, B. J. Somerset

Name: Ben James Phillips
Role: Right-hand bat, right-arm fast-medium bowler
Born: 30 September 1975, Lewisham, London
Height: 6ft 6in **Weight:** 15st
Nickname: Bennyphil, Bus
County debut: 1996 (Kent), 2002 (Northamptonshire)
County cap: 2005 (Northamptonshire)
Place in batting averages: (2006 195th av. 22.39)
Place in bowling averages: (2006 58th av. 31.79)
Parents: Glynis and Trevor
Wife and date of marriage: Sarah Jane, 20 January 2003
Family links with cricket: Father and brother both keen club cricketers for Hayes CC (Kent)
Education: Langley Park School for Boys, Beckenham
Qualifications: 9 GCSEs, 3 A-levels
Overseas tours: Northamptonshire to Grenada 2002

Overseas teams played for: University of Queensland, Australia 1993-94; Cape Technikon Green Point, Cape Town 1994-95, 1996-98; University of Western Australia, Perth 1998-99; Valley, Brisbane 2001-02
Cricket superstitions: 'Arrive at the ground early – hate rushing!'
Cricketers particularly admired: Glenn McGrath, Jason Gillespie
Other sports followed: Football (West Ham United), rugby (Northampton Saints)
Relaxations: 'Enjoy swimming, watching a good movie, and just generally like spending time with family and friends'
Extras: Set Langley Park School record for the fastest half-century, off 11 balls. Represented England U19 Schools 1993-94
Best batting: 100* Kent v Lancashire, Old Trafford 1997
Best bowling: 6-29 Northamptonshire v CUCCE, Fenner's 2006

2007 Season (did not make any first-class or one-day appearances)

Career Performances

	M	Inn	NO	Runs	HS	Avg	100	50	Ct	St	Balls	Runs	Wkts	Avg	BB	5I	10M
Test																	
FC	80	114	17	2009	100 *	20.71	1	11	19	-	10914	5339	176	30.33	6-29	4	-
ODI																	
List A	92	62	19	802	44 *	18.65	-	-	23	-	3774	3008	99	30.38	4-25	-	
20/20 Int																	
20/20	25	20	7	335	41 *	25.76	-	-	10	-	540	727	30	24.23	4-18	-	

PHILLIPS, T. J. — Essex

Name: Timothy (Tim) James Phillips
Role: Left-hand bat, slow left-arm bowler
Born: 13 March 1981, Cambridge
Height: 6ft 1in **Weight:** 13st
Nickname: Pips
County debut: 1999
County cap: 2006
Place in batting averages: 252nd av. 13.78 (2006 193rd av. 22.40)
Place in bowling averages: (2006 121st av. 43.64)
Parents: Carolyn and Martin (deceased)
Marital status: Single
Family links with cricket: 'Father played in Lancashire League then village cricket in Essex. Brother Nick plays for local village, Lindsell'
Education: Felsted School; Durham University
Qualifications: 10 GCSEs, 3 A-levels, BA (Hons) Sport in the Community
Overseas tours: Felsted School to Australia 1995-96; England U19 to Malaysia and (U19 World Cup) Sri Lanka 1999-2000

Cricket moments to forget: '2003 season' (*Out for the whole of the season with cartilage and ligament damage to a knee*)
Cricketers particularly admired: Phil Tufnell
Other sports played: Golf, hockey (Essex Schools U14, U15; East of England U21 trials)
Other sports followed: Rugby union
Favourite band: The Libertines, Coldplay, The White Stripes
Relaxations: 'Music, gigs, socialising, fishing'
Extras: Holmwoods School Cricketer of the Year runner-up 1997 and 1998. Broke Nick Knight's and Elliott Wilson's record for runs in a season for Felsted School, scoring 1213 in 1999. NBC Denis Compton Award 1999. Played for Durham UCCE 2001 and 2002
Best batting: 89 Essex v Worcestershire, Worcester 2005
Best bowling: 5-41 Essex v Derbyshire, Chelmsford 2006

2007 Season

	M	Inn	NO	Runs	HS	Avg	100	50	Ct	St	Balls	Runs	Wkts	Avg	BB	5I	10M
Test																	
FC	10	14	0	193	68	13.78	-	1	4	-	426	246	6	41.00	3-28	-	-
ODI																	
List A	8	6	1	67	21	13.40	-	-	2	-	42	31	0		-	-	
20/20 Int																	
20/20	7	4	0	48	31	12.00	-	-	1	-	12	21	0		-	-	

Career Performances

	M	Inn	NO	Runs	HS	Avg	100	50	Ct	St	Balls	Runs	Wkts	Avg	BB	5I	10M
Test																	
FC	44	60	7	1033	89	19.49	-	3	27	-	6069	3887	81	47.98	5-41	1	-
ODI																	
List A	31	19	8	168	24 *	15.27	-	-	10	-	904	705	31	22.74	5-34	1	
20/20 Int																	
20/20	15	7	2	58	31	11.60	-	-	4	-	159	192	7	27.42	2-11	-	

PIETERSEN, K. P. Hampshire

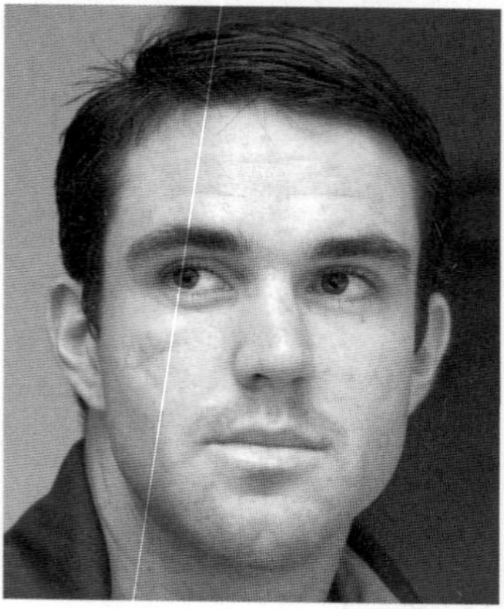

Name: Kevin Peter Pietersen
Role: Right-hand bat, right-arm off-spin bowler
Born: 27 June 1980, Pietermaritzburg, South Africa
Height: 6ft 4in **Weight:** 14st 9lbs
Nickname: KP, Kelv, Kapes
County debut: 2001 (Nottinghamshire), 2005 (Hampshire)
County cap: 2002 (Nottinghamshire), 2005 (Hampshire)
Test debut: 2005
ODI debut: 2004-05
Twenty20 Int debut: 2005
1000 runs in a season: 3
1st-Class 200s: 4
Place in batting averages: 9th av. 62.38 (2006 23rd av. 58.91)
Parents: Jannie and Penny
Wife and date of marriage: Jessica, 29 December 2007
Education: Maritzburg College; University of South Africa
Qualifications: 3 A-levels
Overseas tours: Natal to Zimbabwe 1999-2000, to Australia 2000-01; Nottinghamshire to South Africa 2001, 2002; England A to Malaysia and India 2003-04; England to Zimbabwe (one-day series) 2004-05, to South Africa 2004-05 (one-day series), to Pakistan 2005-06, to India 2005-06, to India (ICC Champions Trophy) 2006-07, to Australia 2006-07, to West Indies (World Cup) 2006-07, to South Africa (World 20/20) 2007-08, to Sri Lanka 2007-08, to New Zealand 2007-08; ICC World XI to Australia (Super Series) 2005-06
Overseas teams played for: Berea Rovers, Durban 1997 – 2001-02; KwaZulu-Natal 1997-98 – 2000-01; Sydney University 2002-03
Career highlights to date: 'Scoring the three centuries in South Africa for England 2005'
Cricket moments to forget: 'Breaking my leg against Glamorgan in August 2002 in an NUL game'
Cricket superstitions: 'Left pad first'
Cricketers particularly admired: Shaun Pollock, Errol Stewart
Other sports played: Golf, swimming ('represented my state in 1992-93'), running
Other sports followed: Formula One (Ferrari), rugby (Natal Sharks)
Player website: www.kevinpietersen.com
Extras: Played for South Africa Schools B 1997. Scored 61* and had figures of 4-141 from 56 overs for KwaZulu-Natal v England XI 1999-2000. Scored 1275 first-

class runs in first season of county cricket 2001. Player of the [ODI] Series v South Africa 2004-05 (454 runs at 151.33, including the fastest hundred for England in ODIs, from 69 balls). Scored maiden Test century (158, including an Ashes record seven sixes) in the fifth Test v Australia at The Oval 2005, winning Man of the Match award. Scored maiden Test double century (226) in the second Test v West Indies at Headingley 2007, winning Man of the Match award. His other international awards include Man of the Match v Australia at Bristol in the NatWest Series 2005 (65-ball 91*), England's Man of the [Test] Series v Sri Lanka 2006, and Man of the Match in the first Test v India at Lord's 2007 (134). Scored 158 in the second Test v Australia at Adelaide 2006-07, in the process sharing with Paul Collingwood (206) in a record fourth-wicket partnership for England in Tests v Australia (310). ECB National Academy 2003-04, 2004-05. ICC Emerging Player of the Year and ICC ODI Player of the Year awards 2005. Appointed MBE in 2006 New Year Honours as part of 2005 Ashes-winning England team. One of *Wisden*'s Five Cricketers of the Year 2006. Autobiography *Crossing the Boundary: The Early Years in My Cricketing Life* published 2006. England 12-month central contract 2007-08. Is married to Liberty X singer Jessica Taylor

Best batting: 254* Nottinghamshire v Middlesex, Trent Bridge 2002

Best bowling: 4-31 Nottinghamshire v DUCCE, Trent Bridge 2003

2007 Season

	M	Inn	NO	Runs	HS	Avg	100	50	Ct	St	Balls	Runs	Wkts	Avg	BB	5I	10M
Test	7	13	0	811	226	62.38	4	1	5	-	78	61	1	61.00	1-41	-	-
FC	7	13	0	811	226	62.38	4	1	5	-	78	61	1	61.00	1-41	-	-
ODI	10	10	2	251	71 *	31.37	-	2	2	-	11	13	1	13.00	1-6	-	
List A	14	14	3	386	71 *	35.09	-	3	2	-	29	35	1	35.00	1-6	-	
20/20 Int	2	2	0	35	19	17.50	-	-	-	-	0	0	0		-	-	
20/20	2	2	0	35	19	17.50	-	-	-	-	0	0	0		-	-	

Career Performances

	M	Inn	NO	Runs	HS	Avg	100	50	Ct	St	Balls	Runs	Wkts	Avg	BB	5I	10M
Test	30	57	2	2898	226	52.69	10	10	19	-	336	262	2	131.00	1-11	-	-
FC	111	185	14	8917	254 *	52.14	31	35	99	-	5050	2904	58	50.06	4-31	-	-
ODI	61	55	11	2277	116	51.75	5	16	24	-	101	106	2	53.00	1-4	-	
List A	167	152	28	5627	147	45.37	10	36	66	-	2031	1791	36	49.75	3-14	-	
20/20 Int	11	11	0	275	79	25.00	-	1	5	-	0	0	0		-	-	
20/20	21	21	0	531	79	25.28	-	3	5	-	108	136	6	22.66	2-9	-	

PIPE, D. J. Derbyshire

Name: David James Pipe
Role: Right-hand bat, wicket-keeper
Born: 16 December 1977, Bradford
Height: 5ft 11in **Weight:** 13st
Nickname: Pipey
County debut: 1998 (Worcestershire), 2006 (Derbyshire)
County cap: 2002 (Worcestershire colours), 2007 (Derbyshire)
50 dismissals in a season: 1
Place in batting averages: 98th av. 36.06 (2006 127th av. 32.18)
Parents: David and Dorothy
Marital status: Single
Family links with cricket: 'My dad and uncle played in the local league'
Education: Queensbury Upper School; BICC
Qualifications: 8 GCSEs, BTEC National in Business and Finance, HND Leisure Management, senior coaching award, Diploma in Personal Training, Diploma in Sports Therapy
Overseas teams played for: Leeming Spartans CC/South Metropolitan Cricket Association, Perth 1998-99; Manly CC, Australia 1999-2004
Career highlights to date: 'Getting first hundred'
Cricket moments to forget: 'Any game we lose'
Cricket superstitions: 'None'
Cricketers particularly admired: Adam Gilchrist, Ian Healy
Young players to look out for: Brett D'Oliveira (Worcestershire Academy), Gary Ballance, Dan Redfern
Other sports followed: Rugby league (Bradford Bulls, Manly Sea Eagles), boxing ('all British fighters'), AFL (West Coast Eagles)
Relaxations: Training
Extras: MCC School of Merit Wilf Slack Memorial Trophy winner 1995. Took eight catches v Hertfordshire at Hertford in the C&G 2001 to set a new NatWest/C&G record for most dismissals in a match by a wicket-keeper. Dick Lygon Award 2002 (Worcestershire Club Man of the Year). Derbyshire Club Man of the Year 2006
Best batting: 133* Derbyshire v Essex, Chelmsford 2007

2007 Season

	M	Inn	NO	Runs	HS	Avg	100	50	Ct	St	Balls	Runs	Wkts	Avg	BB	5I	10M
Test																	
FC	14	21	5	577	133 *	36.06	2	1	42	4	0	0	0		-	-	-
ODI																	
List A	15	14	2	204	83	17.00	-	1	11	3	0	0	0		-	-	
20/20 Int																	
20/20	4	4	0	23	12	5.75	-	-	2	4	0	0	0		-	-	

Career Performances

	M	Inn	NO	Runs	HS	Avg	100	50	Ct	St	Balls	Runs	Wkts	Avg	BB	5I	10M
Test																	
FC	59	88	14	1873	133 *	25.31	3	6	166	18	0	0	0		-	-	-
ODI																	
List A	58	47	10	683	83	18.45	-	3	47	16	0	0	0		-	-	
20/20 Int																	
20/20	25	20	4	154	29 *	9.62	-	-	12	9	0	0	0		-	-	

PLUNKETT, L. E. — Durham

Name: Liam Edward Plunkett
Role: Right-hand bat, right-arm fast bowler
Born: 6 April 1985, Middlesbrough
Height: 6ft 4in **Weight:** 13st
Nickname: Pudsey
County debut: 2003
Test debut: 2005-06
ODI debut: 2005-06
Twenty20 Int debut: 2006
50 wickets in a season: 2
Place in batting averages: 215th av. 20.38 (2006 228th av. 17.16)
Place in bowling averages: 68th av. 30.60 (2006 26th av. 27.15)
Parents: Alan and Marie
Family links with cricket: 'Father played local cricket'
Education: Nunthorpe Comprehensive
Qualifications: 9 GCSEs, volleyball coaching badge
Overseas tours: England U19 to Australia 2002-03, to Bangladesh (U19 World Cup) 2003-04; England to Pakistan 2005-06, to India 2005-06, to Australia 2006-07, to West Indies (World Cup) 2006-07; England Lions to India 2007-08

Overseas teams played for: Adelaide University 2005; Dolphins, South Africa 2007-08
Career highlights to date: 'England debut'
Cricket moments to forget: 'Injury (oblique)' (*Out from July to September 2006 with a damaged oblique muscle*)
Cricket superstitions: 'None'
Cricketers particularly admired: Glenn McGrath
Young players to look out for: Ben Harmison
Other sports played: Golf, swimming
Other sports followed: Football (Middlesbrough, Arsenal)
Favourite band: 'R&B'
Extras: Became only the second bowler to record a five-wicket innings return on Championship debut for Durham, 5-53 v Yorkshire at Headingley 2003. Represented England U19 2003. NBC Denis Compton Award for the most promising young Durham player 2003. ECB National Academy 2004-05 (part-time), 2005-06. Friends Provident Man of the Match award in the semi-final v Essex at Riverside 2007 (4-15/30*)
Opinions on cricket: 'Twenty20 game loaded towards batsmen.'
Best batting: 74* Durham v Somerset, Stockton 2005
Best bowling: 6-74 Durham v Hampshire, Riverside 2004

2007 Season

	M	Inn	NO	Runs	HS	Avg	100	50	Ct	St	Balls	Runs	Wkts	Avg	BB	5I	10M
Test	3	4	1	57	44 *	19.00	-	-	1	-	534	315	7	45.00	3-35	-	-
FC	15	23	5	367	59 *	20.38	-	2	10	-	2663	1530	50	30.60	5-105	1	-
ODI	2	2	0	6	4	3.00	-	-	1	-	120	97	5	19.40	3-59	-	
List A	14	7	2	126	33	25.20	-	-	2	-	655	529	25	21.16	4-15	-	
20/20 Int																	
20/20	1	0	0	0	0		-	-	-	-	24	35	2	17.50	2-35	-	

Career Performances

	M	Inn	NO	Runs	HS	Avg	100	50	Ct	St	Balls	Runs	Wkts	Avg	BB	5I	10M
Test	9	13	2	126	44 *	11.45	-	-	3	-	1538	916	23	39.82	3-17	-	-
FC	55	83	19	1254	74 *	19.59	-	4	23	-	8896	5447	173	31.48	6-74	5	-
ODI	27	24	10	295	56	21.07	-	1	7	-	1291	1260	37	34.05	3-24	-	
List A	68	45	19	569	56	21.88	-	1	13	-	3147	2762	93	29.69	4-15	-	
20/20 Int	1	0	0	0	0		-	-	-	-	24	37	1	37.00	1-37	-	
20/20	11	6	4	29	8	14.50	-	-	4	-	208	277	8	34.62	2-18	-	

POONIA, N. S. Warwickshire

Name: Navdeep (<u>Navi</u>) Singh Poonia
Role: Right-hand bat, right-arm medium bowler
Born: 11 May 1986, Glasgow
Height: 6ft 3in **Weight:** 14st
Nickname: Nav, Sat Nav
County debut: 2006
ODI debut: 2006
Twenty20 Int debut: 2007-08
Parents: Jaipal and Bindy Poonia
Marital status: Single
Family links with cricket: 'Dad played club cricket at Walsall CC'
Education: Moseley Park School; Wolverhampton University
Qualifications: 10 GCSEs, 2 A-levels, Levels 1 and 2 coaching
Overseas tours: Warwickshire Academy to South Africa 2005; Scotland to Bangladesh (one-day series) 2006-07, to Kenya (including ICC World Cricket League) 2006-07, to West Indies (World Cup) 2006-07, to Ireland (Quadrangular Series) 2007, to South Africa (World 20/20) 2007-08
Cricket superstitions: 'None'
Cricketers particularly admired: Sachin Tendulkar, Brian Lara, Allan Donald
Other sports played: Football, badminton
Other sports followed: Football (Man Utd and Glasgow Rangers)
Favourite band: 112, Jagged Edge
Relaxations: 'Playing snooker with mates and cousins'
Extras: Played for Warwickshire Board XI in the 2003 C&G. Cyril Goodway (Warwickshire Old County Cricketers' Association) Trophy U17. Top-scored with 59 on county one-day debut v Nottinghamshire at Edgbaston in the C&G 2006. Has played one-day (including ODI and Twenty20 Int) cricket for Scotland
Best batting: 35 Warwickshire v West Indies A, Edgbaston 2006

2007 Season (did not make any first-class or one-day appearances for his county)

Career Performances

	M	Inn	NO	Runs	HS	Avg	100	50	Ct	St	Balls	Runs	Wkts	Avg	BB	5I	10M
Test																	
FC	1	1	0	35	35	35.00	-	-	-	-	0	0	0		-	-	-
ODI	14	14	0	184	67	13.14	-	1	4	-	0	0	0		-	-	
List A	24	24	0	435	67	18.12	-	2	5	-	0	0	0		-	-	
20/20 Int	2	1	0	4	4	4.00	-	-	-	-	0	0	0		-	-	
20/20	5	4	0	36	19	9.00	-	-	-	-	0	0	0		-	-	

POPE, J. I. Leicestershire

Name: Joel Ian Pope
Role: Right-hand bat, wicket-keeper
Born: 23 October 1988, Ashford, Middlesex
Height: 5ft 7in **Weight:** 10st 2lbs
Nickname: Popey
County debut: No first-team appearance
Parents: Tania and Ian
Marital status: Single
Family links with cricket: 'Uncle (Ben Scott) is wicket-keeper for Middlesex. Dad and Grandad played at club level for Wycombe House'
Education: Whitton Sports College
Qualifications: 9 GCSEs, Level 1 coach
Off-season: 'Club cricket in Australia'
Overseas tours: MCC Young Cricketers to St Kitts and Nevis 2007
Overseas teams played for: Melville CC, Perth 2007-08
Career highlights to date: 'Fielding for England as thirteenth man at Lord's against the West Indies'
Cricket superstitions: 'Put left pad on first'
Cricketers particularly admired: Jack Russell, Alec Stewart, Mike Hussey
Young players to look out for: Bradley Erasmus, Stuart Poynter
Other sports played: Golf, football
Other sports followed: Football (Manchester United)
Favourite band: Oasis
Relaxations: 'Art, music'

Extras: MCC Young Cricketers 2007. Played for Middlesex U10-19, Middlesex Academy and 2nd XI. Plays for Sunbury CC
Opinions on cricket: 'Quick and entertaining – good for the crowds.'

PORTERFIELD, W. T. S. Gloucestershire

Name: William Thomas Stuart Porterfield
Role: Left-hand bat
Born: 6 September 1984, Londonderry, Northern Ireland
Height: 5ft 11in **Weight:** 12st
Nickname: Purdy
County debut: No first-team appearance
ODI debut: 2006
Parents: William and Alison
Marital status: Single
Family links with cricket: Father played for Killyclooney CC
Education: Strabane Grammar School; Leeds Metropolitan University
Qualifications: BA (Hons) Physical Education (2.1)
Off-season: 'Hopefully tour with Ireland to Bangladesh'
Overseas tours: Ireland U19 to Bangladesh (U19 World Cup) 2003-04; Ireland to Scotland (European Championship) 2006, to Kenya (ICC World Cricket League) 2006-07, to West Indies (World Cup) 2006-07, plus various Ireland age-group and A tours
Overseas teams played for: Rush CC, Dublin
Career highlights to date: '2006-07 World Cup in West Indies with Ireland'
Cricket moments to forget: 'Not qualifying for the Twenty20 World Championship in South Africa'
Cricketers particularly admired: Brian Lara, Sachin Tendulkar
Young players to look out for: Eoin Morgan, Paul Stirling
Other sports played: 'Rugby at school; bit of football'
Other sports followed: Football (Manchester United)
Favourite band: Snow Patrol
Relaxations: 'Socialising'
Extras: Played for Bradford/Leeds UCCE in 2004 and 2006. Played for MCC YC 2004-06. Attended ICC Winter Training Camp in South Africa 2006-07. Has represented Ireland in first-class and one-day cricket, including ODIs and C&G/Friends Provident. Man of the Match v Bermuda in Nairobi in the ICC World

Cricket League 2006-07 (112*) and v Bangladesh in Bridgetown in the World Cup 2006-07 (85). Played for MCC in 2007
Best batting: 166 Ireland v Bermuda, Dublin 2007

2007 Season (did not make any first-class or one-day appearances for his county)

Career Performances

	M	Inn	NO	Runs	HS	Avg	100	50	Ct	St	Balls	Runs	Wkts	Avg	BB	5I	10M
Test																	
FC	7	9	0	371	166	41.22	1	1	4	-	0	0	0		-	-	-
ODI	20	20	2	614	112 *	34.11	2	2	6	-	0	0	0		-	-	
List A	32	32	2	965	112 *	32.16	2	5	8	-	0	0	0		-	-	
20/20 Int																	
20/20																	

POTHAS, N. Hampshire

Name: Nicolas (Nic) Pothas
Role: Right-hand bat, wicket-keeper
Born: 18 November 1973, Johannesburg, South Africa
Height: 6ft 1in **Weight:** 13st 7lbs
Nickname: Skeg
County debut: 2002
County cap: 2003
ODI debut: 2000
50 dismissals in a season: 3
Place in batting averages: 42nd av. 46.87 (2006 10th av. 64.86)
Parents: Emmanuel and Penelope
Marital status: Single
Family links with cricket: 'Greek by nationality, therefore clearly none'
Education: King Edward VII High School; Rand Afrikaans University
Overseas tours: South Africa A to England 1996, to Sri Lanka 1998-99, to West Indies 2000-01; Gauteng to Australia 1997; South Africa to Singapore (Singapore Challenge) 2000-01
Overseas teams played for: Transvaal/Gauteng 1993-94 – 2001-02
Career highlights to date: 'First tour for South Africa A. Playing for South Africa'
Cricket superstitions: 'Too many to mention'
Cricketers particularly admired: Ray Jennings, Jimmy Cook, Robin Smith

Other sports played: Hockey (South Africa U21, Transvaal)
Other sports followed: Football (Manchester United)
Favourite band: Counting Crows, Gin Blossoms, Just Jinjer
Relaxations: 'Shopping; designing clothes; sleeping; gym'
Extras: Scored maiden first-class century (147) for South African Students v England tourists at Pietermaritzburg 1995-96. Benson and Hedges Young Player of the Year 1996. Transvaal Player of the Year 1996, 1998. C&G Man of the Match award v Glamorgan at Cardiff 2005 (114*). Scored 139 v Gloucestershire at Cheltenham 2005, in the process sharing with Andy Bichel (138) in a new Hampshire record partnership for the eighth wicket (257). Took seven catches in an innings v Lancashire at Old Trafford 2006, becoming the first Hampshire wicket-keeper to achieve the feat in a first-class match. Made 51 dismissals and scored 973 runs in first-class cricket 2005; 58 dismissals and 973 runs in first-class cricket 2006. Is not considered an overseas player
Best batting: 165 Gauteng v KwaZulu-Natal, Johannesburg 1998-99
Best bowling: 1-16 Hampshire v Middlesex, Lord's 2006

2007 Season

	M	Inn	NO	Runs	HS	Avg	100	50	Ct	St	Balls	Runs	Wkts	Avg	BB	5I	10M
Test																	
FC	15	23	7	750	126 *	46.87	1	5	36	6	0	0	0		-	-	-
ODI																	
List A	17	14	4	373	114	37.30	1	1	18	5	0	0	0		-	-	
20/20 Int																	
20/20	7	5	3	34	23 *	17.00	-	-	3	-	0	0	0		-	-	

Career Performances

	M	Inn	NO	Runs	HS	Avg	100	50	Ct	St	Balls	Runs	Wkts	Avg	BB	5I	10M
Test																	
FC	176	272	50	8825	165	39.75	20	45	490	44	120	63	1	63.00	1-16	-	-
ODI	3	1	0	24	24	24.00	-	-	4	1	0	0	0		-	-	
List A	208	176	61	4114	114 *	35.77	3	22	194	47	0	0	0		-	-	
20/20 Int																	
20/20	33	24	10	316	59	22.57	-	2	16	4	0	0	0		-	-	

71. Which Kent leg-spinner had match figures of 10-175 as England beat South Africa by ten wickets at Lord's in 1947?

POWELL, D. B. L. Hampshire

Name: Daren Brent Lyle Powell
Role: Right-hand bat, right-arm fast-medium bowler
Born: 15 April 1978, St Elizabeth, Jamaica
County debut: 2004 (Derbyshire), 2007 (Hampshire)
Test debut: 2002
ODI debut: 2002-03
Twenty20 Int debut: 2007
Place in batting averages: 269th av. 11.81
Place in bowling averages: 82nd av. 33.36
Overseas tours: West Indies A to Ireland and England 2002, to Canada 2002, to England 2006; West Indies to India 2002-03, to Bangladesh 2002-03, to Sri Lanka 2005, to Australia 2005-06, to New Zealand 2005-06, to Pakistan 2006-07, to England 2007, to South Africa (World 20/20) 2007-08, to South Africa 2007-08, plus other one-day series and tournaments in India, Ireland and Zimbabwe

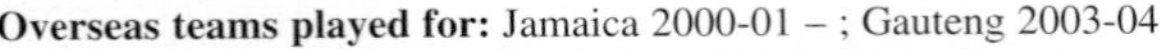

Overseas teams played for: Jamaica 2000-01 – ; Gauteng 2003-04
Extras: Represented West Indies in the 2006-07 World Cup. His match awards include Man of the Match v Bangladesh A in Jamaica in the Busta Cup 2001-02 (3-39/5-37), v West Indies B in Jamaica in the Carib Beer Cup 2002-03 (5-34/2-36) and v England in the third ODI at Trent Bridge 2007 (4-40). Was a temporary overseas player with Derbyshire during the 2004 season; was an overseas player with Hampshire during the 2007 season. Returned innings figures of 10-5-8-4 v Worcestershire at The Rose Bowl 2007
Best batting: 62 West Indies A v Durham, Riverside 2006
Best bowling: 6-49 Derbyshire v DUCCE, Derby 2004

2007 Season

	M	Inn	NO	Runs	HS	Avg	100	50	Ct	St	Balls	Runs	Wkts	Avg	BB	5I	10M
Test	3	5	1	49	36 *	12.25	-	-	-	-	708	437	9	48.55	3-89	-	-
FC	8	12	1	130	36 *	11.81	-	-	1	-	1479	834	25	33.36	4-8	-	-
ODI	3	1	0	1	1	1.00	-	-	1	-	180	131	6	21.83	4-40	-	
List A	10	3	0	4	2	1.33	-	-	3	-	468	445	19	23.42	4-30	-	
20/20 Int	2	0	0	0	0		-	-	1	-	42	63	1	63.00	1-24	-	
20/20	3	1	1	1	1 *		-	-	1	-	61	82	1	82.00	1-24	-	

Career Performances	M	Inn	NO	Runs	HS	Avg	100	50	Ct	St	Balls	Runs	Wkts	Avg	BB	5I	10M
Test	22	34	1	216	36 *	6.54	-	-	1	-	4341	2443	56	43.62	5-25	1	-
FC	75	106	15	1133	62	12.45	-	3	22	-	12389	6677	219	30.48	6-49	6	-
ODI	30	14	3	73	48 *	6.63	-	-	5	-	1578	1206	40	30.15	4-27	-	
List A	66	30	9	171	48 *	8.14	-	-	14	-	3258	2586	101	25.60	5-23	1	
20/20 Int	4	1	1	1	1 *		-	-	2	-	84	125	1	125.00	1-24	-	
20/20	5	2	2	2	1 *		-	-	2	-	103	144	1	144.00	1-24	-	

POWELL, M. J. — Warwickshire

Name: Michael James Powell
Role: Right-hand opening/middle-order bat, right-arm medium bowler
Born: 5 April 1975, Bolton
Height: 5ft 10in **Weight:** 12st 2lbs
Nickname: Arthur, Powelly
County debut: 1996
County cap: 1999
Benefit: 2008
1000 runs in a season: 1
1st-Class 200s: 1
Place in batting averages: 163rd av. 27.50 (2006 174th av. 25.60)
Parents: Terry and Pat
Marital status: Single
Family links with cricket: 'Father loves the game. Brother John played for Warwickshire youth teams'
Education: Lawrence Sheriff Grammar School, Rugby
Qualifications: 6 GCSEs, 2 A-levels, Levels I-III ECB coaching awards
Career outside cricket: Coaching
Overseas tours: England U18 to South Africa 1992-93 (c), to Denmark 1993 (c); England U19 to Sri Lanka 1993-94; England A to West Indies 2000-01
Overseas teams played for: Avendale CC, Cape Town 1994-95, 1996-97, 2000-01; Griqualand West, South Africa 2001-02
Career highlights to date: 'B&H Cup winners 2002. Frizzell County Champions 2004'
Cricket superstitions: 'None'
Cricketers particularly admired: Dermot Reeve, Shaun Pollock, Allan Donald
Young players to look out for: Moeen Ali
Other sports played: Golf, rugby (Warwickshire U16-U18)

Other sports followed: Football
Extras: Captained Warwickshire U14-U19 and England U17 and U18. Became first uncapped Warwickshire player for 49 years to carry his bat, for 70* out of 130 v Nottinghamshire at Edgbaston 1998. Captain of Warwickshire 2001-03
Best batting: 236 Warwickshire v OUCCE, The Parks 2001
Best bowling: 2-16 Warwickshire v Oxford University, The Parks 1998

2007 Season

	M	Inn	NO	Runs	HS	Avg	100	50	Ct	St	Balls	Runs	Wkts	Avg	BB	5I	10M
Test																	
FC	4	6	0	165	82	27.50	-	1	2	-	0	0	0		-	-	-
ODI																	
List A	3	1	0	6	6	6.00	-	-	-	-	0	0	0		-	-	
20/20 Int																	
20/20	4	3	1	6	3	3.00	-	-	2	-	0	0	0		-	-	

Career Performances

	M	Inn	NO	Runs	HS	Avg	100	50	Ct	St	Balls	Runs	Wkts	Avg	BB	5I	10M
Test																	
FC	138	230	11	7022	236	32.06	12	38	99	-	1314	744	11	67.63	2-16	-	-
ODI																	
List A	112	93	15	1967	101 *	25.21	1	5	53	-	824	727	25	29.08	5-40	1	
20/20 Int																	
20/20	15	13	4	200	44 *	22.22	-	-	7	-	0	0	0		-	-	

POWELL, M. J. Glamorgan

Name: Michael John Powell
Role: Right-hand bat
Born: 3 February 1977, Abergavenny
Height: 6ft 1in **Weight:** 14st 8lbs
Nickname: Powelly
County debut: 1997
County cap: 2000
1000 runs in a season: 5
1st-Class 200s: 3
Place in batting averages: 30th av. 50.87 (2006 38th av. 51.03)
Parents: Linda and John
Marital status: Single
Family links with cricket: 'Dad John and Uncle Mike both played for Abergavenny'
Education: Crickhowell Secondary School; Pontypool College
Qualifications: 5 GCSEs, BTEC National Diploma in Sports Science, Level 1 coaching award

Overseas tours: Glamorgan to Cape Town 1999, 2002; England A to Sri Lanka 2004-05
Overseas teams played for: Wests, Brisbane 1996-97; Cornwall CC, Auckland 1998-99, 2000-01
Cricket moments to forget: 'You wouldn't want to forget any of it'
Cricket superstitions: 'None'
Other sports played: Rugby (Crickhowell RFC)
Other sports followed: Rugby (Cardiff)
Relaxations: Eating and sleeping
Extras: Scored 200* on first-class debut v Oxford University at The Parks 1997. Second XI Championship Player of the Year 1997 (1210 runs at 75.63). NBC Denis Compton Award for the most promising young Glamorgan player 2000. Acted as 12th man in the third Test v Sri Lanka at Old Trafford 2002, taking the catch that ended Sri Lanka's second innings. Included in England one-day squad for NatWest Series 2004. ECB National Academy 2004-05
Best batting: 299 Glamorgan v Gloucestershire, Cheltenham 2006
Best bowling: 2-39 Glamorgan v Oxford University, The Parks 1999

2007 Season

	M	Inn	NO	Runs	HS	Avg	100	50	Ct	St	Balls	Runs	Wkts	Avg	BB	5I	10M
Test																	
FC	6	10	2	407	114	50.87	1	4	4	-	0	0	0		-	-	-
ODI																	
List A	5	4	0	118	69	29.50	-	1	3	-	0	0	0		-	-	
20/20 Int																	
20/20																	

Career Performances

	M	Inn	NO	Runs	HS	Avg	100	50	Ct	St	Balls	Runs	Wkts	Avg	BB	5I	10M
Test																	
FC	160	272	25	9852	299	39.88	22	48	98	-	164	132	2	66.00	2-39	-	-
ODI																	
List A	180	169	19	4212	91 *	28.08	-	24	73	-	24	26	1	26.00	1-26	-	
20/20 Int																	
20/20	25	24	2	534	68 *	24.27	-	5	9	-	0	0	0		-	-	

POYNTON, T. J. Derbyshire

Name: Thomas (Tom) James Poynton
Role: Right-hand bat, wicket-keeper
Born: 25 November 1989, Burton-on-Trent, Staffordshire
Height: 5ft 10in **Weight:** 10st 10lbs
Nickname: TP, Poynts
County debut: 2007
Parents: Keith and Sheena
Marital status: 'Long-term relationship – Megan Jacobs'
Family links with cricket: 'Brother plays at same club – Lullington Park CC. Both parents involved in club cricket and keen county supporters'
Education: John Taylor High School; Repton School (Sixth Form)
Qualifications: 11 GCSEs, 'studying 3 A-levels', Level 1 ECB coach
Career outside cricket: Student
Off-season: 'Academy winter training programme; tour to West Indies; ECB National Skill Sets; studying at school'
Overseas tours: Derbyshire Academy to South Africa 2006; Repton School to Grenada 2007
Career highlights to date: 'Making first-class debut for Derbyshire v Middlesex in 2007'
Cricket moments to forget: 'Pair on debut and Ant Botha dislocating my jaw during first first-class innings'
Cricket superstitions: 'None'
Cricketers particularly admired: Ian Healy, Adam Gilchrist, Jack Russell
Young players to look out for: Dan Redfern, Adam Poynton, James Taylor
Other sports played: Football (Repton 1st XI)
Other sports followed: Football (Man Utd)
Favourite band: Craig David, Usher ('Like all music')
Relaxations: 'Music, PlayStation/PC, spending time with my girlfriend'
Extras: Played for Derbyshire U10-U17 and for Midlands U14, U15, U17. Derbyshire Academy since 2004. Played in Bunbury Festival 2005. Derbyshire County Board Young Player of the Year 2006. Represented England U17 2006, 2007. Attended ECB National Skill Sets (wicket-keeping) 2006, 2007. Youngest wicket-keeper to play first-class cricket for Derbyshire

Opinions on cricket: 'Grateful that a number of first-class counties are giving young players an opportunity to play at the highest level possible, reflecting the success of the county academy set-ups.'
Best batting: 2 Derbyshire v Glamorgan, Derby 2007

2007 Season

	M	Inn	NO	Runs	HS	Avg	100	50	Ct	St	Balls	Runs	Wkts	Avg	BB	5I	10M
Test																	
FC	2	3	0	2	2	.66	-	-	3	-	0	0	0		-	-	-
ODI																	
List A	1	0	0	0	0		-	-	2	-	0	0	0		-	-	
20/20 Int																	
20/20	2	1	0	3	3	3.00	-	-	-	2	0	0	0		-	-	

Career Performances

	M	Inn	NO	Runs	HS	Avg	100	50	Ct	St	Balls	Runs	Wkts	Avg	BB	5I	10M
Test																	
FC	2	3	0	2	2	.66	-	-	3	-	0	0	0		-	-	-
ODI																	
List A	1	0	0	0	0		-	-	2	-	0	0	0		-	-	
20/20 Int																	
20/20	2	1	0	3	3	3.00	-	-	-	2	0	0	0		-	-	

72. Which bowler holds the record for the most wickets for South Africa in a five-Test series v England in England (33)?

PRICE, R. W. Worcestershire

Name: Raymond (Ray) William Price
Role: Right-hand bat, slow left-arm bowler
Born: 12 June 1976, Harare, Zimbabwe
Height: 6ft 2in **Weight:** 13st 4lbs
Nickname: Razor
County debut: 2004
County colours: 2004
Test debut: 1999-2000
ODI debut: 2002-03
Place in batting averages: (2006 242nd av. 15.14)
Place in bowling averages: (2006 143rd av. 54.20)
Parents: Tim and Pam
Wife and date of marriage: Julie, 13 July 2003
Children: Ashleigh Rayne
Family links with cricket: Father captained Zimbabwe Schools team
Education: Watershed College, Zimbabwe; Delta Engineering Training Centre
Qualifications: 7 O-levels, 2 A-levels, refrigeration and air conditioning technician
Overseas tours: Zimbabwe A to Sri Lanka 1999-2000, to Kenya 2001-02; Zimbabwe to India 2001-02, to Sri Lanka (ICC Champions Trophy) 2002-03, to Sharjah (Cherry Blossom Sharjah Cup) 2002-03, to England 2003, to Australia 2003-04, to South Africa (SuperSport Challenge) 2007-08, to Pakistan 2007-08
Overseas teams played for: Midlands, Zimbabwe 1999-2000 – 2003-04; Old Hararians
Career highlights to date: 'Six wickets v Australia at Sydney 2003-04. Tendulkar twice in same Test' (*In the second Test v India at Delhi 2001-02*)
Cricket moments to forget: 'Missed stumping off first ball in Test cricket'
Cricket superstitions: 'None'
Cricketers particularly admired: Steve Waugh, Heath Streak, Andy Flower, Sachin Tendulkar, Shane Warne
Young players to look out for: Steve Davies
Other sports played: Tennis, squash, golf
Favourite band: Dire Straits
Relaxations: Fishing, walking
Extras: Took 33 wickets in six Tests 2003-04, including 6-121 in Australia's first innings of the second Test at Sydney and 19 wickets (av. 20.84) in two-Test home series v West Indies. Zimbabwe Cricketer of the Year. Worcestershire One-Day Player of the Year 2005. Is nephew of golfer Nick Price. Left Worcestershire at the end of the 2007 season

Opinions on cricket: 'More Twenty20!'
Best batting: 117* Midlands v Manicaland, Mutare 2003-04
Best bowling: 8-35 Midlands v CFX Academy, Kwekwe 2001-02

2007 Season

	M	Inn	NO	Runs	HS	Avg	100	50	Ct	St	Balls	Runs	Wkts	Avg	BB	5I	10M
Test																	
FC	2	4	1	24	15 *	8.00	-	-	-	-	353	256	4	64.00	2-89	-	-
ODI																	
List A	17	6	3	81	49	27.00	-	-	2	-	686	488	15	32.53	3-27	-	
20/20 Int																	
20/20	7	1	1	1	1 *		-	-	1	-	102	151	2	75.50	1-19	-	

Career Performances

	M	Inn	NO	Runs	HS	Avg	100	50	Ct	St	Balls	Runs	Wkts	Avg	BB	5I	10M
Test	18	30	7	224	36	9.73	-	-	3	-	5135	2475	69	35.86	6-73	5	1
FC	81	128	24	1632	117 *	15.69	1	7	28	-	19892	9239	274	33.71	8-35	15	3
ODI	26	12	5	90	20 *	12.85	-	-	1	-	1328	917	15	61.13	2-16	-	
List A	109	54	16	407	49	10.71	-	-	21	-	5114	3473	104	33.39	4-21	-	
20/20 Int																	
20/20	15	2	1	11	10	11.00	-	-	5	-	264	364	9	40.44	2-13	-	

PRIOR, M. J. — Sussex

Name: Matthew (Matt) James Prior
Role: Right-hand bat, wicket-keeper
Born: 26 February 1982, Johannesburg, South Africa
Height: 5ft 11in **Weight:** 13st
Nickname: MP, Cheese
County debut: 2001
County cap: 2003
Test debut: 2007
ODI debut: 2004-05
Twenty20 Int debut: 2007
1000 runs in a season: 2
1st-Class 200s: 1
Place in batting averages: 119th av. 32.64 (2006 57th av. 46.70)
Parents: Michael and Teresa
Marital status: Engaged
Education: Brighton College, East Sussex
Qualifications: 9 GCSEs, 3 A-levels, Level 1 coaching certificate

Overseas tours: Brighton College to India 1997-98; Sussex Academy to Cape Town 1999; Sussex to Grenada 2001, 2002; England A to Malaysia and India 2003-04, to Sri Lanka 2004-05, to Bangladesh 2006-07; England to Zimbabwe (one-day series) 2004-05, to Pakistan 2005-06, to India 2005-06, to South Africa (World 20/20) 2007-08, to Sri Lanka 2007-08
Cricket moments to forget: 'Falling on to stumps at The Rose Bowl on Sky TV!'
Cricket superstitions: 'Too many to name all of them'
Cricketers particularly admired: Steve Waugh, Alec Stewart, Mushtaq Ahmed, Murray Goodwin
Other sports played: Golf
Other sports followed: Football (Arsenal), golf, rugby
Favourite band: Red Hot Chili Peppers
Relaxations: 'Gym, listening to music'
Extras: Has played for Sussex since U12. Represented England U14-U19, captaining England U17. NBC Denis Compton Award for the most promising young Sussex player 2001, 2002, 2003. Umer Rashid Award for Most Improved [Sussex] Player 2003. ECB National Academy 2003-04, 2004-05, 2006-07. Became first England wicket-keeper to score a century (126*) on Test debut in the first Test v West Indies at Lord's 2007
Best batting: 201* Sussex v LUCCE, Hove 2004

2007 Season

	M	Inn	NO	Runs	HS	Avg	100	50	Ct	St	Balls	Runs	Wkts	Avg	BB	5I	10M
Test	7	12	2	397	126 *	39.70	1	2	20	-	0	0	0		-	-	-
FC	11	19	2	555	126 *	32.64	1	2	31	2	0	0	0		-	-	-
ODI	10	10	0	229	52	22.90	-	1	19	1	0	0	0		-	-	
List A	14	13	0	336	76	25.84	-	2	24	1	0	0	0		-	-	
20/20 Int	2	2	0	47	25	23.50	-	-	-	1	0	0	0		-	-	
20/20	3	3	0	52	25	17.33	-	-	-	1	0	0	0		-	-	

Career Performances

	M	Inn	NO	Runs	HS	Avg	100	50	Ct	St	Balls	Runs	Wkts	Avg	BB	5I	10M
Test	7	12	2	397	126 *	39.70	1	2	20	-	0	0	0		-	-	-
FC	115	182	17	6321	201 *	38.30	15	32	262	21	0	0	0		-	-	-
ODI	22	22	0	469	52	21.31	-	1	23	2	0	0	0		-	-	
List A	147	136	7	3261	144	25.27	3	18	118	22	0	0	0		-	-	
20/20 Int	5	5	0	116	32	23.20	-	-	4	1	0	0	0		-	-	
20/20	29	27	2	663	73	26.52	-	4	26	2	0	0	0		-	-	

PYRAH, R. M. — Yorkshire

Name: Richard (<u>Rich</u>) Michael Pyrah
Role: Right-hand bat, right-arm medium-fast bowler; all-rounder
Born: 1 November 1982, Dewsbury
Height: 6ft **Weight:** 12st 9lbs
Nickname: RP, Pyro
County debut: 2004
Parents: Mick and Lesley
Marital status: Single
Family links with cricket: 'Dad played local cricket in the Central Yorkshire League for Ossett'
Education: Ossett High School; Wakefield College
Qualifications: 10 GCSEs, Level 2 coach
Off-season: 'Working up to New Year; World Cricket Academy, Mumbai, in February'
Overseas tours: Yorkshire to Mumbai 2005

Overseas teams played for: Kaponga CC, New Zealand 2000-01, 2001-02; Taranaki District, New Zealand 2002-03; Campbelltown-Camden Ghosts, Sydney 2004-05
Career highlights to date: 'First first-class hundred. Four wickets in four balls [for Driffield] in 2007. Knocking 12 runs off the final over v Middlesex to win game [in Pro40 2007]'
Cricket moments to forget: 'Dropping a dolly of a catch in front of full crowd at Old Trafford and live on Sky Sports'
Cricket superstitions: 'None'
Cricketers particularly admired: Michael Vaughan, Darren Lehmann, Anthony McGrath
Young players to look out for: Oliver Hannon-Dalby, Adil Rashid
Other sports played: Golf, squash, football (had trials with Bradford City and Sheffield Wednesday)
Other sports followed: Football (Leeds United), rugby league (Leeds Rhinos)
Favourite band: Take That, Girls Aloud
Extras: C&G Man of the Match award for his 5-50 (plus 26 runs) for Yorkshire Board XI v Somerset at Scarborough in the third round 2002. His Bradford League awards include the all-rounders' and bowling averages trophies 2006. Yorkshire Fielder of the Year 2007. Has acted as 12th man for England
Opinions on cricket: 'Second XI cricket should mirror first-team competitions and rules to feed young players into county cricket. There should be a minimum number of English cricketers in each side who are eligible to play Test cricket, e.g. seven or eight.'

Best batting: 106 Yorkshire v LUCCE, Headingley 2007
Best bowling: 1-3 Yorkshire v LUCCE, Headingley 2007

2007 Season

	M	Inn	NO	Runs	HS	Avg	100	50	Ct	St	Balls	Runs	Wkts	Avg	BB	5I	10M
Test																	
FC	1	1	0	106	106	106.00	1	-	-	-	72	41	1	41.00	1-3	-	-
ODI																	
List A	17	10	2	98	24	12.25	-	-	5	-	644	533	22	24.22	3-22	-	
20/20 Int																	
20/20	8	4	0	10	6	2.50	-	-	2	-	54	65	6	10.83	2-8	-	

Career Performances

	M	Inn	NO	Runs	HS	Avg	100	50	Ct	St	Balls	Runs	Wkts	Avg	BB	5I	10M
Test																	
FC	7	11	1	342	106	34.20	1	1	1	-	168	77	4	19.25	1-3	-	-
ODI																	
List A	36	29	4	426	42	17.04	-	-	12	-	932	852	34	25.05	5-50	1	
20/20 Int																	
20/20	16	11	3	110	33 *	13.75	-	-	5	-	72	91	6	15.16	2-8	-	

RAMPRAKASH, M. R. — Surrey

Name: Mark Ravindra Ramprakash
Role: Right-hand bat, right-arm off-spin bowler
Born: 5 September 1969, Bushey, Herts
Height: 5ft 10in **Weight:** 12st 4lbs
Nickname: Ramps, Bloodaxe
County debut: 1987 (Middlesex), 2001 (Surrey)
County cap: 1990 (Middlesex), 2002 (Surrey)
Benefit: 2000 (Middlesex), 2008 (testimonial, Surrey)
Test debut: 1991
ODI debut: 1991
1000 runs in a season: 17
1st-Class 200s: 12
1st-Class 300s: 1
Place in batting averages: 1st av. 101.30 (2006 1st av. 103.54)
Parents: Deonarine and Jennifer

Wife and date of marriage: Van, 24 September 1993
Children: Cara, 1997; Anya, 2002
Family links with cricket: Father played club cricket in Guyana
Education: Gayton High School; Harrow Weald Sixth Form College
Qualifications: 6 O-levels, 2 A-levels, Level 3 cricket coach, Level 2 FA football coach
Overseas tours: England YC to Sri Lanka 1986-87, to Australia (U19 World Cup) 1987-88; England A to Pakistan 1990-91, to West Indies 1991-92, to India 1994-95 (vc); Lion Cubs to Barbados 1993; England to New Zealand 1991-92, to West Indies 1993-94, to Australia 1994-95, to South Africa 1995-96, to West Indies 1997-98, to Australia 1998-99, to South Africa 1999-2000, to Zimbabwe (one-day series) 2001-02, to India and New Zealand 2001-02
Overseas teams played for: Nairobi Jafferys, Kenya 1988; North Melbourne 1989; University of Perth 1996-97; Clico-Preysal, Trinidad 2004
Career highlights to date: 'My two Test hundreds, v West Indies and Australia'
Cricket superstitions: 'Same piece of chewing gum in innings'
Cricketers particularly admired: 'All the great all-rounders'; Alec Stewart
Young players to look out for: Arun Harinath
Other sports played: Football (Corinthian Casuals FC, Arsenal Pro-Celeb XI)
Other sports followed: Football (Arsenal FC)
Favourite band: 'Have lost touch!'
Extras: Voted Best U15 Schoolboy of 1985 by Cricket Society (Sir John Hobbs Silver Jubilee Memorial Prize) and Cricket Society's Most Promising Young Cricketer of the Year 1988. Man of the Match for his 56 in Middlesex's NatWest Trophy final win in 1988, on his debut in the competition. Represented England YC. Cricket Writers' Young Cricketer of the Year 1991. Middlesex captain May 1997 to the end of the 1999 season. Man of the Match in the fifth Test v West Indies at Bridgetown 1997-98 (154). Leading run-scorer in the single-division four-day era of the County Championship with 8392 runs (av. 56.32) 1993-99. Became first player to score a Championship century against all 18 first-class counties with his 110 v Middlesex at Lord's 2003. Surrey Players' Player of the Year 2003, 2004, 2005, 2006, 2007; Surrey Supporters' Player of the Year 2003, 2004. In 2006 became the first English batsman to score 2000 first-class runs in a season since the start of the two-division Championship in 2000, reaching the landmark in a record 20 innings and finishing the season with 2278 runs at an average of 103.54. PCA Player of the Year 2006. Winner, with Karen Hardy, of *Strictly Come Dancing*, December 2006. One of *Wisden*'s Five Cricketers of the Year 2007. Scored century in each innings (196/130*) for the sixth time, v Lancashire at The Oval 2007 to become the first batsman to average more than 100 in consecutive English seasons, finishing with 2026 runs at an average of 101.30. Vice-captain of Surrey 2004-05
Best batting: 301* Surrey v Northamptonshire, The Oval 2006
Best bowling: 3-32 Middlesex v Glamorgan, Lord's 1998

2007 Season

	M	Inn	NO	Runs	HS	Avg	100	50	Ct	St	Balls	Runs	Wkts	Avg	BB	5I	10M
Test																	
FC	15	25	5	2026	266 *	101.30	10	4	13	-	6	18	0		-	-	-
ODI																	
List A	11	10	2	456	142 *	57.00	2	2	3	-	0	0	0		-	-	
20/20 Int																	
20/20	8	8	2	265	85 *	44.16	-	2	3	-	0	0	0		-	-	

Career Performances

	M	Inn	NO	Runs	HS	Avg	100	50	Ct	St	Balls	Runs	Wkts	Avg	BB	5I	10M
Test	52	92	6	2350	154	27.32	2	12	39	-	895	477	4	119.25	1-2	-	-
FC	401	661	84	30659	301 *	53.13	97	134	235	-	4171	2196	34	64.58	3-32	-	-
ODI	18	18	4	376	51	26.85	-	1	8	-	132	108	4	27.00	3-28	-	
List A	379	367	59	12195	147 *	39.59	14	79	127	-	1734	1354	46	29.43	5-38	1	
20/20 Int																	
20/20	34	34	7	977	85 *	36.18	-	7	11	-	0	0	0		-	-	

RANKIN, W. B. — Warwickshire

Name: William Boyd Rankin
Role: Left-hand lower-order bat, right-arm fast-medium bowler
Born: 5 July 1984, Londonderry
Height: 6ft 8in **Weight:** 16st 7lbs
Nickname: Boydo, Stankin
County debut: 2006 (one-day, Derbyshire), 2007 (first-class, Derbyshire)
ODI debut: 2006-07
Place in bowling averages: 58th av. 29.20
Parents: Robert and Dawn
Marital status: Single
Family links with cricket: Both brothers (Robert and David) have played in Ireland age-group teams
Education: Strabane Grammar School; Harper Adams University College
Qualifications: 10 GCSEs, 3 A-levels, Level 1 cricket coaching
Career outside cricket: 'Student and work on home farm'
Off-season: 'Working on family farm; training, and playing in ICL'
Overseas tours: Ireland U19 to Bangladesh (U19 World Cup) 2003-04; Ireland to

Scotland (European Championship) 2006, to Kenya (ICC World Cricket League) 2006-07, to West Indies (World Cup) 2006-07, plus various Ireland age-group and A tours
Career highlights to date: 'Playing in 2006-07 Cricket World Cup, beating Pakistan and Bangladesh and tying with Zimbabwe'
Cricket moments to forget: 'U19 World Cup match against West Indies (2004)' *(Ireland U19 lost by just six runs)*
Cricket superstitions: 'None'
Cricketers particularly admired: Glenn McGrath, Curtly Ambrose
Young players to look out for: Gary Ballance, Daniel Redfern, Eoin Morgan
Other sports played: Rugby, football, badminton, snooker
Other sports followed: Football (Liverpool FC), rugby (Ulster)
Injuries: Out for more than two months with a stress fracture of a fibula
Favourite band: Coldplay, Oasis
Relaxations: 'Shooting'
Extras: Attended European Cricket Academy in Spain. Formerly with Middlesex but made no first-team appearances. Has represented Ireland in first-class and ODI cricket. Left Derbyshire at the end of the 2007 season and has joined Warwickshire for 2008
Opinions on cricket: 'Twenty20 cricket brings good crowds to games, which is good for cricket and clubs. I feel all 2nd XI cricket one-day matches should be coloured clothing and white ball, as this will help get young players used to playing in these conditions; otherwise it's completely new to them when they play first-team cricket.'
Best batting: 3 Derbyshire v Middlesex, Derby 2007
Best bowling: 4-41 Derbyshire v Middlesex, Derby 2007

2007 Season

	M	Inn	NO	Runs	HS	Avg	100	50	Ct	St	Balls	Runs	Wkts	Avg	BB	5I	10M
Test																	
FC	3	4	1	5	3	1.66	-	-	3	-	459	292	10	29.20	4-41	-	-
ODI																	
List A	4	2	1	4	2 *	4.00	-	-	-	-	147	177	3	59.00	2-56	-	
20/20 Int																	
20/20																	

Career Performances

	M	Inn	NO	Runs	HS	Avg	100	50	Ct	St	Balls	Runs	Wkts	Avg	BB	5I	10M
Test																	
FC	4	4	1	5	3	1.66	-	-	3	-	615	382	15	25.46	4-41	-	-
ODI	10	4	3	15	7 *	15.00	-	-	2	-	380	349	12	29.08	3-32	-	
List A	17	8	5	24	7 *	8.00	-	-	2	-	617	603	17	35.47	3-32	-	
20/20 Int																	
20/20																	

RASHID, A. U. Yorkshire

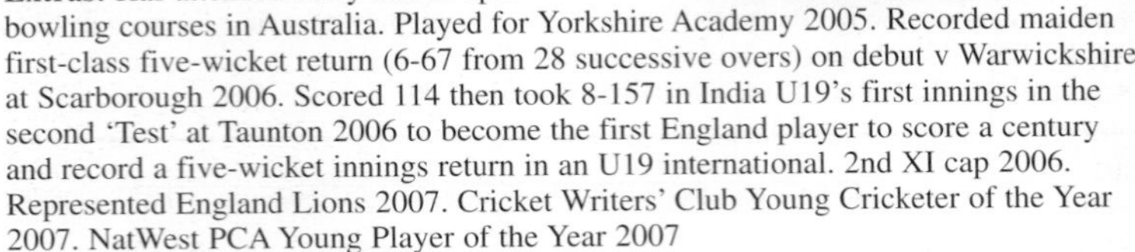

Name: Adil Usman Rashid
Role: Right-hand bat, right-arm leg-break bowler; all-rounder
Born: 17 February 1988, Bradford
Nickname: Dilly
County debut: 2006
Place in batting averages: 50th av. 44.05 (2006 215th av. 19.16)
Place in bowling averages: 121st av. 42.16 (2006 16th av. 25.16)
Family links with cricket: Brothers Amar and Haroon have both played for Bradford/Leeds UCCE
Overseas tours: England A to Bangladesh 2006-07; England Performance Programme to India 2007-08; England Lions to India 2007-08
Extras: Has attended Terry Jenner spin-bowling courses in Australia. Played for Yorkshire Academy 2005. Recorded maiden first-class five-wicket return (6-67 from 28 successive overs) on debut v Warwickshire at Scarborough 2006. Scored 114 then took 8-157 in India U19's first innings in the second 'Test' at Taunton 2006 to become the first England player to score a century and record a five-wicket innings return in an U19 international. 2nd XI cap 2006. Represented England Lions 2007. Cricket Writers' Club Young Cricketer of the Year 2007. NatWest PCA Young Player of the Year 2007
Best batting: 108 Yorkshire v Worcestershire, Kidderminster 2007
Best bowling: 6-67 Yorkshire v Warwickshire, Scarborough 2006

2007 Season

	M	Inn	NO	Runs	HS	Avg	100	50	Ct	St	Balls	Runs	Wkts	Avg	BB	5I	10M
Test																	
FC	17	23	4	837	108	44.05	1	7	9	-	2742	1813	43	42.16	5-88	3	-
ODI																	
List A	3	2	0	3	2	1.50	-	-	2	-	138	117	2	58.50	1-27	-	
20/20 Int																	
20/20																	

Career Performances

	M	Inn	NO	Runs	HS	Avg	100	50	Ct	St	Balls	Runs	Wkts	Avg	BB	5I	10M
Test																	
FC	23	30	5	961	108	38.44	1	8	11	-	3975	2514	69	36.43	6-67	4	-
ODI																	
List A	6	5	0	50	28	10.00	-	-	3	-	270	255	5	51.00	2-63	-	
20/20 Int																	
20/20																	

RAYNER, O. P. — Sussex

Name: Oliver (Ollie) Philip Rayner
Role: Right-hand bat, right-arm off-spin bowler
Born: 1 November 1985, Walsrode, Germany
Height: 6ft 5¼in **Weight:** 16st
Nickname: Mervin, Rocket, Rain-cakes, KP ('Kelvin Pietersen, not Kevin!')
County debut: 2006
Place in bowling averages: 61st av. 29.57
Parents: Mark and Penny
Marital status: Single
Education: St Bede's, The Dicker, Hailsham, East Sussex
Qualifications: 7 GCSEs, 2 A-levels, Level 1 coaching
Overseas tours: Sussex Academy to Sri Lanka 2001, to South Africa 2003
Overseas teams played for: University of Cape Town; Western Province
Cricket moments to forget: 'Chirping at Somerset, then getting a pair!'
Cricketers particularly admired: Andrew Flintoff, Shane Warne, Chris Gayle
Young players to look out for: Tom Smith, Krishna Singh
Other sports played: Football (Eastbourne Town Reserves; Eastbourne United 1st XI)
Other sports followed: Football (Brighton & Hove Albion)
Favourite band: Kanye West, Common, Talib Kwali
Relaxations: 'Bodyboarding, skiing, chilling with mates'
Extras: South of England U15. England Development Squad U19. Sussex 2nd XI Player of the Year 2005. Scored century (101) on first-class debut v Sri Lankans at Hove 2006, batting at No. 8
Best batting: 101 Sussex v Sri Lankans, Hove 2006
Best bowling: 5-68 Sussex v Sri Lanka A, Hove 2007

2007 Season

	M	Inn	NO	Runs	HS	Avg	100	50	Ct	St	Balls	Runs	Wkts	Avg	BB	5I	10M
Test																	
FC	4	5	1	61	35	15.25	-	-	3	-	704	414	14	29.57	5-68	1	-
ODI																	
List A	7	6	2	28	15	7.00	-	-	3	-	216	209	3	69.66	1-31	-	
20/20 Int																	
20/20	5	2	0	5	5	2.50	-	-	-	-	25	47	1	47.00	1-20	-	

Career Performances

	M	Inn	NO	Runs	HS	Avg	100	50	Ct	St	Balls	Runs	Wkts	Avg	BB	5I	10M
Test																	
FC	9	11	2	194	101	21.55	1	-	9	-	1292	762	20	38.10	5-68	1	-
ODI																	
List A	12	10	4	122	61	20.33	-	1	3	-	354	378	6	63.00	1-25	-	
20/20 Int																	
20/20	7	3	0	16	11	5.33	-	-	-	-	49	93	1	93.00	1-20	-	

READ, C. M. W. Nottinghamshire

Name: Christopher (<u>Chris</u>) Mark Wells Read
Role: Right-hand bat, wicket-keeper, county captain
Born: 10 August 1978, Paignton, Devon
Height: 5ft 8in **Weight:** 11st
Nickname: Readie, Reados
County debut: 1997 (one-day, Glos), 1998 (Notts)
County cap: 1999 (Notts)
Test debut: 1999
ODI debut: 1999-2000
Twenty20 Int debut: 2006
1000 runs in a season: 1
50 dismissals in a season: 3
1st-Class 200s: 1
Place in batting averages: 27th av. 52.68 (2006 66th av. 42.76)
Parents: Geoffrey and Carolyn
Wife and date of marriage: Louise, 2 October 2004
Education: Torquay Boys' Grammar School; University of Bath; Loughborough University
Qualifications: 9 GCSEs, 4 A-levels, senior coaching award

Overseas tours: West of England U13 to Netherlands 1991; West of England U15 to West Indies 1992-93; England U17 to Netherlands (International Youth Tournament) 1995; England U19 to Pakistan 1996-97; England A to Kenya and Sri Lanka 1997-98, to Zimbabwe and South Africa 1998-99, to West Indies 2000-01, 2005-06; England to South Africa and Zimbabwe 1999-2000, to Australia 2002-03 (VB Series), to Bangladesh and Sri Lanka 2003-04, to West Indies 2003-04, to South Africa 2004-05, to India (ICC Champions Trophy) 2006-07, to Australia 2006-07; British Universities to South Africa 2002; ECB National Academy to Australia and Sri Lanka 2002-03; England VI to Hong Kong 2005
Career highlights to date: 'Winning Test series v West Indies 2004'
Cricket moments to forget: 'Ducking a slower ball from Chris Cairns in second Test v New Zealand at Lord's 1999'
Cricketers particularly admired: Adam Gilchrist, Bruce French, Alan Knott, Bob Taylor, Jack Russell, Ian Healy
Young players to look out for: James Hildreth
Other sports played: Hockey (Devon U18, U21; West of England U17; South Nottingham)
Other sports followed: Football (Torquay United)
Favourite band: Stereophonics
Relaxations: 'Reading, listening to music, keeping fit and going out with friends'
Extras: Played for Devon 1995-97. Represented England U18 1996 and England U19 1997. Was selected for the England A tour to Kenya and Sri Lanka 1997-98 aged 18 and without having played a first-class game. Recorded eight dismissals on Test debut in the first Test v New Zealand at Edgbaston 1999. Man of the Match in the first ODI v West Indies at Georgetown 2003-04 after striking a match-winning 15-ball 27 including three sixes and a four. ECB National Academy 2005-06. Scored 165* v Essex at Trent Bridge 2007, in the process sharing with David Hussey (275) in a new record fifth-wicket partnership for Nottinghamshire (359). Scored 240 v Essex at Chelmsford 2007, becoming the first Nottinghamshire wicket-keeper to score a double century. Appointed captain of Nottinghamshire for 2008
Best batting: 240 Nottinghamshire v Essex, Chelmsford 2007

2007 Season

	M	Inn	NO	Runs	HS	Avg	100	50	Ct	St	Balls	Runs	Wkts	Avg	BB	5I	10M
Test																	
FC	17	23	4	1001	240	52.68	2	4	42	6	30	35	0		-	-	-
ODI																	
List A	14	11	4	363	68	51.85	-	3	10	2	0	0	0		-	-	
20/20 Int																	
20/20	6	6	3	80	26	26.66	-	-	2	-	0	0	0		-	-	

Career Performances

	M	Inn	NO	Runs	HS	Avg	100	50	Ct	St	Balls	Runs	Wkts	Avg	BB	5I	10M
Test	15	23	4	360	55	18.94	-	1	48	6	0	0	0		-	-	-
FC	190	285	45	7826	240	32.60	11	41	548	30	66	68	0		-	-	-
ODI	36	24	7	300	30 *	17.64	-	-	41	2	0	0	0		-	-	
List A	222	175	44	3702	135	28.25	2	11	224	48	0	0	0		-	-	
20/20 Int	1	1	0	13	13	13.00	-	-	1	-	0	0	0		-	-	
20/20	28	27	7	540	48 *	27.00	-	-	20	3	0	0	0		-	-	

REDFERN, D. J. — Derbyshire

Name: Daniel (Dan) James Redfern
Role: Left-hand bat, occasional right-arm off-spin bowler
Born: 18 April 1990, Shrewsbury
Height: 5ft 9in **Weight:** 10st
Nickname: Panda, Redders, Randy, Rowdy
County debut: 2006 (one-day), 2007 (first-class)
Place in batting averages: 143rd av. 30.00
Parents: Michael and Shirley
Marital status: Single
Family links with cricket: 'Grandfathers, father and brother all played for Leycett CC, Staffs. Brother also plays Shropshire U21'
Education: Adams' Grammar School, Newport, Shropshire
Qualifications: 10 GCSEs, 'doing A-levels'
Off-season: 'Training with Derbyshire Academy'
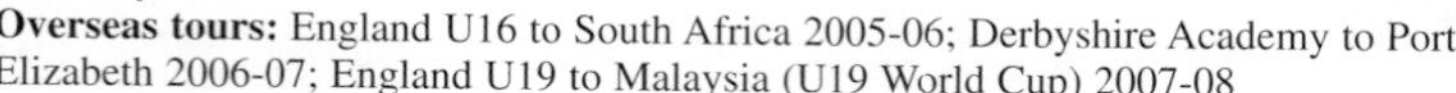
Overseas tours: England U16 to South Africa 2005-06; Derbyshire Academy to Port Elizabeth 2006-07; England U19 to Malaysia (U19 World Cup) 2007-08
Career highlights to date: 'Playing for Derbyshire 1st XI and for England U19 v Pakistan'
Cricket moments to forget: 'Run out by Lou Vincent on Sky [on county one-day debut]'
Cricket superstitions: 'None'
Cricketers particularly admired: Mark Ramprakash
Young players to look out for: Christian Mason, Matt Howard, Gary Ballance, Paul Borrington
Other sports played: Golf ('recreational')
Other sports followed: Football (Stoke City), rugby (Sale Sharks)

Favourite band: The Fratellis
Relaxations: 'Watching sport on TV'
Extras: Has represented England U15, U16, U17 and U19. Neil Lloyd Memorial Trophy for Best Batsman at Bunbury Festival 2005. Made one-day debut for Derbyshire v Worcestershire at Worcester in Pro40 2006, aged 16. Made Minor Counties Trophy debut for Shropshire v Northumberland at Oswestry 2007, scoring 107
Opinions on cricket: 'Longer tea breaks and innings change around.'
Best batting: 51 Derbyshire v Northamptonshire, Derby 2007
Best bowling: 1-7 Derbyshire v Somerset, Derby 2007

2007 Season

	M	Inn	NO	Runs	HS	Avg	100	50	Ct	St	Balls	Runs	Wkts	Avg	BB	5I	10M
Test																	
FC	5	7	1	180	51	30.00	-	1	5	-	114	70	2	35.00	1-7	-	-
ODI																	
List A	5	4	0	54	32	13.50	-	-	-	-	0	0	0			-	-
20/20 Int																	
20/20																	

Career Performances

	M	Inn	NO	Runs	HS	Avg	100	50	Ct	St	Balls	Runs	Wkts	Avg	BB	5I	10M
Test																	
FC	5	7	1	180	51	30.00	-	1	5	-	114	70	2	35.00	1-7	-	-
ODI																	
List A	6	5	0	60	32	12.00	-	-	-	-	0	0	0			-	-
20/20 Int																	
20/20																	

73. Which wicket-keeper-turned-commentator scored his maiden Test century (113*) and then made five dismissals in England's innings of the third Test at Auckland in 1983-84?

REES, G. P. — Glamorgan

Name: Gareth Peter Rees
Role: Left-hand opening bat, right-arm medium-fast 'utility bowler'
Born: 8 April 1985, Swansea
Height: 6ft 1in **Weight:** 14st 2lbs
Nickname: Gums, Nasser, Albert
County debut: 2006
Place in batting averages: 189th av. 23.83
Parents: Peter and Diane
Marital status: Single
Education: Coedcae Comprehensive, Llanelli; Coleg Sir Gar; Bath University
Qualifications: 10 GCSEs, 3 A-levels, Maths and Physics degree (First)
Cricket moments to forget: 'Getting run out by Ryan Watkins'
Cricket superstitions: 'Left pad on first'
Cricketers particularly admired: Brian Lara
Young players to look out for: James Harris
Other sports played: Rugby (Wales U17, Llanelli Scarlets U21)
Other sports followed: Rugby (Llanelli Scarlets, Felinfoel RFC)
Favourite band: Oasis
Relaxations: 'Golf'
Extras: Played for Wales Minor Counties in the 2004 and 2005 C&G and in Minor Counties competitions 2002-07
Best batting: 109 Glamorgan v Derbyshire, Cardiff 2007

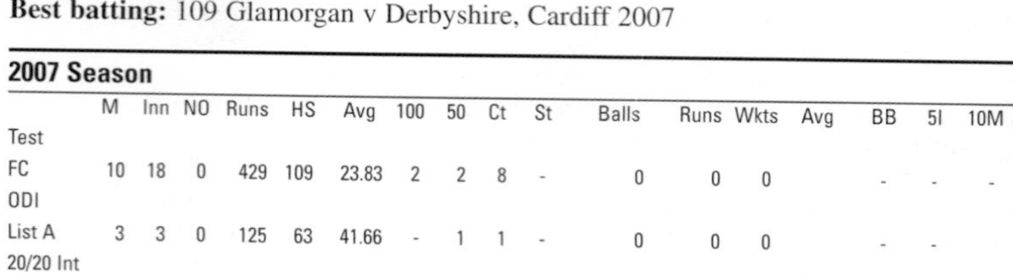

2007 Season

	M	Inn	NO	Runs	HS	Avg	100	50	Ct	St	Balls	Runs	Wkts	Avg	BB	5I	10M
Test																	
FC	10	18	0	429	109	23.83	2	2	8	-	0	0	0		-	-	-
ODI																	
List A	3	3	0	125	63	41.66	-	1	1	-	0	0	0		-	-	
20/20 Int																	
20/20																	

Career Performances

	M	Inn	NO	Runs	HS	Avg	100	50	Ct	St	Balls	Runs	Wkts	Avg	BB	5I	10M
Test																	
FC	13	23	1	513	109	23.31	2	3	9	-	0	0	0		-	-	-
ODI																	
List A	6	6	0	163	63	27.16	-	1	2	-	0	0	0		-	-	
20/20 Int																	
20/20																	

RICHARDSON, A. Middlesex

Name: Alan Richardson
Role: Right-hand bat, right-arm medium bowler
Born: 6 May 1975, Newcastle-under-Lyme, Staffs
Height: 6ft 2in **Weight:** 13st
Nickname: Richo
County debut: 1995 (Derbyshire), 1999 (Warwickshire), 2005 (Middlesex)
County cap: 2002 (Warwickshire), 2005 (Middlesex)
50 wickets in a season: 1
Place in batting averages: 261st av. 13.00
Place in bowling averages: 24th av. 24.21
Parents: Roy and Sandra
Marital status: Single
Family links with cricket: 'Dad captained Little Stoke 3rd XI and now patrols the boundary with pint in hand at the Sid Jenkins Cricket Ground'
Education: Alleyne's High School, Stone; Stafford College of Further Education
Qualifications: 8 GCSEs, 2 A-levels, 2 AS-levels, Level 2 cricket coach
Career outside cricket: Landscape gardener
Overseas tours: Derbyshire to Malaga 1995; Warwickshire to Bloemfontein 2000, to Cape Town 2001, 2002, to Portugal 2003; England Lions to India 2007-08
Overseas teams played for: Northern Natal, South Africa 1994-96; Hawkesbury CC, Sydney 1997-99; Northern Districts, Sydney 1999-2000, 2001-03; Avendale, Cape Town 2000-01; Kyriang Mountains, Australia 2003-04
Career highlights to date: 'Getting capped by both Warwickshire and Middlesex. Doing well on my home debuts'
Cricket moments to forget: 'The whole 2006 season!' (*Out for four weeks with a broken thumb; for the rest of the season with a floating bone in the elbow*)

Cricket superstitions: 'None'
Other sports played: Football, golf, tennis ('all very badly')
Other sports followed: Football (Stoke City)
Favourite band: Josh Rouse, Jeff Buckley, The Housemartins
Extras: *Cricket World* award for best bowling performance in Oxford U19 Festival (8-60 v Devon). Topped Minor Counties bowling averages with Staffordshire 1998 and won Minor Counties bowling award. Most Improved 2nd XI Player 1999. Outstanding Performance of the Year 1999 for his 8-51 v Gloucestershire on home debut. Scored 91 v Hampshire at Edgbaston 2002, in the process sharing with Nick Knight (255*) in a Warwickshire record tenth-wicket stand of 214. Had first innings figures of 7-113 on first-class debut for Middlesex v Nottinghamshire at Lord's 2005
Opinions on cricket: 'Being a cricketer is almost fashionable now, and so attracting young kids into the game shouldn't be a problem. Still think we need longer tea breaks.'
Best batting: 91 Warwickshire v Hampshire, Edgbaston 2002
Best bowling: 8-46 Warwickshire v Sussex, Edgbaston 2002

2007 Season

	M	Inn	NO	Runs	HS	Avg	100	50	Ct	St	Balls	Runs	Wkts	Avg	BB	5I	10M
Test																	
FC	14	13	5	104	24 *	13.00	-	-	5	-	2143	1017	42	24.21	5-50	1	-
ODI																	
List A	4	1	1	2	2 *		-	-	-	-	192	174	4	43.50	2-57	-	
20/20 Int																	
20/20																	

Career Performances

	M	Inn	NO	Runs	HS	Avg	100	50	Ct	St	Balls	Runs	Wkts	Avg	BB	5I	10M
Test																	
FC	92	93	36	642	91	11.26	-	1	25	-	16439	7995	269	29.72	8-46	8	1
ODI																	
List A	61	27	17	104	21 *	10.40	-	-	11	-	2680	2102	57	36.87	5-35	1	
20/20 Int																	
20/20	5	1	1	6	6 *		-	-	1	-	102	120	4	30.00	3-13	-	

74. Which New Zealand captain scored his only Test century (116) v England at Christchurch in 1946-47?

ROBINSON, D. D. J. Leicestershire

Name: Darren David John Robinson
Role: Right-hand bat, leg-spin bowler
Born: 2 March 1973, Braintree, Essex
Height: 5ft 11in **Weight:** 14st
Nickname: Pies, Pie Shop, Robbo
County debut: 1993 (Essex), 2004 (Leicestershire)
County cap: 1997 (Essex), 2007 (Leicestershire)
1000 runs in a season: 3
1st-Class 200s: 1
Place in batting averages: 135th av. 31.30 (2006 138th av. 30.75)
Parents: Dorothy (deceased) and David
Wife and date of marriage: Alyssa, 2 December 2001
Children: Kalli, 20 July 1998; Cameron, 20 May 2000; Evie, 30 October 2002
Family links with cricket: Father club cricketer for Halstead
Education: Tabor High School, Braintree; Chelmsford College of Further Education
Qualifications: 5 GCSEs, BTEC National Diploma in Building and Construction
Career outside cricket: Site investigation and surveying
Overseas tours: England U18 to Canada (International Youth Tournament) 1991; England U19 to Pakistan 1991-92
Overseas teams played for: Waverley, Sydney 1992-94; Eden Roskill CC, Auckland 1995-96
Career highlights to date: 'Every trophy won'
Cricket moments to forget: 'Being bowled out for 57 against Lancashire in the NatWest final [1996]'
Cricket superstitions: 'None'
Cricketers particularly admired: Steve Hale, David Denny
Other sports played: Football, golf, squash
Other sports followed: Golf, football, rugby, swimming
Relaxations: Reading, music
Extras: International Youth Tournament in Canada batting award 1991. Scored two centuries (102/118*) in match v Leicestershire at Chelmsford 2001. Essex Player of the Year 2002. Scored 81 v Australians at Leicester 2005, in the process sharing with Chris Rogers (209) in a record opening partnership for a county against an Australian touring side (247). Acting captain of Leicestershire in the Championship during the first part of the 2007 season. Released by Leicestershire at the end of the 2007 season
Best batting: 200 Essex v New Zealanders, Chelmsford 1999
Best bowling: 1-7 Essex v Middlesex, Chelmsford 2003

2007 Season

	M	Inn	NO	Runs	HS	Avg	100	50	Ct	St	Balls	Runs	Wkts	Avg	BB	5I	10M
Test																	
FC	8	14	1	407	122	31.30	1	1	4	-	48	50	1	50.00	1-48	-	-
ODI																	
List A	5	5	0	89	44	17.80	-	-	-	-	0	0	0		-	-	
20/20 Int																	
20/20																	

Career Performances

	M	Inn	NO	Runs	HS	Avg	100	50	Ct	St	Balls	Runs	Wkts	Avg	BB	5I	10M
Test																	
FC	189	334	16	10489	200	32.98	22	50	156	-	348	449	2	224.50	1-7	-	-
ODI																	
List A	195	186	14	4488	137 *	26.09	4	21	51	-	17	26	1	26.00	1-7	-	
20/20 Int																	
20/20	8	8	1	82	41	11.71	-	-	3	-	0	0	0		-	-	

ROGERS, C. J. L. — Derbyshire

Name: Christopher (Chris) John Llewellyn Rogers
Role: Left-hand bat, leg-spin/right-arm medium bowler
Born: 31 August 1977, Sydney, Australia
Height: 5ft 11in **Weight:** 12st 8lbs
County debut: 2004 (Derbys), 2005 (Leics), 2006 (Northants)
1000 runs in a season: 1
1st-Class 200s: 3
1st-Class 300s: 1
Place in batting averages: 140th av. 30.92 (2006 13th av. 61.81)
Family links with cricket: Father played for New South Wales and became cricket administrator
Overseas tours: Australia A to Pakistan 2007-08
Overseas teams played for: Western Australia 1998-99 –
Extras: Represented Australia U19 1995-96. Has represented Australia A. Scored two centuries (101*/102*) in Pura Cup match v South Australia at Perth 2001-02, winning Man of the Match award. Won three Western Australia awards 2002-03 – Lawrie

Sawle Medal (leading first-class and one-day player), President's Silver Trophy (season's best individual performance – for his 194 v NSW in the Pura Cup), and Excalibur Award (spirit of WA cricket). An overseas player with Derbyshire 2004 but forced to return home early injured; a temporary overseas player with Leicestershire during the 2005 season. Scored 209 v Australians at Leicester 2005, in the process sharing with Darren Robinson (81) in a record opening partnership for a county against an Australian touring side (247). An overseas player with Northamptonshire 2006-07. Scored century and double century (128/222*) in the same match, v Somerset at Taunton 2006, becoming the first Northants batsman to achieve the feat since Allan Lamb in 1992. Pura Cup Player of the Year 2006-07; also named State Player of the Year at the 2007 Allan Border Medal awards. Has rejoined Derbyshire as an overseas player for 2008 as a locum for Mahela Jayawardene
Best batting: 319 Northamptonshire v Gloucestershire, Northampton 2006
Best bowling: 1-16 Northamptonshire v Leicestershire, Northampton 2006
Stop press: Made Test debut in the third Test v India at Perth 2007-08

2007 Season

	M	Inn	NO	Runs	HS	Avg	100	50	Ct	St	Balls	Runs	Wkts	Avg	BB	5I	10M
Test																	
FC	8	14	1	402	138	30.92	1	3	13	-	0	0	0		-	-	-
ODI																	
List A	4	3	0	124	58	41.33	-	1	1	-	0	0	0		-	-	
20/20 Int																	
20/20	7	3	0	38	23	12.66	-	-	4	-	0	0	0		-	-	

Career Performances

	M	Inn	NO	Runs	HS	Avg	100	50	Ct	St	Balls	Runs	Wkts	Avg	BB	5I	10M
Test																	
FC	99	177	10	8074	319	48.34	21	42	98	-	184	106	1	106.00	1-16	-	-
ODI																	
List A	74	71	6	2076	117 *	31.93	2	12	39	-	24	26	2	13.00	2-22	-	
20/20 Int																	
20/20	10	6	0	90	35	15.00	-	-	5	-	0	0	0		-	-	

75. Which current cricket correspondent had match figures of 10-122 as England beat South Africa by eight wickets at Trent Bridge in 1998?

ROSENBERG, M. C. — Leicestershire

Name: Marc Christopher Rosenberg
Role: Right-hand bat, right-arm medium-fast bowler; all-rounder
Born: 10 February 1982, Johannesburg, South Africa
Height: 6ft **Weight:** 12st 10lbs
Nickname: Rosie, Goz
County debut: 2006
Place in batting averages: 225th av. 18.57
Parents: Terry and Carol
Marital status: Single
Education: Kearsney College; Loughborough University
Qualifications: BSc (Hons) Sports Science and Management
Overseas teams played for: North West, South Africa 2004-05
Career highlights to date: 'Debut for Leicestershire'
Cricket superstitions: 'Too many to mention'
Cricketers particularly admired: Errol Stewart, Jonty Rhodes, Michael Vaughan, HD Ackerman
Young players to look out for: James Allenby
Other sports played: Golf, rugby, surfing
Other sports followed: Rugby (Natal Sharks, Leicester Tigers)
Favourite band: Two Tone Deaf, Jack Johnson
Relaxations: 'Surfing'
Extras: Played for Loughborough UCCE 2003-04. Is not considered an overseas player. Released by Leicestershire at the end of the 2007 season
Best batting: 86 North West v Griqualand West, Potchefstroom 2004-05
Best bowling: 1-27 LUCCE v Somerset, Taunton 2004

2007 Season

	M	Inn	NO	Runs	HS	Avg	100	50	Ct	St	Balls	Runs	Wkts	Avg	BB	5I	10M
Test																	
FC	7	8	1	130	64 *	18.57	-	1	2	-	56	45	0		-	-	-
ODI																	
List A	3	0	0	0	0		-	-	-	-	0	0	0		-	-	
20/20 Int																	
20/20																	

Career Performances

	M	Inn	NO	Runs	HS	Avg	100	50	Ct	St	Balls	Runs	Wkts	Avg	BB	5I	10M
Test																	
FC	13	18	2	385	86	24.06	-	2	3	-	129	114	2	57.00	1-27	-	-
ODI																	
List A	6	3	0	29	26	9.66	-	-	1	-	18	17	3	5.66	3-17	-	
20/20 Int																	
20/20																	

ROWE, D. T. Leicestershire

Name: Daniel Thomas Rowe
Role: Right-hand bat, right-arm fast-medium bowler
Born: 22 March 1984, Bridgend, South Wales
Height: 6ft **Weight:** 14st
Nickname: Dragon, Rowey, Rowster
County debut: 2006
Place in bowling averages: 78th av. 32.84
Parents: Paul and Barbara
Marital status: Long-term girlfriend Emma
Family links with cricket: 'Brother played Mid-Glamorgan age groups'
Education: Archbishop McGrath Roman Catholic School; University of Glamorgan, Cardiff
Qualifications: 3 A-levels, BSc Sports and Health Science, Level 1 coaching
Career outside cricket: 'Coaching – nutrition in sport'
Off-season: 'Playing cricket in South Africa'
Overseas tours: Wales U16 to Jersey Festival 2000; Leicestershire CCC to Sri Lanka and India 2007
Overseas teams played for: Varsity Academy, Potchefstroom; International Pros, Potchefstroom 2007
Career highlights to date: '[Championship] debut against Essex CCC, scoring 85 and taking 2-27'
Cricket moments to forget: 'Injury to finger' (*see **Injuries***)
Cricketers particularly admired: Darren Gough, Chris Cairns, Allan Donald
Other sports played: Golf
Other sports followed: Rugby (Tondu, Ospreys), football (Manchester City)
Injuries: Out for eight weeks when 'tore tendons, ligaments and sliced away part of

my knuckle of right index finger during a game of golf when the shaft of the club broke on the downswing'

Favourite band: Linkin Park

Relaxations: 'Golf, cinema, shopping, watching my brother play for Tondu RFC'

Extras: Represented Wales U12-U16, Mid-Glamorgan Schools and Glamorgan U17 and U19. Played for Cardiff UCCE 2004-06. Has also played for Somerset 2nd XI. Scored 85 on Championship debut v Essex at Leicester 2007, batting at No. 9

Best batting: 85 Leicestershire v Essex, Leicester 2007

Best bowling: 5-61 Leicestershire v OUCCE, The Parks 2007

2007 Season

	M	Inn	NO	Runs	HS	Avg	100	50	Ct	St	Balls	Runs	Wkts	Avg	BB	5I	10M
Test																	
FC	5	6	1	137	85	27.40	-	1	-	-	534	427	13	32.84	5-61	1	-
ODI																	
List A	3	2	1	4	2 *	4.00	-	-	-	-	72	95	0		-	-	
20/20 Int																	
20/20																	

Career Performances

	M	Inn	NO	Runs	HS	Avg	100	50	Ct	St	Balls	Runs	Wkts	Avg	BB	5I	10M
Test																	
FC	6	7	1	137	85	22.83	-	1	1	-	588	449	14	32.07	5-61	1	-
ODI																	
List A	4	2	1	4	2 *	4.00	-	-	1	-	102	121	1	121.00	1-26	-	
20/20 Int																	
20/20																	

RUDGE, W. D. Gloucestershire

Name: William (Will) Douglas Rudge

Role: Right-hand lower-order bat, right-arm medium-fast bowler

Born: 15 July 1983, Bristol

Height: 6ft 4in **Weight:** 14st 6lbs

Nickname: Rudgey, Glasseye, Sloth

County debut: 2005

County cap: 2005

Parents: Barry and Susan

Marital status: Single

Family links with cricket: 'Dad played club cricket for Timsbury'

Education: Clifton College

Qualifications: 10 GCSEs, 3 A-levels

Overseas tours: Clifton College to Australia 1997, to Barbados 1999
Overseas teams played for: Albion CC, Tauranga, New Zealand 2001-02; Greeton CC, Tauranga, New Zealand 2002-03; Central CC, Rotorua, New Zealand 2004-05
Career highlights to date: 'Debut v Sussex 2005 at Cheltenham'
Cricket moments to forget: 'Twenty20 v Somerset 2006. They set a new record 250 off their 20 overs'
Cricketers particularly admired: Glenn McGrath, Ian Botham, Curtly Ambrose
Other sports played: Rugby (at school), football (Bristol North West), golf
Other sports followed: Rugby (Bristol), football (Tottenham Hotspur)
Favourite band: The Stone Roses
Relaxations: 'Eating out, golf'
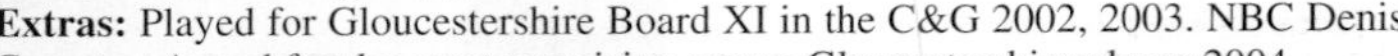
Extras: Played for Gloucestershire Board XI in the C&G 2002, 2003. NBC Denis Compton Award for the most promising young Gloucestershire player 2004
Opinions on cricket: 'Too many Kolpak players [*see page 13*].'
Best batting: 15 Gloucestershire v Surrey, The Oval 2005
Best bowling: 3-46 Gloucestershire v Bangladesh A, Bristol 2005

2007 Season

	M	Inn	NO	Runs	HS	Avg	100	50	Ct	St	Balls	Runs	Wkts	Avg	BB	5I	10M
Test																	
FC	1	2	1	3	3 *	3.00	-	-	1	-	72	40	0		-	-	-
ODI																	
List A	1	1	0	1	1	1.00	-	-	-	-	36	18	2	9.00	2-18	-	
20/20 Int																	
20/20																	

Career Performances

	M	Inn	NO	Runs	HS	Avg	100	50	Ct	St	Balls	Runs	Wkts	Avg	BB	5I	10M
Test																	
FC	10	12	3	47	15	5.22	-	-	4	-	1087	856	16	53.50	3-46	-	-
ODI																	
List A	5	4	1	9	4	3.00	-	-	-	-	167	149	5	29.80	2-1	-	
20/20 Int																	
20/20	3	1	0	1	1	1.00	-	-	-	-	58	105	4	26.25	3-37	-	

RUDOLPH, J. A. Yorkshire

Name: Jacobus (Jacques) Andries Rudolph
Role: Left-hand bat, right-arm leg-spin bowler
Born: 4 May 1981, Springs, South Africa
County debut: 2007
County cap: 2007
Test debut: 2003
ODI debut: 2003
Twenty20 Int debut: 2005-06
1000 runs in a season: 1
1st-Class 200s: 2
Place in batting averages: 18th av. 56.73
Overseas tours: South Africa U19 to Pakistan 1998-99, to Sri Lanka (U19 World Cup) 1999-2000; South Africa A to Zimbabwe 2002-03, to Sri Lanka 2005-06; South Africa to Australia 2001-02, to Bangladesh 2003, to England 2003, to Pakistan 2003-04, to New Zealand 2003-04, to Sri Lanka 2004, to England (ICC Champions Trophy) 2004, to India 2004-05, to West Indies 2004-05, to Australia 2005-06, to Sri Lanka 2006
Overseas teams played for: Northerns B/Northerns 1997-98 – 2003-04; Titans 2003-04 – 2004-05; Eagles 2005-06 –
Extras: Was twice on verge of Test debut – selected for the third Test v India at Centurion 2001-02, only for the match to be stripped of Test status due to the Denness Affair; chosen for the third Test v Australia in Sydney 2001-02, only for his selection to be overruled in favour of Justin Ontong. Man of the Match for his 222* on Test debut in the first Test v Bangladesh in Chittagong 2003; in the process shared with Boeta Dippenaar (177*) in the highest partnership for any wicket for South Africa in Tests (429*). One of *South African Cricket Annual*'s five Cricketers of the Year 2003. Scored second innings 102* to help save the first Test v Australia at Perth 2005-06. Was due to join Derbyshire as an overseas player in 2006 but withdrew with a shoulder problem. Joined Yorkshire in 2007; is not considered an overseas player
Best batting: 222* South Africa v Bangladesh, Chittagong 2003
Best bowling: 5-87 Northerns B v Griqualand West B, Centurion 1998-99
Stop press: Man of the Match v Cape Cobras at Cape Town in the SuperSport Series 2007-08 (94/5-80)

2007 Season

	M	Inn	NO	Runs	HS	Avg	100	50	Ct	St	Balls	Runs	Wkts	Avg	BB	5I	10M
Test																	
FC	15	22	3	1078	220	56.73	4	3	19	-	96	55	0		-	-	-
ODI																	
List A	15	14	2	587	127	48.91	2	2	8	-	13	5	0		-	-	
20/20 Int																	
20/20	8	7	4	126	48 *	42.00	-	-	1	-	90	110	6	18.33	3-20	-	

Career Performances

	M	Inn	NO	Runs	HS	Avg	100	50	Ct	St	Balls	Runs	Wkts	Avg	BB	5I	10M
Test	35	63	7	2028	222 *	36.21	5	8	22	-	664	432	4	108.00	1-1	-	-
FC	117	204	13	8063	222 *	42.21	23	35	93	-	3404	1911	45	42.46	5-87	2	-
ODI	45	39	6	1174	81	35.57	-	7	11	-	24	26	0		-	-	
List A	126	116	20	4385	134 *	45.67	6	27	41	-	275	250	7	35.71	4-40	-	
20/20 Int	1	1	1	6	6 *		-	-	-	-	0	0	0		-	-	
20/20	23	22	6	515	71	32.18	-	3	9	-	121	157	9	17.44	3-16	-	

SADLER, J. L. — Derbyshire

Name: John Leonard Sadler
Role: Left-hand top-order bat, right-arm off-spin bowler
Born: 19 November 1981, Dewsbury
Height: 5ft 11in **Weight:** 12st 7lbs
Nickname: Sads, Chrome, Super
County debut: 2002 (one-day, Yorkshire), 2003 (Leicestershire)
1000 runs in a season: 1
Place in batting averages: 229th av. 17.88 (2006 46th av. 48.76)
Parents: Sue and Mike ('Baz')
Marital status: Single
Family links with cricket: 'Dad played league cricket for 30 years, fielding round the corner with his sun hat on; now coaches. Brothers Dave and Jamie represented Yorkshire Schools and now play local league in Yorkshire CYCL'
Education: St Thomas à Becket RC Comprehensive School, Wakefield
Qualifications: 9 GCSEs, Levels I and II coaching awards

Overseas tours: England U19 to Malaysia and (U19 World Cup) Sri Lanka 1999-2000, to India 2000-01; Yorkshire to Grenada 2002
Overseas teams played for: Tuart Hill, Perth 2001-04
Career highlights to date: 'First first-class century. Winning Twenty20 2004, 2006'
Cricket superstitions: 'None'
Cricketers particularly admired: Robin Smith, Brian Lara, Sachin Tendulkar
Other sports played: Five-a-side football, squash, golf
Other sports followed: Football (Leeds United)
Favourite band: Oasis, Green Day, Michael Jackson
Extras: Played for Yorkshire Schools at all levels; attended Yorkshire Academy; awarded Yorkshire 2nd XI cap. Yorkshire Supporters' Club Young Player of the Year 1998. Represented England U14, U15, U17, U18 and U19. Left Leicestershire at the end of the 2007 season and has joined Derbyshire for 2008
Opinions on cricket: 'The game seems to be getting quicker and more exciting every year, which is great. Twenty20 has helped the longer form, and is no longer a lottery, but shouldn't be overdone. Still the best game in the world but the hardest at times.'
Best batting: 145 Leicestershire v Surrey, Leicester 2003
145 Leicestershire v Sussex, Hove 2003
Best bowling: 1-5 Leicestershire v Middlesex, Southgate 2007

2007 Season

	M	Inn	NO	Runs	HS	Avg	100	50	Ct	St	Balls	Runs	Wkts	Avg	BB	5I	10M
Test																	
FC	10	17	0	304	45	17.88	-	-	7	-	84	95	1	95.00	1-5	-	-
ODI																	
List A	14	14	5	510	113 *	56.66	1	3	1	-	48	33	1	33.00	1-33	-	
20/20 Int																	
20/20	5	4	2	23	14	11.50	-	-	3	-	0	0	0		-	-	

Career Performances

	M	Inn	NO	Runs	HS	Avg	100	50	Ct	St	Balls	Runs	Wkts	Avg	BB	5I	10M
Test																	
FC	52	89	12	2630	145	34.15	3	15	38	-	171	193	2	96.50	1-5	-	-
ODI																	
List A	73	68	11	1507	113 *	26.43	1	6	14	-	48	33	1	33.00	1-33	-	
20/20 Int																	
20/20	37	32	8	467	73	19.45	-	1	13	-	0	0	0		-	-	

76. In which series did South Africa record their first Test match win against England:
a) 1905-06; b) 1907; c) 1924?

SAFFELL, O. H. J. — Derbyshire

Name: Oliver Henry James Saffell
Role: Right-hand bat, right-arm medium-fast bowler
Born: 16 July 1986, Derby
Height: 6ft **Weight:** 13st 6lbs
Nickname: Saff
County debut: 2007
Parents: Richard and Clare
Marital status: Single
Education: De Lisle, Loughborough; University of Derby
Qualifications: 11 GCSEs, 4 A-levels
Off-season: 'Tour with Club Cricket Conference to Australia'
Overseas tours: Club Cricket Conference to Australia 2007-08
Career highlights to date: 'Making debut for Derbyshire'
Cricket moments to forget: 'North Gear Twenty20 final'
Cricketers particularly admired: Andrew Flintoff, Brett Lee
Young players to look out for: Gary Ballance, Dan Redfern, Jack Ratcliffe, Ben Symcox
Other sports played: Rugby (Castle Donington RUFC)
Other sports followed: Rugby (Leicester Tigers)
Extras: Played one first-class match for Derbyshire 2007
Best batting: 35* Derbyshire v CUCCE, Fenner's 2007
Best bowling: 3-37 Derbyshire v CUCCE, Fenner's 2007

2007 Season

	M	Inn	NO	Runs	HS	Avg	100	50	Ct	St	Balls	Runs	Wkts	Avg	BB	5I	10M
Test																	
FC	1	1	1	35	35 *		-	-	-	-	97	59	5	11.80	3-37	-	-
ODI																	
List A																	
20/20 Int																	
20/20																	

Career Performances

	M	Inn	NO	Runs	HS	Avg	100	50	Ct	St	Balls	Runs	Wkts	Avg	BB	5I	10M
Test																	
FC	1	1	1	35	35 *		-	-	-	-	97	59	5	11.80	3-37	-	-
ODI																	
List A																	
20/20 Int																	
20/20																	

SAGGERS, M. J. Kent

Name: Martin John Saggers
Role: Right-hand bat, right-arm fast-medium bowler
Born: 23 May 1972, King's Lynn
Height: 6ft 2in **Weight:** 14st 2lbs
Nickname: Saggs, Saggy Bits, Bits of Aloo, Jurgen Burgen
County debut: 1996 (Durham), 1999 (Kent) (*see **Extras***)
County cap: 2001 (Kent)
Test debut: 2003-04
50 wickets in a season: 4
Place in bowling averages: 26th av. 24.37
Parents: Brian and Edna
Wife and date of marriage: Samantha, 27 February 2004
Children: Ethan, 9 October 2005
Family links with cricket: Grandfather played in the Essex League
Education: Springwood High School; University of Huddersfield
Qualifications: BA (Hons) Architectural Studies International
Overseas tours: Kent to South Africa 2001; England VI to Hong Kong 2002; England to Bangladesh 2003-04
Overseas teams played for: Randburg CC, Johannesburg 1996-98, 2000-04; Southern Suburbs CC, Johannesburg 1998-99
Career highlights to date: 'Winning the Norwich Union League 2001. Making my Test debut in Bangladesh. Taking a wicket with my first delivery in Test cricket on English soil'
Cricket moments to forget: 'Any form of injury'
Cricket superstitions: 'Getting a corner spot in the changing room'

Cricketers particularly admired: Neil Foster, Graham Dilley, Allan Donald, Richard Ellison
Young players to look out for: Neil Dexter, Samuel Jordan
Other sports played: Golf (10 handicap)
Other sports followed: Football (Spurs), 'any form of motor sport'
Favourite band: Nickelback
Extras: Won Most Promising Uncapped Player Award 2000. Joint Kent Player of the Year 2000 (with David Masters). Underwood Award (Kent leading wicket-taker) 2001, 2002, 2003. *Kent Messenger* Group Readers' Player of the Season 2002. Shepherd Neame Award for Best Bowler 2002. Cowdrey Award (Kent Player of the Year) 2002. Scored career best 64 as nightwatchman as Kent scored a then county fourth-innings record 429-5 to beat Worcestershire at Canterbury 2004. Took wicket (Mark Richardson) with his first delivery in Test cricket on English soil, in the second Test v New Zealand at Headingley 2004. Played two first-class, three List A and five Twenty20 matches for Essex on loan 2007
Best batting: 64 Kent v Worcestershire, Canterbury 2004
Best bowling: 7-79 Kent v Durham, Riverside 2000

2007 Season

	M	Inn	NO	Runs	HS	Avg	100	50	Ct	St	Balls	Runs	Wkts	Avg	BB	5I	10M
Test																	
FC	9	8	2	49	16	8.16	-	-	-	-	1426	707	29	24.37	5-39	2	-
ODI																	
List A	10	5	3	6	2 *	3.00	-	-	1	-	459	273	17	16.05	4-25	-	
20/20 Int																	
20/20	5	0	0	0	0		-	-	-	-	102	163	3	54.33	2-34	-	

Career Performances

	M	Inn	NO	Runs	HS	Avg	100	50	Ct	St	Balls	Runs	Wkts	Avg	BB	5I	10M
Test	3	3	0	1	1	.33	-	-	1	-	493	247	7	35.28	2-29	-	-
FC	104	127	34	1059	64	11.38	-	2	26	-	18362	9376	381	24.60	7-79	18	-
ODI																	
List A	122	66	33	299	34 *	9.06	-	-	23	-	5556	4154	166	25.02	5-22	2	
20/20 Int																	
20/20	10	1	0	5	5	5.00	-	-	2	-	186	256	6	42.66	2-14	-	

77. Which Surrey player made his Test comeback with a hundred (124) in the fifth Test v South Africa at The Oval in 2003?

SAKER, N. C. — Surrey

Name: Neil Clifford Saker
Role: Right-hand bat, right-arm fast bowler
Born: 20 September 1984, Tooting, London
Height: 6ft 4in **Weight:** 12st 7lbs
Nickname: Bulby, Sakes
County debut: 2003
Place in batting averages: 265th av. 12.33 (2006 205th av. 21.33)
Place in bowling averages: 125th av. 43.26 (2006 134th av. 46.92)
Parents: Pauline and Steve
Marital status: Single
Family links with cricket: 'Dad played league cricket in Surrey'
Education: Raynes Park High School; Nescot College, Ewell
Qualifications: ECB Level 1 coach, City & Guilds Carpentry
Overseas tours: Guildford CC to Trinidad and Tobago 2001; Surrey U19 to Sri Lanka 2002
Overseas teams played for: Randwick-Petersham, Sydney 2003-04; Blacktown CC, Sydney
Cricket superstitions: 'Bowling marker has to be lying on the grass, not pushed in'
Cricketers particularly admired: Brett Lee, Allan Donald
Young players to look out for: Jade Dernbach, Rory Hamilton-Brown, Danny Miller
Other sports played: Snooker, golf
Other sports followed: Football (Tottenham)
Favourite band: Queen
Relaxations: 'Music, sleeping and eating!'
Extras: First academy player at Surrey to sign full-time professional contract. Attended University of Port Elizabeth International Cricket Academy 2002-03
Best batting: 58* Surrey v Essex, Colchester 2006
Best bowling: 5-76 Surrey v Lancashire, Old Trafford 2007

2007 Season

	M	Inn	NO	Runs	HS	Avg	100	50	Ct	St	Balls	Runs	Wkts	Avg	BB	5I	10M
Test																	
FC	8	9	3	74	19	12.33	-	-	1	-	936	649	15	43.26	5-76	1	-
ODI																	
List A	5	2	0	5	5	2.50	-	-	-	-	210	178	4	44.50	2-35	-	
20/20 Int																	
20/20	2	1	0	0	0	0.00	-	-	-	-	30	44	1	44.00	1-28	-	

Career Performances

	M	Inn	NO	Runs	HS	Avg	100	50	Ct	St	Balls	Runs	Wkts	Avg	BB	5I	10M
Test																	
FC	18	23	4	272	58 *	14.31	-	1	5	-	2159	1578	31	50.90	5-76	1	-
ODI																	
List A	20	9	4	53	22	10.60	-	-	2	-	795	788	18	43.77	4-43	-	
20/20 Int																	
20/20	2	1	0	0	0	0.00	-	-	-	-	30	44	1	44.00	1-28	-	

SALES, D. J. G. Northamptonshire

Name: David John Grimwood Sales
Role: Right-hand bat, right-arm medium bowler
Born: 3 December 1977, Carshalton, Surrey
Height: 6ft **Weight:** 14st 7lbs
Nickname: Jumble
County debut: 1994 (one-day), 1996 (first-class)
County cap: 1999
Benefit: 2007
1000 runs in a season: 5
1st-Class 200s: 6
1st-Class 300s: 1
Place in batting averages: 22nd av. 55.36 (2006 55th av. 46.88)
Parents: Daphne and John
Wife and date of marriage: Abigail, 22 September 2001
Children: James, 11 February 2003; Benjamin David, 3 March 2005; Charlie Matthew, 20 September 2006
Family links with cricket: Father played club cricket
Education: Caterham Boys' School, Surrey

Qualifications: 7 GCSEs, cricket coach
Overseas tours: England U15 to South Africa 1993; England U19 to West Indies 1994-95, to Zimbabwe 1995-96, to Pakistan 1996-97; England A to Kenya and Sri Lanka 1997-98, to Bangladesh and New Zealand 1999-2000, to West Indies 2000-01; Northamptonshire to Grenada 2000
Overseas teams played for: Wellington Firebirds, New Zealand 2001-02
Career highlights to date: '303 not out v Essex [1999]; 104 v Pakistan 2003'
Cricket moments to forget: 'Watching White and Powell for five hours, then getting 0' (*Rob White and Mark Powell shared in a new record Northamptonshire opening partnership of 375 v Gloucestershire at Northampton 2002*)
Cricket superstitions: 'None'
Cricketers particularly admired: Graham Gooch, Steve Waugh
Young players to look out for: Alex Wakely, Graeme White
Other sports followed: Rugby (Northampton Saints), football (Crystal Palace), golf
Favourite band: Coldplay
Relaxations: Fishing and golf
Extras: Sir John Hobbs Silver Jubilee Memorial Prize 1993. Scored 56-ball 70* v Essex at Chelmsford in the Sunday League 1994, aged 16 years 289 days. Scored 210* on Championship debut v Worcs at Kidderminster 1996, aged 18 years 237 days. Became the youngest Englishman to score a first-class triple century (303*) v Essex at Northampton 1999, aged 21 years 240 days. PCA/CGU Young Player of the Year 1999. Man of the Match for Wellington v Canterbury in the final of New Zealand's State Shield at Wellington 2001-02 (62). Captain of Northamptonshire 2004-07
Best batting: 303* Northamptonshire v Essex, Northampton 1999
Best bowling: 4-25 Northamptonshire v Sri Lanka A, Northampton 1999

2007 Season

	M	Inn	NO	Runs	HS	Avg	100	50	Ct	St	Balls	Runs	Wkts	Avg	BB	5I	10M
Test																	
FC	16	29	4	1384	219	55.36	3	7	23	-	6	3	0		-	-	-
ODI																	
List A	14	14	3	755	116 *	68.63	1	8	9	-	0	0	0		-	-	
20/20 Int																	
20/20	7	5	2	144	61 *	48.00	-	2	2	-	0	0	0		-	-	

Career Performances

	M	Inn	NO	Runs	HS	Avg	100	50	Ct	St	Balls	Runs	Wkts	Avg	BB	5I	10M
Test																	
FC	171	272	24	10321	303 *	41.61	20	53	153	-	339	174	9	19.33	4-25	-	-
ODI																	
List A	217	205	28	6020	161	34.01	4	41	100	-	84	67	0		-	-	
20/20 Int																	
20/20	33	31	8	821	78 *	35.69	-	8	18	-	12	23	1	23.00	1-10	-	

SALISBURY, I. D. K. Warwickshire

Name: Ian David Kenneth Salisbury
Role: Right-hand bat, leg-break bowler
Born: 21 January 1970, Moulton, Northampton
Height: 5ft 11in **Weight:** 12st 7lbs
Nickname: Solly, Dingle, Sals
County debut: 1989 (Sussex), 1997 (Surrey)
County cap: 1991 (Sussex), 1998 (Surrey)
Benefit: 2007 (Surrey)
Test debut: 1992
ODI debut: 1992-93
50 wickets in a season: 7
Place in batting averages: 219th av. 19.33 (2006 183rd av. 24.20)
Place in bowling averages: 147th av. 67.72 (2006 30th av. 27.93)
Parents: Dave and Margaret
Wife and date of marriage: Emma Louise, 25 September 1993
Children: Anya-Rose, 10 August 2002
Family links with cricket: 'Dad is vice-president of my first club, Brixworth. He also re-lays cricket squares (e.g. Lord's, Northampton, Leicester)'
Education: Moulton Comprehensive, Northampton
Qualifications: 7 O-levels, NCA coaching certificate
Overseas tours: England A to Pakistan 1990-91, to Bermuda and West Indies 1991-92, to India 1994-95, to Pakistan 1995-96; England to India and Sri Lanka 1992-93, to West Indies 1993-94, to Pakistan 2000-01; World Masters XI v Indian Masters XI November 1996 ('Masters aged 26?')
Overseas teams played for: University of New South Wales, Sydney 1997-2000
Cricketers particularly admired: 'Any that keep performing day in, day out, for both country and county'
Other sports played: 'Most sports'
Other sports followed: Football (Southampton FC, Northampton Town FC), rugby union (Northampton Saints), 'any England team'
Relaxations: 'Spending time with wife Emma; meeting friends and relaxing with them and eating out with good wine'
Extras: In 1992 was named Young Player of the Year by both the Wombwell Cricket Lovers and the Cricket Writers. One of *Wisden*'s Five Cricketers of the Year 1993. Won Bill O'Reilly Medal for Sydney first-grade player of the year 1999-2000. Took 800th first-class wicket (Tim Phillips) v Essex at Croydon 2006. Left Surrey at the end of the 2007 season and has joined Warwickshire for 2008

Best batting: 103 Surrey v Hampshire, The Oval 2007
Best bowling: 8-60 Surrey v Somerset, The Oval 2000

2007 Season

	M	Inn	NO	Runs	HS	Avg	100	50	Ct	St	Balls	Runs	Wkts	Avg	BB	5I	10M
Test																	
FC	6	9	0	174	103	19.33	1	-	4	-	1133	745	11	67.72	4-121	-	-
ODI																	
List A																	
20/20 Int																	
20/20																	

Career Performances

	M	Inn	NO	Runs	HS	Avg	100	50	Ct	St	Balls	Runs	Wkts	Avg	BB	5I	10M
Test	15	25	3	368	50	16.72	-	1	5	-	2492	1539	20	76.95	4-163	-	-
FC	311	400	79	6619	103	20.61	3	23	199	-	54734	28000	853	32.82	8-60	35	6
ODI	4	2	1	7	5	7.00	-	-	1	-	186	177	5	35.40	3-41	-	
List A	249	162	46	1569	59 *	13.52	-	1	89	-	10574	8102	247	32.80	5-30	1	
20/20 Int																	
20/20	22	14	3	94	20	8.54	-	-	7	-	286	361	12	30.08	2-6	-	

SANDERSON, B. W. — Yorkshire

Name: Ben William Sanderson
Role: Right-hand bat, right-arm medium-fast bowler
Born: 3 January 1989, Sheffield
Height: 6ft **Weight:** 13st
Nickname: Sando
County debut: No first-team appearance
Parents: Roy and Lynne
Marital status: Single
Family links with cricket: 'Dad plays for Whitley Hall CC'
Education: Ecclesfield; Sheffield College
Qualifications: Plumber (trade)
Off-season: 'Working'
Career highlights to date: 'Playing for Yorkshire 2nd XI. Winning U17 County Championship two years running'
Cricket moments to forget: 'Getting out on a hat-trick ball'
Cricketers particularly admired: Glenn McGrath, Darren Gough

Young players to look out for: Oliver Hannon-Dalby
Other sports played: Football (Hallam U19)
Other sports followed: Football (Sheffield Wednesday)
Injuries: Out for one month with an ankle injury
Favourite band: Milburn
Relaxations: 'Watching films'
Extras: Yorkshire Academy
Opinions on cricket: 'Glad to see the game moving forward and gaining interest with the public supporters.'

SANGAKKARA, K. C. — Warwickshire

Name: Kumar Chokshanada Sangakkara
Role: Left-hand bat, wicket-keeper, occasional off-break bowler
Born: 27 October 1977, Matale, Sri Lanka
County debut: 2007
Test debut: 2000
ODI debut: 2000
Twenty20 Int debut: 2006
1st-Class 200s: 6
Place in batting averages: 33rd av. 49.60
Overseas tours: Sri Lanka A to South Africa 1999-2000; Sri Lanka to Kenya (ICC Knockout Trophy) 2000-01, to South Africa 2000-01, to England 2002, to South Africa 2002-03, to Africa (World Cup) 2002-03, to West Indies 2003, to Zimbabwe 2004, to Australia 2004, to England (ICC Champions Trophy) 2004, to Pakistan 2004-05, to New Zealand 2004-05, to India 2005-06, to Bangladesh 2005-06, to England 2006, to India (ICC Champions Trophy) 2006-07, to New Zealand 2006-07, to West Indies (World Cup) 2006-07, to South Africa (World 20/20) 2007-08, to Australia 2007-08, plus other one-day series and tournaments in Sharjah, New Zealand, Morocco, Australia, Netherlands and India; Asian Cricket Council XI to Australia (Tsunami Relief) 2004-05, to South Africa (Afro-Asia Cup) 2005-06; FICA World XI to New Zealand 2004-05; ICC World XI to Australia (Super Series) 2005-06
Overseas teams played for: Nondescripts CC, Colombo; Kandurata
Extras: Represented Sri Lanka U19. Scored 287 in the first Test v South Africa at Colombo 2006, in the process sharing with Mahela Jayawardene (374) in a record partnership for any wicket in first-class cricket history (624). His numerous awards include Man of the [ODI] Series v South Africa 2004 and v Bangladesh 2005-06. Was an overseas player with Warwickshire 2007

Best batting: 287 Sri Lanka v South Africa, Colombo (SSC) 2006
Best bowling: 1-13 Sri Lankans v Zimbabwe A, Harare (T) 2003-04
Stop press: Man of the Match in the first Test v England at Kandy 2007-08 (92/152)

2007 Season

	M	Inn	NO	Runs	HS	Avg	100	50	Ct	St	Balls	Runs	Wkts	Avg	BB	5I	10M
Test																	
FC	7	11	1	496	149	49.60	2	2	4	-	0	0	0		-	-	-
ODI																	
List A	11	10	0	349	115	34.90	1	1	3	-	0	0	0		-	-	
20/20 Int																	
20/20																	

Career Performances

	M	Inn	NO	Runs	HS	Avg	100	50	Ct	St	Balls	Runs	Wkts	Avg	BB	5I	10M
Test	67	110	9	5492	287	54.37	14	22	147	20	6	4	0		-	-	-
FC	150	237	19	9417	287	43.19	20	46	302	33	132	74	1	74.00	1-13	-	-
ODI	203	187	23	5866	138 *	35.76	6	40	184	51	0	0	0		-	-	
List A	267	247	30	8260	156 *	38.06	9	56	242	69	0	0	0		-	-	
20/20 Int	8	7	0	138	30	19.71	-	-	3	3	0	0	0		-	-	
20/20	11	10	0	309	93	30.90	-	1	6	3	0	0	0		-	-	

SAQLAIN MUSHTAQ — Surrey

Name: Saqlain Mushtaq
Role: Right-hand bat, off-spin bowler
Born: 29 December 1976, Lahore, Pakistan
Height: 5ft 9in
Nickname: Saqi, Baba
County debut: 1997 (Surrey), 2007 (Sussex)
County cap: 1998 (Surrey)
Test debut: 1995-96
ODI debut: 1995-96
50 wickets in a season: 5
Place in bowling averages: 3rd av. 17.55
Parents: Nasim Akhtar and Mushtaq Ahmed
Wife and date of marriage: Sana ('Sunny') Saqlain, 11 April 2000
Education: Lahore MAO College
Overseas tours: Pakistan U19 to New Zealand 1994-95; Pakistan to Australia 1995-96, to England 1996, to Australia 1996-97, to Sri Lanka 1996-97, to India 1996-97, to South Africa and Zimbabwe 1997-98, to India

1998-99, to Bangladesh (Wills International Cup) 1998-99, to UK, Ireland and Netherlands (World Cup) 1999, to Australia 1999-2000, to West Indies 1999-2000, to Kenya (ICC Knockout Trophy) 2000-01, to New Zealand 2000-01, to England 2001, to Bangladesh 2001-02, to Sharjah (v West Indies) 2001-02, to Sri Lanka and Sharjah (v Australia) 2002-03, to Zimbabwe and South Africa 2002-03, to Africa (World Cup) 2002-03, plus other one-day tournaments in Sri Lanka, Toronto, Sharjah, Kenya, Bangladesh, Singapore and Morocco

Overseas teams played for: PIA 1994-95 – 2003-04; Islamabad 1994-95 – 1997-98; Lahore 2003-04

Other sports played: Squash

Extras: Scored 79 in the first Test v Zimbabwe at Sheikhupura 1996-97, sharing with Wasim Akram (257*) in a world record eighth-wicket partnership in Tests (313). Took only the second hat-trick in World Cup cricket (Olonga, Huckle and Mbangwa), v Zimbabwe at The Oval 1999; it was his second hat-trick in ODIs v Zimbabwe. Topped the English first-class bowling averages in 1999, taking 58 wickets at 11.37 in seven games. One of *Wisden*'s Five Cricketers of the Year 2000. His series and match awards include Man of the [Test] Series v India 1998-99 (including 5-94/5-93 in Pakistan's victory in the first Test in Chennai) and v Zimbabwe 2002-03. Holds record for taking fewest matches to reach 100 ODI wickets (53 matches), 150 (78), 200 (104) and 250 (138), and also for the most ODI wickets in a calendar year (69 in 1997). An overseas player with Surrey 1997-2004 and in August-September 2005. Played for Ireland in the C&G 2006. Joined Sussex for 2007; left Sussex at the end of the 2007 season and has rejoined Surrey for 2008. Is England-qualified

Best batting: 101* Pakistan v New Zealand, Christchurch 2000-01

Best bowling: 8-65 Surrey v Derbyshire, The Oval 1998

2007 Season

	M	Inn	NO	Runs	HS	Avg	100	50	Ct	St	Balls	Runs	Wkts	Avg	BB	5I	10M
Test																	
FC	4	5	1	90	57 *	22.50	-	1	1	-	710	316	18	17.55	5-96	1	-
ODI																	
List A	4	2	1	15	10 *	15.00	-	-	1	-	144	126	3	42.00	1-36	-	
20/20 Int																	
20/20	4	1	0	5	5	5.00	-	-	1	-	96	114	4	28.50	2-22	-	

Career Performances

	M	Inn	NO	Runs	HS	Avg	100	50	Ct	St	Balls	Runs	Wkts	Avg	BB	5I	10M
Test	49	78	14	927	101 *	14.48	1	2	15	-	14070	6206	208	29.83	8-164	13	3
FC	180	247	55	3201	101 *	16.67	1	13	65	-	42254	18342	793	23.12	8-65	57	15
ODI	169	98	38	711	37 *	11.85	-	-	40	-	8770	6275	288	21.78	5-20	6	
List A	322	181	67	1335	38 *	11.71	-	-	80	-	16002	11198	477	23.47	5-20	7	
20/20 Int																	
20/20	7	3	0	10	5	3.33	-	-	2	-	162	201	8	25.12	2-22	-	

SAYERS, J. J. Yorkshire

Name: Joseph (Joe) John Sayers
Role: Left-hand bat, right-arm off-spin bowler
Born: 5 November 1983, Leeds
Height: 6ft **Weight:** 13st
Nickname: Squirrel
County debut: 2003 (one-day), 2004 (first-class)
County cap: 2007
Place in batting averages: 110th av. 33.89 (2006 121st av. 32.77)
Parents: Geraldine and Roger
Marital status: Single
Family links with cricket: 'Father played at school, but otherwise none'
Education: St Mary's RC Comprehensive School, Menston; Worcester College, Oxford University
Qualifications: 12 GCSEs, 4 A-levels, BA Physics (Oxon)
Off-season: 'I intend to tour Antigua and Barbados with London CCC before beginning off-season training with the Yorkshire squad at Headingley'
Overseas tours: Leeds Schools to South Africa 1998; Yorkshire U17 to South Africa 2001; England U17 to Australia 2001
Overseas teams played for: Manly-Warringah, Sydney 2004-05
Career highlights to date: 'Receiving my county cap for Yorkshire'
Cricket superstitions: 'None'
Cricketers particularly admired: Steve Waugh
Young players to look out for: Billy Godleman
Other sports played: Football ('played as goalkeeper for Bradford City AFC for three years'), rowing (Worcester College)
Other sports followed: Rugby league (Leeds Rhinos), rugby union (Leeds Tykes), football
Favourite band: Coldplay
Relaxations: 'Drawing, painting, writing, watching movies'
Extras: Captained England U17 v Australia U17 at Adelaide 2001. Played for Oxford UCCE 2002, 2003, 2004 (captain 2003). Oxford Blue 2002, 2003, 2004. Represented England U19 2002, 2003 (captain in the third 'Test' 2003). Wrote weekly column 'View from the Balcony' for *Yorkshire Post* during the 2006 season. Carried bat for 122* v Middlesex at Scarborough 2006; carried bat again for a 553-minute 149* v Durham at Headingley 2007 and was on the field of play for the entire game

Opinions on cricket: 'The domestic game in England is in good condition with competitive cricket played throughout the season.'
Best batting: 187 Yorkshire v Kent, Tunbridge Wells 2007

2007 Season

	M	Inn	NO	Runs	HS	Avg	100	50	Ct	St	Balls	Runs	Wkts	Avg	BB	5I	10M
Test																	
FC	14	22	3	644	187	33.89	3	1	5	-	0	0	0		-	-	-
ODI																	
List A	1	1	0	17	17	17.00	-	-	-	-	0	0	0		-	-	
20/20 Int																	
20/20																	

Career Performances

	M	Inn	NO	Runs	HS	Avg	100	50	Ct	St	Balls	Runs	Wkts	Avg	BB	5I	10M
Test																	
FC	53	87	8	2739	187	34.67	8	12	26	-	72	54	0		-	-	-
ODI																	
List A	13	13	2	249	62	22.63	-	2	-	-	54	71	1	71.00	1-31	-	
20/20 Int																	
20/20	3	1	0	12	12	12.00	-	-	2	-	0	0	0		-	-	

SCHOFIELD, C. P. — Surrey

Name: Christopher (Chris) Paul Schofield
Role: Left-hand bat, right-arm leg-spin bowler; all-rounder
Born: 6 October 1978, Rochdale
Height: 6ft 2in **Weight:** 12st
Nickname: Schoey
County debut: 1998 (Lancashire), 2006 (Surrey)
County cap: 2002 (Lancashire)
Test debut: 2000
Twenty20 Int debut: 2007-08
Place in batting averages: 248th av. 14.33
Place in bowling averages: 117th av. 40.62
Parents: David and Judith
Marital status: Single
Family links with cricket: Father played with local club team Whittles and brother with local team Littleborough
Education: Wardle High School, Rochdale

Qualifications: 4 GCSEs, NVQ Levels 2 and 3 in Information Technology
Overseas tours: England U17 to Bermuda 1997; England U19 to South Africa (including U19 World Cup) 1997-98; England A to Bangladesh and New Zealand 1999-2000, to West Indies 2000-01; ECB National Academy to Australia 2001-02; England to South Africa (World 20/20) 2007-08; England Performance Programme to India 2007-08
Career highlights to date: 'Two Tests and four Twenty20 games for England'
Cricketers particularly admired: Shane Warne
Young players to look out for: Chris Jordan
Other sports played: Football, golf, snooker ('highest break 124')
Other sports followed: Football (Liverpool FC)
Favourite band: Matchbox Twenty
Relaxations: Listening to music, playing snooker, socialising
Extras: Was part of England U19 World Cup winning squad 1997-98. Won double twice in two years with Littleborough CC (Wood Cup and Lancashire Cup 1997; League and Wood Cup 1998). Won Sir Ron Brierley/Crusaders Scholarship 1998. NBC Denis Compton Award for the most promising young Lancashire player 1998, 1999, 2000. Leading first-class wicket-taker on England A tour to West Indies 2000-01 (22 wickets; av. 26.27). Represented England Lions 2007
Best batting: 99 Lancashire v Warwickshire, Old Trafford 2004
Best bowling: 6-120 England A v Bangladesh, Chittagong 1999-2000

2007 Season

	M	Inn	NO	Runs	HS	Avg	100	50	Ct	St	Balls	Runs	Wkts	Avg	BB	5I	10M
Test																	
FC	6	7	1	86	28	14.33	-	-	3	-	1121	650	16	40.62	5-52	1	-
ODI																	
List A	14	12	3	247	75 *	27.44	-	2	5	-	480	461	17	27.11	4-32	-	
20/20 Int																	
20/20	8	2	1	7	4	7.00	-	-	2	-	150	150	17	8.82	4-12	-	

Career Performances

	M	Inn	NO	Runs	HS	Avg	100	50	Ct	St	Balls	Runs	Wkts	Avg	BB	5I	10M
Test	2	3	0	67	57	22.33	-	1	-	-	108	73	0		-	-	-
FC	76	105	15	2623	99	29.14	-	21	45	-	12177	6293	195	32.27	6-120	5	-
ODI																	
List A	107	78	20	1325	75 *	22.84	-	5	29	-	3138	2721	105	25.91	5-31	1	
20/20 Int	4	4	3	24	9 *	24.00	-	-	1	-	77	92	4	23.00	2-15	-	
20/20	23	15	6	115	27	12.77	-	-	5	-	281	291	25	11.64	4-12	-	

SCOTT, B. J. M. Middlesex

Name: Benjamin (Ben) James Matthew Scott
Role: Right-hand bat, wicket-keeper
Born: 4 August 1981, Isleworth
Height: 'Small' (5ft 9in) **Weight:** 11st 7lbs
Nickname: Scotty
County debut: 2002 (one-day, Surrey), 2003 (first-class, Surrey), 2004 (Middlesex)
County cap: 2007 (Middlesex)
50 dismissals in a season: 1
Place in batting averages: 101st av. 35.36 (2006 216th av. 19.07)
Parents: Terry and Edna
Marital status: Single
Family links with cricket: Father played for the Primitives; brother played local cricket. Nephew Joel Pope is with Leicestershire
Education: Whitton School, Richmond; Richmond College
Qualifications: 9 GCSEs, 3 A-levels studied, ECB Level 1 coach, YMCA Fitness Instructor's Award
Overseas tours: MCC YC to Cape Town 1999-2000; Middlesex to Mumbai, India 2005, 2006
Overseas teams played for: Portland CC, Victoria 1999-2000; Mt Gambia, South Australia 2001-02; South Melbourne CC 2006
Career highlights to date: 'Scoring 101* at Lord's v Northants; just getting there with Nantie Hayward down the other end'
Cricket moments to forget: 'Being the hat-trick for Billy Taylor v Hampshire' (*At The Rose Bowl 2006*)
Cricket superstitions: 'None'
Cricketers particularly admired: Alec Stewart, Jack Russell, Nad Shahid
Young players to look out for: Eoin Morgan, Joel Pope
Other sports played: Golf
Favourite band: Michael Jackson, The Jacksons, Usher
Relaxations: Music, golf, TV
Extras: Middlesex YC cap. Represented ESCA U14 and U15. Played for Development of Excellence XI 1999. Finchley CC Player of the Season 2000
Best batting: 112 Middlesex v Gloucestershire, Bristol 2007

2007 Season

	M	Inn	NO	Runs	HS	Avg	100	50	Ct	St	Balls	Runs	Wkts	Avg	BB	5I	10M
Test																	
FC	11	14	3	389	112	35.36	1	2	23	5	0	0	0		-	-	-
ODI																	
List A	9	5	3	84	54 *	42.00	-	1	9	4	0	0	0		-	-	
20/20 Int																	
20/20	6	4	2	12	5	6.00	-	-	1	6	0	0	0		-	-	

Career Performances

	M	Inn	NO	Runs	HS	Avg	100	50	Ct	St	Balls	Runs	Wkts	Avg	BB	5I	10M
Test																	
FC	45	68	15	1394	112	26.30	2	6	109	16	0	0	0		-	-	-
ODI																	
List A	65	35	12	484	73 *	21.04	-	3	57	20	0	0	0		-	-	
20/20 Int																	
20/20	27	19	10	150	32 *	16.66	-	-	9	12	0	0	0		-	-	

SCOTT, G. M. — Durham

Name: Gary Michael Scott
Role: Right-hand bat, right-arm off-spin bowler; all-rounder
Born: 21 July 1984, Sunderland
Height: 6ft **Weight:** 14st
Nickname: Scotty
County debut: 2001
Place in batting averages: (2006 141st av. 30.61)
Parents: Mary and Michael
Marital status: Single
Children: Megan Mary
Family links with cricket: 'Brother played county U12-15 for Durham'
Education: Hetton Comprehensive
Qualifications: 7 GCSEs
Career outside cricket: 'Golfer'
Off-season: 'Passing driving test and working hard on my game'
Overseas tours: England U17 to Australia 2000-01; Durham to Sharjah and Dubai 2005, to India and Sharjah 2006; Durham Development Team to India 2005
Overseas teams played for: Northern Districts, Adelaide

Career highlights to date: 'Making debut and double promotion 2005'
Cricket moments to forget: 'Dropping catch on TV v Glamorgan capped off a bad game'
Cricketers particularly admired: Mike Hussey, Ottis Gibson, Dale Benkenstein
Young players to look out for: Scott Borthwick, Mark Stoneman
Other sports played: Football (represented Sunderland Schools as a goalkeeper)
Other sports followed: Football (Newcastle Utd)
Injuries: Out for eight weeks of the 2007 season with a stress fracture of the back; for four weeks with a groin injury
Favourite band: Luther Vandross
Relaxations: 'Chilling'
Extras: Sir John Hobbs Silver Jubilee Memorial Prize 1999. C&G Man of the Match award (for Durham Board XI) for his 100 v Herefordshire at Darlington in the 2003 competition. Became youngest person to play first-class cricket for Durham, v Derbyshire at Riverside 2001 aged 17 years and 19 days
Opinions on cricket: 'It's a great game!'
Best batting: 133 Durham v OUCCE, The Parks 2006
Best bowling: 2-39 Durham v Warwickshire, Riverside 2006

2007 Season (did not make any first-class or one-day appearances)

Career Performances

	M	Inn	NO	Runs	HS	Avg	100	50	Ct	St	Balls	Runs	Wkts	Avg	BB	5I	10M
Test																	
FC	17	33	2	891	133	28.74	1	4	10	-	343	296	3	98.66	2-39	-	-
ODI																	
List A	14	13	2	424	100	38.54	1	2	4	-	242	172	7	24.57	2-24	-	
20/20 Int																	
20/20	15	13	2	129	31	11.72	-	-	8	-	96	157	8	19.62	3-27	-	

78. Which former Gloucestershire coach reached both 1000 runs and 100 wickets in Tests in the third Test between England and New Zealand at Edgbaston in 1990?

SHAFAYAT, B. M. Nottinghamshire

Name: Bilal Mustafa Shafayat
Role: Right-hand bat, right-arm medium-fast bowler, occasional wicket-keeper
Born: 10 July 1984, Nottingham
Height: 5ft 7in **Weight:** 10st 7lbs
Nickname: Billy, Muzzy, Our Kid
County debut: 2001 (Nottinghamshire), 2005 (Northamptonshire)
1000 runs in a season: 1
Place in batting averages: 138th av. 31.11 (2006 130th av. 31.67)
Parents: Mohammad Shafayat and Mahfooza Begum
Marital status: Single
Family links with cricket: 'Brother Rashid played for Notts up to 2nd XI and is now playing in Staffordshire Premier (took ten wickets in a game 2003). Uncle Nadeem played for PCC. Father just loves it!'
Education: Greenwood Dale; Nottingham Bluecoat School and Sixth Form College
Qualifications: 9 GCSEs, 2 A-levels, Level 1 coaching
Overseas tours: ZRK to Pakistan 2000; Sparkhill ('Kadeer Ali's dad's academy') to Pakistan; England U17 to Australia 2000-01; England U19 to Australia and (U19 World Cup) New Zealand 2001-02, to Australia 2002-03 (c); Nottinghamshire to South Africa 2002, 2003; England A to Malaysia and India 2003-04
Overseas teams played for: National Bank of Pakistan 2004-05
Career highlights to date: 'Making my first-class debut for Notts v Middlesex (scoring 72). Scoring a hundred and double hundred v India in final U19 "Test" 2002. Scoring crucial hundred v Worcestershire for promotion in Championship. Beating Australia U19 in first "Test" 2002-03, scoring 66, 108 and taking six wickets'
Cricket moments to forget: 'Losing U19 "Test" series to Australia'
Cricketers particularly admired: Sachin Tendulkar, Carl Hooper, Andrew Jackman
Other sports played: Football, badminton, squash, pool
Other sports followed: Football (Liverpool), boxing, snooker
Favourite band: Sean Paul, 50 Cent, Tupac, Nusrat Fateh Ali Khan
Relaxations: 'Praying Namaz; chilling with loved ones'
Extras: Scored 72 on Championship debut v Middlesex at Trent Bridge 2001, aged 16 years 360 days. NBC Denis Compton Award for the most promising young Nottinghamshire player 2001, 2002. Scored record-equalling four 'Test' centuries for England U19. BBC East Midlands Junior Sportsman of the Year 2003. ECB National Academy 2003-04. Left Northamptonshire at the end of the 2006 season and rejoined Nottinghamshire for 2007

Best batting: 161 Northamptonshire v Derbyshire, Derby 2005
Best bowling: 2-25 Northamptonshire v Pakistanis, Northampton 2006

2007 Season

	M	Inn	NO	Runs	HS	Avg	100	50	Ct	St	Balls	Runs	Wkts	Avg	BB	5I	10M
Test																	
FC	12	19	1	560	79	31.11	-	4	15	1	155	100	1	100.00	1-24	-	-
ODI																	
List A	10	10	1	260	104	28.88	1	-	1	-	72	70	4	17.50	2-28	-	
20/20 Int																	
20/20	6	3	0	53	31	17.66	-	-	1	-	30	41	1	41.00	1-23	-	

Career Performances

	M	Inn	NO	Runs	HS	Avg	100	50	Ct	St	Balls	Runs	Wkts	Avg	BB	5I	10M
Test																	
FC	73	125	4	3837	161	31.71	6	22	66	5	626	439	4	109.75	2-25	-	-
ODI																	
List A	88	82	6	1726	104	22.71	1	6	30	2	790	730	24	30.41	4-33	-	
20/20 Int																	
20/20	29	22	2	325	40	16.25	-	-	6	1	120	191	4	47.75	2-13	-	

79. Which Lancashire fast bowler played his final Test (of 70) against South Africa at The Oval in 1965?

SHAH, O. A. Middlesex

Name: Owais Alam Shah
Role: Right-hand bat, off-spin bowler
Born: 22 October 1978, Karachi, Pakistan
Height: 6ft 1in **Weight:** 13st 7lbs
Nickname: Ace, The Mauler
County debut: 1995 (one-day), 1996 (first-class)
County cap: 1999
Benefit: 2008
Test debut: 2005-06
ODI debut: 2001
Twenty20 Int debut: 2007
1000 runs in a season: 7
1st-Class 200s: 1
Place in batting averages: 6th av. 70.93 (2006 96th av. 35.96)
Parents: Jamshed and Mehjabeen
Wife and date of marriage: Gemma, 25 September 2004
Family links with cricket: Father played for his college side
Education: Isleworth and Syon School; Lampton School, Hounslow; Westminster University, Harrow
Qualifications: 7 GCSEs, 2 A-levels
Overseas tours: England U19 to Zimbabwe 1995-96, to South Africa (including U19 World Cup) 1997-98 (c); England A to Australia 1996-97, to Kenya and Sri Lanka 1997-98, to Sri Lanka 2004-05, to West Indies 2005-06; ECB National Academy to Australia 2001-02; England to Zimbabwe (one-day series) 2001-02, to India and New Zealand 2001-02 (one-day series), to Sri Lanka (ICC Champions Trophy) 2002-03, to Australia 2002-03 (VB Series), to India 2005-06, to South Africa (World 20/20) 2007-08, to Sri Lanka 2007-08, to New Zealand 2007-08
Overseas teams played for: University of Western Australia, Perth
Career highlights to date: '[Debut] Test match against India in Mumbai'
Cricket moments to forget: 'Getting a pair in first-class cricket'
Cricketers particularly admired: Viv Richards, Sachin Tendulkar, Mark Waugh
Young players to look out for: Graham Onions, Nick Compton, Eoin Morgan
Other sports played: Snooker
Other sports followed: Football ('like to watch Man Utd play')
Favourite band: 'Too many to mention'
Relaxations: 'Movies, eating out'
Extras: Man of the U17 'Test' series v India 1994. Captained England U19 to success in the 1997-98 U19 World Cup in South Africa, scoring 54* in the final; captain of

England U19 v Pakistan U19 1998. Cricket Writers' Young Player of the Year 2001. Middlesex Player of the Year 2002. Vice-captain of Middlesex 2002 to June 2004. Leading run-scorer in English first-class cricket 2005 (1728 runs; av. 66.46). Made Test debut in the third Test v India at Mumbai 2005-06, scoring 88. Man of the Match in the second Twenty20 Int v West Indies at The Oval 2007 (55*). ECB National Academy 2004-05, 2005-06, 2006-07
Best batting: 203 Middlesex v Derbyshire, Southgate 2001
Best bowling: 3-33 Middlesex v Gloucestershire, Bristol 1999
Stop press: Man of the Match in the second ODI v Sri Lanka in Dambulla 2007-08 (82)

2007 Season

	M	Inn	NO	Runs	HS	Avg	100	50	Ct	St	Balls	Runs	Wkts	Avg	BB	5I	10M
Test	1	2	0	10	6	5.00	-	-	-	-	0	0	0		-	-	-
FC	13	22	6	1135	193	70.93	4	2	10	-	181	137	0		-	-	-
ODI	8	7	1	287	107 *	47.83	1	1	-	-	24	19	1	19.00	1-19	-	
List A	22	21	2	786	107 *	41.36	1	6	3	-	258	238	5	47.60	2-55	-	
20/20 Int	2	2	1	62	55 *	62.00	-	1	-	-	0	0	0		-	-	
20/20	3	3	1	64	55 *	32.00	-	1	-	-	0	0	0		-	-	

Career Performances

	M	Inn	NO	Runs	HS	Avg	100	50	Ct	St	Balls	Runs	Wkts	Avg	BB	5I	10M
Test	2	4	0	136	88	34.00	-	1	1	-	0	0	0		-	-	-
FC	181	306	29	11913	203	43.00	32	60	139	-	1814	1235	21	58.80	3-33	-	-
ODI	26	25	3	581	107 *	26.40	1	3	6	-	24	19	1	19.00	1-19	-	
List A	245	232	29	6781	134	33.40	11	40	82	-	633	611	16	38.18	2-2	-	
20/20 Int	7	7	1	165	55 *	27.50	-	1	-	-	0	0	0		-	-	
20/20	31	31	6	803	79	32.12	-	6	6	-	13	11	1	11.00	1-10	-	

80. Who scored 126 and 94* as England swept to victory over South Africa by seven wickets in the first Test at Port Elizabeth in 2004-05?

SHAHZAD, A. Yorkshire

Name: Ajmal Shahzad
Role: Right-hand bat, right-arm fast bowler; all-rounder
Born: 27 July 1985, Bradford
Height: 6ft **Weight:** 13st 8lbs
Nickname: The Dark Destroyer, AJ
County debut: 2004 (one-day), 2006 (first-class)
Parents: Parveen and Mohammed
Marital status: Single
Family links with cricket: 'Father played in Bradford League'
Education: Bradford Grammar School, Woodhouse Grove School; Leeds Metropolitan University
Qualifications: 9 GCSEs, 4 A-levels
Overseas tours: Schools tours to Scotland and Grenada; England U18 to Netherlands 2003
Career highlights to date: 'Making my debut for Yorkshire and being the first British-born Asian to play for YCCC'
Cricket moments to forget: 'Playing against Ireland in Holland – enough said. Also ripping my side (getting a side strain) in Twenty20 quarter-final in Essex'
Cricket superstitions: 'Put right pad on before left'
Cricketers particularly admired: Wasim Akram, Waqar Younis, Craig White, Anthony McGrath
Young players to look out for: Adam Lyth, Moeen Ali
Other sports played: Badminton (Yorkshire U15-U17), rugby (school), squash (school)
Other sports followed: Rugby league (Bradford Bulls)
Favourite band: Danny Bond, DJ Veteran, Jamie Duggan, DJ Leverton
Relaxations: 'Socialising, gym, study and Islam'
Extras: First British-born Asian to play for Yorkshire first team. Man of the Match in first match representing England – century and 3-22
Best batting: 32* Yorkshire v Sussex, Headingley 2007
Best bowling: 4-22 Yorkshire v Sussex, Headingley 2007

2007 Season

	M	Inn	NO	Runs	HS	Avg	100	50	Ct	St	Balls	Runs	Wkts	Avg	BB	5I	10M
Test																	
FC	6	7	3	65	32 *	16.25	-	-	-	-	556	343	9	38.11	4-22	-	-
ODI																	
List A	3	2	1	9	8 *	9.00	-	-	-	-	138	143	6	23.83	5-51	1	
20/20 Int																	
20/20																	

Career Performances

	M	Inn	NO	Runs	HS	Avg	100	50	Ct	St	Balls	Runs	Wkts	Avg	BB	5I	10M
Test																	
FC	7	8	3	67	32 *	13.40	-	-	-	-	628	388	9	43.11	4-22	-	-
ODI																	
List A	7	6	2	27	11 *	6.75	-	-	-	-	312	279	11	25.36	5-51	1	
20/20 Int																	
20/20	1	1	1	2	2 *		-	-	-	-	18	22	2	11.00	2-22	-	

SHANTRY, A. J. — Glamorgan

Name: Adam John Shantry
Role: Left-hand bat, left-arm swing bowler
Born: 13 November 1982, Bristol
Height: 6ft 2in **Weight:** 13st 8lbs
Nickname: Shants
County debut: 2003 (Northamptonshire), 2005 (one-day, Warwickshire), 2006 (first-class, Warwickshire)
Parents: Brian and Josephine
Marital status: Single
Family links with cricket: 'Father Brian played for Gloucestershire. Brother Jack will be better than me'
Education: The Priory School, Shrewsbury; Shrewsbury Sixth Form College
Qualifications: 11 GCSEs, 4 A-levels, Level 2 coaching
Overseas teams played for: Balwyn, Melbourne 2001-02; Subiaco-Floreat, Perth 2004-05 – 2006-07
Career highlights to date: 'Five-fors against New Zealand and West Indies A'

Cricket moments to forget: 'Giving Tino Best a send-off, forgetting that I still had to bat'
Cricket superstitions: 'Try not to bowl up the hill into the wind on a flat one'
Cricketers particularly admired: Brian Shantry, Mike Smith
Young players to look out for: Jack Shantry, Moeen Ali
Other sports played: Football
Other sports followed: Football (Bristol City)
Favourite band: Feeder, Aiden, The Wurzels
Relaxations: 'Fishing, music'
Extras: England U17 squad. Represented ESCA U18 2001. Radio Shropshire Young Player of the Year 2001. Took 3-8 (including spell of three wickets in five balls before conceding a run) on Championship debut v Somerset at Northampton 2003. Took 5-37 v New Zealanders in 50-over match at Northampton 2004, winning Carlsberg Man of the Match award. His 5-15 v Warwickshire 2nd XI at Kenilworth 2004 included four wickets in four balls (bowled, bowled, lbw, bowled). Took 5-49 on first-class debut for Warwickshire v West Indies A at Edgbaston 2006. Took four wickets in his first four overs on Championship debut for Warwickshire v Sussex at Hove 2007 for innings figures of 4-31. Left Warwickshire at the end of the 2007 season and has joined Glamorgan for 2008
Opinions on cricket: 'Good game.'
Best batting: 38* Northamptonshire v Somerset, Northampton 2003
Best bowling: 5-49 Warwickshire v West Indies A, Edgbaston 2006

2007 Season

	M	Inn	NO	Runs	HS	Avg	100	50	Ct	St	Balls	Runs	Wkts	Avg	BB	5I	10M
Test																	
FC	2	3	0	10	5	3.33	-	-	1	-	198	111	4	27.75	4-31	-	-
ODI																	
List A	2	1	1	1	1 *		-	-	1	-	72	61	1	61.00	1-30	-	
20/20 Int																	
20/20																	

Career Performances

	M	Inn	NO	Runs	HS	Avg	100	50	Ct	St	Balls	Runs	Wkts	Avg	BB	5I	10M
Test																	
FC	8	10	5	76	38 *	15.20	-	-	3	-	832	439	21	20.90	5-49	1	-
ODI																	
List A	9	4	1	26	15	8.66	-	-	6	-	294	228	11	20.72	5-37	1	
20/20 Int																	
20/20	1	0	0	0	0		-	-	-	-	12	31	0		-	-	

SHRECK, C. E. Nottinghamshire

Name: Charles (Charlie) Edward Shreck
Role: Right-hand bat, right-arm fast-medium bowler
Born: 6 January 1978, Truro
Height: 6ft 7in **Weight:** 15st 7lbs
Nickname: Shrecker, Ogre, Stoat, Chough
County debut: 2002 (one-day), 2003 (first-class)
County cap: 2006
50 wickets in a season: 1
Place in bowling averages: 45th av. 27.10 (2006 12th av. 24.78)
Parents: Peter and Sheila
Marital status: Single
Family links with cricket: 'Grandfather watched Southampton'
Education: Truro School
Qualifications: Level 1 coaching
Overseas tours: Cornwall U17 to South Africa 1997; England Lions to India 2007-08
Overseas teams played for: Merewether District CC, NSW 1997-98; Hutt District CC, New Zealand 2000-03; Wellington, New Zealand 2005-06
Cricket moments to forget: 'Being run out off the last ball of the game against Shropshire, walking off – we lost!'
Cricket superstitions: 'None'
Cricketers particularly admired: Viv Richards, Michael Holding, Ian Botham
Young players to look out for: Michael Munday, Carl Gazzard
Relaxations: 'Swimming, music'
Extras: C&G Man of the Match award for his 5-19 for Cornwall v Worcestershire at Truro 2002. Took wicket (Vikram Solanki) with his third ball in county cricket v Worcestershire at Trent Bridge in the NUL 2002, going on to record maiden one-day league five-wicket return (5-35). Took four wickets in six balls, including hat-trick (Smith, Morgan, Weekes), v Middlesex at Lord's 2006. Took 61 first-class wickets in 2006 (including 12-129 v Middlesex at Trent Bridge), having missed the entire 2005 season after undergoing back surgery. Nottinghamshire Player of the Year 2006
Best batting: 19 Nottinghamshire v Essex, Chelmsford 2003
Best bowling: 8-31 Nottinghamshire v Middlesex, Trent Bridge 2006
Stop press: Called up to squad for England Lions tour of India 2007-08

2007 Season

	M	Inn	NO	Runs	HS	Avg	100	50	Ct	St	Balls	Runs	Wkts	Avg	BB	5I	10M
Test																	
FC	11	11	8	4	3	1.33	-	-	6	-	2405	1274	47	27.10	7-35	4	-
ODI																	
List A	9	0	0	0	0		-	-	3	-	420	446	11	40.54	2-37	-	
20/20 Int																	
20/20	3	0	0	0	0		-	-	-	-	49	79	1	79.00	1-40	-	

Career Performances

	M	Inn	NO	Runs	HS	Avg	100	50	Ct	St	Balls	Runs	Wkts	Avg	BB	5I	10M
Test																	
FC	45	51	29	82	19	3.72	-	-	14	-	8532	4931	177	27.85	8-31	14	2
ODI																	
List A	30	9	7	28	9 *	14.00	-	-	8	-	1353	1251	42	29.78	5-19	2	
20/20 Int																	
20/20	15	2	2	1	1 *		-	-	3	-	325	411	16	25.68	3-33	-	

SIDEBOTTOM, R. J. — Nottinghamshire

Name: Ryan Jay Sidebottom
Role: Left-hand bat, left-arm fast bowler
Born: 15 January 1978, Huddersfield
Height: 6ft 4in **Weight:** 14st 7lbs
Nickname: Siddy, Sexual, Jazz
County debut: 1997 (Yorkshire), 2004 (Nottinghamshire)
County cap: 2000 (Yorkshire), 2004 (Nottinghamshire)
Test debut: 2001
ODI debut: 2001-02
Twenty20 Int debut: 2007
50 wickets in a season: 2
Place in batting averages: 243rd av. 15.36 (2006 256th av. 13.87)
Place in bowling averages: 65th av. 29.89 (2006 22nd av. 26.14)
Parents: Arnie and Gillian
Marital status: Single
Family links with sport: Father played cricket for Yorkshire and England and football for Manchester United and Huddersfield Town
Education: King James Grammar School, Almondbury

Qualifications: 5 GCSEs
Overseas tours: England U17 to Netherlands 1995; MCC to Bangladesh 1999-2000; England A to West Indies 2000-01; England to Zimbabwe (one-day series) 2001-02, to Sri Lanka 2007-08, to New Zealand 2007-08; ECB National Academy to Australia 2001-02
Overseas teams played for: Ringwood, Melbourne 1998
Cricketers particularly admired: Darren Gough, Chris Silverwood, Glenn McGrath
Young players to look out for: Joe Sayers
Other sports played: Football (once with Sheffield United), 'all sports'
Other sports followed: 'Love rugby league (any team)', football (Man Utd)
Relaxations: 'Music (R&B), films, clubbing, going out with my team-mates'
Extras: NBC Denis Compton Award for the most promising young Yorkshire player 1999, 2000. Took 5-31 (8-65 in match) for England A v Jamaica at Kingston in the Busta Cup 2000-01, winning the Man of the Match award; topped tour first-class bowling averages (16 wickets; av. 16.81). Made Test debut in the first Test v Pakistan at Lord's 2001 (England's 100th Test at the ground), becoming the tenth player to follow his father into the England Test team. Recalled to Test side after six years for the second Test v West Indies at Headingley 2007, returning match figures of 8-86 (4-42/4-44). England 12-month central contract 2007-08
Best batting: 54 Yorkshire v Glamorgan, Cardiff 1998
Best bowling: 7-97 Yorkshire v Derbyshire, Headingley 2003
Stop press: Man of the [ODI] Series v Sri Lanka 2007-08

2007 Season

	M	Inn	NO	Runs	HS	Avg	100	50	Ct	St	Balls	Runs	Wkts	Avg	BB	5I	10M
Test	6	9	5	107	26 *	26.75	-	-	2	-	1362	618	24	25.75	5-88	1	-
FC	13	17	6	169	26 *	15.36	-	-	3	-	2638	1166	39	29.89	5-88	1	-
ODI	1	1	0	15	15	15.00	-	-	1	-	54	56	2	28.00	2-56	-	
List A	6	2	0	21	15	10.50	-	-	1	-	318	248	3	82.66	2-56	-	
20/20 Int	2	0	0	0	0		-	-	1	-	48	67	3	22.33	2-25	-	
20/20	2	0	0	0	0		-	-	1	-	48	67	3	22.33	2-25	-	

Career Performances

	M	Inn	NO	Runs	HS	Avg	100	50	Ct	St	Balls	Runs	Wkts	Avg	BB	5I	10M
Test	7	10	5	111	26 *	22.20	-	-	2	-	1482	682	24	28.41	5-88	1	-
FC	113	143	42	1193	54	11.81	-	1	42	-	18924	8893	348	25.55	7-97	12	1
ODI	3	2	1	17	15	17.00	-	-	1	-	138	140	4	35.00	2-56	-	
List A	140	60	27	362	32	10.96	-	-	31	-	6073	4342	141	30.79	6-40	2	
20/20 Int	2	0	0	0	0		-	-	1	-	48	67	3	22.33	2-25	-	
20/20	17	5	4	23	12 *	23.00	-	-	5	-	361	410	20	20.50	3-20	-	

SILLENCE, R. J. Worcestershire

Name: Roger John Sillence
Role: Right-hand bat, right-arm fast-medium bowler
Born: 29 June 1977, Salisbury, Wiltshire
Height: 6ft 3in **Weight:** 13st 7lbs
Nickname: Sillo
County debut: 2001 (Gloucestershire), 2006 (Worcestershire)
County cap: 2004 (Gloucestershire), 2006 (Worcestershire colours)
Place in batting averages: 227th av. 18.36 (2006 167th av. 27.05)
Place in bowling averages: 146th av. 62.13 (2006 75th av. 34.43)
Parents: Angela
Marital status: Single
Family links with cricket: Father played cricket
Education: Highbury, Salisbury; Salisbury Art College
Qualifications: 7 GCSEs, ND and HND Graphic Design, ECB Level 2 coach
Career outside cricket: Graphic designer
Overseas teams played for: Napier Old Boys, New Zealand 1997-98; St Augustine's, Cape Town 1998-99; East Keilor, Melbourne 2000-01; Hamersley Carine, Perth 2001-02; South Melbourne 2002-03, 2005-06
Career highlights to date: 'Getting five wickets on debut v Sussex at Hove and then getting 100 on home debut v Derby'
Cricket moments to forget: 'Whenever I drop a catch'
Cricket superstitions: 'Always bowl in a short-sleeved shirt'
Cricketers particularly admired: Mike Smith, Jack Russell
Young players to look out for: Steve Davies
Other sports followed: 'Follow football but not really one team, and look out for my mate who plays AFL for St Kilda'
Favourite band: Jamiroquai, Razorlight, Coldplay
Relaxations: 'Enjoy a good coffee with a slice of carrot cake. Other interests such as design, photography, fashion design, music – the normal same old same old'
Extras: Wiltshire Player of the Year 2000. Recorded maiden first-class five-wicket return (5-97) on debut v Sussex at Hove 2001. Scored maiden first-class century (101) v Derbyshire at Bristol 2002 on home debut, batting at No. 9. Released by Worcestershire at the end of the 2007 season
Best batting: 101 Gloucestershire v Derbyshire, Bristol 2002
Best bowling: 7-96 Worcestershire v Somerset, Taunton 2006

2007 Season

	M	Inn	NO	Runs	HS	Avg	100	50	Ct	St	Balls	Runs	Wkts	Avg	BB	5I	10M
Test																	
FC	10	13	2	202	51 *	18.36	-	1	4	-	1409	932	15	62.13	2-48	-	-
ODI																	
List A	12	7	1	41	16 *	6.83	-	-	6	-	399	367	10	36.70	2-27	-	
20/20 Int																	
20/20	7	6	2	59	21 *	14.75	-	-	3	-	114	199	2	99.50	1-27	-	

Career Performances

	M	Inn	NO	Runs	HS	Avg	100	50	Ct	St	Balls	Runs	Wkts	Avg	BB	5I	10M
Test																	
FC	36	50	3	1068	101	22.72	1	5	12	-	4609	2960	72	41.11	7-96	3	-
ODI																	
List A	32	24	6	400	94	22.22	-	2	12	-	895	871	29	30.03	4-35	-	
20/20 Int																	
20/20	15	14	4	153	22 *	15.30	-	-	5	-	271	424	10	42.40	2-27	-	

SILVERWOOD, C. E. W. Middlesex

Name: Christopher (Chris) Eric Wilfred Silverwood
Role: Right-hand bat, right-arm fast bowler
Born: 5 March 1975, Pontefract
Height: 6ft 1in **Weight:** 12st 9lbs
Nickname: Spoons, Silvers, Chubby
County debut: 1993 (Yorkshire), 2006 (Middlesex)
County cap: 1996 (Yorkshire), 2006 (Middlesex)
Benefit: 2004 (Yorkshire)
Test debut: 1996-97
ODI debut: 1996-97
50 wickets in a season: 2
Place in batting averages: 266th av. 12.22 (2006 244th av. 15.05)
Place in bowling averages: 51st av. 28.22 (2006 17th av. 25.25)
Parents: Brenda
Wife and date of marriage: Victoria, 2006
Family links with cricket: 'Dad played a bit'

Education: Garforth Comprehensive
Qualifications: 8 GCSEs, City and Guilds in Leisure and Recreation
Overseas tours: England A to Kenya and Sri Lanka 1997-98, to Bangladesh and New Zealand 1999-2000, to West Indies 2000-01; England to Zimbabwe and New Zealand 1996-97, to West Indies 1997-98, to Bangladesh (Wills International Cup) 1998-99, to South Africa 1999-2000, to Zimbabwe (one-day series) 2001-02, to Australia 2002-03; England VI to Hong Kong 2002, 2003
Overseas teams played for: Wellington, Cape Town 1993-94, 1995-96
Career highlights to date: 'Making Test debut. Winning the Championship [2001]'
Cricketers particularly admired: Ian Botham, Allan Donald
Other sports played: Karate (black belt), rugby league, athletics (represented Yorkshire)
Other sports followed: Rugby league (Castleford)
Extras: Attended Yorkshire Academy. Represented England U19. C&G Man of the Match awards v Northamptonshire at Northampton 2002 (61/2-35) and v Dorset at Dean Park 2004 (4-18). Took 500th first-class wicket (Andrew Gale) against his old county, Yorkshire, at Southgate 2006, finishing with match figures of 8-64
Best batting: 80 Yorkshire v Durham, Riverside 2005
Best bowling: 7-93 Yorkshire v Kent, Headingley 1997

2007 Season

	M	Inn	NO	Runs	HS	Avg	100	50	Ct	St	Balls	Runs	Wkts	Avg	BB	5I	10M
Test																	
FC	11	10	1	110	30	12.22	-	-	2	-	1564	875	31	28.22	6-49	1	-
ODI																	
List A	2	1	0	23	23	23.00	-	-	-	-	84	100	2	50.00	2-54	-	
20/20 Int																	
20/20																	

Career Performances

	M	Inn	NO	Runs	HS	Avg	100	50	Ct	St	Balls	Runs	Wkts	Avg	BB	5I	10M
Test	6	7	3	29	10	7.25	-	-	2	-	828	444	11	40.36	5-91	1	-
FC	175	231	45	2892	80	15.54	-	9	40	-	28719	15234	564	27.01	7-93	25	1
ODI	7	4	0	17	12	4.25	-	-	-	-	306	244	6	40.66	3-43	-	
List A	192	110	37	1002	61	13.72	-	4	29	-	8626	6145	250	24.58	5-28	1	
20/20 Int																	
20/20	14	8	4	44	13 *	11.00	-	-	4	-	306	398	12	33.16	2-22	-	

SINGH, R. P. Leicestershire

Name: Rudra Pratap (RP) Singh
Role: Right-hand bat, left-arm fast-medium bowler
Born: 6 December 1985, Uttar Pradesh, India
County debut: 2007
County cap: 2007
Test debut: 2005-06
ODI debut: 2005-06
Twenty20 Int debut: 2007-08
Place in batting averages: 264th av. 12.37
Place in bowling averages: 66th av. 30.04
Overseas tours: India U19 to Bangladesh (U19 World Cup) 2003-04; India A to Abu Dhabi (Eurasia Cricket Series) 2006, to Australia (Top End Series) 2006; India to Zimbabwe (Videocon Tri-Series) 2005-06, to Pakistan 2005-06, to West Indies 2006 (one-day series), to Malaysia (DLF Cup) 2006-07, to Bangladesh 2007, to Ireland and Scotland (one-day series) 2007, to England 2007, to South Africa (World 20/20) 2007-08, to Australia 2007-08
Overseas teams played for: Uttar Pradesh, India
Extras: Made first-class debut for India A v New Zealand in Rajkot 2003. Man of the Match on Test debut in the second Test v Pakistan in Faisalabad 2005-06 (4-89/1-75). Also Man of the Match in the sixth ODI v Sri Lanka in Rajkot 2005-06 (4-35) and in the fourth ODI v Pakistan in Multan 2005-06 (4-40). Represented India in the ICC Champions Trophy 2006-07. Recorded maiden Test five-wicket innings return (5-59) in the first Test v England at Lord's 2007. Was an overseas player with Leicestershire at the start of the 2007 season before being called up to the India tours of Bangladesh and subsequently England
Best batting: 41* Indians v Sussex, Hove 2007
Best bowling: 5-33 Uttar Pradesh v Maharashtra, Kolhapur 2004-05

2007 Season

	M	Inn	NO	Runs	HS	Avg	100	50	Ct	St	Balls	Runs	Wkts	Avg	BB	5I	10M
Test	3	4	0	30	17	7.50	-	-	2	-	555	347	12	28.91	5-59	1	-
FC	6	9	1	99	41 *	12.37	-	-	4	-	1093	691	23	30.04	5-59	1	-
ODI	5	4	2	13	12 *	6.50	-	-	1	-	252	222	7	31.71	3-55	-	
List A	6	5	2	13	12 *	4.33	-	-	1	-	294	263	8	32.87	3-55	-	
20/20 Int																	
20/20																	

Career Performances

	M	Inn	NO	Runs	HS	Avg	100	50	Ct	St	Balls	Runs	Wkts	Avg	BB	5I	10M
Test	7	7	2	36	17	7.20	-	-	3	-	1305	822	27	30.44	5-59	1	-
FC	32	41	10	279	41 *	9.00	-	-	13	-	5885	3168	127	24.94	5-33	7	1
ODI	30	12	7	39	12 *	7.80	-	-	8	-	1344	1099	37	29.70	4-35	-	
List A	67	33	12	213	35	10.14	-	-	20	-	3020	2482	89	27.88	5-30	2	
20/20 Int	7	1	1	1	1 *		-	-	1	-	144	152	12	12.66	4-13	-	
20/20	10	4	3	8	4 *	8.00	-	-	2	-	216	251	13	19.30	4-13	-	

SMITH, B. F. — Worcestershire

Name: Benjamin (Ben) Francis Smith
Role: Right-hand bat, right-arm medium bowler
Born: 3 April 1972, Corby
Height: 5ft 9in **Weight:** 11st
Nickname: Turnip, Sven
County debut: 1990 (Leicestershire), 2002 (Worcestershire)
County cap: 1995 (Leicestershire), 2002 (Worcestershire colours)
1000 runs in a season: 7
1st-Class 200s: 3
Place in batting averages: 155th av. 27.95 (2006 91st av. 36.60)
Parents: Keith and Janet
Wife and date of marriage: Lisa, 10 October 1998
Children: Ruby, 6 November 2005
Family links with cricket: Father, grandfather and uncles all played club and representative cricket
Education: Kibworth High School; Robert Smyth, Market Harborough
Qualifications: 5 O-levels, 8 GCSEs, NCA coaching certificate

Off-season: 'Time with family; Level IV coaching award; training hard for 2008 season'
Overseas tours: England YC to New Zealand 1990-91; MCC to Bangladesh 1999-2000; 'numerous pre-season tours to South Africa, Caribbean and Sri Lanka'
Overseas teams played for: Alexandria, Zimbabwe 1990; Bankstown-Canterbury, Sydney 1993-96; Central Hawke's Bay CC, New Zealand 1997-98; Central Districts, New Zealand 2000-02
Career highlights to date: 'Winning 1996 County Championship'
Cricket moments to forget: 'Lord's finals'
Cricketers particularly admired: Viv Richards, David Gower, Steve Waugh
Young players to look out for: Steve Davies
Other sports played: Tennis (Leicestershire aged 12), golf, touch rugby
Other sports followed: Rugby union (Leicester Tigers)
Injuries: Out for two weeks with a broken finger
Favourite band: Coldplay
Relaxations: 'Music, DIY, good wine'
Extras: Cricket Society Young Player of the Year 1991. Vice-captain of Leicestershire 2001. Scored century (137) on first-class debut for Worcestershire v OUCCE at The Parks and another (129) on Championship debut for the county v Gloucestershire at Worcester 2002 to become the first player to achieve this 'double' for Worcestershire. Worcestershire Supporters' Player of the Year 2002. Worcestershire Player of the Year 2003. Scored 187 v Gloucestershire at Worcester 2004, in the process sharing with Graeme Hick (262) in the highest first-class partnership ever made at New Road (417). Scored 203 v Somerset at Taunton 2006, in the process sharing with Graeme Hick (182) in a Worcestershire record partnership for the fourth wicket (330). Captain of Worcestershire 2003 until standing down in August 2004
Best batting: 204 Leicestershire v Surrey, The Oval 1998
Best bowling: 1-5 Leicestershire v Essex, Ilford 1991

2007 Season

	M	Inn	NO	Runs	HS	Avg	100	50	Ct	St	Balls	Runs	Wkts	Avg	BB	5I	10M
Test																	
FC	14	22	2	559	98 *	27.95	-	6	11	-	42	49	0		-	-	-
ODI																	
List A	14	14	4	382	66 *	38.20	-	2	4	-	12	16	0		-	-	
20/20 Int																	
20/20	7	6	0	84	37	14.00	-	-	2	-	0	0	0		-	-	

Career Performances

	M	Inn	NO	Runs	HS	Avg	100	50	Ct	St	Balls	Runs	Wkts	Avg	BB	5I	10M
Test																	
FC	296	463	52	16794	204	40.86	40	83	184	-	653	488	4	122.00	1-5	-	-
ODI																	
List A	364	351	50	9170	115	30.46	2	58	129	-	127	121	2	60.50	1-2	-	
20/20 Int																	
20/20	32	31	2	534	105	18.41	1	1	15	-	0	0	0		-	-	

SMITH, E. T. — Middlesex

Name: Edward (Ed) Thomas Smith
Role: Right-hand bat, right-arm medium bowler, county captain
Born: 19 July 1977, Pembury, Kent
Height: 6ft 2in **Weight:** 13st
Nickname: Smudge
County debut: 1996 (Kent), 2005 (Middlesex)
County cap: 2001 (Kent), 2005 (Middlesex)
Test debut: 2003
1000 runs in a season: 8
1st-Class 200s: 2
Place in batting averages: 15th av. 58.04 (2006 72nd av. 40.30)
Parents: Jonathan and Gillie
Marital status: Single
Family links with cricket: 'Dad wrote *Good Enough?* with Chris Cowdrey'
Education: Tonbridge School; Peterhouse, Cambridge University
Qualifications: 11 GCSEs, 3 A-levels, degree in History
Career outside cricket: Journalism; broadcasting
Overseas tours: England A to Malaysia and India 2003-04

Overseas teams played for: University CC, Perth, Western Australia
Career highlights to date: 'My Test debut'
Cricket moments to forget: 'Getting a pair at Chelmsford 2003'
Cricket superstitions: 'Left pad on first'
Cricketers particularly admired: Steve Waugh, Rahul Dravid
Other sports played: Squash, golf
Other sports followed: Football (Arsenal FC), baseball (New York Mets)
Favourite band: Bob Dylan
Relaxations: 'Listening to music, reading, going to concerts'
Extras: Scored century (101) on first-class debut v Glamorgan 1996; was also the first person to score 50 or more in each of his first six first-class games. Cambridge Blue 1996. Represented England U19. Equalled Kent record of four consecutive first-class centuries with his 108 v Essex at Canterbury 2003. *Kent Messenger* Readers' Player of the Year 2003. Denness Award (Kent leading run-scorer) 2003. Cowdrey Award (Kent Player of the Season) 2003. Slazenger 'Sheer Instinct' award for 2003. Books *Playing Hard Ball* (about baseball) published 2001 and *On and Off the Field* published 2004; series *Peak Performance* (comparing sporting and musical performance) broadcast on Radio 3 2005. Captain of Middlesex since 2007
Best batting: 213 Kent v Warwickshire, Canterbury 2003
Best bowling: 1-60 Middlesex v Sussex, Southgate 2006

2007 Season

	M	Inn	NO	Runs	HS	Avg	100	50	Ct	St	Balls	Runs	Wkts	Avg	BB	5I	10M
Test																	
FC	17	25	4	1219	149 *	58.04	5	4	9	-	6	0	0		-	-	-
ODI																	
List A	17	17	0	522	80	30.70	-	3	3	-	0	0	0		-	-	
20/20 Int																	
20/20	6	6	0	125	66	20.83	-	1	1	-	0	0	0		-	-	

Career Performances

	M	Inn	NO	Runs	HS	Avg	100	50	Ct	St	Balls	Runs	Wkts	Avg	BB	5I	10M
Test	3	5	0	87	64	17.40	-	1	5	-	0	0	0		-	-	-
FC	185	315	19	12392	213	41.86	34	50	82	-	108	119	1	119.00	1-60	-	-
ODI																	
List A	129	126	9	3668	122	31.35	2	25	27	-	0	0	0		-	-	
20/20 Int																	
20/20	23	23	0	513	85	22.30	-	3	5	-	0	0	0		-	-	

SMITH, G. M. Derbyshire

Name: Gregory (Greg) Marc Smith
Role: Right-hand bat, right-arm medium/off-spin bowler; all-rounder
Born: 20 April 1983, Johannesburg, South Africa
Height: 5ft 8½in **Weight:** 11st 5lbs
Nickname: Smithy
County debut: 2006
Place in batting averages: 197th av. 22.61 (2006 158th av. 28.37)
Place in bowling averages: 95th av. 34.45
Parents: Ian and Nadine
Marital status: Single
Family links with cricket: 'Dad used to be financial adviser of the UCB [United Cricket Board of South Africa]'
Education: St Stithians College; UNISA (University of South Africa)
Qualifications: Matriculation, Level 2 coaching certificate
Off-season: 'Relaxing on the beach'
Overseas tours: South Africa U19 to New Zealand (U19 World Cup) 2001-02
Overseas teams played for: Old Edwardians, Johannesburg; Griqualand West 2003-04
Career highlights to date: 'Scoring half-century in U19 World Cup final v Australia'
Cricket moments to forget: 'Getting my first pair'
Cricketers particularly admired: Jacques Kallis, Kevin Pietersen
Young players to look out for: Dan Redfern, Gary Ballance
Other sports played: Golf, tennis
Other sports followed: Football (Arsenal), rugby (Sharks)
Favourite band: Coldplay
Relaxations: 'Spending time with my girlfriend Nicole'
Extras: Represented Gauteng U13, U15, U19. South Africa Academy 2003-04
Opinions on cricket: 'Very good, but I think it would be better and produce better intensity if there weren't so many games in the year.'
Best batting: 86 Derbyshire v Gloucestershire, Derby 2006
Best bowling: 3-31 Derbyshire v Middlesex, Southgate 2007

2007 Season

	M	Inn	NO	Runs	HS	Avg	100	50	Ct	St	Balls	Runs	Wkts	Avg	BB	5I	10M
Test																	
FC	12	20	2	407	74	22.61	-	3	4	-	1285	689	20	34.45	3-31	-	-
ODI																	
List A	16	16	0	424	88	26.50	-	2	4	-	439	374	14	26.71	3-19	-	
20/20 Int																	
20/20	5	5	0	124	79	24.80	-	1	-	-	24	37	0		-	-	

Career Performances

	M	Inn	NO	Runs	HS	Avg	100	50	Ct	St	Balls	Runs	Wkts	Avg	BB	5I	10M
Test																	
FC	26	47	4	945	86	21.97	-	6	9	-	2010	1122	28	40.07	3-31	-	-
ODI																	
List A	30	30	1	705	88	24.31	-	4	12	-	673	660	19	34.73	3-19	-	
20/20 Int																	
20/20	5	5	0	124	79	24.80	-	1	-	-	24	37	0		-	-	

SMITH, T. C. P. Lancashire

Name: Thomas (Tom) Christopher Pascoe Smith
Role: Left-hand bat, right-arm medium-fast bowler; all-rounder
Born: 26 December 1985, Liverpool
Height: 6ft 3in **Weight:** 14st
Nickname: Smudger, Yeti
County debut: 2005
Place in batting averages: (2006 219th av. 18.00)
Place in bowling averages: (2006 50th av. 30.65)
Parents: Mark and Jacqui
Marital status: Single
Family links with cricket: Brother Lancashire U19. Father and stepfather play for local village teams
Education: Parklands High School; Runshaw College
Qualifications: 10 GCSEs, 4 A-levels
Overseas tours: England U19 to India 2004-05; England A to Bangladesh 2006-07
Career highlights to date: 'Contract with Lancs and being picked for National Academy 2005-06'

Cricket moments to forget: 'First-ball duck on my first-class debut'
Cricket superstitions: 'Right pad on first'
Cricketers particularly admired: Andrew Flintoff, Ricky Ponting
Young players to look out for: Karl Brown
Other sports played: Football, golf, swimming
Other sports followed: Football (Liverpool FC)
Favourite band: Oasis, Goo Goo Dolls, Kelly Clarkson
Relaxations: 'Watching films and socialising with friends'
Extras: Represented England U19 2005. ECB National Academy 2005-06, 2006-07
Best batting: 49 Lancashire v Hampshire, Rose Bowl 2006
Best bowling: 4-57 Lancashire v Yorkshire, Headingley 2006

2007 Season

	M	Inn	NO	Runs	HS	Avg	100	50	Ct	St	Balls	Runs	Wkts	Avg	BB	5I	10M
Test																	
FC	6	6	2	119	44	29.75	-	-	4	-	575	351	8	43.87	2-47	-	-
ODI																	
List A	5	3	1	45	30	22.50	-	-	2	-	112	115	2	57.50	2-42	-	
20/20 Int																	
20/20	4	1	0	3	3	3.00	-	-	1	-	52	84	4	21.00	3-15	-	

Career Performances

	M	Inn	NO	Runs	HS	Avg	100	50	Ct	St	Balls	Runs	Wkts	Avg	BB	5I	10M
Test																	
FC	23	26	7	365	49	19.21	-	-	22	-	3113	1509	45	33.53	4-57	-	-
ODI																	
List A	18	9	3	86	30	14.33	-	-	5	-	600	464	16	29.00	3-8	-	
20/20 Int																	
20/20	12	8	3	74	21	14.80	-	-	4	-	204	259	9	28.77	3-15	-	

SMITH, T. M. J. — Sussex

Name: Thomas Michael John Smith
Role: Right-hand bat, slow left-arm orthodox bowler
Born: 29 August 1987, Eastbourne, Sussex
Height: 5ft 9in **Weight:** 11st 7lbs
Nickname: Smudge
County debut: 2006 (one-day), 2007 (first-class)
Parents: Michael and Claudine
Marital status: Single
Education: Seaford Head Community College; Sussex Downs College
Qualifications: NVQ Level 2 in Plumbing
Overseas tours: Sussex Academy to Cape Town 2003, 2005

Cricket moments to forget: 'Semi-dislocating my shoulder in a net a week before I went to Cape Town on a cricket tour'
Cricket superstitions: 'None'
Cricketers particularly admired: Daniel Vettori, Monty Panesar, Mike Yardy
Young players to look out for: Andrew Hodd, Ollie Rayner, Ben Brown
Other sports played: Football (Seaford Town FC), golf
Favourite band: The Subways
Extras: Sussex 2nd XI Player of the Year 2006. Sussex League Young Player of the Year 2006
Opinions on cricket: 'Good that younger players are getting more opportunity and also Twenty20 great competition.'
Best batting: 2 Sussex v Sri Lanka A, Hove 2007
Best bowling: 1-52 Sussex v Sri Lanka A, Hove 2007

2007 Season

	M	Inn	NO	Runs	HS	Avg	100	50	Ct	St	Balls	Runs	Wkts	Avg	BB	5I	10M
Test																	
FC	1	1	0	2	2	2.00	-	-	-	-	78	79	1	79.00	1-52	-	-
ODI																	
List A	2	0	0	0	0		-	-	1	-	72	100	1	100.00	1-64	-	
20/20 Int																	
20/20	1	0	0	0	0		-	-	-	-	0	0	0		-	-	

Career Performances

	M	Inn	NO	Runs	HS	Avg	100	50	Ct	St	Balls	Runs	Wkts	Avg	BB	5I	10M
Test																	
FC	1	1	0	2	2	2.00	-	-	-	-	78	79	1	79.00	1-52	-	-
ODI																	
List A	3	0	0	0	0		-	-	2	-	120	145	3	48.33	2-45	-	
20/20 Int																	
20/20	1	0	0	0	0		-	-	-	-	0	0	0		-	-	

SMITH, W. R. — Durham

Name: William (Will) Rew Smith
Role: Right-hand top-order bat, right-arm off-break bowler, occasional wicket-keeper
Born: 28 September 1982, Luton
Height: 5ft 9in **Weight:** 12st
Nickname: Smudger, Jiggy
County debut: 2002 (Nottinghamshire), 2007 (Durham)
Place in batting averages: 186th av. 23.95 (2006 165th av. 27.38)
Parents: Jim and Barbara
Marital status: Single ('long-term partner – Claire')
Family links with cricket: 'Brother played county age-group; father a cricket "statto"'
Education: Bedford School; Durham University; Staffordshire University
Qualifications: 3 A-levels, BSc Molecular Biology and Biochemistry, Level 2 cricket coach
Career outside cricket: Media and journalism
Off-season: 'My second stint as a student, studying professional sports writing and broadcasting at Staffordshire University'
Overseas tours: British Universities to South Africa 2004; Nottinghamshire to Cape Town; Durham to Cape Town
Overseas teams played for: Gordon DCC, Sydney 2001-02, 2006-07
Career highlights to date: 'Being part of Durham's Friends Provident Trophy winning side'
Cricket moments to forget: 'Any dropped catch – luckily not too many!'
Cricket superstitions: 'None'
Cricketers particularly admired: Graeme Fowler, Stephen Fleming, Dale Benkenstein, Mike Atherton
Young players to look out for: Mark Stoneman, Luke Evans, Scott Borthwick
Other sports played: 'Not much any more – used to play good level hockey and rugby; five-a-side football now!'
Other sports followed: Football (Rushden & Diamonds), rugby (Bedford), horse racing, golf
Favourite band: Editors
Relaxations: 'Music, going to gigs, reading, socialising'
Extras: Represented England U16-U18. Played for Durham UCCE 2003-05 (captain 2004-05). Represented British Universities 2004, 2005 (captain 2005). Nottinghamshire 2nd XI Player of the Year 2005

Opinions on cricket: 'Make sure umpires are source of authority and have final say.'
Best batting: 156 DUCCE v Somerset, Taunton 2005
Best bowling: 3-34 DUCCE v Leicestershire, Leicester 2005

2007 Season

	M	Inn	NO	Runs	HS	Avg	100	50	Ct	St	Balls	Runs	Wkts	Avg	BB	5I	10M
Test																	
FC	12	23	0	551	105	23.95	1	-	7	-	72	46	2	23.00	1-5	-	-
ODI																	
List A	9	9	2	270	103	38.57	1	1	4	-	0	0	0		-	-	
20/20 Int																	
20/20	3	3	1	35	24 *	17.50	-	-	-	-	24	39	1	39.00	1-31	-	

Career Performances

	M	Inn	NO	Runs	HS	Avg	100	50	Ct	St	Balls	Runs	Wkts	Avg	BB	5I	10M
Test																	
FC	41	67	3	1674	156	26.15	3	3	25	-	645	494	8	61.75	3-34	-	-
ODI																	
List A	38	34	3	854	103	27.54	1	6	12	-	0	0	0		-	-	
20/20 Int																	
20/20	24	18	4	269	55	19.21	-	2	13	-	24	39	1	39.00	1-31	-	

SNAPE, J. N. — Leicestershire

Name: Jeremy Nicholas Snape
Role: Right-hand bat, off-spin bowler; all-rounder
Born: 27 April 1973, Stoke-on-Trent
Height: 5ft 8in **Weight:** 12st
Nickname: Snapper
County debut: 1992 (Northamptonshire), 1999 (Gloucestershire), 2003 (Leicestershire)
County cap: 1999 (Gloucestershire), 2003 (Leicestershire)
Testimonial: 2008 (Leicestershire)
ODI debut: 2001-02
Twenty20 Int debut: 2007-08
Place in batting averages: (2006 200th av. 21.90)
Parents: Keith and Barbara
Wife and date of marriage: Joanne, 4 October 2003
Children: Tamsin, 26 September 2005

Family links with cricket: 'Brother Jonathan plays at Rode Park in Cheshire'
Education: Denstone College, Staffordshire; Durham University; Loughborough University
Qualifications: 8 GCSEs, 3 A-levels, BSc Natural Science, MSc Sport Psychology
Career outside cricket: Director of Sporting Edge – performance coaching company (www.thesportingedge.co.uk)
Off-season: 'Working with my clients from Sporting Edge in elite sport and business; completing my testimonial year with Leicestershire'
Overseas tours: England U18 to Canada (International Youth Tournament) 1991 (c); England U19 to Pakistan 1991-92; Durham University to South Africa 1993, to Vienna (European Indoor Championships) 1994; Northamptonshire to Cape Town 1993; Christians in Sport to Zimbabwe 1994-95; Troubadours to South Africa 1997; Gloucestershire to South Africa 1999; England to Zimbabwe (one-day series) 2001-02, to India and New Zealand 2001-02 (one-day series), to Sri Lanka (ICC Champions Trophy) 2002-03, to Australia 2002-03 (VB Series), to South Africa (World 20/20) 2007-08
Overseas teams played for: Petone, Wellington, New Zealand 1994-95; Wainuiamata, Wellington, New Zealand 1995-96; Techs CC, Cape Town 1996-99
Career highlights to date: 'England debut. England ODI in Calcutta – 120,000 people. Twenty20 Cup wins'
Cricket moments to forget: 'Breaking my thumb in Australia 2003 and being ruled out of World Cup'
Cricketers particularly admired: Allan Lamb, Jack Russell
Other sports followed: Rugby (Leicester Tigers)
Relaxations: Travelling, music, cooking, good food and wine
Player website: www.jeremysnape2008.co.uk
Extras: Sir John Hobbs Silver Jubilee Memorial Prize 1988. B&H Gold Award for his 3-34 for Combined Universities v Worcestershire at The Parks 1992. Player of the Tournament at European Indoor 6-a-side Championships 1994. Made ODI debut in the first ODI v Zimbabwe at Harare 2001-02, winning Man of the Match award for his 2-39 and brilliant catch. BBC West Country Sports Cricketer of the Year for 2001. Struck 16-ball 34*, including winning runs, in the Twenty20 Cup final at Edgbaston 2004. Captain of Leicestershire 2006 to the end of August 2007
Opinions on cricket: 'The game seems to be in a fairly healthy state, with divisional cricket working well. Twenty20 has been hugely refreshing, and following a very successful World Cup in South Africa, it has become a global brand. Cricket has never been more widespread internationally, which opens many opportunities. England must now strive for consistently elite performance on the international stage, which will also fuel a more successful domestic competition.'
Best batting: 131 Gloucestershire v Sussex, Cheltenham 2001
Best bowling: 5-65 Northamptonshire v Durham, Northampton 1995

2007 Season

	M	Inn	NO	Runs	HS	Avg	100	50	Ct	St	Balls	Runs	Wkts	Avg	BB	5I	10M
Test																	
FC																	
ODI																	
List A	12	9	3	157	58	26.16	-	2	4	-	402	359	12	29.91	3-41	-	
20/20 Int																	
20/20	5	3	2	31	16	31.00	-	-	1	-	42	51	3	17.00	3-6	-	

Career Performances

	M	Inn	NO	Runs	HS	Avg	100	50	Ct	St	Balls	Runs	Wkts	Avg	BB	5I	10M
Test																	
FC	121	180	31	4194	131	28.14	3	23	74	-	10728	5583	113	49.40	5-65	1	-
ODI	10	7	3	118	38	29.50	-	-	5	-	529	403	13	31.00	3-43	-	
List A	271	218	58	3716	104 *	23.22	1	13	95	-	8381	6482	222	29.19	5-32	1	
20/20 Int	1	1	0	7	7	7.00	-	-	1	-	6	12	0		-	-	
20/20	41	36	14	556	47 *	25.27	-	-	15	-	634	697	36	19.36	4-22	-	

SNELL, S. D. — Gloucestershire

Name: Steven David Snell
Role: Right-hand bat, wicket-keeper
Born: 27 February 1983, Winchester
Height: 6ft **Weight:** 11st 7lbs
Nickname: Snelly, Glove Monkey, Gonzo, Jaws
County debut: 2005
County cap: 2005
Parents: Jonathan and Sandra
Marital status: Single
Family links with cricket: 'Grandad and Dad both keen amateur cricketers. Brothers Rob and Peter both play at Ventnor Cricket Club (the real home of cricket!) on the Isle of Wight'
Education: Sandown High School, Isle of Wight
Qualifications: 10 GCSEs, 2 A-levels, ECB Level 2 cricket coach, FA Level 1 football coach, EBA basketball coach, YMCA fitness instructor
Overseas tours: MCC Young Cricketers to Cape Town 2002, to Lanzarote 2003, to Sri Lanka 2004; MCC B to USA 2004

Overseas teams played for: Hermanus, Cape Town 2001-02; Brighton, Melbourne 2003-05
Career highlights to date: '83* on first-class debut against Bangladesh A'
Cricket moments to forget: 'Breaking my jaw in three places during nets at Lord's'
Cricket superstitions: 'Always have to ask somebody if I have the right shirt on. Bordering on obsessive-compulsive…'
Cricketers particularly admired: Jack Russell, Ian Healy, Jonty Rhodes
Young players to look out for: Will Rudge, Tom Stayt, Ben Woodhouse, Peter Snell
Other sports played: Football, squash ('thought I was half-decent till I played Matt Windows')
Other sports followed: Football (Portsmouth FC)
Favourite band: John Mayer, The Killers
Relaxations: 'Enjoy writing about the game; meals out; lying on Sandown beach on the Isle of Wight'
Extras: Played for Hampshire Board XI in the 2002 C&G. Attended World Cricket Academy, Mumbai 2003; International Cricket Academy, Port Elizabeth 2005
Best batting: 83* Gloucestershire v Bangladesh A, Bristol 2005

2007 Season

	M	Inn	NO	Runs	HS	Avg	100	50	Ct	St	Balls	Runs	Wkts	Avg	BB	5I	10M
Test																	
FC	4	8	0	57	12	7.12	-	-	8	-	0	0	0		-	-	-
ODI																	
List A																	
20/20 Int																	
20/20																	

Career Performances

	M	Inn	NO	Runs	HS	Avg	100	50	Ct	St	Balls	Runs	Wkts	Avg	BB	5I	10M
Test																	
FC	6	12	1	198	83 *	18.00	-	1	12	-	0	0	0		-	-	-
ODI																	
List A	10	8	0	31	17	3.87	-	-	16	-	0	0	0		-	-	
20/20 Int																	
20/20																	

81. Which current Northamptonshire player was left stranded on 99* when his side's final second innings wicket fell in the fourth Test between England and South Africa at Headingley in 2003?

SOLANKI, V. S. — Worcestershire

Name: Vikram Singh Solanki
Role: Right-hand bat, right-arm off-spin bowler, county captain
Born: 1 April 1976, Udaipur, India
Height: 6ft **Weight:** 12st
Nickname: Vik
County debut: 1993 (one-day), 1995 (first-class)
County cap: 1998; colours, 2002
Benefit: 2007
ODI debut: 1999-2000
Twenty20 Int debut: 2005
1000 runs in a season: 3
1st-Class 200s: 2
Place in batting averages: 131st av. 31.42 (2006 59th av. 46.37)
Parents: Mr Vijay Singh and Mrs Florabel Solanki
Marital status: Single
Family links with cricket: 'Father played in India. Brother Vishal is a keen cricketer'
Education: Regis School, Wolverhampton; Open University
Qualifications: 9 GCSEs, 3 A-levels
Overseas tours: England U18 to South Africa 1992-93, to Denmark (ICC Youth Tournament) 1994; England U19 to West Indies 1994-95; Worcestershire CCC to Barbados 1996, to Zimbabwe 1997; England A to Zimbabwe and South Africa 1998-99, to Bangladesh and New Zealand 1999-2000, to West Indies 2000-01, to Sri Lanka 2004-05, to West Indies 2005-06 (c); England to South Africa and Zimbabwe 1999-2000 (one-day series), to Kenya (ICC Knockout Trophy) 2000-01, to Pakistan 2000-01 (one-day series), to Bangladesh and Sri Lanka 2003-04 (one-day series), to Zimbabwe (one-day series) 2004-05, to South Africa 2004-05 (one-day series), to Pakistan 2005-06 (one-day series), to India 2005-06 (one-day series), to South Africa (World 20/20) 2007-08
Overseas teams played for: Midland-Guildford, Perth, Western Australia; Rajasthan, India 2006-07
Career highlights to date: 'Playing for England'
Cricket moments to forget: 'Losing to Scotland (NatWest 1998)'
Cricketers particularly admired: Sachin Tendulkar, Graeme Hick
Other sports played: 'Enjoy most sports'
Relaxations: 'Reading; spending time with family and friends'
Extras: Scored more first-class runs (1339) in 1999 season than any other English player. Scored 106 v South Africa at The Oval in the NatWest Series 2003, winning

the Man of the Match award and sharing with Marcus Trescothick (114*) in a record England opening partnership in ODIs (200). Man of the Match in the third ODI v Zimbabwe at Bulawayo 2004-05 (100*). C&G Man of the Match awards for his 127 (plus three catches and a run-out) in the semi-final v Warwickshire at Edgbaston 2004 and for his 115 in the final v Gloucestershire at Lord's 2004. Captain of Worcestershire since 2005

Best batting: 232 Worcestershire v Surrey, Worcester 2007
Best bowling: 5-40 Worcestershire v Middlesex, Lord's 2004

2007 Season

	M	Inn	NO	Runs	HS	Avg	100	50	Ct	St	Balls	Runs	Wkts	Avg	BB	5I	10M
Test																	
FC	13	21	0	660	232	31.42	1	2	4	-	270	149	1	149.00	1-54	-	-
ODI																	
List A	16	16	1	695	144 *	46.33	2	2	6	-	69	71	2	35.50	1-0	-	
20/20 Int																	
20/20	7	6	0	145	58	24.16	-	1	2	-	0	0	0		-	-	

Career Performances

	M	Inn	NO	Runs	HS	Avg	100	50	Ct	St	Balls	Runs	Wkts	Avg	BB	5I	10M
Test																	
FC	220	362	23	12179	232	35.92	21	66	237	-	6787	3945	84	46.96	5-40	4	1
ODI	51	46	5	1097	106	26.75	2	5	16	-	111	105	1	105.00	1-17	-	
List A	318	291	24	8236	164 *	30.84	13	43	120	-	995	874	26	33.61	4-14	-	
20/20 Int	3	3	0	76	43	25.33	-	-	3	-	0	0	0		-	-	
20/20	22	21	0	666	92	31.71	-	4	15	-	18	36	1	36.00	1-25	-	

SPEARMAN, C. M. — Gloucestershire

Name: Craig Murray Spearman
Role: Right-hand opening bat
Born: 4 July 1972, Auckland, New Zealand
Height: 6ft **Weight:** 13st 7lbs
Nickname: Spears
County debut: 2002
County cap: 2002
Benefit: 2008
Test debut: 1995-96
ODI debut: 1995-96
1000 runs in a season: 3
1st-Class 200s: 2
1st-Class 300s: 1
Place in batting averages: 69th av. 40.47 (2006 64th av. 44.19)

Parents: Murray and Sandra
Wife and date of marriage: Maree, 4 March 2004
Education: Kelston Boys High School, Auckland; Massey University, Palmerston North, New Zealand
Qualifications: Bachelor of Business Studies (BBS; Finance major)
Overseas tours: New Zealand to India and Pakistan (World Cup) 1995-96, to West Indies 1995-96, to Sharjah (Singer Champions Trophy) 1996-97, to Pakistan 1996-97, to Zimbabwe 1997-98, to Australia 1997-98 (CUB Series), to Sri Lanka 1998, to India 1999-2000, to Zimbabwe 2000-01, to Kenya (ICC Knockout Trophy) 2000-01, to South Africa 2000-01; FICA World XI to New Zealand 2004-05
Overseas teams played for: Auckland 1993-96; Central Districts 1996-97 – 2000-01, 2002-03 – 2004-05
Career highlights to date: 'Playing international cricket; Test century; winning ICC Knockout Trophy [2000-01] with New Zealand; winning two C&G finals with Gloucestershire; scoring 341 for Gloucestershire v Middlesex (highest score for Gloucestershire)'
Cricket moments to forget: 'Misfielding on the boundary at the SCG in the fifth over and hearing about it for the next 45 overs'
Cricket superstitions: 'None'
Cricketers particularly admired: Gordon Greenidge
Other sports played: Golf, tennis
Other sports followed: Rugby, golf, football
Favourite band: U2
Relaxations: 'Sleeping'
Extras: Gloucestershire Players' Player of the Year 2002. Scored 123-ball 153 v Warwickshire at Gloucester in the NCL 2003 to set a new individual record score for Gloucestershire in the one-day league. Vice-captain of Gloucestershire 2003. Scored 341, the highest individual score for Gloucestershire in first-class cricket, v Middlesex at Gloucester 2004. C&G Man of the Match award for his 122-ball 143* in the semi-final v Yorkshire at Bristol 2004. Struck century (100) before lunch on first day v Surrey at Bristol 2006. Is England-qualified
Best batting: 341 Gloucestershire v Middlesex, Gloucester 2004
Best bowling: 1-37 Central Districts v Wellington, New Plymouth 1999-2000

2007 Season

	M	Inn	NO	Runs	HS	Avg	100	50	Ct	St	Balls	Runs	Wkts	Avg	BB	5I	10M
Test																	
FC	11	17	0	688	110	40.47	2	3	15	-	0	0	0		-	-	-
ODI																	
List A	9	9	0	248	71	27.55	-	2	4	-	0	0	0		-	-	
20/20 Int																	
20/20	9	9	0	143	86	15.88	-	1	4	-	0	0	0		-	-	

Career Performances

	M	Inn	NO	Runs	HS	Avg	100	50	Ct	St	Balls	Runs	Wkts	Avg	BB	5I	10M
Test	19	37	2	922	112	26.34	1	3	21	-	0	0	0		-	-	-
FC	190	342	15	12642	341	38.66	30	54	186	-	78	55	1	55.00	1-37	-	-
ODI	51	50	0	936	86	18.72	-	5	15	-	3	6	0		-	-	
List A	267	265	7	7326	153	28.39	7	45	100	-	33	43	0		-	-	
20/20 Int																	
20/20	38	34	2	654	88	20.43	-	4	12	-	0	0	0		-	-	

SPRIEGEL, M. N. W. Surrey

Name: Matthew Neil William Spriegel
Role: Left-hand bat, right-arm off-spin bowler; all-rounder
Born: 4 March 1987, Epsom, Surrey
Height: 6ft 3in **Weight:** 13st 8lbs
Nickname: Spriegs
County debut: No first-team appearance
Parents: Geoff and Julie
Marital status: Single
Education: Whitgift School, South Croydon; Loughborough University
Qualifications: 11 GCSEs, 1 AS-level, 3 A-levels, Level 1 ECB coach
Career outside cricket: Student
Off-season: 'In my second year of studying Sports and Exercise Science at Loughborough; going to the World Cricket Academy in Mumbai in January'
Overseas tours: Surrey Academy to Perth 2004, to Cape Town 2005, 2006; British Universities to Pretoria 2007
Overseas teams played for: Subiaco Marist CC, Perth 2005-06

Career highlights to date: 'Taking 7-85 and scoring 96 in the same game for Surrey against Kent in the 2nd XI Championship 2006'
Cricket moments to forget: 'Scoring three ducks in six innings on tour in Perth in 2004'
Cricketers particularly admired: Mark Ramprakash, Alec Stewart
Young players to look out for: Tom Danby, Mike Baer, Brian Williams
Other sports played: Golf, football
Favourite band: Babyshambles
Relaxations: 'Golf'
Extras: Captained Loughborough UCCE 2007
Opinions on cricket: 'It is a very exciting time for domestic cricket, with the success of Twenty20 and introduction of new one-day competitions attracting bigger crowds. The success of the England team in the last few years has raised the profile of the sport and this has filtered down into the county game. It is a great time to be involved in cricket.'
Best batting: 30 LUCCE v Somerset, Taunton 2007
Best bowling: 1-12 LUCCE v Somerset, Taunton 2007

2007 Season (did not make any first-class or one-day appearances for his county)

Career Performances

	M	Inn	NO	Runs	HS	Avg	100	50	Ct	St	Balls	Runs	Wkts	Avg	BB	5I	10M
Test																	
FC	3	6	1	100	30	20.00	-	-	4	-	198	106	3	35.33	1-12	-	-
ODI																	
List A																	
20/20 Int																	
20/20																	

82. Which future England captain scored a century (138) on debut in the fourth Test v South Africa at Headingley in 1951?

SPURWAY, S. H. P. — Somerset

Name: Samuel (Sam) Harold Patrick Spurway
Role: Left-hand bat, wicket-keeper
Born: 13 March 1987, Taunton
Height: 6ft 1in **Weight:** 12st 7lbs
Nickname: Spurs, Speedy
County debut: 2005 (one-day), 2006 (first-class)
Parents: Susan and Colin
Marital status: Single
Family links with cricket: 'Dad and older brother Tom play local cricket'
Education: Wadham Community School; Richard Huish College
Qualifications: 11 GCSEs, 3 A-levels
Overseas tours: West Region to West Indies 2001; Somerset to Cape Town 2006
Career highlights to date: 'Making my debut for Somerset in the International 20:20 v Leicestershire'
Cricket moments to forget: 'Getting three front teeth knocked out whilst playing for my local club side, Ilminster'
Cricket superstitions: 'None'
Cricketers particularly admired: Adam Gilchrist, Tim Crawley
Young players to look out for: Jack Cooper, William Spurway
Other sports played: Football, skittles
Other sports followed: Football (Yeovil and Man Utd)
Extras: Released by Somerset at the end of the 2007 season
Best batting: 83 Somerset v Northamptonshire, Taunton 2006

2007 Season

	M	Inn	NO	Runs	HS	Avg	100	50	Ct	St	Balls	Runs	Wkts	Avg	BB	5I	10M
Test																	
FC	3	4	1	46	44 *	15.33	-	-	9	-	0	0	0		-	-	-
ODI																	
List A																	
20/20 Int																	
20/20																	

Career Performances

	M	Inn	NO	Runs	HS	Avg	100	50	Ct	St	Balls	Runs	Wkts	Avg	BB	5I	10M
Test																	
FC	6	8	1	210	83	30.00	-	1	16	-	0	0	0		-	-	-
ODI																	
List A	4	2	0	31	31	15.50	-	-	4	2	0	0	0		-	-	
20/20 Int																	
20/20	1	1	1	15	15 *		-	-	-	-	0	0	0		-	-	

STAYT, T. P. Gloucestershire

Name: Thomas (Tom) Patrick Stayt
Role: Right-hand bat, right-arm medium-fast bowler
Born: 20 January 1986, Salisbury
Height: 6ft 2in **Weight:** 11st
Nickname: Staytie, Stick
County debut: 2007
County cap: 2007
Parents: Patrick and Jane
Marital status: Single
Family links with cricket: 'Dad plays occasionally for Erlestoke and Coulston Cricket Club and is part-time groundsman'
Education: Lavington School, Market Lavington; St Augustine's Catholic College, Trowbridge; University of Exeter
Qualifications: 1 AS-Level, 3 A-Levels, BA (Hons) Accounting and Finance
Off-season: 'Training in Bristol, working on fitness and skills'
Career highlights to date: 'Making first-class debut at Lord's, August 2007'
Cricket moments to forget: 'Being run out by Chris Taylor without facing a ball on first-class debut at Lord's'
Cricket superstitions: 'Get to the ground early'
Cricketers particularly admired: Jon Lewis, Allan Donald, Courtney Walsh
Young players to look out for: James Campbell, Paul James, James Brown, Andy Fairbairn
Other sports played: 'Will try anything'
Other sports followed: Rugby union (Gloucester)
Favourite band: John Legend
Relaxations: 'Spending time with mates and girlfriend; watching sport'
Best batting: 6 Gloucestershire v Middlesex, Bristol 2007
Best bowling: 3-51 Gloucestershire v Middlesex, Lord's 2007

2007 Season

	M	Inn	NO	Runs	HS	Avg	100	50	Ct	St	Balls	Runs	Wkts	Avg	BB	5I	10M
Test																	
FC	3	3	1	9	6	4.50	-	-	2	-	354	218	4	54.50	3-51	-	-
ODI																	
List A																	
20/20 Int																	
20/20																	

Career Performances

	M	Inn	NO	Runs	HS	Avg	100	50	Ct	St	Balls	Runs	Wkts	Avg	BB	5I	10M
Test																	
FC	3	3	1	9	6	4.50	-	-	2	-	354	218	4	54.50	3-51	-	-
ODI																	
List A																	
20/20 Int																	
20/20																	

STEVENS, D. I. Kent

Name: Darren Ian Stevens
Role: Right-hand top-order bat, right-arm medium bowler
Born: 30 April 1976, Leicester
Height: 5ft 11in **Weight:** 13st 7lbs
Nickname: Stevo
County debut: 1997 (Leicestershire), 2005 (Kent)
County cap: 2002 (Leicestershire), 2005 (Kent)
1000 runs in a season: 1
1st-Class 200s: 1
Place in batting averages: 92nd av. 36.94 (2006 79th av. 39.00)
Place in bowling averages: 37th av. 25.41 (2006 87th av. 36.21)
Parents: Maddy and Bob
Marital status: Single
Family links with cricket: Father and grandfather played league cricket in Leicestershire
Education: Mount Grace High School; John Cleveland College, Hinckley; Hinckley Tech; Charles Klein College

Qualifications: 5 GCSEs, BTEC National in Sports Studies
Off-season: 'Tour to West Indies with London CCC'
Overseas tours: Leicestershire U19 to South Africa 1994-95; Leicestershire to Barbados 1998, to Sri Lanka 1999, to Potchefstroom 2001; ECB National Academy to Australia and Sri Lanka 2002-03; London CCC to West Indies 2007-08
Overseas teams played for: Wanderers CC, Johannesburg, South Africa 1996-97; Rhodes University, Grahamstown, South Africa 1997-98; Fairfield CC, Sydney 1998-99; Hawthorn-Waverley, Melbourne 1999-2000; Taita CC, Wellington, New Zealand 2000-01; Ringwood CC, Melbourne 2001-02
Career highlights to date: 'Winning the 2007 Twenty20'
Cricket moments to forget: 'Losing in my first final in the C&G against Somerset 2001'
Cricket superstitions: 'Left pad first'
Cricketers particularly admired: Ricky Ponting
Young players to look out for: Joe Denly, Sam Northeast
Other sports played: Golf, squash
Other sports followed: Rugby union (Leicester Tigers), football (Dover FC)
Injuries: Out for three weeks with a torn abductor muscle
Favourite band: Snow Patrol
Relaxations: 'Spending time with friends'
Extras: Received painting from Sir Colin Cowdrey on day of maiden first-class 100 (130 in fourth Championship match), v Sussex at Arundel 1999. Won Sir Ron Brierley/Crusaders Scholarship 1999. Included in provisional England squad of 30 for the 2002-03 World Cup. Kent Player of the Year 2005
Best batting: 208 Kent v Glamorgan, Canterbury 2005
Best bowling: 4-36 Kent v Yorkshire, Canterbury 2006

2007 Season

	M	Inn	NO	Runs	HS	Avg	100	50	Ct	St	Balls	Runs	Wkts	Avg	BB	5I	10M
Test																	
FC	11	17	0	628	174	36.94	2	2	7	-	677	305	12	25.41	3-91	-	-
ODI																	
List A	15	14	3	319	85 *	29.00	-	2	1	-	240	153	9	17.00	3-15	-	
20/20 Int																	
20/20	11	7	2	127	46 *	25.40	-	-	2	-	102	86	6	14.33	4-14	-	

Career Performances

	M	Inn	NO	Runs	HS	Avg	100	50	Ct	St	Balls	Runs	Wkts	Avg	BB	5I	10M
Test																	
FC	124	205	13	6344	208	33.04	12	37	102	-	3959	2061	54	38.16	4-36	-	-
ODI																	
List A	177	167	14	4381	133	28.63	3	29	69	-	1475	1186	39	30.41	5-32	1	
20/20 Int																	
20/20	41	36	3	652	69	19.75	-	1	12	-	156	177	9	19.66	4-14	-	

STEYN, D. W. — Warwickshire

Name: Dale Willem Steyn
Role: Right-hand bat, right-arm fast bowler
Born: 27 June 1983, Phalaborwa, South Africa
County debut: 2005 (Essex), 2007 (Warwickshire)
Test debut: 2004-05
ODI debut: 2005-06
Place in bowling averages: 40th av. 25.86
Overseas tours: South Africa A to Sri Lanka 2005-06, to India 2007-08; South Africa to Australia 2005-06 (VB Series), to Sri Lanka 2006, to Ireland (one-day series) 2007, to Zimbabwe (one-day series) 2007-08, to Pakistan 2007-08
Overseas teams played for: Northerns 2003-04; Titans 2004-05 –

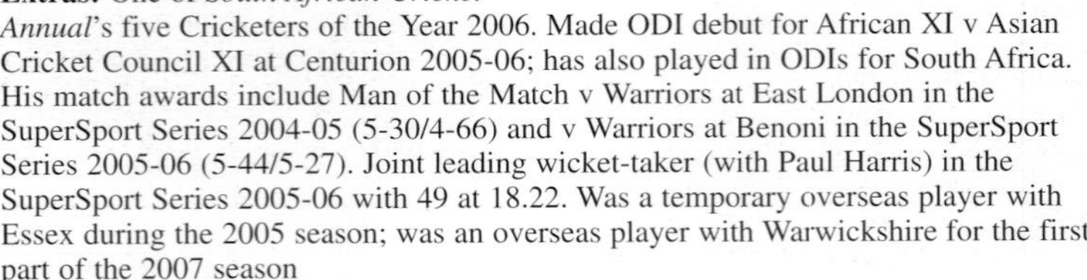

Extras: One of *South African Cricket Annual*'s five Cricketers of the Year 2006. Made ODI debut for African XI v Asian Cricket Council XI at Centurion 2005-06; has also played in ODIs for South Africa. His match awards include Man of the Match v Warriors at East London in the SuperSport Series 2004-05 (5-30/4-66) and v Warriors at Benoni in the SuperSport Series 2005-06 (5-44/5-27). Joint leading wicket-taker (with Paul Harris) in the SuperSport Series 2005-06 with 49 at 18.22. Was a temporary overseas player with Essex during the 2005 season; was an overseas player with Warwickshire for the first part of the 2007 season
Best batting: 82 Essex v Durham, Riverside 2005
Best bowling: 5-27 Titans v Warriors, Benoni 2005-06
Stop press: Made Twenty20 Int debut v New Zealand at Johannesburg 2007-08. Man of the [Test] Series v New Zealand 2007-08 and v West Indies 2007-08

2007 Season

	M	Inn	NO	Runs	HS	Avg	100	50	Ct	St	Balls	Runs	Wkts	Avg	BB	5I	10M
Test																	
FC	7	7	2	145	51	29.00	-	1	-	-	1221	595	23	25.86	5-49	1	-
ODI																	
List A	8	2	0	14	14	7.00	-	-	1	-	366	274	16	17.12	5-29	1	
20/20 Int																	
20/20																	

Career Performances

	M	Inn	NO	Runs	HS	Avg	100	50	Ct	St	Balls	Runs	Wkts	Avg	BB	5I	10M
Test	11	17	6	80	13	7.27	-	-	2	-	2040	1325	42	31.54	5-47	2	-
FC	49	59	17	514	82	12.23	-	2	7	-	9051	5072	178	28.49	5-27	8	1
ODI	7	2	0	4	3	2.00	-	-	-	-	247	262	9	29.11	3-65	-	
List A	47	15	5	39	14	3.90	-	-	6	-	2152	1635	71	23.02	5-20	2	
20/20 Int																	
20/20	12	3	1	6	4 *	3.00	-	-	2	-	252	267	11	24.27	2-10	-	

STOKES, M. S. T. — Hampshire

Name: Mitchell Sam Thomas Stokes
Role: Right-hand bat, right-arm off-spin bowler
Born: 27 March 1987, Basingstoke
Height: 5ft 8in **Weight:** 10st
Nickname: Bram Stoker, Stokesy, Chuckavati
County debut: 2005 (one-day)
Parents: Paul and Janice
Marital status: Single
Education: Cranbourne School, Basingstoke; Basingstoke College of Technology
Qualifications: Level 1 cricket coaching
Overseas tours: West of England U15 to West Indies 2002; England U19 to India 2004-05
Career highlights to date: 'Making 62 against Middlesex in Twenty20 2006. Making debut in both Twenty20 2005 and Pro40 2006 for Hampshire'
Young players to look out for: David Griffiths, Liam Dawson, Adil Rashid
Other sports played: Football (Crystal Palace younger age groups)
Other sports followed: Football (Tottenham Hotspur)
Favourite band: 'Don't have a favourite band but listen to all types of music – R&B, hip hop, indie, old school music'
Relaxations: 'Football, going out with mates, music, poker with the lads'
Extras: Bunbury U15 Festival Bowler of the Tournament 2002. Basingstoke Sportsman of the Year 2005. Released by Hampshire at the end of the 2007 season

2007 Season

	M	Inn	NO	Runs	HS	Avg	100	50	Ct	St	Balls	Runs	Wkts	Avg	BB	5I	10M
Test																	
FC																	
ODI																	
List A	1	1	0	4	4	4.00	-	-	-	-	0	0	0		-	-	
20/20 Int																	
20/20																	

Career Performances

	M	Inn	NO	Runs	HS	Avg	100	50	Ct	St	Balls	Runs	Wkts	Avg	BB	5I	10M
Test																	
FC																	
ODI																	
List A	5	4	0	53	36	13.25	-	-	2	-	24	26	0		-	-	
20/20 Int																	
20/20	14	12	0	179	62	14.91	-	1	4	-	6	14	0		-	-	

STONEMAN, M. D. — Durham

Name: Mark Daniel Stoneman
Role: Left-hand top-order bat, 'right-arm variations'
Born: 26 June 1987, Newcastle upon Tyne
Height: 5ft 11in **Weight:** 12st 5lbs
Nickname: Rocky, Doug
County debut: 2007
Place in batting averages: 184th av. 24.60
Parents: Ian and Pauline
Marital status: Single
Family links with cricket: 'Father played. Grandfather played and was also an umpire'
Education: Whickham Comprehensive School, Gateshead
Qualifications: 11 GCSEs, 3 A-levels
Overseas tours: Durham Development Squad to Mumbai 2004-05; England U19 to Sri Lanka (U19 World Cup) 2005-06
Cricket moments to forget: 'None. All experiences can provide positives and lessons learned'
Cricket superstitions: 'Right pad on first'
Cricketers particularly admired: Brian Lara

Young players to look out for: Mark Turner, Ben Harmison, Karl Turner
Other sports followed: Football (Newcastle United FC)
Favourite band: 'None in particular. Like dance, R&B music'
Relaxations: 'Watching films, socialising with friends'
Extras: Attended Darren Lehmann Talent Squad, Adelaide, January-March 2006. Represented England U19 2006
Best batting: 101 Durham v Sussex, Riverside 2007

2007 Season

	M	Inn	NO	Runs	HS	Avg	100	50	Ct	St	Balls	Runs	Wkts	Avg	BB	5I	10M
Test																	
FC	8	15	0	369	101	24.60	1	1	5	-	0	0	0		-	-	-
ODI																	
List A																	
20/20 Int																	
20/20																	

Career Performances

	M	Inn	NO	Runs	HS	Avg	100	50	Ct	St	Balls	Runs	Wkts	Avg	BB	5I	10M
Test																	
FC	8	15	0	369	101	24.60	1	1	5	-	0	0	0		-	-	-
ODI																	
List A																	
20/20 Int																	
20/20																	

83. Which off-spinning all-rounder batted for more than three hours for 37* to help save the third Test between England and South Africa at Old Trafford in 1998?

STRAUSS, A. J. — Middlesex

Name: Andrew John Strauss
Role: Left-hand bat, left-arm medium bowler
Born: 2 March 1977, Johannesburg, South Africa
Height: 5ft 11in **Weight:** 13st
Nickname: Straussy, Johann, Levi, Mareman, Muppet, Lord Brocket
County debut: 1997 (one-day), 1998 (first-class)
County cap: 2001
Test debut: 2004
ODI debut: 2003-04
Twenty20 Int debut: 2005
1000 runs in a season: 3
Place in batting averages: 118th av. 32.81 (2006 34th av. 52.92)
Parents: David and Dawn
Wife and date of marriage: Ruth, 18 October 2003
Children: Samuel David, December 2005
Education: Radley College; Durham University
Qualifications: 4 A-levels, BA (Hons) Economics

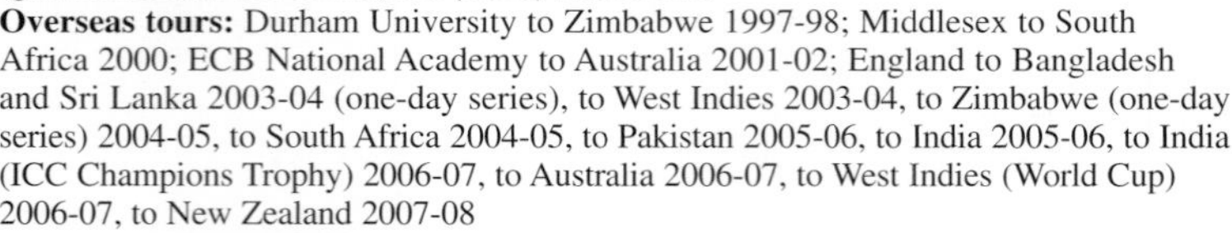

Overseas tours: Durham University to Zimbabwe 1997-98; Middlesex to South Africa 2000; ECB National Academy to Australia 2001-02; England to Bangladesh and Sri Lanka 2003-04 (one-day series), to West Indies 2003-04, to Zimbabwe (one-day series) 2004-05, to South Africa 2004-05, to Pakistan 2005-06, to India 2005-06, to India (ICC Champions Trophy) 2006-07, to Australia 2006-07, to West Indies (World Cup) 2006-07, to New Zealand 2007-08
Overseas teams played for: Sydney University 1998-99; Mosman, Sydney 1999-2001; Northern Districts, New Zealand 2007-08
Cricketers particularly admired: Allan Donald, Brian Lara, Saqlain Mushtaq
Other sports played: Golf (Durham University 1998), rugby (Durham University 1996-97)
Other sports followed: 'Anything with a ball'
Extras: Middlesex Player of the Year 2001. Scored century (112) plus 83 in second innings on Test debut in the first Test v New Zealand at Lord's (his home ground) 2004, winning Man of the Match award. Scored century (100) v West Indies, also at Lord's, in the NatWest Series 2004, in the process sharing with Andrew Flintoff (123) in a new record partnership for England in ODIs (226). Wombwell Cricket Lovers' Society George Spofforth Cricketer of the Year 2004. Captain of Middlesex 2002-04. Scored 126 in the first Test v South Africa at Port Elizabeth 2004-05, achieving feat of scoring a Test century on home and away debuts and becoming first player to score a

Test century in his first innings against each of first three opponents. His other series and match awards include Man of the [Test] Series v South Africa 2004-05 (656 runs at 72.88) and England's Man of the [Test] Series v Pakistan 2006. Vodafone England Cricketer of the Year 2004-05. One of *Wisden*'s Five Cricketers of the Year 2005. Appointed MBE in 2006 New Year Honours as part of 2005 Ashes-winning England team. Has captained England. England 12-month central contract 2007-08
Best batting: 176 Middlesex v Durham, Lord's 2001
Best bowling: 1-16 Middlesex v Nottinghamshire, Lord's 2007

2007 Season

	M	Inn	NO	Runs	HS	Avg	100	50	Ct	St	Balls	Runs	Wkts	Avg	BB	5I	10M
Test	7	13	0	379	96	29.15	-	3	9	-	0	0	0		-	-	-
FC	15	27	0	886	120	32.81	1	6	17	-	36	16	1	16.00	1-16	-	-
ODI																	
List A	7	7	1	214	70	35.66	-	1	7	-	0	0	0		-	-	
20/20 Int																	
20/20	2	2	0	0	0	0.00	-	-	-	-	0	0	0		-	-	

Career Performances

	M	Inn	NO	Runs	HS	Avg	100	50	Ct	St	Balls	Runs	Wkts	Avg	BB	5I	10M
Test	43	81	2	3223	147	40.79	10	11	51	-	0	0	0		-	-	-
FC	142	253	12	9677	176	40.15	23	44	109	-	84	74	2	37.00	1-16	-	-
ODI	78	77	7	2239	152	31.98	2	14	28	-	6	3	0		-	-	
List A	186	179	13	4959	152	29.87	4	33	55	-	6	3	0		-	-	
20/20 Int	3	3	0	51	33	17.00	-	-	1	-	0	0	0		-	-	
20/20	12	12	0	245	60	20.41	-	2	5	-	0	0	0		-	-	

84. Which future cricket administrator made his Test debut v England at Lord's in 1965 and went on to captain South Africa in their last series before isolation (against Australia in 1969-70)?

STREAK, H. H. Warwickshire

Name: Heath Hilton Streak
Role: Right-hand bat, right-arm fast-medium bowler
Born: 16 March 1974, Bulawayo, Zimbabwe
Height: 6ft 1in **Weight:** 15st 5lbs
Nickname: Streaky
County debut: 1995 (Hampshire), 2004 (Warwickshire)
County cap: 2005 (Warwickshire)
Test debut: 1993-94
ODI debut: 1993-94
50 wickets in a season: 1
Place in batting averages: 192nd av. 23.16 (2006 156th av. 28.50)
Place in bowling averages: 145th av. 60.69 (2006 70th av. 33.51)
Parents: Denis and Sheona
Wife and date of marriage: Nadine, 18 August 2000
Children: Holly, 23 December 1992; Charlotte, 14 August 2002; Harry, 5 January 2005
Family links with cricket: 'Father played for Rhodesia and Zimbabwe'
Education: Falcon College, Zimbabwe
Qualifications: 3 A-levels, professional safari guide
Career outside cricket: Safari guide, farming
Overseas tours: Zimbabwe to England 1993, to India (Hero Cup) 1993-94, to Pakistan 1993-94, to New Zealand 1995-96, to India and Pakistan (World Cup) 1995-96, to Sri Lanka 1996, 1997-98, to New Zealand 1997-98, to Malaysia (Commonwealth Games) 1998-99, to Bangladesh (Wills International Cup) 1998-99, to Pakistan 1998-99, to UK, Ireland and Netherlands (World Cup) 1999, to West Indies 1999-2000, to England 2000, to Kenya (ICC Knockout Trophy) 2000-01 (c), to India 2000-01 (c), to New Zealand 2000-01 (c), to Bangladesh 2001-02, to Sri Lanka 2001-02, to India 2001-02, to Sri Lanka (ICC Champions Trophy) 2002-03 (c), to England 2003 (c), to Australia 2003-04 (c), to South Africa 2004-05, plus other one-day tournaments in Australia, South Africa, Sharjah, India and Bangladesh; FICA World XI to New Zealand 2004-05
Overseas teams played for: Matabeleland 1993-94 – 2003-04
Career highlights: 'First Test win v Pakistan for Zimbabwe [1994-95]'
Cricket moments to forget: 'Being bowled out for 38 as a team by Sri Lanka [2001-02]'
Cricket superstitions: 'Nelson – 111'

Cricketers particularly admired: Dennis Lillee, Richard Hadlee, Malcolm Marshall
Other sports played: Rugby (Zimbabwe U19)
Other sports followed: Football (Liverpool), rugby (Natal Sharks)
Favourite band: Bon Jovi
Relaxations: 'Fishing'
Extras: First Zimbabwe player to 100 and 200 wickets in both Tests and ODIs. Has won several ODI awards, including Man of the Match v West Indies at Sydney in the CUB Series 2000-01 (45/4-8) and Man of the Series v Bangladesh 2003-04. His Test awards include Zimbabwe's Man of the Series v England in 2000 and 2003. Captain of Zimbabwe 2000-01 and 2002-04, including the 2002-03 World Cup. An overseas player with Hampshire 1995; an overseas player with Warwickshire 2004-06; is no longer considered an overseas player. Had match figures of 13-158 (7-80/6-78) in his first game for Warwickshire, v Northamptonshire at Edgbaston 2004. Announced retirement from international cricket in October 2005. Captain of Warwickshire 2006, standing down at the start of the 2007 season. Retired at the end of the 2007 season
Opinions on cricket: 'More Twenty20 cricket – exciting and fun for players and spectators.'
Best batting: 131 Matabeleland v Mashonaland CD, Bulawayo (AC) 1995-96
131 Matabeleland v Midlands, Bulawayo 2003-04
Best bowling: 7-55 Matabeleland v Mashonaland, Bulawayo 2003-04

2007 Season

	M	Inn	NO	Runs	HS	Avg	100	50	Ct	St	Balls	Runs	Wkts	Avg	BB	5I	10M
Test																	
FC	11	15	3	278	66	23.16	-	2	-	-	1532	789	13	60.69	3-105	-	-
ODI																	
List A	15	9	4	81	28	16.20	-	-	3	-	549	459	16	28.68	4-37	-	
20/20 Int																	
20/20	8	8	4	77	20	19.25	-	-	1	-	154	151	11	13.72	3-18	-	

Career Performances

	M	Inn	NO	Runs	HS	Avg	100	50	Ct	St	Balls	Runs	Wkts	Avg	BB	5I	10M
Test	65	107	18	1990	127 *	22.35	1	11	17	-	13559	6079	216	28.14	6-73	7	-
FC	175	264	48	5684	131	26.31	6	27	58	-	31117	14352	499	28.76	7-55	17	2
ODI	189	159	55	2942	79 *	28.28	-	13	46	-	9468	7129	239	29.82	5-32	1	
List A	309	245	86	4088	90 *	25.71	-	14	75	-	14741	10994	385	28.55	5-32	1	
20/20 Int																	
20/20	23	19	7	333	59	27.75	-	1	7	-	420	537	24	22.37	3-18	-	

STUBBINGS, S. D. Derbyshire

Name: Stephen David Stubbings
Role: Left-hand bat, right-arm bowler 'all disciplines', occasional wicket-keeper
Born: 31 March 1978, Huddersfield
Height: 6ft 4in **Weight:** 15st
Nickname: Stubbo, Hollywood, Wilton Shagpile, The Plank
County debut: 1997
County cap: 2001
Benefit: 2008
1000 runs in a season: 4
Place in batting averages: 136th av. 31.28 (2006 112th av. 34.06)
Parents: Marie and David
Marital status: Single
Family links with cricket: 'Father and brother both played, as I did, for Delacombe Park Cricket Club in Melbourne, Australia'
Education: Frankston High School; Swinburne University – both Melbourne, Australia
Qualifications: Victorian Certificate of Education (VCE), Level 2 coaching
Overseas tours: Derbyshire to Portugal 2000
Overseas teams played for: Delacombe Park CC, Melbourne 1989-90 – 1993-94; Frankston Peninsula CC, Victoria 1994-95 – 1999-2000, 2002-03 – 2005-06; Kingborough CC, Tasmania 2000-01 – 2001-02
Career highlights to date: '2006 Championship season at Derbyshire'
Cricket moments to forget: '2005 Championship season at Derbyshire'
Cricket superstitions: 'No shaving on first day of a game'
Cricketers particularly admired: Michael DiVenuto
Other sports played: Golf, Aussie Rules, football
Other sports followed: AFL (Essendon Bombers), football (Cambridge United FC)
Favourite band: Powderfinger
Extras: Represented Victoria at all junior levels. Spent two years on the cricket programme at the Victorian Institute of Sport. Scored 135* v Kent at Canterbury 2000, taking part in an unbroken opening partnership of 293 with Steve Titchard (141*); it was the first occasion on which Derbyshire had batted all day without losing a wicket. Derbyshire Player of the Year 2001 and 2006
Best batting: 151 Derbyshire v Somerset, Taunton 2005

2007 Season

	M	Inn	NO	Runs	HS	Avg	100	50	Ct	St	Balls	Runs	Wkts	Avg	BB	5I	10M
Test																	
FC	16	31	3	876	128	31.28	2	2	7	-	0	0	0		-	-	-
ODI																	
List A	6	6	0	91	57	15.16	-	1	1	-	0	0	0		-	-	
20/20 Int																	
20/20																	

Career Performances

	M	Inn	NO	Runs	HS	Avg	100	50	Ct	St	Balls	Runs	Wkts	Avg	BB	5I	10M
Test																	
FC	122	222	11	6755	151	32.01	12	35	55	-	60	79	0		-	-	-
ODI																	
List A	108	101	5	2417	110	25.17	1	13	17	-	0	0	0		-	-	
20/20 Int																	
20/20	9	9	1	186	57	23.25	-	2	4	-	0	0	0		-	-	

STYRIS, S. B. Durham

Name: Scott Bernard Styris
Role: Right-hand bat, right-arm medium-fast bowler; all-rounder
Born: 10 July 1975, Brisbane, Australia
Height: 5ft 10in **Weight:** 11st 4lbs
Nickname: Billy Ray
County debut: 2005 (Middlesex), 2007 (Durham)
County cap: 2006 (Middlesex)
Test debut: 2002
ODI debut: 1999-2000
Twenty20 Int debut: 2004-05
1st-Class 200s: 1
Place in batting averages: 207th av. 21.00 (2006 68th av. 42.31)
Place in bowling averages: (2006 91st av. 37.22)
Parents: Bernie and Heather
Marital status: Partner Nicky
Children: Emison (Emi), 29 May 2006
Family links with cricket: 'Brother/father played club cricket'
Education: Hamilton Boys High School

Overseas tours: New Zealand A to England 2002; New Zealand to India 1999-2000 (one-day series), to Zimbabwe and South Africa 2000-01, to Kenya (ICC Knockout Trophy) 2000-01, to Australia 2001-02 (VB Series), to Pakistan 2002, to West Indies 2002, to Sri Lanka (ICC Champions Trophy) 2002-03, to Africa (World Cup) 2002-03, to Sri Lanka 2003, to India 2003-04, to England 2004, to England (ICC Champions Trophy) 2004, to Bangladesh 2004-05, to Australia 2004-05, to Zimbabwe 2005-06, to South Africa 2005-06, to India (ICC Champions Trophy) 2006-07, to West Indies (World Cup) 2006-07, to South Africa (World 20/20) 2007-08, to South Africa 2007-08, plus one-day tournaments and series in Singapore, Sharjah and Australia
Overseas teams played for: Northern Districts 1994-95 – 2004-05; Auckland 2005-06 –
Career highlights to date: 'Test century on debut'
Cricket moments to forget: 'Any duck, dropped catch'
Cricket superstitions: 'None'
Cricketers particularly admired: Jacques Kallis, Ricky Ponting
Young players to look out for: Kane Williamson (Northern Districts)
Other sports played: Golf
Other sports followed: Rugby (Chiefs), baseball (Oakland), football (Man U)
Favourite band: Green Day, Metallica
Extras: Made Test debut in the second Test v West Indies in Grenada 2002, scoring 107 and 69*. His ODI awards include Man of the Series v Bangladesh 2004-05, Man of the Match in the fourth ODI v West Indies at Port of Spain 2002 (63*/6-25), in the third ODI v Australia at Christchurch 2005-06 (101) and v England at Gros Islet in the 2006-07 World Cup (2-25/87*). Was an overseas player with Middlesex 2005-06; was a temporary overseas player with Durham during the 2007 season
Best batting: 212* Northern Districts v Otago, Hamilton 2001-02
Best bowling: 6-32 Northern Districts v Otago, Gisborne 1999-2000

2007 Season

	M	Inn	NO	Runs	HS	Avg	100	50	Ct	St	Balls	Runs	Wkts	Avg	BB	5I	10M
Test																	
FC	5	10	0	210	48	21.00	-	-	-	-	306	217	4	54.25	2-56	-	-
ODI																	
List A	5	5	1	137	98	34.25	-	1	1	-	144	138	1	138.00	1-44	-	
20/20 Int																	
20/20	3	3	0	58	29	19.33	-	-	-	-	42	52	0		-	-	

Career Performances

	M	Inn	NO	Runs	HS	Avg	100	50	Ct	St	Balls	Runs	Wkts	Avg	BB	5I	10M
Test	27	44	4	1527	170	38.17	5	6	23	-	1900	973	20	48.65	3-28	-	-
FC	114	189	18	5391	212 *	31.52	9	26	88	-	12430	6215	203	30.61	6-32	9	1
ODI	133	114	15	3158	141	31.89	4	19	52	-	4803	3784	116	32.62	6-25	1	
List A	260	229	38	6167	141	32.28	5	40	99	-	9954	7634	263	29.02	6-25	1	
20/20 Int	9	8	0	179	66	22.37	-	1	1	-	90	107	4	26.75	2-33	-	
20/20	35	33	2	805	73 *	25.96	-	5	5	-	616	765	29	26.37	3-25	-	

SUPPIAH, A. V. Somerset

Name: Arul Vivasvan Suppiah
Role: Right-hand bat, left-arm orthodox spin bowler
Born: 30 August 1983, Kuala Lumpur, Malaysia
Height: 6ft **Weight:** 12st 7lbs
Nickname: Ruley, Ja Rule
County debut: 2002
Place in batting averages: (2006 150th av. 29.63)
Parents: Suppiah and Baanumathi
Marital status: Single
Family links with cricket: Brother Rohan Vishnu Suppiah has played cricket for Malaysia
Education: Millfield School; Exeter University
Qualifications: 9 GCSEs, 4 A-levels, BA (Hons) in Accounting and Finance, Level 1 coaching qualification
Overseas tours: Millfield School to South Africa 1997, to Sri Lanka 1999; West of England U15 to West Indies 1998; Malaysia to Sharjah (Asian Cricket Council Trophy) 2000-01, to Nepal (ACC Fast Track Countries Tournament) 2005
Overseas teams played for: Doubleview Carine CC, Perth 2005-06
Career highlights to date: 'Making my first-class debut v West Indies A for Somerset 2002; making my debut in the NUL for Somerset v Durham 2002; being the youngest ever cricketer to play for Malaysia; playing for England through the age groups; maiden first-class hundred for Somerset against Derbyshire 2005'
Cricket moments to forget: 'Being bowled out for a golden duck off the seventh ball of the over'
Cricket superstitions: 'Right pad first'
Cricketers particularly admired: Sachin Tendulkar, Wasim Akram, Marcus Trescothick
Young players to look out for: James Hildreth
Other sports played: Hockey (Somerset U16), badminton (Millfield School 1st team)
Other sports followed: Football (Manchester United)
Favourite band: Red Hot Chili Peppers
Relaxations: 'Starbucks'
Extras: Made debut for Malaysia aged 15. Represented England U14, U15, U17 and U18. Somerset U15 Player of the Year 1998. West of England U15 Player of the Year 1998. Most Promising Sportsman for Malaysia 2000. NBC Denis Compton Award for the most promising young Somerset player 2002

Best batting: 123 Somerset v Derbyshire, Derby 2005
Best bowling: 3-46 Somerset v West Indies A, Taunton 2002

2007 Season

	M	Inn	NO	Runs	HS	Avg	100	50	Ct	St	Balls	Runs	Wkts	Avg	BB	5I	10M
Test																	
FC	1	2	1	92	51	92.00	-	1	2	-	18	5	0		-	-	-
ODI																	
List A	1	1	1	0	0 *		-	-	-	-	18	15	0		-	-	
20/20 Int																	
20/20	2	1	1	8	8 *		-	-	-	-	24	27	1	27.00	1-27	-	

Career Performances

	M	Inn	NO	Runs	HS	Avg	100	50	Ct	St	Balls	Runs	Wkts	Avg	BB	5I	10M
Test																	
FC	25	42	1	1161	123	28.31	1	7	11	-	1129	785	12	65.41	3-46	-	-
ODI																	
List A	35	34	2	821	79	25.65	-	5	13	-	879	780	25	31.20	4-39	-	
20/20 Int																	
20/20	17	9	2	74	18 *	10.57	-	-	7	-	132	182	9	20.22	2-14	-	

SUTCLIFFE, I. J. — Lancashire

Name: Iain John Sutcliffe
Role: Left-hand bat, leg-spin bowler
Born: 20 December 1974, Leeds
Height: 6ft 2in **Weight:** 13st
Nickname: Sutty
County debut: 1995 (Leicestershire), 2003 (Lancashire) (*see* ***Extras***)
County cap: 1997 (Leicestershire), 2003 (Lancashire)
1000 runs in a season: 3
1st-Class 200s: 1
Place in batting averages: 149th av. 29.00 (2006 89th av. 36.82)
Parents: John and Valerie
Marital status: Single
Education: Leeds Grammar School; Oxford University
Qualifications: 10 GCSEs, 4 A-levels, 2.1 PPE degree

Overseas tours: Leeds GS to Kenya; Leicestershire to South Africa, to West Indies, to Sri Lanka
Career highlights to date: 'Championship winner's medal 1998'
Cricketers particularly admired: Brian Lara, David Gower
Other sports played: Boxing (Oxford Blue 1994, 1995; British Universities Light-middleweight Champion 1993)
Other sports followed: Football (Liverpool)
Relaxations: Socialising, cinema
Extras: Played NCA England U14 and NCA Development Team U18/U19. Scored 55 of Leicestershire's first innings total of 96 v Pakistanis at Leicester 2001. Leicestershire vice-captain 2002. Leicestershire Player of the Year 2002. Scored century (102*) v Surrey at Whitgift School in the totesport League 2004, in the process sharing with Mark Chilton (115) in a new Lancashire record opening stand in one-day cricket (223). Played one first-class match for Northamptonshire on loan 2007
Best batting: 203 Leicestershire v Glamorgan, Cardiff 2001
Best bowling: 2-21 Oxford University v Cambridge University, Lord's 1996

2007 Season

	M	Inn	NO	Runs	HS	Avg	100	50	Ct	St	Balls	Runs	Wkts	Avg	BB	5I	10M
Test																	
FC	5	9	2	203	104 *	29.00	1	1	5	-	0	0	0		-	-	-
ODI																	
List A	1	1	0	2	2	2.00	-	-	-	-	0	0	0		-	-	
20/20 Int																	
20/20																	

Career Performances

	M	Inn	NO	Runs	HS	Avg	100	50	Ct	St	Balls	Runs	Wkts	Avg	BB	5I	10M
Test																	
FC	184	294	28	9300	203	34.96	16	50	107	-	447	330	9	36.66	2-21	-	-
ODI																	
List A	123	121	11	3222	105 *	29.29	4	20	27	-	0	0	0		-	-	
20/20 Int																	
20/20	4	3	0	4	4	1.33	-	-	-	-	0	0	0		-	-	

85. Who bowed out of Test cricket after the third Test between England and South Africa at Old Trafford in 1955 with a then world record 236 Test wickets?

SUTTON, A. P. Somerset

Name: Andrew Peter Sutton
Role: Right-hand bat, right-arm medium-fast bowler
Born: 29 November 1985, Worcestershire
Height: 6ft **Weight:** 12st 2lbs
Nickname: Sutts
County debut: No first-team appearance
Parents: Caroline and Alan
Marital status: Single
Family links with cricket: 'Uncle played local cricket. Cousins Dave and Mark played local cricket'
Education: Hanley Castle High School; Worcester College of Technology
Qualifications: Level 2 cricket coach, Level 1 football coach
Off-season: 'Somerset – working hard on fitness and strength'
Overseas teams played for: Bassendean CC, Perth 2005-06; Spotswood CC, Melbourne 2006-07
Career highlights to date: 'Playing at Lord's twice for MCC Young Cricketers and being signed by Somerset'
Cricket superstitions: 'None'
Cricketers particularly admired: Brett Lee, Shane Bond, 'every [MCC] Young Cricketer I have played with'
Young players to look out for: Lee Hodgson, Gary Wilson, Will Gidman, Dawid Malan
Other sports played: Football (Worcester City Academy; semi-pro ages 16-18)
Other sports followed: Rugby, football (Man Utd)
Favourite band: Scouting For Girls
Relaxations: 'Watching films, *Family Guy*; chilling with mates'
Extras: Played for Herefordshire in Minor Counties competitions 2004, 2005. Played for MCC Young Cricketers 2006
Opinions on cricket: 'Twenty20 is the best format for all cricket lovers. More cricket should be played in secondary schools.'

SUTTON, L. D. Lancashire

Name: Luke David Sutton
Role: Right-hand bat, wicket-keeper, 'right-arm rubbish'
Born: 4 October 1976, Keynsham
Height: 5ft 11in **Weight:** 12st 13lbs
Nickname: Sutts
County debut: 1997 (Somerset), 2000 (Derbyshire), 2006 (Lancashire)
County cap: 2002 (Derbyshire), 2007 (Lancashire)
50 dismissals in a season: 1
Place in batting averages: 96th av. 36.68 (2006 37th av. 51.23)
Parents: David and Molly
Wife and date of marriage: Jude, 7 October 2006
Education: Millfield School; Durham University
Qualifications: 9 GCSEs, 4 A-levels, 2.1 degree in Economics, CeMAP 1, 2 and 3, Level 1 coaching
Career outside cricket: 'Running Activate Sport camps'
Overseas tours: Various Somerset Schools tours to Netherlands; West of England U15 to West Indies 1991; Millfield School to Zimbabwe 1993, to Sri Lanka 1994; Durham University to Zimbabwe 1997
Overseas teams played for: UNSW, Sydney 1998-99; Northville, Port Elizabeth, South Africa 1999-2000; Subiaco Marist, Perth 2000-01
Career highlights to date: 'Scoring my highest first-class score to date of 151* in the Roses match at Old Trafford in 2006'
Cricket moments to forget: 'Losing the C&G final and the Championship to Sussex in 2006'
Cricket superstitions: 'Plenty!'
Cricketers particularly admired: Ian Healy, Jack Russell, Alec Stewart, Steve Waugh
Young players to look out for: Tom Smith, Karl Brown, Steven Croft
Other sports followed: Football (Derby County), rugby (Bath)
Relaxations: 'Quality time with family and friends'
Extras: Captained England U15 and also represented England U18 and U19. Won Sir John Hobbs Silver Jubilee Memorial Prize for the U16 Cricketer of the Year in 1992 and the Gray-Nicolls Award for the English Schools Cricketer of the Year in 1995. Voted Derbyshire 2nd XI Player of the Year 2000. NBC Denis Compton Award for the most promising young Derbyshire player 2000, 2001, 2002. Captain of Derbyshire

2004-05. Scored 151* v Yorkshire at Old Trafford 2006, setting a new record for the highest Championship score by a Lancashire wicket-keeper. 'Set up a charity with my brother Noel called Freddie Fright, which raises money for CAH research; CAH (congenital adrenal hyperplasia) is a condition suffered by my nephew Freddie'
Best batting: 151* Lancashire v Yorkshire, Old Trafford 2006

2007 Season

	M	Inn	NO	Runs	HS	Avg	100	50	Ct	St	Balls	Runs	Wkts	Avg	BB	5I	10M
Test																	
FC	15	19	3	587	111	36.68	2	1	42	2	0	0	0		-	-	-
ODI																	
List A	11	8	1	43	22	6.14	-	-	11	5	0	0	0		-	-	
20/20 Int																	
20/20																	

Career Performances

	M	Inn	NO	Runs	HS	Avg	100	50	Ct	St	Balls	Runs	Wkts	Avg	BB	5I	10M
Test																	
FC	115	189	26	5351	151 *	32.82	9	17	261	12	0	0	0		-	-	-
ODI																	
List A	132	114	23	1741	83	19.13	-	6	145	19	0	0	0		-	-	
20/20 Int																	
20/20	16	14	4	306	61 *	30.60	-	1	9	7	0	0	0		-	-	

SWANN, G. P. — Nottinghamshire

Name: Graeme Peter Swann
Role: Right-hand bat, right-arm off-spin bowler
Born: 24 March 1979, Northampton
Height: 6ft **Weight:** 13st
Nickname: G-spot, Besty
County debut: 1997 (one-day, Northants), 1998 (first-class, Northants), 2005 (Notts)
County cap: 1999 (Northants)
ODI debut: 1999-2000
50 wickets in a season: 1
Place in batting averages: 124th av. 32.25 (2006 166th av. 27.30)
Place in bowling averages: 83rd av. 33.40 (2006 125th av. 44.53)
Parents: Ray and Mavis
Marital status: Single
Family links with cricket: Father played Minor Counties cricket for Bedfordshire and Northumberland and also for England Amateurs. Brother was contracted to Northamptonshire and Lancashire. 'Cat is named after Gus Logie'
Education: Sponne School, Towcester

Qualifications: 10 GCSEs, 4 A-levels, Levels 1 and 2 coaching awards, 'London Marathon sub 2hr 45min certificate'
Career outside cricket: 'After-dinner speaking, journalism'
Overseas tours: England U19 to South Africa (including U19 World Cup) 1997-98; England A to Zimbabwe and South Africa 1998-99, to West Indies 2000-01, to Sri Lanka 2004-05; England to South Africa 1999-2000, to Sri Lanka 2007-08, to New Zealand 2007-08; ECB National Academy to Australia 2001-02
Overseas teams played for: Old Colts, Christchurch 2002-03
Career highlights to date: 'Winning County Championship [2005]'
Cricket moments to forget: 'Being hit for an enormous six by Peter Such'
Cricketers particularly admired: Neil Foster, Devon Malcolm
Other sports played: Golf, rugby (Northants U14, U15, U16), football (Old Northamptonians Chenecks FC)
Other sports followed: Football (Newcastle United)
Favourite band: Oasis, The Fratellis, The Stone Roses, The Charlatans
Extras: Played for England U14, U15, U17 and U19. Gray-Nicolls Len Newbery Schools Cricketer of the Year 1996. Took 8-118 for England U19 in second 'Test' v Pakistan U19 1998, the best ever figures for England in an U19 'Test'. Cricket Society's Leading Young All-rounder award 1999, 2002. Man of the Match for England A v Windward Islands in St Lucia in the Busta Cup 2000-01. ECB National Academy 2004-05. Scored 33-ball 59, then took 5-17 v Gloucestershire at Trent Bridge in the Pro40 2007
Best batting: 183 Northamptonshire v Gloucestershire, Bristol 2002
Best bowling: 7-33 Northamptonshire v Derbyshire, Northampton 2003
Stop press: Man of the Match in the third ODI v Sri Lanka in Dambulla 2007-08 (4-34/25)

86. Which left-arm spinner holds the record for the best innings analysis in Tests between England and New Zealand (7-32): a) Tony Lock; b) Hedley Howarth; c) Derek Underwood?

2007 Season

	M	Inn	NO	Runs	HS	Avg	100	50	Ct	St	Balls	Runs	Wkts	Avg	BB	5I	10M
Test																	
FC	16	20	4	516	97	32.25	-	3	15	-	2924	1503	45	33.40	7-100	1	1
ODI																	
List A	14	10	2	220	80	27.50	-	2	7	-	708	465	20	23.25	5-17	1	
20/20 Int																	
20/20	5	5	0	128	61	25.60	-	1	1	-	120	121	10	12.10	3-16	-	

Career Performances

	M	Inn	NO	Runs	HS	Avg	100	50	Ct	St	Balls	Runs	Wkts	Avg	BB	5I	10M
Test																	
FC	157	222	15	5448	183	26.31	4	26	109	-	26284	13254	400	33.13	7-33	15	3
ODI	1	0	0	0	0		-	-	-	-	30	24	0		-	-	
List A	172	135	15	2414	83	20.11	-	13	51	-	6509	4833	172	28.09	5-17	2	
20/20 Int																	
20/20	34	33	3	576	62	19.20	-	2	10	-	750	832	40	20.80	3-16	-	

TAHIR, N. Warwickshire

Name: Naqaash Tahir
Role: Right-hand bat, right-arm fast bowler
Born: 14 November 1983, Birmingham
Height: 5ft 10in **Weight:** 11st
Nickname: Naq, Naqy
County debut: 2004
Place in bowling averages: 50th av. 27.76 (2006 34th av. 28.84)
Parents: Mohammed Amin and Ishrat Nasreen
Marital status: Single
Family links with cricket: 'Dad played club cricket and brother played for Worcestershire and Warwickshire'
Education: Moseley School; Spring Hill College
Qualifications: 3 GCSEs, Level 1 coaching
Overseas tours: Warwickshire U15 to South Africa 1999
Overseas teams played for: Mirpur, Pakistan; Subiaco-Floreat, Perth
Cricket superstitions: 'Putting my pads on in a certain way'

Cricketers particularly admired: Waqar Younis, Wasim Akram, Darren Gough, Brett Lee
Young players to look out for: Moeen Ali
Other sports played: Football
Other sports followed: Football (Man Utd)
Relaxations: 'Watching TV; PlayStation 2'
Extras: Has been Moseley Ashfield U15 Player of the Year, Warwickshire U15 Youth Player of the Year, Warwickshire U19 Players' Player of the Year and Warwickshire U19 Player of the Year (Coney Edmonds Trophy). Had match figures of 8-90 (4-47/4-43) on Championship debut v Worcestershire at Edgbaston 2004
Best batting: 49 Warwickshire v Worcestershire, Worcester 2004
Best bowling: 7-107 Warwickshire v Lancashire, Blackpool 2006

2007 Season

	M	Inn	NO	Runs	HS	Avg	100	50	Ct	St	Balls	Runs	Wkts	Avg	BB	5I	10M
Test																	
FC	11	11	1	87	32	8.70	-	-	-	-	1432	694	25	27.76	4-47	-	-
ODI																	
List A	2	0	0	0	0		-	-	-	-	60	58	1	58.00	1-19	-	
20/20 Int																	
20/20																	

Career Performances

	M	Inn	NO	Runs	HS	Avg	100	50	Ct	St	Balls	Runs	Wkts	Avg	BB	5I	10M
Test																	
FC	31	33	10	368	49	16.00	-	-	2	-	3764	2173	77	28.22	7-107	1	-
ODI																	
List A	9	3	2	2	1 *	2.00	-	-	1	-	276	227	3	75.66	1-19	-	
20/20 Int																	
20/20																	

87. Who made his Test debut for South Africa in the rain-affected first Test v England at Centurion in 1995-96, taking 3-98 bowling second change?

TAYLOR, B. V. Hampshire

Name: Billy Victor Taylor
Role: Left-hand bat, right-arm medium-fast bowler
Born: 11 January 1977, Southampton
Height: 6ft 3in **Weight:** 14st
Nickname: Tav
County debut: 1999 (Sussex), 2004 (Hampshire)
County cap: 2006 (Hampshire)
Place in bowling averages: (2006 47th av. 30.33)
Parents: Jackie and Victor
Marital status: Single
Family links with cricket: 'Learnt from and played cricket with both my brothers, Martin and James'
Education: Bitterne Park; Southampton Tech College; Sparsholt Agricultural College, Hampshire
Qualifications: 5 GCSEs, NVQ Level 2 Carpentry and Joinery, NTPC Tree Surgery, Level 2 coaching
Career outside cricket: 'Tree surgery'
Overseas tours: Sussex/Hampshire to Cyprus 1999; Sussex to Grenada 2002
Overseas teams played for: Central Hawke's Bay, New Zealand 1996-97; Manawatu Foxton CC and Horowhenua rep team, New Zealand 1998-99, 2000-01; Te Puke 2002
Career highlights to date: 'Winning the County Championship in 2003 [with Sussex]. Playing for Hampshire'
Cricket moments to forget: 'Don't want to forget any moments as it's such a great career and too short a one'
Cricket superstitions: 'Have a towel hanging out of back of trousers'
Cricketers particularly admired: Malcolm Marshall, Robin Smith, Mushtaq Ahmed
Other sports played: Golf
Other sports followed: Football (Havant & Waterlooville)
Favourite band: Dido, Black Eyed Peas
Extras: Took 98 wickets in New Zealand club cricket in 1998-99. Sussex 2nd XI Player of the Year 1999, 2000. Took hat-trick (Ormond, Sampson, Giddins) v Surrey at Hove in the B&H and another (G. Flower, Maddy, Malcolm) v Leicestershire at Leicester in the C&G, both in 2002. Took Championship hat-trick (Compton, Weekes, Scott) v Middlesex at The Rose Bowl 2006, finishing with 6-32
Best batting: 40 Hampshire v Essex, Rose Bowl 2004
Best bowling: 6-32 Hampshire v Middlesex, Rose Bowl 2006

2007 Season

	M	Inn	NO	Runs	HS	Avg	100	50	Ct	St	Balls	Runs	Wkts	Avg	BB	5I	10M
Test																	
FC																	
ODI																	
List A	7	2	1	5	4	5.00	-	-	1	-	312	228	6	38.00	3-33	-	
20/20 Int																	
20/20	7	0	0	0	0		-	-	-	-	95	126	5	25.20	2-32	-	

Career Performances

	M	Inn	NO	Runs	HS	Avg	100	50	Ct	St	Balls	Runs	Wkts	Avg	BB	5I	10M
Test																	
FC	53	68	26	431	40	10.26	-	-	6	-	8286	4483	135	33.20	6-32	4	-
ODI																	
List A	118	53	25	182	21 *	6.50	-	-	21	-	5199	3770	148	25.47	5-28	1	
20/20 Int																	
20/20	21	6	5	17	12 *	17.00	-	-	3	-	372	444	17	26.11	2-9	-	

TAYLOR, C. G. — Gloucestershire

Name: Christopher (Chris) Glyn Taylor
Role: Right-hand bat, right-arm off-spin bowler
Born: 27 September 1976, Bristol
Height: 5ft 8in **Weight:** 10st
Nickname: Tales, Tootsie
County debut: 2000
County cap: 2001
1000 runs in a season: 1
Place in batting averages: 79th av. 38.57 (2006 171st av. 26.11)
Place in bowling averages: 79th av. 33.10
Parents: Chris and Maggie
Wife and date of marriage: Sarah, 8 December 2001
Children: Harriet, 2003; Alexandra, 2004; Jonty 2007
Family links with cricket: Father and grandfather both played local club cricket
Education: Colston's Collegiate School, Bristol
Qualifications: GCSEs and A-levels
Overseas teams played for: Harbord CC, Manly, Australia 2000

Cricket moments to forget: 'B&H loss to Surrey at Lord's [2001]'
Cricketers particularly admired: Jonty Rhodes, Mark Waugh
Other sports played: Rugby, hockey (both county level); squash, tennis
Other sports followed: Rugby
Relaxations: Fishing
Extras: Represented England Schools U18. In 1995 won the Cricket Society's A. A. Thomson Fielding Prize and Wetherell Award for Leading All-rounder in English Schools Cricket. Scored maiden first-class century (104) v Middlesex 2000, becoming the first player to score a century at Lord's on Championship debut; also the first player to score a century for Gloucestershire in match that was both first-class and Championship debut. NBC Denis Compton Award for the most promising young Gloucestershire player 2000. Four-day captain of Gloucestershire 2004-05
Best batting: 196 Gloucestershire v Nottinghamshire, Trent Bridge 2001
Best bowling: 4-52 Gloucestershire v Northamptonshire, Northampton 2007

2007 Season

	M	Inn	NO	Runs	HS	Avg	100	50	Ct	St	Balls	Runs	Wkts	Avg	BB	5I	10M
Test																	
FC	15	23	4	733	112 *	38.57	3	2	13	-	546	331	10	33.10	4-52	-	-
ODI																	
List A	14	14	0	255	42	18.21	-	-	9	-	102	98	2	49.00	1-21	-	
20/20 Int																	
20/20	9	9	4	149	48 *	29.80	-	-	4	-	0	0	0		-	-	

Career Performances

	M	Inn	NO	Runs	HS	Avg	100	50	Ct	St	Balls	Runs	Wkts	Avg	BB	5I	10M
Test																	
FC	97	171	11	5335	196	33.34	14	18	68	-	1377	863	16	53.93	4-52	-	-
ODI																	
List A	127	116	16	2231	93	22.31	-	11	49	1	260	227	8	28.37	2-5	-	
20/20 Int																	
20/20	36	32	9	682	83	29.65	-	3	15	-	6	11	0		-	-	

88. Who has amassed the most centuries for New Zealand in Tests against England with five:
a) Martin Crowe; b) Geoff Howarth; c) Glenn Turner?

TAYLOR, C. R. Yorkshire

Name: Christopher (Chris) Robert Taylor
Role: Right-hand top-order bat, right-arm fast-medium 'bouncer' bowler
Born: 21 February 1981, Leeds
Height: 6ft 4in **Weight:** 15st
Nickname: CT
County debut: 2001 (Yorkshire), 2006 (Derbyshire)
Place in batting averages: 153rd av. 28.00 (2006 102nd av. 34.92)
Parents: Phil and Elaine
Wife and date of marriage: Charlotte, 10 February 2007
Family links with cricket: 'Dad slogged a few in the Dales Council League, Mum gave good throw-downs and brother (Moo) is captain of Morley CC in Bradford League'
Education: Benton Park High School, Rawdon
Qualifications: 9 GCSEs, 4 A-levels, qualified cricket coach
Career outside cricket: 'Own my own cricket coaching busness www.procricketcoachingacademy.com in Yorkshire and Derbyshire. Own a cricket bat business www.playinthevcricketbats.com'
Off-season: 'Training hard and working on both my businesses'
Overseas tours: Yorkshire to Grenada 2002
Overseas teams played for: Western Suburbs Magpies, Sydney 1999-2002; Fairfield-Liverpool Lions, Sydney 2003-05
Career highlights to date: 'Winning County Championship with Yorkshire 2001. Becoming first Derbyshire player to score a century on both my four-day and one-day debut for the club'
Cricket moments to forget: 'Pair on Sky in the Roses match 2002!'
Cricket superstitions: 'Too many!'
Cricketers particularly admired: Geoffrey Boycott, Anthony McGrath, Stephen Stubbings
Young players to look out for: Oliver Hannon-Dalby, Jonny Bairstow
Other sports played: Football (goalkeeper; played for Farsley Celtic FC)
Other sports followed: Football ('mighty Everton'), rugby league (Leeds Rhinos)
Injuries: Out for two months with a disc problem in the back
Favourite band: Take That, Bon Jovi
Relaxations: 'Swilling, cricket coaching, listening to Steve Patterson'
Extras: Represented Yorkshire U10-U17. Neil Lloyd Trophy for top run-scorer at

Bunbury Festival 1996. Represented England U15, U17 and U19. Yorkshire CCC Supporters' Club Young Player of the Year 1999. Became first Derbyshire player to score a hundred on both first-class debut (102 v Oxford UCCE at The Parks 2006) and one-day debut (100 v Yorkshire at Headingley in the C&G 2006) for the county. Scored 564 List A runs at 62.66 in 2006 and was named Derbyshire One-Day Player of the Season. Derbyshire Supporters' Player of the Year 2006. Left Derbyshire at the end of the 2007 season and has rejoined Yorkshire for 2008

Opinions on cricket: 'Think we play far too much cricket. Never have chance to refresh and work on key aspects of the game. Still far too many Kolpaks [*see page 13*] and non-English-qualified players in our game – give our young players a chance first!'

Best batting: 121 Derbyshire v Glamorgan, Cardiff 2006

2007 Season

	M	Inn	NO	Runs	HS	Avg	100	50	Ct	St	Balls	Runs	Wkts	Avg	BB	5I	10M
Test																	
FC	4	6	0	168	96	28.00	-	2	4	-	0	0	0		-	-	-
ODI																	
List A	3	3	1	72	34 *	36.00	-	-	-	-	0	0	0		-	-	
20/20 Int																	
20/20	6	5	3	55	28 *	27.50	-	-	4	-	0	0	0		-	-	

Career Performances

	M	Inn	NO	Runs	HS	Avg	100	50	Ct	St	Balls	Runs	Wkts	Avg	BB	5I	10M
Test																	
FC	35	59	3	1492	121	26.64	3	8	22	-	0	0	0		-	-	-
ODI																	
List A	20	19	5	693	111 *	49.50	2	2	7	-	0	0	0		-	-	
20/20 Int																	
20/20	14	12	6	147	28 *	24.50	-	-	4	-	0	0	0		-	-	

TAYLOR, J. E. — Leicestershire

Name: Jerome Everton Taylor
Role: Right-hand bat, right-arm fast bowler
Born: 22 June 1984, St Elizabeth, Jamaica
County debut: 2007
Test debut: 2003
ODI debut: 2003
Twenty20 Int debut: 2005-06
Place in batting averages: 218th av. 19.55
Place in bowling averages: 72nd av. 31.90
Overseas tours: West Indies to Zimbabwe 2003-04, to New Zealand 2005-06, to

Malaysia (DLF Cup) 2006-07, to India (ICC Champions Trophy) 2006-07, to Pakistan 2006-07, to India (one-day series) 2006-07, to England 2007, to Zimbabwe (one-day series) 2007-08, to South Africa 2007-08
Overseas teams played for: Jamaica 2002-03 –
Extras: Recorded maiden Test five-wicket innings return (5-50) at his home ground of Kingston, Jamaica, in the fourth Test v India 2006, following up with 4-45 in the second innings. Became first West Indies bowler to take an ODI hat-trick (M. Hussey, Lee, Hogg) as West Indies beat Australia at Mumbai in the ICC Champions Trophy 2006-07. Represented West Indies in the World Cup 2006-07. His match awards include Man of the Match in the first and second ODIs v Zimbabwe in St John's, Antigua, 2006. Was a temporary overseas player with Leicestershire during August and September 2007

Best batting: 40 Leicestershire v Derbyshire, Leicester 2007
Best bowling: 8-59 Jamaica v Trinidad and Tobago, Port-of-Spain 2002-03
Stop press: Man of the [ODI] Series v Zimbabwe 2007-08

2007 Season

	M	Inn	NO	Runs	HS	Avg	100	50	Ct	St	Balls	Runs	Wkts	Avg	BB	5I	10M
Test	3	5	1	55	23 *	13.75	-	-	1	-	480	360	4	90.00	2-67	-	-
FC	7	11	2	176	40	19.55	-	-	1	-	1044	702	22	31.90	6-35	3	-
ODI																	
List A	6	4	2	45	22	22.50	-	-	2	-	216	210	6	35.00	3-33	-	
20/20 Int																	
20/20																	

Career Performances

	M	Inn	NO	Runs	HS	Avg	100	50	Ct	St	Balls	Runs	Wkts	Avg	BB	5I	10M
Test	13	21	4	164	23 *	9.64	-	-	1	-	2266	1389	35	39.68	5-50	2	-
FC	43	65	14	557	40	10.92	-	-	10	-	6599	3523	140	25.16	8-59	10	2
ODI	35	13	5	65	13	8.12	-	-	9	-	1796	1455	49	29.69	4-24	-	
List A	48	21	9	128	22	10.66	-	-	12	-	2396	1922	67	28.68	4-23	-	
20/20 Int	1	0	0	0	0		-	-	-	-	18	30	2	15.00	2-30	-	
20/20	3	0	0	0	0		-	-	1	-	64	85	7	12.14	5-10	1	

TAYLOR, J. W. A. — Leicestershire

Name: James William Arthur Taylor
Role: Right-hand bat, leg-spin bowler
Born: 6 January 1990, Nottingham
County debut: No first-team appearance
Education: Shrewsbury School
Overseas tours: England U19 to Malaysia (U19 World Cup) 2007-08
Extras: Played for Worcestershire 2nd XI 2006, 2007. Played one match for Shropshire in the Minor Counties Championship 2007. Played for Midlands U17 at ECB U17 Regional Festival at Loughborough 2007. Has represented England U19

TEN DOESCHATE, R. N. — Essex

Name: Ryan Neil ten Doeschate
Role: Right-hand bat, right-arm medium-fast bowler; all-rounder
Born: 30 June 1980, Port Elizabeth, South Africa
Height: 5ft 11in **Weight:** 13st 5lbs
Nickname: Tendo
County debut: 2003
County cap: 2006
ODI debut: 2006
Place in batting averages: 70th av. 40.42 (2006 73rd av. 40.30)
Place in bowling averages: (2006 105th av. 39.82)
Parents: Boudewyn and Ingrid
Marital status: Single
Education: Fairbairn College; University of Cape Town

Qualifications: Business science degree
Overseas tours: Netherlands to Ireland (ICC Trophy) 2005, to Scotland (European Championship) 2006, to South Africa (ICC Associates Tri-Series) 2006-07, to Kenya (ICC World Cricket League) 2006-07, to West Indies (World Cup) 2006-07, to Ireland (Quadrangular Series) 2007
Overseas teams played for: Western Province, South Africa; Bloemendaal, Netherlands; Rockingham-Mandurah, Australia
Career highlights to date: 'Winning totesport in 2005. Getting county cap'
Cricket moments to forget: 'My county debut at Chelmsford'
Cricketers particularly admired: Jacques Kallis, Kepler Wessels
Young players to look out for: Tom Westley, Mervyn Westfield
Other sports played: Rugby
Other sports followed: Football (Arsenal), rugby (Stormers)
Favourite band: Phil Collins
Relaxations: Golf, tennis, reading
Extras: Has played first-class and one-day cricket (including ODIs) for Netherlands. Scored 686 runs (av. 228.66) in the ICC Inter-Continental Cup 2006, recording four consecutive centuries, including twin hundreds (138/100) v Bermuda and a competition record 259* (plus match figures of 6-20/3-92) v Canada, both in Pretoria. His match awards include Man of the Match v Bermuda in Nairobi in the ICC World Cricket League 2006-07 (3-37/109*). Is not considered an overseas player
Best batting: 259* Netherlands v Canada, Pretoria (SCC) 2006
Best bowling: 6-20 Netherlands v Canada, Pretoria (SCC) 2006

2007 Season

	M	Inn	NO	Runs	HS	Avg	100	50	Ct	St	Balls	Runs	Wkts	Avg	BB	5I	10M
Test																	
FC	16	23	2	849	148	40.42	3	3	10	-	717	552	7	78.85	1-13	-	-
ODI																	
List A	15	12	0	225	42	18.75	-	-	5	-	226	200	13	15.38	5-50	1	
20/20 Int																	
20/20	8	7	2	96	26	19.20	-	-	5	-	12	15	0		-	-	

Career Performances

	M	Inn	NO	Runs	HS	Avg	100	50	Ct	St	Balls	Runs	Wkts	Avg	BB	5I	10M
Test																	
FC	36	47	6	2175	259 *	53.04	9	6	19	-	3377	2406	59	40.77	6-20	2	-
ODI	17	16	5	615	109 *	55.90	1	4	7	-	777	654	30	21.80	4-31	-	
List A	70	55	17	1571	109 *	41.34	1	8	26	-	1570	1390	70	19.85	5-50	1	
20/20 Int																	
20/20	29	23	9	363	49 *	25.92	-	-	12	-	133	182	5	36.40	2-27	-	

THOMAS, A. C. Warwickshire

Name: Alfonso Clive Thomas
Role: Right-hand bat, right-arm fast-medium bowler
Born: 9 February 1977, Cape Town, South Africa
County debut: 2007
Twenty20 Int debut: 2006-07
Place in batting averages: 204th av. 21.66
Place in bowling averages: 103rd av. 36.70
Overseas tours: South Africa VI to Hong Kong 2001; South Africa A to Zimbabwe 2004, 2006-07; South Africa to India 2004-05; South Africa Emerging Players to Australia (Cricket Australia Emerging Players Tournament) 2006
Overseas teams played for: Western Province B 1998-99; North West 2000-01 – 2002-03; Northerns 2003-04 – 2005-06; Titans 2003-04 –
Extras: Played for South African Board President's XI v India A 2001-02, for South Africa A v India A 2001-02 and v England XI 2004-05, and for Rest of South Africa v Indians 2006-07. His match awards include Man of the Match v Dolphins at Pietermaritzburg in the SuperSport Series 2006-07 (5-55/2-46) and v Lions at Potchefstroom in the SuperSport Series 2006-07 (4-43/3-67 plus 54). Played for Staffordshire in the C&G 2005. Was a temporary overseas player with Warwickshire during August and September 2007
Best batting: 119* North West v Northerns, Centurion 2002-03
Best bowling: 7-54 Titans v Cape Cobras, Cape Town 2005-06

2007 Season

	M	Inn	NO	Runs	HS	Avg	100	50	Ct	St	Balls	Runs	Wkts	Avg	BB	5I	10M
Test																	
FC	4	7	1	130	42	21.66	-	-	2	-	776	367	10	36.70	4-109	-	-
ODI																	
List A	5	1	1	1	1 *		-	-	1	-	155	161	4	40.25	2-49	-	
20/20 Int																	
20/20																	

Career Performances

	M	Inn	NO	Runs	HS	Avg	100	50	Ct	St	Balls	Runs	Wkts	Avg	BB	5I	10M
Test																	
FC	66	99	23	2151	119 *	28.30	2	8	24	-	12853	5780	228	25.35	7-54	11	1
ODI																	
List A	68	39	16	344	27 *	14.95	-	-	14	-	3110	2526	78	32.38	4-31	-	
20/20 Int	1	0	0	0	0		-	-	-	-	24	25	3	8.33	3-25	-	
20/20	22	6	3	53	27	17.66	-	-	5	-	396	545	18	30.27	3-20	-	

THOMPSON, J. G. Gloucestershire

Name: Jackson Gladwin Thompson
Role: Left-hand bat, right-arm off-spin bowler, occasional wicket-keeper
Born: 7 February 1986, Ozar Township, India
Height: 6ft 4in **Weight:** 16st
Nickname: Jacko
County debut: 2007
County cap: 2007
Parents: Gladwin and Balarojamma
Marital status: Single
Family links with cricket: 'Cousin plays for Mumbai'
Education: St Benedict's Sports College; University of Gloucestershire (studying BSc in Computer Science)
Qualifications: 12 GCSEs, 3 A-levels
Off-season: 'Training; university'
Overseas tours: Oman U17 to Bangladesh (Asia Cricket Council U17 Asia Cup) 2000-01
Cricket moments to forget: 'Misfield on first-class debut for Gloucestershire that went for a boundary'
Cricket superstitions: 'None'
Cricketers particularly admired: Matthew Hayden
Young players to look out for: Isaac Reid, James Campbell
Other sports played: Football ('occasional')
Other sports followed: Football (Arsenal)
Relaxations: 'Internet surfing'
Extras: Played for Gloucestershire Board XI in the 2003 C&G. Gloucestershire CCC Academy Player of the Year 2006
Opinions on cricket: 'Fast, demanding and commercial.'
Best batting: 21 Gloucestershire v Middlesex, Bristol 2007

2007 Season

	M	Inn	NO	Runs	HS	Avg	100	50	Ct	St	Balls	Runs	Wkts	Avg	BB	5I	10M
Test																	
FC	1	2	0	32	21	16.00	-	-	-	-	0	0	0		-	-	-
ODI																	
List A	1	1	0	7	7	7.00	-	-	-	-	0	0	0		-	-	
20/20 Int																	
20/20																	

Career Performances

	M	Inn	NO	Runs	HS	Avg	100	50	Ct	St	Balls	Runs	Wkts	Avg	BB	5I	10M
Test																	
FC	1	2	0	32	21	16.00	-	-	-	-	0	0	0		-	-	-
ODI																	
List A	2	2	0	8	7	4.00	-	-	-	-	0	0	0		-	-	
20/20 Int																	
20/20																	

THORNELY, M. A. — Sussex

Name: Michael Alistair Thornely
Role: Right-hand top-order bat, right-arm medium-fast bowler
Born: 19 October 1987, London
Height: 6ft 1in **Weight:** 13st
Nickname: T-Bone, A-Bomb, Chubs, Thorners
County debut: 2007
Parents: Richard and Jan
Marital status: Single
Family links with cricket: 'Uncle played for Cambridgeshire'
Education: Brighton College
Qualifications: 8 GCSEs, 3 A-levels
Off-season: 'Playing club cricket in Perth for six months'
Overseas tours: Brighton College to Sri Lanka; Sussex Academy to Cape Town 2003, 2005; Sussex to Mumbai 2004
Overseas teams played for: Subiaco Marist CC, Perth 2007-08
Career highlights to date: '150 v Essex 2nd XI for Sussex 2nd XI 2007'

Cricket moments to forget: 'Forgetting my whites for my first county game (U11) and getting a first-ball duck'
Cricket superstitions: 'Not superstitious'
Cricketers particularly admired: Mark Waugh, Michael Vaughan, Kevin Pietersen
Young players to look out for: Matt Machan, Ben Brown, Will Beer
Other sports played: Rugby (Sussex)
Other sports followed: Football (Man United), rugby (Harlequins)
Favourite band: Red Hot Chili Peppers, Razorlight, Justin Timberlake
Relaxations: 'Listening to music, watching movies, seeing friends'
Extras: Scored 1350 runs for Brighton College 2005, including six centuries
Opinions on cricket: 'I like the way the Twenty20 format has affected the longer forms of the game, with players inventing new shots and increasing scoring rates resulting in a more appealing game.'
Best batting: 11 Sussex v Indians, Hove 2007

2007 Season

	M	Inn	NO	Runs	HS	Avg	100	50	Ct	St	Balls	Runs	Wkts	Avg	BB	5I	10M
Test																	
FC	2	3	0	15	11	5.00	-	-	4	-	0	0	0		-	-	-
ODI																	
List A	1	0	0	0	0		-	-	-	-	0	0	0		-	-	
20/20 Int																	
20/20																	

Career Performances

	M	Inn	NO	Runs	HS	Avg	100	50	Ct	St	Balls	Runs	Wkts	Avg	BB	5I	10M
Test																	
FC	2	3	0	15	11	5.00	-	-	4	-	0	0	0		-	-	-
ODI																	
List A	1	0	0	0	0		-	-	-	-	0	0	0		-	-	
20/20 Int																	
20/20																	

89. Which Surrey batsman and future England selector became the first player to score a Test hundred in all seven (at the time) Test-playing countries when he scored 148* v South Africa at Durban in 1964-65?

THORNICROFT, N. D. — Yorkshire

Name: Nicholas (Nick) David Thornicroft
Role: Left-hand bat, right-arm fast bowler
Born: 23 January 1985, York
Height: 5ft 11in **Weight:** 12st 8lbs
Nickname: Thorny, Mad Dog, Harry Potter
County debut: 2002 (*see **Extras***)
Parents: Lyn and David
Marital status: Single
Education: Easingwold School, York
Overseas tours: Yorkshire U16 to Cape Town, to Jersey; England U19 to Australia 2002-03
Career highlights to date: 'Getting Neil Fairbrother as my first first-class wicket'
Cricketers particularly admired: Darren Gough, Brett Lee, Ian Botham, Craig White, Andrew Flintoff
Other sports played: Athletics, football, basketball
Other sports followed: Football (York City FC), horse racing
Relaxations: 'Spending time with family; music; shooting'
Extras: Made first-class debut in Roses match v Lancashire at Old Trafford 2002, aged 17. Represented England U19 2002 and 2003. Played for Essex on loan 2005. Yorkshire 2nd XI cap 2006. Released by Yorkshire at the end of the 2007 season
Best batting: 30 Yorkshire v Nottinghamshire, Headingley 2004
Best bowling: 6-60 Yorkshire v LUCCE, Headingley 2007

2007 Season

	M	Inn	NO	Runs	HS	Avg	100	50	Ct	St	Balls	Runs	Wkts	Avg	BB	5I	10M
Test																	
FC	1	0	0	0	0		-	-	1	-	126	72	6	12.00	6-60	1	-
ODI																	
List A	1	0	0	0	0		-	-	1	-	54	47	1	47.00	1-47	-	
20/20 Int																	
20/20																	

Career Performances

	M	Inn	NO	Runs	HS	Avg	100	50	Ct	St	Balls	Runs	Wkts	Avg	BB	5I	10M
Test																	
FC	8	12	5	54	30	7.71	-	-	2	-	975	615	17	36.17	6-60	1	-
ODI																	
List A	15	7	4	52	20	17.33	-	-	3	-	589	610	17	35.88	5-42	1	
20/20 Int																	
20/20	1	1	1	0	0 *		-	-	-	-	6	20	0		-	-	

THORP, C. D. Durham

Name: Callum David Thorp
Role: Right-hand bat, right-arm fast-medium bowler
Born: 11 January 1975, Perth, Western Australia
Height: 6ft 3in **Weight:** 13st 5lbs
County debut: 2005
Place in batting averages: (2006 229th av. 17.15)
Place in bowling averages: (2006 13th av. 24.82)
Parents: Annette and David
Marital status: Single
Education: Servite College, Western Australia
Overseas teams played for: Western Warriors 2002-03 – 2003-04; Wanneroo DCC
Cricket superstitions: 'Left shoe on first'
Cricketers particularly admired: Mike Hussey
Young players to look out for: Graham Onions, Luke Evans
Other sports followed: AFL (West Coast Eagles), football (West Ham United)
Relaxations: 'Golf'
Extras: Took 4-58 for Western Australia v England XI in two-day match at Perth 2002-03. Attended Commonwealth Bank [Australian] Cricket Academy 2003. Took 5-17 v Scotland at The Grange in the C&G 2006, the best one-day figures for Durham since the county gained first-class status, following up with 100 runs (75/28) and ten wickets (6-55/5-42) in the Championship match v Hampshire at The Rose Bowl later that week. Has British parents and is not considered an overseas player
Best batting: 75 Durham v Hampshire, Rose Bowl 2006
Best bowling: 6-55 Durham v Hampshire, Rose Bowl 2006

2007 Season

	M	Inn	NO	Runs	HS	Avg	100	50	Ct	St	Balls	Runs	Wkts	Avg	BB	5I	10M
Test																	
FC	2	4	1	40	30 *	13.33	-	-	-	-	286	163	6	27.16	3-51	-	-
ODI																	
List A	2	1	0	18	18	18.00	-	-	1	-	93	61	4	15.25	4-30	-	
20/20 Int																	
20/20																	

Career Performances

	M	Inn	NO	Runs	HS	Avg	100	50	Ct	St	Balls	Runs	Wkts	Avg	BB	5I	10M
Test																	
FC	25	39	3	481	75	13.36	-	2	9	-	3613	1889	59	32.01	6-55	2	1
ODI																	
List A	29	18	6	233	52	19.41	-	1	4	-	1335	1010	37	27.29	6-17	1	
20/20 Int																	
20/20	9	6	0	63	13	10.50	-	-	1	-	162	266	3	88.66	2-32	-	

TOMLINSON, J. A. — Hampshire

Name: James Andrew Tomlinson
Role: Left-hand lower-order bat, left-arm fast-medium bowler
Born: 12 June 1982, Winchester
Height: 6ft 2in **Weight:** 13st
Nickname: Tommo, T-Bird, Mr T
County debut: 2002
Place in bowling averages: 116th av. 40.61
Parents: Ian and Janet
Marital status: Single
Family links with cricket: 'Both grandads played at a high level in Yorkshire leagues. Brothers Ralph and Hugh play for Dulwich and South Wilts cricket clubs'
Education: Harrow Way Community School, Andover; Cricklade College, Andover; Cardiff University
Qualifications: 3 A-levels, 2.1 degree in Education and Psychology
Career outside cricket: 'Patient!'
Off-season: 'Rehab, fitness and some sort of work, voluntary and paid'
Overseas teams played for: South Perth 2004-05, 2006-07

Career highlights to date: '6-63 v Derbyshire 2003, 5-78 v Worcestershire 2007 and a very good and crucial caught-and-bowled v Surrey 2007. Any Hampshire win I am involved in'
Cricket moments to forget: 'Any dropped catch'
Cricket superstitions: 'None'
Cricketers particularly admired: Dimitri Mascarenhas, Nic Pothas, Jimmy Adams, Mark Ramprakash, Ryan Sidebottom
Young players to look out for: Benny Howell, Hamza Riazuddin
Other sports played: Darts
Other sports followed: Football (West Ham United)
Injuries: Out for three weeks with impingement of an ankle and a calf tear
Favourite band: Snow Patrol, Scouting For Girls, A-ha
Relaxations: 'Ornithology, wildlife in general'
Extras: Played for Development of Excellence XI (South) 2001. Played for Cardiff UCCE 2002-03. Represented British Universities 2002-03. NBC Denis Compton Award for the most promising young Hampshire player 2003. Cardiff University Sportsperson of the Year award 2003
Opinions on cricket: 'Too many Kolpak players [*see page 13*]. Leave Twenty20 as it is. First-division cricket is excellent. Playing three-day cricket in second team is a waste of time – should be four-day games.'
Best batting: 23 Hampshire v Indians, Rose Bowl 2002
Best bowling: 6-63 Hampshire v Derbyshire, Derby 2003

2007 Season

	M	Inn	NO	Runs	HS	Avg	100	50	Ct	St	Balls	Runs	Wkts	Avg	BB	5I	10M
Test																	
FC	5	4	2	19	9	9.50	-	-	1	-	928	528	13	40.61	5-78	1	-
ODI																	
List A	2	0	0	0	0		-	-	1	-	75	63	2	31.50	2-43	-	
20/20 Int																	
20/20																	

Career Performances

	M	Inn	NO	Runs	HS	Avg	100	50	Ct	St	Balls	Runs	Wkts	Avg	BB	5I	10M
Test																	
FC	22	30	13	95	23	5.58	-	-	6	-	3324	2259	47	48.06	6-63	2	-
ODI																	
List A	20	11	4	15	6	2.14	-	-	3	-	833	651	18	36.16	4-47	-	
20/20 Int																	
20/20	2	1	0	5	5	5.00	-	-	-	-	42	48	1	48.00	1-20	-	

TOOR, K. S. Middlesex

Name: Kabir Singh Toor
Role: Right-hand bat, leg-spin bowler
Born: 30 April 1990, Watford, Hertfordshire
County debut: No first-team appearance
Education: John Lyon School, Harrow
Extras: Made 2nd XI Championship debut 2006. Played for Middlesex U17. Played for South U17 in ECB U17 Regional Festival at Loughborough 2007. Plays for Radlett CC

TREDWELL, J. C. Kent

Name: James Cullum Tredwell
Role: Left-hand bat, right-arm off-spin bowler
Born: 27 February 1982, Ashford, Kent
Height: 5ft 11in **Weight:** 14st 2lbs
Nickname: Tredders, Pingu, Chad
County debut: 2001
County cap: 2007
Place in batting averages: 166th av. 26.70 (2006 255th av. 14.00)
Place in bowling averages: 100th av. 35.69 (2006 85th av. 35.65)
Parents: John and Rosemary
Marital status: Single
Family links with cricket: Father played for Ashford and Folkestone in Kent League
Education: Southlands Community Comprehensive

Qualifications: 10 GCSEs, 2 A-levels, ECB Level 1 coach
Overseas tours: Kent U17 to Sri Lanka 1998-99; Kent to Port Elizabeth 2002; England A to Malaysia and India 2003-04; England Performance Programme to India 2007-08; England to New Zealand 2007-08 (one-day series)
Overseas teams played for: Redlands Tigers, Brisbane 2000-02
Cricket moments to forget: 'Being hit for six in a crucial B&H Cup match v Essex, which probably cost Kent's qualification to next stage'
Cricketers particularly admired: 'All the great spinners'
Extras: Represented England U19 2001 (captain in second 'Test'). Kent Most Improved Player Award 2003. ECB National Academy 2003-04. Took over captaincy of England A in India 2003-04 after Alex Gidman was forced to return home with a hand injury. NBC Denis Compton Award for the most promising young Kent player 2003
Best batting: 116* Kent v Yorkshire, Tunbridge Wells 2007
Best bowling: 6-47 Kent v Surrey, Canterbury 2007

2007 Season

	M	Inn	NO	Runs	HS	Avg	100	50	Ct	St	Balls	Runs	Wkts	Avg	BB	5I	10M
Test																	
FC	14	19	2	454	116 *	26.70	1	2	11	-	2493	1285	36	35.69	6-47	1	-
ODI																	
List A	17	11	4	243	88	34.71	-	2	8	-	765	646	19	34.00	2-20	-	
20/20 Int																	
20/20	11	2	0	13	12	6.50	-	-	5	-	168	187	6	31.16	2-19	-	

Career Performances

	M	Inn	NO	Runs	HS	Avg	100	50	Ct	St	Balls	Runs	Wkts	Avg	BB	5I	10M
Test																	
FC	53	74	9	1407	116 *	21.64	1	5	52	-	8912	5037	127	39.66	6-47	3	1
ODI																	
List A	104	79	26	1051	88	19.83	-	4	50	-	4220	3271	101	32.38	4-16	-	
20/20 Int																	
20/20	37	22	2	246	34	12.30	-	-	12	-	606	782	28	27.92	4-21	-	

90. Who set an England ODI record opening stand of 200 v South Africa at The Oval in the NatWest Series 2003?

TREGO, P. D. Somerset

Name: Peter David Trego
Role: Right-hand bat, right-arm fast-medium/occasional leg-break bowler; all-rounder
Born: 12 June 1981, Weston-super-Mare
Height: 6ft **Weight:** 13st
Nickname: Tregs, Steve the Pirate, Pikey
County debut: 2000 (Somerset), 2003 (Kent), 2005 (Middlesex)
County cap: 2007 (Somerset)
Place in batting averages: 28th av. 52.25 (2006 148th av. 29.80)
Place in bowling averages: 94th av. 34.27 (2006 140th av. 50.78)
Parents: Carol and Paul
Wife and date of marriage: Claire, 8 May 2000
Children: Amelia Ann, 9 July 2001; Davis Paul, 8 February 2005; Dexter, 2007
Family links with cricket: 'Brother on staff at Somerset 1997; unlucky not to get a better go – batter and off-spin bowler'
Education: Wyvern Comprehensive, Weston-super-Mare
Qualifications: 'School of Life'
Career outside cricket: 'Still thinking'
Overseas tours: Somerset to Cape Town 2000, 2001, 2006
Career highlights to date: 'County cap 10 June 2007'
Cricket moments to forget: 'All of 2003'
Cricket superstitions: 'None'
Cricketers particularly admired: Ian Botham, Graham Rose, Justin Langer, Andrew Caddick, Marcus Trescothick, Ian Blackwell
Young players to look out for: James Hildreth, 'my sons'
Other sports played: Football (semi-professional with Weston-super-Mare and Margate FC), golf (Weston-super-Mare first team; 3 handicap)
Other sports followed: Football (Man Utd), golf (Tiger Woods)
Favourite band: Oasis, Queen, Guns N' Roses
Relaxations: 'Shopping and my kids'
Extras: Represented England U19. NBC Denis Compton Award for the most promising young Somerset player 2000. Scored 140 at Taunton 2002 as Somerset, chasing 454 to win, tied with West Indies A. 'I'm very proud of being the first player ever to incur a five-run penalty for replacing Jamie Cox and nobody thinking to tell Mr Dudleston.' 'Played football in the FA Cup on *Match of the Day* – that was cool up

until the part where I was 'megged to let in the goal to send us out; but still got Star Man in the paper.' Left Middlesex at the end of the 2005 season and rejoined Somerset for 2006. Scored 63-ball 78 and took 4-61 v Middlesex at Lord's in the Friends Provident 2007

Opinions on cricket: 'Too much emphasis put on speed of bowling. The vast majority of great/good seam bowlers move the ball sideways. I'm not sure why we always seem to go for 85mph and straight rather than 78-80mph and clever. Why we feel that unless you're rapid you won't cut it at the highest level, I don't know.'

Best batting: 140 Somerset v West Indies A, Taunton 2002

Best bowling: 6-59 Middlesex v Nottinghamshire, Trent Bridge 2005

2007 Season

	M	Inn	NO	Runs	HS	Avg	100	50	Ct	St	Balls	Runs	Wkts	Avg	BB	5I	10M
Test																	
FC	17	22	6	836	130	52.25	2	5	4	-	1719	1131	33	34.27	4-49	-	-
ODI																	
List A	14	13	2	213	78	19.36	-	1	5	-	531	539	19	28.36	5-44	1	
20/20 Int																	
20/20	6	5	1	86	35	21.50	-	-	-	-	108	126	6	21.00	2-28	-	

Career Performances

	M	Inn	NO	Runs	HS	Avg	100	50	Ct	St	Balls	Runs	Wkts	Avg	BB	5I	10M
Test																	
FC	51	74	10	2200	140	34.37	6	10	17	-	5757	3944	97	40.65	6-59	1	-
ODI																	
List A	59	50	9	564	78	13.75	-	1	13	-	1811	1731	57	30.36	5-44	1	
20/20 Int																	
20/20	15	14	3	198	47	18.00	-	-	2	-	206	302	13	23.23	2-17	-	

91. Who became the fourth bowler to reach 300 Test wickets, during the second Test between England and New Zealand at Headingley in 1983: a) Ian Botham; b) Richard Hadlee; c) Bob Willis?

TREMLETT, C. T. Hampshire

Name: Christopher (Chris) Timothy Tremlett
Role: Right-hand bat, right-arm fast-medium bowler
Born: 2 September 1981, Southampton
Height: 6ft 7in **Weight:** 16st 1lb
Nickname: Twiggy, Goober
County debut: 2000
County cap: 2004
Test debut: 2007
ODI debut: 2005
Twenty20 Int debut: 2007-08
Place in batting averages: 147th av. 29.00
Place in bowling averages: 90th av. 33.96 (2006 11th av. 24.55)
Parents: Timothy and Carolyn
Marital status: Single
Family links with cricket: Grandfather [Maurice] played for Somerset and in three Tests for England. Father played for Hampshire and is now director of cricket at the county
Education: Thornden School, Chandlers Ford; Taunton's College, Southampton
Qualifications: 5 GCSEs, BTEC National Diploma in Sports Science, Level 2 coach
Overseas tours: West of England U15 to West Indies 1997; Hampshire U16 to Jersey; England U17 to Northern Ireland (ECC Colts Festival) 1999; England U19 to India 2000-01; ECB National Academy to Australia 2001-02, to Australia and Sri Lanka 2002-03; England VI to Hong Kong 2004; England to Australia 2006-07 (C'wealth Bank Series), to South Africa (World 20/20) 2007-08, to Sri Lanka 2007-08 (one-day series), to New Zealand 2007-08 (one-day series); England Performance Programme to India 2007-08
Cricketers particularly admired: Glenn McGrath, Mark Waugh, Shane Warne
Other sports played: Basketball, volleyball
Other sports followed: Football (Arsenal)
Relaxations: 'Socialising with friends; cinema'
Extras: Took wicket (Mark Richardson) with first ball in first-class cricket v New Zealand A at Portsmouth 2000; finished with debut match figures of 6-91. Represented England U19. NBC Denis Compton Award for the most promising young Hampshire player 2000, 2001. Hampshire Young Player of the Year 2001. Took Championship hat-trick (Ealham, Swann, G. Smith) v Nottinghamshire at Trent Bridge 2005. ECB National Academy 2006-07
Best batting: 64 Hampshire v Gloucestershire, Rose Bowl 2005
Best bowling: 6-44 Hampshire v Sussex, Hove 2005

2007 Season

	M	Inn	NO	Runs	HS	Avg	100	50	Ct	St	Balls	Runs	Wkts	Avg	BB	5I	10M
Test	3	5	1	50	25 *	12.50	-	-	1	-	859	386	13	29.69	3-12	-	-
FC	10	14	6	232	62 *	29.00	-	1	3	-	1907	985	29	33.96	4-47	-	-
ODI	2	2	2	19	19 *		-	-	1	-	102	130	2	65.00	2-57	-	
List A	11	7	3	37	19 *	9.25	-	-	3	-	600	487	12	40.58	2-29	-	
20/20 Int																	
20/20	4	2	1	2	2	2.00	-	-	1	-	66	74	5	14.80	3-12	-	

Career Performances

	M	Inn	NO	Runs	HS	Avg	100	50	Ct	St	Balls	Runs	Wkts	Avg	BB	5I	10M
Test	3	5	1	50	25 *	12.50	-	-	1	-	859	386	13	29.69	3-12	-	-
FC	71	94	28	1247	64	18.89	-	3	19	-	11935	6586	243	27.10	6-44	6	-
ODI	8	5	2	35	19 *	11.66	-	-	1	-	419	395	8	49.37	4-32	-	
List A	95	57	17	373	38 *	9.32	-	-	19	-	4385	3368	137	24.58	4-25	-	
20/20 Int	1	0	0	0	0		-	-	-	-	24	45	2	22.50	2-45	-	
20/20	17	9	3	48	13	8.00	-	-	4	-	342	419	21	19.95	3-12	-	

TRESCOTHICK, M. E. Somerset

Name: Marcus Edward Trescothick
Role: Left-hand bat, right-arm swing bowler, reserve wicket-keeper
Born: 25 December 1975, Keynsham, Bristol
Height: 6ft 3in **Weight:** 14st 7lbs
Nickname: Banger, Tres
County debut: 1993
County cap: 1999
Benefit: 2008
Test debut: 2000
ODI debut: 2000
Twenty20 Int debut: 2005
1000 runs in a season: 1
1st-Class 200s: 2
Place in batting averages: 10th av. 61.04 (2006 159th av. 28.33)
Parents: Martyn and Lin
Wife and date of marriage: Hayley, 24 January 2004
Children: Ellie, April 2005
Family links with cricket: Father played for Somerset 2nd XI; uncle played club cricket

Education: Sir Bernard Lovell School, Bristol
Qualifications: 7 GCSEs
Overseas tours: England U18 to South Africa 1992-93; England U19 to Sri Lanka 1993-94, to West Indies 1994-95 (c); England A to Bangladesh and New Zealand 1999-2000; England to Kenya (ICC Knockout Trophy) 2000-01, to Pakistan and Sri Lanka 2000-01, to Zimbabwe (one-day series) 2001-02, to India and New Zealand 2001-02, to Sri Lanka (ICC Champions Trophy) 2002-03, to Australia 2002-03, to Africa (World Cup) 2002-03, to Bangladesh and Sri Lanka 2003-04, to West Indies 2003-04, to South Africa 2004-05, to Pakistan 2005-06, to India 2005-06, to Australia 2006-07
Overseas teams played for: Melville CC, Perth 1997-99
Cricketers particularly admired: Adam Gilchrist, Andy Caddick
Other sports followed: Golf, football (Bristol City FC)
Relaxations: 'Spending time at home, playing golf'
Extras: Scored more than 1000 runs for England U19. Took hat-trick (Gilchrist, Angel, McIntyre) for Somerset v Young Australia at Taunton 1995. PCA Player of the Year 2000. Sports.com Cricketer of the Year 2001. BBC West Country Sports Sportsman of the Year 2001. One of *Indian Cricket*'s five Cricketers of the Year 2002. Scored 114* v South Africa at The Oval in the NatWest Series 2003, sharing with Vikram Solanki (106) in a record England opening partnership in ODIs (200). Scored century in each innings (105/107) in the second Test v West Indies at Edgbaston 2004. Man of the Match in his 100th ODI v Bangladesh at The Oval in the NatWest Series 2005 (100*). His Test awards include England's Man of the Series v Bangladesh 2005 and Man of the Match in the fifth Test v South Africa at The Oval 2003 (219/69*). His other ODI awards include Man of the Series v West Indies 2003-04 and Man of the Match v Australia at Headingley in the NatWest Challenge 2005 (104*). One of *Wisden*'s Five Cricketers of the Year 2005. Appointed MBE in 2006 New Year Honours as part of 2005 Ashes-winning England team
Best batting: 284 Somerset v Northamptonshire, Northampton 2007
Best bowling: 4-36 Somerset v Young Australia, Taunton 1995

2007 Season

	M	Inn	NO	Runs	HS	Avg	100	50	Ct	St	Balls	Runs	Wkts	Avg	BB	5I	10M
Test																	
FC	16	24	2	1343	284	61.04	4	5	34	-	0	0	0		-	-	-
ODI																	
List A	15	15	0	517	124	34.46	1	5	7	-	0	0	0		-	-	
20/20 Int																	
20/20	4	4	0	138	76	34.50	-	1	-	-	0	0	0		-	-	

Career Performances

	M	Inn	NO	Runs	HS	Avg	100	50	Ct	St	Balls	Runs	Wkts	Avg	BB	5I	10M
Test	76	143	10	5825	219	43.79	14	29	95	-	300	155	1	155.00	1-34	-	-
FC	223	384	20	13570	284	37.28	28	68	274	-	2674	1541	36	42.80	4-36	-	-
ODI	123	122	6	4335	137	37.37	12	21	49	-	232	219	4	54.75	2-7	-	
List A	288	276	23	9373	158	37.04	24	44	111	-	2004	1636	57	28.70	4-50	-	
20/20 Int	3	3	0	166	72	55.33	-	2	2	-	0	0	0		-	-	
20/20	10	10	0	395	76	39.50	-	4	5	-	0	0	0		-	-	

TROTT, I. J. L. Warwickshire

Name: Ian Jonathan Leonard Trott
Role: Right-hand bat, right-arm medium bowler; all-rounder
Born: 22 April 1981, Cape Town, South Africa
Height: 6ft **Weight:** 13st 5lbs
Nickname: Booger
County debut: 2003
County cap: 2005
Twenty20 Int debut: 2007
1000 runs in a season: 3
1st-Class 200s: 1
Place in batting averages: 199th av. 22.52 (2006 71st av. 41.77)
Parents: Ian and Donna
Marital status: Single
Family links with cricket: Father a professional cricket coach. Brother (Kenny Jackson) played for Western Province and Boland. Is related to the late-19th-century Test cricketers Albert (Australia and England) and Harry Trott (Australia)
Education: Rondebosch Boys' High School; Stellenbosch University
Qualifications: Level 2 coaching
Overseas tours: South Africa U15 to England (U15 World Cup) 1996; South Africa U19 to Pakistan 1998-99, to Sri Lanka (U19 World Cup) 1999-2000; England Performance Programme to India 2007-08; England Lions to India 2007-08
Overseas teams played for: Boland 1999-2000 – 2000-01; Western Province 2001-02; Otago 2005-06
Cricket superstitions: 'Personal'
Cricketers particularly admired: Sachin Tendulkar, Adam Hollioake, Steve Waugh
Other sports played: Hockey (Western Province U16, U18, U21), golf
Other sports followed: Football (Tottenham Hotspur)

Favourite band: Roxette, Robbie Williams
Relaxations: 'Music, watching sport'
Extras: Represented South Africa A. Struck 245 on debut for Warwickshire 2nd XI v Somerset 2nd XI at Knowle & Dorridge 2002. Scored century (134) on Championship debut for Warwickshire v Sussex at Edgbaston 2003. Became the first player to bat for the full 20 overs in the Twenty20, for a 54-ball 65* v Gloucestershire at Edgbaston 2003. Represented England Lions 2007
Best batting: 210 Warwickshire v Sussex, Edgbaston 2005
Best bowling: 7-39 Warwickshire v Kent, Canterbury 2003

2007 Season

	M	Inn	NO	Runs	HS	Avg	100	50	Ct	St	Balls	Runs	Wkts	Avg	BB	5I	10M
Test																	
FC	15	22	1	473	84	22.52	-	2	16	-	444	214	2	107.00	2-33	-	-
ODI																	
List A	15	14	4	549	125 *	54.90	2	2	3	-	122	116	2	58.00	2-32	-	
20/20 Int	2	2	0	11	9	5.50	-	-	-	-	0	0	0		-	-	
20/20	5	5	0	148	49	29.60	-	-	1	-	0	0	0		-	-	

Career Performances

	M	Inn	NO	Runs	HS	Avg	100	50	Ct	St	Balls	Runs	Wkts	Avg	BB	5I	10M
Test																	
FC	98	167	15	5770	210	37.96	11	31	100	-	2359	1387	34	40.79	7-39	1	-
ODI																	
List A	117	108	23	3473	125 *	40.85	6	21	37	-	991	934	36	25.94	4-55	-	
20/20 Int	2	2	0	11	9	5.50	-	-	-	-	0	0	0		-	-	
20/20	34	30	7	818	75 *	35.56	-	3	10	-	132	200	7	28.57	2-19	-	

TROUGHTON, J. O. — Warwickshire

Name: Jamie (Jim) Oliver Troughton
Role: Left-hand bat, slow left-arm bowler
Born: 2 March 1979, London
Height: 5ft 11in **Weight:** 13st
Nickname: Troughts
County debut: 2001
County cap: 2002
ODI debut: 2003
1000 runs in a season: 1
Place in batting averages: 59th av. 42.83 (2006 191st av. 22.94)
Parents: Ali and David
Wife and date of marriage: Naomi, 28 September 2002
Children: Eva, February 2007

Family links with cricket: Father was a Middlesex Colt. Great-grandfather Henry Crichton played for Warwickshire. 'Younger brother is a Stratford Panther'
Education: Trinity School, Leamington Spa; Birmingham University
Qualifications: 3 A-levels, BSc Sport & Exercise Psychology, Level 1 coaching
Career outside cricket: 'Work in progress'
Off-season: 'Training/coaching'
Overseas tours: Warwickshire Development of Excellence squad to Cape Town; MCC to Australia and Singapore 2001; ECB National Academy to Australia and Sri Lanka 2002-03
Overseas teams played for: Harvinia CC, Bloemfontein, South Africa 2000; Avendale CC, Cape Town 2001-02; Belville CC, Cape Town 2003-04; Claremont-Nedlands CC, Perth 2004-05
Career highlights to date: 'B&H final 2002, England call-up 2003, county champions 2004, highest first-class score 2007'
Cricket superstitions: 'Don't leave straight ones'
Cricketers particularly admired: Brian Lara, Graham Thorpe, Nick Knight, Ashley Giles
Young players to look out for: Chris Woakes
Other sports played: Football (Stoke City youth player)
Other sports followed: 'Hooked on Manchester United since going to their soccer school aged five'
Injuries: Out for two weeks with an injury to the lower back
Favourite band: Stone Roses, Beatles, Red Hot Chili Peppers
Relaxations: 'Movies, music, going abroad'
Extras: Is grandson of *Dr Who* actor Patrick Troughton; father also an actor. County colours U12-U19. Has represented England U15, U16 and U17. Represented ECB Midlands U19 1998. Has won the Alec Hastilow Trophy and the Coney Edmonds Trophy (Warwickshire awards). Warwickshire 2nd XI Player of the Year 2001. Scored 1067 first-class runs in his first full season 2002. NBC Denis Compton Award for the most promising young Warwickshire player 2002. Warwickshire Young Player and Most Improved Player of the Year 2002
Opinions on cricket: '[Should have] three main competitions – 50-over, Twenty20, four-day. Fewer games, therefore more intensity in those games.'
Best batting: 162 Warwickshire v Worcestershire, Worcester 2007
Best bowling: 3-1 Warwickshire v CUCCE, Fenner's 2004

2007 Season

	M	Inn	NO	Runs	HS	Avg	100	50	Ct	St	Balls	Runs	Wkts	Avg	BB	5I	10M
Test																	
FC	14	19	1	771	162	42.83	3	1	1	-	510	276	2	138.00	1-34	-	-
ODI																	
List A	12	11	1	220	37	22.00	-	-	4	-	60	74	2	37.00	2-35	-	
20/20 Int																	
20/20	8	8	0	114	37	14.25	-	-	6	-	6	12	0		-	-	

Career Performances

	M	Inn	NO	Runs	HS	Avg	100	50	Ct	St	Balls	Runs	Wkts	Avg	BB	5I	10M
Test																	
FC	79	123	9	4338	162	38.05	13	21	30	-	2323	1391	22	63.22	3-1	-	-
ODI	6	5	1	36	20	9.00	-	-	1	-	0	0	0		-	-	
List A	98	87	8	2197	115 *	27.81	2	10	36	-	736	644	25	25.76	4-23	-	
20/20 Int																	
20/20	29	25	1	392	51	16.33	-	1	11	-	90	124	6	20.66	2-10	-	

TUDGE, K. D. Glamorgan

Name: Kyle Daniel Tudge
Role: Right-hand bat, slow left-arm orthodox bowler
Born: 19 March 1987, Newport, Wales
Height: 5ft 10in **Weight:** 13st 2lbs
Nickname: Tudgey
County debut: 2006
Parents: Gerald and Sheila
Marital status: Single
Education: Blackwood Comprehensive (GCSEs), Monmouth Boys School (A-levels); UWIC (University of Wales Institute Cardiff)
Qualifications: 10 GCSEs, 4 AS-levels, 1 A-level, Level 1 cricket coaching
Career highlights to date: 'First-class debut – August 2006, Glamorgan v Worcestershire, Liverpool Victoria Championship'
Cricket moments to forget: 'Duck in first game at Lord's (MCC Young Cricketers 2006)'
Cricket superstitions: 'None'
Cricketers particularly admired: Daniel Vettori, Mike Hussey
Young players to look out for: James Harris

Other sports played: Golf
Other sports followed: Rugby (Neath-Swansea Ospreys), football (Manchester United)
Favourite band: Eminem
Relaxations: 'Films (*Lord of the Rings*, *Star Wars*)'
Extras: Played for Wales Minor Counties in the C&G 2005 and in Minor Counties competitions 2004-07. MCC Young Cricketers 2004-06 (leading wicket-taker 2006). Played for Cardiff UCCE 2007
Best batting: 4 Glamorgan v Worcestershire, Colwyn Bay 2006

2007 Season (did not make any first-class or one-day appearances)

Career Performances

	M	Inn	NO	Runs	HS	Avg	100	50	Ct	St	Balls	Runs	Wkts	Avg	BB	5I	10M
Test																	
FC	1	2	1	7	4	7.00	-	-	-	-	78	58	0		-	-	-
ODI																	
List A	1	1	0	4	4	4.00	-	-	-	-	30	31	0		-	-	
20/20 Int																	
20/20																	

TUDOR, A. J. — Essex

Name: Alexander (Alex) Jeremy Tudor
Role: Right-hand bat, right-arm fast bowler
Born: 23 October 1977, West Brompton, London
Height: 6ft 4in **Weight:** 13st 7lbs
Nickname: Big Al, Bambi, Tudes
County debut: 1995 (Surrey), 2005 (Essex)
County cap: 1999 (Surrey)
Test debut: 1998-99
ODI debut: 2002
Place in batting averages: 271st av. 11.20 (2006 145th av. 30.16)
Place in bowling averages: 99th av. 35.41 (2006 116th av. 42.67)
Parents: Daryll and Jennifer
Marital status: Engaged to Francesca
Children: Sienna
Family links with cricket: Brother was on the staff at The Oval
Education: St Mark's C of E, Fulham; City of Westminster College

Overseas tours: England U15 to South Africa 1992-93; England U19 to Zimbabwe 1995-96, to Pakistan 1996-97; England to Australia 1998-99, to South Africa 1999-2000, to Pakistan 2000-01, to Australia 2002-03; England A to West Indies 2000-01; ECB National Academy to Australia 2001-02, 2002-03
Cricketers particularly admired: Curtly Ambrose, Brian Lara
Other sports followed: Basketball, football (QPR)
Relaxations: Listening to music
Extras: Played for London Schools at all ages from U8. Represented England U17. MCC Young Cricketer. Took 4-89 in Australia's first innings on Test debut at Perth 1998-99; his victims included both Waugh twins. Scored 99* in second innings of the first Test v New Zealand at Edgbaston 1999, bettering the highest score by a nightwatchman for England (Harold Larwood's 98 v Australia at Sydney 1932-33) and winning Man of the Match award. Cricket Writers' Club Young Cricketer of the Year 1999. Recorded match figures of 7-109 in the third Test v Sri Lanka at Old Trafford 2002, winning Man of the Match award
Best batting: 144 Essex v Derbyshire, Chelmsford 2006
Best bowling: 7-48 Surrey v Lancashire, The Oval 2000

2007 Season

	M	Inn	NO	Runs	HS	Avg	100	50	Ct	St	Balls	Runs	Wkts	Avg	BB	5I	10M
Test																	
FC	10	13	3	112	35	11.20	-	-	3	-	1046	602	17	35.41	3-29	-	-
ODI																	
List A	2	2	0	14	9	7.00	-	-	-	-	84	66	2	33.00	1-25	-	
20/20 Int																	
20/20																	

Career Performances

	M	Inn	NO	Runs	HS	Avg	100	50	Ct	St	Balls	Runs	Wkts	Avg	BB	5I	10M
Test	10	16	4	229	99 *	19.08	-	1	3	-	1512	963	28	34.39	5-44	1	-
FC	116	148	31	2601	144	22.23	2	8	34	-	16385	9870	333	29.63	7-48	14	-
ODI	3	2	1	9	6	9.00	-	-	1	-	127	136	4	34.00	2-30	-	
List A	74	50	14	442	56	12.27	-	1	21	-	3187	2501	105	23.81	4-26	-	
20/20 Int																	
20/20																	

92. Who kept Nathan Astle company for nearly three hours in a last-wicket stand that denied England victory in the first Test at Auckland in 1996-97?

TURNER, M. L. Somerset

Name: Mark Leif Turner
Role: Right-hand lower-order bat, right-arm fast-medium bowler
Born: 23 October 1984, Sunderland
Height: 6ft **Weight:** 12st 12lbs
Nickname: Tina, Racing Pigeon, Gimp
County debut: 2005 (Durham), 2007 (Somerset)
Parents: Kenny and Eileen
Marital status: 'Living with partner'
Family links with cricket: 'Brother Ian played county juniors and was a well-respected local player'
Education: Thornhill Comprehensive School
Qualifications: 7 GCSEs, Level 2 coaching
Off-season: 'Aiming to learn some kind of trade. National Skill Sets; South Africa for six weeks with Jimmy Cook after Christmas'
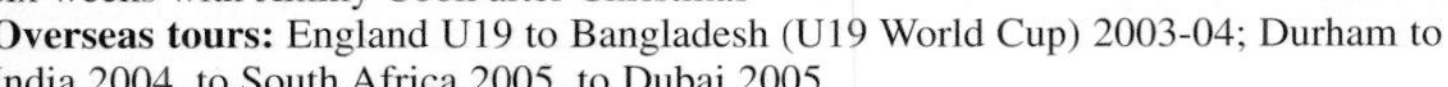
Overseas tours: England U19 to Bangladesh (U19 World Cup) 2003-04; Durham to India 2004, to South Africa 2005, to Dubai 2005
Career highlights to date: 'Being part of the Somerset team that achieved double promotion'
Cricket moments to forget: 'Dropping a dolly on Sky for England U19'
Cricketers particularly admired: Allan Donald, Andrew Caddick, Marcus Trescothick, Sachin Tendulkar, Dale Benkenstein, Keith Parsons
Young players to look out for: James Hildreth, Ben Harmison, Mark Stoneman
Other sports played: Football (junior with Manchester Utd and Sunderland), golf, fishing
Other sports followed: Football (Sunderland AFC)
Favourite band: 'Anything that is neo-soul, old school R&B (Maxwell, Keith Sweat etc.)'
Extras: Represented England U19 2003 and 2004, returning match figures of 9-104 (5-57/4-47) in the second 'Test' v Bangladesh U19 at Taunton 2004
Opinions on cricket: 'Two-division format is good and the difference between the two divisions is becoming stronger.'
Best batting: 57 Somerset v Derbyshire, Taunton 2007
Best bowling: 4-30 Somerset v LUCCE, Taunton 2007

2007 Season

	M	Inn	NO	Runs	HS	Avg	100	50	Ct	St	Balls	Runs	Wkts	Avg	BB	5I	10M
Test																	
FC	3	3	1	63	57	31.50	-	1	1	-	465	312	8	39.00	4-30	-	-
ODI																	
List A	6	4	2	15	11 *	7.50	-	-	-	-	242	220	5	44.00	2-40	-	
20/20 Int																	
20/20	4	3	2	3	2	3.00	-	-	1	-	54	81	1	81.00	1-31	-	

Career Performances

	M	Inn	NO	Runs	HS	Avg	100	50	Ct	St	Balls	Runs	Wkts	Avg	BB	5I	10M
Test																	
FC	6	5	2	82	57	27.33	-	1	1	-	897	564	12	47.00	4-30	-	-
ODI																	
List A	6	4	2	15	11 *	7.50	-	-	-	-	242	220	5	44.00	2-40	-	
20/20 Int																	
20/20	5	3	2	3	2	3.00	-	-	1	-	66	106	1	106.00	1-31	-	

UDAL, S. D. Middlesex

Name: Shaun David Udal
Role: Right-hand bat, off-spin bowler
Born: 18 March 1969, Farnborough, Hampshire
Height: 6ft 2in **Weight:** 14st
Nickname: Shaggy
County debut: 1989 (Hampshire)
County cap: 1992 (Hampshire)
Benefit: 2002 (Hampshire)
Test debut: 2005-06
ODI debut: 1994
50 wickets in a season: 7
Place in batting averages: (2006 245th av. 14.75)
Place in bowling averages: 84th av. 33.50 (2006 117th av. 43.06)
Parents: Robin and Mary
Wife and date of marriage: Emma, 5 October 1991
Children: Katherine Mary, 26 August 1992; Rebecca Jane, 17 November 1995; Jack David, 23 August 2004

Family links with cricket: 'Great-grandfather – MCC; grandfather [G. F. Udal] – Middlesex and Leicestershire; father – Camberley CC for 40 years; brother – captain Camberley CC'
Education: Cove Comprehensive, Farnborough
Qualifications: 8 CSEs, print finisher, company director
Career outside cricket: 'Media – printing company'
Overseas tours: England to Australia 1994-95, to Pakistan 2005-06, to India 2005-06; England A to Pakistan 1995-96; England XI to New Zealand (Cricket Max) 1997; Hampshire to Anguilla 1998, to Cape Town 2001
Overseas teams played for: Hamilton Wickham, Newcastle, NSW 1989-90
Career highlights to date: 'Captain of Hants in C&G final 2005. Being picked for England again aged 36'
Cricket moments to forget: 'Getting out twice as nightwatchman hooking'
Cricket superstitions: 'Left everything on first'
Cricketers particularly admired: Ian Botham, Shane Warne, Robin Smith
Young players to look out for: Chris Benham
Other sports played: Golf (14 handicap), football
Other sports followed: Football (West Ham Utd, Aldershot Town, Eastleigh FC)
Favourite band: Robbie Williams
Relaxations: 'Good food and wine; the odd beer with Peter Ebdon at the snooker club'
Extras: Scored double hundred for Camberley CC in 40-over game. Man of the Match on NatWest debut against Berkshire 1991. Hampshire Cricket Association Player of the Year 1993. Vice-captain of Hampshire 1998-2000. Hampshire Players' Player of the Year 2001, 2002. Skipper of Hampshire in C&G final at Lord's 2005, becoming the first Hampshire-born captain to lift silverware for the county. Had second innings figures of 4-14 as England defeated India in the third Test at Mumbai 2005-06. Leading wicket-taker for Hampshire in one-day cricket. President of Camberley CC. Retired at the end of the 2007 season but later accepted an invitation to join Middlesex for 2008
Opinions on cricket: 'It really is a great game. Keep agents out of affecting young players' attitudes – some get a higher opinion of their abilities and can cause friction between the player and club unnecessarily.'
Best batting: 117* Hampshire v Warwickshire, Southampton 1997
Best bowling: 8-50 Hampshire v Sussex, Southampton 1992

2007 Season

	M	Inn	NO	Runs	HS	Avg	100	50	Ct	St	Balls	Runs	Wkts	Avg	BB	5I	10M
Test																	
FC	5	8	1	34	17 *	4.85	-	-	-	-	901	469	14	33.50	4-138	-	-
ODI																	
List A	14	7	4	52	31	17.33	-	-	4	-	552	447	13	34.38	2-28	-	
20/20 Int																	
20/20																	

Career Performances

	M	Inn	NO	Runs	HS	Avg	100	50	Ct	St	Balls	Runs	Wkts	Avg	BB	5I	10M
Test	4	7	1	109	33 *	18.16	-	-	1	-	596	344	8	43.00	4-14	-	-
FC	260	367	68	6761	117 *	22.61	1	28	116	-	47791	23649	724	32.66	8-50	33	4
ODI	11	7	4	35	11 *	11.66	-	-	1	-	612	400	9	44.44	2-37	-	
List A	371	238	75	2556	78	15.68	-	8	121	-	17083	12530	418	29.97	5-43	1	
20/20 Int																	
20/20	25	18	7	188	37	17.09	-	-	7	-	465	557	25	22.28	3-21	-	

VAAS, W. P. U. J. C. — Middlesex

Name: Warnakulasuriya Patabendige Ushantha Joseph Chaminda Vaas
Role: Left-hand bat, left-arm fast-medium bowler
Born: 27 January 1974, Mattumagala, Sri Lanka
County debut: 2003 (Hampshire), 2005 (Worcestershire), 2007 (Middlesex)
County cap: 2005 (Worcestershire colours), 2007 (Middlesex)
Test debut: 1994
ODI debut: 1993-94
Twenty20 Int debut: 2006-07
Place in bowling averages: 48th av. 27.60 (2006 42nd av. 29.33)
Overseas tours: Sri Lanka U19 to England 1992; Sri Lanka to India 1993-94, to Zimbabwe 1994-95, to South Africa 1994-95, to New Zealand 1994-95, to Pakistan 1995-96, to Australia 1995-96, to India and Pakistan (World Cup) 1995-96, to New Zealand 1996-97, to India 1997-98, to South Africa 1997-98, to Bangladesh (Wills International Cup) 1998-99, to UK, Ireland and Netherlands (World Cup) 1999, to Zimbabwe 1999-2000, to Pakistan 1999-2000, to Kenya (ICC Knockout Trophy) 2000-01, to South Africa 2000-01, to England 2002, to South Africa 2002-03, to Africa (World Cup) 2002-03, to West Indies 2003, to Zimbabwe 2004, to Australia 2004, to England (ICC Champions Trophy) 2004, to Pakistan 2004-05, to New Zealand 2004-05, to India 2005-06, to England 2006, to India (ICC Champions Trophy) 2006-07, to New Zealand 2006-07, to West Indies (World Cup) 2006-07, to South Africa (World 20/20) 2007-08, to Australia 2007-08, plus numerous other one-day series and tournaments in Sharjah, Singapore, West Indies, Kenya, India, Pakistan, Australia, Bangladesh, New Zealand and Morocco; ICC World XI to Australia (Tsunami Relief) 2004-05; FICA World XI to New Zealand 2004-05

Overseas teams played for: Colts CC, Sri Lanka 1990-91 –
Extras: Man of the Match for his 8-19 v Zimbabwe in the LG Abans Triangular Series at Colombo 2001-02, a new world's best analysis for ODIs; his figures included a hat-trick (Carlisle, Wishart, Taibu) as Zimbabwe were bowled out for 38. Took hat-trick (Hannan Sarkar, Mohammad Ashraful, Ehsanul Haque) with the first three balls of the match (four wickets in first over) v Bangladesh at Pietermaritzburg in the World Cup 2002-03, finishing with 6-25 and winning Man of the Match award. His other international awards include Man of the [Test] Series v South Africa 2004 and Man of the Match (jointly with Brian Lara) in the third Test v West Indies at Colombo 2001-02 (7-120/7-71). An overseas player with Hampshire in the latter part of the 2003 season; an overseas player with Worcestershire for the early part of the 2005 season; an overseas player with Middlesex 2007
Best batting: 134 Colts v Burgher, Colombo (SSC) 2004-05
Best bowling: 7-54 Western Province v Southern Province, Colombo (RPS) 2004-05

2007 Season

	M	Inn	NO	Runs	HS	Avg	100	50	Ct	St	Balls	Runs	Wkts	Avg	BB	5I	10M
Test																	
FC	7	8	3	277	79	55.40	-	2	2	-	972	552	20	27.60	5-126	1	-
ODI																	
List A	9	6	3	76	30 *	25.33	-	-	1	-	412	302	9	33.55	2-17	-	
20/20 Int																	
20/20																	

Career Performances

	M	Inn	NO	Runs	HS	Avg	100	50	Ct	St	Balls	Runs	Wkts	Avg	BB	5I	10M
Test	98	142	28	2684	100 *	23.54	1	11	30	-	20952	9321	319	29.21	7-71	11	2
FC	175	235	49	4661	134	25.05	4	20	53	-	33359	15216	618	24.62	7-54	26	3
ODI	300	203	67	1910	50 *	14.04	-	1	59	-	14701	10260	383	26.78	8-19	4	
List A	353	238	81	2472	62 *	15.74	-	3	73	-	17068	11863	453	26.18	8-19	4	
20/20 Int	6	2	1	33	21	33.00	-	-	-	-	132	128	6	21.33	2-14	-	
20/20	7	3	1	45	21	22.50	-	-	-	-	132	128	6	21.33	2-14	-	

93. Which Yorkshire batsman was left on 98*, just two runs short of his 100th first-class century, when England beat South Africa by nine wickets at Old Trafford in 1951?

VAN DER WATH, J. J. Northamptonshire

Name: Johannes Jacobus van der Wath
Role: Right-hand bat, right-arm fast-medium bowler; all-rounder
Born: 10 January 1978, Newcastle, Natal, South Africa
County debut: 2005 (Sussex), 2007 (Northamptonshire)
ODI debut: 2005-06
Twenty20 Int debut: 2005-06
Place in batting averages: 150th av. 28.83
Place in bowling averages: 21st av. 23.67
Education: Ermelo High School
Overseas tours: South Africa A to Sri Lanka 2005-06, to Zimbabwe 2006-07; South Africa to Australia 2005-06 (VB Series), to Sri Lanka 2006, to Zimbabwe (one-day series) 2007-08

Overseas teams played for: Easterns 1995-96 – 1996-97; Free State 1997-98 – 2003-04; Eagles 2004-05 – 2006-07

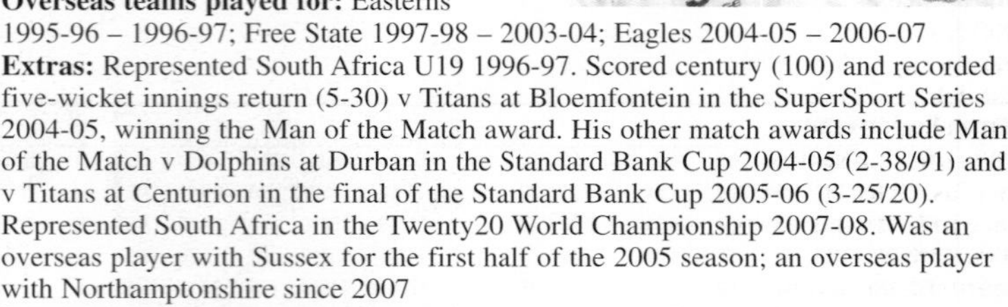

Extras: Represented South Africa U19 1996-97. Scored century (100) and recorded five-wicket innings return (5-30) v Titans at Bloemfontein in the SuperSport Series 2004-05, winning the Man of the Match award. His other match awards include Man of the Match v Dolphins at Durban in the Standard Bank Cup 2004-05 (2-38/91) and v Titans at Centurion in the final of the Standard Bank Cup 2005-06 (3-25/20). Represented South Africa in the Twenty20 World Championship 2007-08. Was an overseas player with Sussex for the first half of the 2005 season; an overseas player with Northamptonshire since 2007
Best batting: 113* Free State v KwaZulu-Natal, Bloemfontein 2001-02
Best bowling: 6-27 Eagles v Dolphins, Durban 2006-07

2007 Season

	M	Inn	NO	Runs	HS	Avg	100	50	Ct	St	Balls	Runs	Wkts	Avg	BB	5I	10M
Test																	
FC	10	15	3	346	94	28.83	-	3	3	-	1441	805	34	23.67	6-49	2	-
ODI																	
List A	7	6	4	126	45 *	63.00	-	-	1	-	365	310	8	38.75	4-40	-	
20/20 Int																	
20/20	7	4	2	78	48 *	39.00	-	-	-	-	113	145	3	48.33	2-40	-	

Career Performances

	M	Inn	NO	Runs	HS	Avg	100	50	Ct	St	Balls	Runs	Wkts	Avg	BB	5I	10M
Test																	
FC	70	110	19	2228	113 *	24.48	2	13	25	-	11937	5831	217	26.87	6-27	11	-
ODI	10	8	2	89	37 *	14.83	-	-	3	-	526	551	13	42.38	2-21	-	
List A	117	93	28	1805	91	27.76	-	11	29	-	5062	4080	148	27.56	4-31	-	
20/20 Int	8	4	1	45	21	15.00	-	-	-	-	186	231	8	28.87	2-31	-	
20/20	38	26	7	286	48 *	15.05	-	-	1	-	731	913	36	25.36	2-8	-	

VAN JAARSVELD, M. Kent

Name: Martin van Jaarsveld
Role: Right-hand top-order bat, right-arm off-spin bowler
Born: 18 June 1974, Klerksdorp, South Africa
Height: 6ft 2in **Weight:** 12st 12lbs
Nickname: Jarre
County debut: 2004 (Northamptonshire), 2005 (Kent)
County cap: 2005 (Kent)
Test debut: 2002-03
ODI debut: 2002-03
1000 runs in a season: 3
1st-Class 200s: 3
Place in batting averages: 46th av. 45.95 (2006 48th av. 48.68)
Parents: Leon and Isobel
Wife and date of marriage: Jill, 6 May 2005
Education: Warmbads High School; University of Pretoria
Qualifications: BComm (Financial Management)
Off-season: Captain of the Titans in South Africa
Overseas tours: South Africa A to Sri Lanka 1998, to Zimbabwe 2002-03, to Australia 2002-03; South Africa Academy to Zimbabwe 1998-99; South Africa to England 2003, to New Zealand 2003-04, to Sri Lanka 2004, to England (ICC Champions Trophy) 2004, to India 2004-05
Overseas teams played for: Northern Transvaal/Northerns Titans 1994-95 – 2003-04; Titans 2004-05 –
Career highlights to date: 'Playing for South Africa. Being chosen as one of the five Cricketers of the Year in South Africa 2002'
Cricket moments to forget: 'Losing the NatWest Series final [playing for South Africa] at Lord's, July 2003'

Cricket superstitions: 'Left pad first when padding up'
Cricketers particularly admired: Gary Kirsten, Michael Atherton
Young players to look out for: Neil Dexter, Joe Denly
Other sports played: Golf, tennis
Other sports followed: Rugby (Blue Bulls), football (Blackburn Rovers)
Favourite band: Snow Patrol
Relaxations: 'Spending time with friends and family'
Extras: Scored 182* and 158* v Griqualand West at Centurion 2001-02, becoming only the second batsman to record two 150s in the same match in South Africa. Player of the SuperSport Series 2001-02 (934 runs at 84.90); also topped South African first-class averages 2001-02 (1268 runs at 74.58). One of *South African Cricket Annual*'s five Cricketers of the Year 2002. Was an overseas player with Northamptonshire 2004. Scored a century in each innings (118/111) on first-class debut for Kent, v Warwickshire at Canterbury 2005, becoming the first Kent debutant to achieve the feat. Scored 168 v Surrey at Tunbridge Wells 2005, in the process sharing with Robert Key (189) in a new Kent record third-wicket partnership (323). Retired from international cricket in February 2005. Is no longer considered an overseas player. Leading run-scorer in the SuperSport Series 2006-07 with 828 runs (av. 55.20)
Opinions on cricket: 'I think the standard of county cricket, with the inclusion of overseas players and the odd Kolpak player [*see page 13*], is very strong and although there is a lot of resistance I do think the English game has benefited from it.'
Best batting: 262* Kent v Glamorgan, Cardiff 2005
Best bowling: 2-17 Kent v Hampshire, Rose Bowl 2007

2007 Season

	M	Inn	NO	Runs	HS	Avg	100	50	Ct	St	Balls	Runs	Wkts	Avg	BB	5I	10M
Test																	
FC	15	23	1	1011	166	45.95	5	3	17	-	122	68	5	13.60	2-17	-	-
ODI																	
List A	17	15	2	428	86 *	32.92	-	3	16	-	210	169	7	24.14	3-43	-	
20/20 Int																	
20/20	11	10	3	148	42 *	21.14	-	-	8	-	12	9	1	9.00	1-9	-	

Career Performances

	M	Inn	NO	Runs	HS	Avg	100	50	Ct	St	Balls	Runs	Wkts	Avg	BB	5I	10M
Test	9	15	2	397	73	30.53	-	3	11	-	42	28	0	-	-	-	-
FC	177	300	28	12291	262 *	45.18	36	56	241	-	1691	873	23	37.95	2-17	-	-
ODI	11	7	1	124	45	20.66	-	-	4	-	31	18	2	9.00	1-0	-	
List A	209	192	28	6289	123	38.34	8	41	123	-	968	827	21	39.38	3-43	-	
20/20 Int																	
20/20	52	48	9	1089	76 *	27.92	-	8	35	-	66	92	4	23.00	2-19	-	

VAN JAARSVELD, V. B. — Warwickshire

Name: Vaughn Bernard van Jaarsveld
Role: Left-hand bat, right-arm medium bowler
Born: 2 February 1985, Johannesburg, South Africa
Nickname: Hulk, Rabbit
County debut: 2007 (one-day)
Overseas tours: South Africa U15 to England (U15 World Cup) 2000; South Africa U19 to Bangladesh (U19 World Cup) 2003-04; South Africa Academy to Pakistan 2005-06
Overseas teams played for: Gauteng 2002-03 – 2004-05; Lions 2003-04 –
Extras: Played for NF Oppenheimer's XI v Pakistanis 2002-03 and v West Indians 2003-04. Represented Rest of South Africa v Indians 2006-07 and v Pakistanis 2006-07.

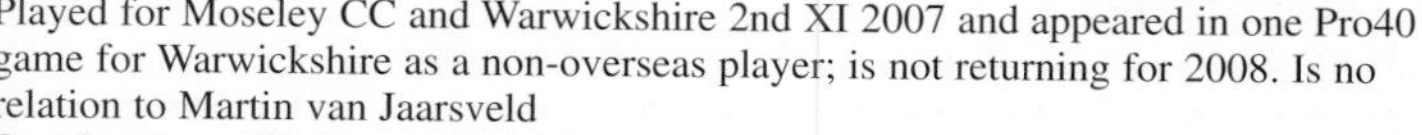

Played for Moseley CC and Warwickshire 2nd XI 2007 and appeared in one Pro40 game for Warwickshire as a non-overseas player; is not returning for 2008. Is no relation to Martin van Jaarsveld
Best batting: 159 Lions v Dolphins, Pietermaritzburg 2006-07

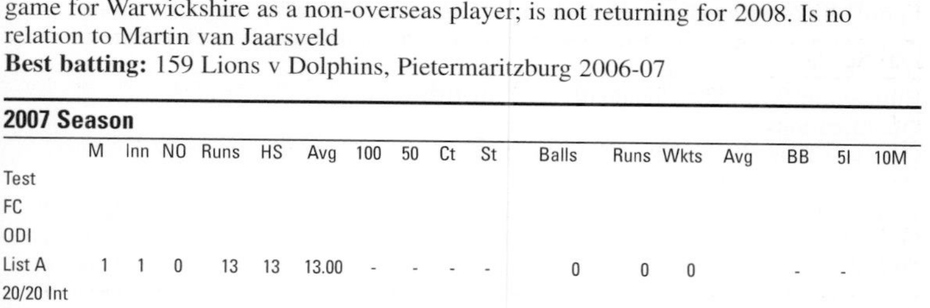

2007 Season

	M	Inn	NO	Runs	HS	Avg	100	50	Ct	St	Balls	Runs	Wkts	Avg	BB	5I	10M
Test																	
FC																	
ODI																	
List A	1	1	0	13	13	13.00	-	-	-	-	0	0	0		-	-	
20/20 Int																	
20/20																	

Career Performances

	M	Inn	NO	Runs	HS	Avg	100	50	Ct	St	Balls	Runs	Wkts	Avg	BB	5I	10M
Test																	
FC	30	51	4	1814	159	38.59	4	15	32	-	18	11	0		-	-	-
ODI																	
List A	40	34	7	903	81	33.44	-	7	11	-	18	17	0		-	-	
20/20 Int																	
20/20	21	19	3	452	64	28.25	-	3	7	-	0	0	0		-	-	

VAUGHAN, M. P. Yorkshire

Name: Michael Paul Vaughan
Role: Right-hand bat, off-spin bowler
Born: 29 October 1974, Eccles, Manchester
Height: 6ft 2in **Weight:** 11st 7lbs
Nickname: Frankie, Virgil
County debut: 1993
County cap: 1995
Benefit: 2005
Test debut: 1999-2000
ODI debut: 2000-01
Twenty20 Int debut: 2005
1000 runs in a season: 4
Place in batting averages: 48th av. 44.58 (2006 149th av. 29.66)
Parents: Graham John and Dee
Wife and date of marriage: Nichola, September 2003
Children: Tallulah Grace, 4 June 2004; Archie, December 2005
Family links with cricket: Father played league cricket for Worsley CC. Brother plays for Sheffield Collegiate. Mother is related to the famous Tyldesley family (Lancashire and England)
Education: Silverdale Comprehensive, Sheffield
Qualifications: 7 GCSEs
Overseas tours: Yorkshire to West Indies 1994, to South Africa 1995, to Zimbabwe 1996; England U19 to India 1992-93, to Sri Lanka 1993-94 (c); England A to India 1994-95, to Australia 1996-97, to Zimbabwe and South Africa 1998-99 (c); England to South Africa 1999-2000, to Pakistan and Sri Lanka 2000-01, to India and New Zealand 2001-02, to Australia 2002-03, to Africa (World Cup) 2002-03, to Bangladesh and Sri Lanka 2003-04 (c), to West Indies 2003-04 (c), to Zimbabwe (one-day series) 2004-05 (c), to South Africa 2004-05 (c), to Pakistan 2005-06 (c), to India 2005-06 (c), to Australia 2006-07 (C'wealth Bank Series; c), to West Indies (World Cup) 2006-07 (c), to Sri Lanka 2007-08 (Test c), to New Zealand 2007-08 (Test c)
Cricketers particularly admired: Darren Lehmann, 'all the Yorkshire and England squads'
Other sports played: Football (Baslow FC), golf (10 handicap)
Other sports followed: Football (Sheffield Wednesday), all golf
Relaxations: Most sports. 'Enjoy a good meal with friends'
Extras: Maurice Leyland Batting Award 1990; Cricket Society's Most Promising Young Cricketer 1993; A. A. Thompson Memorial Trophy 1993. Scored 1066 runs in first full season of first-class cricket 1994. Captained England U19. PCA Player of the

Year 2002. Highest-scoring batsman in Test cricket for the calendar year 2002 (1481 runs). One of *Wisden*'s Five Cricketers of the Year 2003. Topped Pricewaterhouse Coopers rankings for Test batsmen in early summer 2003. Vodafone Cricketer of the Year 2002-03. Scored century in each innings (103/101*) in the first Test v West Indies at Lord's 2004. His international awards include England's Man of the [Test] Series v India 2002 (615 runs at 102.50) and Man of the [Test] Series v Australia 2002-03 (633 runs at 63.30), as well as Man of the Match v Australia at Edgbaston in the ICC Champions Trophy 2004 (86/2-42 plus run-out). England one-day captain from May 2003 to June 2007 and England Test captain since July 2003; led England to a Test series win over Australia in 2005, their first Ashes success for 18 years, and was appointed OBE in 2006 New Year Honours. Book *A Year in the Sun* published 2003. Scored century (103) in the second Test v West Indies at his home ground of Headingley 2007 on his return to Test cricket after 18 months out through injury. England 12-month central contract 2007-08
Best batting: 197 England v India, Trent Bridge 2002
Best bowling: 4-39 Yorkshire v Oxford University, The Parks 1994

2007 Season

	M	Inn	NO	Runs	HS	Avg	100	50	Ct	St	Balls	Runs	Wkts	Avg	BB	5I	10M
Test	6	11	1	546	124	54.60	2	1	2	-	24	18	0		-	-	-
FC	12	19	2	758	124	44.58	2	3	2	-	72	47	0		-	-	-
ODI																	
List A	4	4	0	141	95	35.25	-	1	5	-	96	81	1	81.00	1-37	-	
20/20 Int																	
20/20																	

Career Performances

	M	Inn	NO	Runs	HS	Avg	100	50	Ct	St	Balls	Runs	Wkts	Avg	BB	5I	10M
Test	70	126	9	5141	197	43.94	17	15	39	-	960	555	6	92.50	2-71	-	-
FC	242	426	27	15307	197	38.36	41	64	108	-	9282	5189	114	45.51	4-39	-	-
ODI	86	83	10	1982	90 *	27.15	-	16	25	-	796	649	16	40.56	4-22	-	
List A	274	265	25	6920	125 *	28.83	3	43	87	-	3303	2538	78	32.53	4-22	-	
20/20 Int	2	2	0	27	27	13.50	-	-	-	-	0	0	0		-	-	
20/20	2	2	0	27	27	13.50	-	-	-	-	0	0	0		-	-	

94. Which Kent swing bowler dismissed Mark Richardson with his first ball in Test cricket on English soil in the second Test between England and New Zealand at Headingley in 2004?

VOGES, A. C. — Hampshire

Name: Adam Charles Voges
Role: Right-hand bat, left-arm wrist-spin bowler
Born: 4 October 1979, Subiaco, Perth, Australia
Height: 6ft 1in
Nickname: Kenny
County debut: 2007 (one-day)
ODI debut: 2006-07
Overseas tours: Australia U19 to England 1999; Australian Cricket Academy to Bangladesh 2000-01, to South Africa 2006-07, to Zimbabwe 2006-07 (c); University of Western Australia to India 2006-07; Australia to New Zealand (one-day series) 2006-07; Australia A to Pakistan 2007-08
Overseas teams played for: Western Australia 2002-03 –

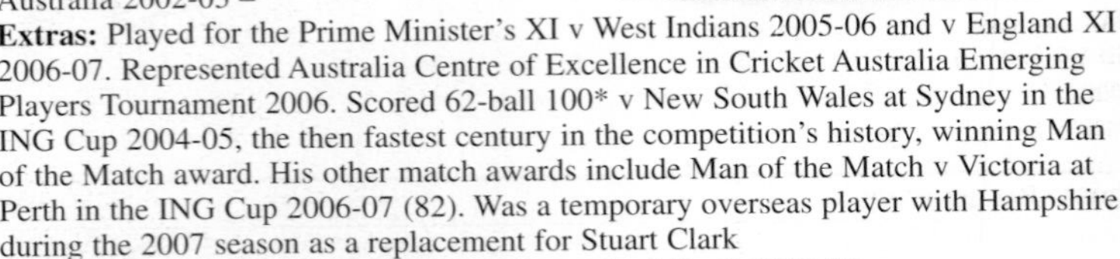

Extras: Played for the Prime Minister's XI v West Indians 2005-06 and v England XI 2006-07. Represented Australia Centre of Excellence in Cricket Australia Emerging Players Tournament 2006. Scored 62-ball 100* v New South Wales at Sydney in the ING Cup 2004-05, the then fastest century in the competition's history, winning Man of the Match award. His other match awards include Man of the Match v Victoria at Perth in the ING Cup 2006-07 (82). Was a temporary overseas player with Hampshire during the 2007 season as a replacement for Stuart Clark
Best batting: 178 Western Australia v Queensland, Perth 2005-06
Best bowling: 4-92 Western Australia v South Australia, Adelaide 2006-07
Stop press: Made Twenty20 Int debut v New Zealand at Perth 2007-08

2007 Season

	M	Inn	NO	Runs	HS	Avg	100	50	Ct	St	Balls	Runs	Wkts	Avg	BB	5I	10M
Test																	
FC																	
ODI																	
List A																	
20/20 Int																	
20/20	7	7	1	106	66 *	17.66	-	1	5	-	18	18	3	6.00	2-4	-	

Career Performances

	M	Inn	NO	Runs	HS	Avg	100	50	Ct	St	Balls	Runs	Wkts	Avg	BB	5I	10M
Test																	
FC	31	52	9	1777	178	41.32	6	5	40	-	1134	672	15	44.80	4-92	-	-
ODI	1	1	1	16	16 *		-	-	1	-	18	33	0		-	-	
List A	33	33	7	1122	100 *	43.15	1	9	8	-	528	495	9	55.00	2-27	-	
20/20 Int																	
20/20	13	13	2	352	74 *	32.00	-	3	6	-	69	116	6	19.33	2-4	-	

WAGG, G. G. — Derbyshire

Name: Graham Grant Wagg
Role: Right-hand bat, left-arm fast-medium bowler
Born: 28 April 1983, Rugby
Height: 6ft **Weight:** 12st 5lbs
Nickname: Waggy, DC, Caveman
County debut: 2002 (Warwickshire), 2006 (Derbyshire)
County cap: 2007 (Derbyshire)
50 wickets in a season: 1
Place in batting averages: 137th av. 31.17 (2006 181st av. 24.38)
Place in bowling averages: 87th av. 33.67 (2006 95th av. 37.66)
Parents: John and Dawn
Marital status: Single
Family links with cricket: 'Dad played and coached in local leagues in Rugby'
Education: Ashlawn School, Rugby; Warwickshire College (Sports Science)
Qualifications: Level 1 cricket coach ('coached in South Africa and Holland')
Overseas tours: Warwickshire Development tour to South Africa 1998, to West Indies 2000; England A to Malaysia and India 2003-04
Overseas teams played for: Hams Tech, East London, South Africa 1999; HBS, Netherlands
Career highlights to date: 'Winning our first match for Derby at Derby for four years. Getting 6-38 against Somerset [at Taunton 2006] to win us the game'
Cricket moments to forget: 'Bowling at Cameron White at Derby when he made 260 in no time, but they still lost (ha, ha)'
Cricketers particularly admired: Cameron White, Andy Flower
Young players to look out for: Travis Birt
Other sports played: Snooker, fishing, football, rugby

Other sports followed: Football (Man United), snooker (Ronnie O'Sullivan)
Relaxations: 'Casino, snooker, partying'
Extras: Represented England U16, U17, U18, U19 as well as Development of Excellence (Midlands) XI. Scored 42* from 50 balls, 51 from 57 balls and took 4-43 on first-class debut v Somerset at Edgbaston 2002. NBC Denis Compton Award for the most promising young Warwickshire player 2003. ECB National Academy 2003-04
Opinions on cricket: 'Is getting a very aggressive game and the standard and the pace it's played is brill.'
Best batting: 94 Derbyshire v Surrey, Derby 2006
Best bowling: 6-38 Derbyshire v Somerset, Taunton 2006

2007 Season

	M	Inn	NO	Runs	HS	Avg	100	50	Ct	St	Balls	Runs	Wkts	Avg	BB	5I	10M
Test																	
FC	15	21	4	530	82	31.17	-	4	7	-	2952	1785	53	33.67	5-119	2	-
ODI																	
List A	13	10	1	150	45	16.66	-	-	2	-	594	567	19	29.84	4-36	-	
20/20 Int																	
20/20	6	5	1	45	15	11.25	-	-	4	-	88	100	4	25.00	2-16	-	

Career Performances

	M	Inn	NO	Runs	HS	Avg	100	50	Ct	St	Balls	Runs	Wkts	Avg	BB	5I	10M
Test																	
FC	34	50	7	1131	94	26.30	-	7	12	-	5281	3415	100	34.15	6-38	3	-
ODI																	
List A	50	37	3	546	45	16.05	-	-	12	-	1751	1702	52	32.73	4-36	-	
20/20 Int																	
20/20	25	21	3	265	27	14.72	-	-	7	-	328	453	18	25.16	3-24	-	

WAGH, M. A. — Nottinghamshire

Name: Mark Anant Wagh
Role: Right-hand bat, off-spin bowler
Born: 20 October 1976, Birmingham
Height: 6ft 2in **Weight:** 13st
Nickname: Waggy
County debut: 1997 (Warwickshire), 2007 (Nottinghamshire)
County cap: 2000 (Warwickshire)
1000 runs in a season: 4
1st-Class 200s: 1
1st-Class 300s: 1
Place in batting averages: 25th av. 54.58 (2006 151st av. 29.45)
Parents: Mohan and Rita

Marital status: Single
Education: King Edward's School, Birmingham; Keble College, Oxford
Qualifications: BA degree, Level 2 coaching award
Overseas tours: Warwickshire U19 to South Africa 1992; ECB National Academy to Australia 2001-02
Career highlights to date: '315 at Lord's 2001'
Cricket moments to forget: 'Too many to mention'
Cricketers particularly admired: Andy Flower
Young players to look out for: Moeen Ali
Favourite band: Dido

Extras: Oxford Blue 1996-98; Oxford University captain 1997. Scored maiden first-class century (116) for Oxford University v Glamorgan at The Parks 1997, following up with another hundred (101) in the second innings. His 315 v Middlesex at Lord's 2001 is the equal second highest individual Championship score made at Lord's behind Jack Hobbs's 316* in 1926 (although Percy Holmes's 315 in 1925 was unbeaten). C&G Man of the Match award for his 102* v Kent at Edgbaston 2004. Included in preliminary England one-day squad of 30 for ICC Champions Trophy 2004
Best batting: 315 Warwickshire v Middlesex, Lord's 2001
Best bowling: 7-222 Warwickshire v Lancashire, Edgbaston 2003

2007 Season

	M	Inn	NO	Runs	HS	Avg	100	50	Ct	St	Balls	Runs	Wkts	Avg	BB	5I	10M
Test																	
FC	17	26	2	1310	152	54.58	3	11	2	-	72	33	2	16.50	2-6	-	-
ODI																	
List A	14	14	2	599	81	49.91	-	7	6	-	0	0	0		-	-	
20/20 Int																	
20/20	3	2	0	39	24	19.50	-	-	-	-	0	0	0		-	-	

Career Performances

	M	Inn	NO	Runs	HS	Avg	100	50	Ct	St	Balls	Runs	Wkts	Avg	BB	5I	10M
Test																	
FC	157	260	22	9387	315	39.44	23	45	73	-	8643	4600	100	46.00	7-222	2	-
ODI																	
List A	83	79	7	2099	102 *	29.15	1	16	18	-	1096	862	25	34.48	4-35	-	
20/20 Int																	
20/20	18	15	0	288	56	19.20	-	1	5	-	75	106	5	21.20	2-16	-	

WAINWRIGHT, D. J. Yorkshire

Name: David John Wainwright
Role: Left-hand bat, left-arm orthodox spin bowler
Born: 21 March 1985, Pontefract
Height: 5ft 9in **Weight:** 9st 6lbs
Nickname: Wainers
County debut: 2004
Parents: Paul and Debbie
Marital status: Single
Family links with cricket: 'Grandfather (Harry Heritage) represented Yorkshire Schoolboys 1950-51'
Education: Hemsworth High School; Hemsworth Arts and Community College; Loughborough University
Qualifications: 10 GCSEs, 3 A-levels, Sports Science and Physics degree, Level 2 coaching
Overseas tours: Yorkshire U15 to South Africa 2000
Overseas teams played for: Grovedale CC, Geelong, Melbourne 2006-07
Career highlights to date: 'Winning at Lord's in BUSA final for Loughborough'
Cricketers particularly admired: Brian Lara, Daniel Vettori
Young players to look out for: Chris Murtagh, Richard Morris
Other sports played: Football, golf
Other sports followed: Football (Liverpool FC)
Favourite band: Will Smith, Leona Lewis
Relaxations: Listening to music
Extras: Best bowling award at Bunbury Festival for North of England U15. Played for Loughborough UCCE 2005-06. Represented British Universities 2005-06
Opinions on cricket: 'Introduction of one overseas player is good for younger players to be given an opportunity to play first-class cricket.'
Best batting: 62 Yorkshire v Bangladesh A, Headingley 2005
Best bowling: 4-48 LUCCE v Worcestershire, Kidderminster 2005

2007 Season

	M	Inn	NO	Runs	HS	Avg	100	50	Ct	St	Balls	Runs	Wkts	Avg	BB	5I	10M
Test																	
FC	1	1	1	46	46 *		-	-	1	-	114	74	2	37.00	2-72	-	-
ODI																	
List A	10	4	1	33	26	11.00	-	-	1	-	288	234	9	26.00	2-30	-	
20/20 Int																	
20/20	7	2	0	3	2	1.50	-	-	2	-	138	128	8	16.00	3-6	-	

Career Performances

	M	Inn	NO	Runs	HS	Avg	100	50	Ct	St	Balls	Runs	Wkts	Avg	BB	5I	10M
Test																	
FC	10	12	3	274	62	30.44	-	1	7	-	1379	766	22	34.81	4-48	-	-
ODI																	
List A	12	4	1	33	26	11.00	-	-	1	-	354	293	9	32.55	2-30	-	
20/20 Int																	
20/20	7	2	0	3	2	1.50	-	-	2	-	138	128	8	16.00	3-6	-	

WAKELY, A. G. Northamptonshire

Name: Alexander (Alex) George Wakely
Role: Right-hand bat, right-arm off-spin bowler; batting all-rounder
Born: 3 November 1988, Hammersmith, London
Height: 6ft 2in **Weight:** 13st 7lbs
Nickname: Wakers, Big Al
County debut: 2007
Place in batting averages: 205th av. 21.12
Parents: Jan and John
Marital status: Single
Family links with cricket: 'Father played club and representative cricket. Uncle umpired first-class cricket for ten years'
Education: Bedford School
Qualifications: 11 GCSEs, 3 A-levels
Career outside cricket: 'Golf'
Off-season: 'England to U19 World Cup, Malaysia (captain)'
Overseas tours: Bedford School to Australia 2003; England U16 to South Africa 2004; England U19 to Malaysia 2006-07, to Malaysia (U19 World Cup) 2007-08 (c)

Career highlights to date: '108 for England U19 to beat Sri Lanka 2007' (*HSBC Invitational 1st Tri-Series 2006-07, Kuala Lumpur*)
Cricket moments to forget: 'Diving for a ball on Championship debut and losing my trousers (still get letters about it)'
Cricket superstitions: 'None'
Cricketers particularly admired: Ricky Ponting, Rob Bailey, Keith Pont
Young players to look out for: Billy Godleman, Tom Westley
Other sports played: Golf (6 handicap), hockey (regional and GB trials), football (Meppershall FC), rugby (school 1st XV)
Other sports followed: Rugby (Northampton Saints), football (Luton Town)
Favourite band: Timbaland
Relaxations: 'Friends, family'
Extras: Bunbury Scholarship for Batting 2004. Played for Bedfordshire in the 2005 C&G. Northamptonshire Young Player of the Year 2006. Represented England U19 2007. Scored 66 on first-class debut v Somerset at Taunton, following up with 55 in second match v Nottinghamshire at Northampton 2007
Opinions on cricket: 'More Twenty20 should be played. Younger players from counties should have more of a chance.'
Best batting: 66 Northamptonshire v Somerset, Taunton 2007
Best bowling: 2-62 Northamptonshire v Somerset, Taunton 2007

2007 Season

	M	Inn	NO	Runs	HS	Avg	100	50	Ct	St	Balls	Runs	Wkts	Avg	BB	5I	10M
Test																	
FC	4	8	0	169	66	21.12	-	2	1	-	174	127	3	42.33	2-62	-	-
ODI																	
List A	2	2	0	14	14	7.00	-	-	-	-	18	14	2	7.00	2-14	-	
20/20 Int																	
20/20																	

Career Performances

	M	Inn	NO	Runs	HS	Avg	100	50	Ct	St	Balls	Runs	Wkts	Avg	BB	5I	10M
Test																	
FC	4	8	0	169	66	21.12	-	2	1	-	174	127	3	42.33	2-62	-	-
ODI																	
List A	3	3	0	17	14	5.66	-	-	1	-	18	14	2	7.00	2-14	-	
20/20 Int																	
20/20																	

WALKER, M. J. Kent

Name: Matthew (<u>Matt</u>) Jonathan Walker
Role: Left-hand bat
Born: 2 January 1974, Gravesend
Height: 5ft 6in **Weight:** 13st
Nickname: Walks, Pumba
County debut: 1992-93
County cap: 2000
Benefit: 2008
1000 runs in a season: 3
1st-Class 200s: 1
Place in batting averages: 67th av. 40.72 (2006 14th av. 61.69)
Parents: Richard and June
Wife and date of marriage: Claudia, 25 September 1999
Children: Charlie Jack, 20 November 2002; Lexie, 19 January 2007
Family links with cricket: 'Dad played Kent and Middlesex 2nd XIs and was on Lord's groundstaff. Grandfather kept wicket for Kent. Mum was women's cricket coach'
Education: King's School, Rochester
Qualifications: 9 GCSEs, 2 A-levels, advanced cricket coaching certificate
Career outside cricket: PE teacher
Overseas tours: Kent U17 to New Zealand 1990-91; England U19 to Pakistan 1991-92, to India 1992-93 (c); Kent to Zimbabwe 1993
Career highlights to date: 'Captaining England U19. Winning Norwich Union League 2001'
Cricket moments to forget: 'Losing Lord's B&H final v Surrey 1997'
Cricket superstitions: 'None'
Cricketers particularly admired: Darren Lehmann, Nick Knight, Mark Ramprakash
Young players to look out for: Alex Blake, Neil Dexter
Other sports played: Hockey (England U14-U21 [captain U15-U17]), rugby (Kent U18)
Other sports followed: Football (Charlton Athletic), hockey (Gore Court HC)
Favourite band: Razorlight, Arctic Monkeys, Jeff Buckley
Relaxations: 'Music and films'
Extras: Captained England U16 cricket and hockey teams in same year. Sir John Hobbs Silver Jubilee Memorial Prize for outstanding U16 cricketer 1989. Captained England U19 1993. Woolwich Kent League's Young Cricketer of the Year 1994. Scored 275* against Somerset in 1996 – the highest ever individual score by a Kent batsman at Canterbury. Ealham Award for Fielding Excellence 2003, 2004, 2005.

Cowdrey Award (Kent Player of the Year) 2004, 2006. Vice-captain of Kent 2005. Denness Award (Kent leading run-scorer) 2006. Scored century in each innings (142/157) v Lancashire at Canterbury 2007. Became an Eminent Roffensian 1995

Opinions on cricket: 'The game is in great shape and domestic cricket is as competitive as ever.'

Best batting: 275* Kent v Somerset, Canterbury 1996

Best bowling: 2-21 Kent v Middlesex, Canterbury 2004

2007 Season

	M	Inn	NO	Runs	HS	Avg	100	50	Ct	St	Balls	Runs	Wkts	Avg	BB	5I	10M
Test																	
FC	12	18	0	733	157	40.72	3	2	6	-	12	10	1	10.00	1-10	-	-
ODI																	
List A	15	11	1	276	83	27.60	-	2	6	-	0	0	0		-	-	
20/20 Int																	
20/20	10	8	0	161	45	20.12	-	-	1	-	0	0	0		-	-	

Career Performances

	M	Inn	NO	Runs	HS	Avg	100	50	Ct	St	Balls	Runs	Wkts	Avg	BB	5I	10M
Test																	
FC	177	291	31	9674	275*	37.20	25	40	121	-	1822	1081	21	51.47	2-21	-	-
ODI																	
List A	250	227	34	5497	117	28.48	3	34	69	-	886	740	30	24.66	4-24	-	
20/20 Int																	
20/20	37	35	6	745	58*	25.68	-	1	3	-	0	0	0		-	-	

WALKER, N. G. E. — Leicestershire

Name: Nicholas (Nick) Guy Eades Walker

Role: Right-hand bat, right-arm fast-medium bowler

Born: 7 August 1984, Enfield

Height: 6ft 2in **Weight:** 14st 2lbs

Nickname: Walks, Wak

County debut: 2004 (Derbyshire), 2006 (Leicestershire)

Place in batting averages: 190th av. 23.83

Place in bowling averages: 124th av. 43.16 (2006 84th av. 35.57)

Parents: Amanda and Martin

Marital status: Single

Family links with cricket: 'Brothers play local village cricket'

Education: Haileybury Imperial Service College; Durham University ('two terms')

Qualifications: Level 2 cricket coach

Career outside cricket: 'Property'

Off-season: 'Buying property'

Overseas tours: Haileybury to South Africa 2000; Leicestershire to Sri Lanka and India 2007
Overseas teams played for: South Perth, Western Australia 2001-02; Macquarie University, Sydney 2004-05
Career highlights to date: 'Winning 2006 Twenty20 trophy with Leicestershire'
Cricket moments to forget: 'Being sacked from Derbyshire'
Cricket superstitions: 'None'
Cricketers particularly admired: Jimmy Adams (West Indies), Devon Malcolm
Young players to look out for: Nathan Buck, Shiv Thakor
Other sports played: Hockey (Broxbourne 1st XI), football (Haileybury Hermits), squash
Other sports followed: Rugby (Leicester Tigers)
Injuries: Out for two weeks with an injured disc
Favourite band: Michael Jackson
Relaxations: 'Television'
Extras: Struck 57-ball 80 (highest first-class score by a Derbyshire No. 11) in his third Championship innings, then recorded maiden first-class five-wicket return (5-68), both v Somerset at Derby 2004. Struck 24-ball fifty (ending with 63*), batting at No. 11 v Leicestershire at Oakham School 2004. NBC Denis Compton Award for the most promising young Derbyshire player 2004
Opinions on cricket: 'Need more time off in between games. Too many Kolpaks [*see page 13*] infiltrating our game.'
Best batting: 80 Derbyshire v Somerset, Derby 2004
Best bowling: 5-59 Leicestershire v Somerset, Leicester 2006

2007 Season

	M	Inn	NO	Runs	HS	Avg	100	50	Ct	St	Balls	Runs	Wkts	Avg	BB	5I	10M
Test																	
FC	8	11	5	143	31	23.83	-	-	4	-	1026	777	18	43.16	4-70	-	-
ODI																	
List A	10	6	0	71	26	11.83	-	-	5	-	372	352	7	50.28	3-60	-	
20/20 Int																	
20/20	4	1	1	1	1*		-	-	-	-	42	53	3	17.66	2-24	-	

Career Performances

	M	Inn	NO	Runs	HS	Avg	100	50	Ct	St	Balls	Runs	Wkts	Avg	BB	5I	10M
Test																	
FC	31	40	11	558	80	19.24	-	3	13	-	4106	2834	67	42.29	5-59	2	-
ODI																	
List A	30	21	2	189	43	9.94	-	-	13	-	792	740	23	32.17	4-26	-	
20/20 Int																	
20/20	8	3	2	25	16 *	25.00	-	-	-	-	102	110	7	15.71	3-19	-	

WALLACE, M. A. — Glamorgan

Name: Mark Alexander Wallace
Role: Left-hand bat, wicket-keeper
Born: 19 November 1981, Abergavenny
Height: 5ft 10in **Weight:** 11st 9lbs
Nickname: Wally, Wash, Grom, Screech, Kyle, Marcellus
County debut: 1999
County cap: 2003
50 dismissals in a season: 2
Place in batting averages: 181st av. 24.77 (2006 143rd av. 30.34)
Parents: Ryland and Alvine
Wife and date of marriage: Lucy, 28 October 2007
Family links with cricket: 'Father plays for Wales Over 50'
Education: Crickhowell High School; Staffordshire University
Qualifications: 10 GCSEs, 2 A-levels, Level 2 coach, 'studying for a degree in journalism'
Career outside cricket: 'Hopefully journalism'
Off-season: 'Studying; getting married; forgetting summer of 2007'
Overseas tours: England U19 to New Zealand 1998-99, to Malaysia and (U19 World Cup) Sri Lanka 1999-2000, to India 2000-01; ECB National Academy to Australia 2001-02, to Australia and Sri Lanka 2002-03; MCC to New Zealand and Papua New Guinea 2007
Overseas teams played for: Port Adelaide, South Australia 2001-02; Redlands Tigers, Brisbane 2004-06
Career highlights to date: 'Academy tours. Winning one-day league 2002 and 2004'
Cricket moments to forget: 'Summer 2007'

Cricketers particularly admired: Ian Healy, Adam Gilchrist, Chris Read, Matt Elliott, Keith Piper
Young players to look out for: James Harris, Imran Hassan
Other sports played: Golf, touch rugby ('playmaker')
Other sports followed: Football (Merthyr Tydfil FC), rugby (Cardiff Blues)
Favourite band: Stereophonics, Shania Twain
Relaxations: 'Golf, TV'
Extras: Represented England U17. Represented England U19 1998, 1999 and 2000 (captain for second 'Test' 2000). Made first-class debut v Somerset at Taunton 1999 aged 17 years 287 days – youngest ever Glamorgan wicket-keeper. NBC Denis Compton Award 1999. Captained ECB National Academy to innings victory over Commonwealth Bank [Australian] Cricket Academy at Adelaide 2001-02. Byron Denning Glamorgan Clubman of the Year Award 2003. Captained Glamorgan v Somerset at Taunton 2007 in the absence of David Hemp
Opinions on cricket: 'The impact of Twenty20 on the world game may have an irretrievably negative impact on Test and first-class cricket. It may soon be so financially rewarding to play Twenty20 that many players will play it exclusively and not bother playing the traditional forms.'
Best batting: 128 Glamorgan v Gloucestershire, Bristol 2007

2007 Season

	M	Inn	NO	Runs	HS	Avg	100	50	Ct	St	Balls	Runs	Wkts	Avg	BB	5I	10M
Test																	
FC	16	27	0	669	128	24.77	2	1	40	6	0	0	0		-	-	-
ODI																	
List A	14	13	3	232	37 *	23.20	-	-	10	3	0	0	0		-	-	
20/20 Int																	
20/20	6	5	1	115	35 *	28.75	-	-	2	-	0	0	0		-	-	

Career Performances

	M	Inn	NO	Runs	HS	Avg	100	50	Ct	St	Balls	Runs	Wkts	Avg	BB	5I	10M
Test																	
FC	118	195	16	4909	128	27.42	6	24	313	22	0	0	0		-	-	-
ODI																	
List A	113	88	18	1205	48	17.21	-	-	115	26	0	0	0		-	-	
20/20 Int																	
20/20	33	25	9	376	35 *	23.50	-	-	12	5	0	0	0		-	-	

WALTERS, S. J. Surrey

Name: Stewart Jonathan Walters
Role: Right-hand bat, right-arm slow-medium/leg-spin bowler
Born: 25 June 1983, Mornington, Victoria, Australia
Height: 6ft **Weight:** 12st 13lbs
Nickname: Roadie
County debut: 2005 (one-day), 2006 (first-class)
Place in batting averages: 209th av. 20.72 (2006 163rd av. 27.66)
Parents: Stewart and Sue
Wife and date of marriage: Jacki, 24 February 2006
Family links with cricket: 'Father played'
Education: Guildford Grammar School, Perth, Western Australia
Career outside cricket: Fitness trainer
Off-season: 'Grade cricket in Perth'
Overseas teams played for: Midland-Guildford CC, Perth; Perth CC
Career highlights to date: 'Playing with Test match players'
Cricket superstitions: 'Throw to Ramps'
Cricketers particularly admired: Ali Brown
Young players to look out for: Chris Jordan
Other sports played: Australian Rules football (AFL)
Other sports followed: Australian Rules (Collingwood)
Injuries: 'Back problem – stops me bowling fast'
Relaxations: 'Swimming, poker'
Extras: Captain of Western Australia U17 for two years
Opinions on cricket: 'Simple game made complicated by idiots, me being one of them.'
Best batting: 70 Surrey v Durham, The Oval 2007
Best bowling: 1-4 Surrey v Durham, Riverside 2007

2007 Season

	M	Inn	NO	Runs	HS	Avg	100	50	Ct	St	Balls	Runs	Wkts	Avg	BB	5I	10M
Test																	
FC	8	12	1	228	70	20.72	-	1	9	-	48	28	1	28.00	1-4	-	-
ODI																	
List A	4	4	0	24	13	6.00	-	-	1	-	51	52	1	52.00	1-12	-	
20/20 Int																	
20/20	3	1	0	18	18	18.00	-	-	2	-	0	0	0		-	-	

Career Performances

	M	Inn	NO	Runs	HS	Avg	100	50	Ct	St	Balls	Runs	Wkts	Avg	BB	5I	10M
Test																	
FC	11	18	1	394	70	23.17	-	2	12	-	204	97	3	32.33	1-4	-	-
ODI																	
List A	19	17	4	215	32 *	16.53	-	-	6	-	135	135	2	67.50	1-12	-	
20/20 Int																	
20/20	10	5	1	39	18	9.75	-	-	7	-	12	17	0		-	-	

WARNE, S. K. — Hampshire

Name: Shane Keith Warne
Role: Right-hand bat, leg-spin bowler, county captain
Born: 13 September 1969, Ferntree Gully, Victoria, Australia
Height: 6ft **Weight:** 13st 12lbs
Nickname: Warney
County debut: 2000
County cap: 2000
Test debut: 1991-92
ODI debut: 1992-93
50 wickets in a season: 5
Place in batting averages: 221st av. 19.15 (2006 135th av. 30.91)
Place in bowling averages: 62nd av. 29.58 (2006 25th av. 27.08)
Parents: Keith and Brigite
Marital status: Single
Children: Brooke, 10; Jackson, 8; Summer, 6
Education: Mentone Grammar School; Hampton High School
Overseas tours: Australia YC to West Indies 1990; Australia B to Zimbabwe 1991-92; Australia to Sri Lanka 1992, to New Zealand 1992-93, to England 1993, to South

Africa 1993-94, to Pakistan 1994-95, to West Indies 1994-95, to India, Pakistan and Sri Lanka (World Cup) 1995-96, to South Africa 1996-97, to England 1997, to India 1997-98, to West Indies 1998-99, to UK, Ireland and Netherlands (World Cup) 1999, to Sri Lanka 1999, to Zimbabwe 1999-2000, to New Zealand 1999-2000, to India 2000-01, to England 2001, to South Africa 2001-02, to Sri Lanka (ICC Champions Trophy) 2002-03, to Sri Lanka and Sharjah (v Pakistan) 2002-03, to Sri Lanka 2003-04, to India 2004-05, to New Zealand 2004-05, to England 2005, to South Africa 2005-06, to Bangladesh 2005-06, plus other one-day series and tournaments in Sharjah, Sri Lanka, Pakistan, New Zealand, India, South Africa and Kenya; FICA World XI to New Zealand 2004-05
Overseas teams played for: St Kilda, Victoria; Victoria 1990-91 – 2006-07
Career highlights to date: '1999 World Cup and being selected for Australia'
Cricket moments to forget: 'Losing to the West Indies by one run in 1992-93 season in Adelaide'
Cricket superstitions: 'I eat pizza the night before I bowl'
Cricketers particularly admired: Sachin Tendulkar, Brian Lara, Ian Chappell, Glenn McGrath
Other sports played: AFL, golf, tennis
Other sports followed: AFL (St Kilda), football (Chelsea)
Favourite band: Rogue Traders, Bruce Springsteen
Relaxations: 'Yoga and kids'
Extras: One of *Wisden*'s Five Cricketers of the Year 1994, one of *South African Cricket Annual*'s five Cricketers of the Year 1994, and one of *Indian Cricket*'s five Cricketers of the Year 1996; voted one of *Wisden*'s Five Cricketers of the Century 2000. Voted Australia's ODI Player of the Year at the inaugural Allan Border Medal awards January 2000. Took hat-trick (DeFreitas, Gough, Malcolm) in the second Test v England at Melbourne 1994-95. Man of the Match in his 100th Test, v South Africa at Cape Town 2001-02 (2-70/6-161). Has won numerous other Test awards, among them Man of the Series v England 1993 (34 wickets; av. 25.79), v Pakistan in Colombo and Sharjah 2002-03 (27 wickets; av. 12.66) and Australia's Man of the Series v England 2005 (40 wickets; av. 19.92). Has also won numerous ODI awards, including Man of the Match in the 1999 World Cup semi-final v South Africa at Edgbaston (4-29) and final v Pakistan at Lord's (4-33). Has captained Australia in ODIs; retired from ODI cricket in 2003 (bar one match for ICC World XI 2004-05). Took 1000th first-class wicket (Hamish Marshall) in the first Test v New Zealand at Christchurch 2004-05. Was Hampshire's overseas player in 2000; rejoined Hampshire as an overseas player and as captain in 2004. Leading wicket-taker in English first-class cricket 2005 (87; av. 22.50). BBC Overseas Sports Personality of the Year 2005. Leading Test wicket-taker for the calendar year 2005 (96; av. 22.02). Named Australia's Test Player of the Year at the 2006 Allan Border Medal awards. Awarded honorary doctorate for services to cricket by Southampton Solent University at The Rose Bowl 2006 on his 37th birthday. Took 5-39 in England's first innings of the fourth Test at Melbourne 2006-07, in the process becoming the first bowler to take 700 Test wickets when he dismissed Andrew Strauss. Retired from Test cricket after the fifth Test v England at Sydney 2006-07

Best batting: 107* Hampshire v Kent, Canterbury 2005
Best bowling: 8-71 Australia v England, Brisbane 1994-95

2007 Season

	M	Inn	NO	Runs	HS	Avg	100	50	Ct	St	Balls	Runs	Wkts	Avg	BB	5I	10M
Test																	
FC	15	19	0	364	50	19.15	-	1	17	-	2629	1479	50	29.58	6-83	5	1
ODI																	
List A	14	11	6	60	18 *	12.00	-	-	7	-	720	554	21	26.38	3-16	-	
20/20 Int																	
20/20																	

Career Performances

	M	Inn	NO	Runs	HS	Avg	100	50	Ct	St	Balls	Runs	Wkts	Avg	BB	5I	10M
Test	145	199	17	3154	99	17.32	-	12	125	-	40705	17995	708	25.41	8-71	37	10
FC	301	404	48	6919	107 *	19.43	2	26	264	-	74830	34449	1319	26.11	8-71	69	12
ODI	194	107	29	1018	55	13.05	-	1	80	-	10642	7541	293	25.73	5-33	1	
List A	311	200	41	1879	55	11.81	-	1	126	-	16419	11642	473	24.61	6-42	3	
20/20 Int																	
20/20	2	2	0	12	12	6.00	-	-	-	-	48	51	1	51.00	1-29	-	

WATERS, H. T. — Glamorgan

Name: Huw Thomas Waters
Role: Right-hand bat, right-arm medium-fast bowler
Born: 26 September 1986, Cardiff
Height: 6ft 2in **Weight:** 13st 5lbs
Nickname: Muddy
County debut: 2005
Place in batting averages: 274th av. 10.87
Place in bowling averages: 137th av. 49.40 (2006 56th av. 31.66)
Parents: Valerie and Donald
Marital status: Single
Family links with cricket: 'Long line of club cricketers, most notably Big Don, a stalwart of the old 3 Counties League'
Education: Llantarnam CS; Monmouth School
Qualifications: 8 GCSEs, 'a couple of A-levels – somehow!', Level 2 cricket coach
Overseas tours: West Region to West Indies 2002; Wales U16 to Jersey 2002;

Monmouth School to St Lucia 2003; England U19 to Bangladesh 2005-06, to Sri Lanka (U19 World Cup) 2005-06
Career highlights to date: 'Making debut. Taking my first five-for'
Cricketers particularly admired: Glenn McGrath
Young players to look out for: 'Our academy boys'
Other sports played: Football ('mainly during warm-ups')
Other sports followed: Football (Man United)
Favourite band: Coldplay, 'any indie rock'
Relaxations: 'Pro Evo Soccer, listening to music, watching films, chilling out with friends'
Extras: Played for Wales Minor Counties in the C&G 2005 and in Minor Counties competitions 2004-07
Opinions on cricket: 'Gaining more interest due to Twenty20. Should just have one one-day competition. Glad only one overseas – means youngsters get more of a chance.'
Best batting: 34 Glamorgan v Kent, Canterbury 2005
Best bowling: 5-86 Glamorgan v Somerset, Taunton 2006

2007 Season

	M	Inn	NO	Runs	HS	Avg	100	50	Ct	St	Balls	Runs	Wkts	Avg	BB	5I	10M
Test																	
FC	10	16	8	87	33	10.87	-	-	4	-	1209	741	15	49.40	4-76	-	-
ODI																	
List A	9	6	3	14	8	4.66	-	-	-	-	366	417	8	52.12	3-47	-	
20/20 Int																	
20/20																	

Career Performances

	M	Inn	NO	Runs	HS	Avg	100	50	Ct	St	Balls	Runs	Wkts	Avg	BB	5I	10M
Test																	
FC	22	36	17	135	34	7.10	-	-	5	-	2478	1453	38	38.23	5-86	1	-
ODI																	
List A	11	7	3	22	8	5.50	-	-	-	-	456	477	8	59.62	3-47	-	
20/20 Int																	
20/20																	

95. Which current county director of cricket made his Test debut in the third Test between England and New Zealand at Lord's in 1978, taking a wicket with his fourth delivery?

WATKINS, R. E. Glamorgan

Name: Ryan Edward Watkins
Role: Left-hand bat, right-arm medium-fast bowler, occasional wicket-keeper
Born: 9 June 1983, Abergavenny, Monmouthshire
Height: 6ft **Weight:** 14st 2lbs
Nickname: Tets, Maverick, Big Red, Commando, Wokka
County debut: 2003 (one-day), 2005 (first-class)
Place in batting averages: 259th av. 13.23 (2006 185th av. 24.08)
Place in bowling averages: 119th av. 41.10 (2006 138th av. 48.52)
Parents: Huw and Gaynor
Wife and date of marriage: Lisa, 16 October 2005
Family links with cricket: 'Father and brother keen club cricketers'
Education: Pontllanfraith Comprehensive School; Crosskeys College
Qualifications: Level 2 coach, qualified tyre and exhaust fitter, 'Working Safely' Level 1 qualified
Career outside cricket: 'Working for Crownford, a leading training and consultancy firm. Or police officer'
Off-season: 'Commandos tour to Egypt, October 2007; becoming Number 1 trainer at Glamorgan CCC; Guernsey 2007'
Overseas tours: Glamorgan to Guernsey 2006, 2007
Overseas teams played for: North Balwyn CC, Victoria, Australia 2003
Career highlights to date: 'Being voted Man of the Match in the Glamorgan v Nottinghamshire end-of-season football victory. Glamorgan Young Player of the Year 2006'
Cricket moments to forget: 'Being relegated from division one of the Pro40 2006. Any game we get a chance to win and don't take it'
Cricket superstitions: 'Right pad on first'
Cricketers particularly admired: Andrew Flintoff, Matthew Hayden, Yuvraj Singh
Young players to look out for: Tom Baker, James Harris
Other sports played: Football (Ynysddu Welfare FC)
Other sports followed: Football (Tottenham Hotspur), rugby (Cardiff Blues), 'Markham Tigers'
Injuries: Out for whole pre-season with an ankle injury; for two weeks with a thigh strain; ongoing groin problem

Favourite band: 50 Cent
Relaxations: 'Playing golf; walking my dog; spending time with my wife; mocking Gareth Rees'
Extras: Played for Wales Minor Counties in Minor Counties competitions 2003-07. Took five catches in an innings v Gloucestershire at Cheltenham 2006, equalling Glamorgan record. Glamorgan Young Player of the Year 2006
Opinions on cricket: 'More preparation time should be given between games. Do away with 40-over competition – as it isn't played at international level, what is it preparing you for? Too many Kolpak players [*see page 13*] coming into the game.'
Best batting: 87 Glamorgan v Essex, Cardiff 2006
Best bowling: 4-40 Glamorgan v Worcestershire, Worcester 2006

2007 Season

	M	Inn	NO	Runs	HS	Avg	100	50	Ct	St	Balls	Runs	Wkts	Avg	BB	5I	10M
Test																	
FC	8	13	0	172	30	13.23	-	-	3	-	597	411	10	41.10	4-89	-	-
ODI																	
List A	4	4	1	95	39	31.66	-	-	-	-	89	107	2	53.50	1-22	-	
20/20 Int																	
20/20	6	1	1	1	1 *		-	-	3	-	108	145	7	20.71	3-33	-	

Career Performances

	M	Inn	NO	Runs	HS	Avg	100	50	Ct	St	Balls	Runs	Wkts	Avg	BB	5I	10M
Test																	
FC	27	47	2	857	87	19.04	-	2	15	-	2204	1458	32	45.56	4-40	-	-
ODI																	
List A	18	15	3	215	39	17.91	-	-	1	-	518	571	13	43.92	2-25	-	
20/20 Int																	
20/20	9	2	2	7	6 *		-	-	5	-	138	194	9	21.55	3-33	-	

WESSELS, M. H. — Northamptonshire

Name: Mattheus Hendrik (Riki) Wessels
Role: Right-hand bat, wicket-keeper
Born: 12 November 1985, Nambour, Australia
Height: 5ft 10½in **Weight:** 11st 7lbs
Nickname: Weasel
County debut: 2005
Place in batting averages: 134th av. 31.35 (2006 189th av. 23.53)
Parents: Kepler and Sally
Marital status: Engaged
Family links with cricket: 'Dad' (*Kepler Wessels played Test and ODI cricket for Australia and South Africa between 1982-83 and 1994-95*)

Education: Woodridge College, Port Elizabeth
Off-season: 'Playing club cricket, coaching, surfing and drinking'
Overseas teams played for: Pirates CC, Port Elizabeth
Cricket moments to forget: 'Getting my first and last pair; tearing my hamstring going for a run'
Cricket superstitions: 'None'
Cricketers particularly admired: Justin Langer
Young players to look out for: Alex Wakely
Other sports played: Hockey, archery
Other sports followed: Football (Spurs)
Favourite band: Linkin Park
Extras: Northamptonshire Academy Players' Player of the Year 2004. Northamptonshire Young Player of the Year (Frank Rudd Trophy) 2004. Made first-class debut for MCC v West Indians at Arundel 2004. Scored maiden first-class century (102) v Somerset at Northampton 2005 after coming to the wicket on a hat-trick ball

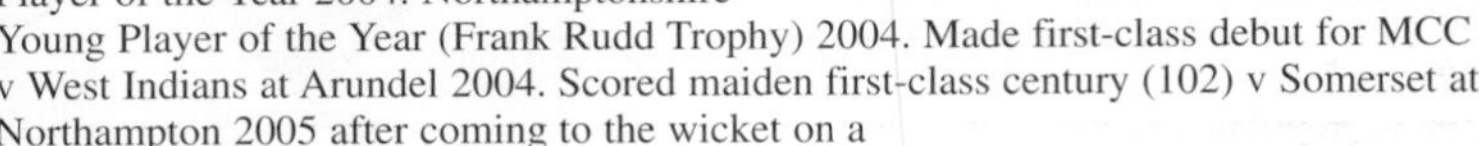

Best batting: 107 Northamptonshire v Durham, Riverside 2005

2007 Season

	M	Inn	NO	Runs	HS	Avg	100	50	Ct	St	Balls	Runs	Wkts	Avg	BB	5I	10M
Test																	
FC	11	18	1	533	97	31.35	-	3	28	2	0	0	0		-	-	-
ODI																	
List A	12	12	2	230	52	23.00	-	1	8	-	0	0	0		-	-	
20/20 Int																	
20/20	7	3	0	54	30	18.00	-	-	2	3	0	0	0		-	-	

Career Performances

	M	Inn	NO	Runs	HS	Avg	100	50	Ct	St	Balls	Runs	Wkts	Avg	BB	5I	10M
Test																	
FC	36	60	6	1534	107	28.40	3	7	82	8	0	0	0		-	-	-
ODI																	
List A	38	34	6	634	80	22.64	-	2	31	-	0	0	0		-	-	
20/20 Int																	
20/20	23	16	4	264	49 *	22.00	-	-	8	9	0	0	0		-	-	

WESTFIELD, M. S.   Essex

Name: Mervyn (Merv) Simon Westfield
Role: Right-hand bat, right-arm fast bowler
Born: 5 May 1988, Romford
Height: 6ft 1in **Weight:** 12st
Nickname: Swerve
County debut: 2005
Parents: Pamela and Mervyn
Marital status: Single
Family links with cricket: 'Dad used to play cricket and my older brother played for Essex for a couple of years'
Education: The Chafford School, Rainham; Havering College
Qualifications: 8 GCSEs, Level 1 coaching
Overseas tours: England U16 to South Africa 2004-05; England U19 to Malaysia 2006-07
Career highlights to date: 'Taking four wickets against Somerset and scoring 32 runs as well in 2006'
Cricketers particularly admired: Andy Flower, Andy Bichel
Young players to look out for: Maurice Chambers, Tom Westley, Adil Rashid
Other sports followed: Football (Manchester United)
Favourite band: TOK
Relaxations: 'Socialising with friends, listening to music'
Extras: Wanstead U11 Young Player of the Year 1997. Wanstead U11 All-Rounder of 1998. Havering District U13 Best Innings 2000. MCC Cricketer of the Year 2003, 2004. *Daily Telegraph* Bunbury Scholar 2003 (Best Fast Bowler; scholarship entailed a week's training with England A)
Best batting: 32 Essex v Somerset, Southend 2006
Best bowling: 4-72 Essex v Somerset, Southend 2006

2007 Season

	M	Inn	NO	Runs	HS	Avg	100	50	Ct	St	Balls	Runs	Wkts	Avg	BB	5I	10M
Test																	
FC	1	1	1	4	4 *		-	-	-	-	78	64	0		-	-	-
ODI																	
List A																	
20/20 Int																	
20/20																	

Career Performances

	M	Inn	NO	Runs	HS	Avg	100	50	Ct	St	Balls	Runs	Wkts	Avg	BB	5I	10M
Test																	
FC	5	7	3	45	32	11.25	-	-	1	-	444	334	7	47.71	4-72	-	-
ODI																	
List A	2	2	2	6	4 *		-	-	1	-	36	38	0		-	-	
20/20 Int																	
20/20																	

WESTLEY, T. Essex

Name: Thomas (Tom) Westley
Role: Right-hand top-order bat, right-arm off-spin bowler
Born: 13 March 1989, Cambridge
Height: 6ft 2in
Nickname: Spongebob, Pup
County debut: 2006 (one-day), 2007 (first-class)
Place in batting averages: 129th av. 31.85
Parents: Ade and Mags
Family links with cricket: 'Dad has played village club cricket in Cambridgeshire, along with uncle and brother'
Education: Linton Village College; Hills Road Sixth Form College (both Cambridge)
Overseas tours: England U16 to South Africa 2004-05; England U19 to Malaysia (U19 World Cup) 2007-08
Cricket moments to forget: 'King pair against Surrey 2nd XI 2005'
Cricket superstitions: 'Mark my crease three times before every over and after every boundary'
Cricketers particularly admired: Steve Waugh, Sachin Tendulkar, Andy Flower, Alastair Cook
Young players to look out for: Mervyn Westfield, Adam Wheater
Other sports followed: Football (Newcastle United)
Extras: Played for MCC 2007. Represented England U19 2007
Best batting: 72 Essex v Somerset, Chelmsford 2007
Best bowling: 1-24 MCC v Sri Lanka A, Arundel 2007

2007 Season

	M	Inn	NO	Runs	HS	Avg	100	50	Ct	St	Balls	Runs	Wkts	Avg	BB	5I	10M
Test																	
FC	6	9	2	223	72	31.85	-	1	3	-	30	24	1	24.00	1-24	-	-
ODI																	
List A	2	2	0	37	36	18.50	-	-	-	-	0	0	0		-	-	
20/20 Int																	
20/20																	

Career Performances

	M	Inn	NO	Runs	HS	Avg	100	50	Ct	St	Balls	Runs	Wkts	Avg	BB	5I	10M
Test																	
FC	6	9	2	223	72	31.85	-	1	3	-	30	24	1	24.00	1-24	-	-
ODI																	
List A	3	2	0	37	36	18.50	-	-	-	-	0	0	0		-	-	
20/20 Int																	
20/20																	

WESTON, W. P. C. — Derbyshire

Name: William Philip Christopher Weston
Role: Left-hand bat, left-arm medium bowler
Born: 16 June 1973, Durham City
Height: 6ft 4in **Weight:** 14st
Nickname: Tickle, Weso
County debut: 1991 (Worcestershire), 2003 (Gloucestershire), 2007 (Derbyshire)
County cap: 1995; colours, 2002 (both Worcestershire), 2004 (Gloucestershire)
1000 runs in a season: 4
1st-Class 200s: 1
Place in batting averages: 260th av. 13.20 (2006 76th av. 39.60)
Parents: Michael and Kate (deceased)
Wife and date of marriage: Sarah, 30 September 2000
Family links with sport: Brother Robin played for Durham, Derbyshire and Middlesex. Father played Minor Counties cricket for Durham (and rugby union for England)
Education: Durham School
Qualifications: 9 GCSEs, 4 A-levels, Diploma in Business and Management

Overseas tours: England U18 to Canada (International Youth Tournament) 1991 (vc); England YC to New Zealand 1990-91; England U19 to Pakistan 1991-92 (c); Worcestershire to Zimbabwe 1996
Overseas teams played for: Melville, Perth 1992-94, 1996-97; Swanbourne, Perth 1995-96
Career highlights to date: '2004 C&G final'
Cricket superstitions: 'Not really'
Cricketers particularly admired: Ian Botham
Other sports played: 'Have a go at most sports'
Other sports followed: Rugby union, football (Sunderland AFC)
Favourite band: U2
Relaxations: 'Spending time with my lovely wife; travelling, films, hanging out with friends'
Extras: Represented England YC 1991 and England U19 1992 (Man of the Series). Cricket Society's Most Promising Young Cricketer 1992. Worcestershire Uncapped Player of the Year 1992. C&G Man of the Match award for his 106 v Netherlands at Amstelveen 2004. Scored century (110*) in the C&G final v Worcestershire at Lord's 2004
Best batting: 205 Worcestershire v Northamptonshire, Northampton 1997
Best bowling: 2-39 Worcestershire v Pakistanis, Worcester 1992
Stop press: Retired during the 2007-08 off-season

2007 Season

	M	Inn	NO	Runs	HS	Avg	100	50	Ct	St	Balls	Runs	Wkts	Avg	BB	5I	10M
Test																	
FC	9	15	0	198	38	13.20	-	-	5	-	12	12	0		-	-	-
ODI																	
List A	7	7	0	269	78	38.42	-	3	1	-	0	0	0		-	-	
20/20 Int																	
20/20																	

Career Performances

	M	Inn	NO	Runs	HS	Avg	100	50	Ct	St	Balls	Runs	Wkts	Avg	BB	5I	10M
Test																	
FC	237	417	34	12789	205	33.39	24	64	133	-	1013	670	5	134.00	2-39	-	-
ODI																	
List A	199	184	13	4385	134	25.64	4	24	45	-	6	2	1	2.00	1-2	-	
20/20 Int																	
20/20	7	5	2	167	73 *	55.66	-	1	3	-	0	0	0		-	-	

WESTWOOD, I. J. Warwickshire

Name: Ian James Westwood
Role: Left-hand opening bat, right-arm off-spin bowler
Born: 13 July 1982, Birmingham
Height: 5ft 8in **Weight:** 11st
Nickname: Westy, Wezzo
County debut: 2003
Place in batting averages: 80th av. 38.55 (2006 67th av. 42.50)
Parents: Ann and Dave
Marital status: Single
Family links with cricket: 'Brother played Warwickshire Youth cricket'
Education: Wheelers Lane, Kings Heath; Solihull Sixth Form College
Qualifications: 10 GCSEs, BTEC Sports Science, Level 2 cricket coaching
Off-season: 'Coaching'
Overseas tours: Warwickshire Development squad to Cape Town 1998
Overseas teams played for: Hawkesbury CC, Sydney 2001-02; University CC, Perth 2005-06
Career highlights to date: 'First Championship century for Warwickshire'
Cricket moments to forget: 'Too many to mention'
Cricket superstitions: 'None'
Cricketers particularly admired: Nick Knight, Brian Lara
Other sports played: Football (Coleshill Town FC 2001; Moseley Mariners FC)
Other sports followed: Football (Birmingham City)
Injuries: Out for three weeks with a cracked rib
Favourite band: Fleetwood Mac
Relaxations: 'Music, socialising, poker, friends and family'
Extras: Scored 250* v Worcestershire 2nd XI at Barnt Green 2003, sharing with Jonathan Trott (248) in an opening partnership of 429; also took 6-104 in Worcestershire 2nd XI's only innings
Opinions on cricket: 'Cricket has become much more professional in the last few years and will continue to grow with the introduction of Twenty20 etc.'
Best batting: 178 Warwickshire v West Indies A, Edgbaston 2006
Best bowling: 2-46 Warwickshire v Kent, Edgbaston 2006

2007 Season

	M	Inn	NO	Runs	HS	Avg	100	50	Ct	St	Balls	Runs	Wkts	Avg	BB	5I	10M
Test																	
FC	14	22	2	771	116	38.55	2	5	8	-	41	26	1	26.00	1-9	-	-
ODI																	
List A	12	12	0	248	44	20.66	-	-	2	-	6	9	0		-	-	
20/20 Int																	
20/20	3	1	1	1	1 *		-	-	1	-	0	0	0		-	-	

Career Performances

	M	Inn	NO	Runs	HS	Avg	100	50	Ct	St	Balls	Runs	Wkts	Avg	BB	5I	10M
Test																	
FC	40	70	9	2305	178	37.78	5	12	19	-	245	171	4	42.75	2-46	-	-
ODI																	
List A	25	22	4	434	55	24.11	-	1	4	-	186	148	2	74.00	1-28	-	
20/20 Int																	
20/20	10	5	5	33	19 *		-	-	2	-	48	78	5	15.60	3-29	-	

WHARF, A. G. B. — Glamorgan

Name: Alexander (Alex) George Busfield Wharf
Role: Right-hand bat, right-arm fast-medium bowler; all-rounder
Born: 4 June 1975, Bradford
Height: 6ft 4in **Weight:** 15st
Nickname: Gangster
County debut: 1994 (Yorks), 1998 (Notts), 2000 (Glamorgan)
County cap: 2000 (Glamorgan)
ODI debut: 2004
50 wickets in a season: 1
Place in batting averages: 116th av. 33.00 (2006 142nd av. 30.53)
Place in bowling averages: 98th av. 35.05 (2006 142nd av. 51.73)
Parents: Jane and Derek
Wife and date of marriage: Shelley Jane, 1 December 2001
Children: Tristan Jack Busfield Wharf, 15 November 1997; Alf Alexander Busfield Wharf, 30 June 2001

Family links with cricket: Father played local cricket and brother Simon plays local cricket
Education: Buttershaw Upper School, Bradford; Thomas Danby College, Leeds
Qualifications: 6 GCSEs, City & Guilds in Sports Management, NCA coaching award, junior football coaching award
Overseas tours: England to Zimbabwe (one-day series) 2004-05, to South Africa 2004-05 (one-day series); England VI to Hong Kong 2005; England A to West Indies 2005-06; various pre-season tours with Yorkshire, Nottinghamshire and Glamorgan
Overseas teams played for: Somerset West, Cape Town 1993-95; Johnsonville CC, Wellington, New Zealand 1996-97; Universities, Wellington 1998-99
Cricket moments to forget: 'Too many to mention'
Cricket superstitions: 'None'
Cricketers particularly admired: Ian Botham
Other sports played: Football
Other sports followed: Football (Manchester United, Bradford City)
Relaxations: 'Spending time with family and friends, movies, PlayStation 2, eating (too much), TV, gym, football'
Extras: Took hat-trick (Wagg, Knight, Pretorius) v Warwickshire at Edgbaston in the totesport League 2004. Had figures of 6-5 v Kent at Cardiff in the totesport League 2004 (match reduced to 25 overs a side). Made ODI debut v India at Trent Bridge in the NatWest Challenge 2004, taking a wicket in each of his first three overs, finishing with 3-30 and winning Man of the Match award
Best batting: 128* Glamorgan v Gloucestershire, Bristol 2007
Best bowling: 6-59 Glamorgan v Gloucestershire, Bristol 2005

2007 Season

	M	Inn	NO	Runs	HS	Avg	100	50	Ct	St	Balls	Runs	Wkts	Avg	BB	5I	10M
Test																	
FC	15	26	4	726	128 *	33.00	3	1	7	-	1856	1262	36	35.05	4-16	-	-
ODI																	
List A	12	11	0	116	23	10.54	-	-	5	-	510	547	19	28.78	4-45	-	
20/20 Int																	
20/20	5	2	2	14	9 *		-	-	1	-	74	122	4	30.50	2-26	-	

Career Performances

	M	Inn	NO	Runs	HS	Avg	100	50	Ct	St	Balls	Runs	Wkts	Avg	BB	5I	10M
Test																	
FC	111	170	26	3333	128 *	23.14	6	13	60	-	15671	10045	272	36.93	6-59	5	1
ODI	13	5	3	19	9	9.50	-	-	1	-	584	428	18	23.77	4-24	-	
List A	141	99	19	1323	72	16.53	-	1	42	-	6006	5128	170	30.16	6-5	1	
20/20 Int																	
20/20	23	14	6	126	19	15.75	-	-	3	-	459	716	31	23.09	4-39	-	

WHEATER, A. J. — Essex

Name: Adam Jack Wheater
Role: Right-hand bat, wicket-keeper
Born: 13 February 1990, Whipps Cross, London
County debut: No first-team appearance (*see* ***Extras***)
Extras: Played for Essex U17. Made 2nd XI Championship debut 2006. Played for South U17 in ECB U17 Regional Festival at Loughborough 2007. Played for Essex v Derbyshire in the Twenty20 Floodlit Cup 2007 but has yet to appear for the county in first-class cricket or a major domestic one-day competition. Has played for England U19. Plays for Saffron Walden CC

WHEELDON, D. A. — Worcestershire

Name: David Antony Wheeldon
Role: Left-hand bat, leg-spin bowler
Born: 12 April 1989, Staffordshire
County debut: No first-team appearance
Extras: Made 2nd XI Championship debut 2006. Played for Staffordshire in the Minor Counties Championship 2006

WHELAN, C. D. — Worcestershire

Name: Christopher (Chris) David Whelan
Role: Right-hand bat, right-arm fast bowler
Born: 8 May 1986, Liverpool
Height: 6ft 2in **Weight:** 13st
Nickname: R-Kid, Wheelo, Scouse
County debut: 2004 (one-day, Middlesex), 2005 (first-class, Middlesex)
Parents: Sue and Dave
Marital status: Single
Family links with cricket: 'Dad was an accomplished left-hand opening bat'
Education: St Margaret's High School, Liverpool
Qualifications: 11 GCSEs, 3 A-levels, Level 1 coaching
Overseas tours: Middlesex to Mumbai 2004-05, 2005-06
Overseas teams played for: Randwick-Petersham, Sydney 2005-06
Career highlights to date: 'Playing at Lord's – Pro40 debut'
Cricket superstitions: 'Clean socks every session'
Cricketers particularly admired: Brett Lee
Young players to look out for: Chris Wright, Eoin Morgan
Other sports played: Football, golf
Other sports followed: Football (Everton)
Favourite band: G. Love & Special Sauce
Relaxations: 'Internet poker; DVDs'
Extras: Merseyside Young Sports Personality of the Year 2004-05. Left Middlesex at the end of the 2007 season and has joined Worcestershire for 2008
Opinions on cricket: 'Too many Kolpaks [*see page 13*] getting in the way of young English players. The gulf between the standard of cricket played in the two divisions is becoming greater.'
Best batting: 9* Middlesex v Hampshire, Rose Bowl 2005
Best bowling: 2-13 Middlesex v OUCCE, The Parks 2007

2007 Season

	M	Inn	NO	Runs	HS	Avg	100	50	Ct	St	Balls	Runs	Wkts	Avg	BB	5I	10M
Test																	
FC	1	1	0	0	0	0.00	-	-	-	-	55	31	4	7.75	2-13	-	-
ODI																	
List A	3	2	0	5	4	2.50	-	-	-	-	72	89	0		-	-	
20/20 Int																	
20/20																	

Career Performances

	M	Inn	NO	Runs	HS	Avg	100	50	Ct	St	Balls	Runs	Wkts	Avg	BB	5I	10M
Test																	
FC	3	3	1	10	9 *	5.00	-	-	-	-	305	213	11	19.36	2-13	-	-
ODI																	
List A	5	4	0	11	6	2.75	-	-	-	-	150	172	1	172.00	1-43	-	
20/20 Int																	
20/20																	

WHITE, C. — Yorkshire

Name: Craig White
Role: Right-hand bat, right-arm fast-medium bowler
Born: 16 December 1969, Morley, Yorkshire
Height: 6ft 1in **Weight:** 11st 11lbs
Nickname: Chalky, Bassey
County debut: 1990
County cap: 1993
Benefit: 2002
Test debut: 1994
ODI debut: 1994-95
Place in batting averages: 182nd av. 24.77 (2006 78th av. 39.04)
Parents: Fred Emsley and Cynthia Anne
Wife and date of marriage: Elizabeth Anne, 19 September 1992
Family links with cricket: Father played for Pudsey St Lawrence
Education: Flora Hill High School; Bendigo Senior High School (both Victoria, Australia)
Overseas tours: Australia YC to West Indies 1989-90; England A to Pakistan 1995-96, to Australia 1996-97; England to Australia 1994-95, to India and Pakistan

(World Cup) 1995-96, to Zimbabwe and New Zealand 1996-97, to South Africa and Zimbabwe 1999-2000 (one-day series), to Kenya (ICC Knockout Trophy) 2000-01, to Pakistan and Sri Lanka 2000-01, to India and New Zealand 2001-02, to Australia 2002-03, to Africa (World Cup) 2002-03
Overseas teams played for: Victoria, Australia 1990-91; Central Districts, New Zealand 1999-2000
Cricketers particularly admired: Graeme Hick, Mark Waugh, Brian Lara
Other sports followed: Leeds RFC, motocross, golf, tennis
Relaxations: Playing guitar, reading, gardening and socialising
Extras: Man of the Match in the second ODI v Zimbabwe at Bulawayo 1999-2000 (5-21/26). Took National League hat-trick (Fleming, Patel, Masters) v Kent at Headingley 2000. Scored 93 in the first Test at Lahore 2000-01, in the process sharing with Graham Thorpe (118) in a new record sixth-wicket partnership for England in Tests v Pakistan (166). Scored maiden Test century (121) in the second Test v India at Ahmedabad 2001-02, winning Man of the Match award. C&G Man of the Match award for his 4-35 and 78-ball 100* in the semi-final v Surrey at Headingley 2002. Captain of Yorkshire 2004-06
Best batting: 186 Yorkshire v Lancashire, Old Trafford 2001
Best bowling: 8-55 Yorkshire v Gloucestershire, Gloucester 1998

2007 Season

	M	Inn	NO	Runs	HS	Avg	100	50	Ct	St	Balls	Runs	Wkts	Avg	BB	5I	10M
Test																	
FC	11	18	0	446	117	24.77	1	2	4	-	36	11	0		-	-	-
ODI																	
List A	14	12	1	189	49	17.18	-	-	4	-	24	28	0		-	-	
20/20 Int																	
20/20	8	8	0	181	47	22.62	-	-	1	-	0	0	0		-	-	

Career Performances

	M	Inn	NO	Runs	HS	Avg	100	50	Ct	St	Balls	Runs	Wkts	Avg	BB	5I	10M
Test	30	50	7	1052	121	24.46	1	5	14	-	3959	2220	59	37.62	5-32	3	-
FC	276	438	57	12395	186	32.53	21	62	167	-	21286	11260	395	28.50	8-55	11	-
ODI	51	41	5	568	57 *	15.77	-	1	12	-	2364	1726	65	26.55	5-21	1	
List A	355	316	44	7122	148	26.18	5	28	99	-	11575	8462	337	25.10	5-19	3	
20/20 Int																	
20/20	31	29	0	544	55	18.75	-	2	8	-	70	132	1	132.00	1-22	-	

WHITE, C. L. Somerset

Name: <u>Cameron</u> Leon White
Role: Right-hand bat, leg-spin bowler
Born: 18 August 1983, Bairnsdale, Victoria, Australia
Height: 6ft 1½in **Weight:** 14st 2lbs
Nickname: Whitey
County debut: 2006
County cap: 2007
ODI debut: 2005-06
Twenty20 Int debut: 2006-07
1000 runs in a season: 2
1st-Class 200s: 2
Place in batting averages: 5th av. 72.20 (2006 21st av. 59.50)
Place in bowling averages: 77th av. 32.75 (2006 137th av. 48.20)
Overseas tours: Australia U19 to New Zealand (U19 World Cup) 2001-02; Australia A to Pakistan 2005-06, 2007-08; Australia to Zimbabwe (one-day series) 2003-04, to India 2004-05, to New Zealand (one-day series) 2005-06
Overseas teams played for: Victoria 2000-01 –

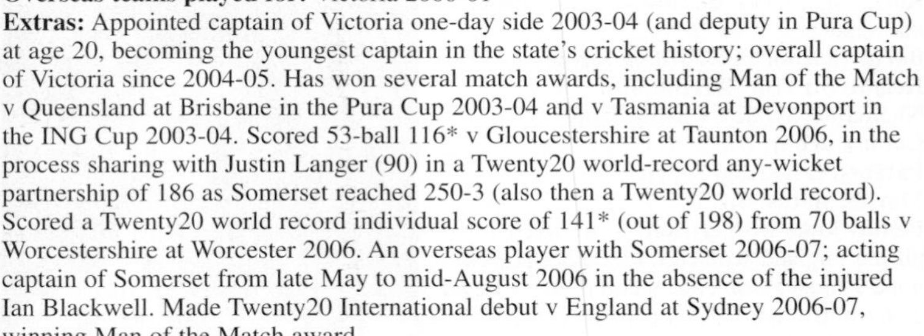

Extras: Appointed captain of Victoria one-day side 2003-04 (and deputy in Pura Cup) at age 20, becoming the youngest captain in the state's cricket history; overall captain of Victoria since 2004-05. Has won several match awards, including Man of the Match v Queensland at Brisbane in the Pura Cup 2003-04 and v Tasmania at Devonport in the ING Cup 2003-04. Scored 53-ball 116* v Gloucestershire at Taunton 2006, in the process sharing with Justin Langer (90) in a Twenty20 world-record any-wicket partnership of 186 as Somerset reached 250-3 (also then a Twenty20 world record). Scored a Twenty20 world record individual score of 141* (out of 198) from 70 balls v Worcestershire at Worcester 2006. An overseas player with Somerset 2006-07; acting captain of Somerset from late May to mid-August 2006 in the absence of the injured Ian Blackwell. Made Twenty20 International debut v England at Sydney 2006-07, winning Man of the Match award
Best batting: 260* Somerset v Derbyshire, Derby 2006
Best bowling: 6-66 Victoria v Western Australia, Melbourne 2002-03

2007 Season

	M	Inn	NO	Runs	HS	Avg	100	50	Ct	St	Balls	Runs	Wkts	Avg	BB	5I	10M
Test																	
FC	12	19	4	1083	241	72.20	5	3	7	-	1072	655	20	32.75	4-28	-	-
ODI																	
List A	10	10	0	340	65	34.00	-	4	4	-	226	236	6	39.33	3-37	-	
20/20 Int																	
20/20	8	8	1	190	68	27.14	-	2	2	-	90	103	5	20.60	3-16	-	

Career Performances

	M	Inn	NO	Runs	HS	Avg	100	50	Ct	St	Balls	Runs	Wkts	Avg	BB	5I	10M
Test																	
FC	83	136	17	4809	260*	40.41	12	19	79	-	9996	5876	155	37.90	6-66	2	1
ODI	16	10	3	157	45	22.42	-	-	5	-	174	201	4	50.25	1-5	-	
List A	99	82	11	2290	126*	32.25	3	13	39	-	2819	2553	69	37.00	4-15	-	
20/20 Int	1	1	1	40	40*		-	-	2	-	12	11	1	11.00	1-11	-	
20/20	23	23	6	847	141*	49.82	2	5	7	-	268	373	17	21.94	3-8	-	

WHITE, G. G. — Northamptonshire

Name: Graeme Geoffrey White
Role: Right-hand bat, slow left-arm bowler; all-rounder
Born: 18 April 1987, Milton Keynes
Height: 5ft 11in **Weight:** 10st
Nickname: Whitey, Chalky, Pony
County debut: 2006
Parents: David and Sophie
Marital status: Single
Family links with cricket: Sister Rachel played England Women U17. Father played good standard club cricket and is also a Level 2 coach. Brother Russell played county U11
Education: Stowe School, Buckingham
Qualifications: 9 GCSEs, 1 AS-level, 3 A-levels, coaching Level 2
Overseas tours: Stowe School to India 2004; England U19 to Sri Lanka (U19 World Cup) 2005-06
Career highlights to date: 'Representing my country at the U19 World Cup in Sri Lanka in 2006 and reaching the semi-finals'

Cricket moments to forget: 'Getting hit for five sixes in one over playing for Stowe School (they kept going further!)'
Cricket superstitions: 'Putting pads on from the top down'
Cricketers particularly admired: Bishan Bedi, Phil Tufnell, Daniel Vettori
Young players to look out for: Russell White, Moeen Ali, Andy Miller
Other sports played: Badminton, hockey, football
Other sports followed: Football ('big Manchester United fan')
Favourite band: Kings of Leon, Bloc Party
Relaxations: 'Like listening to music. Playing PS2'
Extras: Represented England U15, U17 and U19. Dorothy Radd Shield (Northamptonshire) 2003. Colin Shillington Award (Stowe School) 2005
Best batting: 65 Northamptonshire v Glamorgan, Colwyn Bay 2007
Best bowling: 2-35 Northamptonshire v CUCCE, Fenner's 2007

2007 Season

	M	Inn	NO	Runs	HS	Avg	100	50	Ct	St	Balls	Runs	Wkts	Avg	BB	5I	10M
Test																	
FC	3	2	0	71	65	35.50	-	1	1	-	372	142	3	47.33	2-35	-	-
ODI																	
List A	5	3	0	16	14	5.33	-	-	3	-	174	145	4	36.25	2-44	-	
20/20 Int																	
20/20	4	0	0	0	0		-	-	1	-	30	70	1	70.00	1-10	-	

Career Performances

	M	Inn	NO	Runs	HS	Avg	100	50	Ct	St	Balls	Runs	Wkts	Avg	BB	5I	10M
Test																	
FC	5	5	0	108	65	21.60	-	1	1	-	528	221	3	73.66	2-35	-	-
ODI																	
List A	5	3	0	16	14	5.33	-	-	3	-	174	145	4	36.25	2-44	-	
20/20 Int																	
20/20	4	0	0	0	0		-	-	1	-	30	70	1	70.00	1-10	-	

96. Whose return to the country of his birth brought him 454 runs, three centuries and the Man of the Series award when England and South Africa contended the ODI rubber in 2004-05?

WHITE, R. A. Northamptonshire

Name: Robert (Rob) Allan White
Role: Right-hand bat, leg-spin bowler
Born: 15 October 1979, Chelmsford, Essex
Height: 5ft 11in **Weight:** 11st 7lbs
Nickname: Chalky, Toff, Zorro, Whitey, Lamb
County debut: 2000
1st-Class 200s: 1
Place in batting averages: 91st av. 37.31 (2006 198th av. 22.15)
Parents: Dennis and Ann
Marital status: Single
Family links with cricket: 'Grandfather on Essex committee for many years. Dad flailed the willow and brother travels the local leagues high and low'
Education: Stowe School, Buckingham; St John's College, Durham University; Loughborough University
Qualifications: 9 GCSEs, 3 A-levels
Cricket moments to forget: 'Franklyn Rose telling me my mates had bet £10 that he couldn't injure me, as I walked out to play Lashings'
Cricketers particularly admired: Ian Botham, Viv Richards, Steve Waugh
Other sports played: Badminton, squash, golf, kabaddi
Other sports followed: Football (West Ham), rugby (Northampton Saints)
Extras: Northamptonshire League Young Player of the Year and Youth Cricketer of the Year 1999. Northamptonshire Young Player of the Year (Frank Rudd Trophy) 2001. Played for Loughborough UCCE 2001, 2002 and 2003. Recorded the highest maiden century in the history of English first-class cricket (277, including a hundred before lunch on the first day), v Gloucestershire at Northampton 2002 in his fifth first-class match. NBC Denis Compton Award for the most promising young Northamptonshire player 2002. Represented British Universities 2003
Best batting: 277 Northamptonshire v Gloucestershire, Northampton 2002
Best bowling: 2-30 Northamptonshire v Gloucestershire, Northampton 2002

2007 Season

	M	Inn	NO	Runs	HS	Avg	100	50	Ct	St	Balls	Runs	Wkts	Avg	BB	5I	10M
Test																	
FC	13	22	3	709	108	37.31	1	3	9	-	234	188	2	94.00	1-35	-	-
ODI																	
List A	13	13	1	265	56	22.08	-	1	2	-	6	9	0		-	-	
20/20 Int																	
20/20	7	4	1	38	14	12.66	-	-	-	-	0	0	0		-	-	

Career Performances

	M	Inn	NO	Runs	HS	Avg	100	50	Ct	St	Balls	Runs	Wkts	Avg	BB	5I	10M
Test																	
FC	55	94	7	2653	277	30.49	3	11	33	-	1120	800	14	57.14	2-30	-	-
ODI																	
List A	53	51	2	984	101	20.08	1	4	10	-	54	55	2	27.50	2-18	-	
20/20 Int																	
20/20	20	17	1	317	66	19.81	-	2	3	-	0	0	0		-	-	

WHITE, W. A. Derbyshire

Name: Wayne Andrew White
Role: Right-hand bat, right-arm fast-medium bowler; all-rounder
Born: 22 April 1985, Derby
Height: 6ft 2in **Weight:** 13st
Nickname: Chalky, Stix, Philip Schofield
County debut: 2005
Place in batting averages: 277th av. 10.16
Place in bowling averages: 104th av. 38.58
Parents: John and Sharon
Marital status: Single
Family links with cricket: 'Brother U13 Midlands/Derbyshire'
Education: John Port School, Etwall; Nottingham University
Qualifications: 11 GCSEs, 4 A-levels, BA Politics
Career outside cricket: 'Semi-professional footballer; internet business – darts-store.com'
Off-season: 'Gym, football, golf, possible trip to Melbourne'
Career highlights to date: 'First wicket for Derbyshire – Anthony McGrath; and 5-87 v Northamptonshire [2007]'

Cricket moments to forget: '0-107 in the first innings of my debut against Yorkshire'
Cricketers particularly admired: Mike Hendrick, Graeme Welch, Andy Caddick
Young players to look out for: Jake Needham
Other sports played: Football (Gresley Rovers, Burton Albion, Mickleover Sports, Derby County), golf
Other sports followed: Football (Derby County, LA Galaxy)
Favourite band: Arctic Monkeys, Stone Roses
Relaxations: 'Internet, Xbox 360, spread betting'
Extras: Scored 76 and took 7-18 on club cricket debut for Swarkestone
Opinions on cricket: 'Scrap Pro40. One hour for lunch.'
Best batting: 19* Derbyshire v Surrey, Derby 2006
Best bowling: 5-87 Derbyshire v Northamptonshire, Northampton 2007

2007 Season

	M	Inn	NO	Runs	HS	Avg	100	50	Ct	St	Balls	Runs	Wkts	Avg	BB	5I	10M
Test																	
FC	4	6	0	61	19	10.16	-	-	3	-	678	463	12	38.58	5-87	1	-
ODI																	
List A	9	7	3	61	25	15.25	-	-	4	-	365	336	5	67.20	1-23	-	
20/20 Int																	
20/20																	

Career Performances

	M	Inn	NO	Runs	HS	Avg	100	50	Ct	St	Balls	Runs	Wkts	Avg	BB	5I	10M
Test																	
FC	7	10	2	106	19 *	13.25	-	-	3	-	1157	826	23	35.91	5-87	1	-
ODI																	
List A	11	7	3	61	25	15.25	-	-	4	-	455	437	7	62.42	1-23	-	
20/20 Int																	
20/20																	

WIGLEY, D. H. — Northamptonshire

Name: David Harry Wigley
Role: Right-hand bat, right-arm fast-medium bowler
Born: 26 October 1981, Bradford, Yorkshire
Height: 6ft 3in **Weight:** 14st
Nickname: Wiggy, Wiggers, Wigs
County debut: 2002 (Yorkshire), 2003 (Worcestershire), 2006 (Northamptonshire)
County colours: 2003 (Worcestershire)
Place in batting averages: 200th av. 22.30
Place in bowling averages: 47th av. 27.52 (2006 124th av. 44.22)
Parents: Max and Judith

Marital status: Single
Family links with cricket: Father played league cricket in Liverpool Competition, Bradford League and Durham Senior League
Education: St Mary's RC Comprehensive, Menston; Loughborough University
Qualifications: 9 GCSEs, 3 A-levels, degree in Sport and Exercise Science, ECB Level I coaching
Off-season: 'Working in the commercial department of Cadbury Schweppes plc'
Overseas tours: British Universities to Cape Town 2004
Overseas teams played for: Gormandale CC, Victoria 2001; Mount Lawley CC, Perth 2004-05
Career highlights to date: 'Taking my first five-for in first-class cricket against Pakistan'
Cricket moments to forget: 'Losing Uni final at Lord's 2004 in last over'
Cricket superstitions: 'Must turn to left to run in and bowl'
Cricketers particularly admired: Darren Gough, Andrew Flintoff
Young players to look out for: Moeen Ali
Other sports played: Golf, rugby ('used to play to decent standard; gave up at 16')
Other sports followed: Football (Leeds United), rugby (Llanelli Scarlets)
Relaxations: 'Music, films, golf'
Extras: Played for ECB Schools v Sri Lanka U19 2000. Yorkshire U19 Bowling Award 2000. Played for Loughborough UCCE 2002-04 (captain 2004), taking 5-52 v Oxford in the UCCE One-Day Challenge at Lord's and 5-71 v Hampshire at The Rose Bowl 2002. Represented British Universities 2003 and (as captain) 2004
Opinions on cricket: 'Probably play too much county cricket, not allowing enough time for recovery and practice.'
Best batting: 70 Northamptonshire v Middlesex, Northampton 2007
Best bowling: 5-77 Northamptonshire v Pakistanis, Northampton 2006

2007 Season

	M	Inn	NO	Runs	HS	Avg	100	50	Ct	St	Balls	Runs	Wkts	Avg	BB	5I	10M
Test																	
FC	10	13	3	223	70	22.30	-	2	6	-	1374	936	34	27.52	3-10	-	-
ODI																	
List A	7	3	0	18	10	6.00	-	-	2	-	186	218	5	43.60	1-16	-	
20/20 Int																	
20/20																	

Career Performances

	M	Inn	NO	Runs	HS	Avg	100	50	Ct	St	Balls	Runs	Wkts	Avg	BB	5I	10M
Test																	
FC	29	36	10	398	70	15.30	-	2	15	-	4116	2858	80	35.72	5-77	1	-
ODI																	
List A	21	10	0	32	10	3.20	-	-	4	-	714	752	15	50.13	4-37	-	
20/20 Int																	
20/20	2	1	0	1	1	1.00	-	-	-	-	30	33	1	33.00	1-8	-	

WILLIAMS, R. E. M. — Middlesex

Name: Robert (Robbie) Edward Morgan Williams
Role: Right-hand bat, right-arm fast-medium bowler
Born: 19 January 1987, Pembury, Kent
Height: 6ft **Weight:** 13st 2lbs
County debut: 2007
Place in bowling averages: 114th av. 40.30
Parents: Gail and Tim
Marital status: Single
Education: Marlborough College; Durham University
Qualifications: 3 A-levels
Overseas tours: Marlborough College to South Africa 2003
Overseas teams played for: Corrimal, Wollongong 2005-06
Career highlights to date: 'Taking five wickets on Championship debut'
Cricket moments to forget: 'Leaving a ball and getting stumped at the Bunbury Festival when nine down and three balls from a draw'
Cricket superstitions: 'Batsmen can be jinxed'
Cricketers particularly admired: Brett Lee
Young players to look out for: Laurie Evans, Steven Finn
Other sports played: Rugby (Marlborough College 1st XV), hockey (Marlborough College 1st XI)
Other sports followed: Rugby union (Leicester Tigers)
Favourite band: Pendulum
Relaxations: 'Sudoku, yoga, table tennis'
Extras: Played for Durham UCCE 2007, taking 5-70 v Lancashire at Durham. Played for MCC 2007. Took 5-112 on Championship debut v Essex at Chelmsford 2007

Best batting: 15 Middlesex v Essex, Chelmsford 2007
Best bowling: 5-70 DUCCE v Lancashire, Durham 2007

2007 Season

	M	Inn	NO	Runs	HS	Avg	100	50	Ct	St	Balls	Runs	Wkts	Avg	BB	5I	10M
Test																	
FC	5	8	4	30	15	7.50	-	-	2	-	796	524	13	40.30	5-70	2	-
ODI																	
List A	1	0	0	0	0		-	-	-	-	36	49	0		-	-	
20/20 Int																	
20/20																	

Career Performances

	M	Inn	NO	Runs	HS	Avg	100	50	Ct	St	Balls	Runs	Wkts	Avg	BB	5I	10M
Test																	
FC	5	8	4	30	15	7.50	-	-	2	-	796	524	13	40.30	5-70	2	-
ODI																	
List A	1	0	0	0	0		-	-	-	-	36	49	0		-	-	
20/20 Int																	
20/20																	

WILLOUGHBY, C. M. — Somerset

Name: Charl Myles Willoughby
Role: Left-hand bat, left-arm fast-medium bowler
Born: 3 December 1974, Cape Town, South Africa
Height: 6ft 3in **Weight:** 12st 12lbs
Nickname: Puppy, Harry
County debut: 2005 (Leicestershire), 2006 (Somerset)
County cap: 2005 (Leicestershire), 2007 (Somerset)
Test debut: 2003
ODI debut: 1999-2000
50 wickets in a season: 2
Place in bowling averages: 31st av. 24.67 (2006 20th av. 25.56)
Parents: David and Belinda
Wife and date of marriage: Nicky, 17 April 2004
Children: Cole, 18 October 2006

Family links with cricket: 'Father played club cricket'
Education: Wynberg Boys' High School; Stellenbosch University and UNISA
Off-season: 'Rest in Cape Town; relax with wife and son'
Overseas tours: South Africa Academy to Zimbabwe 1998-99; South Africa A to West Indies 2000, to Zimbabwe 2004; South Africa to Sharjah (Coca-Cola Sharjah Cup) 1999-2000, to Bangladesh 2003, to England 2003
Overseas teams played for: Boland 1994-95 – 1999-2000; Western Province 2000-01 – 2003-04; Western Province Boland 2003-04 – 2004-05; Cape Cobras 2005-06 – 2006-07
Career highlights to date: 'Test and ODI debuts. Four wickets in four balls in first-class match v Dolphins'
Cricket moments to forget: 'Dislocating my shoulder diving on boundary'
Cricketers particularly admired: Graeme Smith, Andrew Flintoff, Wasim Akram
Young players to look out for: JP Duminy, Stuart Broad
Other sports followed: Rugby (Stormers)
Favourite band: Coldplay
Relaxations: 'Movies and time with my wife'
Extras: Played for Berkshire in the NatWest 2000. Took four wickets in four balls v Dolphins at Durban in the Supersport Series 2005-06; the feat was spread over two innings and consisted of a hat-trick (Mhlongo, Gobind, Hayward) plus the wicket of Watson with his first ball of the second innings. Has won several match awards, including Man of the Match for South Africa A v Barbados at Bridgetown 2000 (6-24) and for Leicestershire v Somerset at Leicester in the C&G 2005 (6-16; the best one-day return by a Leicestershire bowler). An overseas player with Leicestershire 2005. Is no longer considered an overseas player
Best batting: 47 Somerset v Worcestershire, Taunton 2006
Best bowling: 7-44 Somerset v Gloucestershire, Taunton 2006

2007 Season

	M	Inn	NO	Runs	HS	Avg	100	50	Ct	St	Balls	Runs	Wkts	Avg	BB	5I	10M
Test																	
FC	16	12	7	58	23 *	11.60	-	-	2	-	2776	1530	62	24.67	5-33	5	-
ODI																	
List A	13	5	2	11	11	3.66	-	-	1	-	595	435	17	25.58	5-33	1	
20/20 Int																	
20/20	4	1	1	0	0 *		-	-	-	-	90	103	6	17.16	2-21	-	

Career Performances

	M	Inn	NO	Runs	HS	Avg	100	50	Ct	St	Balls	Runs	Wkts	Avg	BB	5I	10M
Test	2	0	0	0	0		-	-	-	-	300	125	1	125.00	1-47	-	-
FC	160	185	81	606	47	5.82	-	-	36	-	32460	15044	608	24.74	7-44	27	3
ODI	3	2	0	0	0	0.00	-	-	-	-	168	148	2	74.00	2-39	-	
List A	178	53	28	123	12 *	4.92	-	-	24	-	8672	5987	223	26.84	6-16	5	
20/20 Int																	
20/20	45	10	8	20	11	10.00	-	-	7	-	995	1114	50	22.28	4-9	-	

WILSON, G. C. Surrey

Name: Gary Craig Wilson
Role: Right-hand bat, wicket-keeper, very occasional right-arm medium bowler
Born: 5 February 1986, Belfast
Height: 5ft 10in **Weight:** 13st 2lbs
Nickname: Gaz, Wils
County debut: No first-team appearance
ODI debut: 2007
Parents: George and Iris
Marital status: 'Unmarried'
Family links with cricket: 'Dad played league cricket in Ireland'
Education: Methodist College, Belfast
Qualifications: 10 GCSEs, 3 A-levels, gym instructor Level 2, FA Level 1
Career outside cricket: 'Bit of coaching'
Overseas tours: Ireland U19 to Bangladesh (U19 World Cup) 2003-04, to Sri Lanka (U19 World Cup) 2005-06; Ireland A to UAE (EurAsia Series) 2006, plus various Ireland age-group and Ireland A tours

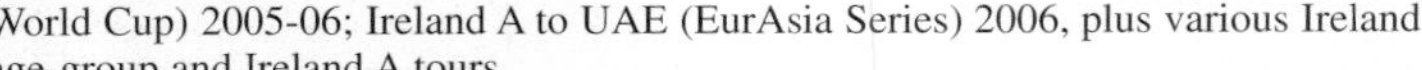

Overseas teams played for: Portland Colts CC, Melbourne 2004-05; Durbanville CC, Cape Town 2006-07
Career highlights to date: 'Playing first game of U19 World Cup in Bangladesh; beating Scotland in the Inter-Continental Cup by three runs; being signed by Surrey'
Cricket moments to forget: 'Being beaten by three wickets by New Zealand in U19 World Cup 2005-06 after scoring 304; being beaten by four runs by England in the same World Cup; pair on debut for Surrey 2nd XI'
Cricket superstitions: 'Left pad first'
Cricketers particularly admired: Alec Stewart, Brian Lara, Mark Boucher
Young players to look out for: Gary Kidd, William Porterfield, Paul Stirling
Other sports played: Rugby, football, golf ('badly')
Other sports followed: Football (Man United), rugby (Ireland)
Favourite band: 'Any really'
Extras: Player of the Tournament at European U19 Championship 2003 and 2004. MCC Young Cricketer 2005-06. Has represented Ireland in first-class and one-day cricket, including an ODI and the 2006 C&G and 2007 Friends Provident; has also represented Ireland A in one-day (List A) cricket
Opinions on cricket: 'A lot of cricket being played in England – good for the advertising of the game; wouldn't fancy being a quick bowler, though.'
Best batting: 11 Ireland v Scotland, Aberdeen 2005

2007 Season (did not make any first-class or one-day appearances for his county)

Career Performances

	M	Inn	NO	Runs	HS	Avg	100	50	Ct	St	Balls	Runs	Wkts	Avg	BB	5I	10M
Test																	
FC	4	5	1	24	11	6.00	-	-	6	-	0	0	0		-	-	-
ODI	1	1	0	13	13	13.00	-	-	-	-	0	0	0		-	-	
List A	11	10	0	219	58	21.90	-	3	11	1	0	0	0		-	-	
20/20 Int																	
20/20																	

WISEMAN, P. J. Durham

Name: Paul John Wiseman
Role: Right-hand bat, right-arm off-spin bowler
Born: 4 May 1970, Auckland, New Zealand
Nickname: Whiz
County debut: 2006
Test debut: 1998
ODI debut: 1997-98
Place in batting averages: 212th av. 20.57
Place in bowling averages: 64th av. 29.84
Overseas tours: New Zealand Academy to South Africa 1997; New Zealand A to India 2001-02, to South Africa 2004-05, to Sri Lanka 2005-06; New Zealand to Zimbabwe 1997-98, to Sri Lanka 1998, to Malaysia (Commonwealth Games) 1998-99, to Bangladesh (Wills International Cup) 1998-99, to India 1999-2000, to Zimbabwe 2000-01, to Kenya (ICC Knockout Trophy) 2000-01, to South Africa 2000-01, to Australia 2001-02, to Sri Lanka 2003, to India 2003-04, to Bangladesh 2004-05, to Australia 2004-05, plus other one-day tournaments and series in Sharjah, Singapore and Namibia
Overseas teams played for: Auckland 1991-92 – 1993-94; Otago 1994-95 – 2000-01; Canterbury 2001-02 – 2005-06
Extras: Has played cricket in the Lancashire Leagues for Rishton (1999), Haslingden (2005) and Milnrow (2005); and for Walkden in the Bolton League (2006). Man of the Match in the first Test v Zimbabwe at Bulawayo 2000-01 (5-90/3-54). His 9-13 (16.4-9-13-9) for Canterbury v Central Districts in the State Championship at Christchurch 2004-05 is the second best innings return in New Zealand first-class

cricket history. Joined Durham towards the end of the 2006 season. Holds a British passport and is not considered an overseas player
Best batting: 130 Canterbury v Northern Districts, Hamilton 2005-06
Best bowling: 9-13 Canterbury v Central Districts, Christchurch (VG) 2004-05

2007 Season

	M	Inn	NO	Runs	HS	Avg	100	50	Ct	St	Balls	Runs	Wkts	Avg	BB	5I	10M
Test																	
FC	13	19	5	288	44	20.57	-	-	6	-	1731	955	32	29.84	5-65	1	-
ODI																	
List A	6	2	1	14	13	14.00	-	-	-	-	227	208	10	20.80	3-18	-	
20/20 Int																	
20/20	4	1	0	0	0	0.00	-	-	-	-	36	33	2	16.50	1-10	-	

Career Performances

	M	Inn	NO	Runs	HS	Avg	100	50	Ct	St	Balls	Runs	Wkts	Avg	BB	5I	10M
Test	25	34	8	366	36	14.07	-	-	11	-	5660	2903	61	47.59	5-82	2	-
FC	170	232	49	3775	130	20.62	2	13	78	-	33110	15113	449	33.65	9-13	18	4
ODI	15	7	5	45	16	22.50	-	-	2	-	450	368	12	30.66	4-45	-	
List A	119	82	19	967	65 *	15.34	-	2	28	-	4741	3387	82	41.30	4-45	-	
20/20 Int																	
20/20	7	1	0	0	0	0.00	-	-	2	-	96	113	8	14.12	2-20	-	

WOAKES, C. R. — Warwickshire

Name: Christopher (<u>Chris</u>) Roger Woakes
Role: Right-hand bat, right-arm fast-medium bowler
Born: 2 March 1989, Birmingham
Height: 6ft 2in **Weight:** 12st 6lbs
Nickname: Woakesy, Jokes, Cheetah
County debut: 2006
Parents: Roger and Elaine
Marital status: Single
Family links with cricket: 'Stepbrothers played club cricket'
Education: Barr Beacon Language School, Walsall
Qualifications: 7 GCSEs, 3 A-levels, Level 1 cricket coaching
Career outside cricket: 'Have not got a clue'

Overseas tours: Warwickshire Academy to Cape Town 2005; England U19 to Malaysia (U19 World Cup) 2007-08
Career highlights to date: 'Making Championship debut and representing England U19 v Pakistan 2007'
Cricket superstitions: 'Always turn to my left at end of bowling run-up'
Young players to look out for: Liam Dawson, Tom Lewis, James Harris
Other sports played: Football, golf, snooker
Other sports followed: Football (Aston Villa)
Favourite band: Feeder, Snow Patrol
Relaxations: 'Snooker, golf, music'
Extras: Played for Herefordshire in Minor Counties competitions 2006-07. England U17 squad 2006. Represented England U19 2007
Opinions on cricket: 'Too much county cricket is played. Pro40 competition should be scrapped as we do not play it at international level.'
Best batting: 14* Warwickshire v Surrey, Edgbaston 2007
Best bowling: 2-64 Warwickshire v West Indies A, Edgbaston 2006

2007 Season

	M	Inn	NO	Runs	HS	Avg	100	50	Ct	St	Balls	Runs	Wkts	Avg	BB	5I	10M
Test																	
FC	1	2	1	23	14 *	23.00	-	-	1	-	118	90	1	90.00	1-42	-	-
ODI																	
List A	1	0	0	0	0		-	-	-	-	0	0	0			-	-
20/20 Int																	
20/20																	

Career Performances

	M	Inn	NO	Runs	HS	Avg	100	50	Ct	St	Balls	Runs	Wkts	Avg	BB	5I	10M
Test																	
FC	2	3	1	27	14 *	13.50	-	-	4	-	256	192	4	48.00	2-64	-	-
ODI																	
List A	1	0	0	0	0		-	-	-	-	0	0	0			-	-
20/20 Int																	
20/20																	

97. In which season did England and New Zealand contest their first Test series against one another: a) 1913-14; b) 1929-30; c) 1938-39?

WOOD, G. L. — Yorkshire

Name: Gregory (Greg) Luke Wood
Role: Left-hand bat, wicket-keeper
Born: 2 December 1988, Dewsbury, West Yorkshire
Height: 5ft 11in **Weight:** 12st 5lbs
Nickname: Tiger, Mowgli
County debut: 2007 (one-day)
Parents: Shaun and Joan
Marital status: Single
Family links with cricket: 'Brother Daniel played Yorkshire and England Schools; now Barnsley CC and Mildura Settlers CC'
Education: Queen Elizabeth's Grammar School (QEGS), Wakefield
Qualifications: A-levels
Off-season: 'U19 World Cup in Malaysia'
Overseas tours: England U16 to South Africa 2005 (c); England U19 to Bangladesh 2005-06, to Sri Lanka (U19 World Cup) 2005-06, to Malaysia 2006-07 (c), to Malaysia (U19 World Cup) 2007-08
Career highlights to date: 'Captaining England U19. Making Yorkshire debut'
Cricket moments to forget: 'Being hit through the grille whilst batting, resulting in nearly 40 stitches in my lip!'
Cricketers particularly admired: Ricky Ponting, Richard Blakey
Young players to look out for: Adam Lyth
Other sports played: Golf, rugby (captained school to national finals)
Other sports followed: Football (Leeds United)
Injuries: Out for four weeks with injury to face (*see above*)
Favourite band: Take That, The Calling
Extras: Scored 139* for QEGS v Leeds Grammar 2005, sharing with brother Daniel (also 139*) in ECB schools record first-wicket partnership (300*). Played for Yorkshire Academy 2005-07. Represented England U19 and captained ECB Development of Excellence XI 2006
Opinions on cricket: 'As I have not been in the professional game that long it would be premature for me to say; however, I have enjoyed everything I have experienced so far.'

2007 Season

	M	Inn	NO	Runs	HS	Avg	100	50	Ct	St	Balls	Runs	Wkts	Avg	BB	5I	10M
Test																	
FC																	
ODI																	
List A	1	1	0	26	26	26.00	-	-	-	-	0	0	0		-	-	
20/20 Int																	
20/20																	

Career Performances

	M	Inn	NO	Runs	HS	Avg	100	50	Ct	St	Balls	Runs	Wkts	Avg	BB	5I	10M
Test																	
FC																	
ODI																	
List A	1	1	0	26	26	26.00	-	-	-	-	0	0	0		-	-	
20/20 Int																	
20/20																	

WOOD, M. J. Nottinghamshire

Name: Matthew James Wood
Role: Right-hand bat, right-arm off-spin bowler
Born: 30 September 1980, Exeter
Height: 5ft 11in **Weight:** 12st 6lbs
Nickname: Woody, Gran, Moo
County debut: 2001 (Somerset)
County cap: 2005 (Somerset)
1000 runs in a season: 1
1st-Class 200s: 1
Place in batting averages: (2006 190th av. 23.03)
Parents: James and Trina
Marital status: Single
Family links with cricket: Father is chairman of Devon Cricket Board
Education: Exmouth College; Exeter University
Qualifications: 10 GCSEs, 2 A-levels, ECB Level 3 coach
Career outside cricket: Coach
Overseas tours: West of England U15 to West Indies 1995
Overseas teams played for: Doubleview CC, Perth 2001, 2002

Career highlights to date: 'Winning the Twenty20 Cup and scoring 297 v Yorkshire'
Cricket moments to forget: 'Getting a pair v Essex 2005'
Cricket superstitions: 'None'
Cricketers particularly admired: Marcus Trescothick
Other sports followed: Football (Liverpool FC), horse racing
Relaxations: Golf
Extras: NBC Denis Compton Award for the most promising young Somerset player 2001. Scored century in each innings (106/131) v Surrey at Taunton 2002. Somerset Player of the Year 2002. Scored 297 v Yorkshire at Taunton 2005, the fifth highest individual score in Somerset's history. Vice-captain of Somerset July 2005-2006. Left Somerset at the end of the 2007 season and has joined Nottinghamshire for 2008
Best batting: 297 Somerset v Yorkshire, Taunton 2005

2007 Season

	M	Inn	NO	Runs	HS	Avg	100	50	Ct	St	Balls	Runs	Wkts	Avg	BB	5I	10M
Test																	
FC	2	3	0	55	35	18.33	-	-	1	-	0	0	0		-	-	-
ODI																	
List A	2	2	0	13	10	6.50	-	-	-	-	0	0	0		-	-	
20/20 Int																	
20/20	6	6	0	184	88	30.66	-	1	2	-	0	0	0		-	-	

Career Performances

	M	Inn	NO	Runs	HS	Avg	100	50	Ct	St	Balls	Runs	Wkts	Avg	BB	5I	10M
Test																	
FC	76	132	6	4375	297	34.72	9	27	26	-	85	68	0		-	-	-
ODI																	
List A	75	71	4	1948	129	29.07	2	13	12	-	0	0	0		-	-	
20/20 Int																	
20/20	29	29	0	859	94	29.62	-	5	5	-	0	0	0		-	-	

98. Who became the first South African wicket-keeper to achieve the double of 1000 runs and 100 dismissals in Tests when he stumped Geoff Pullar at The Oval in 1960?

WOOD, M. J. — Glamorgan

Name: Matthew James Wood
Role: Right-hand opening bat, off-spin bowler
Born: 6 April 1977, Huddersfield
Height: 5ft 9in **Weight:** 12st
Nickname: Ronnie, Chuddy
County debut: 1997 (Yorkshire)
County cap: 2001 (Yorkshire)
1000 runs in a season: 4
1st-Class 200s: 3
Place in batting averages: (2006 223rd av. 17.70)
Parents: Roger and Kathryn
Marital status: Single
Family links with cricket: 'Father played for local team Emley. Mum made the teas and sister Caroline scored'
Education: Shelley High School and Sixth Form Centre
Qualifications: 9 GCSEs, 2 A-levels, NCA coaching award
Overseas tours: England U19 to Zimbabwe 1995-96; Yorkshire CCC to West Indies 1996-97, to Cape Town 1997, 1998; MCC to Kenya 1999, to Bangladesh 1999-2000; ECB National Academy to Australia 2001-02
Overseas teams played for: Somerset West CC, Cape Town 1994-95; Upper Hutt United CC, New Zealand 1997-98; Mosman Park, Western Australia 2000-01; Mosman CC, Sydney 2004-05
Career highlights to date: 'Being on the pitch as fielding 12th man for England series win v South Africa at Headingley [1998]. Winning the Championship in 2001 and winning the C&G 2002 at Lord's'
Cricket moments to forget: 'Most of the 2002 season'
Cricket superstitions: 'Not any more'
Cricketers particularly admired: Darren Lehmann, Matthew Maynard, Stephen Fleming, Michael Vaughan
Other sports played: Football (Kirkburton FC)
Other sports followed: Football (Liverpool FC)
Favourite band: Atomic Kitten
Relaxations: 'Socialising, eating out, golf, DIY'
Extras: Represented England U17. Attended Yorkshire Academy. Scored 1000 first-class runs in first full season 1998. Yorkshire Coach's Player of the Year, Yorkshire Club Player of the Year and Yorkshire Players' Player of the Year 2003. Set a new Yorkshire record individual score in the NatWest/C&G (160 from 124 balls) v Devon

at Exmouth 2004, winning Man of the Match award. Vice-captain of Yorkshire 2003-04. Left Yorkshire during the 2007 season and has joined Glamorgan for 2008
Best batting: 207 Yorkshire v Somerset, Taunton 2003
Best bowling: 1-4 Yorkshire v Somerset, Headingley 2003

2007 Season

	M	Inn	NO	Runs	HS	Avg	100	50	Ct	St	Balls	Runs	Wkts	Avg	BB	5I	10M
Test																	
FC	1	1	0	23	23	23.00	-	-	-	-	6	4	0		-	-	-
ODI																	
List A	1	1	0	0	0	0.00	-	-	-	-	0	0	0		-	-	
20/20 Int																	
20/20																	

Career Performances

	M	Inn	NO	Runs	HS	Avg	100	50	Ct	St	Balls	Runs	Wkts	Avg	BB	5I	10M
Test																	
FC	129	224	20	6820	207	33.43	16	30	113	-	78	43	2	21.50	1-4	-	-
ODI																	
List A	146	135	14	3271	160	27.03	5	14	57	-	66	76	3	25.33	3-45	-	
20/20 Int																	
20/20	15	15	3	328	96 *	27.33	-	2	11	-	18	32	2	16.00	1-11	-	

WRIGHT, B. J. — Glamorgan

Name: Ben James Wright
Role: Right-hand bat, right-arm medium bowler
Born: 5 December 1987, Fulwood, Preston
Height: 5ft 8in **Weight:** 11st
Nickname: Kevin, Space, Bej
County debut: 2006
Place in batting averages: 213th av. 20.56
Parents: Julia and Peter
Marital status: Single
Education: Cowbridge Comprehensive
Qualifications: 11 GCSEs
Overseas tours: West of England U15 to West Indies 2003; England U16 to South Africa 2004; England U19 to Bangladesh 2005-06, to Sri Lanka (U19 World Cup) 2005-06, to Malaysia 2006-07

Cricket moments to forget: 'Watching my dad bat and get a not out'
Cricket superstitions: 'All left kit goes on before right'
Cricketers particularly admired: Matthew Maynard
Young players to look out for: 'All the Glamorgan youngsters'
Other sports played: Rugby (Wales U16)
Other sports followed: Football (Man Utd), rugby (Leicester Tigers)
Favourite band: 'All R&B'
Relaxations: 'Spending time with girlfriend and watching TV'
Extras: Sir John Hobbs Memorial Prize 2003. A.A. Thomson Fielding Prize 2003. BBC *Test Match Special* U15 Young Cricketer of the Year Award 2003. Played for Wales Minor Counties in Minor Counties competitions 2005-06. Represented England U19 2006, 2007. Scored maiden first-class century (108) v Leicestershire at Leicester 2007 aged 19, becoming the youngest Glamorgan centurion since Matthew Maynard in 1985
Best batting: 108 Glamorgan v Leicestershire, Leicester 2007
Best bowling: 1-14 Glamorgan v Essex, Chelmsford 2007

2007 Season

	M	Inn	NO	Runs	HS	Avg	100	50	Ct	St	Balls	Runs	Wkts	Avg	BB	5I	10M
Test																	
FC	11	18	2	329	108	20.56	1	1	13	-	132	89	2	44.50	1-14	-	-
ODI																	
List A	13	12	0	227	61	18.91	-	1	2	-	48	53	0			-	-
20/20 Int																	
20/20	6	5	4	100	35 *	100.00	-	-	1	-	0	0	0			-	-

Career Performances

	M	Inn	NO	Runs	HS	Avg	100	50	Ct	St	Balls	Runs	Wkts	Avg	BB	5I	10M
Test																	
FC	12	19	2	401	108	23.58	1	2	15	-	132	89	2	44.50	1-14	-	-
ODI																	
List A	14	13	0	264	61	20.30	-	1	2	-	48	53	0			-	-
20/20 Int																	
20/20	6	5	4	100	35 *	100.00	-	-	1	-	0	0	0			-	-

99. Whose 643-minute 185* saved England from defeat in the second Test v South Africa at Johannesburg in 1995-96?

WRIGHT, C. J. C. Essex

Name: Christopher (Chris) Julian Clement Wright
Role: Right-hand bat, right-arm fast-medium bowler
Born: 14 July 1985, Chipping Norton, Oxfordshire
Height: 6ft 3in **Weight:** 12st
Nickname: Wrighty, Baron
County debut: 2004 (Middlesex)
Parents: Alan and Nikki
Marital status: Single
Family links with cricket: 'Dad plays for Hampshire Over 50s'
Education: Eggars School, Alton; Alton College; Anglia Polytechnic University
Qualifications: 11 GCSEs, 4 A-levels
Career outside cricket: 'Family business – Hygienics Limited'
Overseas tours: Cambridge UCCE to Grenada 2004
Overseas teams played for: Tamil Union C&AC, Colombo 2005-06
Career highlights to date: 'Middlesex debut v Yorkshire. First match at Lord's'
Cricket moments to forget: 'Relegation for Middlesex'
Cricket superstitions: 'Not really; they make people crazy'
Young players to look out for: Chris Whelan, Eoin Morgan, Billy Godleman, Steve Finn
Other sports played: Basketball
Other sports followed: Football (Arsenal), basketball (Dallas Mavericks)
Relaxations: 'Table football, poker, eating out, films'
Extras: Played for Cambridge UCCE 2004-05. Represented British Universities 2005. Left Middlesex at the end of the 2007 season and has joined Essex for 2008
Opinions on cricket: 'Game needs to avoid too much tampering – i.e. super subs etc.'
Best batting: 76 CUCCE v Essex, Fenner's 2005
Best bowling: 2-21 Middlesex v Glamorgan, Swansea 2007

2007 Season

	M	Inn	NO	Runs	HS	Avg	100	50	Ct	St	Balls	Runs	Wkts	Avg	BB	5I	10M
Test																	
FC	2	2	0	15	12	7.50	-	-	-	-	168	107	3	35.66	2-21	-	-
ODI																	
List A	5	2	2	25	21 *		-	-	-	-	228	232	4	58.00	3-29	-	
20/20 Int																	
20/20																	

Career Performances

	M	Inn	NO	Runs	HS	Avg	100	50	Ct	St	Balls	Runs	Wkts	Avg	BB	5I	10M
Test																	
FC	18	25	3	444	76	20.18	-	2	5	-	2224	1624	23	70.60	2-21	-	-
ODI																	
List A	21	13	7	69	21 *	11.50	-	-	3	-	846	754	15	50.26	3-21	-	
20/20 Int																	
20/20	4	1	1	1	1 *		-	-	2	-	78	109	3	36.33	2-24	-	

WRIGHT, D. G. Glamorgan

Name: Damien Geoffrey Wright
Role: Right-hand bat, right-arm fast-medium bowler; all-rounder
Born: 25 July 1975, Casino, NSW, Australia
Height: 6ft 1½in
Nickname: Moves
County debut: 2003 (Northamptonshire), 2007 (Glamorgan)
50 wickets in a season: 1
Overseas tours: Australia A to South Africa 2002-03
Overseas teams played for: Tasmania 1997-98 –
Injuries: Out for three weeks with a thigh injury; from early July onwards with an ankle injury
Extras: Played for Scotland in the 2002 C&G, winning two Man of the Match awards. Has also won several match awards in Australia, including Man of the Match v Victoria at Melbourne in the ING Cup 2001-02 (4-23/40) and v Queensland at Brisbane in the Pura Cup 2003-04 (4-30/3-33 plus 60). Has represented Australia A. Tasmania's leading wicket-taker in the Pura Cup 2002-03 (31 wickets; av. 27.25) and

(jointly with Andrew Downton) 2003-04 (37; 26.49). Tasmanian Player of the Year 2002-03. Named in Australia's initial squad of 30 for the 2002-03 World Cup. Was a member of Tasmania's first Pura Cup winning side 2006-07, taking 5-13 in NSW's second innings in the final in Hobart (having also taken 3-38 in the first innings and scored 67 and 47). Was an overseas player with Northamptonshire in 2003 (temporary) and 2005; was an overseas player with Glamorgan during the 2007 season but was forced to return home early through injury

Best batting: 111 Tasmania v Victoria, Hobart 2004-05

Best bowling: 8-60 Northamptonshire v Yorkshire, Headingley 2005

2007 Season

	M	Inn	NO	Runs	HS	Avg	100	50	Ct	St	Balls	Runs	Wkts	Avg	BB	5I	10M
Test																	
FC	1	2	0	1	1	.50	-	-	1	-	96	60	3	20.00	3-60	-	-
ODI																	
List A	2	2	0	2	1	1.00	-	-	-	-	38	46	0		-	-	
20/20 Int																	
20/20	6	5	0	67	31	13.40	-	-	1	-	96	123	3	41.00	1-8	-	

Career Performances

	M	Inn	NO	Runs	HS	Avg	100	50	Ct	St	Balls	Runs	Wkts	Avg	BB	5I	10M
Test																	
FC	86	133	21	2689	111	24.00	1	13	40	-	17518	8249	271	30.43	8-60	8	-
ODI																	
List A	90	70	20	867	55	17.34	-	4	20	-	4567	3160	113	27.96	5-37	1	
20/20 Int																	
20/20	16	13	2	165	38 *	15.00	-	-	2	-	301	372	12	31.00	3-17	-	

100. When the players were each asked to select a piece of music to accompany them to the wicket in the ODI series between England and New Zealand in 1996-97, who chose 'How Much is that Doggie in the Window?'

WRIGHT, L. J. — Sussex

Name: Luke James Wright
Role: Right-hand bat, right-arm medium-fast bowler; all-rounder
Born: 7 March 1985, Grantham
Height: 6ft **Weight:** 13st
Nickname: Wrighty
County debut: 2003 (Leicestershire), 2004 (Sussex)
County cap: 2007 (Sussex)
ODI debut: 2007
Twenty20 Int debut: 2007-08
Place in batting averages: 34th av. 49.57 (2006 206th av. 20.86)
Place in bowling averages: 129th av. 44.21 (2006 99th av. 38.80)
Parents: Keith and Anna
Marital status: Single
Family links with cricket: 'Father very keen cricketer (Level 2 coach).' Brother Ashley played for Leicestershire
Education: Belvoir High School, Bottesford; Ratcliffe College, Leicester; Loughborough University
Qualifications: 8 GCSEs, National Diploma in Sports Science and Sports Massage, ECB Level 1 coaching
Overseas tours: Leicestershire U13 to South Africa; Leicestershire U15 to South Africa; England U19 to Australia 2002-03, to Bangladesh (U19 World Cup) 2003-04; England A to West Indies 2005-06; England to South Africa (World 20/20) 2007-08, to Sri Lanka 2007-08 (one-day series), to New Zealand 2007-08 (one-day series); England Performance Programme to India 2007-08
Cricket superstitions: 'Too many to name'
Cricketers particularly admired: Andrew Flintoff, Jacques Kallis
Other sports played: Football, hockey, squash, tennis
Other sports followed: Football (Newcastle United)
Favourite band: Kelly Clarkson
Relaxations: Music, cinema, going out
Extras: NBC Denis Compton Award for the most promising young Leicestershire player 2002. Took the first ever hat-trick for England U19 in one-day cricket, v South Africa U19 at Hove 2003. Scored maiden first-class century (100) on Sussex debut v Loughborough UCCE at Hove 2004. ECB National Academy 2004-05 (part-time), 2005-06. Leading run-scorer in the Twenty20 2007 with 346 runs (av. 43.25), including 45-ball 103 v Kent at Canterbury and 48-ball 98 v Hampshire at Hove. Made ODI debut in the sixth ODI v India at The Oval 2007, scoring 50

Best batting: 100 Sussex v LUCCE, Hove 2004
Best bowling: 3-33 Sussex v Surrey, Hove 2005
Stop press: Forced to return home from England Performance Programme in India 2007-08 with a foot injury

2007 Season

	M	Inn	NO	Runs	HS	Avg	100	50	Ct	St	Balls	Runs	Wkts	Avg	BB	5I	10M
Test																	
FC	11	13	6	347	61	49.57	-	3	3	-	1011	619	14	44.21	3-117	-	-
ODI	2	2	0	50	50	25.00	-	1	1	-	12	11	0		-	-	
List A	14	12	0	375	125	31.25	1	2	2	-	289	337	2	168.50	1-20	-	
20/20 Int																	
20/20	9	9	1	346	103	43.25	1	1	4	-	90	164	3	54.66	2-35	-	

Career Performances

	M	Inn	NO	Runs	HS	Avg	100	50	Ct	St	Balls	Runs	Wkts	Avg	BB	5I	10M
Test																	
FC	32	43	9	915	100	26.91	1	6	16	-	3062	1729	43	40.20	3-33	-	-
ODI	2	2	0	50	50	25.00	-	1	1	-	12	11	0		-	-	
List A	71	51	9	814	125	19.38	1	2	20	-	2360	2054	52	39.50	4-12	-	
20/20 Int	5	5	0	43	24	8.60	-	-	2	-	0	0	0		-	-	
20/20	34	25	3	476	103	21.63	1	1	15	-	438	584	27	21.62	3-17	-	

YARDY, M. H. — Sussex

Name: Michael (Mike) Howard Yardy
Role: Left-hand bat, left-arm medium/spin bowler, county vice-captain
Born: 27 November 1980, Pembury, Kent
Height: 6ft **Weight:** 14st 2lbs
Nickname: Yards, Paolo
County debut: 1999 (one-day), 2000 (first-class)
County cap: 2005
ODI debut: 2006
Twenty20 Int debut: 2006
1000 runs in a season: 1
1st-Class 200s: 1
Place in batting averages: 81st av. 38.52 (2006 39th av. 50.77)
Parents: Beverly and Howard
Wife and date of marriage: Karin, October 2005

Children: Syenna Lucienne, 24 December 2006
Family links with cricket: 'Brother plays for local team'
Education: William Parker School, Hastings
Qualifications: 5 GCSEs, 2 A-levels, ECB Level 1 coach, Sports Psychology diploma
Overseas tours: Sussex Academy to Barbados 1997; Sussex to Grenada 2001, 2002; England A to West Indies 2005-06, to Bangladesh 2006-07 (c); England to India (ICC Champions Trophy) 2006-07; England Lions to India 2007-08 (c)
Overseas teams played for: Cape Town CC 1999
Cricket superstitions: 'Loads – all secret'
Cricketers particularly admired: 'All those who have reached the pinnacle of their careers'
Other sports followed: Football (West Ham)
Favourite band: Bluetones
Relaxations: 'Watching West Ham; relaxing with my wife'
Extras: Played for Sussex U15, U16 and U19. Represented England U17. Attended Sussex Academy. Sussex Most Improved Player 2001. His 257 v Bangladeshis at Hove 2005 is the highest individual score for Sussex against a touring side; also took 5-83 in Bangladeshis' second innings. Scored 159* v Warwickshire at Hove 2006, in the process sharing with Murray Goodwin (214*) in a new Sussex record partnership for the third wicket (385*). ECB National Academy 2005-06, 2006-07. Vice-captain of Sussex since 2007
Best batting: 257 Sussex v Bangladeshis, Hove 2005
Best bowling: 5-83 Sussex v Bangladeshis, Hove 2005

2007 Season

	M	Inn	NO	Runs	HS	Avg	100	50	Ct	St	Balls	Runs	Wkts	Avg	BB	5I	10M
Test																	
FC	13	21	2	732	125	38.52	2	5	11	-	309	181	4	45.25	2-32	-	-
ODI	1	1	0	19	19	19.00	-	-	-	-	36	29	0		-	-	
List A	11	10	1	128	40	14.22	-	-	6	-	367	301	6	50.16	2-28	-	
20/20 Int	2	1	1	23	23 *		-	-	1	-	42	65	1	65.00	1-35	-	
20/20	5	4	2	43	23 *	21.50	-	-	2	-	66	97	2	48.50	1-9	-	

Career Performances

	M	Inn	NO	Runs	HS	Avg	100	50	Ct	St	Balls	Runs	Wkts	Avg	BB	5I	10M
Test																	
FC	85	144	15	4978	257	38.58	11	23	66	-	2334	1304	20	65.20	5-83	1	-
ODI	6	5	1	49	19	12.25	-	-	1	-	252	135	4	33.75	3-24	-	
List A	118	105	15	1747	98 *	19.41	-	8	49	-	2935	2322	68	34.14	6-27	1	
20/20 Int	3	2	2	47	24 *		-	-	2	-	60	85	2	42.50	1-20	-	
20/20	23	18	8	320	68 *	32.00	-	1	9	-	270	328	9	36.44	2-15	-	

YASIR ARAFAT Kent

Name: Yasir Arafat Satti
Role: Right-hand bat, right-arm fast bowler
Born: 12 March 1982, Rawalpindi, Punjab, Pakistan
Height: 5ft 9½in **Weight:** 11st 11lbs
Nickname: Yas
County debut: 2006 (Sussex), 2007 (Kent)
County cap: 2006 (Sussex), 2007 (Kent)
ODI debut: 1999-2000
Twenty20 Int debut: 2007-08
Place in batting averages: 141st av. 30.75 (2006 65th av. 43.33)
Place in bowling averages: 76th av. 32.66 (2006 14th av. 24.85)
Parents: M. Idrees (father)
Marital status: Single
Family links with cricket: 'Father plays club cricket'
Education: Gordon College, Rawalpindi
Overseas tours: Pakistan U15 to England (U15 World Cup) 1996; Pakistan U19 to Australia 1997-98, to Sri Lanka (U19 World Cup) 1999-2000; Pakistan A to UAE (UAE National Day Tournament) 1999-2000, to Kenya 2000, to Sri Lanka 2001, 2004-05, to UAE (EurAsia Cricket Series) 2006; Pakistan to Sharjah (ARY Gold Cup) 2000-01, to India (ICC Champions Trophy) 2006-07, to West Indies (World Cup) 2006-07, to South Africa (World 20/20) 2007-08, to India 2007-08
Overseas teams played for: Rawalpindi 1997-98, 2000-01 – 2001-02, 2003-04 – 2005-06; Pakistan Reserves 1999-2000; Khan Research Laboratories 1999-2000 – 2004-05, 2006-07 – ; REDCO 1999-2000; National Bank of Pakistan 2005-06
Career highlights to date: 'Playing for Pakistan'
Cricket moments to forget: 'Nil'
Cricket superstitions: 'Nil'
Other sports played: Football
Other sports followed: Football (Real Madrid)
Relaxations: 'Watching movies and music'
Extras: Pakistan domestic Player of the Year 2003-04. Played for Clydesdale CC, Scotland 2001-06 and for Scotland in the totesport and C&G 2004-05. Became fourth bowler in history of first-class cricket to take five wickets in six balls, for Rawalpindi v Faisalabad at Rawalpindi in the Quaid-e-Azam Trophy 2004-05; his feat, spread across two innings, included a hat-trick. Was an overseas player with Sussex from June to September 2006; was an overseas player with Kent 2007

Best batting: 122 Kent v Sussex, Canterbury 2007
Best bowling: 7-102 Rawalpindi v Sialkot, Sialkot 2001-02
Stop press: Made Test debut in the third Test v India at Bangalore 2007-08

2007 Season

	M	Inn	NO	Runs	HS	Avg	100	50	Ct	St	Balls	Runs	Wkts	Avg	BB	5I	10M
Test																	
FC	10	13	1	369	122	30.75	2	-	2	-	1433	882	27	32.66	5-63	1	-
ODI																	
List A	10	6	2	44	26 *	11.00	-	-	1	-	495	386	18	21.44	3-20	-	
20/20 Int																	
20/20	11	4	3	19	7	19.00	-	-	1	-	195	280	14	20.00	3-24	-	

Career Performances

	M	Inn	NO	Runs	HS	Avg	100	50	Ct	St	Balls	Runs	Wkts	Avg	BB	5I	10M
Test																	
FC	120	183	23	4234	122	26.46	3	23	41	-	19659	11238	492	22.84	7-102	28	3
ODI	7	5	1	48	27	12.00	-	-	1	-	234	233	4	58.25	1-28	-	
List A	154	115	29	1856	87	21.58	-	7	31	-	7374	5868	240	24.45	6-24	3	
20/20 Int	4	4	2	46	17	23.00	-	-	1	-	78	103	2	51.50	1-31	-	
20/20	31	23	7	276	49	17.25	-	-	3	-	607	843	36	23.41	4-21	-	

YOUNUS KHAN Yorkshire

Name: Mohammad Younus Khan
Role: Right-hand bat, leg-break bowler, occasional wicket-keeper
Born: 29 November 1977, Mardan, Pakistan
County debut: 2005 (Nottinghamshire), 2007 (Yorkshire)
County cap: 2007 (Yorkshire)
Test debut: 1999-2000
ODI debut: 1999-2000
Twenty20 Int debut: 2006
1st-Class 200s: 7
Place in batting averages: 39th av. 48.47 (2006 9th av. 65.57)
Overseas tours: Pakistan to Sharjah (Coca-Cola Sharjah Cup) 1999-2000, to West Indies 1999-2000, to Sri Lanka 2000, to New Zealand 2000-01, to England 2001, to Bangladesh 2001-02, to Sharjah (v West Indies) 2001-02, to Sri Lanka (ICC Champions Trophy) 2002-03, to Sri Lanka and

Sharjah (v Australia) 2002-03, to Zimbabwe and South Africa 2002-03, to Africa (World Cup) 2002-03, to New Zealand 2003-04, to Australia 2004-05, to India 2004-05, to West Indies 2004-05, to Sri Lanka 2005-06, to England 2006, to India (ICC Champions Trophy) 2006-07 (c), to South Africa 2006-07, to West Indies (World Cup) 2006-07, to South Africa (World 20/20) 2007-08, to India 2007-08, plus other one-day tournaments in Abu Dhabi, Singapore, Sharjah, Australia, Morocco, Kenya, Sri Lanka, England, Netherlands and India

Overseas teams played for: Peshawar/Peshawar Panthers; Habib Bank 1999-2000 –

Extras: Took a Test innings record for a substitute of four catches v Bangladesh in the Asian Test Championship 2001-02. His match and series awards include Man of the Match in the third Test v India at Bangalore 2004-05 (267/84*), Man of the [Test] Series v India 2005-06 and Man of the [ODI] Series v England 2006. Vice-captain of Pakistan since the tour to India of 2004-05. Was an overseas player with Nottinghamshire from July to September 2005; was an overseas player with Yorkshire 2007. Scored century and double century (106/202*) and returned career best bowling figures (4-52) in the same match v Hampshire at The Rose Bowl 2007

Best batting: 267 Pakistan v India, Bangalore 2004-05

Best bowling: 4-52 Yorkshire v Hampshire, Rose Bowl 2007

2007 Season

	M	Inn	NO	Runs	HS	Avg	100	50	Ct	St	Balls	Runs	Wkts	Avg	BB	5I	10M
Test																	
FC	13	19	2	824	217 *	48.47	3	-	11	-	515	342	8	42.75	4-52	-	-
ODI																	
List A	11	8	0	248	100	31.00	1	-	5	-	136	144	2	72.00	2-43	-	
20/20 Int																	
20/20	2	2	0	55	40	27.50	-	-	-	-	18	32	2	16.00	2-32	-	

Career Performances

	M	Inn	NO	Runs	HS	Avg	100	50	Ct	St	Balls	Runs	Wkts	Avg	BB	5I	10M
Test	53	95	6	4291	267	48.21	12	19	64	-	264	169	2	84.50	1-24	-	-
FC	121	196	21	8713	267	49.78	27	35	133	-	1591	1011	20	50.55	4-52	-	-
ODI	151	146	18	3988	144	31.15	2	26	80	-	97	106	1	106.00	1-24	-	
List A	190	181	24	5009	144	31.90	4	32	102	-	569	535	18	29.72	3-5	-	
20/20 Int	11	10	0	176	51	17.60	-	1	7	-	22	18	3	6.00	3-18	-	
20/20	20	19	4	396	51	26.40	-	1	9	-	52	83	5	16.60	3-18	-	

ZONDEKI, M. — Warwickshire

Name: Monde Zondeki
Role: Right-hand bat, right-arm fast bowler
Born: 25 July 1982, King William's Town, South Africa
County debut: No first-team appearance
Test debut: 2003
ODI debut: 2002-03
Twenty20 Int debut: 2005-06
Education: Dale College, South Africa
Overseas tours: South Africa U19 to New Zealand 2000-01; South Africa A to Sri Lanka 2005-06; South Africa to England 2003, to West Indies 2004-05, to Australia 2005-06 (VB Series)
Overseas teams played for: Border 2000-01 – 2004-05; Warriors 2004-05; Cape Cobras 2005-06 – ; has also played for Western Province and Eastern Cape
Extras: Made ODI debut v Sri Lanka in the fifth ODI at Bloemfontein 2002-03, taking a wicket (Marvan Atapattu) with his first ball in international cricket. Represented South Africa in the 2002-03 World Cup. Made Test debut in the fourth Test v England at Headingley 2003, scoring 59 and sharing with Gary Kirsten in a record-equalling eighth-wicket partnership for South Africa in Tests (150). His match awards include Man of the Match in the second Test v Zimbabwe at Centurion 2004-05 (3-66/6-39). Represented African XI v Asian Cricket Council XI in the Afro-Asia Cup 2005-06. Is nephew of the late South African government minister Steve Tshwete
Best batting: 59 South Africa v England, Headingley 2003
Best bowling: 6-39 South Africa v Zimbabwe, Centurion 2004-05
Stop press: Man of the Match for South Africa A v West Indians at East London 2007-08 (5-39/3-61)

2007 Season (did not make any first-class or one-day appearances)

Career Performances

	M	Inn	NO	Runs	HS	Avg	100	50	Ct	St	Balls	Runs	Wkts	Avg	BB	5I	10M
Test	5	4	0	82	59	20.50	-	1	1	-	692	438	16	27.37	6-39	1	-
FC	55	80	23	508	59	8.91	-	1	18	-	8813	4767	149	31.99	6-39	3	-
ODI	11	3	2	4	3 *	4.00	-	-	3	-	456	414	8	51.75	2-46	-	
List A	64	23	9	98	23	7.00	-	-	11	-	2738	2237	78	28.67	6-37	2	
20/20 Int	1	1	0	0	0	0.00	-	-	-	-	18	41	1	41.00	1-41	-	
20/20	7	2	1	1	1 *	1.00	-	-	1	-	118	172	4	43.00	2-19	-	

OTHER REGISTERED PLAYERS

WATKINSON, M. Lancashire

Name: Michael (Mike) Watkinson
Role: Right-hand bat, right-arm medium or off-spin bowler
Born: 1 August 1961, Westhoughton, Greater Manchester
County debut: 1982
County cap: 1987
Benefit: 1996
Extras: Man of the Match in the first Refuge Assurance Cup final 1988 and for his 50 plus 2-37 in B&H Cup final 1990. Lancashire captain 1994-97, leading the county to one NatWest and two B&H titles. Lancashire Player of the Year 1995. Played four Tests and one ODI for England 1995 – 1995-96. Cricket Manager at Lancashire since 2002; retired as player but registration retained
Best batting: 161 Lancashire v Essex, Old Trafford 1995
Best bowling: 8-30 Lancashire v Hampshire, Old Trafford 1994

YATES, G. Lancashire

Name: Gary Yates
Role: Right-hand bat, right-arm off-spin bowler
Born: 20 September 1967, Ashton-under-Lyne
County debut: 1990
County cap: 1994
Benefit: 2005
Extras: Scored century (106) on Championship debut v Nottinghamshire at Trent Bridge 1990. Assistant Coach at Lancashire but registration retained
Best batting: 134* Lancashire v Northamptonshire, Old Trafford 1993
Best bowling: 6-64 Lancashire v Kent, Old Trafford 1999

THE UMPIRES

BAILEY, R. J.

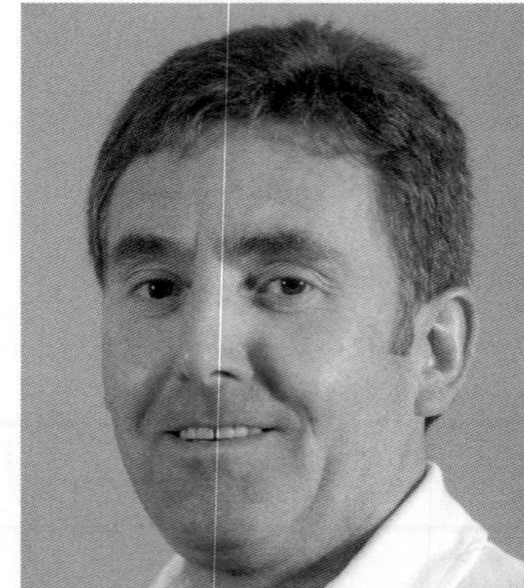

Name: Robert (Rob) John Bailey
Born: 28 October 1963, Biddulph, Stoke-on-Trent
Height: 6ft 3in
Nickname: Bailers
Wife and date of marriage: Rachel, 11 April 1987
Children: Harry, 7 March 1991; Alexandra, 13 November 1993
Family links with cricket: 'Son Harry plays for Northampton Saints CC'
Education: Biddulph High School
Career outside cricket: Rob Bailey Ceramics ('promotional mugs etc.')
Other sports played: Badminton (county schools)
Other sports followed: 'All football clubs that I supply mugs to!'
Appointed to 1st-Class list: 2006
Counties as player: Northamptonshire, Derbyshire
Role: Right-hand bat, off-spin bowler
County debut: 1982 (Northamptonshire), 2000 (Derbyshire)
County cap: 1985 (Northamptonshire), 2000 (Derbyshire)
Benefit: 1993 (Northamptonshire)
Test debut: 1988
ODI debut (matches): 1984-85 (4)
1000 runs in a season: 13
1st-Class 200s: 4
One-Day 100s: 9
One-Day 5 w. in innings: 1
Overseas tours: England to Sharjah 1984-85, 1986-87, to India 1988-89 (cancelled), to West Indies 1989-90
Overseas teams played for: Rhodes University, Grahamstown, South Africa 1982-83; Uitenhage CC, South Africa 1983-85; Fitzroy CC, Melbourne 1985-86; Gosnells CC, Perth 1987-88
Highlights of playing career: 'Loved all of it'
Extras: Won three consecutive NatWest Man of the Match awards 1995 and three consecutive B&H Gold Awards 1996. Northamptonshire captain 1996-97. In 1999 became sixth player to pass 20,000 first-class runs for Northamptonshire
Best batting: 224* Northamptonshire v Glamorgan, Swansea 1986
Best bowling: 5-54 Northamptonshire v Nottinghamshire, Northampton 1993

First-Class Career Performances

	M	Inn	NO	Runs	HS	Avg	100	Ct	St	Runs	Wkts	Avg	BB	5I	10M
Test	4	8	0	119	43	14.87	-	-	-						
FC	374	628	89	21844	224*	40.52	47	272	-	5144	121	42.51	5-54	2	-

BAINTON, N. L.

Name: Neil Laurence Bainton
Born: 2 October 1970, Romford, Essex
Height: 5ft 8in
Wife and date of marriage: Kay, 25 October 1997
Family links with cricket: Father played and umpired club cricket
Education: Ilford County High School
Career outside cricket: 'Postman'
Off-season: 'Postman in Braintree, Essex'
Other sports followed: Football (West Ham 'and whichever local team my mate plays for!')
Appointed to 1st-Class list: 2006
Highlights of umpiring career: 'Being appointed to first-class list'
Players to watch for the future: Billy Godleman, Tom Westley
County as player: Did not play first-class cricket
Highlights of playing career: 'Playing for South of England U15 at England Schools Festival 1986'

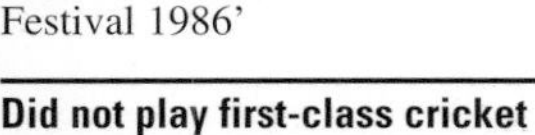

Did not play first-class cricket

BENSON, M. R.

Name: Mark Richard Benson
Born: 6 July 1958, Shoreham, Sussex
Height: 5ft 10in
Nickname: Benny
Wife and date of marriage: Sarah Patricia, 20 September 1986
Children: Laurence, 16 October 1987; Edward, 23 June 1990
Education: Sutton Valence School
Other sports played: Bridge, golf, swimming, cycling
Relaxations: Bridge, golf
Appointed to 1st-Class list: 2000
International panel: 2004-2006
Elite panel: 2006 –
Tests umpired: 21 (plus 6 as TV umpire)
ODIs umpired: 61 (plus 24 as TV umpire)
Twenty20 Ints umpired: 8 (plus 3 as TV umpire)
Other umpiring honours: Stood in the C&G Trophy final 2003. Umpired in the 2006-07 World Cup and the Twenty20 World Championship 2007-08
County as player: Kent
Role: Left-hand bat
County debut: 1980
County cap: 1981
Benefit: 1991
Test debut: 1986
ODI debut (matches): 1986 (1)
1000 runs in a season: 11
1st-Class 200s: 1
One-Day 100s: 5
Overseas tours: None
Highlights of playing career: '257 v Hampshire. Winning Sunday League as captain of Kent. Two 90s to win a game against Hampshire with Malcolm Marshall bowling. One of only four cricketers in the history of Kent to have scored more than 10,000 runs and have an average in excess of 40 [in a completed career]'
Extras: Scored 1000 runs in first full season. Kent captain 1991-95
Best batting: 257 Kent v Hampshire, Southampton 1991
Best bowling: 2-55 Kent v Surrey, Dartford 1986

First-Class Career Performances

	M	Inn	NO	Runs	HS	Avg	100	Ct	St	Runs	Wkts	Avg	BB	5I	10M
Test	1	2	0	51	30	25.50	-	-	-						
FC	292	491	34	18387	257	40.23	48	140	-	493	5	98.60	2-55	-	-

BURGESS, G. I.

Name: Graham Iefvion Burgess
Born: 5 May 1943, Glastonbury, Somerset
Education: Millfield School
Appointed to 1st-Class list: 1991
ODIs umpired: 2 as TV umpire
County as player: Somerset
Role: Right-hand bat, right-arm medium bowler
County debut: 1966
County cap: 1968
Testimonial: 1977
One-Day 5 w. in innings: 2
Extras: Played Minor Counties cricket for Wiltshire 1981-82 and for Cambridgeshire 1983-84
Best batting: 129 Somerset v Gloucestershire, Taunton 1973
Best bowling: 7-43 Somerset v Oxford University, The Parks 1975

First-Class Career Performances

	M	Inn	NO	Runs	HS	Avg	100	Ct	St	Runs	Wkts	Avg	BB	5I	10M
Test															
FC	252	414	37	7129	129	18.90	2	120	-	13543	474	28.57	7-43	18	2

COWLEY, N. G. C.

Name: Nigel Geoffrey Charles Cowley
Born: 1 March 1953, Shaftesbury, Dorset
Height: 5ft 6½in
Marital status: Divorced
Children: Mark Antony, 14 June 1973; Darren James, 30 October 1976
Family links with cricket: Darren played Hampshire Schools U11, U12, U13; Natal Schools 1993, 1994, 1995; and toured India with South Africa U19 1996
Education: Duchy Manor, Mere, Wiltshire
Other sports played: Golf (8 handicap)
Other sports followed: Football (Liverpool FC)
Appointed to 1st-Class list: 2000
Counties as player: Hampshire, Glamorgan
Role: Right-hand bat, off-spin bowler
County debut: 1974 (Hampshire), 1990 (Glamorgan)
County cap: 1978 (Hampshire)
Benefit: 1988 (Hampshire)
1000 runs in a season: 1
50 wickets in a season: 2
One-Day 5 w. in innings: 1
Overseas tours: Hampshire to Barbados 1985, 1986, 1987, to Dubai 1989
Overseas teams played for: Paarl CC 1982-83; Amanzimtoti 1984-96 (both South Africa)
Extras: Played for Dorset 1972. NatWest Man of the Match award
Best batting: 109* Hampshire v Somerset, Taunton 1977
Best bowling: 6-48 Hampshire v Leicestershire, Southampton 1982

First-Class Career Performances

	M	Inn	NO	Runs	HS	Avg	100	Ct	St	Runs	Wkts	Avg	BB	5I	10M
Test															
FC	271	375	62	7309	109*	23.35	2	105	-	14879	437	34.04	6-48	5	-

DUDLESTON, B.

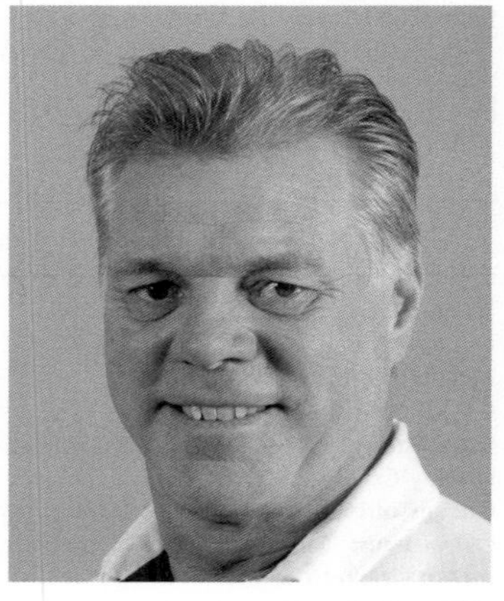

Name: Barry Dudleston
Born: 16 July 1945, Bebington, Cheshire
Height: 5ft 9in
Nickname: Danny
Wife and date of marriage: Louise Wendy, 19 October 1994
Children: Sharon Louise, 29 October 1968; Matthew Barry, 12 September 1988; Jack Nicholas, 29 April 1998
Family links with cricket: 'Dad was a league cricketer'
Education: Stockport School
Career outside cricket: Managing director of Sunsport Ltd
Other sports played: Golf
Other sports followed: All sports
Relaxations: Bridge, red wine
Appointed to 1st-Class list: 1984
First appointed to Test panel: 1991
Tests umpired: 2 (plus 4 as TV umpire)
ODIs umpired: 4 (plus 6 as TV umpire)
Other umpiring honours: Stood in C&G final 2001 and B&H final 2002; also officiated at the inaugural Twenty20 finals day at Trent Bridge 2003, including standing in the final, and at Twenty20 finals day 2006 at Trent Bridge
Players to watch for the future: Stuart Broad
Counties as player: Leicestershire, Gloucestershire
Role: Right-hand opening bat, slow left-arm bowler, occasional wicket-keeper
County debut: 1966 (Leicestershire), 1981 (Gloucestershire)
County cap: 1969 (Leicestershire)
Benefit: 1980 (Leicestershire)
1000 runs in a season: 8
1st-Class 200s: 1
One-Day 100s: 4
Overseas tours: Kent (as guest player) to West Indies 1972; D.H. Robins' XI to West Indies 1973; Wisden XI to West Indies 1984; MCC to Kenya 1993
Overseas teams played for: Rhodesia/Zimbabwe-Rhodesia 1976-80
Highlights of playing career: 'Winning County Championship [with Leicestershire]'
Extras: Played for England U25. Holder with John Steele of the highest first-wicket partnership for Leicestershire, 390 v Derbyshire at Leicester in 1979. Fastest player in Rhodesian cricket history to 1000 first-class runs in Currie Cup; second fastest ever in Currie Cup

Best batting: 202 Leicestershire v Derbyshire, Leicester 1979
Best bowling: 4-6 Leicestershire v Surrey, Leicester 1972

First-Class Career Performances

	M	Inn	NO	Runs	HS	Avg	100	Ct	St	Runs	Wkts	Avg	BB	5I	10M
Test															
FC	295	501	47	14747	202	32.48	32	234	7	1365	47	29.04	4-6	-	-

EVANS, J. H.

Name: Jeffrey (Jeff) Howard Evans
Born: 7 August 1954, Llanelli
Height: 5ft 8in
Children: Rhian; Siân
Education: Llanelli Boys Grammar School; Dudley College of Education
Career outside cricket: Supply teaching
Off-season: 'Supply teaching. Umpiring in Indian Cricket League'
Other sports followed: 'Most sports, rugby in particular'
Relaxations: 'Walking, keeping fit'
Appointed to 1st-Class list: 2001
Other umpiring honours: Toured Namibia and Uganda 2004-05 with MCC (as umpire)
Highlights of umpiring career: 'First Championship match – Yorkshire v Somerset at Headingley 2001'
Players to watch for the future: Ravi Bopara
Cricket moments to forget: 'Any error of judgement!'
County as player: Did not play first-class cricket. Played league cricket in South Wales as a right-hand bat
Extras: Coach to Welsh Schools Cricket Association team on tour to Australia 1993. Taught in the Gwendraeth Grammar School – 'the old "outside-half factory"'
Opinions on cricket: 'Would like to see more honesty throughout the game!'

Did not play first-class cricket

GARRATT, S. A.

Name: Stephen (Steve) Arthur Garratt
Born: 5 July 1953, Nottingham
Height: 6ft 2in
Nickname: Trigger
Wife and date of marriage: Marion, 1975
Children: Mark, 25; Chris, 23; Farris (grandson), 3
Family links with cricket: 'Father Arthur played local club cricket in Nottingham'
Education: Arnold County High School, Nottingham
Career outside cricket: Retired police officer
Off-season: 'Taking holidays with my wife'
Other sports played: Rugby union, football
Other sports followed: 'All sports'
Relaxations: 'Walk on the beach at Whitby'
Appointed to 1st-Class list: 2008
Highlights of umpiring career: 'Appointment to first-class reserve list, April 2003. Appointment to first-class full list, April 2008'
County as player: Did not play first-class cricket

Did not play first-class cricket

GOULD, I. J.

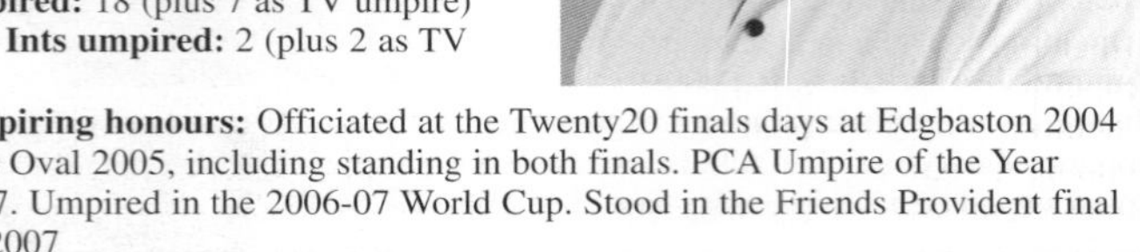

Name: Ian James Gould
Born: 19 August 1957, Taplow, Bucks
Height: 5ft 7in
Nickname: Gunner
Wife and date of marriage: Joanne, 27 September 1986
Children: Gemma; Michael; George
Education: Westgate Secondary Modern, Slough
Other sports played: Golf
Other sports followed: Football (Arsenal), racing
Appointed to 1st-Class list: 2002
International panel: 2006 –
Tests umpired: 4 as TV umpire
ODIs umpired: 18 (plus 7 as TV umpire)
Twenty20 Ints umpired: 2 (plus 2 as TV umpire)
Other umpiring honours: Officiated at the Twenty20 finals days at Edgbaston 2004 and at The Oval 2005, including standing in both finals. PCA Umpire of the Year 2005, 2007. Umpired in the 2006-07 World Cup. Stood in the Friends Provident final at Lord's 2007
Players to watch for the future: Ollie Rayner
Counties as player: Middlesex, Sussex
Role: Left-hand bat, wicket-keeper
County debut: 1975 (Middlesex), 1981 (Sussex)
County cap: 1977 (Middlesex), 1981 (Sussex)
Benefit: 1990 (Sussex)
ODI debut (matches): 1982-83 (18)
Overseas tours: England YC to West Indies 1976; D.H. Robins' XI to Canada 1978-79; International XI to Pakistan 1980-81; England to Australia and New Zealand 1982-83; MCC to Namibia
Overseas teams played for: Auckland 1979-80
Highlights of playing career: 'Playing in the World Cup'
Extras: Represented England in the 1983 World Cup. Retired from county cricket in 1991
Best batting: 128 Middlesex v Worcestershire, Worcester 1978
Best bowling: 3-10 Sussex v Surrey, The Oval 1989

First-Class Career Performances

	M	Inn	NO	Runs	HS	Avg	100	Ct	St	Runs	Wkts	Avg	Best	5I	10M
Test															
FC	297	399	63	8756	128	26.06	4	536	67	365	7	52.14	3-10	-	-

HARRIS, M. J.

Name: Michael John Harris
Born: 25 May 1944, St Just-in-Roseland, Cornwall
Height: 6ft 1in
Nickname: Pasty
Wife and date of marriage: Danielle Ruth, 10 September 1969
Children: Jodie; Richard
Education: Gerrans Comprehensive
Career outside cricket: Sports teacher
Other sports followed: Squash, golf
Appointed to 1st-Class list: 1998
Counties as player: Middlesex, Nottinghamshire
Role: Right-hand bat, leg-break bowler, wicket-keeper
County debut: 1964 (Middlesex), 1969 (Nottinghamshire)
County cap: 1967 (Middlesex), 1970 (Nottinghamshire)
1000 runs in a season: 11
1st-Class 200s: 1
One-Day 100s: 3
Overseas teams played for: Eastern Province 1971-72; Wellington 1975-76
Extras: Shared Middlesex then record first-wicket partnership of 312 with Eric Russell v Pakistanis at Lord's 1967. Scored nine centuries in 1971 to equal Nottinghamshire county record for a season, scoring two centuries in a match twice and totalling 2238 runs at an average of 50.86
Best batting: 201* Nottinghamshire v Glamorgan, Trent Bridge 1973
Best bowling: 4-16 Nottinghamshire v Warwickshire, Trent Bridge 1969

First-Class Career Performances

	M	Inn	NO	Runs	HS	Avg	100	Ct	St	Runs	Wkts	Avg	BB	5I	10M
Test															
FC	344	581	58	19196	201*	36.70	41	288	14	3459	79	43.78	4-16	-	-

HARTLEY, P. J.

Name: Peter John Hartley
Born: 18 April 1960, Keighley, Yorkshire
Height: 6ft
Nickname: Jack
Wife and date of marriage: Sharon, 12 March 1988
Children: Megan, 25 April 1993; Courtney, 25 July 1995
Family links with cricket: Father played local league cricket
Education: Greenhead Grammar School, Keighley; Bradford College
Off-season: 'Skiing'
Other sports played: Golf (2 handicap)
Other sports followed: Football (Chelsea)
Relaxations: 'Walking, any sport'
Appointed to 1st-Class list: 2003
International panel: 2006 – (as TV umpire)
Tests umpired: 5 as TV umpire
ODIs umpired: 1 (plus 6 as TV umpire)
Twenty20 Ints umpired: 2 (plus 2 as TV umpire)
Other umpiring honours: Officiated at Twenty20 finals day 2006 at Trent Bridge, including standing in the final. Umpired his first ODI in 2007 – England v India, The Oval
Highlights of umpiring career: 'Above [ODI], and umpired Friends Provident final 2007'
Counties as player: Warwickshire, Yorkshire, Hampshire
Role: Right-hand bat, right-arm fast-medium bowler
County debut: 1982 (Warwickshire), 1985 (Yorkshire), 1998 (Hampshire)
County cap: 1987 (Yorkshire), 1998 (Hampshire)
Benefit: 1996 (Yorkshire)
50 wickets in a season: 7
One-Day 5 w. in innings: 5
Overseas tours: Yorkshire pre-season tours to Barbados 1986-87, to South Africa 1991-92, 1992-93, to Zimbabwe
Overseas teams played for: Melville, New Zealand 1983-84; Adelaide, Australia 1985-86; Harmony and Orange Free State, South Africa 1988-89
Highlights of playing career: 'Hat-trick and taking 9-41 in same game'
Extras: His 9-41 v Derbyshire at Chesterfield 1995 contained a spell of five wickets in nine balls, including a hat-trick (DeFreitas, Harrison, Cork). Returned 8-65, his best figures for Hampshire, against Yorkshire, his former county, at Basingstoke 1999.

Recorded his highest B&H score (32*) and best one-day analysis (5-20) v Sussex at Hove 2000. Retired from county cricket at the end of the 2000 season
Best batting: 127* Yorkshire v Lancashire, Old Trafford 1988
Best bowling: 9-41 Yorkshire v Derbyshire, Chesterfield 1995

First-Class Career Performances

	M	Inn	NO	Runs	HS	Avg	100	Ct	St	Runs	Wkts	Avg	BB	5I	10M
Test															
FC	232	283	66	4321	127*	19.91	2	68	-	20635	683	30.21	9-41	23	3

HOLDER, J. W.

Name: John Wakefield Holder
Born: 19 March 1945, Barbados
Height: 5ft 11in
Nickname: Benson
Wife's name: Glenda
Children: Christopher, 1968; Nigel, 1970
Education: Combermere High School, Barbados; Rochdale College
Other sports followed: Football (Manchester United)
Relaxations: 'Regular visits to the gym trying to keep fit. Love watching wildlife programmes on TV and travel'
Appointed to 1st-Class list: 1983
First appointed to Test panel: 1988
Tests umpired: 11 (plus 5 as TV umpire)
ODIs umpired: 19 (plus 3 as TV umpire)
Other umpiring honours: Umpired in Nehru Cup in India and in Pakistan v India Test series 1989-90. Umpired in Pepsi Champions Trophy, Sharjah 1993-94 and Masters Cup, Sharjah 1995-96. MCC tours to Kenya 1999, 2002 and to Greece 2003 (as umpire). Has stood in Refuge Assurance Cup, B&H Cup and NatWest Trophy finals and in C&G Trophy final 2002. Officiated at the inaugural Twenty20 finals day at Trent Bridge 2003, including standing in the final, and at finals day at The Oval 2005
Highlights of umpiring career: 'Ashes Test at Lord's in 2001'
County as player: Hampshire
Role: Right-hand bat, right-arm fast bowler
County debut: 1968
50 wickets in a season: 1
Highlights of playing career: 'Taking 6-7 against International Cavaliers in 1968'

Extras: Championship hat-trick v Kent at Southampton 1972. Retired from county cricket in 1972
Best batting: 33 Hampshire v Sussex, Hove 1971
Best bowling: 7-79 Hampshire v Gloucestershire, Gloucester 1972

First-Class Career Performances

	M	Inn	NO	Runs	HS	Avg	100	Ct	St	Runs	Wkts	Avg	BB	5I	10M
Test															
FC	47	49	14	374	33	10.68	-	12	-	3415	139	24.56	7-79	5	1

HOLDER, V. A.

Name: Vanburn Alonza Holder
Born: 8 October 1945, St Michael, Barbados
Height: 6ft 3in
Nickname: Vanny
Wife and date of marriage: Chris, 19 July 1980
Children: James, 2 September 1981
Education: St Leonard's Secondary Modern; Community High
Off-season: 'Relaxing'
Other sports followed: Football (Liverpool)
Relaxations: Music, doing crosswords
Appointed to 1st-Class list: 1992
ODIs umpired: 2 as TV umpire
County as player: Worcestershire
Role: Right-hand bat, right-arm fast-medium bowler
County debut: 1968
County cap: 1970
Benefit: 1979
Test debut: 1969
ODI debut (matches): 1973 (12)
50 wickets in a season: 9
One-Day 5 w. in innings: 3
Overseas tours: West Indies to England 1969, 1973, 1975 (World Cup), 1976, to India, Sri Lanka and Pakistan 1974-75, to Australia 1975-76, to India and Sri Lanka 1978-79 (vc); Rest of the World to Pakistan 1973-74
Overseas teams played for: Barbados 1966-78
Extras: Made his debut for Barbados in the Shell Shield competition in 1966-67. Won John Player League 1973 and County Championship 1974 with Worcestershire. Played in West Indies 1975 World Cup winning side

Best batting: 122 Barbados v Trinidad, Bridgetown 1973-74
Best bowling: 7-40 Worcestershire v Glamorgan, Cardiff 1974

First-Class Career Performances

	M	Inn	NO	Runs	HS	Avg	100	Ct	St	Runs	Wkts	Avg	BB	5I	10M
Test	40	59	11	682	42	14.20	-	16	-	3627	109	33.27	6-28	3	-
FC	311	354	81	3559	122	13.03	1	98	-	23183	948	24.45	7-40	38	3

ILLINGWORTH, R. K.

Name: Richard Keith Illingworth
Born: 23 August 1963, Greengates, near Bradford, Yorkshire
Height: 5ft 11in
Nickname: Harry, Lucy, Illy
Wife and date of marriage: Anne Louise, 20 September 1985
Children: Miles, 28 August 1987; Thomas, 20 April 1989
Family links with cricket: Father played Bradford League
Education: Salts GS
Off-season: 'Coaching'
Other sports played: Golf
Other sports followed: Football (Leeds), rugby league (Bradford Bulls), rugby union (Worcester)
Relaxations: 'Watching my two sons playing sport; cooking; wine tasting'
Appointed to 1st-Class list: 2006
Players to watch for the future: Dan Redfern (Derbyshire), Neil Pinner (Worcestershire Academy)
Counties as player: Worcestershire, Derbyshire
Role: Right-hand bat, left-arm orthodox spin bowler
County debut: 1982 (Worcestershire), 2001 (Derbyshire)
County cap: 1986 (Worcestershire)
Benefit: 1997 (Worcestershire)
Test debut: 1991
ODI debut (matches): 1991 (25)
50 wickets in a season: 5
One-Day 5 w. in innings: 2

Overseas tours: England A to Kenya and Zimbabwe 1989-90, to Pakistan and Sri Lanka 1990-91; England to New Zealand and Australia (World Cup) 1991-92, to South Africa 1995-96, to India and Pakistan (World Cup) 1995-96
Overseas teams played for: Brisbane Colts 1982-83; Zingari, Pietermaritzburg, South Africa 1984-85, 1988-89; University/St Heliers, New Zealand 1986-88; Natal 1988-89; Abahani, Bangladesh 1994
Highlights of playing career: 'Playing for England. Being part of many Worcestershire trophy wins. Wicket [Phil Simmons of West Indies] with first ball in Test cricket'
Cricket moments to forget: 'None, apart from getting out for nought or dropping catches (of which there were a few)'
Extras: Scored three centuries batting as a nightwatchman. First Worcestershire bowler to take a one-day hat-trick, v Sussex at Hove in the Sunday League 1993. Retired from county cricket at the end of the 2001 season
Best batting: 120* Worcestershire v Warwickshire, Worcester 1987
Best bowling: 7-50 Worcestershire v Oxford University, The Parks 1985

First-Class Career Performances

	M	Inn	NO	Runs	HS	Avg	100	Ct	St	Runs	Wkts	Avg	BB	5I	10M
Test	9	14	7	128	28	18.28	-	5	-	615	19	32.36	4-96	-	-
FC	376	435	122	7027	120*	22.45	4	161	-	26213	831	31.54	7-50	27	6

JESTY, T. E.

Name: Trevor Edward Jesty
Born: 2 June 1948, Gosport, Hampshire
Height: 5ft 9in
Nickname: Jets
Wife and date of marriage: Jacqueline, 12 September 1970
Children: Graeme Barry, 27 September 1972; Lorna Samantha, 7 November 1976
Family links with cricket: Daughter played for England XI 2000
Education: Privett County Secondary Modern, Gosport
Other sports followed: Football (Arsenal)
Relaxations: Gardening, reading
Appointed to 1st-Class list: 1994
ODIs umpired: 3 as TV umpire
Counties as player: Hampshire, Surrey, Lancashire
Role: Right-hand bat, right-arm medium bowler

County debut: 1966 (Hampshire), 1985 (Surrey), 1988 (Lancashire)
County cap: 1971 (Hampshire), 1985 (Surrey), 1990 (Lancashire)
Benefit: 1982 (Hampshire)
ODI debut (matches): 1982-83 (10)
1000 runs in a season: 10
50 wickets in a season: 2
1st-Class 200s: 2
One-Day 100s: 7
Overseas tours: International XI to West Indies 1982; joined England tour to Australia 1982-83; Lancashire to Zimbabwe 1989
Overseas teams played for: Border, South Africa 1973-74; Griqualand West 1974-76, 1980-81; Canterbury, New Zealand 1979-80
Highlights of playing career: 'Winning Championship with Hampshire in 1973. Playing against Australia for England in one-day match on 1982-83 tour'
Extras: One of *Wisden*'s Five Cricketers of the Year 1983
Best batting: 248 Hampshire v Cambridge University, Fenner's 1984
Best bowling: 7-75 Hampshire v Worcestershire, Southampton 1976

First-Class Career Performances

	M	Inn	NO	Runs	HS	Avg	100	Ct	St	Runs	Wkts	Avg	BB	5I	10M
Test															
FC	490	777	107	21916	248	32.71	35	265	1	16075	585	27.47	7-75	19	-

JONES, A. A.

Name: Allan Arthur Jones
Born: 9 December 1947, Three Bridges, Sussex
Height: 6ft 3in
Nickname: Jonah
Wife and date of marriage: Stephanie, 11 December 2004
Children: Clare, 4 July 1979
Education: St John's College, Horsham
Career outside cricket: 'Selling golf holidays and villas in Spain'
Off-season: 'Enjoying life'
Other sports played: Golf
Other sports followed: Football (Arsenal)
Relaxations: 'Reading, visiting castles etc.'
Appointed to 1st-Class list: 1985
First appointed to Test panel: 1996
Tests umpired: 3 as TV umpire
ODIs umpired: 1 (plus 4 as TV umpire)
Other umpiring honours: Has umpired at Hong Kong Sixes. Stood in the C&G final 2005 at Lord's; also at Twenty20 finals day 2006 at Trent Bridge, including in the final. Former chairman of the First-Class Umpires' Association
Highlights of umpiring career: 'C&G final 2005'
Counties as player: Sussex, Somerset, Middlesex, Glamorgan
Role: Right-hand bat, right-arm fast bowler
County debut: 1964 (Sussex), 1970 (Somerset), 1976 (Middlesex), 1980 (Glamorgan)
County cap: 1972 (Somerset), 1976 (Middlesex)
50 wickets in a season: 4
One-Day 5 w. in innings: 5
Overseas teams played for: Northern Transvaal 1971-72; Orange Free State 1976-77
Highlights of playing career: '9-51 v Sussex 1972'
Cricket moments to forget: 'Being hit by Norman McVicker of Leicestershire for two sixes off last two balls of the match to lose the game'
Extras: Won two Championship medals with Middlesex (1976 and 1977). Was on stand-by for England tour of India 1976-77. Represented MCC v Australians 1977. Was the first person to play for four counties
Opinions on cricket: 'Too many technicalities used for bowling, instead of teaching basics.'
Best batting: 33 Middlesex v Kent, Canterbury 1978
Best bowling: 9-51 Somerset v Sussex, Hove 1972

First-Class Career Performances

	M	Inn	NO	Runs	HS	Avg	100	Ct	St	Runs	Wkts	Avg	BB	5I	10M
Test															
FC	214	216	68	799	33	5.39	-	50	-	15414	549	28.07	9-51	23	3

KETTLEBOROUGH, R. A.

Name: Richard Allan Kettleborough
Born: 15 March 1973, Sheffield
Height: 5ft 10in
Nickname: Ketts
Wife and date of marriage: Lucy, 6 October 2007
Family links with cricket: 'Dad played league cricket'
Education: Worksop College; Airedale and Wharfdale College
Career outside cricket: Groundsman
Off-season: 'Sorting out the wedding and working on the new house'
Other sports played: Football
Other sports followed: Football (Sheffield Wednesday FC)
Relaxations: 'Socialising with friends and walking the dogs'
Appointed to 1st-Class list: 2006
Other umpiring honours: Stood in the International 20:20 Club Championship 2005
Highlights of umpiring career: 'Above, and all the first-class matches in which I have stood'
Players to watch for the future: Adil Rashid, Stuart Broad
Counties as player: Yorkshire, Middlesex
Role: Left-hand bat
County debut: 1994 (Yorkshire), 1998 (Middlesex)
Overseas tours: England U18 to Canada 1991; Yorkshire to South Africa 1994, to Zimbabwe 1995, to West Indies 1996; MCC to Hong Kong 2000, to Kenya 2001, to Australia 2002-03, to UAE 2004, to Namibia and Uganda 2005, to India 2006
Overseas teams played for: Somerset West, Cape Town 1993-94; Constantia, Cape Town 2003
Highlights of playing career: 'Yorkshire debut 1994. Maiden first-class hundred v Essex 1996. Winning National Club Knockout with Sheffield Collegiate 2000'
Cricket moments to forget: '1998 and 1999 in London'

Extras: MCC Young Cricketer of the Year 1988. Yorkshire Young Player of the Year 1996
Opinions on cricket: 'Reduce the number of non-English-qualified players in county cricket.'
Best batting: 108 Yorkshire v Essex, Headingley 1996
Best bowling: 2-26 Yorkshire v Nottinghamshire, Scarborough 1996

First-Class Career Performances

	M	Inn	NO	Runs	HS	Avg	100	Ct	St	Runs	Wkts	Avg	BB	5I	10M
Test															
FC	33	56	6	1258	108	25.16	1	20	-	243	3	81.00	2-26	-	-

LEADBEATER, B.

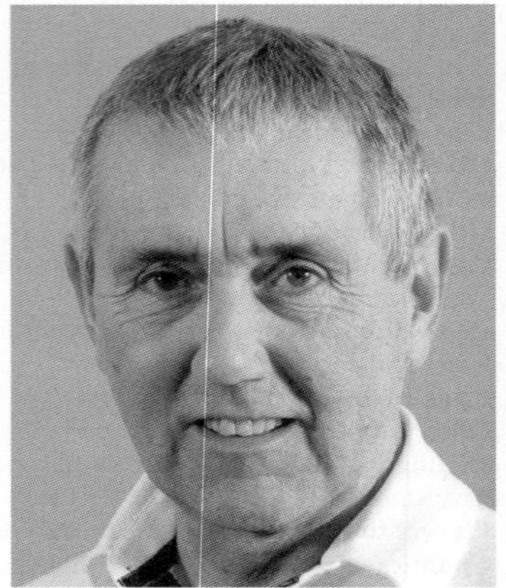

Name: Barrie Leadbeater
Born: 14 August 1943, Leeds
Height: 6ft
Nickname: Leady
Wife and date of marriage: Penny, 8 April 2006
Children: Richard Barrie, 23 November 1972; Michael Spencer, 21 March 1976; Daniel Mark Ronnie, 19 June 1981
Family links with cricket: 'My father played works cricket'
Education: Harehills County Secondary, Leeds
Career outside cricket: HGV Class 1 driver
Off-season: 'Nothing'
Other sports played: Golf, snooker, darts, table tennis
Other sports followed: Rugby league (Leeds Rhinos), football (Leeds United)
Relaxations: 'Reading, going to the pub, running and gym'
Appointed to 1st-Class list: 1981
Tests umpired: 2 as TV umpire
ODIs umpired: 5 (plus 2 as TV umpire)
Other umpiring honours: Stood in 1983 World Cup. Four A tours with MCC. Has stood in several domestic semi-finals. Former chairman of the First-Class Umpires' Association
Highlights of umpiring career: 'Every game'
County as player: Yorkshire
Role: Right-hand bat, right-arm medium bowler, slip fielder

County debut: 1966
County cap: 1969
Benefit: 1980 (joint benefit with G.A. Cope)
Overseas tours: Duke of Norfolk's XI to West Indies 1969-70
Overseas teams played for: Johannesburg Municipals 1978-79
Highlights of playing career: 'Man of the Match, Gillette Cup final 1969 v Derbyshire. Overseas tour (above)'
Cricket moments to forget: 'I've forgotten'
Extras: Took part in London Marathon 1997, 1998, 2000. Retired from county cricket in 1979 and played social cricket
Opinions on cricket: 'Pleased to see the governing body is at last reducing the number of overseas players, which should give young home-grown players more of a chance, and improve England.'
Best batting: 140* Yorkshire v Hampshire, Portsmouth 1976
Best bowling: 1-1 Yorkshire v Middlesex, Headingley 1971

First-Class Career Performances

	M	Inn	NO	Runs	HS	Avg	100	Ct	St	Runs	Wkts	Avg	BB	5I	10M
Test															
FC	147	241	29	5373	140*	25.34	1	82	-	5	1	5.00	1-1	-	-

LLONG, N. J.

Name: Nigel James Llong
Born: 11 February 1969, Ashford, Kent
Height: 6ft
Nickname: Nidge
Wife and date of marriage: Melissa, 20 February 1999
Children: Andrew Stuart, 30 August 2002; Matthew James, 14 December 2004
Family links with cricket: Father and brother played local club cricket
Education: North School for Boys, Ashford
Off-season: Coaching – Duke of York School, Dover
Other sports followed: Football (Arsenal), 'generally most sports'
Relaxations: Fishing
Appointed to 1st-Class list: 2002
International panel: 2004-2006 as TV umpire; 2006 –
Tests umpired: 2 (plus 9 as TV umpire)

ODIs umpired: 13 (plus 14 as TV umpire)
Twenty20 Ints umpired: 10 (plus 3 as TV umpire)
Other umpiring honours: Officiated at Twenty20 finals days at Edgbaston 2004, including standing in the final, and 2007. Stood in his first Test match in January 2008 – the first Test between New Zealand and Bangladesh at Dunedin
Highlights of umpiring career: 'Umpired at Twenty20 World Championship, South Africa 2007-08'
County as player: Kent
Role: Left-hand bat, right-arm off-spin bowler
County debut: 1991
County cap: 1993
One-Day 100s: 2
Overseas tours: Kent to Zimbabwe 1993
Overseas teams played for: Ashburton, Melbourne 1988-90, 1996-97; Green Point, Cape Town 1990-95
Highlights of playing career: 'B&H final 1997. Sunday League winners 1995. First Championship hundred, Lord's 1993'
Cricket moments to forget: 'Sunday League [1993], last match against Glamorgan at Canterbury – lost the match and were runners-up. Plus not making the most of my ability'
Extras: Kent Young Player of the Year 1992. Man of the Match in 2nd XI Trophy semi-final and final 1999. Retired from county cricket in September 1999 and played for Norfolk in 2000
Opinions on cricket: 'Umpires watch every ball of a game. It's amazing how little their opinions are valued!'
Best batting: 130 Kent v Hampshire, Canterbury 1996
Best bowling: 5-21 Kent v Middlesex, Canterbury 1996

First-Class Career Performances

	M	Inn	NO	Runs	HS	Avg	100	Ct	St	Runs	Wkts	Avg	BB	5I	10M
Test															
FC	68	108	11	3024	130	31.17	6	59	-	1259	35	35.97	5-21	2	-

LLOYDS, J. W.

Name: Jeremy William Lloyds
Born: 17 November 1954, Penang, Malaya
Height: 5ft 11in
Nickname: Jerry
Wife and date of marriage: Janine, 16 September 1997
Children: Kaeli, 16 November 1991
Family links with cricket: Father played cricket in Malaya. Brother Chris played for Somerset 2nd XI
Education: Blundell's School, Tiverton
Career outside cricket: Coaching and setting up Western Province Youth Programme 1992-95 in South Africa
Off-season: 'Getting a job'
Other sports played: Golf (6 handicap)
Other sports followed: Golf, football (Tottenham Hotspur), American football (San Francisco 49ers), Formula One and saloon car racing, rugby (Gloucester)
Relaxations: 'Reading, music and spending time at home with my family'
Appointed to 1st-Class list: 1998
International panel: 2002-2004 as TV umpire; 2004-2006
Tests umpired: 5 (plus 10 as TV umpire)
ODIs umpired: 18 (plus 22 as TV umpire)
Twenty20 Ints umpired: 1
Other umpiring honours: Stood in the C&G final 2006. Officiated at Twenty20 finals day at Edgbaston 2007
Counties as player: Somerset, Gloucestershire
Role: Left-hand bat, off-spin bowler
County debut: 1979 (Somerset), 1985 (Gloucestershire)
County cap: 1982 (Somerset), 1985 (Gloucestershire)
1000 runs in a season: 3
Overseas tours: Somerset to Antigua 1982; Gloucestershire to Barbados 1985, to Sri Lanka 1987
Overseas teams played for: St Stithian's Old Boys, Johannesburg 1978-79; Toombull DCC, Brisbane 1980-82; North Sydney District 1982-83; Alberton, Johannesburg 1984; Preston CC, Melbourne 1986; Orange Free State 1987; Fish Hoek CC, Cape Town 1988-92
Highlights of playing career: 'Winning 1983 NatWest final'
Extras: Highest score in Brisbane Premier League 1980-81 (165). Britannic Player of the Month July 1987. Gloucestershire Player of the Year 1987. Leading run-scorer in Western Province Cricket League 1988, 1989

Opinions on cricket: 'Would take too long. I would suggest that by having central contracts we are creating elitism. Batsmen must be allowed to bat and bowlers to bowl whenever possible. Net bowling/batting is never quite the same.'
Best batting: 132* Somerset v Northamptonshire, Northampton 1982
Best bowling: 7-88 Somerset v Essex, Chelmsford 1982

First-Class Career Performances

	M	Inn	NO	Runs	HS	Avg	100	Ct	St	Runs	Wkts	Avg	BB	5I	10M
Test															
FC	267	408	64	10679	132*	31.04	10	229	-	12943	333	38.86	7-88	13	1

MALLENDER, N. A.

Name: Neil Alan Mallender
Born: 13 August 1961, Kirk Sandall, Doncaster
Height: 6ft
Nickname: Ghostie
Marital status: Divorced
Children: Kirstie, 19; Dominic, 16; Jacob, 11
Education: Beverley Grammar School
Off-season: 'Trying to keep fit'
Other sports played: Golf (2 handicap)
Other sports followed: 'Most sports'
Relaxations: 'Watching sport; music'
Appointed to 1st-Class list: 1999
International panel: 2002-2004
Tests umpired: 3 (plus 5 as TV umpire)
ODIs umpired: 22 (plus 10 as TV umpire)
Other umpiring honours: Went with MCC to umpire in Namibia March/April 2001. PCA Umpire of the Year 2001, 2002, 2003, 2004, 2006. Stood in the 2002-03 World Cup. Umpired the 2004, 2005 and 2006 C&G Trophy finals. Officiated at Twenty20 finals day at Edgbaston 2007, including standing in the final
Highlights of umpiring career: 'First ODI at Lord's, England v Pakistan – and game went to the last ball'
Players to watch for the future: Steve Finn, Chris Jordan
Counties as player: Northamptonshire, Somerset
Role: Right-hand bat, right-arm fast-medium bowler
County debut: 1980 (Northamptonshire), 1987 (Somerset)
County cap: 1984 (Northamptonshire), 1987 (Somerset)
Benefit: 1994 (Somerset)
Test debut: 1992

50 wickets in a season: 6
One-Day 5 w. in innings: 3
Overseas tours: England YC to West Indies 1979-80
Overseas teams played for: Kaikorai, Dunedin, New Zealand; University, Wellington, New Zealand; Otago, New Zealand 1983-84 – 1992-93
Highlights of playing career: 'Test debut at Headingley'
Extras: Represented England YC 1980-81. Took 5-50 on Test debut v Pakistan at Headingley in 1992. Retired from county cricket in 1996
Best batting: 100* Otago v Central Districts, Palmerston North 1991-92
Best bowling: 7-27 Otago v Auckland, Auckland 1984-85

First-Class Career Performances

	M	Inn	NO	Runs	HS	Avg	100	Ct	St	Runs	Wkts	Avg	BB	5I	10M
Test	2	3	0	8	4	2.66	-	-	-	215	10	21.50	5-50	1	-
FC	345	396	122	4709	100*	17.18	1	111	-	24654	937	26.31	7-27	36	5

ROBINSON, R. T.

Name: Robert Timothy (Tim) Robinson
Born: 21 November 1958, Sutton-in-Ashfield, Nottinghamshire
Height: 6ft
Nickname: Robbo
Marital status: Divorced
Children: Philip; Alex
Family links with cricket: 'Father, uncles all played local cricket'
Education: Dunstable GS; High Pavement GS; Sheffield University
Career outside cricket: 'Accountancy. Sports promotions'
Off-season: 'Self-employed, doing above'
Other sports played: Golf, squash
Other sports followed: Golf, rugby, football
Appointed to 1st-Class list: 2007
County as player: Nottinghamshire
Role: Right-hand opening bat
County debut: 1978
County cap: 1983
Benefit: 1992
Test debut: 1984-85
ODI debut (matches): 1984-85 (26)
1000 runs in a season: 14

1st-Class 200s: 3
One-Day 100s: 9
Overseas tours: England to India and Sri Lanka 1984-85, to West Indies 1985-86, to India and Pakistan (World Cup) 1987-88, to Pakistan 1987-88, to New Zealand and Australia 1987-88, plus two one-day tournaments in Sharjah; unofficial England XI to South Africa 1989-90
Highlights of playing career: '175 v Aussie, home Test debut 1985' (*In the first Test at Headingley*)
Cricket moments to forget: 'Retiring from first-class cricket'
Extras: One of *Wisden*'s Five Cricketers of the Year 1986. Second in the list of Nottinghamshire first-class run-scorers behind George Gunn. Captain of Nottinghamshire 1988-95. Retired from county cricket at the end of the 1999 season
Opinions on cricket: 'Should become more spectator-orientated.'
Best batting: 220* Nottinghamshire v Yorkshire, Trent Bridge 1990
Best bowling: 1-22 Nottinghamshire v Northamptonshire, Northampton 1982

First-Class Career Performances

	M	Inn	NO	Runs	HS	Avg	100	Ct	St	Runs	Wkts	Avg	BB	5I	10M
Test	29	49	5	1601	175	36.38	4	8	-	0	0		-	-	-
FC	425	739	85	27571	220*	42.15	63	257	-	289	4	72.25	1-22	-	-

SHARP, G.

Name: George Sharp
Born: 12 March 1950, West Hartlepool, County Durham
Height: 5ft 11in
Nickname: Sharpy
Wife and date of marriage: Audrey, 14 September 1974
Children: Gareth James, 27 June 1984
Education: Elwick Road Secondary Modern, Hartlepool
Career outside cricket: Watching all sports
Off-season: Working as joint director of GSB Loams Ltd for soils and top dressing
Other sports played: Golf (8 handicap)
Other sports followed: Football (Newcastle Utd and Middlesbrough), rugby (Northampton Saints)
Relaxations: Golf; 'spend a lot of time in the gym during the off-season'
Appointed to 1st-Class list: 1992

International panel: 1996-2002
Tests umpired: 15 (plus 1 as TV umpire)
ODIs umpired: 31 (plus 13 as TV umpire)
Other umpiring honours: Has umpired three B&H finals and one NatWest final and stood in the inaugural C&G final 2001 and the 2002 final; also officiated at the inaugural Twenty20 finals day at Trent Bridge 2003, at finals day 2005 at The Oval and at finals day 2006 at Trent Bridge. Has stood in four overseas tournaments, including the Singer Cup (India, Sri Lanka, Pakistan) in Singapore 1995-96 and the Singer Champions Trophy (Pakistan, Sri Lanka, New Zealand) in Sharjah 1996-97
County as player: Northamptonshire
Role: Right-hand bat, wicket-keeper
County debut: 1967
County cap: 1973
Benefit: 1982
Overseas tours: England Counties XI to Barbados and Trinidad 1975
Best batting: 98 Northamptonshire v Yorkshire, Northampton 1983
Best bowling: 1-47 Northamptonshire v Yorkshire, Northampton 1980

First-Class Career Performances

	M	Inn	NO	Runs	HS	Avg	100	Ct	St	Runs	Wkts	Avg	BB	5I	10M
Test															
FC	306	396	81	6254	98	19.85	-	565	90	70	1	70.00	1-47	-	-

STEELE, J. F.

Name: John Frederick Steele
Born: 23 July 1946, Stafford
Height: 5ft 10in
Nickname: Steely
Wife and date of marriage: Susan, 17 April 1977
Children: Sarah Jane, 2 April 1982; Robert Alfred, 10 April 1985
Family links with cricket: Uncle Stan played for Staffordshire. Brother David played for Northamptonshire, Derbyshire and England. Cousin Brian Crump played for Northamptonshire and Staffordshire
Education: Endon School, Stoke-on-Trent; Stafford College
Other sports followed: Football (Stoke City, Port Vale), golf
Relaxations: Music and walking

Appointed to 1st-Class list: 1997
Counties as player: Leicestershire, Glamorgan
Role: Right-hand bat, slow left-arm bowler
County debut: 1970 (Leicestershire), 1984 (Glamorgan)
County cap: 1971 (Leicestershire), 1984 (Glamorgan)
Benefit: 1983 (Leicestershire)
1000 runs in a season: 6
One-Day 100s: 1
One-Day 5 w. in innings: 4
Overseas teams played for: Springs HSOB, Northern Transvaal 1971-73; Pine Town CC, Natal 1973-74, 1982-83; Natal 1975-76, 1978-79
Extras: Played for England U25. Was voted Natal's Best Bowler in 1975-76. First-wicket record partnership for Leicestershire of 390 with Barry Dudleston v Derbyshire at Leicester 1979. Won two Man of the Match Awards in the Gillette Cup and four in the Benson and Hedges Cup. Won the award for the most catches in a season in 1984
Best batting: 195 Leicestershire v Derbyshire, Leicester 1971
Best bowling: 7-29 Natal B v Griqualand West, Umzinto 1973-74
7-29 Leicestershire v Gloucestershire, Leicester 1980

First-Class Career Performances

	M	Inn	NO	Runs	HS	Avg	100	Ct	St	Runs	Wkts	Avg	BB	5I	10M
Test															
FC	379	605	85	15053	195	28.94	21	414	-	15793	584	27.04	7-29	16	-

WILLEY, P.

Name: Peter Willey
Born: 6 December 1949, Sedgefield, County Durham
Height: 6ft 1in
Nickname: Will, 'many unprintable'
Wife and date of marriage: Charmaine, 23 September 1971
Children: Heather Jane, 11 September 1985; David, 28 February 1990
Family links with cricket: Father played local club cricket in County Durham
Education: Seaham Secondary School, County Durham
Other sports followed: All sports
Relaxations: 'Dog-walking, keeping fit (??), fishing'
Appointed to 1st-Class list: 1993
International panel: 1996-2003
Tests umpired: 25 (plus 7 as TV umpire)
ODIs umpired: 34 (plus 16 as TV umpire)
Other umpiring honours: Stood in the 1999 and 2002-03 World Cups, in the 1999 Benson and Hedges Super Cup final and in the 2004 C&G Trophy final. Officiated at Twenty20 finals days at The Oval 2005 and Edgbaston 2007, including standing in

both finals. Chairman of the First-Class Umpires' Association
Counties as player: Northamptonshire, Leicestershire
Role: Right-hand bat, off-break bowler
County debut: 1966 (Northamptonshire), 1984 (Leicestershire)
County cap: 1971 (Northamptonshire), 1984 (Leicestershire)
Benefit: 1981 (Northamptonshire)
Test debut: 1976
ODI debut (matches): 1977 (26)
1000 runs in a season: 10
50 wickets in a season: 2
1st-Class 200s: 1
One-Day 100s: 9
Overseas tours: England to Australia and India 1979-80, to West Indies 1980-81, 1985-86; unofficial England XI to South Africa 1981-82
Overseas teams played for: Eastern Province, South Africa 1982-85
Cricket moments to forget: 'First ball in first-class cricket (v Cambridge University), bowled – thought it can only get better'
Extras: Became youngest player ever to play for Northamptonshire, at 16 years 180 days, v Cambridge University in 1966. Leicestershire captain 1987. Played for Northumberland in 1992. Offered membership of the ICC Elite Panel of umpires in 2002 but declined because of the amount of time the appointment would require away from his family
Opinions on cricket: 'Too much "robot" coaching from nine-year-olds to county standard. Players don't seem to be allowed individual batting styles or bowling actions. Bowling actions changed in case of injury. Too much time spent looking at video analysis and training instead of more time spent in nets. Seems bowling length and line (Pollock, McGrath) is a thing of the past.'
Best batting: 227 Northamptonshire v Somerset, Northampton 1976
Best bowling: 7-37 Northamptonshire v Oxford University, The Parks 1975

First-Class Career Performances

	M	Inn	NO	Runs	HS	Avg	100	Ct	St	Runs	Wkts	Avg	BB	5I	10M
Test	26	50	6	1184	102*	26.90	2	3	-	456	7	65.14	2-73	-	-
FC	559	918	121	24361	227	30.56	44	235	-	23400	756	30.95	7-37	26	3

APPENDICES

Roll of Honour 2007
First-class Averages 2007
Index of Players by County

ROLL OF HONOUR 2007

LV COUNTY CHAMPIONSHIP

Division One

		P	W	L	D	T	Bt	Bl	Pts
1	Sussex (I/1)	16	7	3	6	0	37	43	202
2	Durham (I/7)	16	7	5	4	0	38	47	197.5
3	Lancashire (I/2)	16	5	2	9	0	40	44	190
4	Surrey (II/1)	16	5	4	7	0	41	40	178
5	Hampshire (I/3)	16	5	3	8	0	32	43	177
6	Yorkshire (I/6)	16	4	4	8	0	49	38	175
7	Kent (I/5)	16	3	5	8	0	43	36	153
8	Warwickshire (I/4)	16	2	5	9	0	40	35	139
9	Worcestershire (II/2)	16	1	8	7	0	18	35	95

The bottom two counties were relegated to Division Two for the 2008 season. Positions in 2006 in brackets.

Division Two

		P	W	L	D	T	Bt	Bl	Pts
1	Somerset (II/9)	16	10	1	5	0	65	41	266
2	Nottinghamshire (I/8)	16	6	3	7	0	60	43	214.5
3	Middlesex (I/9)	16	6	2	8	0	35	43	192.5
4	Essex (II/3)	16	6	4	6	0	40	36	182
5	Northamptonshire (II/6)	16	5	5	6	0	44	38	176
6	Derbyshire (II/5)	16	3	5	8	0	30	44	147
7	Gloucestershire (II/7)	16	3	5	8	0	32	37	139.5
8	Leicestershire (II/4)	16	2	8	6	0	32	35	115
9	Glamorgan (II/8)	16	1	9	6	0	26	37	92.5

The top two counties were promoted to Division One for the 2008 season. Positions in 2006 in brackets.

The following sides incurred points deductions for slow over rates in 2007: Durham 1.5, Surrey 1, Derbyshire 1, Essex 2, Glamorgan 0.5, Gloucestershire 3.5, Leicestershire 4, Middlesex 1.5, Nottinghamshire 0.5. Glamorgan also incurred an 8-point deduction for a sub-standard pitch for their match v Middlesex, 23 May 2007.

NATWEST PRO40 LEAGUE

Division One

		P	W	L	NR	T	Pts
1	Worcestershire (II/2)	8	6	1	0	1	13
2	Nottinghamshire (I/4)	8	4	2	0	2	10
3	Lancashire (I/6)	8	3	1	0	4	10
4	Hampshire (II/3)	8	4	3	0	1	9
5	Sussex (I/3)	8	3	3	0	2	8
6	Gloucestershire (II/1)	8	2	4	0	2	6
7	Northamptonshire (I/2)	8	2	4	1	1	6
8	Warwickshire (I/5)	8	2	5	0	1	5
9	Essex (I/1)	8	1	4	1	2	5

Worcestershire were champions and the bottom three counties were relegated to Division Two for the 2008 season, Northamptonshire (I/7) after a play-off with Middlesex (II/3). Positions in 2006 in brackets.

Division Two

		P	W	L	NR	T	Pts
1	Durham (I/8)	8	6	2	0	0	12
2	Somerset (II/7)	8	5	2	0	1	11
3	Middlesex (I/9)	8	5	3	0	0	10
4	Surrey (II/4)	8	5	3	0	0	10
5	Kent (II/5)	8	5	3	0	0	10
6	Yorkshire (II/9)	8	4	3	0	1	9
7	Leicestershire (II/6)	8	3	4	0	1	7
8	Derbyshire (II/8)	8	1	7	0	0	2
9	Glamorgan (I/7)	8	0	7	0	1	1

The top three counties (see note above) were promoted to Division One for the 2008 season. Positions in 2006 in brackets.

FRIENDS PROVIDENT TROPHY

Winners: Durham **Runners-up:** Hampshire

TWENTY20 CUP

Winners: Kent **Runners-up:** Gloucestershire
Semi-finalists: Lancashire, Sussex

2007 AVERAGES (all first-class matches)

BATTING AVERAGES

Qualifying requirements: 6 completed innings and an average of over 10.00

	Name	*M*	*Inn*	*NO*	*Runs*	*HS*	*Avg*	*100*	*50*
1	MR Ramprakash	15	25	5	2026	266 *	101.30	10	4
2	DJ Hussey	13	17	2	1259	275	83.93	4	5
3	SM Katich	13	23	6	1284	221	75.52	3	8
4	S Chanderpaul	7	12	3	670	136 *	74.44	2	5
5	CL White	12	19	4	1083	241	72.20	5	3
6	OA Shah	13	22	6	1135	193	70.93	4	2
7	MJ DiVenuto	13	25	5	1329	204 *	66.45	3	9
8	SG Law	14	22	2	1277	206	63.85	3	9
9	KP Pietersen	7	13	0	811	226	62.38	4	1
10	ME Trescothick	16	24	2	1343	284	61.04	4	5
11	DC Nash	7	10	3	426	103 *	60.85	3	0
12	AJ Bichel	8	12	4	482	148	60.25	2	2
13	RS Bopara	12	18	2	960	229	60.00	3	4
14	SP Fleming	11	17	1	930	243	58.12	4	2
15	ET Smith	17	25	4	1219	149 *	58.04	5	4
16	SR Tendulkar	4	7	0	399	171	57.00	1	2
17	RWT Key	15	25	3	1250	182	56.81	5	4
18	JA Rudolph	15	22	3	1078	220	56.73	4	3
19	MJ North	5	10	0	565	109	56.50	3	2
20	JL Langer	16	23	1	1231	315	55.95	3	3
21	DM Benkenstein	16	28	5	1278	117	55.56	3	8
22	DJG Sales	16	29	4	1384	219	55.36	3	7
23	MW Goodwin	15	27	5	1214	205 *	55.18	4	5
24	AN Cook	11	20	0	1094	142	54.70	5	3
25	MA Wagh	17	26	2	1310	152	54.58	3	11
26	JC Hildreth	17	26	2	1270	163	52.91	4	6
27	CMW Read	17	23	4	1001	240	52.68	2	4
28	PD Trego	17	22	6	836	130	52.25	2	5
29	LJ Evans	4	8	1	365	133 *	52.14	1	2
30	MJ Powell (Gm)	6	10	2	407	114	50.87	1	4
31	MA Carberry	13	24	3	1067	192 *	50.80	5	3
32	SR Patel	14	20	1	963	176	50.68	4	5
33	KC Sangakkara	7	11	1	496	149	49.60	2	2
34	LJ Wright	11	13	6	347	61	49.57	0	3
35	RS Dravid	5	10	4	295	67 *	49.16	0	3
36	PA Nixon	13	21	3	879	126	48.83	2	5
37	PJ Horton	14	25	2	1116	152	48.52	3	5

	Name	M	Inn	NO	Runs	HS	Avg	100	50
38	TT Bresnan	16	21	7	679	126 *	48.50	3	2
39	Younus Khan	13	19	2	824	217 *	48.47	3	0
40	L Klusener	16	26	5	1013	122	48.23	2	5
41	NJ Edwards	17	26	0	1251	212	48.11	2	8
42	N Pothas	15	23	7	750	126 *	46.87	1	5
43	DL Maddy	14	20	3	796	148 *	46.82	4	2
44	CJ Adams	15	24	2	1030	193	46.81	3	3
45	A McGrath	14	22	2	931	188 *	46.55	3	6
46	M van Jaarsveld	15	23	1	1011	166	45.95	5	3
47	GR Napier	10	10	3	317	125	45.28	1	1
48	MP Vaughan	12	19	2	758	124	44.58	2	3
49	VVS Laxman	11	18	2	713	103	44.56	2	5
50	AU Rashid	17	23	4	837	108	44.05	1	7
51	JN Batty	15	25	3	965	154 *	43.86	4	3
52	PD Collingwood	8	15	1	614	128	43.85	2	3
53	SC Ganguly	4	7	1	263	79	43.83	0	2
54	NJ Dexter	8	10	2	350	86	43.75	0	3
55	RS Morton	5	8	0	347	201	43.37	1	1
56	DKH Mitchell	5	8	2	260	112	43.33	1	1
57	MJ Brown	16	29	4	1078	126 *	43.12	3	5
58	TR Ambrose	16	23	3	862	251 *	43.10	1	4
59	JO Troughton	14	19	1	771	162	42.83	3	1
60	GA Hick	15	24	1	963	110	41.86	2	6
61	N Boje	4	7	1	251	125	41.83	1	1
62	MTG Elliott	4	6	0	251	95	41.83	0	2
63	JL Denly	16	27	3	1003	115 *	41.79	2	6
64	DJ Bravo	4	7	0	291	56	41.57	0	2
65	HJH Marshall	13	21	1	817	123	40.85	3	3
66	GW Flower	11	16	1	611	203	40.73	2	1
67	MJ Walker	12	18	0	733	157	40.72	3	2
68	JHK Adams	11	20	1	773	110	40.68	1	5
69	CM Spearman	11	17	0	688	110	40.47	2	3
70	RN ten Doeschate	16	23	2	849	148	40.42	3	3
71	RR Montgomerie	17	29	1	1129	195	40.32	2	7
72	APR Gidman	17	29	4	1003	130	40.12	3	5
73	MA Butcher	14	21	2	752	179	39.57	2	2
74	TT Samaraweera	4	7	0	277	79	39.57	0	2
75	JP Crawley	15	27	5	866	113 *	39.36	1	6
76	AJ Hodd	14	21	5	628	123	39.25	2	2
77	ID Blackwell	15	19	2	667	141	39.23	1	5
78	EC Joyce	14	20	2	704	106	39.11	1	4
79	CG Taylor	15	23	4	733	112 *	38.57	3	2
80	IJ Westwood	14	22	2	771	116	38.55	2	5
81	MH Yardy	13	21	2	732	125	38.52	2	5

	Name	M	Inn	NO	Runs	HS	Avg	100	50
82	TR Birt	13	24	1	884	162	38.43	2	5
83	BL Hutton	4	7	1	230	118	38.33	1	0
84	B-A Godleman	15	24	2	842	113 *	38.27	1	6
85	KJ Coetzer	14	26	3	880	153 *	38.26	2	2
86	MDK Perera	4	8	2	229	57	38.16	0	1
87	IR Bell	9	14	1	491	109 *	37.76	1	4
88	JER Gallian	17	25	0	940	178	37.60	2	4
89	JS Foster	15	23	1	827	204	37.59	1	5
90	KD Karthik	6	12	0	448	91	37.33	0	5
91	RA White	13	22	3	709	108	37.31	1	3
92	DI Stevens	11	17	0	628	174	36.94	2	2
93	GP Hodnett	15	25	1	886	168	36.91	2	6
94	TJ New	16	29	3	957	125	36.80	1	8
95	SC Moore	15	25	1	882	143	36.75	2	3
96	LD Sutton	15	19	3	587	111	36.68	2	1
97	AP Davies	7	12	6	220	54	36.66	0	1
98	DJ Pipe	14	21	5	577	133 *	36.06	2	1
99	U Afzaal	8	16	0	570	73	35.62	0	5
100	MB Loye	8	14	2	427	105 *	35.58	1	1
101	BJM Scott	11	14	3	389	112	35.36	1	2
102	WI Jefferson	5	9	0	316	73	35.11	0	1
103	DA Mascarenhas	10	16	2	489	90	34.92	0	3
104	GO Jones	15	21	3	623	106 *	34.61	2	3
105	SD Peters	16	30	2	966	112	34.50	3	4
106	SM Ervine	7	10	2	276	103 *	34.50	1	1
107	DL Hemp	15	25	1	827	152 *	34.45	1	5
108	J Allenby	16	26	4	755	93	34.31	0	5
109	AGR Loudon	16	24	1	782	105	34.00	3	2
110	JJ Sayers	14	22	3	644	187	33.89	3	1
111	JN Gillespie	12	13	5	270	123 *	33.75	1	0
112	DJ Birch	4	7	0	236	130	33.71	1	1
113	AR Crook	5	9	1	269	72	33.62	0	2
114	MS Dhoni	6	10	1	302	92	33.55	0	3
115	Kadeer Ali	16	28	1	903	140	33.44	2	4
116	AGB Wharf	15	26	4	726	128 *	33.00	3	1
117	GL Brophy	13	19	1	593	100 *	32.94	1	2
118	AJ Strauss	15	27	0	886	120	32.81	1	6
119	MJ Prior	11	19	2	555	126 *	32.64	1	2
120	RSC Martin-Jenkins	15	22	6	521	99	32.56	0	2
121	SA Newman	15	25	0	812	124	32.48	1	5
122	EJG Morgan	5	7	0	227	76	32.42	0	3
123	JD Middlebrook	17	24	6	583	127	32.38	1	3
124	GP Swann	16	20	4	516	97	32.25	0	3
125	D Ramdin	5	8	0	258	131	32.25	1	1

	Name	M	Inn	NO	Runs	HS	Avg	100	50
126	BJ Hodge	8	13	2	354	156 *	32.18	1	0
127	MG Dighton	7	14	1	418	68	32.15	0	2
128	PS Jones	13	12	4	255	114	31.87	1	1
129	T Westley	6	9	2	223	72	31.85	0	1
130	PA Jaques	10	17	0	541	124	31.82	2	1
131	VS Solanki	13	21	0	660	232	31.42	1	2
132	CH Gayle	5	8	1	220	52	31.42	0	1
133	SM Davies	16	27	3	753	87	31.37	0	4
134	MH Wessels	11	18	1	533	97	31.35	0	3
135	DDJ Robinson	8	14	1	407	122	31.30	1	1
136	SD Stubbings	16	31	3	876	128	31.28	2	2
137	GG Wagg	15	21	4	530	82	31.17	0	4
138	BM Shafayat	12	19	1	560	79	31.11	0	4
139	MJ Lumb	16	25	0	775	89	31.00	0	8
140	CJL Rogers	8	14	1	402	138	30.92	1	3
141	Yasir Arafat	10	13	1	369	122	30.75	2	0
142	MJ Nicholson	12	12	4	240	48 *	30.00	0	0
143	DJ Redfern	5	7	1	180	51	30.00	0	1
144	W Jaffer	6	12	1	327	62	29.72	0	3
145	AJ Hall	7	10	1	264	77	29.33	0	2
146	C Kieswetter	14	16	3	377	93	29.00	0	3
147	CT Tremlett	10	14	6	232	62 *	29.00	0	1
148	Mansoor Amjad	9	13	2	319	105 *	29.00	1	1
149	IJ Sutcliffe	5	9	2	203	104 *	29.00	1	1
150	JJ van der Wath	10	15	3	346	94	28.83	0	3
151	V Chopra	16	26	3	649	86	28.21	0	5
152	MJ Chilton	14	24	2	616	115	28.00	1	2
153	CR Taylor	4	6	0	168	96	28.00	0	2
154	Azhar Mahmood	3	6	0	168	69	28.00	0	1
155	BF Smith	14	22	2	559	98 *	27.95	0	6
156	AW Gale	6	8	0	223	68	27.87	0	2
157	CD Nash	17	30	0	835	89	27.83	0	7
158	NR Prowting	3	6	0	167	78	27.83	0	1
159	HD Ackerman	15	26	0	723	153	27.80	3	1
160	JGE Benning	8	11	1	277	51	27.70	0	1
161	KS Lokuarachchi	3	6	0	166	45	27.66	0	0
162	OD Gibson	15	23	2	578	71	27.52	0	4
163	MJ Powell (Wa)	4	6	0	165	82	27.50	0	1
164	RN Grant	8	13	0	350	79	26.92	0	2
165	CP Murtagh	3	6	0	161	107	26.83	1	0
166	JC Tredwell	14	19	2	454	116 *	26.70	1	2
167	SP Crook	10	16	3	344	60	26.46	0	2
168	SJ Adshead	13	18	1	447	99	26.29	0	3
169	A Jacobs	6	9	2	184	55	26.28	0	1

	Name	M	Inn	NO	Runs	HS	Avg	100	50
170	JK Maunders	13	22	0	575	97	26.13	0	4
171	JC Morris	5	10	0	259	67	25.90	0	2
172	GJ Batty	14	22	3	487	84	25.63	0	3
173	P Mustard	17	31	2	743	76	25.62	0	4
174	BW Harmison	9	16	2	358	101	25.57	1	2
175	DG Cork	13	17	4	329	48 *	25.30	0	0
176	GT Park	4	7	0	177	61	25.28	0	2
177	JHP Hooper	3	6	0	151	79	25.16	0	1
178	CW Henderson	10	13	0	326	81	25.07	0	1
179	MA Ealham	13	16	4	300	74 *	25.00	0	2
180	RDB Croft	16	26	2	595	115	24.79	1	1
181	MA Wallace	16	27	0	669	128	24.77	2	1
182	C White	11	18	0	446	117	24.77	1	2
183	GJ Muchall	12	22	1	520	66	24.76	0	4
184	MD Stoneman	8	15	0	369	101	24.60	1	1
185	DJ Balcombe	5	8	2	144	29	24.00	0	0
186	WR Smith	12	23	0	551	105	23.95	1	0
187	MA Hardinges	9	15	1	335	104	23.92	1	1
188	DS Lucas	9	13	4	215	37	23.88	0	0
189	GP Rees	10	18	0	429	109	23.83	2	2
190	NGE Walker	8	11	5	143	31	23.83	0	0
191	ML Pettini	17	27	1	604	86 *	23.23	0	6
192	HH Streak	11	15	3	278	66	23.16	0	2
193	R Clarke	10	14	1	301	68 *	23.15	0	2
194	AD Brown	9	14	2	277	69	23.08	0	3
195	PJ Franks	11	13	1	275	92	22.91	0	1
196	NJP O'Brien	8	13	2	249	109	22.63	1	0
197	GM Smith	12	20	2	407	74	22.61	0	3
198	G Chapple	12	16	1	338	88	22.53	0	2
199	IJL Trott	15	22	1	473	84	22.52	0	2
200	DH Wigley	10	13	3	223	70	22.30	0	2
201	CC Benham	9	14	0	312	76	22.28	0	1
202	NRD Compton	11	18	0	399	67	22.16	0	3
203	PJW Young	3	6	0	132	54	22.00	0	1
204	AC Thomas	4	7	1	130	42	21.66	0	0
205	AG Wakely	4	8	0	169	66	21.12	0	2
206	Hassan Adnan	11	21	2	399	63	21.00	0	2
207	SB Styris	5	10	0	210	48	21.00	0	0
208	R McLaren	15	18	5	272	54 *	20.92	0	1
209	SJ Walters	8	12	1	228	70	20.72	0	1
210	PJ Wilshaw	3	6	0	124	38	20.66	0	0
211	DS Smith	5	8	0	165	42	20.62	0	0
212	PJ Wiseman	13	19	5	288	44	20.57	0	0
213	BJ Wright	11	18	2	329	108	20.56	1	1

	Name	M	Inn	NO	Runs	HS	Avg	100	50
214	CD Hopkinson	10	17	0	347	83	20.41	0	2
215	LE Plunkett	15	23	5	367	59 *	20.38	0	2
216	JWM Dalrymple	12	17	2	305	57	20.33	0	1
217	AG Botha	16	23	1	447	101	20.31	1	2
218	JE Taylor	7	11	2	176	40	19.55	0	0
219	IDK Salisbury	6	9	0	174	103	19.33	1	0
220	SJ Croft	11	19	2	328	65	19.29	0	2
221	SK Warne	15	19	0	364	50	19.15	0	1
222	M Kartik	12	15	4	209	35 *	19.00	0	0
223	TD Groenewald	8	9	2	133	41 *	19.00	0	0
224	D Ganga	5	9	1	152	49	19.00	0	0
225	MC Rosenberg	7	8	1	130	64 *	18.57	0	1
226	N Peng	3	6	0	111	65	18.50	0	1
227	RJ Sillence	10	13	2	202	51 *	18.36	0	1
228	JE Anyon	14	16	5	199	37 *	18.09	0	0
229	JL Sadler	10	17	0	304	45	17.88	0	0
230	DJ Jacobs	4	8	0	143	56	17.87	0	1
231	TJ Murtagh	14	16	1	267	40	17.80	0	0
232	G Onions	14	17	5	213	41	17.75	0	0
233	RAG Cummins	5	9	3	104	34 *	17.33	0	0
234	DD Masters	11	16	2	242	46	17.28	0	0
235	JP Maher	8	15	0	252	55	16.80	0	1
236	SJ Cook	12	14	5	151	50 *	16.77	0	1
237	DD Cherry	7	12	0	198	48	16.50	0	0
238	RMR Brathwaite	4	7	1	99	76 *	16.50	0	1
239	JAR Harris	9	14	2	196	87 *	16.33	0	1
240	RJ Kirtley	7	8	2	98	51	16.33	0	1
241	GR Breese	5	10	1	145	53	16.11	0	1
242	D Gough	14	15	1	219	50	15.64	0	1
243	RJ Sidebottom	13	17	6	169	26 *	15.36	0	0
244	DO Brown	3	6	0	92	43	15.33	0	0
245	Naved-ul-Hasan	14	18	1	251	75	14.76	0	1
246	SJ Harmison	12	16	5	162	30	14.72	0	0
247	Danish Kaneria	13	16	1	216	65	14.40	0	1
248	CP Schofield	6	7	1	86	28	14.33	0	0
249	SP Jones	4	7	1	86	39	14.33	0	0
250	BSM Warnapura	3	6	0	86	44	14.33	0	0
251	NJ Lamb	3	6	0	84	32	14.00	0	0
252	TJ Phillips	10	14	0	193	68	13.78	0	1
253	Harbhajan Singh	6	7	1	82	29	13.66	0	0
254	LC Parker	5	6	0	81	49	13.50	0	0
255	EJ Foster	3	6	0	81	34	13.50	0	0
256	SI Mahmood	10	14	3	148	41	13.45	0	0
257	MJ Hoggard	13	11	2	121	61	13.44	0	1

	Name	M	Inn	NO	Runs	HS	Avg	100	50
258	AR Caddick	16	13	2	147	51	13.36	0	1
259	RE Watkins	8	13	0	172	30	13.23	0	0
260	WPC Weston	9	15	0	198	38	13.20	0	0
261	A Richardson	14	13	5	104	24 *	13.00	0	0
262	J Lewis	8	8	1	91	42 *	13.00	0	0
263	MA Davies	11	13	5	102	35 *	12.75	0	0
264	RP Singh	6	9	1	99	41 *	12.37	0	0
265	NC Saker	8	9	3	74	19	12.33	0	0
266	CEW Silverwood	11	10	1	110	30	12.22	0	0
267	Mushtaq Ahmed	15	17	3	170	54	12.14	0	1
268	MA Richards	4	6	0	72	26	12.00	0	0
269	DBL Powell	8	12	1	130	36 *	11.81	0	0
270	T Lungley	15	21	6	169	30 *	11.26	0	0
271	AJ Tudor	10	13	3	112	35	11.20	0	0
272	ID Fisher	3	6	0	67	41	11.16	0	0
273	Kabir Ali	14	19	0	211	39	11.10	0	0
274	HT Waters	10	16	8	87	33	10.87	0	0
275	PG Dixey	4	8	0	84	25	10.50	0	0
276	J Ormond	7	10	2	83	25 *	10.37	0	0
277	WA White	4	6	0	61	19	10.16	0	0
278	SR Clark	6	9	2	71	17	10.14	0	0

BOWLING AVERAGES
Qualifying requirements: 10 wickets taken

	Name	M	Balls	Runs	Wkts	Avg	BB	5I	S/R
1	MK Munday	3	264	192	14	13.71	8-55	1	18.85
2	DJG Sammy	2	435	178	12	14.83	7-66	1	36.25
3	Saqlain Mushtaq	4	710	316	18	17.55	5-96	1	39.44
4	Harbhajan Singh	6	1705	686	37	18.54	6-57	3	46.08
5	M Muralitharan	8	2355	952	51	18.66	6-72	5	46.17
6	JL Clare	2	296	203	10	20.30	5-90	1	29.60
7	AJ Bichel	8	1306	842	41	20.53	7-36	3	31.85
8	OD Gibson	15	2879	1660	80	20.75	10-47	4	35.98
9	MJ Hoggard	13	1667	856	40	21.40	5-32	2	41.67
10	RSC Martin-Jenkins	15	1794	771	36	21.41	5-67	1	49.83
11	ST Finn	3	437	239	11	21.72	4-51	0	39.72
12	G Chapple	12	2191	1027	47	21.85	7-53	1	46.61
13	Danish Kaneria	13	3365	1643	74	22.20	7-95	7	45.47
14	AA Noffke	3	748	335	15	22.33	6-68	1	49.86
15	SJ Harmison	12	2180	1184	53	22.33	6-87	3	41.13
16	DD Masters	11	1966	924	41	22.53	6-60	3	47.95
17	AR Caddick	16	3251	1733	75	23.10	7-30	4	43.34
18	SP Kirby	11	1876	961	41	23.43	5-41	3	45.75

	Name	M	Balls	Runs	Wkts	Avg	BB	5I	S/R
19	SR Patel	14	624	329	14	23.50	4-68	0	44.57
20	D Gough	14	1726	876	37	23.67	6-47	3	46.64
21	JJ van der Wath	10	1441	805	34	23.67	6-49	2	42.38
22	Z Khan	4	998	521	22	23.68	5-75	1	45.36
23	N Boje	4	817	382	16	23.87	6-110	1	51.06
24	A Richardson	14	2143	1017	42	24.21	5-50	1	51.02
25	MA Davies	11	1756	824	34	24.23	7-59	1	51.64
26	MJ Saggers	9	1426	707	29	24.37	5-39	2	49.17
27	Kabir Ali	14	2393	1369	56	24.44	8-50	3	42.73
28	CJ Jordan	5	835	490	20	24.50	3-42	0	41.75
29	R McLaren	15	1896	1079	44	24.52	5-24	1	43.09
30	JAR Harris	9	1487	811	33	24.57	7-66	2	45.06
31	CM Willoughby	16	2776	1530	62	24.67	5-33	5	44.77
32	TJ Murtagh	14	1778	1044	42	24.85	6-87	1	42.33
33	GJ-P Kruger	4	510	324	13	24.92	5-62	1	39.23
34	M Kartik	12	2787	1273	51	24.96	6-21	3	54.64
35	SCJ Broad	6	964	602	24	25.08	5-67	2	40.16
36	SR Clark	6	1052	602	24	25.08	7-82	1	43.83
37	DI Stevens	11	677	305	12	25.41	3-91	0	56.41
38	Murtaza Hussain	2	568	282	11	25.63	4-126	0	51.63
39	Mushtaq Ahmed	15	4013	2310	90	25.66	7-72	8	44.58
40	DW Steyn	7	1221	595	23	25.86	5-49	1	53.08
41	U Welagedara	4	586	338	13	26.00	5-45	1	45.07
42	T Lungley	15	2615	1555	59	26.35	5-20	3	44.32
43	MS Panesar	12	2785	1413	53	26.66	6-65	4	52.54
44	CG Greenidge	8	1098	752	28	26.85	5-54	1	39.21
45	CE Shreck	11	2405	1274	47	27.10	7-35	4	51.17
46	DL Maddy	14	996	409	15	27.26	5-63	1	66.40
47	DH Wigley	10	1374	936	34	27.52	3-10	0	40.41
48	WPUJC Vaas	7	972	552	20	27.60	5-126	1	48.60
49	MA Ealham	13	1954	886	32	27.68	4-37	0	61.06
50	N Tahir	11	1432	694	25	27.76	4-47	0	57.28
51	CEW Silverwood	11	1564	875	31	28.22	6-49	1	50.45
52	NM Carter	3	514	283	10	28.30	5-62	1	51.40
53	KJ Dean	10	1602	659	23	28.65	5-24	1	69.65
54	PJ Foster	3	474	318	11	28.90	4-26	0	43.09
55	HMRKB Herath	4	585	319	11	29.00	3-39	0	53.18
56	Naved-ul-Hasan	14	2265	1454	50	29.08	5-106	2	45.30
57	AP Palladino	7	641	350	12	29.16	4-44	0	53.41
58	WB Rankin	3	459	292	10	29.20	4-41	0	45.90
59	MJ Nicholson	12	2268	1289	44	29.29	5-89	1	51.54
60	AG Botha	16	3318	1619	55	29.43	6-101	3	60.32
61	OP Rayner	4	704	414	14	29.57	5-68	1	50.28
62	SK Warne	15	2629	1479	50	29.58	6-83	5	52.58

	Name	M	Balls	Runs	Wkts	Avg	BB	5I	S/R
63	ID Blackwell	15	1947	860	29	29.65	3-8	0	67.13
64	PJ Wiseman	13	1731	955	32	29.84	5-65	1	54.09
65	RJ Sidebottom	13	2638	1166	39	29.89	5-88	1	67.64
66	RP Singh	6	1093	691	23	30.04	5-59	1	47.52
67	OJ Newby	9	1066	670	22	30.45	3-44	0	48.45
68	LE Plunkett	15	2663	1530	50	30.60	5-105	1	53.26
69	JTA Bruce	14	2117	1199	39	30.74	5-64	2	54.28
70	JD Lewry	14	2089	1017	33	30.81	4-81	0	63.30
71	SI Mahmood	10	1623	955	30	31.83	4-21	0	54.10
72	JE Taylor	7	1044	702	22	31.90	6-35	3	47.45
73	DA Mascarenhas	10	1140	481	15	32.06	4-33	0	76.00
74	DA Cosker	11	1830	939	29	32.37	5-69	1	63.10
75	FH Edwards	3	538	392	12	32.66	5-112	1	44.83
76	Yasir Arafat	10	1433	882	27	32.66	5-63	1	53.07
77	CL White	12	1072	655	20	32.75	4-28	0	53.60
78	DT Rowe	5	534	427	13	32.84	5-61	1	41.07
79	CG Taylor	15	546	331	10	33.10	4-52	0	54.60
80	G Onions	14	2377	1490	45	33.11	8-101	2	52.82
81	JM Anderson	9	1905	1067	32	33.34	5-42	2	59.53
82	DBL Powell	8	1479	834	25	33.36	4-8	0	59.16
83	GP Swann	16	2924	1503	45	33.40	7-100	1	64.97
84	SD Udal	5	901	469	14	33.50	4-138	0	64.35
85	RDB Croft	16	3601	1877	56	33.51	6-44	5	64.30
86	SJ Cook	12	1456	740	22	33.63	6-35	1	66.18
87	GG Wagg	15	2952	1785	53	33.67	5-119	2	55.69
88	DG Cork	13	2165	1011	30	33.70	3-39	0	72.16
89	G Keedy	10	1635	813	24	33.87	5-159	1	68.12
90	CT Tremlett	10	1907	985	29	33.96	4-47	0	65.75
91	TT Bresnan	16	2124	1157	34	34.02	4-10	0	62.47
92	PJ Franks	11	1582	1090	32	34.06	3-28	0	49.43
93	DA Griffiths	5	603	411	12	34.25	4-46	0	50.25
94	PD Trego	17	1719	1131	33	34.27	4-49	0	52.09
95	GM Smith	12	1285	689	20	34.45	3-31	0	64.25
96	A Kumble	5	1234	690	20	34.50	3-32	0	61.70
97	JN Gillespie	12	1431	803	23	34.91	3-40	0	62.21
98	AGB Wharf	15	1856	1262	36	35.05	4-16	0	51.55
99	AJ Tudor	10	1046	602	17	35.41	3-29	0	61.52
100	JC Tredwell	14	2493	1285	36	35.69	6-47	1	69.25
101	AR Adams	4	823	501	14	35.78	4-74	0	58.78
102	SP Crook	10	1390	831	23	36.13	4-56	0	60.43
103	AC Thomas	4	776	367	10	36.70	4-109	0	77.60
104	WA White	4	678	463	12	38.58	5-87	1	56.50
105	L Klusener	16	2595	1280	33	38.78	5-40	2	78.63
106	A Nel	4	734	391	10	39.10	3-62	0	73.40

	Name	M	Balls	Runs	Wkts	Avg	BB	5I	S/R
107	S Sreesanth	5	1063	550	14	39.28	3-53	0	75.92
108	J Lewis	8	901	472	12	39.33	5-41	1	75.08
109	RAG Cummins	5	890	512	13	39.38	5-60	1	68.46
110	DS Lucas	9	1212	751	19	39.52	5-49	1	63.78
111	CW Henderson	10	2115	1035	26	39.80	5-56	2	81.34
112	GJ Batty	14	2937	1523	38	40.07	6-106	3	77.28
113	AJ Harris	6	1182	762	19	40.10	4-69	0	62.21
114	REM Williams	5	796	524	13	40.30	5-70	2	61.23
115	PS Jones	13	1527	1055	26	40.57	6-61	1	58.73
116	JA Tomlinson	5	928	528	13	40.61	5-78	1	71.38
117	CP Schofield	6	1121	650	16	40.62	5-52	1	70.06
118	AJ Hall	7	978	610	15	40.66	5-59	1	65.20
119	RE Watkins	8	597	411	10	41.10	4-89	0	59.70
120	JF Brown	14	2723	1235	30	41.16	5-47	1	90.76
121	AU Rashid	17	2742	1813	43	42.16	5-88	3	63.76
122	R Clarke	10	929	633	15	42.20	3-57	0	61.93
123	JD Middlebrook	17	2051	1020	24	42.50	4-53	0	85.45
124	NGE Walker	8	1026	777	18	43.16	4-70	0	57.00
125	NC Saker	8	936	649	15	43.26	5-76	1	62.40
126	CD Collymore	4	822	478	11	43.45	3-58	0	74.72
127	RJ Logan	7	1134	656	15	43.73	3-38	0	75.60
128	J Allenby	16	1262	662	15	44.13	5-125	1	84.13
129	LJ Wright	11	1011	619	14	44.21	3-117	0	72.21
130	RS Bopara	12	842	533	12	44.41	3-60	0	70.16
131	JE Anyon	14	2245	1424	32	44.50	4-55	0	70.15
132	DE Bollinger	7	1146	713	16	44.56	4-82	0	71.62
133	V Banerjee	11	2093	1178	26	45.30	4-38	0	80.50
134	RJ Kirtley	7	1110	567	12	47.25	4-44	0	92.50
135	DJ Balcombe	5	755	479	10	47.90	3-58	0	75.50
136	AP Davies	7	804	542	11	49.27	4-46	0	73.09
137	HT Waters	10	1209	741	15	49.40	4-76	0	80.60
138	MA Hardinges	9	1290	822	16	51.37	3-59	0	80.62
139	J Ormond	7	1134	640	12	53.33	2-42	0	94.50
140	ND Doshi	5	1046	697	13	53.61	6-111	1	80.46
141	Mansoor Amjad	9	968	645	12	53.75	3-16	0	80.66
142	JWM Dalrymple	12	1191	689	12	57.41	3-86	0	99.25
143	MN Malik	14	2254	1470	25	58.80	3-94	0	90.16
144	GR Napier	10	901	589	10	58.90	3-55	0	90.10
145	HH Streak	11	1532	789	13	60.69	3-105	0	117.84
146	RJ Sillence	10	1409	932	15	62.13	2-48	0	93.93
147	IDK Salisbury	6	1133	745	11	67.72	4-121	0	103.00

THE PRIMARY CLUB

PO Box 12121, Saffron Walden
Essex CB10 2ZF
Telephone: 01799 586507
e-mail: secretary@primaryclub.org
website: www.primaryclub.org

Derek Underwood, the patron of the Primary Club, qualified f membership in some style in 1965. Playing for Kent against th South Africans he was out first ball twice in the same match.

However, members do not have to be playing Test or coun cricket when the ultimate disaster strikes in order to qualify fo the club. As long as you are out first ball at ANY level of cricke you are eligible to join The Primary Club.

Why join? The Primary Club is a charity (Registered Charity No. 285285) and all profits from subscriptions, donations and the range of items for sale (ties, sweaters, shirts, mugs, umbrellas, etc.) go to pay for sporting and recreational facilities for the blind and partially sighted. All the club's workers are volunteers.

For many of us sport is an important part of our every day lives; for the blind and partially sighted, sport can mean so much more. The confidence and sense of achievement they get from mastering a physical skill helps them a great deal ir tackling the problems of their lives.

MEMBERSHIP APPLICATION

Name

Address

Joining subscription:	
To include City tie – £20	
To include Club tie – £20	
To include City & Club tie – £30	
To include 100% silk tie (City) – £30	
To include 100% silk tie (Country) – £30	
To include Bow tie – £20	
Lady, to include brooch – £15	
DONATION	
REMITTANCE TO 'THE PRIMARY CLUB' £	

Registered Charity No. 285285

The value of your remittance to The Prim Club can be increased by 28p for every £ you give under Gift Aid tax reclaim arrangements, *at no extra cost to you*. To enable the Club to benefit from this scheme, please sign and date the declaration below, provided that you pay income tax, or capital gains tax, of an amount equal to the tax to be reclaimed.

I wish The Primary Club to reclaim tax or all donations I make on or after the date this declaration.

Signed **Date**

It would be of great benefit to the Club if yo pay future donations by banker's standing order. Please tick the box and a form will be sent to you. ☐

INDEX OF PLAYERS BY COUNTY

*denotes not registered for the 2008 season. Where a player is known to have moved in the off-season he is listed under his new county.

DERBYSHIRE

DURHAM

ESSEX

GLAMORGAN

INDEX OF PLAYERS BY COUNTY

DAVIES, A.P.*
ELLIOTT, M.T.G.*
GILLESPIE, J.N.
GRANT, R.N.
HARRIS, J.A.R.
HARRISON, A.J.*
HARRISON, D.S.
HEMP, D.L.
MAHER, J.P.*
MAYNARD, T.L.
O'SHEA, M.P.
OWEN, W.T.
PENG, N.*
POWELL, M.J.
REES, G.P.
SHANTRY, A.J.
TUDGE, K.D.
WALLACE, M.A.
WATERS, H.T.
WATKINS, R.E.
WHARF, A.G.B.
WOOD, M.J.
WRIGHT, B.J.
WRIGHT, D.G.*

GLOUCESTERSHIRE

ADSHEAD, S.J.
ALI, KADEER
BANERJEE, V.
BROWN, D.O.
EDMONDSON, B.M.*
FISHER, I.D.
GIDMAN, A.P.R.
GITSHAM, M.T.
GREENIDGE, C.G.
HARDINGES, M.A.
HODNETT, G.P.
IRELAND, A.J.
KIRBY, S.P.
LEWIS, J.
MARSHALL, H.J.H.
NORTH, M.J.
PORTERFIELD, W.T.S.
RUDGE, W.D.
SNELL, S.D.
SPEARMAN, C.M.
STAYT, T.P.
TAYLOR, C.G.
THOMPSON, J.G.

HAMPSHIRE

ADAMS, J.H.K.
BALCOMBE, D.J.
BENHAM, C.C.
BROWN, M.J.
BRUCE, J.T.A.
BURROWS, T.G.
CARBERRY, M.A.
CLARK, S.R.*
CRAWLEY, J.P.
DAWSON, L.A.
ERVINE, S.M.
GRIFFITHS, D.A.
HOWELL, B.A.C.
LAMB, G.A.
LATOUF, K.J.
LUMB, M.J.
MASCARENHAS, D.A.
MORRIS, R.K.
PIETERSEN, K.P.
POTHAS, N.
POWELL, D.B.L.*
STOKES, M.S.T.*
TAYLOR, B.V.
TOMLINSON, J.A.
TREMLETT, C.T.
VOGES, A.C.*
WARNE, S.K.

KENT

AZHAR MAHMOOD
BLAKE, A.J.
COOK, S.J.
DENLY, J.L.
DEXTER, N.J.
DIXEY, P.G.
GOODMAN, J.E.
ILES, J.A.
JONES, G.O.
JOSEPH, R.H.
KEY, R.W.T.
KHAN, A.
MALINGA, S.L.*
MCLAREN, R.
MORKEL, M.*
NORTHEAST, S.A.
PARSONS, T.W.
PATEL, M.M.
SAGGERS, M.J.
STEVENS, D.I.
TREDWELL, J.C.
VAN JAARSVELD, M.
WALKER, M.J.
YASIR ARAFAT*

LANCASHIRE

ANDERSON, J.M.
BROWN, K.R.
CHAPPLE, G.
CHEETHAM, S.P.*
CHILTON, M.J.
CORK, D.G.

INDEX OF PLAYERS BY COUNTY

LEICESTERSHIRE

MIDDLESEX

NORTHAMPTONSHIRE

INDEX OF PLAYERS BY COUNTY

NOTTINGHAMSHIRE

ADAMS, A.R.*
BROAD, S.C.J.
CLOUGH, G.D.
EALHAM, M.A.
FERLEY, R.S.
FLEMING, S.P.*
FOOTITT, M.H.A.
FRANCIS, S.R.G.*
FRANKS, P.J.
HALES, A.D.
HARRIS, A.J.
HUSSEY, D.J.
JEFFERSON, W.I.
PATEL, S.R.
READ, C.M.W.
SHAFAYAT, B.M.
SHRECK, C.E.
SIDEBOTTOM, R.J.
SWANN, G.P.
WAGH, M.A.
WOOD, M.J.

SOMERSET

BANKS, O.A.C.
BLACKWELL, I.D.
CADDICK, A.R.
DURSTON, W.J.
EDWARDS, N.J.
FRANCIS, J.D.
GAZZARD, C.M.
HILDRETH, J.C.
JONES, P.S.
KIESWETTER, C.
LANGER, J.L.
LETT, R.J.
MUNDAY, M.K.
PARSONS, K.A.
PHILLIPS, B.J.
SPURWAY, S.H.P.*
SUPPIAH, A.V.
SUTTON, A.P.
TREGO, P.D.
TRESCOTHICK, M.E.
TURNER, M.L.
WHITE, C.L.*
WILLOUGHBY, C.M.

SURREY

AFZAAL, U.
BATTY, J.N.
BENNING, J.G.E.
BROWN, A.D.
BUTCHER, M.A.
CLINTON, R.S.
COLLINS, P.T.
DERNBACH, J.
EVANS, L.J.
HARBHAJAN SINGH*
HARINATH, A.
JORDAN, C.J.
KING, S.J.
MAGOFFIN, S.J.*
MEAKER, S.C.
MOHAMMAD AKRAM*
MOHAMMAD ASIF
MURTAGH, C.P.
MURTAZA HUSSAIN
NEWMAN, S.A.
NICHOLSON, M.J.*
ORMOND, J.
RAMPRAKASH, M.R.
SAKER, N.C.
SAQLAIN MUSHTAQ
SCHOFIELD, C.P.
SPRIEGEL, M.N.W.
WALTERS, S.J.
WILSON, G.C.

SUSSEX

ADAMS, C.J.
AGA, R.G.
BEER, W.A.T.
BROWN, B.C.
DAVIS, M.J.G.
GOODWIN, M.W.
GREEN, J.A.G.*
HAMILTON-BROWN, R.J.
HODD, A.J.
HOPKINSON, C.D.
KIRTLEY, R.J.
LEWRY, J.D.
LIDDLE, C.J.
MARTIN-JENKINS, R.S.C.
MONTGOMERIE, R.R.*
MUSHTAQ AHMED
NASH, C.D.
PRIOR, M.J.
RAYNER, O.P.
SMITH, T.M.J.
THORNELY, M.A.
WRIGHT, L.J.
YARDY, M.H.

WARWICKSHIRE

AMBROSE, T.R.
ANYON, J.E.
BARNES, M.W.*
BELL, I.R.
BOTHA, A.G.
BROWN, D.R.*

INDEX OF PLAYERS BY COUNTY

WORCESTERSHIRE

YORKSHIRE

QUIZ ANSWERS

1. MJK Smith; Peter van der Merwe
2. Graeme Smith
3. Alan Melville
4. Monde Zondeki
5. Peter Kirsten
6. George Lohmann
7. Chris Adams
8. Chris Cairns
9. Glenn Turner
10. Eddie Barlow
11. Martin Bicknell
12. Phil Tufnell
13. Jack Russell
14. Denis Compton's
15. Nathan Astle
16. Bruce French, Bill Athey, Bob Taylor, Bobby Parks
17. Eric and Athol Rowan
18. Stephen Fleming
19. Kent, Sussex, Northamptonshire, Warwickshire and Lancashire respectively
20. Fanie de Villiers
21. James Kirtley
22. Middlesex (Vintcent van der Bijl)
23. Alec Stewart
24. Ken Palmer
25. Lance Klusener
26. Trevor Bailey's
27. Gary Kirsten
28. Lance Cairns
29. Paul Adams's
30. Stephen Harmison
31. Herbert Sutcliffe
32. Jeff and Martin Crowe
33. Len Hutton
34. Marcus Trescothick
35. Peter Pollock
36. Michael Atherton; Kepler Wessels
37. Alex Tudor
38. Sydney Barnes
39. 1990
40. Arthur Milton and MJK Smith
41. Ian Botham
42. Andrew Caddick
43. David Gower
44. Brian Close
45. Nasser Hussain
46. Colin Bland
47. Herby Wade
48. John Crawley
49. Mark Greatbatch
50. Kabir Ali
51. Daniel Vettori
52. Graham Gooch's
53. Geoff Griffin
54. Devon Malcolm
55. Jacques Kallis
56. Jack MacBryan
57. C. Aubrey Smith
58. Nasser Hussain
59. Bruce Mitchell
60. Steve Rhodes
61. Martin Donnelly
62. Michael Atherton
63. Darren Gough's
64. Jackie McGlew
65. Peter Lever and Ken Shuttleworth
66. John Edrich's
67. Matthew Hoggard
68. Mark Butcher
69. Andrew Flintoff
70. Graeme Pollock
71. Doug Wright
72. Allan Donald
73. Ian Smith
74. Walter Hadlee
75. Angus Fraser
76. 1905-06 (first Test)
77. Graham Thorpe
78. John Bracewell
79. Brian Statham
80. Andrew Strauss
81. Andrew Hall
82. Peter May
83. Robert Croft
84. Ali Bacher
85. Alec Bedser
86. Derek Underwood
87. Shaun Pollock
88. Martin Crowe
89. Ken Barrington
90. Vikram Solanki and Marcus Trescothick
91. Bob Willis
92. Danny Morrison
93. Len Hutton
94. Martin Saggers
95. John Emburey
96. Kevin Pietersen's
97. 1929-30
98. John Waite
99. Michael Atherton's
100. Jack Russell